GEORGE M. HAMMELL, D.D.
Editor "The Passing of the Saloon."

THE PASSING OF THE SALOON

AN AUTHENTIC AND OFFICIAL PRESENTATION OF THE ANTI-LIQUOR CRUSADE IN AMERICA

GEORGE M. HAMMELL, D. D.
EDITOR-IN-CHIEF

Author
"BIBLE BRILLIANTS OR MOTHER'S HOME BIBLE STORIES"

Professor of Economics and Sociology in the
American Temperance University, 1899-1902
Editor "*The New Voice*," 1905-1906

WITH NUMEROUS CONTRIBUTORS

ILLUSTRATED

COPYRIGHT 1908
BY
OSCAR B. TODHUNTER

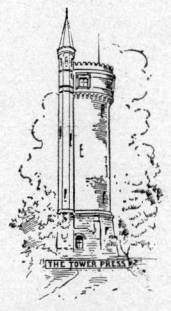

*"I have set thee for a tower, and
a fortress among my people."*

TO

THE BRAVE WOMEN AND MEN

LIVING AND DEAD

WHOSE NOBLE PURPOSE AND CEASELESS ENDEAVOR

HAVE MADE POSSIBLE

THE PASSING OF THE SALOON

THIS VOLUME

IS DEDICATED

LIST OF CONTRIBUTORS

Who have written for, or been quoted in, "THE PASSING OF THE SALOON."

THEODORE ALVORD,
Superintendent Anti-Saloon League, West Virginia.

MRS. J. B. AMMERMAN,
President Woman's Christian Temperance Union, Texas.

MRS. ELIZABETH PRESTON ANDERSON,
President W. C. T. U., North Dakota.

JOHN M. ARTERS,
District Superintendent Peninsula District A. S. L., Delaware.

LOUIS ALBERT BANKS, D. D.,
Minister, Author, Lecturer.

REV. W. C. BARBER,
Superintendent A. S. L., Iowa.

SAMUEL J. BARROWS,
President International Prison Commission.

REV. R. H. BENNETT, D. D.,
Superintendent A. S. L., Virginia.

JAMES W. BODLEY,
Ex-Chairman Prohibition State Committee, Virginia.

MRS. E. C. BODWELL,
President (East) W. C. T. U., Washington.

GENERAL WILLIAM BOOTH.

AARON M. BRAY,
Chairman Prohibition State Committee, Idaho.

BISHOP PHILLIPS BROOKS.

A. M. BROWN,
Economist.

MRS. HENRIETTA BROWN,
President W. C. T. U., Oregon.

MRS. M. MCCLELLAN BROWN, Ph. D.,
Grand Chief Templar, Ohio I. O. G. T.

HENRY A. BUCHTEL,
Governor of Colorado.

JAMES M. BUCKLEY, D. D., LL.D.,
Editor, Author, Lecturer.

MARSHALL BULLITT,
Attorney.

J. FRANK BURKE,
Superintendent A. S. L., New Jersey.

AMOS W. BUTLER,
Secretary Charities and Corrections, Indiana.

JUDGE BUTLER,
Of Illinois.

W. G. CALDERWOOD,
Secretary Prohibition State Committee, Minnesota.

THOMAS M. CAMPBELL,
Governor of Texas.

WILL CARLTON,
Author and Editor.

REV. J. B. CARNS, D. D.,
Superintendent A. S. L., Nebraska.

EUGENE W. CHAFIN,
Prohibition Candidate for President, 1908.

ERVIN S. CHAPMAN, D. D., LL.D.
Superintendent A. S. L., California.

LORD CHESTERFIELD.

REV. A. B. CHURLEY,
Superintendent A. S. L., Rhode Island.

MAMIE M. CLAFLIN,
Editor and Publisher, "Union Worker," W. C. T. U., Nebraska.

SIR ANDREW CLARK,
Physician, London, England.

WILLIAM T. COBB,
Governor of Maine.

RICHARD COBDEN,
English Economist.

JOHN B. COFFIN,
Chairman Prohibition State Committee, Florida.

REV. CHAS. L. COLLINS,
Superintendent A. S. L., Florida.

D. LEIGH COLVIN, M. A.,
President The Intercollegiate Prohibition Association, 1899-1908.

BRAXTON B. COMER,
Governor of Alabama.

R. M. COOPER,
Chairman Prohibition State Committee, Delaware.

J. B. CRANFILL, D. D.,
Editor, Author, Reformer.

JOHN W. CUMMINGS,
Treasurer National Temperance Society, New York.

MRS. W. E. CURRAH,
President W. C. T. U., Montana.

VOLNEY B. CUSHING,
Author and Lecturer, Maine.

JOHN C. CUTLER,
Governor of Utah.

LIST OF CONTRIBUTORS.

Theodore L. Cuyler, D. D.

Huram W. Davis,
Chairman Prohibition State Committee, Kentucky.

Rev. R. L. Davis,
State Organizer A. S. L., North Carolina.

Rev. S. H. Davis,
Superintendent A. S. L., Massachusetts.

William M. O. Dawson,
Governor of West Virginia.

Judge Alton G. Dayton.

T. B. Demaree,
Member National Prohibition Committee, Kentucky.

Samuel Dickie,
Ex-Chairman Prohibition National Committee.

Harris Dickson, LL.B.,
Author and Lawyer; Judge Municipal Court, Vicksburg, Mississippi.

Neal Dow.

Father Doyle,
Roman Catholic Clergyman.

Mrs. Marion H. Dunham,
President W. C. T. U., Iowa.

Richard T. Ely, Ph. D.,
Author "An Introduction to Political Economy."

Frances H. Ensign,
President W. C. T. U., Ohio.

James L. Ewin,
Corresponding Secretary A. S. L. of America, Washington, D. C.

Frank H. Farris,
Attorney.

Franz V. Feldman,
Economist.

C. J. Ferguson,
Superintendent A. S. L., Vermont.

Joseph W. Folk,
Governor of Missouri.

Bishop Cyrus D. Foss.

Rev. L. S. Fuller,
Superintendent A. S. L., Utah, Wyoming, and Nevada.

Mrs. Frances Joseph Gaudet,
President (Willard) W. C. T. U., Louisiana.

Mrs. Ella M. George,
President W. C. T. U., Pennsylvania.

Col. T. M. Gilmore,
President National Model License League.

William E. Gladstone.

Robert B. Glenn,
Governor of North Carolina.

Henry W. Grady,
Editor and Orator.

Rev. W. M. Grafton, Ph. D.,
Superintendent A. S. L., South Dakota.

Mrs. Frances W. Graham,
President W. C. T. U., New York.

Horace Greeley.

Mrs. Mary E. Green,
President W. C. T. U., Hawaii.

Mrs. Hester T. Griffith,
President W. C. T. U., Southern California.

Rev. W. T. Groom,
Superintendent A. S. L., Montana.

Edwin C. Hadley,
Chairman Kansas Prohibition Committee.

Edward Everett Hale,
Author, Minister, Reformer.

W. R. Hamilton,
Superintendent A. S. L., Tennessee.

Hon. J. Frank Hanly,
Governor of Indiana.

Rev. T. M. Hare,
Superintendent A. S. L., District of Columbia.

Rev. John L. Harley,
Superintendent A. S. L., South Carolina.

Andrew L. Harris,
Governor of Ohio.

Charles N. Haskell,
Governor of Oklahoma.

Rev. W. W. Havens,
Superintendent A. S. L., New Mexico.

L. E. Hawk,
Chairman Prohibition State Committee, Ohio.

George S. Hawke, LL.B.,
Prohibition Candidate for Attorney General, Ohio.

A. R. Heath,
Statistician, Editor.

Finley C. Hendrickson,
Attorney, Member National Prohibition Committee, Maryland.

Mrs. Nettie P. Hershiser,
President W. C. T. U., Nevada.

Edward W. Hoch,
Governor of Kansas.

Mrs. Clara C. Hoffman,
Late W. C. T. U. Lecturer.

Wilford B. Hoggatt,
Governor of Alaska.

Mrs. Silena Moore Holman,
President W. C. T. U., Tennessee.

Rev. U. G. Humphrey,
Superintendent A. S. L., Wisconsin.

Robert G. Ingersoll,
Orator, Freethinker.

E. E. Israel,
Chairman Prohibition State Committee, Louisiana.

John Jay,
Jurist.

Samuel Johnson, D. D.,
Minister, Author.

LIST OF CONTRIBUTORS.

WILLIAM E. JOHNSON,
United States Special Agent for the Suppression of the Liquor Traffic among the Indians.

LIEF JONES, M. P.

SAM P. JONES,
Preacher, Lecturer, Revivalist.

ARCHBISHOP JOHN J. KEANE.

MRS. HARRIET B. KELLS,
President W. C. T. U., Mississippi.

RUDYARD KIPLING,
Poet and Author.

REV. J. R. KNODELL,
Assistant Superintendent A. S. L., Oregon.

MRS. JANETTE HILL KNOX,
Editor "Our Message," Massachusetts W. C. T. U.

LEMUEL L. LAUGHLIN,
Chairman Prohibition State Committee, Wyoming.

REV. BROOKS LAWRENCE,
Superintendent A. S. L., Alabama.

ABRAHAM LINCOLN.

MRS. LILAH D. LINDSEY,
President W. C. T. U., Oklahoma (Indian Territory).

C. J. LITTLE, D. D., LL.D.,
President Garrett Biblical Institute.

JOHN D. LONG,
Ex-Secretary of the Navy.

MARTIN LUTHER.

REV. J. D. MCALISTER,
Field Secretary A. S. L., Virginia.

WILLIAM MCKINLEY.

REV. E. E. MCLAUGHLIN,
Superintendent A. S. L., Colorado.

GEORGE F. MAGOUN, D. D.,
Minister, Author.

CARDINAL MANNING.

MISS ELIZABETH MARCH,
President W. C. T. U., North Carolina.

MRS. LULU A. MARKWELL,
President W. C. T. U., Arkansas.

SENATOR MATTINGLY.

SEBASTIAN G. MESSMER,
Archbishop of Milwaukee.

E. J. MOORE,
Superintendent A. S. L., Missouri.

A. H. MORRILL,
Chairman Prohibition State Committee, New Hampshire.

REV. G. W. MORROW,
Superintendent A. S. L., Michigan.

CARRY A. NATION,
Reformer, Author, Lecturer.

S. E. NICHOLSON,
Superintendent A. S. L., Pennsylvania.

EDMOND F. NOEL,
Governor of Mississippi.

ROBERT NORRIS,
Secretary State Temperance Union, Kansas.

C. E. OWEN,
Superintendent A. S. L., Maryland.

LAFOREST J. PAIGE,
Secretary A. S. L., Vermont.

REV. N. A. PALMER,
Superintendent A. S. L., Minesota.

ROBERT H. PATTON,
Attorney.

MRS. E. E. PETERSON,
President (Thurman) W. C. T. U., Texas.

CARRINGTON A. PHELPS,
Author.

WENDELL PHILLIPS.

CHARLES S. PIERCE,
Student, Orator.

CLARENCE E. PITTS,
Chairman Prohibition State Committee, New York.

MRS. MARGARET B. PLATT,
President W. C. T. U., Washington.

JUDGE CHARLES A. POLLOCK,
Representative A. S. L., North Dakota.

TERENCE V. POWDERLY.

J. C. PRICE,
President National Afro-American League.

REV. R. W. RAYMOND,
Superintendent A. S. L., Washington.

ELISHA T. READ,
Chairman Prohibition State Committee, Rhode Island.

O. A. REINHARDT,
Chairman Prohibition State Committee, Colorado.

J. B. RICHARDS,
Associate Superintendent A. S. L., Georgia.

REV. B. F. RILEY, D. D., LL. D.,
Superintendent A. S. L., Texas.

REV. J. H. ROBBINS, D. D.,
Superintendent A. S. L., New Hampshire.

THEODORE ROOSEVELT.

MRS. LOUISE S. ROUNDS,
W. C. T. U. Lecturer.

JOHN RUSKIN.

REV. H. H. RUSSELL, D. D.,
Founder A. S. L. of America; Superintendent A. S. L., New York.

MRS. LULU L. SHEPARD,
President W. C. T. U., Utah.

JAMES K. SHIELDS,
Superintendent A. S. L., Illinois.

E. S. SHUMAKER,
Superintendent A. S. L., Indiana.

MRS. CLINTON SMITH,
President W. C. T. U., District of Columbia.

LIST OF CONTRIBUTORS.

HOKE SMITH,
  Governor of Georgia.
REV. S. A. SMITH,
  Superintendent A. S. L., Louisiana.
REV. J. C. SOLOMON,
  Superintendent A. S. L., Georgia.
BEN H. SPENCE,
  Secretary Ontario Branch Dominion Alliance, Canada.
H. H. SPOONER,
  Secretary Temperance Union, Connecticut.
MRS. JOSEPH SPROTT,
  President W. C. T. U., South Carolina.
FRED. D. L. SQUIRES,
  Editor Associated Prohibition Press, Chicago.
REV. D. J. STARR, D. D.,
  Chaplain, Ohio Penitentiary.
MRS. LILLIAN M. N. STEVENS,
  President National W. C. T. U.
MRS. KATHERINE LENT STEVENSON,
  President W. C. T. U., Massachusetts.
CORA FRANCES STODDARD,
  Corresponding Secretary Scientific Temperance Federation, Boston.
JOHN L. SULLIVAN.
REV. E. A. TABOR,
  Superintendent A. S. L., California.
JOHN W. THOMAS,
  Chairman Prohibition State Committee, Arizona.
OSCAR B. TODHUNTER,
  Editor and Publisher.
R. F. TRAVELICK,
  President National Labor Union.
C. W. TRICKETT,
  Attorney General, Kansas.

T. DEQUINCY TULLY,
  Secretary Law Enforcement Society, New York City.
REV. AUGUST F. WALLIS,
  Secretary A. S. L., Louisiana.
PERE G. WALLMO,
  Author.
FRED. M. WARNER,
  Governor of Michigan.
BOOKER T. WASHINGTON.
AARON S. WATKINS, D. D.,
  Clergyman, Educator; Prohibition Candidate for Vice-President, 1908.
HENRY WATTERSON,
  Editor, Lecturer.
JOHN WESLEY.
J. W. WEST,
  Superintendent A. S. L., Kentucky.
WAYNE B. WHEELER,
  Superintendent A. S. L., Ohio.
MRS. MARY S. WHITNEY,
  President W. C. T. U., Hawaii.
CANON WILBERFORCE.
MRS. KATE E. WILKINS,
  President W. C. T. U., Louisiana.
HENRY SMITH WILLIAMS, M. D., LL.D.,
  Specialist in Nervous and Mental Diseases.
BISHOP L. B. WILSON, D. D., LL.D.,
  President Anti-Saloon League of America.
COL. W. S. WITHAM,
  Chairman Prohibition State Committee, Georgia.
JOHN G. WOOLLEY, A. M., LL.D.,
  Author, Orator, Editor; Prohibition Candidate for President, 1900.
CARROLL D. WRIGHT.
LUKE WRIGHT,
  Secretary of War.

TABLE OF CONTENTS.

	PAGES
LIST OF CONTRIBUTORS	iii-vi
LIST OF PORTRAITS	xi-xii
PROLOGUE	xiii-xvi

By GEORGE M. HAMMELL, *Editor.*

INTRODUCTION .... xvii-xxii

By OSCAR B. TODHUNTER.

CHAPTER I.
THE INDICTMENT OF THE SALOON.

A Statement of the Case against the American Dramshop in the Open Court of Public Opinion by Representative Reformers, corroborated by Advocates of License and Automatic Laws for Regulating the Liquor Traffic........ 1-14

CHAPTER II.
EVIDENCE FROM EXPERIENCE AND OBSERVATION.

Testimony against the Saloon offered by a Citizen Reformer after Hand-to-Hand Conflict, and by Students of the Individual, Social, Economic and Political Effects of the Liquor Traffic................................... 15-30

CHAPTER III.
"CHRISTIAN" SALOONS vs. CHRISTIAN MISSIONS.

A Study of the Obstacles to Christian Propagandism Created by the World-wide Expansion of a Commercial Paganism Protected by so-called Christian Nations 31-41

CHAPTER IV.
THE SALOON AN ECONOMIC VAMPIRE.

A Statistical Arraignment of the Liquor Traffic as a Destroyer, not only of Economic Wealth, but of the Wealth-Producer—based upon comparisons of Authoritative Analyses of Industrial Conditions as found in "wet" and "dry" Territory 42-52

CHAPTER V.
PHYSIOLOGICAL EFFECTS OF ALCOHOL.

By HENRY SMITH WILLIAMS, M.D., LL.D.

A Scientific Statement of the Effects of Alcohol as a Narcotic Irritant, or Anaesthetic, Based Upon the Most Recent Laboratory Experiments, Written by one of the most Famous Nerve-Disease Specialists in the United States 53-68

CHAPTER VI.
SALOON SINS AS SEEN BY A SUFFERER.

The Confession of a Victim of the Liquor Traffic Corroborating the Arraignment of the Saloon by Temperance Agitators and Prohibition Law Makers. 69-79

CHAPTER VII.

THE SALOON AN OUTLAW.

By GEORGE S. HAWKE, LL.B, *Prohibition Candidate for Attorney General, Ohio, 1908.*

A Digest of Judicial Decisions Against the Retail Traffic in Intoxicating Liquors, Rendered by the United States Supreme Court, and other Courts, Establishing the Contention that the Saloon has no Common Law Right to Exist in the American Commonwealth.............................. 80-103

CHAPTER VIII.

HEROES AND MARTYRS.

Life Sketches of Temperance and Prohibition Reformers Who Have Consecrated the Cause of the Great Reform by the Hazard of Life Itself on the Fields of Duty..104-130

CHAPTER IX.

EDUCATIONAL ORGANIZATIONS.

The National Temperance Society—*By* JOHN W. CUMMINGS, *Treasurer.*
The Scientific Temperance Federation—*By* CORA FRANCES STODDARD, *Corresponding Secretary.*
The Independent Order of Good Templars—*By* MRS. M. MCCLELLAN BROWN, Ph. D., *Grand Chief Templar, Ohio, I. O. G. T.*
The Catholic Total Abstinence Union.
A Summary of Educative Forces Co-operating with Political Agencies for the Overthrow of the Saloon...131-142

CHAPTER X.

THE WOMAN'S CHRISTIAN TEMPERANCE UNION.

By MRS. LILLIAN M. N. STEVENS, *President.*

A Résumé of Methods Employed in Abolishing the Saloon by the Greatest Woman's Organization in the World....................................143-152

CHAPTER XI.

FRANCES ELIZABETH WILLARD.

By The EDITOR, AND FELLOW-WORKERS AND PATRIOTS.

An Appreciation of the Best-Loved Woman of Her Time—the Uncrowned Queen of American Womanhood..153-161

CHAPTER XII.

THE NATIONAL PROHIBITION PARTY.

By SAMUEL DICKIE, LL. D., *President of Albion College, Michigan, Chairman of the National Prohibition Committee,* 1888-1900.

The History of the Only Political Organization in the United States Pledged to Administer Government in Harmony with Public Sentiment and Supreme Court Decisions Against the Saloon............................162-171

CHAPTER XIII.

THE INTERCOLLEGIATE PROHIBITION ASSOCIATION.

By D. LEIGH COLVIN, *President* 1899-1908.

A Young Man's Story of One of the Most Significant Movements Among the Young Men of the American Republic..................................172-182

CHAPTER XIV.

THE ANTI-SALOON LEAGUE—PURPOSE AND METHODS.

By BISHOP LUTHER B. WILSON, D. D., *President.*

An Official Statement of the Attitude and Policy of the Most Effective Non-partisan Organization of Modern Times Arrayed Against the Retail Liquor Traffic 183-185

CONTENTS.

PAGES

CHAPTER XV.
THE ANTI-SALOON LEAGUE—ORIGIN AND PERSONNEL.
By LOUIS ALBERT BANKS, D. D.

A Historical and Character Sketch of "The Federated Church in Action Against the Saloon"...186-195

CHAPTER XVI.
THE TEMPERANCE TIDAL WAVE.
By SAMUEL J. BARROWS, *President International Prison Commission.*

A Survey of the Worldwide Movement Against the Liquor Traffic by a Distinguished Penologist 196-203

CHAPTER XVII.
THE TEMPERANCE TIDAL WAVE—(CONTINUED).
By SAMUEL J. BARROWS, *President International Prison Commission*..........204-215

CHAPTER XVIII.
THE GREATEST PROBLEM SINCE SLAVERY.
By CARRINGTON A. PHELPS.

An Analysis of Factors Involved in the Liquor Problem in the United States...216-223

CHAPTER XIX.
LIQUOR'S FIGHT AGAINST PROHIBITION.
By CARRINGTON A. PHELPS.

Methods Employed by the Various Liquor Organizations to Maintain Their Trade Against the Moral Sentiment of the People Embodied in Prohibitory Legislation—A Disclosure of Fraud, Terrorism, Boycott.................224-234

CHAPTER XX.
THE SOUTHLAND'S WINNING FIGHT.
By HARRIS DICKSON, *Judge of the Municipal Court, Vicksburg, Miss.*

A Historical and Political Study of the Various Social, Political and Educational Influences Which Have Cooperated in Placing the Saloon in the South Under Ban of Law...235-241

CHAPTER XXI
THE W. C. T. U. IN ACTION.

Field Reports From State Officers Describing the Operations of the "Do-everything" Policy in All the Commonwealths................................242-252

CHAPTER XXII.
THE PROHIBITION PARTY AT WORK.

Reports of Campaigns in the Various States Furnished by State Officials......253-264

CHAPTER XXIII.
SYMPHONY OF THE STATES.

History of the Movement Against the Saloon in Its Various Phases, Compiled From Statements Furnished by Representatives of the W. C. T. U., the Prohibition Party, and the Anti-Saloon League, and Other Temperance and Reform Organizations.......................................265-282

CHAPTER XXIV.
SYMPHONY OF THE STATES—(CONTINUED).   283-299

CONTENTS.

CHAPTER XXV.

THE CLEANSING OF KANSAS CITY, KANSAS.
By C. W. TRICKETT, *Assistant Attorney General, Kansas.*

A Chapter in the Life of an Official, Who Performed the Duties of His Office, and Demonstrated the Possibility of Closing Saloons by Enforcement of Law 300-317

CHAPTER XXVI.

CARRY A. NATION—THE HEROINE OF THE HATCHET.

The History of a Citizen Militant Without a Vote, Who, in Exercise of a Common Law Right, Aroused a Whole Commonwealth to Action and Immortalized Herself as a Successor of the Ancient Prophets—With an Introductory Appreciation by Will Carlton............................318-326

CHAPTER XXVII.

FIGHTING FIREWATER.

A Story of War Against Liquor Sellers Conducted by William E. Johnson, Special Agent of the United States Government for the Suppression of the Traffic in Intoxicating Liquor Among the Nation's Wards—Compiled from Official Sources 327-339

CHAPTER XXVIII.

THE NEGRO PROBLEM AND THE LIQUOR PROBLEM.

Prohibition and the Negro—By BOOKER T. WASHINGTON, *President Tuskegee Institute.*
The Negro and Prohibition—By J. C. PRICE, *President National Afro-American League.*
The Colored Anti-Saloon League of America—By REV. C. W. MCCOLL, *President.*
Work Among the Negroes in Texas—By MRS. ELIZA E. PETERSON, *President Thurman W. C. T. U.*
Willard W. C. T. U., Louisiana—By MRS. FRANCES JOSEPH GAUDET, *President.*
A Contribution to the Solution of Social and Economic Problems Based on Recognition of Personal Rights and National Duties....................340-352

CHAPTER XXIX.

"UNCLE SAM," THE BIG BARTENDER.

A Plain Statement of Facts Showing the Anomalous Relation that Exists Between the Federal Government and the Liquor Traffic in All Its Phases...353-363

CHAPTER XXX.

ON TO WASHINGTON.

A Plea for National Prohibition as the Only Solution of the Liquor Problem in the United States...364-378

CHAPTER XXXI.

THE ANTI-LIQUOR FIGHT IN CANADA.
By BEN H. SPENCE, *Secretary Ontario Branch The Dominion Alliance.*

An Official Report of the Campaign Against the Liquor Traffic in the Imperial United Provinces of North America.....................................379-392

CHAPTER XXXII.

SIGNS OF THE TIMES.

Optimistic Fore-views of the Movements Against the Saloon Inspired by Faith in the Universal Desire to Realize the Ideals of the Church, the Home, and the State..393-408

CHRONOLOGICAL HISTORY OF THE GREAT REFORM 409-415
BIBLIOGRAPHY..417-426
INDEX...427-437

LIST OF PORTRAITS.

Name	Opposite Page
Allen, Rev. W. Z.	274
Anderson, Mrs. Elizabeth P.	148
Anderson, William H.	130
Armor, Mrs. Mary Harris	148
Arters, Rev. John M.	296
Artman, Judge Samuel R.	98
Atkins, Mrs. Florence Ewell	22
Baily, Joshua L.	132
Bain, George W.	118
Baker, Rev. Purley A.	402
Baldwin, Francis E.	304
Barber, Rev. W. C., B. D.	274
Barnes, Mrs. M. R.	346
Barnes, Mrs. Mary Wilder	312
Batten, Samuel Z.	230
Benjamin, Mrs. A. S.	252
Bettys, F. H.	26
Bidwell, John	166
Black, James	166
Blakesley, Raphael H.	172
Blanchard, Mrs. Lucy S.	84
Boole, Mrs. Ella	160
Bristol, Rev. I. B.	210
Brooks, J. A.	168
Brown, Mrs. Henrietta	40
Brown, Mrs. McClellan, Ph. D.	140
Bullock, Mrs. H. L.	242
Burchenal, Caleb E.	296
Burke, Hon. John	18
Burke, Dr. W. M.	210
Burt, Mrs. Mary Towne	32
Calderwood, W. G.	88-258
Calkins, Mrs. Emor L.	252
Carmack, Hon. Edward W.	128
Carns, Rev. J. B., Ph. D.	280
Carroll, George W.	168
Cartland, Mrs. Mary E.	124
Chafin, Hon. Eugene W.	254
Chapman, Rev. Ervin S.	80
Chown, Rev. S. D., D. D.	386
Clark, Dr. Billy James	102
Coates, A. U.	262
Cobb, Hon. William T.	18
Codding, J. K.	46
Coffin, Hon. John P.	218
Coffin, Mrs. John P.	218
Cohen, Mrs. M. E.	372
Colored W. C. T. U. Officers	346
Colvin, D. Leigh	172
Comer, Hon. Braxton B.	4
Cool, Rev. James W., D. D.	286
Couch, Earl E.	26
Cox, W. D.	88
Crafts, Mrs. W. F.	372
Cranfill, J. B.	168-258
Crosby, Mrs. Hannah E.	364
Crumpton, Rev. W. B., D. D.	224
Cuyler, Theodore L., D. D. LL. D.	106
Daniel, William	168
Davis, Huram W.	262
Davis, Samuel H.	190
Dickie, Samuel	162-258
Dodge, Hon. William E.	136
Dorr, Mrs. Sara J.	84
Dow, Neal	166
Dunham, Mrs. Marion H.	112
Dunn, Rev. James B., D. D.	136
Durkee, Rev. J. H.	130
Edwards, Mrs. Milton H.	58
Emig, Mrs. Clayton E.	364
Ensign, Miss Frances H.	40
Eugene, Miss Cora L.	346
Fairchild, Mrs. C. A. G.	242
Finch, John B.	118
Fisk, Clinton B.	166
Fosdick, Hon. Frederick	190
Fry, Mrs. Susanna M. D.	150
Fuller, Rev. Louis S.	204
Gandier, Rev. D. M.	210
Garbutt, Mrs. Mary Alderman	290
Gaudet, Mrs. Frances Joseph	346
Gibson, Joseph	380
Gilchrist, Miss Christianna G.	256
Glenn, Hon. Robert B.	14
Gordon, Miss Anna A.	150
Grafton, W. M.	204
Graham, Mrs. Cora D.	242
Graham, Mrs. Frances W.	32
Grandfield, Mrs. Charles P.	372
Griffith, Mrs. Hester T.	290
Guile, J. M.	92
Hadley, Edwin E.	178
Hammell, George M., D. D.	Frontispiece
Hanly, Hon. J. Frank	402
Hare, Rev. T. M.	286
Harley, Rev. J. L.	236
Harris, Hon. Andrew L.	402
Haskell, Hon. Charles N.	14
Hawk, Leslie E.	178
Hawke, Hon. George S.	80
Hawley, Mrs. Antoinett Arnold	198
Heald, Mrs. Frances Beveridge	232
Hendrickson, Finley C.	258
Hillyer, Rev. J. L. D.	184
Hilton, J. W., A. M.	280
Hinshaw, Virgil G.	172
Hoch, Hon. Edward W.	10
Hoelscher, Gustave	172
Holman, Mrs. Silena Moore	22
Howard, Clinton N.	102
Humphrey, Ulysses G.	64
Hungerford, Mrs. Adrianna	198
Intercollegiate Prohibition Association Officers and Orators	172

LIST OF PORTRAITS.

	OPPOSITE PAGE
Johnson, Hale	168
Johnson, William E.	326
Jones, Charles R.	258
Jones, Evert L.	172
Jones, Sam P.	102
Kells, Mrs. Harriet B.	124
Knodell, Rev. J. R.	76
LaChance, Mrs. Imogene F. H.	266
Lancaster Campground Group	402
Lawrence, Rev. Brooks	224
Lawson, Mrs. W. A.	230
Levering, Joshua	166
Lewis, John B., Jr.	88
Lewis, Jonathan S.	88
Lincoln, Abraham	106
Lindsey, Mrs. Lilah D.	248
Lough, F. W.	262
McCalmont, David B.	178
McColl, Rev. C. W.	340
McGregor, Bradford	170
McKinney, Mrs. Alice Cary	140
McLaughlin, Rev. E. E.	92
McNeill, James	102
McWhirter, Felix T.	258
Mandigo, Mrs. Della R.	246
Manierre, Alfred L.	304
March, Miss Elizabeth	140
Markwell, Mrs. Lulu A.	248
Marshall, John	46
Marter, G. F.	386
Martin, Hon. John B.	70
Mead, Rev. Charles H.	162
Mesch, Fred, Jr.	172
Metcalf, H. B.	168
Morrill, Rev. A. H., D. D.	178
Morris, Mrs. F. E. W., A. M.	346
Munns, Mrs. Margaret C.	214
Nation, Mrs. Carry A.	318
Neal, Miss Minnie E.	112
Nesbitt, Mrs. Annetta	232
Nicholson, S. E.	300
Noel, Hon. Edmond F.	10
Norris, Robert	46
Nutter, Mrs. S. C.	312
Oates, John A.	236
Odle, M. S., LL. B.	274
Pennington, Levi T.	172
Peterson, Mrs. Eliza E.	346
Pierce, Charles Scroggin	172
Pitts, Clarence E.	26
Platt, Mrs. Margaret B.	214
Plimpton, Mrs. S. W.	290
Presidential Candidates, Prohibition Party	166
Prohibition Party Executive Committee	258
Raymond, Rev. R. W.	76
Reinhardt, O. A.	98

	OPPOSITE PAGE
Richards, J. B.	184
Riley, Dr. B. F.	64
Robbins, Miss Annie A.	40
Robinson, Mrs. J. W.	364
Russell, Howard H.	186
Russell, Rev. John	168-170
St. John, John P.	166
Sampson, Mrs. Mary C.	290
Schalber, William	304
Scholpp, Rev. C. J. C.	304
Scovell, Mrs. Bessie Laythe	246
Shea, Hon. John T.	326
Shearer, Rev. J. C., D. D.	380
Shelton, Mrs Emma Sanford	372
Shepard, Mrs. Lulu Loveland	112
Shields, James Kurtz	64
Sibley, Mrs. Jennie Hart	58
Smith, Mrs. Clinton	364
Smith, Green Clay	166
Smith, Hon. Hoke	4
Solomon, Rev. J. C., A. M.	184
Spence, F. S.	386
Spooner, H. H.	190
Starrett, Mrs. Emma L.	282
Stearns, John N.	132
Stevens, A. A.	258
Stevens, Mrs. Lillian M. N.	142
Stewart, Gideon T.	168
Stewart, Oliver W.	258
Stockwell, George E., D. D.	70
Swallow, Silas C.	166
Taylor, Thomas E.	340
Tenney, Mrs. Ellen L.	242
Thomas, Mrs. Luella E.	266
Thompson, Mrs. Anna	266
Thompson, H. A.	168
Tiffany, Dr. E. L.	26
Todhunter, Oscar B.	XVI
Trickett, Hon. C. W.	300
Vice-Presidential Candidates, Prohibition Party	168
Warner, Harry S.	172
Watkins, Hon. Aaron S.	254
Way, Mrs. Charity	290
Welch, Mrs. Belle M.	246
Westcott, Mrs. S. M.	372
Wetlaufer, Dr. Ellen J.	230
Wheeler, Hon. Wayne B.	402
Wilbur, Mrs. S. D.	266
Wilkins, Mrs. Kate E.	140
Will, Miss Glenn	194
Willard, Frances E.	152
Willard Memorial	156
Williams, Henry Smith, M. D.	52
Wilson, Alonzo E.	262
Wilson, Bishop Luther B.	402
Wolfenbarger, A. G.	258
Woolley, John G.	166
Wright, Hon. Seaborn	402

PROLOGUE.

By George M. Hammell, *Editor*.

I HAVE undertaken to tell the story of the *passing of the saloon*—the story of what the French call a *débâcle*, a downfall. I believe that the saloon will cease to exist, and that there are moral, political, social and economic forces now operating, which will speedily destroy it. As surely as the Third Empire was doomed to pass at Sedan, so surely the Empire of the Saloon is destined to pass on the field of crucial conflict between the forces that make for good and the forces that make for evil.

Long before the Prussian armies crushed the troops of Napoleon the Little and bore their king to be crowned Emperor in the palace of the French monarchs at Versailles, it was predicted that God had decreed the downfall of the rotten régime of Napoleon and Eugenie. In the nature of things it could not live.

And so I predict the downfall of the Liquor Power. It is written in the eternal nature of things that such an evil must die. It must be overcome by good, that the Nation may live.

Against the traffic in intoxicating liquors a widespread final movement has been inaugurated. As never before, universal moral sentiment, always averse to the sale of strong drink, is expressing itself in effective legislation, and the police powers of the state at last are being exercised for the purpose which they were instituted to fulfil—the protection of the commonwealth against its foes, and the suppression of this prime source of crime and misery. Public opinion in England, France, Germany, Sweden, Finland, Russia, Switzerland, Canada and the United States, is advancing to the destruction of a system which the God of nations and the highest convictions of mankind have branded fatal to human life and progress.

Heretofore, there have been "movements" against the saloon, which, for a time, mayhap, augured victory. But the saloon survived. It will be said that the anti-liquor agitation of which this book is the story and apology, will also fail; that the wave will recede, "spume sliding down the baffled decuman," as Lowell says in "The Cathedral." But the world today is too far on in the processes of sound moral and political evolution to retreat from the point of vantage gained in the combat between the allied agencies that make for law and order, and the forces that make for anarchy and death.

The so-called "temperance wave" of 1904-1908 is not a mere rise of fanatical sentiment, destined to fall back into the depths of bigotry from which it is said to spring. It is rather an upheaval of profound moral convictions, registering itself in the enactment of constitutions and statutes based upon Eternal Laws of Good. It is the product of a deepening sense of social responsibility for the child of nobody, the spawn of the tenement, the cadger and the drunkard, the divorced wife, the criminal, the maniac and the pauper. And society sees as never before, and even the saloon sees as never before, the fire-finger of Fate that writes its doom on crumbling walls.

For many a year, since the days of Father Theobald Mathew to the days of John B. Gough, there have been prophetic souls that saw to the slimy depths of the vile trade in drink; but society and the state did not see. The seers reported their vision. Like Dante they entered the world of nameless woes, and drew flame pictures of the social purgatories and hells. At last the eye of the world has been won, and the heart and conscience of mankind responds to the eye's new sense of truth.

This volume is a record; it is also a prophecy. It reports achievement; it utters a prediction. Born of loyalty to the public welfare, it is a contribution to the Campaign for Universal Brotherhood. Against its facts and arguments there can be no logic, even as against the Ten Laws of Moses there can be no legislation. It deals with an Eternal Issue. When the campaign of 1908 has closed, and the question of the presidential succession has been settled, this volume will stand as the Text Book of a Campaign which will never end until the saloon has been put under the ban of law and public opinion from Portland to Honolulu, and from St. Augustine to the Klondike.

And when its ideals shall have been realized, we venture the hope that it will find a place among the *purpose* books of the world, to be cherished in honor and read with joy in homes which no saloon can ever blight and no fear of the liquor traffic will ever disturb.

It is not partisan nor sectional. Its appeal is made not merely to those who are in the fight against the saloon, but to brewers, distillers and saloonkeepers, in the hope that before the people, in the renaissance of their lost powers, shall abolish the "trade," they may escape the impending catastrophe.

The saloonkeeper is a fungoid growth on the social body. Personally, even if he himself be a total abstainer, he is *persona non grata* in society. Industry and commerce repudiate him, and the labor lodge blackballs him. Boys have no ambition to become retailers of intoxicating **liquors.** A schoolteacher of fifty years' experience, familiar with schoolboys' hopes, writes me that he has never known a boy who aspired to preside at a saloon bar. Why? The vocation is in disrepute.

The retail liquor trade is despised of all men. The politician uses it, but he snubs it. The brewer and the distiller exploit it for the sake of the profit, but they flay it for the evils that grow out of it. At their conventions, the retailer is mercilessly denounced by every speaker on the platform. At a recent meeting the attacks were so hot that, at last, the President of the Retailers' Association resented them, and bolted the convention until the organizers offered apology.

It is for this ostracized member of society, as well as for the drunkard and his family, that the great reform is being carried on. When the saloon has passed, the saloonkeeper will not be compelled to work eighteen hours a day, seven days a week. He will have a chance to earn his bread out in the light of day, a producer of goods of economic value, an honored member of society, a true citizen of a saloonless state.

The triumphs of 1907 and 1908 show that the adroit method of forcing one or the other of the dominant political parties to adopt the "temperance" issue is, at the present stage, the most successful in securing immediate results. That is to say, the methods so long practiced successfully by the liquor interests have been adopted and operated by the anti-liquor forces, and the liquor league has been outwitted at its own game. For, in any real test by popular vote, there is in every state a majority of men who, when the direct issue is made, prefer and will vote for law and order. Democrats, republicans, prohibitionists, socialists, Christians and infidels, will work and vote together against the saloon whenever they find a practical way to mobilize their forces. They have grown weary of forever confronting the hostile influence of the saloon whenever they attempt to do anything for the public good. And they can defeat any public candidate who stands in their way.

And so it is happening that, in like manner as there has long been a "saloon vote," so now there is a "temperance vote" which, while it may not always or even often be a "prohibition party" vote, is yet playing sad havoc with many pre-election plans in the national and state campaigns of this current year.

The Real Issue of 1908 is a People's issue, as the battle of Mission Ridge was a soldiers' battle. With instant recognition of advantage, the rank and file thought faster and saw farther than the officers, and acted without orders.

The people, the voters, at last, under the prod of conscience, are doing some of their own political thinking and are making a fight on their own account. Ignoring tariff and other convention-made issues, they are seeing that, until the field is cleared of the dramshop, there is no hope of real prosperity, nor of that governmental administration which guarantees the protection of the home and the family against the destructive forces that are so well illustrated in the saloon and its allied institutions. The day of the "Boss" is passing because the day of the saloon is passing. Voters can no longer be lined up under a mere pretentious promise of a "full dinner pail" and "sound money." They are recognizing the real issues, and, mindful of their own welfare, have sounded the slogan, "The saloon out of politics, and politics out of the saloon!" And the saloon is going out for good.

For the sake of the Great Reform I have been in jail. The Liquor League seized me in the name of Law, and for thirty days held me a prisoner-at-large in the streets of Cincinnati until I appeared in court and made defense. Ten years have passed. The Liquor League is not as strong as it then was, and its agent, who threatened to thrash me "within an inch of death," lies buried in a dishonored grave.

Circumstances, tragic with coincidence, bring me again into the firing line of the anti-liquor forces. I most sincerely desire that the story of the *Passing of the Saloon* may be an inspiration to the grand army of workers engaged in the war. Without their generous and self-sacrificing assistance the compilation of this book could not have been accomplished. So far as possible, credit has been given to all who have assisted. But my hope is that they may receive their higher reward in the complete triumph of the great cause they have done so much to aid.

To my friend and collaborator, Oscar B. Todhunter, is due the credit of conceiving and planning "THE PASSING OF THE SALOON," and providing for its publication. Familiar with philanthropic and reform movements, as well as with the practical process of bookmaking and book publishing, he has made possible what might otherwise have remained as dreams and hopes.

CINCINNATI, December, 1908.

OSCAR B. TODHUNTER,
Who planned "THE PASSING OF THE SALOON."

INTRODUCTION.

By Oscar B. Todhunter.

WHEN the pioneer American colonists set up their democratic form of government, based upon the declaration of the equality of all men, and their inherent right to life, liberty, and the pursuit of happiness, they, at the same time, admitted to their midst the two greatest enemies to equality, life, liberty and happiness, that men have known. Rum and slavery were firmly implanted upon American soil long before the first starry banner was unfurled to the breezes of heaven.

These twin evils were early recognized. The traders who brought ship-loads of slaves to America carried cargoes of rum to Africa. Anti-slavery and anti-liquor agitation were features of the Revolutionary period. Two very conservative pioneer reform societies were formed at that time: the one, a "Society for the relief of free negroes unlawfully held in bondage;" the other, "To restrain the too free use of ardent spirits."

In 1775, the first outright abolition society was formed, with Benjamin Franklin as president, and Dr. Benjamin Rush, a Quaker, as secretary.

Just ten years later, in 1785, this same Dr. Benjamin Rush published his famous essay on "The Effects of Ardent Spirits on the Human Body and Mind." This marked the beginning, in English-speaking countries, of the formal discussion of the drink evil. It is remarkable that, as one man, in the person of Dr. Rush, was so prominently identified with the beginning of these two great reforms, so another man, three quarters of a century later, Abraham Lincoln, was equally active in the promotion of both, and the final settlement of one, of these great movements. And this twin interest was charcteristic of nearly all the reformers and philanthropists of that long period of agitation.

In these days of the enactment and enforcement of prohibitory laws in so many states, it is interesting to recall that the possibility and desirability of the legal prohibition of the manufacture of intoxicating liquor was recognized by the first Continental Congress, which in 1777 passed the following resolution:

"*Resolved*, That it be recommended to the several Legislatures in the United States immediately to pass laws the most effectual for putting an immediate stop to the pernicious practice of distilling grain, by which the most extensive evils are likely to be derived if not quickly prevented."

In 1790, as a result of the essay of Dr. Rush, there was prepared a "Memorial of the College of Physicians to the Senate of the United States Congress" deprecating the use of ardent spirits and recommending the imposition of high duties upon their importation.

Four years later, in 1794, the Quakers presented to Congress the first anti-slavery petition.

From that time, agitation against both evils continued along closely parallel lines. Various "anti" societies were formed, prominent advocates arose, periodicals made their appearance, and propaganda machinery multiplied.

In 1808, what is claimed to have been the first "Temperance Society" was formed at Moreau, New York.

At an early date the movement along both lines began to take on a political aspect.

In November, 1839, a number of Abolitionists met at Warsaw, New York, and organized a political Anti-Slavery party with a platform consisting of a single plank, as follows:

"*Resolved*, That in our judgment every consideration of duty and expediency which ought to control the action of Christian freemen requires of the Abolitionists of the United States to organize a distinct and independent political party, embracing all the necessary means for nominating candidates for office and sustaining them by public suffrage."

This was about sixty-four years after the organization of the first Abolition society.

So, likewise, in 1872, sixty-four years after the Moreau "Temperance Society" was formed, the Prohibition party held its first national nominating convention.

Following each of these incipient political movements arose the now well-worn cries of "third party," and "abolition don't abolish," and "prohibition don't prohibit." The leaders alike in both reforms, both before and after the political phase began, were subjected to unmeasured personal persecution, and political, social and ecclesiastical ostracism, became the victims of mobs, many reaching the apotheosis of martyrdom. On the one hand are Garrison, and Phillips, and Sumner, and Lovejoy, and Lincoln, and on the other Haddock, and Gambrell, and St. John, and Leonard, and Swallow—heading long lists that in history will constitute the nation's double roll of honor.

In like manner as Dr. Benjamin Rush was instrumental in inaugurating both the anti-slavery and the anti-liquor reforms, so nearly every later patriot was interested in both. Had Gerritt Smith, Charles Sumner,

Henry Wilson, Abraham Lincoln, Wendell Phillips and Horace Greeley no name in the anti-slavery cause, their fame would still be secure as anti-liquor advocates.

In the fifties, both reforms were ripe for fruition. The nature of slavery was such that the catastrophe in connection therewith was first precipitated, and the Civil War came on. Had this not happened, it is strongly probable that at that period the general prohibition of the liquor traffic would have gone into effect.

But, as a result of the anti-slavery war, the anti-liquor crusade, for the time, fell into abeyance. Moreover, the nation, driven to extremity by the stress of war, made the fatal mistake of imposing a tax upon the manufacture of liquor as a means of revenue. Seizing upon the nation's need, the distillers and brewers soon so entrenched themselves under the protection of the government that they have never since, until now, nearly fifty years after the war, been seriously disturbed. They have successfully resisted all efforts for a half century to repeal the internal revenue law, although it was adopted originally only to cover a temporary war emergency.

Having made Uncle Sam the chief partner in and beneficiary of the business, the liquor trade flourished enormously, and assumed an importance and an arrogance most astonishing. It forced the whole population into submission, and for a decade following the war, anti-liquor agitation was very mild and ineffective. From the war days up to this day, it has ruled the dominant political parties with an iron hand, dictating their policies and enforcing their acquiescence, so much so that, in this year of grace, 1908, we see the two historic parties afraid to mention the liquor question in their platforms, and their candidates, though men of temperate personal habits and strong convictions, with hands on their mouths, bowing in abject silence before the great liquor Moloch.

Following the war, however, the sleeping conscience of the people on this subject began to be aroused again, and the modern crusade, now reaching its happy consummation, set in. A generation has passed since the war, bearing with it happily the animosities and prejudices aroused by that great struggle. Now a mighty home-loving people, standing shoulder to shoulder, north and south, have joined hands for the eradication of the second and remaining of the two giant evils implanted and permitted upon our soil in the days of our forefathers. As human slavery, the offspring of greed and selfishness, was swept from this fair land in a baptism of blood, so also now the twin progeny of greed and selfishness, the enslaving trade in liquor, must pass away in a warfare less bloody but no less unrelenting.

As New England, in the olden days famous for rum, led in the agitation which freed the country from the curse of slavery, so now it is appropriately significant that the Southland, former seat of slavery, leads in the movement to free the country from the curse of rum.

It is everywhere conceded that it is the arrogance of the liquor trade that has led to its final undoing. It is the popular feeling against the modern American saloon, its ways and its influence, as an institution, rather than active sentiment against the beverage use of liquor that is causing such a rapid spread of dry territory.

The word "saloon," as applied to American drinking-places, is an unwarranted misapplication and perversion of a word of elegant and cultured origin. It comes from the French *salon*, which means (Standard Dictionary): "specifically, in Paris, the periodic social reunion, under the auspices of some distinguished woman, of noted persons." This elegant word is stolen by the liquor trade in the United States, and applied to "A place devoted to the retailing and drinking of intoxicating liquor; a grog-shop."

This parasitic pervert has recognized neither legal nor moral bounds or restraints. Encouraged by its alliance and partnership with the Federal government under the Internal Revenue laws, and with many states and municipalities under license laws and ordinances, the liquor trade pushed the retail shops into a prominence and a recklessness before unknown.

In the olden days, the serving of liquors and dram-drinking possessed the characteristics of hospitality, and the custom was common in most households. In those times, the retail trade in liquor was conducted as a hospitable and incidental adjunct of general stores or the taverns then so common. But gradually the trade developed, until practically the entire retail business was found in places conducted especially for that purpose, and where no other goods except tobacco were sold. The idea of hospitality and accommodation of customers disappeared, and the business was "run for all there is in it." The dram-shops became places which no decent woman could enter and where children could not be admitted. They furnished no convenience or accommodations except such as catered to the incidental wants and vices of drinkers and served to increase the attractions of which the bar is the center. Gradually, free lunches, billiards, pool-tables, cards, dice and other gambling paraphernalia were introduced. Finally, the modern saloon was evolved with all its gorgeous equipment and lavish attractions.

Then followed the arrogance and presumption of the trade. The saloon demanded rights and privileges never thought of in connection with any other line of business. It preëmpted choice locations, and dominated trade, industry and politics. Its entire equipment, management and associations were for the one purpose of enticing and ensnaring customers with the design of absorbing their money and time, and was not giving in return any useful or even harmless article.

The vicious and demoralizing character of the modern saloon is known of all men. Its evils are fully set forth in this book.

At last the public conscience is so aroused that the death knell of this institution has sounded. The saloon is passing. In the last twelve months, as shown by Federal internal revenue returns, dram-shops have passed at the rate of about twenty-five per day. Placed side by side, the buildings would present a frontage of fifty miles. Based upon the estimated average annual saloon receipts, this indicates a saving of $45,000,-000 for this one year, which has been turned into channels of legitimate trade.

This book is not a history in the ordinary book or library sense. It attempts only a panoramic presentation of a mighty conflict in progress. It sketches in outline the causes of the war, the forces aligned, the methods of warfare, the progress of the battle, the gains and the losses and the signs and prospects of victory.

Some day the full story of the overthrow of the American liquor traffic will be told, and it will be the record of the mightiest moral crusade in history. That story will include the history of the different organizations and individuals now and heretofore enlisted in the great warfare against liquor. This will constitute a library of absorbing interest. But the time is not yet.

In this book, the officers and soldiers on the firing line themselves tell the story of their trials and triumphs. The book possesses special interest and value, largely because the busiest and most earnest set of people on earth have snatched the time to contribute to its contents.

There is also an aim to make the book an arsenal filled with the munitions of war, a source from which all workers can, like David the shepherd boy, draw the smooth stones of hard facts to hurl in the sling of faith and confidence full into the forehead of the giant liquor Goliath.

Having had some part in the planning and preparation of "THE PASSING OF THE SALOON," the writer has been most profoundly impressed with the extent and thoroughness of the organization of the anti-liquor forces, and the courage, patience and self-sacrificing spirit of the workers. There is no point so remote that there is not some lonesome but faithful soldier on guard. The leaders are able and the discipline perfect. It is a volunteer army, serving a high purpose without hope of reward. Such a fighting force is absolutely invincible. No one can read the vast volume of correspondence that has come to the editor from the field since the book was announced, without the absolute conviction of speedy, complete and lasting victory. While there are different organizations, armies, divisions and battalions in the field, yet all are so welded together by a common hope and purpose that there is practical harmony and unity of effort everywhere.

Almost without exception all anti-liquor advocates and organizations stand upon the platform: "Total abstinence for the individual—total prohibition for the state." The first plank requires educational effort, and has had most prominence in the past. The second plank demands political effort, and is most prominent to-day.

The men and women most active in the powerful anti-saloon movement of the present are the children of the days of the Woman's Crusade of one generation ago, and they are moved by the powerful impress of that wonderful uprising, and of the educational work of the past two generations. As the great temperance army moves from educational to political lines of action, there may develop slight inharmonies and differences. But all will rally for the final engagement.

In practice it has proved good policy to set each one to cleaning up his own door yard. This is the advantage of district option. It puts the responsibility upon local residents. Few people desire a saloon next door to their own residences. In a district contest they commit themselves against the saloon. They are then ready to support township, county, and state prohibition in turn, and finally will rally for the grand onslaught for national prohibition.

It is increasingly evident that dry territory cannot be fully protected until the federal government adopts new internal revenue and interstate commerce regulations and practices. To this end the anti-liquor forces must take active part in congressional elections, and bring full pressure to bear upon congress.

Finally, the federal government must abandon its internal revenue system and get out of the liquor business, and a prohibition amendment must be added to the federal constitution.

To the accomplishment of these ends the Grand Army is moving.

Change dates, places, names, words, phrases and conditions, and the anti-liquor fight in progress in America today is a repetition of the rebuilding of the wall in Jerusalem by Nehemiah and his followers. Workers, read anew that old story, and, under its inspiration, go forth to battle to the end. "And so builded we the wall."

CHAPTER I.

THE INDICTMENT OF THE SALOON.

TEMPERANCE speakers and writers often are accused of fanatical misrepresentation and exaggeration when they describe the evil character of the saloon and the drink traffic. It is well, therefore, to see what some of the men engaged in the liquor business, and others who speak for or before them, think of their calling.

An open meeting of "The National Model License League," an organization made up of men engaged in the manufacture and sale of intoxicating liquors, was held at Louisville, Kentucky, January, 1908. From its official minutes the following extracts are quoted:

T. M. Gilmore, President, said:

"The handwriting is on the wall. I will say to you that the press and the people of this country have decided that the laws of this country shall be obeyed as the laws of Europe are obeyed. Our trade today is on trial before the bar of public sentiment, and, unless it can be successfully defended before that bar from every possible standpoint, I want to see it go down forever. As long as the present status of the saloon remains, all of the laws that society can pass will neither compel obedience to law, except spasmodically, nor take the liquor dealer out of politics. The purpose of The Model License League is to assist society to bring about the absolute and automatic enforcement of the laws, and the only way, in our opinion, that this can be accomplished is by changing the status of the saloon license. We know by long experience that high license compels the handling of inferior and of imitation goods. High license never has benefited society.

"We hold that our business is either right or wrong. If it is wrong, it ought to be wiped out root and branch."

An extract from a letter by Archbishop Messmer, of Milwaukee, was read:

"The fact cannot be denied that what is called the American saloon —for it is a specifically American institution—as generally conducted, has been a source of untold misery and sin. The material ruin of tens of thousands of families, and the moral ruin of tens of thousands of young men and women, can be traced to the saloon, while its public influence in Church and State has been positively harmful. It is this universal fact, not fanaticism, that has caused a tidal wave of prohibition to roll over the land."

Marshall Bullitt, attorney, in an address, said:

"The politicians use the saloon to carry out their ends, and the saloons in turn use their influence for the purpose of getting political power, and thus the whole thing acts and reacts and interacts, and the result is that feeling which grows up and which arouses the people to make a fight upon the saloon interests.

"There is rising in this country a class of people who have made up their minds that, if there is but one way to make the saloons stay out of politics, and that is to crush them, they are going to do it.

"Why is it that prohibitionists are exerting this big influence? I believe that it is because of the injurious influence that the saloon exercises in each political community. Each community has found for itself, through a sad experience, that the most injurious element in the political life of such communities is the effect of the saloon, and the people have made up their minds that they are not going to stand longer for the influence of the saloon in politics."

Mr. T. DeQuincy Tully, Secretary of the Law Enforcement Society of New York City, an invited speaker, said:

"The liquor men in New York City do not want the law enforced; *i. e.*, they have not been wanting it enforced. Nine-tenths of our difficulties in the way of dealing with crime, with corruption, political and otherwise, arises from the lawless saloon."

Hon. Frank H. Farris, in an address, said:

"Disreputable men in the liquor business, wherever you find them, are the most active men in the politics of their neighborhood or their city. And they have been enabled, by the forming of political alliances, ofttimes by being candidates for office, to maintain themselves and to keep these practices going—gambling and gross immorality. The result has been that the moral conscience of the people has become aroused, and men who believe as firmly in the doctrine of self-rights and personal liberty as you and I, have gone out and lifted up their hands and voices against the traffic purely from local causes, and to remove these evils."

Other quotations, even more striking and significant, might be given from this pamphlet. The attack upon the character of the saloon became so fierce indeed, that the President of the Retail Dealers' Association arose in protest, and with a part of his membership left the hall. Afterwards, overtures and apologies were extended, and they were coaxed back into the meeting.

A large library might be filled with notable utterances from all kinds of sources in condemnation of the saloon. In this chapter a number of these have been compiled, selected somewhat at random. They are so diverse in origin, so widely distributed in time, place and station, as to constitute a fair reflection of the universal verdict of intelligent humanity in reference to this greatest of evils. They indicate the reason why the saloon is passing.

Joshua L. Baily, reformer, Philadelphia:

"That the revenue of the state may be greatly increased by higher license we do not attempt to deny. But the price would be the sacrifice of honor and virtue, 'the price of blood,' the best blood of the State—the blood of our young men. It would be infamous even should her revenue be increased tenfold thereby. Will anyone say that the crime of Judas would have been less infamous had he received three hundred instead of thirty pieces of silver?"

George W. Bain, lecturer:

"For every dollar paid the school to cultivate the intellect of this country, nine dollars are paid the saloon to blight that intellect."

Henry Ward Beecher:

"Every year I live increases my conviction that the use of intoxicating drinks is a greater destroying force to life and virtue than all other physical evils combined."

Roswell A. Benedict, author, "MALEFACTORS OF WEALTH."

"There are only two trusts which this country needs to fear—the Whisky Trust and the Importing Trust. The first swindles the laborer out of his money, and the second swindles him out of his employment."

Andrew Carnegie, to young men:

"I am not a temperance lecturer in disguise, but a man who knows and tells you what observation has proved to him; and I say to you that you are more likely to fail in your career from acquiring the habit of drinking liquor than from any of the other temptations likely to assail you. You may yield to almost any other temptation and reform, but from the insane thirst for liquor, escape is almost impossible. I have known of but few exceptions to this rule."

Senator Carmack, of Tennessee:

"I am weary of saloon domination. I am weary of the saloon's open alliance with vice, its open contempt of law. I am weary of a condition of things where the man whose business it is to make the laws must hold his office by consent of the man whose business it is to break the laws."

Joseph Chamberlain:

"If there is in the whole of this business any single encouraging feature, it is bound to be found in the gathering impatience of the people at the burden which they are bound to bear, and their growing indignation and sense of shame and disgrace which this imposes upon them. The fiery serpent of drink is destroying our people, and now they are awaiting with longing eyes the uplifting of the remedy."

Ervin S. Chapman, D. D., LL. D.:

"Our national Supreme Court has adjudged the liquor traffic inherently immoral and harmful to human interests, and has declared that to engage in that traffic is not one of the rights of American citizenship. We cannot remain at the point to which that decision lifts us, but that court must go forward to the inevitable adjudication that civil government can not grant that traffic any legal protection, or standing."

Lord Chesterfield:

"Luxury, my lords, is to be taxed, but vice prohibited. Let the difficulty in the law be what it may, would you lay a tax upon a breach of the Ten Commandments? Government should not, for revenue, mortgage the morals and health of the people."

Sir Andrew Clark, the great London physician:

"I am speaking solemnly and carefully in the presence of truth, and I tell you that I am considerably within the mark when I say to you that, going the round of my hospital wards today, seven out of every ten owed their ill health to alcohol."

Richard Cobden:

"The temperance cause is the foundation of all social and political reform."

Neal Dow:

"The liquor traffic exists in this country only by the sufferance of the Christian churches. They are masters of the situation so far as the abolition of the traffic is concerned. When they say 'Go,' and vote 'Go,' it will go. The saloon would destroy the church if it could; the church could destroy the saloon if it would."

Gladstone's reply to the London brewers:

"Gentlemen, you need not give yourselves any trouble about the revenue. The question of revenue must never stand in the way of needed reforms. But give me a sober population, not wasting their earnings in strong drink, and I shall know where to obtain the revenue."

Horace Greeley:

"To sell rum for a livelihood is bad enough, but for a whole community to share the responsibility and guilt of such a traffic seems a worse bargain than that of Eve or Judas."

Henry W. Grady:

"The saloon is the mortal enemy of peace and order, the despoiler of men and terror of women, the cloud that shadows the face of children, the demon that has dug more graves and sent more souls unshrived to judgment than all the pestilences that have wasted life since God sent the plagues to Egypt, and all the wars since Joshua stood before Jericho."

HON. BRAXTON B. COMER, Governor of Alabama.

HON. HOKE SMITH, Governor of Georgia.

GOVERNORS OF PROHIBITION STATES.

Edward Everett Hale:

"If anybody will take charge of all Boston's poverty and crime which results from drunkenness, the South Congregational Church, of which I have the honor to be the minister, will alone take charge of all the rest of the poverty which needs relief in the city of Boston."

Robert G. Ingersoll:

"I am aware that there is a prejudice against any man engaged in the manufacture of alcohol. I believe from the time it issues from the coiled and poisoned worm in the distillery until it enters into the hell of death, dishonor and crime, that it dishonors everybody who touches it—from its source to where it ends. I do not believe anybody can contemplate the subject without becoming prejudiced against the liquor crime. All we have to do, gentlemen, is to think of the wrecks on either side of the stream, of the suicides, of the insanity, of the poverty, of the ignorance, of the destitution, of the little children tugging at the faded and withered breasts, of weeping and despairing wives asking for bread, of the man of genius it has wrecked—the men struggling with imaginary serpents produced by the devilish thing.

"And when you think of the jails, of the almshouses, of the asylums, of the prisons, of the scaffolds upon either bank, I do not wonder that every thoughtful man is prejudiced against the damned stuff called alcohol. It breaks the father's heart, it bereaves the doting mother, extinguishes natural affection, erases conjugal love, blots out filial attachments, blights paternal hope, and brings down weary age in sorrow to the grave. It produces weakness, not health; death, not life. It makes wives widows; children orphans; fathers fiends; and all of them paupers and beggars! It feeds rheumatism, nurses gout, welcomes epidemics, invites cholera, imports pestilences and embraces consumption. It covers the land with idleness, misery and crime. It fills your jails, supplies your almshouses and demands your asylums. It crowds your penitentiaries and furnishes victims to your scaffolds. It engenders controversies, fosters quarrels, and cherishes riots. It is the lifeblood of the gambler, the prop of the highwayman and the support of the midnight incendiary. It countenances the liar, respects the thief, esteems the blasphemer. It violates obligations, reverences fraud and honors infamy. It deforms benevolence, hates love, scorns virtue and slanders innocence. It incites the father to butcher his helpless offspring, helps the husband to massacre his wife, and the child to grind the patricidal ax.

"It burns up man, consumes woman, desolates and devastates life, curses God, despises heaven. It suborns witnesses, nurses perjury, defies the jury box and stains the judicial ermine. It bribes votes, disqualifies voters, corrupts elections, pollutes our institutions and endangers governments. It degrades the citizen, debases the legislator, dishonors the statesman and disarms the patriot. It brings shame, not honor; terror, not safety; despair, not hope; misery, not happiness; and with the malevolence of a fiend it calmly surveys its frightful desolation, and, unsatisfied with havoc, it poisons felicity, kills peace, ruins morals, blights confidence, slays reputation and wipes out national honor; then curses the world and laughs at its ruin. It does all that and more. It murders the soul. It is the sum of all villainies, the father of all crime, the mother of all abominations, the devil's best friend and man's worst enemy."

John Jay:

"To tax a thing is to tolerate it, and vice in its nature is not a thing to be tolerated."

Samuel Johnson, D. D.:

"To support government by propagating vice, is to support it by a means which destroys the end for which it was originally established, and for which its continuance is to be desired. If the expense of the government cannot be defrayed but by corrupting the morals of the people, I shall without scruple declare that money ought not to be raised, nor the designs of the government supported."

Sam Jones:

"I've seen a man and a dog go into a saloon, and in an hour the man would get beastly drunk and stagger out like a hog, while the dog would come out and walk away like a gentleman."

Rudyard Kipling:

"Then, recanting previous opinions, I became a Prohibitionist. Better it is that a man should go without his beer in public places, and content himself with swearing at the narrow-mindedness of the majority; better it is to poison the inside with the very vile temperance drinks, and to buy lager furtively at back doors, than to bring temptation to the lips of young fools such as the four I have seen. I understand now why the preacher rages against drink. I have said: 'There is no harm in it taken moderately,' and yet my own demand for beer helped directly to send these two girls reeling down the dark street to—God alone knows what end. If liquor is worth drinking, it is worth taking a little trouble to come at—such trouble as a man will undergo to compass his own desires. It is not good that we should let it lie before the eyes of children, and I have been a fool in writing to the contrary."

Abraham Lincoln:

"The liquor traffic is a cancer in society, eating out the vitals and threatening destruction, and all attempts to regulate it will not only prove abortive, but will aggravate the evil. There must be no more attempts to regulate the cancer. It must be eradicated, not a root must be left behind; for, until this is done all classes must continue in danger of becoming victims of strong drink.

"If it is a crime to make a counterfeit dollar, it is ten thousand times a worse crime to make a counterfeit man."

Hon. John D. Long, Ex-Secretary of the Navy:

"The dynamite of modern civilization."

Martin Luther:

"Whoever first brewed beer has prepared a pest for Germany. I have prayed to God that he would destroy the whole brewing industry. I have often pronounced a curse on the brewer. All Germany could live on the barley that is spoiled and turned into a curse by the brewer."

William McKinley:

"By legalizing this traffic we agree to share with the liquor seller the responsibilities and evils of his business. Every man who votes for license becomes of necessity a partner to the liquor traffic and all its consequences—the most degrading and ruinous of all human pursuits."

Wendell Phillips:

"No one supposes that law can make men temperate; but law can shut up these bars and dram-shops, which facilitate and feed intemperance, which double our taxes and treble the perils to property and life."

Theodore Roosevelt:

"The friends of the saloonkeepers denounce their opponents for not treating the saloon business like any other. The best answer to this is that the business is not like any other business, and that the actions of the saloonkeepers themselves conclusively prove this to be the case. The business tends to produce criminality in the population at large and law breaking among the saloonkeepers themselves. When the liquor men are allowed to do as they wish, they are sure to debauch, not only the body social, but the body politic also.

"The most powerful saloonkeeper controlled the politicians and the police, while the latter in turn terrorized and blackmailed all other saloonkeepers. If the American people do not control it, it will control them."

John Ruskin:

"The encouragement of drunkenness for the sake of the profit on the sale of drink is certainly one of the most criminal methods of assassination for money hitherto adopted by the bravos of any age or country."

Socrates:

"While the intemperate man inflicts evil upon his friends, he brings far more upon himself. Not only to ruin his family, but also to bring ruin on his body and soul, is the greatest wrong any man can commit."

John L. Sullivan, on his fiftieth birthday:

"Here I am, fifty years old as time is computed, but a centenarian in experience. Most sporting men are fifty in experience at twenty. What would I do if it were all to be gone over again? Why, I would cut out the grape juice, and I would lay by for that rainy day that comes into the lives of most men sometime. I have come to realize that to live life well our care should not be so much to live long, as to live right—and remember in all cases to let liquor alone. I quit drinking in 1905. I have never signed the pledge, but made up my mind to get on the water wagon, and I am going to stay there. I feel fine."

Henry Watterson:

"Every office, from the President's down, is handed out over the saloon counter."

St. Louis *Christian Advocate*:

"Rev. George Warren, chaplain of the Missouri penitentiary, says that out of 2,279 convicts in the prison 85 per cent. came there directly through the influence of liquor, and that 5 per cent. of the remainder came there indirectly from the same cause. That is, 2,000 of the convicts in the Missouri penitentiary are the result of the licensed liquor traffic in that state."

Louis Albert Banks, D. D.:

"But high license, you cry. What difference does the size of the license make in the case? Do you suppose the brandy that makes a man's heart beat thirteen times a minute faster than it ought under low license, will only make it beat five times too often under high license? Do you suppose the Bourbon whisky that, under a license fee of a hundred dollars, eats holes in a man's throat and stomach, and makes him from lips to stomach one raw, burning sore, will become mild and healing if the tax be raised to a thousand dollars? Will beer that clogs a man's liver and rots his kidneys when drunk over a pine table in a saloon that pays fifty dollars a quarter, suddenly become healthful when poured from a silver pitcher over a marble table in a saloon that pays three hundred dollars a quarter? Will the drunken brute beat his wife and kick his children the more gently when made drunk under high license than he would under low license? Out on all such nonsense! The stronger and the more elaborate your license system may be, the more thoroughly it intrenches the saloon as a disease-and-crime-scattering center in the community."

General Booth:

"Nine-tenths of our poverty, squalor, vice and crime spring from this poisonous tap-root. Society, by its habits, customs and laws has greased the slope down which these poor creatures slide to perdition."

Phillips Brooks:

"If we should sweep intemperance out of our country there would be hardly poverty enough left to give healthy exercise to our charitable impulses."

James M. Buckley, Editor *Christian Advocate*:

"The fatal defect of the saloon, as a means of gratifying the social instinct, is that it depraves the tastes of its habitués so that they prefer bad society to good. The saloon is an insuperable obstacle to the growth of good society. No frequenter of the saloon loves his home, if he has one. The habitual frequenter of the saloon rarely desires a home, or is possessed of the qualifications to make one happy. The existence of the saloon is a disgrace to the American people."

Father Doyle, of New York:

"Of all the evils that have cursed mankind, crushed woman's heart, sent youth to destruction, driven virtue to the haunts of shame and paved the pathway to hell, there is nothing that can compare with the evil of intoxicating drink."

Bishop Cyrus D. Foss:

"As a Christian minister I oppose drink, because it opposes me. The work I try to do, it undoes. It is an obstacle to the spread of the gospel; nay, it is an enemy which assails the gospel, and whose complete success would drive the gospel from the earth."

Archbishop Ireland:

"The great cause of social crime is drink. The great cause of poverty is drink. When I hear of a family broken up and ask the cause—drink. If I go to the gallows and ask its victim the cause, the answer—drink. Then I ask myself in perfect wonderment, Why do not men put a stop to this thing?"

Archbishop John J. Keane:

"As a man and a Christian, I say, 'Damn the saloon!' If I could cause the earth to open and swallow up every saloon in the world, I would feel that I was doing humanity a blessing. We must protest against this thing! It has no redeeming feature. It is bad for the home, for humanity, for the Church and for the country. The thing we must do is to set our faces against it with the positive determination to conquer it."

Cardinal Manning:

"For thirty years I have been priest and bishop in London, and now I approach my eightieth year. I have learned some lessons, and the first thing is this: The chief bar to the working of the Holy Spirit of God in the souls of men and women is intoxicating drink. I know no antagonist to that Holy Spirit more direct, more subtle, more stealthy, more ubiquitous than intoxicating drink."

John Wesley:

"All who sell liquors in the common way to any that will buy are poisoners-general. They murder his Majesty's subjects by wholesale; neither does their eye pity nor spare. They drive them to hell like sheep. And what is their gain? Is it not the blood of these men? Who, then, would envy their large estates and sumptuous palaces? A curse is in the midst of them. The curse of God is in their gardens, their groves—a fire that burns in the nethermost hell. Blood, blood, is there! The foundation, the floors, the walls, the roof are stained with blood."

Canon Wilberforce:

"The deriving of vast sums for the revenue from the bitter sufferings and grinding pauperism of the people is a terrible offense. If Judas had received one thousand pounds instead of thirty pieces of silver, would that have justified his conduct?"

Governor Henry A. Buchtel, Colorado:

"When you consider the unspeakable damage which comes from the open saloon, you cannot avoid making haste to enact a law which will make possible the exclusion of the open saloon from those districts where the majority of the people are squarely opposed to it."

Governor B. B. Comer, Alabama:

"Before I entered upon my official duties as governor, while a strong temperance man, I was in no sense of the word a prohibitionist; but after a year as chief executive, I am an intense prohibitionist, having been made so by the mothers, wives and children who have come to my office for the purpose of securing pardon or stay of execution for their sons, husbands or fathers, who have been sentenced for murder committed in nearly all cases while they were under the influence of whisky."

Governor John Cutler, Utah:

"It is a foregone conclusion that the morals of a community are improved by a decreased sale of strong drink. The revenues of the state are increased, because temperance leads to frugality and thrift, which lead to property accumulation by the citizens."

Governor William O. Dawson, West Virginia:

"The saloon furnishes the scene and the atmosphere where bribery is easy and secure, rallies the venal voters who constitute the bosses' power, is the refuge of criminals, protects vice, affords gamblers a shield and the patronage of inexperienced youth, and is a place where the opponents of every movement for civic betterment gather to devise fraud to beat it. To emblazon this responsibility of the saloon is the immediate next task of the saloon's enemies."

Governor E. W. Hoch, Kansas:

"With you I rejoice in the rapid progress of prohibition sentiment. It looks as if an old prediction of mine will come true sooner than I expected it would: the prediction that the time would come when it would be thought as incredible that a civilized, Christian people ever tolerated a saloon, as that a civilized, Christian people ever tolerated human slavery.

"The devil never invented a bigger lie than that revenue from illegitimate sources is necessary to the financial success of any town or city."

Governor J. W. Folk, Missouri:

"It is a business the natural tendency of which is toward lawlessness, and the time has come when it will either run the politics of the state or be run out of the politics of the state."

HON. EDWARD W. HOCH,
Governor of Kansas.

HON. E. F. NOEL,
Governor of Mississippi.

GOVERNORS OF PROHIBITION STATES.

Governor R. B. Glenn, North Carolina:

"I say to you deliberately, after thirty years' experience as an attorney and as a prosecuting officer in the courts, that I am firmly of the opinion that sixty per cent. of crime is directly the result of strong drink and ninety-five per cent. is indirectly caused by indulgence in strong drink. Can we then, in the face of such an appalling array, hesitate to say where we stand?"

Governor J. Frank Hanly, Indiana:

"Personally, I have seen so much of the evils of the traffic in the last four years, so much of its economic waste, so much of its physical ruin, so much of its mental blight, so much of its tears and heartache, that I have come to regard the business as one that must be held and controlled by strong and effective laws. I bear no malice toward those engaged in the business, but I hate the traffic. I hate its every phase. I hate it for its intolerance. I hate it for its arrogance. I hate it for its hypocrisy. I hate it for its cant and craft and false pretenses. I hate it for its commercialism. I hate it for its avarice. I hate it for its sordid love of gain at any price. I hate it for its domination in politics. I hate it for its corrupting influence in civic affairs. I hate it for its incessant effort to debauch the suffrage of the country; for the cowards it makes of public men.

"I hate it for its utter disregard of law. I hate it for its ruthless trampling of the solemn compact of state constitutions. I hate it for the load it straps to labor's back; for the palsied hand it gives to toil; for its wounds to genius; for the tragedies of its might-have-beens. I hate it for the human wrecks it has caused. I hate it for the almshouses it peoples; for the prisons it fills; for the insanity it begets; for its countless graves in potters' fields. I hate it for the mental ruin it imposes upon its victims; for its spiritual blight; for its moral degradation. I hate it for the crimes it has committed. I hate it for the homes it has destroyed. I hate it for the hearts it has broken. I hate it for the malice it has planted in the hearts of men; for its poison, for its bitterness, for the dead sea fruit with which it starves their souls.

"I hate it for the grief it causes womanhood—the scalding tears, the hopes deferred, the strangled aspirations, its burdens of want and care.

"I hate it for its heartless cruelty to the aged, the infirm and the helpless; for the shadow it throws upon the lives of children; for its monstrous injustice to blameless little ones.

"I hate it as virtue hates vice, as truth hates error, as righteousness hates sin, as justice hates wrong, as liberty hates tyranny, as freedom hates oppression.

"I hate it as Abraham Lincoln hated slavery. And as he sometimes saw in prophetic visions the end of slavery and the coming of the time when the sun should shine and the rain should fall upon no slave in the republic, so I sometimes seem to see the end of this unholy traffic; the coming of the time when, if it does not wholly cease to be, it shall find no safe habitation anywhere beneath Old Glory's stainless stars."

Governor Hoke Smith, Georgia:

"It is absolutely impossible to have a permanent, decent municipal government where the saloon dominates municipal politics. The elimination of the saloon will help municipal politics everywhere."

Governor Edmond F. Noel, Mississippi:

"The saloons, the nursery of crime, the fruitful soil for the germination of successive crops of drunkards, and the worst enemy of home, of wife and child, should be speedily closed."

D. J. Starr, Chaplain Ohio Penitentiary:

"The records show that 1,250 persons have been received into this institution during the last eighteen months. Of these 930 acknowledge themselves to have been intemperate."

Amos W. Butler, Secretary Charities and Corrections, Indiana:

"A large majority of the cases of crime in Indiana is traceable to strong drink, and a large part of our idiocy, insanity and pauperism results from the same cause."

New York State Commission on Prisons:

"During the year there were 28,519 commitments to the jails, and 3,615 to the penitentiaries for intoxication. It would appear that one-half of the convictions in the criminal courts of the state are for this single offense."

Massachusetts Bureau of Labor:

"In other words, 84.41 per cent. of all the 26,672 crimes were due to intemperate habits, and 82 per cent. were committed while the criminal was under the influence of liquor."

Terence V. Powderly, Grand Master Workman of the Knights of Labor:

"The most damning curse to the laborers is that which gurgles from the neck of the bottle."

R. F. Travelick, President National Labor Union:

"The use of liquor and its influences have done more to darken labor's homes, dwarf its energies and chain it hand and foot to the wheels of corporate aggression, than all other influences combined."

Carroll D. Wright, United States Commissioner of Labor:

"I have looked into a thousand homes of the working people of Europe; I do not know how many in this country. In every case so far as my observation goes, drunkenness was at the bottom of the misery, and not the industrial system or the industrial surrounding of the men and their families."

Judge Butler, of Cairo, Illinois, at the close of a murder trial:

"The case at bar is the seventy-sixth murder case I have tried, either as state's attorney or as judge, during the past nineteen years. I have kept a careful record of each case, and I have to say that in seventy-five out of the seventy-six, liquor was the exciting cause."

Judge Alton G. Dayton, Federal Court, Parkersburg, W. Va.:

"I have said it, and I again proclaim it, that no man can be engaged in the sale of liquor and be honest. He will take the last dollar of a drunken man, kick him out and send him on to a drunkard's grave. He studies dishonesty, and comes into court and perjures himself to avoid punishment. We don't license any man to rob, steal or murder, but you can take the licensed saloons generally of the country, and the murders committed under the sale of liquor will average one murder for every saloon in the country."

State Senator Mattingly, high license champion of Indiana:

"Fully ninety per cent. of all crime can be justly traced to the use of intoxicating liquor."

California *Voice*:

"The maudlin song of a drunken student is no funnier than the contortions of a drowning man. We do not laugh at a fire. Why should we laught at hell-fire in a man?"

Indianapolis *News*:

"The saloon is a running sore on the body politic. It is a vicious, contagious, dangerous plague spot. There is not room for it and liberty both to live. One or the other must go."

London *Times*:

"The use of strong drink produces more idleness, crime, disease, want, misery, than all other causes put together."

The *News-Free-Press*, Lafayette, Colorado:

"A good man or a bad man in such a business has embarked for hell. He will violate the most sacred obligation one man owes to the peace, happiness, the health and the future of another. That business will soon end the career of a bad man, and in the end make a dishonest, skulking, lawbreaking liar and thief of a good man."

The South Dakota *Issue*:

"A man first resorts to wine to stimulate his wits; later, he has to resort to his wits to get his wine. When his wits at last forsake him, he cleans out spittoons in the saloon to get his drinks."

Emperor of China:

"It is true I cannot prevent the introduction of the glowing poison. Gain-seeking and corrupt men will, for profit and sensuality, defeat my wishes; but nothing will induce me to derive a revenue from the misery and vice of my people."

Queen of Madagascar:

"I cannot consent, as your queen, to take revenue from the sale of liquor, which destroys the souls and bodies of my subjects."

Charles Buxton, Member of Parliament:

"Drink is the parent of crime. It would not be too much to say that if all drinking of fermented liquors could be done away with, crime of every kind would fall to a fourth of its present amount."

Lief Jones, Member of Parliament:

"I recently met the finished article of the liquor trade. He was lying in the gutter. He had no hat: the hat trade was suffering. His coat was full of holes: the tailoring trade was suffering. He had no shirt: the hosiery trade was suffering. He was dirty: the soap trade was suffering. Indeed, I can hardly mention an industry which was not affected by that man's insobriety."

Bonfort's Wine and Spirit Circular, September 10, 1908:

"Saloons have been run in violation of law and decency until it looks as if they are doomed to extinction, except in the largest cities. A sufficient percentage have been disorderly, have sold to intoxicated men, have sold to women and to minors, have conducted gambling adjuncts, have kept open after legal hours and on Sundays, etc., to create a hostile sentiment that has crystallized into a war of extermination, and the saloon as a factor in society would seem to be doomed. We realize that this is a big admission, but the facts demand the admission, that our trade may properly grasp the situation.

"If the saloon cannot be successfully defended, if the cry of personal liberty will not save it, then let it go."

HON. ROBERT B. GLENN,
Governor of North Carolina.

HON. CHARLES N. HASKELL,
Governor of Oklahoma.

GOVERNORS OF PROHIBITION STATES.

CHAPTER II.

EVIDENCE FROM EXPERIENCE AND OBSERVATION.

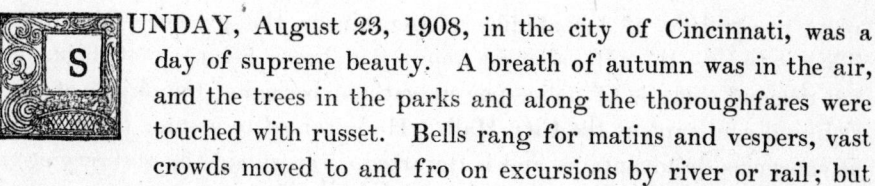

I.

SUNDAY, August 23, 1908, in the city of Cincinnati, was a day of supreme beauty. A breath of autumn was in the air, and the trees in the parks and along the thoroughfares were touched with russet. Bells rang for matins and vespers, vast crowds moved to and fro on excursions by river or rail; but in the lower districts of the city there was almost unwonted quiet.

Near Government Square, however, the heart of the city's life, is a nest of high-class saloons: the "Mecca," the "Foucar," the "Bismarck." To call them *dram-shops*, no doubt, would excite indignation in the minds of their proprietors; they are *cafés, bufféts!* However, they confess the class to which they belong; for, on that Sunday, their front doors were closed and patrons slunk in and out of side doors. For the most part these were young men—many of them minors, and all well-dressed. Hour after hour the cash register jingled its bell, in defiance of law, and the proprietors dared the magistrates to do their duty. And the magistrates? They acted under instructions to make no arrests. The mayor had been elected to nullify the Sunday-closing laws and the police followed instructions.

A few squares south on the river front is the "Silver Moon," a "low dive" in a region reputed to be the "Bad Lands" of Cincinnati. Not a policeman was visible, and negroes—of the Atlanta and Springfield type—had possession. There was little disorder. In fact, there was more apparent conformity to the Sunday-closing law than at the "respectable" saloons.

The astonishing phase of the situation, however, was the failure of the police to do their duty. They were not on the streets as on other days. They had abdicated to the saloons. Sunday seemed a day of truce with the devil! Mayor and chief of police surrendered to the saloonkeeper rather than disturb the political situation. Under the cloudless sky of that perfect summer day the magistrates of Cincinnati were teaching boyhood and girlhood that law may be violated with impunity—if the offenders be saloonkeepers and their friends—and that men sworn to enforce law, may violate their oaths of office with impunity—if they conspire with the saloon.

The condition that existed in this one city on this one Sunday is duplicated in this and many other cities on every Sunday in the year, and year after year. And the astonishing and alarming feature is that such a situation attracts little or no notice, and is accepted by *good* law-abiding citizens as a matter of course. They are cowed and trained to silence.

On this Sunday there was no riot, no conflict between "authorities" and "anarchists," but there existed a condition which bodes evil—the complete prostration of law-abiding citizenship in the presence of sedition. That is to say, the anti-saloonist knows that law is being violated, but can not demand exercise of police powers without becoming the object of aversion and contempt at the City Hall. He is forced to assume the initiative at enormous disadvantage, and is thwarted on every side by the very agencies that nominally are organized to aid him. He becomes a mere spectator of crime, a helpless *particeps criminis*. And when, on some evil day the "mob" sweeps the streets, he becomes one of the "innocent victims" of the compromise between the City Hall and the Saloon.

II.

Theodore Roosevelt once said: "When the liquor men are allowed to do as they wish, they are sure to debauch, not only the body social, but the body politic also." Well, in 1907, according to Internal Revenue Reports, there were 236,448 citizens of the American commonwealth who were engaged in the business of retailing intoxicating liquors, a business which, as Mr. Roosevelt also says, "does not stand well in comparison with other occupations." Every man of the 236,448 transacts business under restraint. If allowed to do as his trade wishes he would rot the body politic and the body social, until government would lapse into anarchy and society into chaos. There is no other occupation in the whole category against which Mr. Roosevelt would or could make such a charge, and no body of citizens engaged in other lines who would not hold him responsible for libel for uttering a sentiment so derogatory to character.

Suppose Mr. Roosevelt had said: "There are 255,526 bookkeepers in the United States. When they are allowed to do as they wish, they are sure to debauch, not only the body social, but the body politic also." Would the bookkeepers have cast their votes for him for president of the United States? Suppose that Mr. Roosevelt had said: "There are 111,-942 clergymen in the United States. When they are allowed to do as they wish, they are sure to debauch, not only the body social, but the body politic also." Everybody knows that such a charge would have no foundation in fact. It would have no foundation in fact if brought against the 74,907 bakers, the 114,212 butchers, the 31,242 candlestick-makers—all honorable men who have, and can have, no other wish than the good of the republic and the welfare of society.

But the liquor dealers, unlike all others, stand accused of evil designs, and dare not resent the charge. So far as their business alone is concerned, if they could, they would strike down organized government. They have done better, however, and have taken the government into partnership, because they can use government for the purpose of protecting their business. Political parties which do not antagonize them are supported at the ballot-box and in legislatures. Their vote is the index of what they want in politics. On the face of it, it does not differ from the vote of the bakers, the butchers, the bishops and the candlestick-makers, but by combination with theirs it counts for perpetuating that compromise under which the government of the United States shares in the spoils of the liquor traffic, instead of abolishing it. It is the price that anarchy pays for a truce with the powers that be.

III.

The saloon pleads guilty. It admits the truth of all that has been legally and properly alleged against it. Charged with causing drunkenness, it answers—guilty. Charged with disturbing the peace of home—guilty. Charged with the promotion of vice—guilty. Charged with murder—guilty. The saloon pleads guilty, but does not confess guilt. If the people exercised the people's powers, the saloon would cease to exist under execution of adverse sentence. This is one of the discoveries that Dr. L. M. D. Haynes made when he went to Albany in March, 1908, as representative of the people before the State Excise Commission, in conference with advocates of "personal liberty." He writes:

"I will note some things which I learned. First, initiative and referendum are greatly needed in this and all other states. We have grown up in this state believing that our system of government is well nigh perfect. We are beginning to see that this is a mistake. Our system of legislation removes from the people the power of the direct vote, and confers it upon a few. This few, in committee, may or may not do the will of the people. If, however, by towns, cities or counties, we could provide our own laws; if the legislature were obliged to refer all laws to the people before they were enacted, the people would have voice in their own government. In Montana and Oklahoma the constitution guarantees initiative and referendum. In twenty other states the matter is under consideration. It should be taken up in New York state, where, as a matter of fact, twenty-five or thirty undesirable citizens in the lower wards of New York City are really blocking the wheels of moral progress."

The initiative and referendum may not secure all that men will get when the kingdom of God comes, but it is better than administration by brewers and distillers in the name of "personal liberty." The world may not become paradise on the day after the last saloon is put out of commission, but the Kingdom of the People will not come until all the lost powers of democracy are restored. Methods employed by the pro-saloonist organizers and agitators are undemocratic; they are the familiar methods of the boycotter, the anarchist, the terrorist. Anti-saloonists are willing to go to the people on an issue; pro-saloonists evade challenge to fair discussion, and use the mails and the channels of darkness to compel neutrality by threats of destroying business.

IV.

The saloon, let us confess, is not a spider's web. Its keeper is not a spider, hungry for fly's blood, a man who deliberately has set a trap for an unwary fellowman. On the contrary, he is a husband who has a wife and family to support, a man who perhaps attends the services of a church, a man who votes with the Best Citizens, and contributes to the public treasury. He is not a burglar, nor a thief, nor a murderer. He is not necessarily a bad soul, even if not a saint, and his saloon may not be the worst place in the neighborhood, even if it may not be the best. But he is a factor of a system, and the system, impartially judged, is radically bad. He is neither better nor worse than his system, and, unconsciously, absorbs its worst features under pressure of the competition which compels him to sell all that he can, as long as he can, to as many people as he can.

I once knew a saloonkeeper, a quiet, white-haired old man who sold groceries in the front of his shop and intoxicating liquors in the back. On Sundays the front of the shop was closed, but customers had access by a side door. Had the side door been closed, they would have gone to the saloon on the corner. As others violated the Sunday-closing law, this old man conformed to custom, on the ground that the law infringed upon personal liberty.

For the same reason he sold to minors. But he sold once too often, and a seventeen-year-old boy who bought drink at his bar, became dead drunk for the first time on a Saturday night, and died in bed before daybreak of Sunday. An inquest was held, and it was ascertained that the boy had belonged to a club organized for the purpose of getting drunk, one of scores of similar clubs in the city. Witnesses testified that he had bought whisky, "cheap" whisky, at the old man's bar. The old man himself, having been subpoenaed, testified that he had sold whisky to many

HON. WILLIAM T. COBB,
Governor of Maine.

HON. JOHN BURKE,
Governor of North Dakota.

GOVERNORS OF PROHIBITION STATES.

boys, and that he probably had sold to the boy who had died. He knew that the law prohibited sale to minors? Yes, but he chose to take the risk.

And that is the difference between a saloonkeeper and a spider, and the boy and the fly. A spider does not cater to an appetite. And a fly is not tempted; the web is simply in his way, and he gets caught on the wing. But a saloonkeeper caters to an appetite, an abnormal appetite. A boy is tempted, and when he drinks he takes big risks.

Well, the old man sold whisky and the boy drank it and died. And the coroner rendered a verdict of death from "alcoholism," after one physician had testified that alcohol *per se* is a poison, and another that it is not. However, the boy was buried and the old man was brought to trial before the police judge on a charge of selling liquor to minors. He belonged to the Liquor Dealers' Association, and the Association's lawyer defended him. Of course, he plead "Not guilty." The records of the coroner's court were not accessible, and the case was tried *de novo* before a police court jury consisting of men whose names were proposed by members of the city council, two-thirds of whom were either saloonkeepers or their allies. Neighbors of the accused testified that he was a model of all virtues, and the accused repudiated the confessions that he had made before the coroner. After seven minutes' deliberation he was acquitted.

V.

Having followed this case through various ramifications, I studied another which involved the welfare of boys and girls. On a Washington's birthday nine hundred pupils of a public school were invited to attend a *kaffee-klatsch*, held in a clubroom attached to a mammoth brewery. Having discovered that laws against gambling were being violated, and that the door to the bar was open, I entered complaint at police headquarters and demanded enforcement of law. The police officials, instead of performing their duty tipped off information to the proprietor of the clubroom, and I was threatened with arrest for "disturbing the peace." My companion, agent for the Law and Order League, was hustled out of the place, and I was left to protect myself against a policeman who had been drinking at the bar and was in a state of intoxication.

It seemed proper that I should demand exercise of discipline; and so I charged the policeman with intoxication while on duty, a charge which he personally never denied; but the Liquor League scented an opportunity to railroad two meddling citizens to the penitentiary and organized a defense which exonerated the officer, despite the fact that the president of the police commissioners was convinced of the truth of the charge. The officer having been exonerated, retaliated by charging me with perjury and

I was tried on that charge. It was easy to prove not guilty and the case was dismissed.

At the time, I was at the head of a state movement against the saloon in Ohio and as such was placed between the upper and the nether millstones of antagonism and threatened with double extinction—the loss of my living and the loss of my life. I can understand why the agent of the brewers entered my office and threatened to strike me dead, but I can never quite understand why a brother member of the church should propose to drive me from a position on a religious journal because I had become a leader of a movement which, in principle, the church had endorsed. But so it was. And it happened that, in the same room, I was confronted by men, who, divided in everything else, were united in their opposition to me—as a fanatic who believed that the State ought to do its duty!

VI.

In the autumn of 1887, the great railroad riots occurred in the city of Chicago. It was observed that a very large percentage of the rioters were boys from sixteen to twenty years of age; that their headquarters were in the liquor shops, and that nearly all were spurred on to their vicious work by the influence of intoxicating liquor.

And it was also observed that, when President Cleveland, overriding the protests of Governor Altgeld, sent Federal troops to Chicago with orders to shoot rioters, he issued no instructions to shoot the keepers of the liquor shops. The rioters were "conspiring to obstruct the movement of the United States mails" and must be killed, if necessary, to guarantee the right of free communication. The keepers of the liquor shops had conspired to prey upon the depraved appetites of ill bred, ill trained, ungoverned and ungovernable boys—the offspring of the Chicago slums, the birth of the under world—but they had paid the city license and the Federal tax and, besides, had votes which would be needed at the next election. And so, though the mayor ordered them to close up during the street fighting, there was no serious effort to enforce the decree and no serious intention on the part of the saloonkeepers to obey the proclamation. All the stuff of a riot lay in the liquor shops and the police knew it before a torch was set to the property of the railroads. The police knew the boys who were surging to and fro through the streets wild with drink and lust for loot, and with anarchistic hate of authority and wealth. But, in violation of law, they had allowed them free run of the saloon because they "could make no case against the saloonkeeper for selling intoxicating liquors to minors. . . . ."

The years passed. In the winter of 1905-1906, there was a high carnival of crime in Chicago. All the city dailies shrieked with horror at the reign of terror in the streets. Footpads were everywhere. Women were not safe on the boulevards. Nobody was safe. The police force was wholly insufficient. The city council struggled with the question and voted that the saloon license was not "high" enough. The fee was lifted to a thousand dollars per year and the police force was increased.

In the meantime, one murderer was tried, found guilty and hanged. But the dive keepers paid the higher fee and the "dives" continued. There followed another carnival of crime—because, though there are laws prohibiting the sale of whisky to minors, the police are instructed to make no arrests unless the case is too serious to ignore or involves no peril to the administration!

Boys today in that city are thronging the saloons as they did in 1887, learning the lessons of anarchism as they learned them then. The "United Societies" are inspiring them with contempt for law. And when the next battle breaks out in the streets of Chicago, observers will note that large numbers of boys between sixteen and twenty will be taking part in the fight and that their headquarters will be in the saloons.

VII.

In the catalogue of "Capital Sins" specified by the Catholic Church, the act of "defrauding one's neighbor" ranks sixth. The saloon is guilty of this sin a hundred times over, as a study of facts and figures will show. For it thrives in largest numbers in the poor districts of a city, under pretense of supplementing the deficiencies of an impoverished home life. Moreover, it assumes to return to labor a larger yield than other industries.

Now sociologists have discovered that the home life of a city is at its lowest stage where saloons multiply. There is no just reason why there should not be places in every village, town and city, where men, women and children may meet to eat and drink together, to discuss news and issues, to read magazines and papers, to gaze upon fair pictures and to listen to beautiful music—without guzzling intoxicating drink. When the liquor traffic has been abolished and the enemies of society who have organized it have been driven to legitimate and far happier occupations, a substitute for the saloon may be found. But it will not be the old dram-shop under another name.

Economists have discovered that a comparison of great industries of equal capital shows that the liquor industry pays a lower rate per cent. of wage on capital employed, uses a smaller percentage of raw material and shows less product value than other manufacturing interests. Statistics show that the liquor industry might be abolished without injury to the labor market of the United States. Not only so, they show also that if the laboring men of the country should invest that part of their earnings now spent for liquor in iron and steel, in lumber, in leather, in paper and printing, in vehicles for land transportation, they would take up all labor thrown out by the cessation of the drink manufacture. And the same results appear in comparative study of those industries which contribute most directly to the economic life of the household, the results being almost identical, whether the basis of investigation be the reports of a city, a state or the nation.

But let us take a concrete illustration of this "sixth capital sin," the act of defrauding one's neighbor. Here is a current item from a daily paper:

"Knock-out drops, it is believed, had been administered to ———, a lumberman of ———, who, when awakened from a sound sleep on the steps of a house on Smith street, tried to subdue two policemen. He said he took a drink in a saloon, and remembers nothing afterward. He claimed he had $300, but the money was gone when he was arrested."

"Knock-out drops" constitute an important part of the "low" saloon's stock in trade. A customer asks for a beer or a whisky and gets a drug which renders him an unconscious victim for the holdups who infest the place. When he recovers consciousness he finds that he has been robbed. He reports the robbery to the police, but "there is no evidence" against the saloonkeeper. There is no evidence against anybody. It is useless to involve the city in the expense of attempting to locate the criminal. The victim only knows that he has been drugged and robbed. And the dive lies in wait for the next victim.

This incident, one of many such reported in the daily press, offers an opportunity to the liquor associations to refute the truth of the story told by the unfortunate patron of the saloon. But when the stranger within our gates goes into a saloon and is knocked out and robbed there is no investigation and the saloon's good standing remains unaffected. The unfortunate visitor gets no sympathy from the police, whom he begins to suspect of being "in" with the saloonkeeper. Nor does he get much comfort from the "practical temperance man," who informs him that the saloon is "regulated" by a "tax," and that he alone is to blame for his misfortune. He ought to know better than to buy drink of a saloonkeeper whom he doesn't know, in a city where he is a stranger. How the poor fellow gets back to his home the newspaper fails to report.

Meanwhile, the saloonkeeper and his pals do not care. They are $300 ahead and proof against interference. The "customer" has no redress. He is one of the victims of the saloon, and has paid the prompt penalty of trusting a fellow citizen who, having gone into the business of

MRS. SILENA M. HOLMAN,
President, Tennessee W. C. T. U.

MRS. FLORENCE EWELL ATKINS,
Secretary, Tennessee Y. W. C. T. U.

trafficking in intoxicating liquors, has paid his taxes—and sold out his conscience.

VIII.

On Sunday, August 16, 1908, the Rev. W. F. McElroy, pastor of the Laurel Methodist Episcopal Church, Springfield, Illinois, referring to the horrible riot in that city, said to his people:

"The crimes committed are violations of the law, but the mob is very little worse in this respect than the Mayor and the City Council. We have laws which they entirely trampled under foot. One of these is the law that saloons should be closed on Sunday and at 12 o'clock at night. Instead, they have been running wide open seven days in the week both day and night. The crimes that the black men committed are the product of these lawless places, and so is the mob spirit."

The people understood. There had been a riot. Two score houses had been burned. Stores had been looted. Two men had been killed; seventy-five had been injured. A negro had been hanged and his body riddled with bullets. The militia had been called out and the mob had been dispersed.

But Springfield, home of Abraham Lincoln, had been mob-ruled. Even then, in spite of the militia, it was mob-ruled. The terror of the tragedy still hung over the city and the preacher justly arraigned the city authorities, the mayor and the council. And, back of the city and the mayor, were the state and the governor.

Governor, mayor and council knew that all the saloons in Springfield violated law. The saloons in the so-called "levee" or "bad lands," the negro quarter, were no worse than others and no worse than the authorities that tolerated them for the sake of the three thousand votes that were always in the market. Three thousand votes constitute a possible balance of power. When they have a definite cash and political value in the open market in a campaign they may not be alienated without serious risk. And so the divekeepers and three thousand floaters—negroes and whites—defied the law, together with the governor, the mayor and the city council.

Here is the constitution of the State of Illinois, Article V, Section 6:

"The supreme executive power shall be vested in the governor, who shall take care that the laws be faithfully executed."

Here is Section 14 of the same:

"The governor shall be commander-in-chief of the military and naval forces of the state (except when they shall be called into the service of the United States), and may call out the same to execute the laws, suppress insurrection, and repel invasion."

These quotations are still further emphasized by the following paragraph in the Criminal Code, Hurd's Revised Statutes of Illinois (1903 Edition), Chapter 38, Section 256n, page 664, "Duty of Governor," which reads:

"Whenever there is in any city, town or county a tumult, riot, mob or body of men acting together by force, with attempt to commit a felony, or to offer violence to persons or property, or by force or violence to break or resist the laws of the state, *or when such tumult, riot or mob is threatened,* and the fact is made to appear to the Governor, it shall be his duty to order such military force as he may deem necessary to aid the civil authorities in suppressing such violence and executing the law."

The Governor knew that the laws were not faithfully executed and the "bad lands" knew that the Governor was afraid to do his duty.

The Springfield riot was not a sudden frenzy, before which students of social phenomena stand dumb. It had its birth in the saloons of the city. Nobody denies that. Eugene W. Chafin, resident of Illinois, and Prohibitionist, who was in the heart of the riot and almost one of its innocent victims, was not dealing in invective when he said:

"Whisky caused the Springfield riot. Whisky caused the negro to commit the outrage which instigated the riots. The mob, which sought to avenge the wronged woman, was composed of a simple lot of saloon loafers. They were young men, and they all seemed to be drunk. I could smell their breath when they were on the platform. Whisky was the cause of it all. In Springfield the negroes have 3,000 votes. The big political parties think they hold the balance of power, and both parties, seeking the negro vote, get down to the level of Whisky Row.

"The effect of this outrage ought to be the same as that of the race riots in Atlanta, Georgia. They caused Georgia to vote for prohibition, and I believe that the state of Illinois will do the same. The riots in Springfield and the resultant damage will cost the city more money than it will receive in license revenues in a year.

"During local prohibition campaigns in different towns in the last year I spoke about three hundred times for no license. When I spoke at Springfield I said, as I did in nearly every other town, that the cities that voted to retain the saloons would get the criminal element of the colored population of the South. And that is coming true. The criminal element, not only of the colored population but of the white population, is centering in the saloon towns of this state.

"Springfield got what it voted for. Every man of sense knew when he voted for license that he was voting for crime, and murder, and debauchery, and mob law—just what they have now been reaping in Springfield. The same will be true of other cities, especially Chicago, which, if the laws are not obeyed, will have some of these days, a much worse riot than occurred in Springfield."

Citizens of Illinois see clearly, and are not guilty of treason when they speak as follows:

"The weight of this occurrence rests hard on the city administration," declared the Rev. W. N. Tobie, of Springfield, from his pulpit in the Douglas Avenue Methodist Church, Sunday, August 16.

The *Chicago Daily News* said:

"The authorities have permitted the most brazen violation of the law by the saloons and the dives. One kind of lawlessness breeds another. It is not strange that the mob laughed in the mayor's face when he tried to plead for law and order. The administration has sown the wind and reaped the whirlwind. A mob which murders, burns and loots, is a logical result of long temporizing with vice and harboring of the vicious. Investigation will show that the mob's leading spirits were saloon loafers and other worthless and dangerous characters."

"The riots are due directly to non-enforcement of the law for years in Springfield. The town had tolerated wholesale vice, which had demoralized the population," commented Shelby M. Singleton, Secretary of the Citizens' Association of Chicago.

"I have found in nine cases out of ten that rioting and murder is a result of the cheap liquor sold in the saloons after hours and on Sunday. It is a commercial proposition, not a religious one," testified Assistant State's Attorney James J. Barbour, of Chicago.

The tap root of riot is in the saloon. All the conditions of mob rule exist in any community where the officialism makes common cause with the constituency of the dram-shop. Then, when the rabble breaks loose, it laughs at the Governor, who pleads for obedience to law in the name of God (whose name he had taken in vain in his oath of office), and in the threat of a gatling gun (which he dare not use), for the chief magistrate of the commonwealth is in office by suffrage of the saloon, and the saloon holds three thousand votes in the "bad lands" for sale to the highest bidder.

IX.

The saloon is under suspended sentence. When Chelsea was swept by fire in the spring days of 1908, the first act of the city government was to order saloons in East Boston and sections of Charlestown adjoining to close their doors under penalty of forfeiting license. There was no discussion of the "food value" of alcohol, although thousands of Chelseans were hungry; no discussion of the social value of the "poor man's club," although thousands of families were without pleasant homes. There was no time for discussing the old taunt, "prohibition won't prohibit." A crisis had come and the civil authorities wielded the power that they possessed, and prohibition did prohibit.

It was so in San Francisco during the awful April days of 1906. The liquor dealers would have carried on their business, though the earth moved into the sea and the fire swept earth and heaven. But the authorities issued orders forbidding the sale of intoxicating drink and the soldiers were instructed to shoot violators of the order as they would shoot an enemy in battle. Saloons were closed and the liquor destroyed. There was no debate then on the merits of the liquor traffic as a source of revenue, or the medicinal qualities of alcohol. The saloonkeeper was put under ban unceremoniously and kept there. The hour had come when it was recognized that the public safety demanded the suppression of the saloon. Nothing is more significant in the newspaper reports of the summary methods of dealing with the liquor traffic than the universal favor with which absolute prohibition was received. Even the anarchist had no red flag in the air. Paternal government of the most stalwart kind had become imperative.

There are persons who say that the earthquake was as good in its moral results as a general revival of religion, even though it bleached hair in an hour and shattered nerves and destroyed homes and human life. And not the least important feature of the moral awakening was the suppression of the saloon by the army of the United States. There was not even a local option vote on the issue. The city of San Francisco was under martial law and for once martial law and moral law became one.

X.

Inasmuch as the presidential election of 1908 will be well out of the way before this book goes into general circulation, it is permissible to make allusion to two incidents which well illustrate the powerful influence which the liquor interest wields in political circles. It so happens that these occurrences, while somewhat personal in character, indicate the enforced attitude of the two gentlemen sufficiently eminent to be the honored candidates of their respective parties for the presidency.

When preparations for the publication of "THE PASSING OF THE SALOON" were begun, a modest "Agents Wanted" advertisement was inserted in a number of leading newspapers, preliminary to the organization of the field for a canvass for the book. Among the papers selected as mediums for this advertisement was the *Commoner*, of Lincoln, Nebraska, published and edited by William J. Bryan, candidate at the head of the national Democratic ticket. The *Commoner* was selected on account of its large

CLARENCE E. PITTS,
Chairman New York Prohibition State Committee.

EARL E. COUCH,
Member New York Prohibition State Committee.

FREEMAN H. BETTYS,
Member New York Prohibition State Committee.

DR. E. L. TIFFANY,
State Superintendent, Venango Work, New York.

circulation, especially in the Democratic states which had already adopted prohibition or were agitating for its adoption. It was thought to be a good medium for such an advertisement. The advertisement was forwarded, with check for its payment, through an advertising agency. After a few days, the advertisement and check were returned to the agency, with a note from the publisher declining to insert the advertisement as "not being suitable" to the columns of the *Commoner*. When informed of this, the manager of the TOWER PRESS addressed a letter to the editor and publisher of the *Commoner*, protesting against the discrimination against the advertisement, and stating that the same advertisement had been accepted by the leading daily newspapers and the leading religious and temperance papers of the country. The manager stated, also, that he personally was greatly surprised at the attitude of the *Commoner*, the more so since he himself had long been a subscriber for the paper, and had twice bolted the Prohibition and the Republican tickets to vote for the editor of the *Commoner* as candidate for President. A reply was received stating:

"The reason your advertisement was turned down was because it was discussing what is a political subject at this time, and inasmuch as the national platform which we are supporting made no reference to it, and to prevent the possibility of injecting any new issues into the campaign, we have declined to accept advertising on both sides of the question. If we succeed in enacting into law the principles for which Mr. Bryan is now contending, we will then be in a better position to take up new issues than we would to attempt to do it now.   CHARLES W. BRYAN."

On the 17th day of September, 1908, Mrs. Carry A. Nation happened to be in Cincinnati. Desiring to call upon Hon. William H. Taft, candidate for President on the Republican ticket, and at that time at the home of his brother in this city, she asked the editor of "THE PASSING OF THE SALOON" to accompany her upon the visit. Upon being admitted to the presence of Mr. Taft, Mrs. Nation asked him the following questions:

"What is your attitude toward the canteen?"
"What is your attitude toward the saloon?"

Mr. Taft was evidently embarrassed by the presentation of these questions. He responded, saying:

"Madam, I cannot discuss these questions. I am engaged in a national campaign. I am dealing with national issues."

Mr. Taft then turned to the editor and said: "I must ask you to terminate this interview," and abruptly left the room.

There can be no doubt that, privately and personally, these two gentlemen agree in sentiment with the great body of earnest, intelligent, patriotic citizens of this country that the liquor issue is the most important issue before the people. They certainly knew in the midst of their campaigns, which on both sides were apathetic to an astonishing degree, that the liquor question was the one live issue at the present time before the American people, an issue which aroused their most earnest enthusiasm and endeavor as so emphatically illustrated in the various state and local prohibition campaigns then in progress. Nevertheless, each of them, when brought face to face with this live question was paralyzed, hidebound and tongue-tied on account of the partisan political conditions by which he was controlled.

THE SOLUTION.

"There can be no prohibition in this country other than national prohibition," said the Hon. Frank H. Farris, of St. Louis, Mo., at the Model License League Convention, Louisville, Ky. Is he not right? License, high or low, has failed to solve the saloon problem. Taxation has failed to solve it. Local option has failed to solve it. The dispensary system has been tried and found wanting. The Gothenburg system has failed. The Woman's Crusade did not solve it. Moral suasion has not ended it.

"Saloons that would perish in the first breath of a regenerated Christian election," says John G. Woolley, "cordially close their doors to pay respect to the revival." Why? "Because the evangelist and the saloonkeeper are indistinguishable twins at the general election, and the saloonkeeper knows that in the aftermath of the revival his business will not suffer."

State prohibition has not solved the liquor problem, not even in Maine. "We cannot settle it here in Maine," says Holman Day; "we've given it up. We can merely do the best that poor human nature will let us do."

One thing remains to be done in dealing with this "poor human nature" that sets itself against the welfare of the state, and that is to enact national laws and to employ the Federal powers for the purpose of abolishing the traffic. With a President who shall judge it necessary and expedient to rid the country of an institution which threatens the safety of the republic, it will be possible to use the regular army and to call the militia of the several states into the actual service of the United States for the high purpose of protecting the home against an enemy which submits to nothing but superior force. Hon. Eugene W. Chafin, one of the presidential candidates in 1908 said:

"If I am elected President of the United States, if I have a Congress that will pass a prohibitory law, and if there are any communities that refuse to obey the law, and if the civil authorities are unable to enforce it, I shall use the power conferred upon me by the constitution and call out the militia, the standing army and the navy, and enforce prohibition in every inch of territory under the American flag."

If national prohibition cannot solve the liquor problem, if all the forces arrayed against the saloon cannot destroy it, anarchy is inevitable and the darkest predictions of the republic's bitterest foes will have been fulfilled.

There are, however, two classes of men and women whose activities combine to save the Union and lift it to a higher level. The "instructed critics of the press" and the "philanthropic reformers who tell upon the multitudes through the churches" James Bryce calls them in "THE AMERICAN COMMONWEALTH." "Their influence is not an ebbing tide." It is a flowing tide, and it flows toward the enactment of laws by Congress and the exercise of powers by the chief executive, in harmony with the decision of the nation's supreme court, that "statistics show a greater amount of crime and misery attributable to the use of ardent spirits obtained at retail liquor saloons than to any other source." If the states cannot solve the liquor problem, the nation can and will.

The goal of all anti-saloon movements in the United States is the amendment of the Federal Constitution so as to prohibit the manufacture, sale, importation, exportation or transportation of alcoholic liquors for beverage purposes and to provide, by appropriate legislation, for its enforcement. Only one political party in the country has as yet declared itself in favor of submitting this amendment to the states and employing the legislative and executive powers of government so as to accomplish this purpose. But this party's dominant issue is fast becoming dominant for all parties, under the pressure and push of conditions which are convincing all citizens devoted to the Great Reform that the liquor traffic cannot be successfully and finally overthrown until the Federal Government shall divorce itself from the great evil, and employ its powers, not in collecting for itself revenue from a traffic which is "the most prolific of all sources of crime and misery," but in suppressing it, if necessary, at the point of the bayonet and the mouth of the gun.

For the history of anti-saloon legislation in the various states proves that commonwealth action cannot be depended upon wholly. It has been demonstrated in more than one instance that the expressed wish of the people may be reversed, not by act of the voting body itself, but by the shrewd manipulation of party managers personally interested in restoring the saloon to its lost place of power; or it may be nullified by the law-defying and conscienceless traffic, which from without the state limits still imposes itself upon an unwilling people.

As shown elsewhere, prior to the outbreak of the war between the states, sixteen states had either enacted prohibitory laws or adopted constitutional prohibition amendments. These prohibition states were found east, west, north and south. Then came the conflict of '61 and a war debt. On a fateful day, representatives of the liquor industry, seeing their opportunity, proposed the imposition of a special tax upon the manufacture and sale of intoxicating liqour. On the face of it, their act appeared beneficent and patriotic; it was, in fact, the product of a shrewd sense of self-protection. If the liquor dealers wished to save the Union, it was because they also wished to save their business. It is said that Mr. Lincoln opposed the measure, but he was assured that the excise tax was "only a war measure," and would be repealed when the Confederacy had been destroyed and the powers of the Federal government restored. Appomattox came and went, but the special tax remained, and Mr. Lincoln's fear has been realized. "If the traffic becomes rooted in the revenues of the Republic," he said, "it will give us more trouble than human slavery."

There is reason to believe that in the hour of triumph, when the Union had been saved, Lincoln foresaw another gigantic struggle: the conflict between the whisky trust and the people. For Colonel Merwin, who had known him since the Washingtonian days of 1842, says that only the day before his assassination he said, "The next snarl to straighten out is the liquor question." It is known that Lincoln was a prohibitionist. His early life was as distinguished for his activity in the temperance field as in the anti-slavery cause.

There may be doubt as to the policy which he would have pursued had he lived. Possibly he would have disappointed radical prohibitionists of the Greeley type. But it is more than possible that he would have sought to abolish the internal revenue tax upon liquors, and would have advocated a constitutional amendment providing for the prohibition of the manufacture and sale and of the importation, exportation and transportation of alcoholic liquors as a beverage. He doubtless would have been one of the leaders in the Great Reform.

For us who love the Union which he suffered and died to preserve, there can be no higher task than that of finishing the work which he so nobly began in the days of his young manhood. To him it was given to smite the shackles from a race in bondage. To us comes the call to free the nation from a bondage baser than that of human slavery, and lead it on to the great day when the land which is free from *slaves* shall be free from *saloons*.

CHAPTER III.

"CHRISTIAN" SALOONS VS. CHRISTIAN MISSIONS.

ONE of the founders of the Christian religion queried: "Doth a fountain send forth at the same place sweet water and bitter?" Were he living in the United States in the year of our Lord, 1908, he might puzzle much over the answer to his question. He would see a Christian nation sending forth missionaries to propagate the religion he taught, and also representatives of the liquor industry to sow the seeds of vice, crime, pauperism, disease and death.

Of course, advocates of the religion of the Christ differ among themselves as to the essential meaning of His example and teaching, as they relate to the "temperance" question. There are those who plead His miracle at Cana as an argument for moderate wine-drinking at weddings—and elsewhere! The president of "The Model License League," who, it is said, is a member of a Christian church, is of opinion that the doctrines of total abstinence and prohibition have no warrant, in view of the wine-making act of the divine Master. And, indeed, the attitude of the Christian sects is so at variance with the propaganda of total abstainers and political prohibitionists that it may be said that the Christian church has no definite program on the question.

When one considers that in the United States there is and can be no official acknowledgment of the Christian or any other form of religion, and that the so-called Christian church is split up into innumerable sects more or less at war with one another, we may well inquire, Is this a Christian nation? By their fruits ye shall know them. Righteousness exalteth a nation, but sin is a reproach to any people. In its relation to the liquor traffic, is the United States bearing the fruits of a Christian nation? Is the nation exalted by its righteousness or shamed by its sin? Instead of abolishing the liquor traffic, the chief source of misery for its people, the nation has gone into partnership with it, and appropriates to itself the chief share of its proceeds.

What fruits does this people bear? Is the nation exalted for its righteousness or is it a reproach among the peoples of the earth?

Nominally, of course, ours is a Christian people and is so known to the world. Indeed, we take pride in our churches, our benevolences, our missions. But what impression does so-called Christendom make upon the non-Christian, the "heathen" world? When the simple-minded heathen beholds the same Christian ship sailing, let us say, from Boston, and bringing into his port, in the same cargo, Bibles and beer, the gospel and grog, salvation and the saloon, is it surprising that he does not at once accept and grow enthusiastic over the new religion? And when he sees our Christian nation put enough money into one battle-ship to supply Bibles to all the heathen of the world, and beholds a great fleet of these mighty engines of warfare and carnage moving in stately procession around the globe, is it surprising that he doubts the honesty and consistency of the professed followers of the Prince of Peace?

It is our proud American boast that "Trade follows the Flag." One branch of *trade* usually manages to keep a little ahead of the flag. In a thousand instances, the first starry banner to float to the breeze in a new camp or a new country has been nailed to some shack of a saloon. The liquor which has been and is poured by millions of gallons into Africa and Asia is from the vats and stills of Christendom. Missionaries of Mohammedanism or Islamism, in Africa, the East Indies and India, make much of the "argument of contrast." The follower of Mohammed may be a polygamist and a slavemaster, but he does not use, touch or sell alcohol. He does not go forth carrying the Koran in one hand and a "cocktail" in the other. When the Mohammedan gains the mastery of a country, the wineshop goes out; when the Christian acquires sovereignty, the saloon comes in. Trade follows the flag. Missionaries of the Prophet point to the drunkenness prevalent among Christians and to the destructive drink traffic they introduce among the natives, and deride the claim of Christianity to exclusive descent from Heaven. They quote in contrast and enforce the teachings of the Koran, which explicitly forbid the use of wine, and which commands abstinence as a positive and necessary virtue.

William Elliot Griffis, eminent as a missionary to the Japanese, says: "Providentially, this feature of Mohammedanism has been a great blessing to a large part of mankind, and it should provoke Christians to the good work of at least staying the flood of intoxicants that issues from the distilleries in Christian lands for the bestializing of the uncivilized races of Africa and Asia." In spite of heathen protest, Mohammedan taunt and missionary appeal, wherever the American flag goes the traffic of the dramshop goes. Wherever the missionary goes with his gospel the "merchant" goes with his gin. And so the missionary has a double battle to fight. He points to the *Book*, but the heathen man points to the *Bottle*, and debates the consistency of a civilization which gives birth to both Religion and Rum.

The "insular possessions" of the United States have been overrun by

MRS. FRANCES W. GRAHAM,
President, New York W. C. T. U.

MRS. MARY TOWNE BURT,
President, 1882-1898, New York W. C. T. U.

vendors of American beer and forced to accept a trade that an aroused social sentiment everywhere is condemning as a menace to social order and progress. In the Philippines, in Hawaii, in Porto Rico, the emissary of the church has been placed in an attitude of uncompromising hostility to the saloon, or he has been compelled to adopt the policy of non-committalism, after the manner of the clergy in the home church. Lest he be charged with treason, he has suppressed the truth. And so the church at home and abroad, lulled or forced into quiescence, has abandoned the field of temperance reform to the organizers of the Woman's Christian Temperance Union, the campaigners of the Prohibition party, and the superintendents of the Anti-Saloon League.

A review of foreign mission fields, dating back some years, serves to illustrate how the imported vice of drunkenness was then, had been before, and still is, the chief obstacle in the way of mission work. The following story of the strife against liquor in mission work in foreign countries is taken substantially from "CHRISTIAN MISSIONS AND SOCIAL PROGRESS," by Rev. James S. Dennis, D. D.

Great honor is due to the world-wide efforts of the Woman's Christian Temperance Union, which has sent to the foreign fields a succession of accomplished missionary advocates of temperance, to quicken devotion to principles and promote helpful adjustment of forces. Organized societies in Christian lands, having in view the protection of native races from the ravages of strong drink, have also accomplished a valuable service. The latter agencies are represented by a "United Committee for the Prevention of the Demoralization of the Native Races by the Liquor Traffic," a committee composed of representatives from twenty-one societies of a missionary, philanthropic or temperance character. The story of the great Polyglot Petition of the World's Woman's Christian Temperance Union is well known. It was the testimony of Frances E. Willard, the originator of the plan, that the organization of which she was the president, had been greatly aided by missionaries in all parts of the world, whose sympathy and practical coöperation had been of the highest value. Her own words of testimony are notable: "It is needless to say that, but for the intelligent and consecutive work of foreign missionaries, the World's Woman's Christian Temperance Union, now a living, organic force, would be merely a plan on paper."

The "Aborigines' Protection Society" of England is giving careful attention to the drink traffic in Africa, as appears from its reports. Its keen sense of responsibility and full recognition of the enormous dangers of the situation, appear in its memorials to the British Government, its public meetings, special literature and practical efforts to stay the surging ravages of the evil. The time limit of the general act of the Brussels

Conference has now expired and it will be the urgent aim of this and other organizations interested in the subject to secure some more effective action dealing with the liquor problem in Africa.

In foreign fields, with hardly an exception, Christian missions find their chief fight must be directed against "Christian" intoxicants, and have organized bands and societies for the advancement of temperance work and the restoration of the fallen, and are endeavoring through every channel of influence to restrict the manufacture and sale of intoxicants and to prevent their use by native converts. The cause of temperance has its place in the program of all missionary conferences. It is advocated in the papers and periodicals issued for circulation among natives and has an honored prominence in all mission literature.

In an examination more in detail of the status in different mission fields, we may well turn our attention first to Africa. A noble personality, singularly wise and heroic, arises at once to greet us out of the deep shadow of what is fast becoming a rum-cursed continent. It is Khama, the native South African chief and Christian convert, who has exercised his authority in prohibiting the drink traffic within his domains. In 1895, with two other African chiefs, he paid a visit to England, the purpose of which was to secure the maintenance of existing political relations with the British Government and also to request its good offices in protecting his country from the threatened invasion of liquor. In this he seems happily to have succeeded, at least for the time being, having received the express commendation of the Queen in approval of his sturdy hostility to the entrance of intoxicants among his people, and being assured of the support of Her Majesty's government in the endeavor to maintain his remarkable position on this question. A dispatch to the British authorities, previously written by this wise-hearted chief, is a unique state paper, and indicates the high watermark of Christian statecraft where full play has been given to the moral power of missions. These are Khama's words:

"It were better for me that I should lose my country than that it should be flooded with drink. Lobengula never gives me a sleepless night, but to fight against drink is to fight against demons, not against men. I dread the white man's drink more than all the assegais of the Matabele, which kill men's bodies and it is quickly over; but drink puts devils into men and destroys both bodies and souls forever. Its wounds never heal. I pray your Honor never to ask me to open even a little door to drink."

It would be well for Christendom if some of our foreign mission converts could have a hand in the legislation against the traffic which is so sadly needed outside of Africa. The heroic struggle of Khama still goes on, but, as European demands grow exacting, he finds his opposition more difficult to maintain. Will those who profess to represent civilization at last strike down the hero who is struggling to save his people from the power of a desolating scourge?

In passing, we may contrast the principles which govern Khama with those that have controlled the neighboring Boer government in the Transvaal, where the licensing of the drink traffic and the freedom with which a native can obtain intoxicants have produced a shocking prevalence of drunkenness. It is reported that twenty-five per cent. of the total number of native employés in the mining industry are rendered unfit for work every day by liquor; and, in an independent report, dated June 20, 1893, from the manager of the Salisbury mine, it is stated that "Nearly half the natives were drunk or incapacitated from the effects of the big drunk on Saturday." For the same reason a high percentage of fatal accidents is recorded, and it is asserted that, "The amount spent yearly on drink by natives on the Rand cannot be estimated at less than a million and a half pounds, and it more probably amounts to two millions." We leave it to the judgment of the reader as to whether the policy of Khama would not only be the more Christian but also the more civilized attitude on the part of the government.

In other sections of South Africa a strenuous warfare is waged under missionary leadership to check this terrible evil. The Committee on Temperance of the Synod of the Free Church Mission in South Africa presented in 1896 a telling report, based upon detailed inquiry, showing the almost unanimous attitude of opposition on the part of native congregations to the traffic in intoxicants, and the prevalence of total abstinence to a remarkable extent among all church members. In some churches this requirement is made a condition of membership. In an account of temperance efforts among the Zulus, it is stated that, through the length and breadth of the missions of the American Board, total abstinence is a fundamental rule of admission to church membership. Work on behalf of temperance is successfully conducted in the Natal Mission of the American Board and in the Kaffraria Mission of the United Presbyterian Church of Scotland. Concerning the policy of the missions around Lake Nyassa similar statements regarding the temperance movement might be given. "At all the stations," writes the Rev. Donald Fraser, of the Livingstonia Mission of the Free Church of Scotland, "the Christians have of their own accord met and pronounced against the drinking of beer. They see that drunkenness has been followed by murder, uncleanness and foolish talking, and that the whole country is being devastated in order to raise the beer crop, so they have agreed together and said, 'We will neither make beer nor drink it.' "

As foreign intoxicants have not yet penetrated to the interior sections of the continent, where access is difficult, the question of temperance has not assumed the importance in the Church Missionary Society's work in Uganda which we may expect it will later when the completion of the railway shall make that region accessible to traders. It is interesting to note, however, that already temperance societies are being formed among the Christian natives, with a view to the restriction among them of the use of indigenous intoxicants. Mr. R. H. Leakey, of Koki, in Uganda, reports that "About ninety per cent. of the adults are more or less addicted to drinking, but happily nearly all the Christians are total abstainers."

The whole West Coast of the Continent, in practical defiance of the Brussels Act of 1890-91, has been cursed by the desolations of the rum traffic. This Act professed to regulate the supply of spirituous liquors to natives in different parts of Africa, but it has proved to be so inoperative that its efficiency has been of little value, especially along the coast-line and in sections of the Congo Valley. The interior regions, either on account of difficulty of access or government prohibition (as in the Niger territories and part of the Congo State), are little touched by the scourge.

The Christian, London, said: "Mr. Chamberlain has given the matter of the liquor traffic on the coast of Africa great consideration, and finds that eighty per cent. of the total revenue of the Niger Coast Protectorate and sixty per cent. of the revenue of the Gold Coast and Lagos are derived from the liquor trade." There is reason to hope that the British Foreign Office will make a successful effort to secure an international agreement with a view to the limitation of the traffic. Sir George T. Goldie, K. C. M. G., President of the Royal Niger Company, says that he has "long been convinced that the whole African movement will end in failure, unless European spirits are practically excluded." He characterizes the rum traffic as "by far the most important topic of the day."

Throughout all the mission of the West Coast of Africa there is a vigilant and vigorous temperance movement to arrest ravages of this dread enemy of the African. In the Congo Valley, the missions of the American Baptist Missionary Union have instituted severe prohibitive measures upon the subject of intemperance, requiring total abstinence of all church members. "We fought for temperance," says the Rev. Henry Richards, in a report of his station, Banza Manteka, "and now we have a strictly temperance church."

If we pass to Egypt and the northern coast of the Continent, we find missions to be the same saving power and almost the only thoroughgoing and consistent influence in favor of abstinence. It may be said, in fact, that Christian missions in Africa are fighting the battle of temperance with zeal, and that they represent a most important phase of organized effort in that direction.

In the neighboring Island of Madagascar we discover the Malagasy Christian Woman's Temperance Society, with its fine record of courageous and devoted service on behalf of sobriety. The French commander had hardly established himself as the military master of the island, when, to his surprise, he was visited by a deputation of native Christian women, not in a spirit of fear with a timid plea for mercy and forbearance, but as representing the Madagascar Branch of the World's Woman's Christian Temperance Union, to thank him for his stringent regulations concerning the sale of intoxicants. "As regards temperance," writes the Rev. James Sibree (L. M. S.), of Antananarivo, "a large number of people have now taken the pledge, and there is a body of women workers who are earnest and zealous in holding meetings for the cause." Where is there, by the way, a temperance society which for its size can present a more inspiring and creditable report than that issued from the busy headquarters of the Malagasy Christian Woman's Temperance Society?

In the South Sea Islands "the fight against intemperance has been resolutely waged by our missionaries." This legend might stand for all mission work in the South Seas, from the time of John Williams, when European traders began their nefarious introduction of intoxicants. There is no darker stain on the history of commerce than the persistent efforts of traders to purchase the native products with ardent spirits. In this they were only too successful and the disease of drunkenness swept over the islands. Nearly everywhere the work was thrown back and "but for these little handfuls of true and faithful Christians the whole race might have gone back into savagery." From that time onward to the present, temperance, strict and uncompromising, has been the watchword of missions in the Pacific Islands. In Apia, Samoa, which is popularly known among the sailors of the South Seas as the "Hell of the Pacific," the London Missionary Society has opened a coffee house and free reading-room especially for foreign sailors. There are flourishing Gospel Temperance and Christian Endeavor Societies in connection with the Apia church.

In the Gilbert Islands, where the American Board is at work, one of the group, Butaritari, has a Christian king. In his realm "strict temperance laws are enforced among the natives, but the white foreigners keep an open saloon in defiance of law." No wonder that the writer of the above sentence asks, "Who are the pagans?" The king appealed to the English, who have assumed a protectorate over the islands, to help him in executing his law against the foreign transgressors. In the Caroline Islands a notable temperance status among the natives had been established before the Spanish occupation in 1887. Of Pingelap it was said that liquor was "banished from the island." The Rev. E. T. Doane wrote concerning Ponape, before the coming of the Spaniards, that the making of intoxicating drinks and the traffic in the same had ceased.

In the New Zealand House of Representatives a young Maori chief, who represents his race, has been pushing for legislation that will protect his fellow countrymen. He pleads for the following striking clause to be added to the Licensing Act of the colony: "That no intoxicating liquor be sold or given to any man of the native race, and that no license be renewed or fresh license be granted within a mile of Maori-land." A petition, in regard to which it is stated that it was signed by thirty of the chiefs and over sixty other representative natives, was recently addressed to the Maori Parliament, which, in response, forwarded an official appeal to the New Zealand Government, urging the addition of the foregoing clause. At the Centenary of the London Missionary Society, the Rev. James Chalmers, one of its missionaries in New Guinea, made an earnest plea for the entire suppression of the liquor traffic among native races, and reported from his own field that Sir William Macgregor, the excellent Governor of New Guinea, was strictly enforcing his prohibitive law against the selling or giving of strong drink to the natives.

On our way to Japan we touch at the Island of Formosa for a word of information from Dr. MacKay, of the Canadian Presbyterian Mission. "On the east coast of Formosa," he says, "I have planted a dozen churches amongst drunken aborigines. The change in the villages since has been amazing. The heathen Chinese around have a common saying that 'the aborigines are now men and women.'"

The Rev. W. Gauld, also of the Canadian Presbyterian Mission, reports that there is great improvement in the native Christian community with reference to temperance. Among the non-Christian population of the island, both Chinese and aborigines, except where mission influence has gained the upper hand, there is unhappily an increasing tendency to drunkenness, especially in the ports where foreign liquors are offered for sale.

In Japan there is a vigorous temperance movement, which is not by any means confined to Christian circles. The history of Christianity in the empire, however, shows that it has taken a pronounced and leading part in advocacy of this reform, and, in the opinion of those who have long resided there, it is the source and promoter of temperance ideas among all classes. The Rev. Albert Arnold Bennett (A. B. M. U.), of Yokohama, wrote, in 1895, that there were four principal Christian temperance societies in Japan, the Yokohama, Tokyo, Hokkaido and Teikoku, with an average membership of about 2,500 each, and also about eighty others in which the membership averaged seventy-five each, making a total of about 16,000 members. In *The Japan Evangelist* for September,

1897, mention is made of six Christian temperance organizations. Later, steps were taken to form a union of temperance societies by the appointment of a Central Committee with Dr. Soper, of the Methodist Episcopal Mission, as President. A further organization into a national alliance, including all the temperance societies of the empire, was also effected.

There is also a Buddhist temperance society, which is said to number about 30,000 members, half of whom bind themselves to total abstinence and the remainder take the same pledge either for a limited time or with special reference to certain Buddhist ceremonies during which drink habits are prevalent. These larger societies issue periodicals of their own. The zealous apostle of temperance in the Hokkaido, or "Northland" of Japan, is Mr. Kazutaka Ito, the first convert to Christianity in Sapporo. The pioneer temperance society in that northern island was organized by Christian converts and Mr. Ito was elected its president. Among the Ainu, who are especially given to drink, it has now a branch and the movement has spread throughout the Hokkaido, being represented by many auxiliaries.

Christian laborers in the employ of the Japanese railways organized Industrial Temperance Societies. Interesting accounts are given in some of the Japanese periodicals of earnest and sustained efforts on the part of many prominent native Christians to establish and foster temperance organizations. Besides the work of Mr. Ito, previously referred to, zealous service was rendered by Mrs. Yajima, Vice-President of the Central Committee, who was active in the formation of the first *Kyofukwai*, or temperance union, in Japan, and was its first president; by Mr. Miyama, who is called "the John B. Gough of Japan," and by Mr. Taro Ando, of Tokyo, who established a monthly temperance journal and himself became active in this special reform. We read also of the organization by Miss Elizabeth Russell of the Methodist Mission, of a Young Woman's Christian Temperance Union in the boarding-school for girls at Nagasaki. This Union numbered one hundred and eighty members at the start. There are still others at Kobe and in the Bancho Girls' School at Tokyo.

Here is a significant incident reported by Rev. Albert Arnold Bennett, writing from Yokohama. In speaking of a number of recent baptisms, he says: "One of the five baptized last Sunday had been away four years studying the manufacture of wines and other liquors, and expected to do quite a business in that line. We feared his faith would not hold out when he was told he must give up such trade if he became a Christian, but he did stop and is now seeking a business that will not work ruin."

It is of interest to note in this connection an historical fact reported by Rev. D. S. Spencer, of Nagoya: "At the time of concluding commercial treaties with the Tokugawa Government, the American representative,

Mr. Townsend Harris, earnestly advised the Japanese Government to restrict the importation of opium to fifteen pounds per boat, and to put thirty per cent. duty on imported liquor. Japan profited by following his advice, since the result has been largely to keep out opium and greatly to reduce the quantity of imported liquors. Nevertheless, the amount of imported liquors has steadily increased from year to year."

Now let us contemplate a picture that comes nearer home and is more up to date. The following recital of facts, written for "THE PASSING OF THE SALOON" by a Woman's Christian Temperance Union organizer and lecturer, is not lessened in value because its author chooses to be anonymous. It corroborates all that has been published on this subject in the various organs of the Woman's Christian Temperance Union and other periodicals. It is printed here, not to disgrace the United States, but to aid in creating a public sentiment which shall compel the government to discontinue its policy of licensing and protecting this horrible traffic in the insular possessions, and in the Canal Zone, and if we are to clean up abroad we must begin by cleaning up at home.

"When I entered Manila, Philippine Islands, in November, 1899, there were, perhaps, two thousand native saloons in small rooms and nipa huts, where *vino*, the native wine, was sold, and food as well. The natives usually took food and a small amount of wine with it. But when the hue and cry was raised throughout the United States about the number of saloons that lined the streets of Manila, something had to be done. So a commission was appointed to investigate. They visited the native saloons, drank of their wine (they were seen drinking it) to see if the *vino* were pure wine or not. If the commissioners decided the wine to be pure (it usually seemed the man who had the most money had the purest wine), the place remained open. If they decided the wine to be impure, the place was closed.

"This action greatly reduced the number of native saloons, from perhaps two thousand to six hundred, in the city of Manila. But immediately in their stead arose our larger, more attractive American saloons. Soon I saw on the streets of Manila, at the side of open doors, life-size paintings of the figure we call 'Uncle Sam' holding a beer glass in his hand, to advertise *'Our Uncle Sam's Saloon.'* I have seen over another doorway a big, glorious American eagle advertising *'Our American Eagle Saloon.'* Stretched across the street was a large banner with the word *'Expansion'* on it, to advertise another such place.

"Our stars and stripes were not only floating over these places, but, through the open door and windows could be seen the bars draped in 'Old Glory,' where they were dealing out death. I could but wonder what the

MRS. HENRIETTA BROWN,
President Oregon W. C. T. U.

MISS ANNA A. ROBBINS,
National Organizer and Lecturer of the
W. C. T. U.

MISS FRANCES H. ENSIGN,
President Ohio W. C. T. U.

natives would think Americans could be, since all they saw advertised that was peculiarly American was the *American Saloon.*

"In the year and a half I was there, I saw just one native man drunk. Asking a friend, a surgeon in the army, what he had seen, he replied that he had seen only one native man drunk, and he had been made drunk on American whisky. Soldiers have told me that they forced the natives to get drunk to see how 'funny' they acted!

"One American saloon, that started across the narrow street from the first Christian mission opened in Manila, was made viler than others and more attractive to the natives by the exhibition of life-size paintings on the walls of nude women in various positions. Before the saloon was opened, however, one of the missionaries found out what was going on and appealed to officials until the pictures were removed.

"As the result of all this, I have been told by men who have recently returned from Manila that it is now common to see natives lying around the streets drunk.

"Upon one of the city streets there was a saloon with an American flag floating over it, the porch festooned in red, white and blue. The bars were draped in 'Old Glory' and one of the bartenders in this flag-decorated American saloon was a woman, supposed to be American. As we passed down that street we could see her standing in the doorway under the stars and stripes, a degraded-looking woman. But she stood there, smoking her cigar, cursing and swearing, enticing young men into the place of vice. As I saw her I remembered that here was a great people that knew very little about the United States. Many of the native Filipinos did not know that there was such a country as the United States. But now, as they passed down the street and saw the woman under the flag, they pointed to her as 'one of the American women!' And, as there were only a few women in the islands to represent American womanhood, she was to them a typical figure. I was not proud of her, nor of the vicious conditions which were introduced and protected by our 'Christian' nation.

"While the American saloons and houses of ill-fame by the hundreds were flourishing in Manila, leading American soldiers and young native men and women into sin, there were *only ten American missionaries* in and around the city, struggling to teach the doctrines of the 'free religion,' as the natives call Protestantism, and to present the 'Christ' as he is known in the true church."

CHAPTER IV.

THE SALOON AN ECONOMIC VAMPIRE.

NO serious defense of the dram-shop has ever been based upon moral grounds. The most fiery advocate of "personal liberty," according to the conception of the brewers' and distillers' boycotting association, has never presumed to say that the retail traffic in intoxicating liquors contributes to moral progress, either of the individual or of society. It is quite true that Lyman Abbott, and the *Outlook* school oppose the state's exercise of police power in suppressing it on the ground that character matures under temptation, and that there should be no arbitrary restraint upon the liberty of one man to subject another to moral test. The same argument has been used by liquor journal editors—without attempting to prove that a bad man may become good under the direct influence of the saloon, or a good man may become morally better.

There have been authors, however, who have defended the existence of the saloon as a social necessity in the life of the American workingman—or as a Poor Man's Club. Even the *Journal of Sociology,* published by the University of Chicago, has discussed its social value in the tenement-house region—and an occasional editorial in some newspaper solemnly endorses the dram-shop as a factor in the pleasure life of handicapped toilers.

Perhaps the most widely offered defense of the saloon, however, is based upon its alleged value as a producer of wealth—a factor in business. It is vociferously asserted by the literary agents of the Brewers' and Distillers' Prosperity League that if the saloon be destroyed, widespread calamity must ensue. Cartoons are exhibited showing the alarming effects caused by prohibition cloud-bursts in the grain fields—or by a fanatical administration of Puritan laws in a thriving town. Pictures of vacant buildings are hung everywhere, for the purpose of producing the impression that Anti-Saloon Leagueism has caused an exodus of desirable citizens—and that grass is growing rank in places where the saloon-keeper has closed his doors. Statistics are paraded, proving by vast arrays of figures, that prosperity goes out at one door when prohibition enters at another—and that "business" dies under the blight of an anti-liquor victory.

This argument weighs somewhat heavily in the minds of people who can see only the debit side of a cash account or the credit side of a property account, as some specific case may chance to affect them personally. It seems to be conclusive, because it is made to appear to be a transcript of government reports. But usually it is adduced by people whose standard of truth is a standard of personal comfort.

Now, it will not be denied even by the most extreme advocate of prohibition on moral grounds, that, if the saloon is necessary to business it ought to be protected. If it can be proved that the liquor traffic really is a producer of honest wealth, the Prohibition party ought to disband and the Anti-Saloon League dissolve as soon as the fact has been established. For "business" is at the foundation of social life. As far back as the human race has any record of its own history, there has been no social life of any kind without some form of business. As social life has become complex business has become complex, and as the wants of society have increased business has become more and more essential to its demands. It no longer satisfies mere needs but ministers to wants which may be artificial but contributory to the love of comfort or beauty, ease or luxury.

Business, in its last definition, is a system of manufacture and exchange, organized to supply the members of society with food, clothing and shelter. It is the *service* of *life*. Food is derived from all parts of the globe for the purpose of maintaining life, or contributing to the productive energy and pleasure of life. Clothing is made, not simply to preserve internal heat, but to charm the eye; and shelter is provided, not simply to shield against the weather, but to surround the family with the most beautiful and comfortable environment. There have been hermits who have cut out all luxuries; rarely a Henry D. Thoreau, who, in the midst of society, attempts to reduce existence to the last simplicities of food, clothing and shelter. But Thoreaus have been few. And the expansion of civilization has created wants wherever it has planted a better conception of the moral ends of being.

Now, what place does the saloon occupy in the actual economics of society?

To answer this question, suppose that society is in the process of organizing itself. As the blacksmith, the physician, the schoolmaster, the artist, apply for places in the community, each is able to demonstrate a reason for his admission. The functions of blacksmith, physician, schoolmaster, artist, commend themselves, for each contributes his measure to the common wealth. But the maker or vendor of intoxicating liquors as a beverage can find no place in an economic society, for he cannot show that in any way he is engaged in the production of any useful commodity. He adds nothing to wealth. Unlike the other members of society, he does not produce corn, or a house, or a piece of cloth, or a chair, or in any way contribute directly to the welfare of the members of society. To be admitted, he must coöperate in some way in developing the capacities of human life to their higher degrees. And so actors, musicians, ministers of religion, educators, painters, engravers, sculptors, have been recognized as "Knights of Labor," because they render service to the higher life of the world. Destroy them and the level of life falls. Nature would be less winsome, because her interpreters had ceased to show beauties; life would be less gracious, because the arts had vanished away.

But the "business" of the dram-shop, the traffic in intoxicating liquors, does not offer anything essential to *life*. Its stock in trade is not food. It does not contribute to the production of clothing. It puts no roofs over the heads of its customers. On the contrary, its patrons are reduced to and remain in economic conditions which render the purchase of clothing and of all necessities of life difficult and finally impossible. The typical product of the saloon, recognized as such everywhere, is not the society man, arrayed in broadcloth and fine linen, or the sturdy workman clothed in substantial garb, but the ragged waif, the man of the slums, a non-producer whom society must support.

It is beyond all doubt, that *if* a saloonkeeper were admitted to a new community life, the tailor and dressmaker, the grocer, the merchant, the manufacturer, would immediately feel the pressure of his competition. They feel it now, but they have been taught to attribute slackness of trade to other causes than the trade in intoxicants and so do not recognize the real evil. What is true of the tailor and dressmaker is true of the housebuilder. The typical product of the saloon is a man without a home of his own. He cannot buy drink and a home at the same time. He becomes a mere renter, and a renter of the lowest type of house. He descends to the tenement house, and at last to the *poorhouse*.

Of course not all men who drink at saloon bars go down to the depths. But the legitimate product of the saloon is the drunkard. And the drunkard is worse than a bandit, because society combines against the bandit, and even may kill him; but it is bound to care for the drunkard, for he is the product of an institution which it tolerates.

The saloonkeeper, having gained entrance to the social body, coins money. He grows rich, has a residence in the best streets, is influential in "practical politics",—and violates law with impunity. The police protect his place of business against fanatics, and the governor of the state declines faithful execution of the laws which would banish him quickly from the community. His cash register rings its bell from 5 A. M. to 1 A. M., or longer, seven days in the week, on election days, holy days, holidays, Sundays. He pays special taxes,—mulct taxes, license fees, excise,—and gloats over the fact that he contributes at least one-fourth of the nation's income—and thus bribes and stifles the public conscience.

Business? He's in "business," of course. But what is his stock in trade? It is a drug, a poison, which he sells as a beverage, and which *creates an appetite for itself*, an unnatural craving which, at last, becomes uncontrollable. The typical patron of the dram-shop is never satisfied. His thirst is never quenched. "Even if I knew I should go to hell the next moment," said poor Steve Hulse, "I could not resist the temptation to drink." That is not extreme; it is the legitimate result of the drink habit. The bread-buyer buys what he needs and quits when he gets enough, without a struggle to control a ravenous appetite. The meat-buyer buys what he needs and quits eating when his hunger is satisfied. The patron of business in all its legitimate domains is normally sane. The merchant cannot induce him to buy again, *again* and AGAIN, because his appetite has become a raging fire. But in the case of the saloonkeeper's customer, the more he buys the more he wants.

The opponent of the liquor traffic opposes each particular saloon, because all saloons constitute a system. The Mutual Protective Association, says the Louisville *Evening Post*, was vociferous a year ago in declaring for orderly saloons, the cancellation of licenses for disorderly houses and the separation of the saloon from political influences. But, when all licenses expired and applications for renewal were being considered, a regular battery of lawyers appeared to defend every saloonkeeper whose license was imperiled. One saloon is like another, and like all others, even though one is a "café" and the other a "dive."

The problem which confronts society is not that of keeping out an institution which has never been in, but of expelling an institution which has grown up with it, and now, to some, seems to be essential to its business life. But there is no reason to doubt that, if by some edict of the powers that be, all saloons, everywhere in the United States, should be closed at midnight, December 31, 1908, never to re-open, and that, if on New Year's Day, 1909, all men who had intended to "drink" would deposit in bank the money they had expected to spend on that one day in the saloon, there would be a fund of at least $5,000,000 subject to the demand of those who had been temporarily thrown out of employment by the sudden end of the dram-shop *régime*. At the same rate, January would not have passed before the legitimate enterprises would absorb resources hitherto wasted on intoxicating liquors, and, before the year had passed, the glass blowers would have orders enough and to spare for jars and bottles for jams and pickles and preserves to meet the increased demands for food; and, before the harvests had been garnered, the two per cent. of farm products that had gone to the brewery and distillery would be absorbed by families which, under the saloon *régime*, had always been underfed. It would be demonstrated that the real cause of "hard times" is the expenditure of earnings for that which breeds or develops crime, insanity, pauperism, divorce and other social and economic forms of disease.

When that better time comes, it will be seen by all, as is now so clearly seen by a comparatively few students of economic society, that the liquor dealer is, economically, worse than a thief; because, though a thief may steal all the money that a man may have, he leaves the man himself intact. As Oliver W. Stewart says, "The saloonkeeper is morally worse than a thief, because he not only takes money for which he gives no equivalent, but incapacitates the man himself for service as a member of economic society." This is not harsh judgment. For, when the saloonkeeper has at last shut up shop and taken his money out of the till, he has in possession the representative of values for which he has passed no equivalent over his bar. Men have gone from his shop poorer in pocket and at a lower value to society than when they came in. His offense is that he has coöperated with his fellow-traffickers to degrade his patrons, to place them on a lower economic plane. Because this is true, society possesses the right to suppress a traffic which affects the economic activities and conditions of those who refuse either to sell intoxicating liquors or to drink them. This right is not denied. Its exercise would solve the liquor problem, because it would remove conditions that reduce or destroy the economic powers of the commonwealth.

E. J. Wheeler, the well known writer and editor, says:

"It is a demonstrable fact that whereas $1,000,000 of capital invested in the manufacture of liquor gives employment to 285 persons, the same amount invested in any one of the other ten leading industries of the nation gives employment on an average to 876 persons (Census of 1880). If the money, therefore, were invested in other forms of industry, it would give employment to three times as many men, and pay two and one-half times as much as now in wages."

Below are estimates and figures derived from various sources. While no such summaries can be regarded as absolutely correct, and while amounts reached by different estimators may not exactly agree, yet the general agreement and trend is so uniform that the statistical showing and argument is unanswerable.

In 1900, a capital of $447,836,072, invested in the manufacture of malt and distilled liquors, employed 43,254 persons. That is to say, in twenty years, liquor capital had lost two-thirds of its employing capacity. For while, in 1880, one million of capital employed 285 persons, in 1900 it employed only 97 persons. Perhaps the brewers and distillers can

ROBERT NORRIS,
Secretary Kansas State Temperance Union.

JOHN MARSHALL,
Attorney Kansas State Temperance Union.

J. K. CODDING,
President Kansas State Temperance Union.

account for this decrease, and also explain the fact that while a million of capital invested in general industrial enterprises employed 540 persons, the same amount of capital in the liquor industry employed less than 100. On an equal basis the liquor industry should have employed at least 582 persons per million of capital.

In 1900, the liquor industry paid $57,656 in wages for every million of capital invested. At the same time, the total capital invested in all manufactures paid $234,467 per million. Perhaps the brewers and distillers can explain this great disparity in wage-paying capacity of the liquor industry.

In 1900, a million of capital invested in the liquor industry purchased $139,959 worth of raw material. At the same time, a million of capital in all industries averaged the purchase of $278,957 of raw material. Or, putting the figures in another form, while the manufacturing establishments of the United States purchased $7,377,907,079 worth of raw material, the liquor industry purchased $66,822,712 worth, or only *nine-tenths of one per cent!*

Again, a million of capital invested in the production of malt and distilled liquors, produced a commercial value of $698,887. But a million invested in general industrial enterprise created a product value of $1,311,285.

Comparing the malt liquor industry, with a capital of $415,284,468, with the wool manufacturing industry, with capital of $415,075,713, it appears that the liquor industry employed only 39,532 persons while the wool industry employed 264,021 persons.

The following estimates are worked up from the official reports of industries in the city of Chicago for one year. If, instead of spending $2,000,000,000 for intoxicating liquors, the people of the United States would buy with it more of the necessities of life, business in other lines would increase as follows:

The annual purchase of flour would increase $3,600,000; groceries, $10,000,000; milk, $400,000; stoves, $16,000,000; coal would increase $16,000,000; wall paper, $200,000; carpets, $200,000; furniture, $20,000,000; clothing, $16,000,000; hats, $2,400,000; shoes (adults'),$2,400,000; shoes (children's), $3,000,000; hose, $1,000,000; flannel, $200,000; cotton goods. $200,000; wagons, $1,000,000; houses, $15,000,000.

Besides these amounts added to the usual investment in such articles, the people would still have $20,000,000, say for public improvements, and $4,000,000 for a national health department.

That the basis upon which these colossal amounts are estimated is rational is shown by the reports of the Cincinnati Chamber of Commerce, according to which the people of Cincinnati and vicinity spent more than fourteen million dollars for beer alone in the year ending December 31, 1907.

The latest Federal statistics on the economic phases of the liquor traffic are for the year 1905. Only industries employing an aggregate capital of over $400,000,000 are considered here. The table below shows the number of wage-earners employed for each million dollars invested.

    Cotton manufactures........................648
    Wool manufactures..........................636
    Lumber manufactures.......................463
    Iron and steel manufactures..................426
    Distilled and malt liquors.................... 96

Of twenty-seven selected industries, tabulated and compared by a government statistician, the Turpentine and Rosin industry, capitalized at only $11,847,495, employed 41,864 persons, and paid out $8,393,483, almost as many employes as were reported by the entire liquor industry, and one-third the wages. That is to say, the turpentine and rosin manufacturers, on one thirty-seventh of the capital employed by liquor manufacturers gave employment to almost as many persons, and, on every million invested, paid $699,456 in wages, as compared with the $61,516 paid by brewers and distillers.

The following table, also from government reports of 1905, shows wages paid per million dollars in industries capitalized at more than four hundred million dollars:

    Iron and steel manufactures.............$238,272
    Wool manufactures 222,889
    Cotton manufactures 185,631
    Lumber manufactures 171,261
    Distilled and malt liquors................ 61,516

The total capital invested in the Liquor Industry (1905) was $575,576,169. This is less than five per cent. of the total capital employed in the United States in all productive industries.

The total number of men employed by the Liquor Industry was 55,407. This is less than two per cent. of the total labor force employed in all productive industries.

The total wages paid by the Liquor Industry was $38,201,476. This is less than two per cent. of the aggregate wages paid by all productive industries.

The Liquor Industry used $106,230,871 of material. This is less than two per cent. of materials used by all productive industries.

In the light of such figures as the above, and in the face of the common knowledge of all persons at all familiar with the liquor traffic, the whole argument as to its alleged industrial value seems extremely absurd, as much so, indeed, as that of the old woman who bought eggs at a cent apiece and sold them at 10 cents a dozen, and explained that she expected to make her profit off of her big business. The liquor business, measured in dollars and cents, is indeed a big business, but, unfortunately, the bigger it is the more society loses.

If the people of the United States instead of consuming intoxicating liquors were to purchase goods, economic goods, the capital invested in production of beer and whisky would necessarily be shifted, but it would not be annihilated. And when placed in other industries it would not only employ all persons now employed in breweries and distilleries, but it would take up the large body of the unemployed.

The diversion of $2,000,000,000 a year, worse than wasted in the purchase of liquor, into channels of productive industry, would prevent panics, in spite of predatory financiers, and avert commercial depression, in spite of destructive competition. This would not only counterbalance the losses caused by abolition of the liquor traffic, but would produce an economic condition of prosperity not even dreamed of during the best days of "high tariff" and "sound money."

ADDENDUM.

NOTE.—*Just as this book is going to press we are fortunate in receiving from Mr. A. R. Heath, the well known writer, editor and statistician, the following memorandum of a study he is now making of the Federal statistics of the drink traffic. The results of this study will be recognized at once as one of the most notable contributions yet made to current economic and sociologic science.*

The facts given are of the very greatest interest to every business man and every wage-earner. They indicate beyond dispute that the prohibition policy put into general practice, will prove the emancipation of both labor and capital, and the basis of general and permanent prosperity, in addition to the great moral uplift of society.—G. M. H.

By A. R. HEATH.

Permanence is a most significant factor in the net results of any policy of government. As the years and decades pass, wherever a certain policy remains settled and uniform, all the conditions and interests of society become adjusted and "geared" to that policy, so that finally the combined whole is a crystallized and harmonious force.

So with prohibition on the one side and license on the other. Either policy if permanent will compel the adjustment to its own standard of all economic conditions. If drinking means waste and loss, the license states will show it; if sobriety means thrift, then the state of Maine, for instance, the prohibition state of longest experience, it will be fair to assume, will show it.

Maine, with its fifty years' record of prohibition, therefore, is taken as a definite unit of representation of that policy, and the other states— the license states—may be compared with the record which Maine presents. Of course I recognize that there have been at times treachery and evasion in the way of failure to enforce the law in that state. But I find that these evasions have almost exclusively had cities of over 8,000 for their field, and in Maine these are few and contain less than one-fourth the people. The great mass of both territory and population has been practically without the liquor traffic for half a century. We accept Maine for purposes of this comparison.

States differ in natural conditions of the business interests, which Maine supports, the mechanics and workingmen, as well as the stores, banks and so on, which she maintains, with records of like enterprises in other states.

In comparing Maine with Massachusetts, for instance, Maine had, in 1900, a per capita wealth of $982, while Massachusetts had $1,553. It is evident that the citizen of the latter state, having greater wealth, had proportionately greater purchasing power, had greater ability to patronize stores and employ workingmen. The ratio is as 1.58 to 1.00. To complete the comparison, we will bear in mind that, while Maine had 694,466 population, Massachusetts had 2,805,346.

In other words, Massachusetts had 4.04 times as many people whose needs had to be met, and on the other hand, 4.04 times as many people with means to supply those needs; while, as above seen, each person had a purchasing power of 1.58 as compared with Maine's 1.00. By multiplying these two factors, we have 6.38 as the "ratio" which Massachusetts bore to Maine in the census year, 1900, the date of the latest figures available for our use. This illustrates how the "ratio" for each state is ascertained from data furnished by the census.

The United States census names vocations of more than 370 kinds, divided into state totals. It tells how many carpenters there were in 1900 in each state, how many masons, how many banks, how many groceries, and so on. It is of great value to us at this point. (One item not given therein is "Business Concerns" found in the Statistical Abstract, and furnished the government by Dun & Company.)

Maine had 8,627 merchants and dealers (except wholesale). Massachusetts should have had 6.38 times as many, or 55,040; but she only had 40,994, a shortage of 14,046, or nearly 26 per cent.

Maine's citizens thus spend their money so wisely, and with such thrift that they support retail merchants to a much greater extent proportionately than does Massachusetts. The latter state falls nearly 26 per cent. short of Maine's standard. The prohibition state supports retail trade far better than does this license state. The same holds good in comparing Maine with many other states.

Ohio had $1,207 per capita wealth and 4,157,545 population. Her ratio to Maine is 7.36. Maine had 14,661 business concerns in 1900; Ohio, 84,478. Ohio should have had 107,904, a shortage of 23,426, or nearly 22 per cent.

Let us see for a moment what this shortage meant to the business interests of the State of Ohio. If Ohio had measured up to the standard of Maine, it would have meant approximately 23,000 additional stores, warerooms, factories and offices rented or built; many thousands of clerks, salesmen and saleswomen, stenographers, typewriters, mechanics, workingmen, superintendents, managers, commercial travelers, etc., employed; enormous amounts used for freight, cartage, railroad fares, raw material and partly finished material; homes needed for all these thousands of employés; their deposited savings in banks, trust companies, building and loan associations and their purchases of real estate, provisions, shoes, clothing, etc.; carfare to and from business, more support for schools and churches and a general stimulus to trade of every description. When Ohio gets ready for whole-hearted prohibition, here will be a part of the benefits to her business men. Can they ignore such results?

Pennsylvania's "ratio" is 13.66. Maine had 8,938 carpenters. Pennsylvania employed 56,300, when she should have employed 122,071; shortage, 65,771 or 54 per cent. In a single state, therefore, *over half* the carpenters were starved out of employment at their trade!

This is not exceptional. In Illinois, also, there is a shortage of more than half. In California, 15,916 are employed, when there should be 42,187; in Massachusetts, 33,011, instead of 57,024, and so on.

Labor is hard hit by the liquor traffic. Those figures prove what vast benefits would come if these lacking hundreds of thousands of carpenters were employed, and thus a fair support obtained for them and their families. They show conclusively that increased labor would be required to build thousands of new homes, erect additions to old homes, create more taxable property, meet the expansion of trade by these carpenters and their families in stores, on cars, and in all the relations of life.

As the inevitable result of this demand in nearly or quite every state for scores of thousands of additional carpenters, there would be an immediate and significant increase in wages. Now, the men who are starved out from that trade because liquor snatches the millions of dollars which would otherwise be paid them for wages, gravitate on lines of local least resistance to other trades already overcrowded, and thus help to keep down wages there, with semi-starvation for all. These facts prove that, under prohibition, the situation would be directly reversed. Thinking workingmen should consider these facts. They are typical. In scores and scores of vocations, prohibition is labor's best friend, and the discovery I here set forth proves that fact over and over.

There is practically no end to the illustrations which can be given along business and labor lines, showing by concrete figures how prohibition works as an economic benefit. I call attention to one more fact, one relative to banking. Maine is largely a "backwoods state," sparsely settled and with considerable lumbering. It would be expected that banking and brokerage would be left to states richer and more densely populated. Yet it is true that all the bankers and brokers in "Continental United States" number 73,315. Maine has 570. The "ratio" of the country as a whole to Maine is 129.765. Therefore, if the entire country measured up to Maine's standard in bankers and brokers, it would have 73,966. So the rural state of Maine is a little ahead on that line, one generally supposed to pertain to city life. Thrifty people require banking conveniences.

There seems to be no escape from the conclusion we reach. The prohibition state of Maine sets an example of thrifty and wise use of means which places her far in the van of progress. If other states would reach her standard they should adopt the prohibition policy which has set her in the van. This subject is commended earnestly to men of foresight in the business and labor world.

HENRY SMITH WILLIAMS, M. D., LL. D.

CHAPTER V.

PHYSIOLOGICAL EFFECTS OF ALCOHOL.

By Henry Smith Williams, M. D., LL.D.

NOTE.—*The following article appeared in* MCCLURE'S MAGAZINE, *and is reprinted here by the courteous permission of the editor and publisher. It is the latest word of science on the effects of alcohol upon the individual in health and sickness, and settles forever all possible question as to the evil effects of alcohol upon the human system, under all circumstances.*—G. M. H.

SOME very puzzling differences of opinion about the use of alcoholic beverages find expression. This is natural enough, since alcohol is a very curious drug and the human organism a very complex mechanism. The effects of this drug upon this mechanism are often very mystifying. Not many persons are competent to analyze these effects in their totality. Still fewer can examine any of them quite without prejudice. But in recent years a large number of scientific investigators have attempted to substitute knowledge for guesswork as to the effects of alcohol, through the institution of definite experiments. Some have tested its effects on the digestive apparatus; others, its power over the heart and voluntary muscles; still others, its influence upon the brain. On the whole, the results of these experiments are singularly consistent. Undoubtedly they tend to upset a good many time-honored preconceptions. But they give better grounds for judgment as to what is the rational attitude toward alcohol than have hitherto been available.

The traditional rôle of alcohol is that of a stimulant. It has been supposed to stimulate digestion and assimilation; to stimulate the heart's action; to stimulate muscular activity and strength; to stimulate the mind. The new evidence seems to show that, in the final analysis, alcohol stimulates none of these activities; that its final effect is everywhere depressive and inhibitory (at any rate as regards higher functions) rather than stimulative; that, in short, it is properly to be classed with the anaesthetics and narcotics. The grounds for this view should be of interest to every user of alcohol; of interest, for that matter, to every citizen, considering that more than one thousand million gallons of alcoholic beverages are consumed in the United States each year.

I shall attempt to describe some of the more significant observations and experiments in sufficient detail to enable the reader to draw his own conclusions. To make room for this, I must deal with other portions of the testimony in a very summary manner. As regards digestion, for example, I must be content to note that the experiments show that alcohol does indeed stimulate the flow of digestive fluids, but that it also tends to interfere with their normal action; so that ordinarily one effect neutralizes the other. As regards the action of the heart, I shall merely state that the ultimate effect of alcohol is to depress, in large doses to paralyze, that organ. These, after all, are matters that concern the physician rather than the general reader.

The effect of alcohol on muscular activity has a larger measure of popular interest; indeed, it is a question of the utmost practicality. The experiments show that alcohol does not increase the capacity to do muscular work, but distinctly decreases it. Doubtless this seems at variance with many a man's observation of himself; but the explanation is found in the fact that alcohol blurs the judgment. As Voit remarks, it gives, not strength, but, at most, the feeling of strength. A man may think he is working faster and better under the influence of alcohol than he would otherwise do; but rigidly conducted experiments do not confirm this opinion. "Both science and the experience of life," says Dr. John J. Abel, of Johns Hopkins University, "have exploded the pernicious theory that alcohol gives any persistent increase of muscular power. The disappearance of this universal error will greatly reduce the consumption of alcohol among laboring men. It is well understood by all who control large bodies of men engaged in physical labor that alcohol and effective work are incompatible."

It is even questionable whether the energy derived from the oxidation of alcohol in the body can be directly used at all as a source of muscular energy. Such competent observers as Schumberg and Scheffer independently reached the conclusion that it cannot. Dr. Abel inclines to the same opinion. He suggests that "alcohol is not a food in the sense in which fats and carbohydrates are food; it should be defined as an easily oxidizable drug with numerous untoward effects which inevitably appear when a certain minimum dose is exceeded." He thinks that alcohol should be classed "with the more or less dangerous stimulants and narcotics, such as hasheesh, tobacco, etc., rather than with truly sustaining foodstuffs." Some of the grounds for this view will appear presently, as we now turn to examine the alleged stimulating effects of alcohol upon the mental processes.

The celebrated physicist Von Helmholtz, one of the foremost thinkers of the nineteenth century, declared that the very smallest quantity of alcohol served effectively, while its influence lasted, to banish from his mind all possibility of creative effort; all capacity to solve an abstruse problem. The results of recent experiments in the field of physiological psychology convince one that the same thing is true in some measure of every other mind capable of creative thinking. Certainly all the evidence goes to show that no mind is capable of its best efforts when influenced by even small quantities of alcohol. If any reader of these words is disposed to challenge this statement, on the strength of his own personal experience, I would ask him to reflect carefully as to whether what he has been disposed to regard as a stimulant effect may not be better explained along lines suggested by these words of Professor James: "The reason for craving alcohol is that it is an anaesthetic even in moderate quantities. It obliterates a part of the field of consciousness and abolishes collateral trains of thought."

The experimental evidence that tends to establish the position of alcohol as an inhibitor and disturber rather than a promoter of mental activity has been gathered largely by German investigators. Many of their experiments are of rather a technical character, aiming to test the basal operations of mind. Others, however, are eminently practical, as we shall see. The earliest experiments, made by Exner in Vienna so long ago as 1873, aimed to determine the effect of alcohol upon the so-called reaction-time. The subject of the experiment sits at a table, with his finger upon a telegraph key. At a given signal—say a flash of light—he releases the key. The time that elapses between signal and response—measured electrically in fractions of a second—is called the simple or direct reaction-time. This varies for different individuals, but is relatively constant, under given conditions, for the same individual. Exner found, however, that when an individual had imbibed a small quantity of alcohol, his reaction-time was lengthened, though the subject believed himself to be responding more promptly than before.

These highly suggestive experiments attracted no very great amount of attention at the time. Some years later, however, they were repeated by several investigators, including Dietl, Vintschgau and, in particular, Kraepelin and his pupils. It was then discovered that, in the case of a robust young man, if the quantity of alcohol ingested was very small, and the tests were made immediately, the direct reaction-time was not lengthened, but appreciably shortened instead. If, however, the quantity of alcohol was increased, or if the experiments were made at a considerable interval of time after its ingestion, the reaction-time fell below the normal, as in Exner's experiments.

Subsequent experiments tested mental processes of a somewhat more complicated character. For example, the subject would place each hand on a telegraph key, at right and left. The signals would then be varied, it being understood that one key or the other would be pressed promptly accordingly as a red or a white light appeared. It became necessary, therefore, to recognize the color of the light and to recall which hand was to be moved at that particular signal; in other words, to make a choice not unlike that which a locomotive engineer is required to make when he encounters an unexpected signal light. The tests showed that after the ingestion of a small quantity of alcohol—say a glass of beer—there was a marked disturbance of the mental processes involved in this reaction. On the average, the keys were released more rapidly than before the alcohol was taken, but the wrong key was much more frequently released than under normal circumstances. Speed was attained at the cost of correct judgment. Thus, as Dr. Stier remarks, the experiment shows the elements of two of the most significant and persistent effects of alcohol, namely, the vitiating of mental processes and the increased tendency to hasty or incoördinate movements. Stated otherwise, a leveling down process is involved whereby the higher function is dulled, the lower function accentuated.

Equally suggestive are the results of some experiments devised by Ach and Maljarewski to test the effects of alcohol upon the perception and comprehension of printed symbols. The subject was required to read aloud a continuous series of letters or meaningless syllables or short words, as viewed through a small slit in a revolving cylinder. It was found that after taking a small quantity of alcohol, the subject was noticeably less able to read correctly. His capacity to repeat, after a short interval, a number of letters correctly read, was also much impaired. He made more omissions than before, and tended to substitute words and syllables for those actually seen. It is especially noteworthy that the largest number of mistakes were made in the reading of meaningless syllables; that is to say, in the part of the task calling for the highest or most complicated type of mental activity.

Another striking illustration of the tendency of alcohol to impair the higher mental processes was given by some experiments instituted by Kraepelin to test the association of ideas. In these experiments, a word is pronounced, and the subject is required to pronounce the first word that suggests itself in response. Some very interesting secrets of the sub-conscious personality are revealed thereby, as was shown, for example, in a series of experiments conducted last year at Zürich by Dr. Frederick Peterson, of New York. But I cannot dwell on these here. Suffice it for our purpose that the possible responses are of two general types. The suggested word being, let us say, "book," the subject may (1) think of some word associated logically with the idea of a book, such as "read" or "'leaves"; or he may (2) think of some word associated merely through similarity of sound, such as "cook" or "shook." In a large series of tests, any given individual tends to show a tolerably uniform proportion between the two types of association; and this ratio is in a sense explicative of his type of mind. Generally speaking, the higher the intelligence, the higher will be the ratio of logical to merely rhymed associations. Moreover, the same individual will exhibit more associations of the logical type when his mind is fresh than when it is exhausted, as after a hard day's work.

In Kraepelin's experiments, it appeared that even the smallest quantity of alcohol had virtually the effect of fatiguing the mind of the subject, so that the number of his rhymed responses rose far above the normal. That is to say, the lower form of association of ideas was accentuated, at the expense of the higher. In effect, the particular mind experimented upon was always brought for the time being to a lower level by the alcohol.

When a single dose of alcohol is administered, its effects gradually disappear, as a matter of course. But they are far more persistent than might be supposed. Some experiments conducted by Fürer are illuminative as to this. He tested a person for several days, at a given hour, as to reaction-time, the association of ideas, the capacity to memorize and facility in adding. The subject was then allowed to drink two litres of beer in the course of a day. No intoxicating effects whatever were to be discovered by ordinary methods. The psychological tests, however, showed marked disturbance of all the reactions, a diminished capacity to memorize, decreased facility in adding, etc., not merely on the day when the alcohol was taken, but on succeeding days as well. Not until the third day was there a gradual restoration to complete normality; although the subject himself—and this should be particularly noted—felt absolutely fresh and free from after effects of alcohol on the day following that on which the beer was taken.

Similarly, Rüdin found the effects of a single dose of alcohol to persist, as regards some forms of mental disturbance, for twelve hours, for other forms twenty-four hours and for yet others thirty-six hours and more. But Rüdin's experiments bring out another aspect of the subject, which no one who considers the alcohol question in any of its phases should overlook: the fact, namely, that individuals differ greatly in their response to a given quantity of the drug. Thus, of four healthy young students who formed the subjects of Rüdin's experiment, two showed very marked disturbance of the mental functions for more than forty-eight hours, whereas the third was influenced for a shorter time and the fourth was scarcely affected at all. The student who was least affected was not, as might be supposed, one who had been accustomed to take alcoholics habitually, but, on the contrary, one who for six years had been a total abstainer.

Noting thus that the effects of a single dose of alcohol may persist for two or three days, one is led to inquire what the result will be if the dose is repeated day after day. Will there then be a cumulative effect, or will the system become tolerant of the drug and hence unresponsive? Some experiments of Smith, and others of Kurz and Kraepelin have been directed toward the solution of this all-important question. The results of the experiments show a piling up of the disturbing effects of alcohol. Kurz and Kraepelin estimate that after giving eighty grams per day to an individual for twelve successive days, the working capacity of that individual's mind was lessened by from twenty-five to forty per cent. Smith found an impairment of the power to add, after twelve days, amounting to forty per cent.; the power to memorize was reduced by about seventy per cent.

Forty to eighty grams of alcohol, the amounts used in producing these astounding results, is no more than the quantity contained in one or two litres of beer or in a half-bottle to a bottle of ordinary wine. Professor Aschaffenburg, commenting on these experiments, points the obvious moral that the so-called moderate drinker, who consumes his bottle of wine as a matter of course each day with his dinner—and who doubtless would declare that he is never under the influence of liquor—is in reality never actually sober from one week's end to another. Neither in bodily nor in mental activity is he ever up to what should be his normal level.

That this fair inference from laboratory experiments may be demonstrated in a thoroughly practical field, has been shown by Professor Aschaffenburg himself, through a series of tests made on four professional typesetters. The tests were made with all the rigor of the psychological laboratory (the experimenter is a former pupil of Kraepelin), but they were conducted in a printing office, where the subjects worked at their ordinary desks, and in precisely the ordinary way, except that the copy from which the type was set was always printed, to secure perfect uniformity. The author summarizes the results of the experiments as follows:

"The experiment extended over four days. The first and third days were observed as normal days, no alcohol being given. On the second and fourth days each worker received thirty-five grams—a little more than one ounce of alcohol, in the form of Greek wine. A comparison of the results of work on normal and on alcoholic days showed, in the case of one of the workers, no difference. But the remaining three showed greater or less retardation of work, amounting in the most pronounced case to almost fourteen per cent. As typesetting is paid for by measure, such a worker would actually earn ten per cent. less on days when he consumed even this small quantity of alcohol."

In the light of such observations, a glass of beer or even the cheapest bottle of wine is seen to be an expensive luxury. To forfeit ten per cent. of one's working efficiency is no trifling matter in these days of strenuous

MRS. MILTON H. EDWARDS,
Corresponding Secretary, Georgia W. C. T. U.

MRS. JENNIE HART SIBLEY,
Honorary President, Georgia W. C. T. U.

competition. Perhaps it should be noted that the subjects of the experiment were all men habituated to the use of liquor, one of them being accustomed to take four glasses of beer each week day, and eight or ten on Sundays. This heaviest drinker was the one whose work was most influenced in the experiment just related. The one whose work was least influenced was the only one of the four who did not habitually drink beer every day; and he drank regularly on Sundays. It goes without saying that all abstained from beer during the experiment. We may note, further, that all the men admitted that they habitually found it more difficult to work on Mondays, after the over-indulgence of Sunday, than on other days, and that they made more mistakes on that day. Aside from that, however, the men were by no means disposed to admit, before the experiment, that their habitual use of beer interfered with their work. That it really did so could not well be doubted after the experiment.

Some doubly significant observations as to the practical effects of beer and wine in dulling the faculties were made by Bayer, who investigated the habits of 591 children in a public school in Vienna. These pupils were ranked by their teachers into three groups, denoting progress as "good," "fair" or "poor," respectively. Bayer found, on investigation, that 134 of these pupils took no alcoholic drink; that 164 drank alcoholics very seldom; but that 219 drank beer or wine once daily; 71 drank it twice daily, and three drank it with every meal. Of the total abstainers, 42 per cent. ranked in the school as "good," 49 per cent. as "fair" and 9 per cent. as "poor." Of the occasional drinkers, 34 per cent. ranked as "good," 57 per cent. as "fair" and 9 per cent. as "poor." Of the daily drinkers, 28 per cent. ranked as "good," 58 per cent. as "fair" and 14 per cent. as "poor." Those who drank twice daily ranked 25 per cent. "good," 58 per cent. "fair" and 18 per cent. "poor." Of the three who drank thrice daily, one ranked as "fair" and the other two as "poor." Statistics of this sort are rather tiresome, but these will repay a moment's examination. As Aschaffenburg, from whom I quote them, remarks, detailed comment is superfluous: the figures speak for themselves.

Neither in England nor America, fortunately, would it be possible to gather statistics comparable to these as to the effects of alcohol on growing children; for the Anglo-Saxon does not believe in alcohol for the child, whatever his view as to its utility for adults. The effects of alcohol upon the growing organism have, however, been studied here with the aid of subjects drawn from lower orders of the animal kingdom. Professor C. F. Hodge, of Clark University, gave alcohol to two kittens, with very striking results. "In beginning the experiment," he says, "it was remarkable how quickly and completely all the higher psychic characteristics of both the kittens dropped out. Playfulness, purring, cleanliness and care of coat, interest in mice, fear of dogs, while normally developed before the experiment began, all disappeared so suddenly that it could hardly be explained otherwise than as a direct influence of the alcohol upon the higher centers of the brain. The kittens simply ate and slept, and could scarcely have been less active had the greater part of their cerebral hemisphere been removed by the knife."

Professor Hodge's experiments extended also to dogs. He found that the alcoholized dogs in his kennel were lacking in spontaneous activity and in alertness in retrieving a ball. These defects must be in part explained by lack of cerebral energy, in part by weakening of the muscular system. Various other symptoms were presented that showed the lowered tone of the entire organism under the influence of alcohol; but perhaps the most interesting phenomenon was the development of extreme timidity on the part of all the alcoholized dogs. The least thing out of the ordinary caused them to exhibit fear, while their kennel companions exhibited only curiosity or interest. "Whistles and bells, in the distance, never ceased to throw them into a panic in which they howled and yelped while the normal dogs simply barked." One of the dogs even had "paroxysms of causeless fear with some evidence of hallucination. He would apparently start at some imaginary object, and go into fits of howling."

The characteristic timidity of the alcoholized dogs did not altogether disappear even when they no longer received alcohol in their diet. Timidity had become with them a "habit of life." As Professor Hodge suggests, we are here apparently dealing with "one of the profound psychological causes of fear, having wide application to its phenomena in man. Fear is commonly recognized as a characteristic feature in alcoholic insanity, and *delirium tremens* is the most terrible form of fear psychosis known." The development of the same psychosis, in a modified degree, through the continued use of small quantities of alcohol, emphasizes the causal relation between the use of alcohol and the genesis of timidity. It shows how pathetically mistaken is the popular notion that alcohol inspires courage; and to anyone who clearly appreciates the share courage plays in the battle of life, it suggests yet another lamentable way in which alcohol handicaps its devotees.

It is perhaps hardly necessary to cite further experiments directly showing the depressing effects of alcohol, even in small quantities, upon the mental activities. Whoever examines the evidence in its entirety will scarcely avoid the conclusion reached by Smith, as the result of his experiments already referred to, which Dr. Abel summarizes thus: "One-half to one bottle of wine, or two to four glasses of beer a day, not only counteract the beneficial effects of 'practice' in any given occupation, but also depress every form of intellectual activity; therefore, every man who, according to his own notions, is only a moderate drinker places himself by this indulgence on a lower intellectual level and opposes the full and complete utilization of his intellectual powers." I content myself with repeating that, to the thoughtful man, the beer and the wine must seem dear at such a price.

To anyone who may reply that he is willing to pay this price for the sake of the pleasurable emotions and passions that are sometimes permitted to hold sway in the absence of those higher faculties of reason which alcohol tends to banish, I would suggest that there is still another aspect of the account which we have not as yet examined. We have seen that alcohol may be a potent disturber of the functions of digestion, of muscular activity, and of mental energizing. But we have spoken all along of function and not of structure. We have not even raised a question as to what might be the tangible effects of this disturber of functions upon the physical organism through which these functions are manifested. We must complete our inquiry by asking whether alcohol, in disturbing digestion, may not leave its mark upon the digestive apparatus. Whether in disturbing the circulation it may not put its stamp upon heart and blood vessels; whether in disturbing the mind it may not leave some indelible record on the tissues of the brain.

Stated otherwise, the question is this: Is alcohol a poison to the animal organism? A poison being, in the ordinary acceptance of the word, an agent that may injuriously affect the tissues of the body, and tend to shorten life.

Students of pathology answer this question with no uncertain voice. The matter is presented in a nutshell by the Professor of Pathology at Johns Hopkins University, Dr. William H. Welch, when he says: "Alcohol in sufficient quantities is a poison to all living organisms, both animal and vegetable." To that unequivocal pronouncement there is, I believe, no dissenting voice, except that a word-quibble was at one time raised over the claim that alcohol in exceedingly small doses might be harmless. The obvious answer is that the same thing is true of any and every poison whatsoever. Arsenic and strychnine, in appropriate doses, are recognized by all physicians as admirable tonics; but no one argues in consequence that they are not virulent poisons.

Open any work on the practice of medicine quite at random, and whether you chance to read of diseased stomach or heart or blood vessels or liver or kidneys or muscles or connective tissues or nerves or brain—it is all one: in any case you will learn that alcohol may be an active factor in the causation, and a retarding factor in the cure, of some, at least, of the important diseases of the organ or set of organs about which you are reading. You will rise with the conviction that alcohol is not merely a poison, but the most subtle, the most far-reaching and, judged by its ultimate effects, incomparably the most virulent, consequently the most to be dreaded, of all poisons.

Here are a few corroborative facts, stated baldly, almost at random: Rauber found that a ten per cent. solution of alcohol "acted as a definite protoplasmic poison to all forms of cell life with which he experimented—including the hydra, tapeworms, earthworms, leeches, crayfish, various species of fish, Mexican axolotl, and mammals, including the human subject." Berkely found, in four rabbits out of five in which he had induced chronic alcohol poisoning, fatty degeneration of the heart muscle. This condition, he says, "seems to be present in all animals subject to a continual administration of alcohol in which sufficient time between the doses is not allowed for complete elimination." Cowan finds that alcoholic cases "bear acute diseases badly, failure of the heart always ensuing at an earlier period than one would anticipate." Bollinger found the beer-drinkers of Munich so subject to hypertrophied or dilated hearts as to justify Liebe in declaring that "one man in sixteen in Munich drinks himself to death."

Dr. Sims Woodhead, Professor of Pathology in the University of Cambridge, says of the effect of alcohol on the heart: "In addition to the fatty degeneration of the heart that is so frequently met with in chronic alcoholics, there appears in some cases to be an increase of fibrous tissue between the muscle fibers, accompanied by wasting of these tissues. . . . Heart failure, one of the most frequent causes of death in people of adult and advanced years, is often due to fatty degeneration, and a patient who suffers from alcoholic degeneration necessarily runs a much greater risk of heart failure during the course of acute fevers or from overwork, exhaustion and an overloaded stomach and the like, than does the man with a strong, healthy heart, unaffected by alcohol or similar poisons."

It must be obvious that these words give a clue to the agency of alcohol in shortening the lives of tens of thousands of persons with whose decease the name of alcohol is never associated in the minds of their friends or in the death certificates.

Dr. Woodhead has this to say about the blood vessels: "In chronic alcoholism in which the poison is acting continuously over a long period, a peculiar fibrous condition of the vessels is met with; this, apparently, is the result of a slight irritation of the connective tissue of the walls of these vessels. The wall of the vessel may become thickened throughout its whole extent or irregularly, and the muscular coat may waste away as a new fibrous or scar-like tissue is formed. The wasting muscles may undergo fatty degeneration, and, in these, lime salts may be deposited; the rigid, brittle, so-called pipe-stem vessels are the result." Referring to these degenerated arteries, Dr. Welch says: "In this way alcoholic excess may stand in a causative relation to cerebral disorders, such as apoplexy and paralysis, and also the diseases of the heart and kidneys."

From our present standpoint it is particularly worthy of remark that Professor Woodhead states that this calcification of the blood vessels is likely to occur in persons who have never been either habitual or occasional drunkards, but who have taken only "what they are pleased to call 'moderate' quantities of alcohol." Similarly, Dr. Welch declares that "alcoholic diseases are certainly not limited to persons recognized as drunkards. Instances have been recorded in increasing number in recent years of the occurrence of diseases of the circulatory, renal and nervous systems, reasonably or positively attributable to the use of alcoholic liquors, in persons who never became really intoxicated and were regarded by themselves and by others as 'moderate drinkers.'"

"It is well established," adds Dr. Welch, "that the general mortality from diseases of the liver, kidney, heart, blood vessels and nervous system is much higher in those following occupations which expose them to the temptation of drinking than in others." Strumpell declares that chronic inflammation of the stomach and bowels is almost exclusively of alcoholic origin; and that when a man in the prime of life dies of certain chronic kidney affections, one may safely infer that he has been a lover of beer and other alcoholic drinks. Similarly, cirrhosis of the liver is universally recognized as being, nine times in ten, of alcoholic origin. The nervous affections of like origin are numerous and important, implicating both brain cells and peripheral fibers.

Without going into further details as to the precise changes that alcohol may effect in the various organs of the body we may note that these pathological changes are everywhere of the same general type. There is an ever-present tendency to destroy the higher form of cells—those that are directly concerned with the vital processes—and to replace them with useless or harmful connective tissue. "Whether this scar tissue formation goes on in the heart, in the kidneys, in the liver, in the blood vessels, or in the nerves," says Woodhead, "the process is essentially the same, and it must be associated with the accumulation of poisonous or waste products in the lymph spaces through which the nutrient fluids pass to the tissues. The contracting scar tissue of a wound has its exact homologue in the contracting scar tissue that is met with in the liver, in the kidney and in the brain."

It is not altogether pleasant to think that one's bodily tissues—from the brain to the remotest nerve fibril, from the heart to the minutest arteriole—may perhaps be undergoing day by day such changes as these. Yet that is the possibility which every habitual drinker of alcoholic beverages—"moderate drinker" though he be—must face. This is an added toll that does not appear in the first price of the glass of beer or bottle of wine, but it is a toll that may refuse to be overlooked or ignored in the final accounting.

In connection with experiments in rendering animals and men immune from certain contagious diseases through inoculation with specific serums, Delearde, working in Calmette's laboratory in Lille, showed that alcoholized rabbits are not protected by inoculation, as normal ones are, against hydrophobia. Moreover, he reports the case of an intemperate man, bitten by a mad dog, who died notwithstanding anti-rabic treatment, whereas a boy of thirteen, much more severely bitten by the same dog on the same day, recovered under treatment. Delearde strongly advises anyone bitten by a mad dog to abstain from alcohol, not only during the anti-rabic treatment but for some months thereafter, lest the alcohol counteract the effects of the protective serum.

Similar laboratory experiments have been made by Laitenan, who became fully convinced that alcohol increases the susceptibility of animals to splenic fever, tuberculosis and diphtheria. Dr. A. C. Abbott, of the University of Pennsylvania, made an elaborate series of experiments to test the susceptibility of rabbits to various micro-organisms causing pus-formation and blood poisoning. He found that the normal resistance of rabbits to infection from this source was in most cases "markedly diminished through the influence of alcohol when given daily to a stage of acute intoxication." "It is interesting to note," Dr. Abbott adds, "that the results of inoculation of the alcoholized rabbits with the erysipelas coccus correspond in a way with clinical observations on human beings addicted to the excessive use of alcohol when infected by this organism."

Additional confirmation of the deleterious effects of alcohol in this connection was furnished by the cats and dogs of Professor Hodge's experiments, already referred to. All of these showed peculiar susceptibility to infectious diseases, not only being attacked earlier than their normal companions, but also suffering more severely. This accords with numerous observations on the human subject; for example, with the claim made some years ago by McCleod and Milles that Europeans in Shanghai who used alcohol showed increased susceptibility to Asiatic cholera, and suffered from a more virulent type of the disease. Professor Woodhead points out that many of the foremost authorities now concede the justice of this view, and unreservedly condemn the giving of alcohol, even in medicinal doses, to patients suffering from cholera or from various other acute diseases and intoxications, including diphtheria, tetanus, snake-bite and pneumonia, as being not merely useless but positively harmful. Even when the patient has advanced far toward recovery from an acute infectious disease, it is held still to be highly unwise to administer alcohol, since this may inter-

DR. B. F. RILEY,
Superintendent Anti-Saloon League of
Texas.

JAMES KURTZ SHIELDS,
Superintendent Anti-Saloon League of
Illinois.

ULYSSES G. HUMPHREY,
Superintendent Anti-Saloon League of
Wisconsin.

fere with the beneficent action of the anti-toxins that have developed in the tissues of the body, and in virtue of which the disease has been overcome.

Not many physicians, perhaps, will go as far as Dr. Muirhead, of Edinburgh, who at one time claimed that he had scarcely known of a death in a case of pneumonia uncomplicated by alcoholism; but almost every physician will admit that he contemplates with increased solicitude every case of pneumonia thus complicated. Equally potent, seemingly, is alcohol in complicating that other ever-menacing lung disease, tuberculosis. Dr. Crothers long ago asserted that inebriety and tuberculosis are practically inter-convertible conditions; a view that may be interpreted in the words of Dr. Dickinson's Baillie Lecture: "We may conclude, and that confidently, that alcohol promotes tubercle, not because it begets the bacilli, but because it impairs the tissues, and makes them ready to yield to the attacks of the parasites." Dr. Brouardel, at the Congress for the Study of Tuberculosis, in London, was equally emphatic as to the influence of alcohol in preparing the way for tuberculosis, and increasing its virulence; and this view has now become general—curiously reversing the popular impression, once held by the medical profession as well, that alcohol is antagonistic to consumption.

Corroborative evidence of the baleful alliance between alcohol and tuberculosis is furnished by the fact that in France the regions where tuberculosis is most prevalent correspond with those in which the consumption of alcohol is greatest. Where the average annual consumption was 12.5 litres per person, the death rate from consumption was found by Baudron to be 32.8 per thousand. Where alcoholic consumption rose to 35.4 litres, the death rate from consumption increased to 107.8 per thousand. Equally suggestive are facts put forward by Guttstadt in regard to the causes of death in the various callings in Prussia. He found that tuberculosis claimed 160 victims in every thousand deaths of persons over twenty-five years of age. But the number of deaths from this disease per thousand deaths among gymnasium teachers, physicians and Protestant clergyman, for example, amounted, respectively, to 126, 113 and 76 only; whereas the number rose, for hotel keepers, to 237; for brewers, to 344, and for waiters, to 556. No doubt several factors complicate the problem here, but one hazards little in suggesting that a difference of habit as to the use of alcohol was the chief determinant in running up the death rate due to tuberculosis from 76 per thousand at one end of the scale to 556 at the other.

Pneumonia and tuberculosis combined account for one-fifth of all deaths in the United States, year by year. In the light of what has just been shown, it would appear that alcohol here has a hand in the carrying off of untold thousands with whose untimely demise its name is not officially associated. I may add that certain German authorities, including, for example, Dr. Liebe, present evidence—not as yet demonstrative—to show that cancer must also be added to the list of diseases to which alcohol predisposes the organism.

If additional evidence of the all-pervading influence of alcohol is required, it may be found in the thought-compelling fact that the effects are not limited to the individual who imbibes the alcohol, but may be passed on to his descendants. The offspring of alcoholics show impaired vitality of the most deep-seated character. Sometimes this impaired vitality is manifested in the non-viability of the offspring; sometimes in deformity; very frequently in neuroses, which may take the severe forms of chorea, infantile convulsions, epilepsy or idiocy. In examining into the history of 2,554 idiotic, epileptic, hysterical or weak-minded children in the institution at Bicetre, France, Bourneville found that over 41 per cent. had alcoholic parents. In more than 9 per cent. of the cases, it was ascertained that one or both parents were under the influence of alcohol at the time of procreation,—a fact of positively terrifying significance, when we reflect how alcohol inflames the passions while subordinating the judgment and the ethical scruples by which these passions are normally held in check. Of similar import are the observations of Bezzola and of Hartmann that a large proportion of the idiots and the criminals in Switzerland were conceived during the season of the year when the customs of the country—"May-fests," etc.—lead to the disproportionate consumption of alcohol.

Experimental evidence of very striking character is furnished by the reproductive histories of Professor Hodge's alcoholized dogs. Of 23 whelps born in four litters to a pair of tipplers, 9 were born dead, 8 were deformed, and only 4 were viable and seemingly normal—meantime, a pair of normal kennel companions produced 45 whelps of which 41 were viable and normal—a percentage of 90.2 against 17.4 per cent. of viable alcoholics. Professor Hodge points out that these results are strikingly similar to the observation of Demme on the progeny of ten alcoholic as compared with ten normal families of human beings. The ten alcoholic families produced 57 children, of whom 10 were deformed, 6 idiotic, 6 choreic or epileptic, 25 non-viable and only 10, or 17 per cent. of the whole, were normal. The ten normal families produced 61 children, two of whom were deformed, 2 pronounced "backward," though not suffering from disease, and 3 non-viable, leaving 54, or 88.5 per cent., normal.

As I am writing this article, the latest report of the Craig Colony for Epileptics, at Sonyea, New York, chances to come to my desk. Glancing at the tables of statistics, I find that the superintendent, Dr. Spratling, reports a history of alcoholism in the parents of 313 out of 950 recent cases. More than 22 per cent. of these unfortunates are thus suffering from the mistakes of their parents. Nor does this by any means tell the whole story, for the report shows the 577 additional cases—more than 60 per cent. of the whole—suffer from "neuropathic heredity"; which means that their parents were themselves the victims of one or another of those neuroses that are peculiarly heritable, and that unquestionably tell, in a large number of cases, of alcoholic indulgence on the part of their progenitors. "Even to the third and fourth generation," said the wise Hebrew of old; and the laws of heredity have not changed since then.

I cite the data from this report of the Epileptic Colony, not because its record is in any way exceptional, but because it is absolutely typical. The mental image that it brings up is precisely comparable to that which would arise were we to examine the life histories of the inmates of any institution whatever where dependent or delinquent children are cared for, be it idiot asylum, orphanage, hospital or reformatory. The same picture, with the same insistent moral, would be before us could we visit a clinic where nervous diseases are treated; or—turning to the other end of the social scale—could we sit in the office of a fashionable specialist in nervous diseases and behold the succession of neurotics, epileptics, paralytics and degenerates that come day by day under his observation. It is this picture, along with others which the preceding pages may in some measure have suggested, that comes to mind and will not readily be banished when one hears advocated "on physiological grounds" the regular use of alcoholic drinks, "in moderation." A vast number of the misguided individuals who were responsible for all this misery never did use alcohol except in what they believed to be strict "moderation"; and of those that did use it to excess, there were few indeed who could not have restricted their use of alcohol to moderate quantities, or have abandoned its use altogether, had not the drug itself made them its slaves by depriving them of all power of choice. Few men indeed are voluntary inebriates.

It does not fall within the scope of my present purpose to dwell upon the familiar aspect of the effects of alcohol suggested by the last sentence. It requires no scientific experiments to prove that one of the subtlest effects of this many-sided drug is to produce a craving for itself, while weakening the will that could resist that craving. But beyond noting that this is precisely in line with what we have everywhere seen to be the typical effect of alcohol—the weakening of higher functions and faculties, with corresponding exaggeration of lower ones—I shall not comment here upon this all too familiar phase of the alcohol problem. Throughout this paper I have had in mind the hidden cumulative effects of relatively small quantities of alcohol rather than the patent effects of excessive indulgence. I have had in mind the voluntary "social" drinker, rather than the drunkard. I have wished to raise a question in the mind of each and every habitual user of alcohol in "moderation" who chances to read this article, as to whether he is acting wisely in using alcohol habitually in any quantity whatever.

If in reply the reader shall say: "There is some quantity of alcohol that constitutes actual moderation; some quantity that will give me pleasure and yet not menace me with these evils," I answer thus:

Conceivably that is true, though it is not proved. But in any event, no man can tell you what the safe quantity is—if safe quantity there be—in any individual case. We have seen how widely individuals differ in susceptibility. In the laboratory some animals are killed by doses that seem harmless to their companions. These are matters of temperament that as yet elude explanation. But this much I can predict with confidence: whatever the "safe" quantity of alcohol for you to take, you will unquestionably at times exceed it. In a tolerably wide experience of men of many nations, I have never known an habitual drinker who did not sometimes take more alcohol than even the most liberal scientific estimate could claim as harmless. Therefore, I believe that you must do the same.

So I am bound to believe, on the evidence, that if you take alcohol habitually in any quantity whatever, it is to some extent a menace to you. I am bound to believe, in the light of what science has revealed: (1) that you are tangibly threatening the physical structures of your stomach, your liver, your kidneys, your heart, your blood vessels, your nerves, your brain; (2) that you are unequivocally decreasing your capacity for work in any field, be it physical, intellectual, or artistic; (3) that you are in some measure lowering the grade of your mind, dulling your higher esthetic sense, and taking the finer edge off your morals; (4) that you are distinctly lessening your chances of maintaining health and attaining longevity; and (5) that you may be entailing upon your descendants yet unborn a bond of incalculable misery.

Such I am bound to believe, is the probable cost of your "moderate" indulgence in alcoholic beverages. Part of that cost you must pay in person; the balance will be the heritage of future generations. As a mere business proposition: Is your glass of beer, your bottle of wine, your high-ball, or your cocktail worth such a price?

CHAPTER VI.

SALOON SINS AS SEEN BY A SUFFERER.

NOTE.—*In* THE INDEPENDENT *for September* 10, 1908, *there appeared the following article which possesses the highest value as evidence against the saloon. Much of the hostility to that institution is based upon its visible effects upon the individual and social life. Few of the temperance orators and advocates have known the inside of the saloon, but this contributor had personal experience. In a note to the editor of* THE INDEPENDENT, *he says:* "*I am not a writer, and am not aware whether the inclosed strictly personal experiences and observations have any value for the public or not. During the present discussion of the astounding 'dry movement', however, it has occurred to me that if there is any subject on earth on which I am competent to write, it should be that whose name heads the enclosed article. If original information gathered at first hand depends for its value upon the amount of money spent to secure it, said article should be a valuable one. A perusal of the article will convey the reason why it must be published anonymously, if at all." The article is reproduced here by permission.*—G. M. H.

ON reviewing a rich and variegated personal experience of saloons, which extends from New York to Denver, the feature that stands out most prominently in my recollection as true of all of them is the hard, listless, unfeeling type of men who keep saloons. Saloonkeepers are all alike, and they are all of this type. The keeper of a swagger place on Broadway is of just the same type as the keeper of a humble little joint in Orange, N. J., only that he is harder. The *bonhomie*, the good fellowship, supposed by some to prevail among saloon habitués, is totally lacking in saloonkeepers. There is plenty of it of the artificial variety when a man has money, but a man may spend a hundred dollars in a saloon one night, and have the saloonkeeper refuse to give him a drink the next morning when he is suffering for it, or give it to him in such a way as to spoil the drink. I never knew a saloonkeeper who was really a good fellow.

Saloonkeepers as a class are of a different type from the grocers and other tradesmen around them, a harder, tougher type, singularly impervious to human sympathy or interest in any matter whatever except the coin. Even when pleasant young fellows who are like anybody else go into the business they lapse into this type in a few years. I have in mind two young men who a few years ago were semi-professional athletes, very popular, very jolly, cheerful, and good company. They went into the saloon business, and both today are typical saloonkeepers, hard, sneering, *blasé*, saturnine.

There is a reason for all this. One sees a lot of human nature in trade, even behind the ribbon counter. The saloonkeeper sees worse and more of it than anybody else. Everybody is trying to stick the saloonkeeper. I have known men who would never think of beating a board or grocery bill who would unhesitatingly hang up the saloonkeeper.

Nobody feels any conscience about the matter. It is almost impossible for any saloonkeeper to collect a bill without taking legal measures. And they hesitate very much about doing this—first, because the judge doesn't greet them with open arms; more largely because it renders them unpopular and hurts their business. I knew a saloonkeeper in Denver who would attach a man's wages for a bill, but it made him so unpopular that he finally went out of business. The saloonkeeper feels that every man's hand is against him, that he is despised and looked down upon, and that hardens him; something, I suppose, as it does the prostitute.

He is not equally hard everywhere, however. In New Jersey the saloonkeepers are the most human, the most like other men, of any place where it has been my pleasure and privilege to make their acquaintance. They are harder in New York, in Denver; and they are hardest in Kansas City of any place I have known. I have seen a saloonkeeper lean his elbows on his bar in Kansas City and watch two men beat up another and say not a word. Nothing of that kind could happen in Orange. A fight is stopped instantly. Many saloonkeepers give away a great deal of liquor. The most successful saloonkeeper who ever lived in a large Eastern city is said to have given away more drinks than many men sold. It was purely advertising on his part, and very cheap and good advertising. He became famous locally, and his place was always crowded. I must say, however, that I never saw the thing referred to in the following clipping. In the recent campaign in Alabama an effective argument widely used in pamphlets and newspaper advertisements by the anti-saloon party consisted of a brief speech by the opposition, from which we quote:

"Men who drink liquor, like others, will die, and if there is no appetite created, our counters will be empty, as will be our money drawers. . . . It will be needful, therefore, that missionary work be done among the boys, and I make the suggestion, gentlemen, that nickels expended in treats to the boys now will return in dollars to your tills after the appetites have been formed. Above all things, create appetites."

I never saw that done, although I have known saloonkeepers who, in my opinion, would be quite capable of it, if they were capable of such a long look ahead. And I never saw any enticing of young girls into wine

HON. JOHN B. MARTIN,
Member, National Committee, Prohibition Party,
Candidate for Governor of Ohio, 1908.

GEORGE E. STOCKWELL, D. D.,
Prohibition Party Candidate for Governor of New York, 1903.

rooms to ruin them, though I have no doubt such things are done. Of course, girls have got to take their first drink some time, but I must confess that I never saw a girl in a wine-room who looked to me as if she were getting her first drink. Different places are very different about that, as well as other things. In Denver, when I was there, the saloons were full of disreputable women, drinking with the men right at the bar. One would come up and nudge you and say, "How's things for a drink?" The barkeeper would say, "Yes, go on, throw a drink into her." It cost twenty-five cents at the cheapest to treat a woman there. If one took a five-cent drink and gave her the same, the bill was twenty-five cents. Of this the house kept a dime and gave her a check for fifteen, which she cashed in at the end of the evening. At this period in Denver gambling was all under cover. One couldn't get a game unless he knew where to go. In Pueblo, 120 miles away in the same state, not a woman was to be seen in the saloons, but games were running full blast in every one, from the humblest dive to the most extravagant layout. I suppose some difference in city ordinances or in public sentiment made the difference.

In New York it is not at all customary for women to mix with the men in the saloon proper, although one is occasionally seen there for a moment. But the wine-rooms back of the saloon are always full of women in the evening. The price for treating one of them is the same as in Denver, twenty-five cents for the cheapest drink. But the girl gets nothing: the house takes it all. The New York saloons consider that they pay the girls by giving them a safe place where they can come in off the street and be out of the way of the police.

In my experience, laws, and particularly enforcement, make a very great difference in the conduct of saloons. In Orange, N. J., for instance, I have heard a saloonkeeper more than once refuse to sell to a minor who certainly looked to me to be twenty-one years old. Nothing but law produced this. There are also no games run by the saloons in Orange. If there were no state law against gambling in New Jersey, I do not know as there would be faro layouts and other games, as in Western saloons. There never have been in Orange. But there would be slot machines in every saloon, as there were a few years ago. In these slot machines, which are run by a syndicate, one puts in a nickel, with the possibility of drawing out up to twenty nickels. The saloonkeepers "holler" sadly because these have been taken out. One told me that his slot machine used to be worth $100 a Sunday, half of which went to the syndicate and half to him. His patronage was nearly all colored. Negroes are very fond of these machines. They were, however, in the very highest grade saloons in great number and variety. I have seen high grade saloons throughout the country fairly lined with them, and they collect probably more money in such places than in the colored saloons. The patrons do not plunge on them, like the colored brother. They put in a nickel to see what it will do and then run along. But as nickels are so much more plentiful among this class and the transient trade is so large, the collections are undoubtedly heavy. In Orange some saloonkeepers kept these in a side room, covered with a curtain, or in a cupboard or closet, after the gambling law began to be enforced.

It is true also that there is practically no Sunday selling today in Orange under the enforcement of the "bishops'" law by Sheriff Frank H. Sommer, of Essex county. Saloons close on the stroke of midnight, Saturday, and the bar remains exposed to view all day Sunday. As a result, I know one place in Orange where I can get a drink Sunday, in a saloonkeeper's flat over his saloon. Others may know of another place, but the Sunday saloon business is practically closed.

The saloonkeepers resent this fiercely. They refer to Sheriff Sommer in the most unprintable language; many of his deputies have been assaulted, and I can truthfully say that I do not think there is a saloonkeeper in Orange who would not be glad to hear that he had been assassinated. This is not at all strange, for Sunday was their big day. Many of them would rather close all the rest of the week and open Saturday night and Sunday. One man told me that before the "bishops" law went into effect he was taking in $250 a Sunday in his saloon, which sum had been lifted bodily out of his weekly receipts. He says he is not making expenses, that he paid $3,000 for the place and cannot sell it at any price, and that he sees nothing but to throw up his license and quit, $3,000 out of pocket and livelihood gone. There are many subtle phases of this Sunday closing question. As every one knows, the Oranges are dormitory towns, filled with rich New Yorkers and the professional and trades people who serve them. But in Orange proper there is also an industrial population—the hatters in what is known as the Valley. These hatters are great patrons of the saloon, although they seldom drink anything but beer.

One of these hatters said to me the other day: "This Sunday closing law is turning me from a beer drinker into a whisky drinker." He went on to explain that because it was so easy to carry home one or two quart bottles of whisky Saturday night he was taking that instead of beer. "Before Sunday closing," said he, "my kids never saw me take a drink. They've seen me drunk twice on Sunday since." He also said that the law was turning houses into saloons. A number of men put together and order cases of beer sent to one house. Then they go there to drink and play cards on Sunday. The bottling business has certainly increased in Orange since the present *régime* began. I know personally of two saloonkeepers who have given up their business and gone into the bottling, delivering at the houses; and there are others. Nevertheless, there must be a great deal less drinking, for there is not a saloonkeeper in Orange who wears a smiling face.

The closing sharp at midnight has more to do with this than the Sunday closing. It is pretty hard for an Orange Valley hatter to get outside enough beer before midnight to make him drunk, and if a man gets home before he is thoroughly soused, he gives up what is left in his pockets to his wife or his people. Parents are getting board money who didn't before, and wives are spending more for shoes and grub and such like vanities. And the fellows themselves have more loose change in their clothes through the week. They have admitted that to me. The hatter's drinking is very light through the week. Four or five beers a day will cover it till Saturday night.

Aside from the saloonkeeper's financial anxiety at this epoch, he has a moral grudge against the community. He says: "The rich people, with cellars full of wine and liqueurs that they can souse in all the time, want to keep the poor man from buying a pint of beer of Sunday." This is perfectly true; *i. e.*, it is true that the rich man can and does drink when he pleases. There is a certain club with which I am quite as familiar as I am with the hatters' saloons. The men who support it do so in order to have a place where they can drink and play cards exclusively with their own class. It is merely a saloon, a restricted, coöperative saloon. It draws its revenues from precisely the same sources as the saloon: from drinks, cigars and cards. The restaurant is run by a separate management. The club rents rooms, but so also do many saloonkeepers. The food, drinks and tobacco consumed at this club are more expensive than at the saloon; the talk is also of more expensive things; that is all the difference. The club members also drink more than the hatters. They drink more steadily throughout the week, and they drink harder drinks. There is, however, far less drunkenness. The reasons for this, pursued to their end, lead one to a consideration of the whole difference between the two classes of men; and a comparative study of the drinking habits of club men and working men results in most interesting discoveries. In the first place, the club man is better nourished than the hatter. That makes a great difference in the effect the liquor has. In the second place, he distributes his liquor evenly over seven days instead of crowding it into one. But there is more than this. With the typical club man there is not only no drunkenness, but no thought of drunkenness. Such a thing doesn't enter his scheme of life at all. The great body of the men I have in mind are in the active occupation of making money, either in good salaried positions or in their own business. Such a man will commonly take a whisky and soda at 10 in the morning, and another before luncheon. Before dinner he will take a cocktail. With dinner he will drink wines; and during the evening he will take perhaps a couple of whiskies with seltzer. Of course, there is a difference in the drinks; some take more wines or brandies, but a great deal more whisky is drunk than anything else. By the time he goes to bed such a man has been stimulated all day; he has taken a great deal more alcohol into his system than the hatter, and yet he has not even approached intoxication. He has drunk scientifically, so to speak. He has imbibed for a specific purpose; for stimulant, not for intoxication.

Now the workingman when he starts in on his Saturday night time, drinks to get drunk. His intention is to drink until he gets that happy feeling which makes him think he would not exchange places with Rockefeller. There is nothing else on earth which can give him that feeling, and he wants the feeling. He wants the world and its cares and brutalities to fade away and leave him feeling like a prince. I have seen that in the Eastern factory operative, and I have seen it in the Leadville miner. I remember particularly one Christmas at Leadville in the late '90's. The saloons frequented by miners were full of a crazy, howling mob, singing, yelling, waving bottles, jumping on faro tables and dancing among the chips. In one corner stood a giant in the last stages before jimjams. He brandished a chair about his head and laid out everybody who came near him. Guns had to be used and a rush made before he was secured. I particularly remember a big miner with a red shirt and a red beard, who had just enough when he came in to make him dignified. He stepped up to the bar, raised his hand, and "Give 'em all a drink," he said, with the dignity of a duke; "Give 'em all a drink." It was a time when all the miners were coming in with money in their clothes, and many were giving similar orders. So the whole house was treated. When it was all over Red Shirt said solemnly to the barkeeper: "Well, it's on you; I haven't got a cent." The next minute he hit the floor. These men drank to get drunk. It was their deliberate intention. And they were a very dangerous crowd, for they were of a reckless, fearless, lawless type that one doesn't find among factory operatives, and nearly all of them carried guns. Now in any club I ever knew anything about there were a few older men—but only a very few—who had crossed the line and become drunkards. They would take liquor to their rooms and drink alone; soak themselves. They were on their way to dipsomania, or already there, and irreclaimable. Such men have occasionally to be fired out of every club. They become uninhabitable, so to speak. There is also a set of young fellows, having their first fling, who drink for exactly the same purpose as the workingman: to get that happy feeling. They also become intoxicated. But the solid mass of successful men who make up club membership and keep the clubs going, never get drunk; never drink to get drunk; and if the young fellows graduate into the same class, they stop getting drunk, too, and get their drinking down to a scientific routine. Such men work at high pressure, hard and fast, in business hours; and they drink in order to work harder and go faster and get the pressure higher. They drink for stimulus. This is the difference, as I have seen it, between clubmen's drinking and workingmen's drinking; and it leads me to the irresistible conclusion that the workingman never grows up mentally. He remains mentally immature, like the young fellows at the club, of whom I have spoken. He doesn't get past that stage; does not acquire the will power, the force, to subordinate his desire for a present good time to the demands of health, reputation and business. Or, perhaps, he never, like the young clubman, sees the prizes of life within his grasp if he keeps straight. He knows instinctively, if not through logical reasoning, that there is nothing ahead of him but a dead succession of monotonous days, and that the only good times he will ever have are those he gets as he goes along. And we must add to this fact that when the workingman gets drunk it is always in public, where everybody knows all about it; which is not true of the clubman. At all events, the difference between the two is not in any sense a moral difference. It is a difference in brains, in temperament, in self-control, a difference in what they see that they can get out of life. The clubman drinks more and spends more for his drinks than the workingman. Of course, in using these terms I speak only of drinking men. Not all business men frequent clubs, and not all workingmen frequent saloons.

Now it is a question whether the public has anything to do with any club. Men who drink there can afford to drink; drink themselves into their graves, if they like. It is not likely that the clubman's family will ever come to charity or his children be deprived of proper care or education because of his drinking. I don't know that society has any business interfering with any vice or habit which does not entail a specific burden on society. There is this deeper fact, however, that just so long as men of wealth, power and influence in their respective communities, are drinking men, no sincere help can be expected from them in the control or extermination of saloon evils. I have seen drinking in their clubs prosecuting attorneys, judges, other men whose business it is to see that laws are enforced. The inference is obvious.

A long course of observation in many towns has convinced me that the hours between midnight and 6 A. M. are the most dangerous in the twenty-four for the saloon to keep open. It is during those hours that a man gets so drunk that he goes to sleep in low-grade saloons and wakes up in the alley, robbed of his money and perhaps of his clothes. It is in those hours that the majority of fights, thefts and killings occur in saloons. It is in those hours that a man gets so drunk that he doesn't go home that night, and as a consequence perhaps not for several nights; and then perhaps to find himself out of a job and his wife gone home to her people. And those six hours on Saturday night—or Sunday morning—are the most dangerous in the whole week. If the saloon closes at twelve, almost any man will go home if he has a home to go to. And if he goes home then, he may lie around the house Sunday, and go to the saloon late in the day or not at all. If I were obliged to choose between the two, I would close from 12 to 6 A. M., Sunday, rather than later in the day. Any community would get a return out of all proportion to the effort involved, by compelling closing during those hours Saturday night, and proportionately greater, of course, by closing those hours every night. In this connection I believe a universal custom of a Monday instead of a Saturday pay night would have an economic value to society greater than any other one thing equally small and easy to accomplish.

Whether it is just or expedient to exterminate the saloon altogether or not, we certainly have a right to regulate, since we regulate other occupations. The first and most important of all regulations is to close absolutely and inviolably, throughout the whole United States, every night at twelve. It is nonsense to say it cannot be done. If the police give the order, it will be done; and if the people of this republic cannot control their police forces they are unworthy of self-government. One necessary feature of any such law is that every bar must be exposed to full view during closed hours.

Saloon conditions in Kansas City, Mo., are the worst I ever saw among the third-rate saloons; the saloonkeepers the most brutalized, the saloons the most lawless and unregulated. It is an all-night town, the saloons never closed from one year's end to another. Men lie all over the saloon floors asleep all night, and of course their clothes are gone through regularly. "Strong-arm" work is a regular thing. In this one man catches another by the back of the neck with one hand and claps the other over his mouth. Then a pal goes through the victim. The saloonkeepers know this is going on all the time.

In connection with saloon life in the West I want to mention "short changing." In many places in the West they run dance halls or concert halls in connection with the saloon, and the customer at these sits down at a table and is served by a waiter. It is a regular part of the system for these waiters to bring a man less change than he is entitled to when he pays his bill. They never try this on a crowd that comes in together. They try it on one fellow alone, or perhaps two, particularly when they seem to be half soused, so that they will not notice their change. If the victim shows himself in the least hostile, he is pounced upon by bouncer and waiters, beaten, kicked and thrown out. If he applies to a policeman, the latter will

REV. J. R. KNODELL,
Assistant Superintendent, Anti-Saloon League of Oregon.

REV. R. W. RAYMOND,
Superintendent, Anti-Saloon League of Washington.

laugh and say, "Run along, little boy"; or, if he insists, will tap him over the head with his club.

I imagine it is conditions like these—the appurtenances of saloons rather than the actual drink itself—which has given the present prohibition movement in this country its strength. Many drinking men have grown to hate the whole business and the way it is conducted, and, despairing of ever regulating it, have concluded that the only way to get back at it is to put it out of existence. One other thing I believe is influencing such men is the awful nature of the beer sold over the bar. It has changed abominably in my time, and my experience doesn't go back very many years. A barkeeper who had grown gray in the business told me that the beer would not keep three days in the kegs; that they had to be extremely careful to order only the exact amount necessary, as, if they had only one keg too much, it would spoil. Another said to me, "I sell beer all day, but I never drink a glass of it; it isn't fit to drink." It is a burning shame that if the government permits its manufacture it does not compel a pure product. There is no doubt that the hops in America go into beer. But there is so much beer and so few hops that the latter are used only in special brands such as one finds in clubs—brands that cost ten cents for a small bottle at wholesale. In the common saloons a "scuttle," which holds as much as three of these bottles, can be had for five cents, which shows the kind of stuff the workingmen are pouring into their unhappy stomachs.

Now as to the deepest part of the whole question: the reason for the saloon's attraction. It is not the drink simply. A man could just as well order the stuff to his house and drink there. As a matter of fact, not one man in a hundred drinks alone at home; and when he does, he is a gone duck. He never recovers. It is the social side of it, and the gang, or clique, element. A certain bunch of fellows gets to going to a saloon to play cards or other games, not necessarily gambling, of an evening; to talk, sing, tell stories, have a good time generally. They are not drunkards, or crooks or toughs. They are honest working boys, or young fellows in salaried positions. Here is where the drink comes in. One treats, then another. Each must hold up his end and treat in his turn. After awhile they begin to feel happy. Cares clear away. The world begins to look cheerful. They forget their troubles. They are having a good time. A fellow could take a soft drink each time and some of them do. But he isn't enjoying himself like the rest. The world is just the same to him. The songs and stories don't seem uproariously good. After awhile they get stupid; he gets tired and goes home. I have seen many a man start in on the soft drink plan. One of two things invariably happened to him. Either he began to drink alcoholics, or he pulled out altogether and stopped going to saloons. Soft drinks don't make a man happy. It's the liquor makes a man think he is having a gloriously good time. After awhile he wakes up and finds the taste for liquor fixed on him; he can't get along without it; he's got the appetite, which, in nine cases out of ten, he did not have to start with.

It is this good time that makes drunkards; makes it of men who have not the slightest taste for liquor when they begin; who even dislike it and are made sick by it. Neither a boy brought up in a total abstinence home, nor the boy accustomed to wine at every meal, is safe. The latter boy, like the former, may reach youth without the taste for liquor. He has never drunk enough at the family table to acquire the appetite. There has been no temptation there to over-indulgence. But neither method protects the boy when he gets into a bunch that gets its good times in this way. There are mighty few things in this world that give a man, particularly a workingman, who lives a sordid, ugly life, the happy feeling that comes from liquor in a social crowd. It is not the taste of the drink at first, it is the happy feeling it gives him. By the time he has got sense enough to see the consequences, the appetite is too often fixed upon him. Then it becomes a physical as well as a moral and economic question.

The woman's side of this question has often been written up from the standpoint of the wife and mother. I do not know, however, as I have ever seen brought out the fact that the saloon prevents many women from marrying at all. A young man who has got into the way of going to the saloon every night, in such a clique as I have described, finds his amusement and entertainment that way. He doesn't go to call on girls, he doesn't spend evenings at their houses, take them to dances, shows and so on. Other fellows may get their fun out of this sort of thing, but not he. And if he does see a girl to whom he would like to pay a little attention, he has no money and no good clothes. His system cuts girls out of lots of good times and entertainments, which would not cost men nearly as much as they spend in saloons.

The above description, of course, is of the workingman's saloon, the "poor man's club." In the high-grade saloons there is a chillier and more formal atmosphere. These places have their habitués, like the other, but the very fact that they are expensive and attractive places implies that they cannot depend on local trade like the little neighborhood joints, but cater to a big transient custom, which keeps them filled with men who are strangers to each other. In these places there is no noise, no disturbance of any description. In some of them there are not even chairs. And yet they are tougher than the workingman's saloon; tougher because of the wine-rooms in behind filled with women; still tougher because of the private rooms upstairs where men who are known to the place may take women to drink. I have in mind now high-class saloons in New York. Such a place has a quiet, unobtrusive, concentrated toughness quite lacking in the workingman's little neighborhood joint.

Harking back to the workingman's saloon once more, the kind I have described as the resort of cliques of friends, I want to depose my honest belief that if the custom of treating could be absolutely done away with, drunkenness would almost cease. Any man who begins the evening sober, and especially if he has not yet acquired the taste for liquor, will, if he drinks nothing but what he pays for himself, wait awhile between drinks. If, when the bunch sits down to play each man would order his own drink, he would not order another unless he really wanted it. He would play along and talk along happily enough, without drinking any great amount. Four or five in the evening would be enough; he would get sleepy and go home in a reasonable hour. But with the custom of every man treating in turn, as they invariably do, the drinks come around so fast that they are fairly poured into a man. He gets happy very soon, and then he gets drunk, and then he gets the appetite fastened on him.

Now, in combating the saloon, I want to register my sincere conviction that there is nothing that will take a saloon bunch away from the saloon except baseball. The masses are crazy over baseball. They like it better than the theater, better than any show, better than the saloon. On Sundays all through summer, when baseball games are running, the saloons are emptied. And the men are not only not drinking, they are also saving money and sitting out in the open air. I believe Sunday baseball is the strongest enemy the saloon has got among saloon habitués. The churches fight Sunday amusements, and are particularly earnest against Sunday baseball; and I confess that baseball makes a lot of noise. Nevertheless, baseball is a perfectly clean, decent, innocent amusement, and I solemnly register my belief that among drinking workingmen it is the saloon's only competitor.

CHAPTER VII.

THE SALOON AN OUTLAW.

By George S. Hawke, LL. B.,

Prohibition Candidate (1908) for Attorney General of Ohio.

NOWHERE have the charges against the traffic in intoxicating liquor had more pronounced and unequivocal expression than in the formal findings of the courts of the United States. Beginning with that august body, the Supreme Court of the United States, and following down through the various Federal and State courts, there is an unbroken line of decisions which leaves the saloon no legal standing whatever.

For instance, the courts have declared—

That a citizen has no inherent right to traffic in intoxicants;

That no state or municipality can be compelled to license or permit the traffic;

That a license, if issued, is not a contract, and does not bind the state on the one hand, or confer special rights upon the traffic on the other;

That the traffic is inimical to public health, morals and safety;

That it is the chief source of crime, vice and misery;

That a license may be canceled at any time without redress;

That, wherever prohibition goes into effect, whether by constitutional amendment, state law or municipal ordinance, or local option by popular vote or otherwise, the traffic has no vested right to be protected, and the dealer has no ground for damages;

That personal liberty is limited by public welfare.

Some courts hold that the saloon is a common nuisance, and as such may be abated at any time.

There are also decisions presenting other phases of the question. But, taking the findings of the courts as a whole, it may be stated in general terms that—

No saloon in the United States today has any legal right to exist. All of them may be closed permanently by the enforcement of existing laws, and the application of established precedents.

In the last analysis, good law must always conform to good common

HON. GEORGE S. HAWKE,
Candidate Attorney-General, Ohio Prohibition Party, 1908.

REV. ERVIN S. CHAPMAN, D. D., LL. D.
Superintendent, Anti-Saloon League of California.

sense. Common sense has its basis in the lessons derived from common human experience. So, by common consent, no member of a community is permitted to scatter poison about, to store gunpowder among residences, to spread a contagious disease, or to perform any act or to engage in any occupation or traffic that imperils the welfare of the community.

And so it happens that, as the race becomes more and more aware from experience of the evil effects of intoxicants, the sentiment against their manufacture and sale becomes more decided, and finds higher and clearer expression in ordinances, laws and court decisions. The higher sentiment of the present day regarding the traffic in intoxicating liquors is clearly expressed in a decision read by Justice Field of the Supreme Court of the United States, in which it is declared that:

"The police power of the State is fully competent to regulate the business, to mitigate its evils, or to suppress it entirely. There is no inherent right in a citizen to sell intoxicating liquor by retail; it is not a privilege of a citizen of the State or of a citizen of the United States."

Judge Samuel R. Artman, of Indiana, says:

"The United States Supreme Court has used the expression, 'There is no inherent right in a citizen to thus sell intoxicating liquor,' no less than twelve different times. And almost every state supreme court of the Union has declared that no person has an inherent right to keep a saloon. The cases in which such declarations have been made are so numerous that it would be a test of time, eyes and digests to collect and cite all of them, and to do so would serve no useful purpose. It is sufficient to say that the declaration has been made by the Supreme Courts of the States of Indiana, Illinois, South Carolina, Idaho, Iowa, Virginia, Alabama, South Dakota, Arkansas, Delaware, Kansas, Georgia, Pennsylvania, New York, North Carolina, New Jersey, Maryland, District of Columbia and perhaps others."

In this chapter is given a digest of the more important decisions of the various State and Federal courts on the subject of the manufacture and sale of liquor.

STATE PROHIBITION OF THE LIQUOR TRAFFIC CONSTITUTIONAL.

In *License Cases*, 46 U. S. 504 (How), Chief Justice Taney said:

"But I do not understand the law of Massachusetts and Rhode Island as interfering with the trade in ardent spirits while the article remains a part of foreign commerce, and is in the hands of the importer, in the cask or vessel in which the laws of Congress authorized it to be imported. These State laws act altogether upon the retail or domestic traffic within their respective borders. They act upon the article after it has passed the line of foreign commerce, and has become a part of the general mass of property in the State. These laws may, indeed, discourage imports, and diminish the price which ardent spirits would otherwise bring. But, although a State is bound to receive and to permit the sale by the importer of any article of merchandise which Congress authorizes to be imported, it is not bound to furnish a market for it nor to abstain from the passage of any law which it may deem necessary or advisable to guard the health or morals of its citizens, although such law may discourage importation, or diminish the profits of the importer, or lessen the revenue of the general government. And if any State deems the retail and internal traffic in ardent spirits injurious to its citizens, and calculated to produce idleness, vice or debauchery, I see nothing in the Constitution of the United States to prevent it from regulating and restraining the traffic, or from *prohibiting it altogether*, if it thinks proper."

LEGISLATURE CANNOT BARGAIN AWAY THE POLICE POWER OF A STATE.

Stone vs. Mississippi, 101 U. S. 814, *Syllabus*:—"In 1867, the legislature of Mississippi granted a charter to a lottery company for twenty-five years in consideration of a stipulated sum in cash, an annual payment of a further sum, and a percentage of receipts from the sale of tickets. A provision of the Constitution adopted in 1868 declares that 'the legislature shall never authorize any lottery, nor shall the sale of lottery tickets be allowed, nor shall any lottery heretofore authorized be permitted to be drawn, or tickets therein to be sold.' Held—

"1. That this provision is not in conflict with Section 10, Article I, of the Constitution of the United States, which prohibits a state from 'passing a law impairing the obligation of contracts'.

"2. That such a charter is in legal effect nothing more than a license, to enjoy the privilege covered for the time and on the terms specified, subject to future legislative or constitutional control or withdrawal.

"3. The legislature cannot by chartering a lottery company defeat the will of the people of the State authoritatively expressed, in relation to the continuance of such business in their midst."

Chief Justice Waite said:—"All agree that the legislature cannot bargain away the police power of a State. Irrevocable grants of property and franchises may be made, if they do not impair the supreme authority to make laws for the right government of the State; but no legislature can curtail the power of its successors to make such laws as they may deem proper in matters of police."

"Many attempts have been made in this court and elsewhere to define the police power but never with entire success. It is always easier to determine whether a particular case comes within the general scope of the power, than to give an abstract definition of the power itself which will be in all respects accurate. No one denies, however, that it extends to all matters affecting the public health or the public morals."

"No legislature can bargain away the public health or the public morals. The people themselves cannot do it, much less their servants. The supervision of both these subjects of governmental power is continuing in its nature, and they are to be dealt with as the special exigencies of the moment may require. Government is organized with a view to their preservation, and cannot divest itself of the power to provide for them.

For this purpose the largest legislative discretion is allowed, and the discretion cannot be parted with any more than the power itself."

PROHIBITORY LIQUOR LAWS IMPAIR NO OBLIGATION OF CONTRACT.

Beer Company vs. Massachusetts, 97 U. S. 25, *Syllabus*:—"The question raised in this case is whether the charter of the Beer Company, which was granted in 1828, contains any contract the obligation of which was impaired by the prohibitory liquor law of Massachusetts, passed in 1869.

"The Company under its charter, has no greater right to manufacture or sell malt liquors than individuals possess, nor is it exempt from any legislative control therein to which they are subject.

"All rights are held subject to the police power of the State; and if the public morals require the discontinuance of any manufacture or traffic, the legislature may provide for its discontinuance, notwithstanding individuals or corporations may thereby suffer inconvenience.

"As the police power of a State extends to the protection of the lives, health and property of her citizens, the maintenance of good order, and the preservation of the public morals, the legislature cannot, by any contract, divest itself of the power to provide for these objects.

"As a measure of police regulations, a state law prohibiting the manufacture and sale of intoxicating liquors is not repugnant to any clause of that Constitution."

PROHIBITION LEGISLATION DOES NOT INFRINGE ANY RIGHT SECURED BY THE CONSTITUTION OF THE UNITED STATES.

Mugler vs. Kansas and *Kansas vs. Ziebold,* 123 U. S. Reports, 623, *Syllabus*:—"State legislation which prohibits the manufacture of spirituous, malt, vinous, fermented or other intoxicating liquors within the limits of the State, to be sold or bartered for general use as a beverage, does not necessarily infringe any right, privilege or immunity secured by the Constitution of the United States, or by the Amendments thereto.

"The prohibition by the State of Kansas, in its constitution and bylaws, of the manufacture or sale within the limits of the State of intoxicating liquors for general use there as a beverage, is fairly adapted to the end of protecting the community against the evils which result from excessive use of ardent spirits; and is not subject to the objection that, under the guise of police regulations, the State is aiming to deprive the citizen of his constitutional rights.

"Lawful State legislation, in the exercise of the police powers of the State, to prohibit the manufacture and sale within the State of spirituous, malt, vinous, fermented, or other intoxicating liquors, to be used as a beverage, may be enforced against persons who, at the time, happen to own property whose chief value consists in its fitness for such manufacturing purposes, without compensating them for the diminution in its value resulting from such prohibitory enactments.

"A prohibition upon the use of property for purposes that are declared by valid legislation to be injurious to the health, morals or safety of the community, is not an appropriation of property for the public benefit, in a sense in which a taking of property by the exercise of the State's power of eminent domain is such a taking or appropriation.

"The destruction in the exercise of the police power of the State of property used, in violation of law, in maintaining a public nuisance, is not a taking of property for public use, and does not deprive the owner of it without due process of law.

"A State has constitutional power to declare that any place kept and maintained for the illegal manufacture and sale of intoxicating liquors shall be deemed a common nuisance, and be abated; and at the same time to provide for the indictment and trial of the offender.

"There is nothing in the provisions of Section 13 of the Statutes of the State of Kansas of March 7, 1885, amendatory of the Act of February 19, 1881, so far as they apply to the proceedings reviewed in these cases, which is inconsistent with the constitutional guarantees of liberty and property; and the equity power conferred by it to abate a public nuisance without a trial by jury is in harmony with settled principles of equity jurisprudence.

"If the provision that, in a prosecution by indictment or otherwise, the State need not in the first instance prove that the defendant has not the permit required by the Statute, as in any application to the proceeding in equity authorized by the Statute of Kansas of 1881, as amended in 1885, it does not deprive him of the presumption that he is innocent of any violation of law; and does him no injury, as, if he has such permit, he can produce it."

Mugler vs. Kansas, 123 U. S. 623:—"It is not necessary, for the sake of justifying the State legislation now under consideration, to array the appalling statistics of misery, pauperism and crime which have their origin in the use or abuse of ardent spirits. For we cannot shut out of view the facts, within the knowledge of all, that the public health, the public morals and the public safety may be endangered by the general use of intoxicating drinks; nor the fact established by statistics accessible to everyone, that the idleness, disorder, pauperism and crime existing in the country are, in some degree at least, traceable to this evil."

THE RIGHT TO SELL INTOXICANTS CANNOT BE CLAIMED AS A COMMON LAW RIGHT.

The People ex rel. Morrison vs. Cregier, 138 Illinois Reports, p. 401: —"While it is true that anterior to any statute on the subject, the right to engage in the business of selling intoxicating liquors was a right recognized and protected by the rules of common law, and stood substantially upon the same footing with other commercial pursuits, the rules of the common law in that respect have long since been abrogated by statute, and are no longer in force. The Dram-Shop Act, which so far as this matter is concerned only took the place of similar legislation which had been long on our statute books, declares the business of selling intoxicating liquors in quantities less than one gallon to be criminal, except so far as it is expressly authorized and made lawful by license. The tendency of the

MRS. LUCY S. BLANCHARD,
President, Woman's Parliament of Southern California.

MRS. SARA J. DORR,
President, Northern California W. C. T. U.

liquor traffic is so completely shown by all human experience, that from an early day said traffic has been subjected in this state to the surveillance and control of the police power, and we presume such has been the case in most if not all civilized communities. The right therefore to engage in this business and to be protected by law in its prosecution can no longer be claimed as a common law right, but is a right which can be exercised only in the manner and upon the terms which the statute prescribes. The refusal to license deprives no man of any personal or property right, but merely deprives him of a privilege which it is in the discretion of the municipal authorities to grant or withhold. It also follows that to adopt the policy of prohibition requires no affirmative act on the part of the authorities authorized to provide for granting licenses. Mere non-action on their part of itself results in prohibition."

POWER TO LICENSE LIQUOR TRAFFIC DORMANT.

Idem, Syllabus:—"1. The statute confers upon municipal corporations the power to license, regulate and prohibit the sale of intoxicating liquors, those powers being given, not in the alternative, but cumulatively, and to be exercised concurrently whenever the municipal authorities, in their discretion, see fit to exercise them.

"2. The power to license, regulate and prohibit the sale of intoxicating liquors must be exercised by a city or village by means of an ordinance passed by the proper municipal authorities. The mere legislative grant of this power does not, of itself, authorize the corporate authorities to issue licenses. The power is dormant, until called into exercise by appropriate municipal legislation."

THE RIGHT TO SELL INTOXICATING LIQUOR NOT AN INALIENABLE RIGHT.

Sherlock vs. Stuart, 96 Michigan, 193, part of *Syllabus*:—"1. No one possesses a natural, inalienable or constitutional right to keep a saloon for the sale of intoxicating liquors (citing Black, *Intox. Liq.*, Secs. 46-48).

"2. The principle upon which is based the regulation of the liquor traffic is found in the police power of the State.

"3. The restrictions and conditions which may be imposed upon the liquor traffic are entirely within the discretion of the people, acting through the legislature; and they have the right to prohibit the low, vicious and the criminal from engaging in it."

A LICENSE TO ENGAGE IN THE LIQUOR TRAFFIC NOT A CONTRACT.

State vs. Gerhardt, 145 Indiana Reports, 439; part of *Syllabus*:— "A license to engage in the liquor traffic is not a contract or grant, but a mere permit, and the applicant who receives it does so with the knowledge that it is at all times within the control of the legislature."

Part of *Court's Opinion*, 450:—"As preliminary to a decision of the questions herein involved it may be proper to call attention to the rule by which this court is controlled in the determination of the constitutionality of any particular law, and also to the extent to which the police power of the state may be invoked to sustain a legislative act. As to the expediency or wisdom of a statute, we have no concern; that is a question lodged wholly within the discretion of the legislature. The court cannot declare a statute unconstitutional and void solely on the grounds of unjust and oppressive provisions, or because it is supposed to violate the natural, social or political rights of the citizen, unless it can be shown that such injustice is prohibited, or such rights guaranteed or protected by the constitution.

"It is said, and properly so, that the courts are not the guardians of the rights of the people, except as those rights are secured by constitutional provisions which come within judicial cognizance. An act of the legislature comes to us as the will of the sovereign power. In the first instance, the members of that body must be deemed to be the judges of their own constitutional authority. The state's executive, and each member of its general assembly, take an oath to support the constitution, both federal and state, and as these can only be supported by obeying and enforcing their provisions, we must presume that these duties were discharged by our law makers in the passage of the particular act in question, and by the Governor when he officially gave to it his sanction and approval. For these reasons and others, all presumptions as to its validity must be indulged in its favor, and it is only when made to appear clearly, palpably, and plainly, and in such a manner as to leave no reasonable doubt or hesitation in our minds, that a statute violates some provisions of the constitution that we can consistently declare it void. This rule has been repeatedly affirmed by this court, and by other courts generally, throughout the nation.

"The police power of a state is recognized by the courts to be one of wide sweep. It is exercised by the state in order to promote the health, safety, comfort, morals and welfare of the public. The right to exercise this power is said to be inherent in the people in every free government. It is not a grant, derived from or under any written constitution. It is not, however, without limitation, and it cannot be invoked so as to invade the fundamental rights of a citizen. As a general proposition, it may be asserted that it is the province of the legislature to decide when the exigency exists for the exercise of this power, but as to what are the subjects which come within it, is evidently a judicial question."

A LICENSE TO SELL LIQUORS GIVES NO VESTED RIGHT.

Board of Excise vs. Barrie, 34 N. Y., 657; part of *Syllabus*:—"The legislature has the constitutional right to regulate and control the traffic in intoxicating liquors; a license to sell liquors gives no vested right which is within the protection of the constitution; it is not a contract."

A LAW PROHIBITING TRAFFIC IN INTOXICATING LIQUORS VIOLATES NO CONSTITUTIONAL RESTRAINTS.

Idem, p. 666:—"A law prohibiting the indiscriminate traffic in intoxicating liquors, and placing the trade under public regulation, to prevent abuse in their sale and use, violates no constitutional restraints. Is it not an absurd proposition that such a law, by its own mere force, deprives any person of his liability or property, within the meaning of the constitution, or that it infringes upon either of these secure private rights?"

PROHIBITORY LAWS VIOLATE NO RIGHTS IN PROPERTY.

Idem, p. 667:—"These licenses to sell liquors are not contracts between the state and the persons licensed, giving the latter vested rights, protected on general principles and by the constitution of the United States, against subsequent legislation; nor are they property, in any legal or constitutional sense. They have neither the qualities of a contract nor of property, but are merely temporary permits to do what otherwise would be an offense against a general law. They form a portion of the internal police system of the state; are issued in the exercise of its police powers and are subject to the discretion of the state government, which may modify, revoke, or continue them, as it may deem fit."

People vs. Village of Crotty, 93 Illinois Reports, 180; *Syllabus*:— "An incorporated village being a municipal corporation, can properly do only such acts as the law enables it to perform, and, being a creature of the law, it can exercise the powers conferred upon it only in the manner provided by law.

"The mere grant of power by the legislature to a municipal corporation to license, regulate and prohibit the sale of intoxicating liquors, will not, of itself, authorize its authorities to issue a license. This power is a dormant one, and affords no authority to issue licenses until called into life and put into operation by appropriate legislation by the municipalities."

CLAIM FOR COMPENSATION CANNOT BE MAINTAINED BY BREWERS IN A PROHIBITION STATE.

During the October term, 1887, three cases came up by appeal to the Supreme Court of the United States, two in error from the Supreme Court of the State of Kansas, and one, on appeal, from the Circuit Court of the United States for the District of Kansas.

Opinion of Justice Harlan, p. 653:—"These cases involve an inquiry into the validity of certain statutes of Kansas relating to the manufacture and sale of intoxicating liquors. The first two are indictments charging Mugler, the plaintiff in error, in one case with having sold, and in the other with having manufactured, spirituous, vinous, malt, fermented and intoxicating liquors in Saline county, Kansas, without having the license or permit required by the statute. The defendant, having been found guilty, was fined in each case $100, and ordered to be committed to the county jail until the fine was paid. Each judgment was affirmed by the Supreme Court of Kansas, and thereby it is contended the defendant was denied rights, privileges and immunities guaranteed by the Constitution of the United States.

"The third case (*Kansas vs. Ziebold & Hagelin*) was commenced by petition filed in one of the courts of the state. The relief sought is:

"1. That the group of buildings constituting the brewery of the defendants, partners, as Ziebold & Hagelin, in Atchison county, Kansas, be adjudged a common nuisance, and the sheriff, or other proper officer, directed to shut up or abate the same.

"2. That the defendants be enjoined from using or permitting to be used, the said premises as a place where intoxicating liquors may be sold, bartered or given away, or kept for barter, sale or gift, otherwise than by authority of the law.

"The defendants answered, denying the allegations of the petition and averring:

"1. That said buildings were erected by them prior to the adoption by the people of Kansas of the Constitutional Amendment prohibiting the manufacture and sale of intoxicating liquors for other than medicinal, scientific and mechanical purposes, and before the passage of the prohibitory liquor statute of that state.

"2. That they were erected for the purpose of manufacturing beer, and cannot be put to any other use; and, if not so used, they will be of little value.

"3. That the statute under which said suit was brought is void under the Fourteenth Amendment of the Constitution of the United States.

Page 656:—"The facts necessary to a clear understanding of the questions common to these cases are the following:

"Mugler and Ziebold & Hagelin were engaged in manufacturing beer at their respective establishments (constructed specially for that purpose) for several years prior to the adoption of the Constitutional Amendment of 1880. They continued in such business in defiance of the Statute of 1881, and without having the required permit. Nor did Mugler have a license or permit to sell beer. The single sale of which he was found guilty, occurred in the State, and after May 1, 1881, that is, after the Act of February 19, 1881, took effect, and was of beer manufactured before its passage.

"The buildings and machinery constituting these breweries are of little value if not used for the purpose of manufacturing beer; that is to say, if the statutes are enforced against the defendants the value of their property will be very materially diminished. The general question in each case is whether the foregoing statutes of Kansas are in conflict with that clause of the Fourteenth Amendment, which provides that—

"'No state shall make or enforce any law which shall abridge the privileges or immunities of citizens of the United States, nor shall any state deprive any person of life, liberty or property, without due process of law.'

"That legislation by a state prohibiting the manufacture within her limits of intoxicating liquors, to be there sold or bartered for general use as a beverage, does not necessarily infringe any right, privilege or immunity secured by the Constitution of the United States, is made clear by the decisions of this court, rendered before and since the adoption of

JONATHAN S. LEWIS,
Chairman Massachusetts Prohibition State Committee.

W. D. COX,
Chairman Wisconsin Prohibition State Committee.

W. G. CALDERWOOD,
Secretary Minnesota Prohibition State Committee.

JOHN B. LEWIS, Jr.,
Member National Committee, Prohibition Party, Massachusetts.

the Fourteenth Amendment, to some of which, in view of questions to be presently considered, it will be well to refer."

In determining the question it became necessary to inquire whether there was any conflict between the exercise by Congress of its power to regulate commerce with foreign countries, or among the several states, and the exercise by a state of what are called police powers. Although the members of the court did not fully agree as to the grounds upon which the decision should be placed, they were unanimous in holding that the statutes then under examination were not inconsistent with the Constitution of the United States, or with any act of Congress.

Page 659:—"It is, however, contended that, although the state may prohibit the manufacture of intoxicating liquors for sale or barter within her limits, for general use as a beverage, 'No convention or legislature has the right, under our form of government, to prohibit any citizen from manufacturing for his own use, or for export, or storage, any article of food or drink not endangering or affecting the rights of others.' The argument made in support of the first branch of this proposition, briefly stated, is:

"That in the implied contract between the state and the citizen, certain rights are reserved by the latter which are guaranteed by the constitutional provision protecting persons against being deprived of life, liberty or property, without due process of law, and with which the state cannot interfere; that among those rights is that of manufacturing for one's own use either food or drink; and that while, according to the doctrines of the Commune, the state may control the tastes, appetites, habits, dress, food and drink of the people, our system of government, based upon the individuality and intelligence of the citizen, does not claim to control him, except as to his conduct toward others, leaving him the sole judge as to all that only affects himself.

"It will be observed that the proposition, and the argument made in support of it, equally concede that the right to manufacture drink for personal use is subject to the condition that such manufacture does not endanger or affect the rights of others. If such manufacture does prejudicially affect the rights and interests of the community, it follows, from the very premises stated, that society has the power to protect itself, by legislation, against the injurious consequences of that business. As was said in *Munn vs. Illinois*, 94 U. S. 124: 'While power does not exist with the whole people to control rights that are purely and exclusively private, government may require each citizen to so conduct himself, and so use his own property, as not unnecessarily to injure another.'

"By whom, or by what authority, is it to be determined whether the manufacture of particular articles of drink will injuriously affect the public? Under our system that power is lodged with the legislative branch of the government. There are of necessity limits beyond which legislation cannot rightfully go. While every possible presumption is to be indulged in favor of the validity of a statute, the courts must obey the constitution rather than the law-making department of government. They are at liberty to look at the substance of things. If, therefore, a statute, purporting to have been enacted to protect the public health, the public morals, or the public safety, has no real or substantial relations to those objects, or is a palpable invasion of rights secured by the fundamental law, it is the duty of the courts to so adjudge, and thereby give effect to the constitution.

"Keeping in view these principles, it is difficult to perceive any ground for the judiciary to declare that the prohibition by Kansas of the manufacture or sale within her limits of intoxicating liquors for general use as a beverage, is not fairly adapted to the end of protecting the community against the evils which confessedly result from the excessive use of ardent spirits.

"If, therefore, a state deems the absolute prohibition of the manufacture and sale within her limits of intoxicating liquors for other than medicinal, scientific and manufacturing purposes, to be necessary to the peace and security of society, the courts cannot, without usurping legislative functions, override the will of the people as thus expressed by their chosen representatives. They have nothing to do with the mere policy of legislation. Indeed, it is a fundamental principle in our institutions, indispensable to the preservation of public liberty, that one of the separate departments of government shall not usurp powers committed by the constitution to another department. And so, if, in the judgment of the legislature, the manufacture of intoxicating liquors for the maker's own use as a beverage, would tend to cripple, if it did not defeat, the effort to guard the community against the evils attending the excessive use of such liquors, it is not for the courts, upon their views as to what is best and safest for the community, to disregard the legislative determination of that question.

"Power which states have of prohibiting such use by individuals of their property as will be prejudicial to the health, morals, or safety of the public, cannot be burdened with a condition that the state must compensate such individual owners for pecuniary losses they sustain by reason of their not being permitted by a noxious use of their property to inflict injury upon the community. The exercise of the police power by the destruction of property which is itself a public nuisance, or the prohibition of its use in a particular way, whereby its value becomes depreciated, is very different from taking property for public use, or from depriving a person of his property without due process of law. In the one case, a nuisance only is abated; in the other, unoffending property is taken away from the innocent owner.

"It is true that, when the defendants in these cases purchased or erected their breweries, the laws of the state did not forbid the manufacture of intoxicating liquors. But the state did not thereby give any assurance, or come under any obligation, that its legislation upon that subject would remain unchanged. Indeed, as was said in *Stone vs. Mississippi*, 101 U. S., the supervision of the public health and the public morals is a governmental power, 'continuing in its nature,' and 'to be dealt with as the special exigencies of the moment may require'; and that, 'for this purpose, the largest legislative discretion is allowed, and the discretion cannot be parted with any more than the power itself.'

"It is contended in the case that the entire scheme of Section 13, Act of 1885, is an attempt to deprive persons who come within its provisions of their property and liberty without due process of law.

"It is said that by the section of the Act of 1885 the legislature, finding a brewery within the state in actual operation, without notice, trial or hearing, by the mere exercise of its arbitrary caprice declares it to be a common nuisance, and then prescribes the consequences which are to follow by judicial mandate required by the statute.

"This is a formidable arraignment of the legislation of Kansas and, if it were founded upon a just interpretation of its statutes, the court would have no difficulty in declaring that they could not be enforced without infringing the constitutional rights of the citizen.

"But these statutes have no such scope, and are not attended with any such results as the defendants suppose. The court is not required to give effect to a legislative 'decree' or 'edict,' unless every enactment by the lawmaking power of a state is to be so characterized.

"It is not declared that every establishment is to be deemed a common nuisance, because it may have been maintained prior to the passage of the statute as a place for manufacturing intoxicating liquors. The statute is prospective in its operation; that is, it does not put the brand of a common nuisance upon any place, unless, after its passage, that place is kept and maintained for purposes declared by the legislature to be injurious to the community. Nor is the court required to adjudge any place to be a common nuisance simply because it is charged by the state to be such. It must first find it to be of that character; that is, must ascertain, in some legal mode, whether, since the statute was passed, the place in question has been, or is being, so used as would make it a common nuisance.

Page 672:—"Equally untenable is the proposition that proceedings in equity for the purposes indicated in the thirteenth section of the statute are inconsistent with the due process of law.

"As to the objection that the statute makes no provision for a jury trial in cases like this, it is sufficient to say that such a mode of trial is not required in suits in equity brought to enjoin a public nuisance.

"It cannot be denied that the defendants kept and maintained a place that is within the statutory definition of a common nuisance. Their petition for the removal of the cause from the state court, and their answer to the bill, admitted every fact necessary to maintain this suit, if the statute under which it was brought was constitutional.

"Touching the provision that in prosecutions, by indictment or otherwise, the state need not, in the first instance, prove that the defendant has the permit required by the statute, we may remark that, if it has any application to a proceeding like this, it does not deprive him of the presumption that he is innocent of any violation of law. It is only a declaration that, when the state has proved that the place described is kept and maintained for the manufacture or sale of intoxicating liquors, such manufacture or sale being unlawful except for specified purposes, and then only under a permit, the prosecution need not prove a negative, namely, that the defendant has not the required license or permit. If the defendant has such license or permit, he can easily produce it, and thus overthrow the *prima facie* case established by the state.

"A portion of the argument in behalf of the defendants is to the effect that the statutes of Kansas forbid the manufacture of intoxicating liquors to be exported, or to be carried to other states, and upon that ground are repugnant to the clause of the constitution of the United States giving Congress power to regulate commerce with foreign nations and among the several states. We need only say upon this point that there is no intimation in the record that the beer which the respective defendants manufactured was intended to be carried out of the state or to foreign countries. And, without expressing an opinion as to whether such facts would have constituted a good defense, we observe that it will be time enough to decide a case of that character when it shall come before us.

"For the reasons stated, we are of opinion that the judgments of the Supreme Court of Kansas have not denied to Mugler, the plaintiff in error, any right, privilege, or immunity secured to him by the Constitution of the United States, and its judgment, in each case, is accordingly affirmed.

"We are also of opinion that the Circuit Court of the United States erred in dismissing the bill of the State against Ziebold & Hagelin. The decree in that case is reversed and the cause remanded, with direction to enter a decree granting to the state such relief as the Act of March 7, 1885, authorizes."

When the Constitution of the United States of America was framed there existed an inter-relation of "States" since impossible. Thirteen sovereign, free and independent commonwealths, which had been leagued together for common defense, security of liberties, mutual and general welfare, dissolved the Confederation and organized a "more perfect union." When the Constitutional Convention provided for a grant of power to Congress for the purpose of regulating commerce among the States, it is evident that the constitution-makers had no intention to force a traffic of any kind upon an unwilling State. While the constituent States surrendered certain rights, they retained their "police powers" undiminished, and these involved rights of self-protection against any form of commerce which should imperil the peace or health of their citizen subjects. It was upon questions of interstate commerce that the Confederation of 1778 had split; it was the purpose of the Union of 1787 to regulate that commerce, so as to free it from the burdens of tariff that had hampered its development.

As the new States were created they entered the Union with constitutions providing for the exercise of self-protective police powers. To these powers the Supreme Court concedes the right to abolish the liquor traffic —a right which the Federal government may not impair in the name of "regulating" commerce. For, if the term "regulate" does not involve the abolition or prohibition of a traffic, neither does it imply the creation of such traffic where a State has outlawed it. When a State, by law, pro-

J. M. GUILE,
Treasurer and State Attorney, Anti-Saloon League of Nebraska.

REV. E. E. McLAUGHLIN,
Superintendent, Anti-Saloon League of Colorado.

hibits a traffic, there is no "interstate commerce" in the interdicted commodity—and, therefore, no commerce to "regulate"—for it takes two parties to constitute trade.

THE RIGHT TO SELL INTOXICATING LIQUORS BY RETAIL NOT INALIENABLE.

Crowley vs. Christensen, 137 United States Reports 86—Henry Christensen, a saloonkeeper of San Francisco, was arrested upon the charge of having carried on the business of selling intoxicating liquors without the license required by the ordinance of the city and county. In order to secure a license, it was necessary for the applicant first to secure the written consent of a majority of the Board of Police Commissioners of the city and county of San Francisco, or the written recommendation of not less than twelve citizens of San Francisco, owning real estate in the block in which said business was to be carried on.

The Police Commissioners having withdrawn their consent to the further issue of a license to him, he continued business without it, and was arrested.

The Circuit Court of the United States held that the ordinance made the business of the saloonkeeper depend upon the arbitrary will of others, and in that respect denied to him the equal protection of the laws. This judgment was reversed by the Supreme Court of the United States.

Part of *Syllabus*:—"The sale of spirituous and intoxicating liquors by retail and in small quantities may be regulated, or may be absolutely prohibited by state legislation without violating the constitution or laws of the United States."

After stating the case as above, Justice Field delivered the opinion of the Court, page 89:—"It is undoubtedly true, that it is the right of every citizen of the United States to pursue any lawful trade or business, under such restrictions as are imposed upon all persons of the same age, sex and condition. But the possession and enjoyment of all rights are subject to such reasonable conditions as may be deemed by the governing authority of the country essential to the safety, health, peace, good order and morals of the community. Even liberty itself, the greatest of all rights, is not unrestricted license to act according to one's own will. It is only freedom from restraint under conditions essential to equal enjoyment of the same right by others. It is liberty regulated by law. The right to acquire, enjoy and dispose of property is declared in the constitutions of several states to be one of the inalienable rights of man. But this declaration is not held to preclude the legislature of any state from passing laws respecting the acquisition, enjoyment and disposition of property. What contracts respecting its acquisition and disposition shall be valid, and what void and voidable; when they shall be in writing, and when they may be made orally, and by what instruments it may be conveyed or mortgaged, are subjects of constant legislation. And as to the enjoyment of property, the rule is general that it must be accompanied with such limitations as will not impair the equal enjoyment by others of their property. *Sic utere tuo ut alienum non laedas,* is a maxim of universal application.

"For the pursuit of any lawful trade or business, the law imposes similar conditions. Regulations respecting them are almost infinite, varying with the nature of the business. Some occupations by the noise made in their pursuit, some by the odors they engender and some by the dangers accompanying them, require regulation as to the locality in which they shall be conducted. Some because of the dangerous character of the articles used, manufactured or sold require, also, special qualifications in the parties permitted to use, manufacture or sell them. All this is but common knowledge, and would hardly be mentioned were it not for the position often taken, and vehemently pressed, that there is something wrong in principle and objectionable in similar restrictions, when applied to the business of selling by retail, in small quantities, spirituous and intoxicating liquors. It is urged that, as the liquors are used as a beverage, and the injury following them, if taken in excess, is voluntarily inflicted and is confined to the party offending, their sale should be without restrictions, the contention being that what a man shall drink, equally with what he shall eat, is not properly matter for legislation.

"There is in this position an assumption of a fact which does not exist, that when liquors are taken in excess the injuries are confined to the party offending. The injury, it is true, first falls upon him in his health, which habit undermines; in his morals, which it weakens, and in the self-abasement, which it creates. But, as it leads to neglect of business and waste of property and general demoralization, it affects those who are immediately connected with and dependent upon him. By the general concurrence of opinion of every civilized and Christian community, there are few sources of crime and misery to society equal to the dram-shop, where intoxicating liquors, in small quantities, to be drunk at the time, are sold indiscriminately to all parties applying. The statistics of every state show a greater amount of crime and misery attributable to the use of ardent spirits obtained at these retail liquor saloons than to any other source. The sale of such liquors in this way has therefore been, at all times, by the courts of every state, considered as the proper subject of legislative regulation. Not only may a license be exacted from a keeper of the saloon, before a glass of his liquors can be disposed of, but restrictions may be imposed as to the class of persons to whom they may be sold, and the hours of the day and the days of the week on which the saloon may be opened. Their sale in that form may be absolutely prohibited. It is a question of public expediency and public morality, and not of federal law. The police power of the state is fully competent to regulate the business, to mitigate its evils or to suppress it entirely. *There is no inherent right in a citizen to thus sell intoxicating liquors by retail; it is not a privilege of a citizen of the state or a citizen of the United States.* As it is a business attended with danger to the community, it may, as already said, be entirely prohibited, or be permitted under such conditions as will limit to the utmost its evils. The manner and extent of regulation rest in the discretion of the governing authority. That authority may vest in such officers as it may deem proper, the power of passing upon application for permission to carry it on, and to issue license for that purpose. It is a matter of legislative will only. As in many other cases, the officers may not always exercise the power conferred upon them with wisdom or justice to the parties affected. But that is a matter which does not affect the authority of the state; or one which can be brought under the cognizance of the courts of the United States."

LIQUOR NOT TO BE PLACED ON THE SAME FOOTING WITH ORDINARY COMMODITIES OF LIFE.

The Supreme Court of South Carolina, in the case of *The State ex rel. George vs. Aiken,* 26 L. R. A. 345, said:—"Liquor, in its nature, is dangerous to the morals, good order, health and safety of the people, and is not to be placed upon the same footing with the ordinary commodities of life, such as corn, wheat, cotton, potatoes, etc."

DRUNKENNESS PRODUCES AT LEAST FOUR-FIFTHS OF CRIME THE TESTIMONY OF THOSE WHO ADMINISTER CRIMINAL LAW.

The Supreme Court of Kansas, in the case of *Durien vs. State,* 80 Pac. 987, said:—"The commodity in controversy is intoxicating liquor. The article is one whose moderate use even is taken into account by actuaries of insurance companies, and which bars employment in classes of service involving prudent and careful conduct—an article conceded to be fraught with such contagious peril to society that it occupies a different status before the courts and the legislatures from other kinds of property, and places traffic in it upon a different plane from other kinds of business. It is still the prolific source of disease, misery, pauperism, vice and crime. Its power to weaken, corrupt, debauch and slay human character and human life is not destroyed or impaired because it may be susceptible of some innocent uses, or may be used with propriety on some occasions. The health, morals, peace and safety of the community at large are still threatened."

Judge Gookins, in the case of *Beebe vs. The State,* 6 Ind. 542, said: —"That drunkenness is an evil, both to the individual and to the state, will probably be admitted. That its legitimate consequences are disease and destruction to the mind and body, will also be granted. That it produces from four-fifths to nine-tenths of all the crimes committed is the united testimony of those judges, prison-keepers, sheriffs and others engaged in the administration of the criminal law, who have investigated the subject. That taxation to meet the expenses of pauperism and crime, falls upon and is borne by the people, follows as a matter of course. That its tendency is to destroy the peace, safety and well-being of the people, to secure which the first article in the Bill of Rights declares all free governments are instituted, is too obvious to be denied."

THE RIGHT TO PURSUE A LAWFUL BUSINESS AN INALIENABLE RIGHT.

In *Butchers' Union Slaughter House Co. vs. Crescent City Live Stock Landing Co.*, 111 U. S. 746, Justice Field said:—"Among the inalienable rights, as proclaimed in the Declaration of Independence, 'is the right of men to pursue any lawful business or avocation, in any manner not inconsistent with the equal rights of others, which may increase their property or develop their faculties, so as to give them their highest enjoyment.' The common business and callings of life, the ordinary trades and pursuits, which are innocent in themselves, and have been followed in all communities from time immemorial, must, therefore, be free in this country, to all alike, upon the same terms. The right to pursue them without let or hindrance, except that which is applied to all persons of the same age, sex and conditions, is a distinguishing privilege of citizens of the United States, and an essential element of that freedom which they claim as their birthright."

In the same case Justice Bradley used the following language: "The right to follow any of the common occupations of life is an inalienable right; it was formulated as such under the phrase 'pursuit of happiness' in the Declaration of Independence, which commenced with the fundamental proposition that 'All men are created equal; that they are endowed by their Creator with certain inalienable rights; that among these are life, liberty, and the *pursuit of happiness.*' This right is a large ingredient in the civil liberty of the citizen."

A LICENSE THE GRANT OF A SPECIAL PRIVILEGE.

In *State vs. Frame*, 39 Ohio State 413, the Supreme Court of Ohio said:—"A license is essentially the granting of a special privilege to one or more persons, not enjoyed by citizens generally, or, at least, not enjoyed by a class of citizens to which the licensee belongs." (This is a saloon license case.)

POLICE POWER INCLUDES EVERYTHING ESSENTIAL TO PUBLIC SAFETY, HEALTH AND MORALS.

In *Lawton vs. Steele*, 152 U. S. 133, the United States Supreme Court said:—"The extent and limits of what is known as the police power have been a fruitful subject of discussion in the appellate courts of nearly every state in the Union. It is universally conceded to include everything essential to the public safety, health and morals, and to justify the destruction of a house falling to decay or otherwise endangering the lives of passers-by; the demolition of such as are in the path of a conflagration; the slaughter of diseased cattle; the destruction of decayed or unwholesome food; the prohibition of wooden buildings in cities; the regulation of railways and other means of public conveyance, and of interments in burial grounds; the restriction of objectionable trades to certain localities; the compulsory vaccination of children; the confinement of the insane, or those afflicted with contagious diseases; the restraint of vagrants, beggars and habitual drunkards; the suppression of obscene publications and houses of ill fame; and the prohibition of gambling houses, and places where intoxicating liquors are sold."

THE IOWA MULCT LAW UNCONSTITUTIONAL.

The Iowa "mulct" law was enacted in 1894. It provided for an annual tax of $600 to be assessed against "every person, partnership or corporation, *other than pharmacists holding permits*, engaged in selling or keeping for sale any intoxicating liquors."

After having been in operation fourteen years it was pronounced null and void by Judge Smith McPherson, of the United States Circuit Court.

Liquor legislation in Iowa has had a varied history. In 1855, a prohibitory law was enacted but repealed in 1858. Thirty years passed. A constitutional amendment was submitted to the people and adopted by a "substantial majority," as Fehlandt says in his "CENTURY OF DRINK REFORM IN THE UNITED STATES." But the Supreme Court pronounced the vote unconstitutional on the ground that three words appeared in the text of the amendment as submitted to the people which were not found in the Journal of the General Assembly.

This decision aroused the temperance people of the state to such a pitch and climax of revolt that they threatened to hold the party in power responsible for failure to carry out the evident desire of the majority of the citizen voters. Under this potent influence, the legislature of 1884 enacted a prohibition law. Ten years later a mulct or tax law was enacted, practically nullifying the law of 1884, by permitting the traffic in intoxicating liquors on payment of an assessment of $600.

Thus it appears the "tax" law of 1894, popularly known as the "mulct law," was a mere subterfuge. The legislature, having power to strengthen the law of 1884, and the magistracy of the state having authority to enforce it to the letter, compromised on a so-called "tax."

On the same day on which Judge McPherson handed down this decision, he denied to the United Breweries of New Jersey an injunction restraining the Civic Federation of Davenport, Iowa, from interfering with one of its saloons in Princeton, Iowa, holding, in effect, that to enjoin the Federation would be similar to an injunction of the police powers of the state; also, that the Iowa law does not legalize the sale of liquor, merely making it conditional—the law of 1884 forbidding the sale of liquors, except by "persons holding permits" for specified purposes.

If the Iowa tax law had no constitutional basis and was in actual contravention of an unrepealed statute, there is reason to think that the Ohio liquor tax law, known as the Dow-Aiken law, is also null and void, and will be so pronounced by an unprejudiced tribunal. For, though

Iowa has a prohibitory law, Ohio has a constitution that prohibits license. The Iowa law contemplates the continuance of a business which has been placed under ban of law, the Ohio law contemplates the continuance of a business which the state refuses to permit. In either case, the legislature compromises with an illegal business, despite the fact that both in Ohio and Iowa the people had voted by large majority in favor of amending the state constitution so as to prohibit the business of trafficking in intoxicating liquors. In Iowa, the tax was assessed as a "mulct" or pecuniary forfeiture as a punishment for violating law. In Ohio, it was assessed to provide against "evils" resulting from a business to which the state denies a license.

TRANSPORTATION OF LIQUOR FROM ONE LOCAL OPTION COUNTY TO ANOTHER ILLEGAL.

Kentucky vs. Adams Express Company. Judgment against defendant affirmed on appeal, September 23, 1908.

Justice O'Rear discussed the difference between a person and a corporation, and showed how a corporation is humanized under the law, and held that, while the person indicted is a stock company, it was not intended that such an artificial person should be embraced within such exceptions of the bill as are designed for natural purposes. He said:

"The liquor was shipped from Mercer county to Springfield, in Washington county, all of which territory is wholly within the state of Kentucky. There was nothing to indicate the contents of the package and the consignee was a painter. The evidence indicates that the object of shipping the goods in that way was to deceive.

"Common carriers ought to obey the law like other persons, not merely in keeping the statute while breaking its spirit, but both in letter and spirit as others are expected to do. Agents employed by corporations ought to inquire and act on knowledge, probabilities, information, experiences, judgment, inferred facts from established facts, as men generally do in similar matters when thinking and acting for themselves. In this way a corporation is humanized and is made to see, hear, know, exercise care, skill, judgment, prudence, and is made amenable to the laws when the intent, motive, knowledge, etc., are elements of wrong."

THE RETAIL SALE OF INTOXICATING LIQUORS CANNOT BE LEGALLY LICENSED.

Albert Soltau vs. Schuyler Young, 20 Judicial Circuit Court, Indiana. Samuel R. Artman, Judge.

At the January session, 1907, of the Board of County Commissioners of Marion County, Albert Soltau filed his application for a license to sell intoxicating liquors at retail in the Tenth Ward of the city of Indianap-

O. A. REINHARDT,
Chairman Colorado Prohibition State Committee.

HON. SAMUEL R. ARTMAN,
Judge, Twentieth Judicial Court, Indiana.

olis. Schuyler Young and William J. Trefz, voters of said ward, appeared before said board and filed their remonstrance. Such proceedings were had before the board that a license was granted to the applicant, and, from this order of the board the remonstrators appealed to the Marion Circuit Court. From that court the case came to Judge Artman's court on a change of venue.

Judge Artman said:—"Waiving all questions as to the form and sufficiency of the demurrer, the ultimate question for decision in this case is whether or not the sale of intoxicating liquors, at retail, for beverage purposes, can be legally licensed.

"The court has no inclination to evade or side-step this proposition. The conclusions at which it has arrived have been reached after long, patient and mature deliberation, and the most careful consideration that the court is capable of giving the question.

"The position of this court then is this: The highest judicial authority of the state has declared a less injurious business inherently unlawful, and beyond the power of the state to delegate to it a legal existence, and this court is now asked, in the face of this declaration, to hold that the business, which has been declared by the highest judicial authority in the nation to be the most unlawful business in any state, can be given a legal existence by the state, for a fixed consideration. This court will not walk into this dilemma. The law should be harmonious.

"In the case of *Commonwealth vs. Douglass,* 100 Ky. 116, 24 S. W. Rep. 233; 66 Am. St. Rep. 328, the Court of Appeals of Kentucky distinguished the exercise of the police power from contract obligations, holding that a license to conduct a lottery was not a contract, but an attempted delegation of a right, which the state could not grant, because a lottery is vicious and demoralizing in the community. I quote from this opinion the following:

" 'The reason for this distinction must be apparent to all; for, when we consider that honesty, morality, religion and education are the main pillars of the state, and for the protection and promotion of which government was instituted among men, it at once strikes the mind that the government, through its agents, cannot throw off these trust duties by selling, bartering or giving them away. The preservation of the trust is essential to the happiness and welfare of the beneficiaries, which the trustees have no power to sell or give away. If it be conceded that the state can give, sell and barter any one of them, it follows that it can thus surrender its control of all, and convert the state into dens of bawdy houses, gambling shops, and other places of vice and demoralization, provided the grantees paid for the privileges, and thus deprive the state of its power to repeal the grants and all control of the subjects as far as the grantees are concerned; and the trust duty of protecting and fostering the honesty, health, morals and good order of the state would be cast to the winds, and vice and crime would triumph in their stead. Now it seems to us that the essential principles of self-preservation forbid that the commonwealth should possess a power so revolting, because destructive of the main pillars of government.

" 'The power of the state to grant a license to carry on any species of gambling, with the privilege of revoking the same at any time, has an unwholesome effect upon the community, and tends to make honest men revolt at the injustice of punishing others for engaging in like vices. We have, for instance, at this day, men confined in the state penitentiary for setting up and carrying on gambling shops whose tendencies are not much more demoralizing, if any, than the licensed lottery operator, who goes free under the protection of the law. The one wears a felon's garb, and the other is protected by license, which he claims is an irrevocable contract bcause he has paid for the privilege. The privilege ought never to be granted, and under the present constitution can never be. As said, to impress the privilege with the idea of contract because it was paid for, might fill the whole state, and especially the cities, with gambling shops and enterprises, protected by contract, and the few gamblers that might not be thus protected and who would be liable to be punished for gambling, would not be, because it would strike the honest man as unjust to punish the poor wretch for doing that which was made lawful for others to do by paying for the privilege.'

"To the same effect is the holding of the United States Supreme Court in the case of *Stone vs. Mississippi*, 101 U. S. 814, in which the court said: 'The question is, therefore, directly presented, whether, in view of these facts, the legislature of a state can, by the charter of a lottery company, defeat the will of the people, authoritatively expressed, in relation to the further continuance of such business in their midst. We think it cannot. No legislature can bargain away the public health or the public morals. The people themselves cannot do it, much less their servants. The supervision of both of these subjects of governmental power is continuing in its nature, and they are to be dealt with as the special exigencies of the moment may require. Government is organized with a view to their preservation, and cannot divest itself of the power to provide for them. For this purpose, the largest legislative discretion is allowed, and the discretion cannot be parted with any more than the power itself.'

"To the same effect in Ritter's *Moral and Civil Law*, Chapt. X; *People ex rel, vs. Squire, etc.*, 15 N. E. 820, and cases there cited.

"In view of these holdings, based, as they certainly are, upon good reason and sound common sense, it must be held that the state cannot, under the guise of a license, delegate to the saloon business a legal existence, because, to hold that it can, is to hold that the state may sell and delegate the right to make widows and orphans, the right to break up homes, the right to create misery and crime, the right to make murderers, the right to produce idiots and lunatics, the right to fill orphanages, poor-houses, insane asylums, jails and penitentiaries, and the right to furnish subjects for the hangman's gallows.

"The Supreme Court of Indiana, the Supreme Courts of many other states, and the Supreme Court of the United States, have already so far passed the middle of the stream upon the question involved in this case, that return would now be more difficult than to go over. To go over is merely to draw the natural, logical and inevitable conclusion from the declarations and judgments of the courts. To return would mean either to abandon the adjudication that the saloon business is unlawful at common law, or to hold that a business which has been adjudged by the courts to be unlawful at common law, because it naturally and inherently endangers the health, comfort, safety, morals and welfare of the people, may be legalized for money. Some court may so hold in this case, but it will not be done by this court. If it is done by any court, it must be done by the court that has already held the business to be unlawful, because of its inherently destructive effects upon society.

"With due appreciation of the responsibility of the occasion, conscious of my obligation, under my oath to Almighty God and to my fellowman, I cannot, by a judgment of this court, authorize the granting of a saloon license, and the demurrer to the amended remonstrance is, therefore, overruled, the amended remonstrance is sustained, and the application is dismissed at the costs of the applicant."

A RETAIL LIQUOR SALOON IS WITHIN ITSELF A PUBLIC NUISANCE.—
FINDING REVERSED.

On April 13, 1907, in the Circuit Court of Hamilton County, Indiana, in the case of the *State of Indiana vs. Edward Sopher*, Judge Ira W. Christian rendered an opinion holding that a retail liquor saloon is within itself a public nuisance, and that the statute authorizing the licensing of the saloon, is unconstitutional, and, therefore, that the saloon license was no defense. This opinion was rendered upon a motion to quash the affidavit.

Following the rendition of the opinion, the defendant applied for and was granted a change of venue from Judge Christian. Reed Holloman, former Prosecuting Attorney of the Boone Circuit Court, was appointed Special Judge to try the case. The trial was held on the 11th day of May, 1907, and, upon proof of the operation of the saloon, the judge found the defendant guilty of maintaining a public nuisance.

On June 25, 1907, only forty days after the case was filed in the Supreme Court, a decision, which had apparently been made before the case was filed in that court, was announced, in the Sopher case, reversing the decision of the trial court.

MUNICIPALITIES HAVE POWER TO REGULATE THE SALOON.

The Dow law of 1886 (83 Ohio Laws, 161) provided that, "Any municipal corporation shall have full power to *regulate, restrain and prohibit* ale, beer and porter houses, and other places where intoxicating liquors are sold at retail, etc." As to the validity of the Dow Law (Section 4364-20, Revised Statutes), see *Madden vs Smeltz*, 2 C. C. 168; *Van Wert vs. Brown*, 47 O. S. 477.

These two leading cases, and *Alliance vs. Joyce*, 49 O. S. 7, held that the council of a municipality in the State of Ohio had the right by ordinance to *prohibit saloons* within the boundaries of the municipality. This Dow law was amended in 1902, by what is known as the Beal Local Option Law (95 Ohio Laws, 87). The above section of the Revised Statutes (4364-20) was amended by the Beal Law, and now reads as follows:

"Any municipal corporation shall have full power to *regulate* the selling, furnishing, or giving away of intoxicating liquors as a beverage, and places where intoxicating liquors are sold, furnished or given away as a beverage, except as provided for in Section 4361 20c of this act. (1902, 95 v. 87)."

Under the original Section 4364-20, a municipal corporation had full power to "regulate, restrain and *prohibit*"; while under the present statute of the Beal Law, the corporation has full power only to "*regulate the selling.*" The words "restrain and prohibit" in the original Dow Law have been dropped in the Beal Law. Under the general powers of municipalities as given in the Municipal Code, Section 7, Clause 5 (96 Ohio Laws, 22), municipalities are given the powers "*to regulate.*"

This brings us to consider the meaning of the word "regulate." For consideration of the scope of the word "regulate" see *Brown v. Van Wert*, 4 C. C. 407-411, and the same case, 47 Ohio State, 477; also *Bronson vs. Oberlin*, 41 O. S. 476, 483.

The Court's opinion, p. 483:—"Whether the legislature could confer the power to prohibit the sale of intoxicating liquors, or whether the council by ordinance could prohibit with this power conferred, are questions not involved in this case. The question simply is, What power did this act confer? We are of the opinion that it did not give authority to prohibit. As expressed in the body of the law, it was a power to provide against the evils resulting from the sale of intoxicating liquors. Section 16, Article II. of the Constitution, provides that the subject of a bill pending before the General Assembly shall be clearly expressed in its title. The title of the law under consideration is 'An act authorizing certain incorporated villages to regulate the sale of intoxicating liquors therein.' Considering the words of this act, together with its title, we conclude that the power conferred was to regulate the sale of intoxicating liquors, and to provide against evils resulting therefrom, but not to prohibit. We are confirmed in this conclusion from the fact that in previous legislation the word 'prohibit' has been used when that was the object sought, and not alone the words 'to regulate' and 'to provide against evils.'"

An examination of the Supreme Court Reports since the enactment of the Beal Law of 1902, fails to discover that the Court has passed upon Section 4364-20 as revised by the Beal Law, in which a municipal corporation has power "to regulate the selling"; but, following the opinion in the case of *Bronson vs. Oberlin*, 41 O. S. 476, from which case the above quotation is made, it would appear that it is not possible under the present

SAM P. JONES,
Evangelist and Lecturer.

DR. BILLY JAMES CLARK,
Organizer First Temperance Society in U. S.

JAMES McNEILL,
Member New York Prohibition State Committee.

CLINTON N. HOWARD,
Lecturer.

law, for the council of a municipal corporation in Ohio by ordinance to prohibit places where intoxicating liquors are sold at retail.

The legislature of any state has the constitutional power to prohibit the sale of liquor or beer by retail. The courts say that it is no longer an open question. *Kettering vs. Jacksonville*, 50 Ills. 39:

"Such a law is subject only to the laws of the United States regulating imports, and these protect it only in the hands of the importer, in the original cask or package. Though a state is bound to admit an article thus imported under the laws of Congress, it is not bound to find a market for its sale. When sold by the importer in the original cask or package, or when broken up for retail sale, it becomes subject to the state laws; and may be taxed, or the sale prohibited."

To the same effect see rulings in—

State vs. Allmond, 2 Houst. (Del.) 612.
Mason vs. Luncortes, 4 Bush (Ky.) 406.
Perdue vs. Ellis, 18 Ga. 586.
Dorman vs. State, 34 Ala. 216.
Lincoln vs. Smith, 27 Vt. 328.
State vs. Robinson, 49 Me. 285.
People vs. Hawley, 3 Mich. 330.
People vs. Collins, 3 Mich. 343.

CHAPTER VIII.

HEROES AND MARTYRS.

THE Great Reform has its confessors and martyrs, heroes and saints—fearless women and men, who, in the face of universal drink-habits, with their attendant product of moral lethargy, uttered protest against defiant custom, and raised the standards of total abstinence for the individual, and prohibition as the policy of the state. Some of them emerged triumphant from the thralldom of drunkenness; others were aroused to effort by observation of the appalling effects of the drink traffic. Some ascended from the so-called "lower classes"; others appeared as representatives of the aristocracy.

From all the churches, or from the un-churched world, they came to bear their witness against drink and the dram-shops. Denounced as visionary, fanatic, insane, they assailed the demon drink in speech fiery with hate of the trade, and hot with pity for the trader and his victim. Many of their names long have been written on grave-stones,—but they are engraved in the hearts of a grateful multitude, who, in the days of the New Movement against the saloon, fulfil duty because of their splendid inspiration. In some Hall of Fame the Pioneers of the Great Reform will find fit memorial, when, at last, the Great Republic shall have freed itself from all complicity with the infamous traffic of the dram-shop. Untainted by compromise, clean of hand and heart, they are the blessed and canonized, whose names the allied enemies of the saloon invoke in the midst of the mightiest battle of the modern age.

Working alone, in the first days of their career, their propaganda became magnetic. They founded societies and orders, and inaugurated world-wide movements which today bear rich fruit to their memories.

THEOBALD MATHEW.

Alone in the church at midnight a young Franciscan friar, Theobald Mathew, had a vision. He saw a priest standing on the altar steps—the figure of Father Donovan, who had been one of his closest friends—dead for many years. He addressed the ghost—and received replies. Indeed, Father Mathew was wont to say afterward, that his commission to preach total abstinence was conferred upon him during that memorable interview. At any rate, it was soon after the midnight vision that he sent for William Martin, the Quaker, who had first urged upon him the obligation of advocating total abstinence, and signed the Quaker's pledge.

"The news that Father Mathew had joined the teetotalers," says Katherine Tynan in her delightful biography, "was received at first with incredulous amazement, by the better classes at all events." But when the poor folk heard that their beloved father confessor and spiritual director had signed the pledge, they thronged his meetings, and in less than three months he had enrolled twenty-five thousand people in Cork alone. In five months, a hundred and thirty thousand; in nine, a hundred and fifty thousand; and by January, 1839, two hundred thousand had taken the vow of total abstinence from intoxicating drink. The Franciscan Friary became the goal of pilgrimages from Kerry, Waterford, Limerick, Clare, Tipperary and Galway.

In December, 1839, Father Mathew began his temperance mission at Limerick. "With a serious and solemn purpose in their minds," runs the record, "the people rushed towards him, as if possessed by a frenzy. They struggled and fought their way through living masses, through every obstacle, until they found themselves in his presence, at his feet, listening to his voice, receiving his blessing, repeating after him the words which emancipated them, as they felt, from sin, sorrow and temptation." From Limerick to Waterford, to Maynooth, to Parsonstown, to Dublin. In 1841, he went to Ulster, stronghold of Orangeism. Here he triumphed as in the South among his own Catholics. "It is amazing," wrote Maria Edgeworth, "and proves the power of moral and religious influence beyond any other example on record in history. I consider Father Mathew the greatest benefactor to this country; the most true friend to Irishmen and to Ireland. Everywhere he went, wherever the coach stopped, he was surrounded by a crowd of the poor, the blind, the lame, the afflicted. He rained silver on such a crowd." To the imaginative Irish, he was a saint, a miracle-worker. The writer adds: "One thing he could not prevent the people from believing, and that was that his administration of the pledge carried with it a miraculous power of resisting temptation; this was, doubtless, a potent factor in the overwhelming tide of his success."

In August, 1842, Father Mathew extended his mission to Glasgow. A year later he went to England. Everywhere the fruits of his mission showed themselves by a lessening of crime, by an increased prosperity and happiness in the homes of the people, by a greater diligence on the part of the workers, by the quietness and order of the streets.

Unfortunately, Father Mathew's Temperance movement, much against his will, became entangled with Daniel O'Connell's Repeal movement. When the good friar returned to Cork, he said:

"What we should pray for is the growth of common sense. When the English get the common sense to give us justice, and we get the common sense to be content with justice and stop quarreling among ourselves, there will be fair days for the Old Country yet."

But the fair days never came. The Repeal movement was crushed by British troops, and the Temperance movement suffered with it and lost its glory. The famine of 1846 smote the Old Country, and Father Mathew's work went down with a million dead peasants.

In 1849 he came to the United States. Seven years before he had signed a declaration in favor of abolition, never expecting to see America. This act, performed in good faith, became an embarrassment to him. He wished to preserve his movement free from politics, with the result that abolitionists grew cool and pro-slavery men suspicious. However, he visited twenty-five states, administered the pledge in more than three hundred towns and cities, and added more than half a million names to the long muster roll of his disciples.

He was now sixty years old. He returned to Ireland only to see signs everywhere of the failure of a movement that had begun so gloriously. He abandoned the Friary, associated with the splendid days of his apostleship, and went to live with a brother at Lehenagh House near Cork. Touching little stories are told of his last days—days dark with sense of failure and fear of Ireland's future. He died December 8, 1856 —and fifty thousand men, women and children followed him to his grave.

Channing said: "Here is a minister who deserves to be canonized, and whose name should be placed in the calendar not far below Apostles."
—G. M. H.

JUSTIN EDWARDS.

Justin Edwards was the ablest organizer and promoter of the original temperance movement in America. From 1829 to 1836 he was General Secretary of the American Temperance Society, and foremost among its founders in 1826. His reports, compiled as "Permanent American Temperance Documents," have become classic sources of information in regard to the early history of the reform, and his addresses and tracts contributed immeasurably to the creation and maintenance of temperance sentiment. Of his "Temperance Manual" 193,625 copies were distributed prior to 1857.

The radical position taken from the first by Edwards and his associates is shown in the declaration made in the Temperance Society's constitution, that the principal object of the organization was, not the recla-

THEODORE L. CUYLER, D. D.

ABRAHAM LINCOLN.

mation and reformation of the inebriate, but the prevention of intemperance.

During Dr. Edward's career as Corresponding Secretary and General Agent of the original American Temperance Society, he inaugurated a movement in Washington, D. C., which resulted in establishing the Congressional Temperance Society, and he organized, in 1830, one of the earliest temperance societies in Canada.

SAMUEL FRAIZER.

Samuel Fraizer was one of the earliest pioneers of temperance and total abstinence in the West. In 1834, he and five of his neighbors organized a total abstinence society, thereby pledging themselves not to have any intoxicating drinks at their house-raisings, log-rollings and other gatherings. Out of this organization grew a strong temperance society, which exerted a great influence for good throughout that region. Soon after the formation of that society he began to preach and lecture, and devoted nearly forty years of his life to the cause of temperance. He was an eloquent speaker, a man of fine presence and goodly countenance, a bold and energetic worker, and wherever he went he shed the light of the gospel of temperance. He was for years what might be called a temperance circuit-rider, going everywhere in spite of bad weather and bad roads, to lecture and circulate total abstinence pledges in the worst neighborhoods he could find. He had a fine voice for singing, and an important feature of his work was to teach children to sing temperance songs from books which he always carried with him. He was also a very good composer and prepared both the words and music of several of the best temperance songs published at that time.

In 1859, he removed from Indiana to Jasper county, Iowa, where he began anew his pioneer work in the cause of temperance. From this time his field of labor really extended from Iowa through Illinois to his old home in Indiana; and there are now living thousands of young and middle-aged men who signed the pledge for the first time in response to his teachings.—*The Cyclopaedia of Temperance and Prohibition.*

LUCRETIA MOTT.

Lucretia Mott, daughter of Thomas Coffin, was a pioneer Abolitionist, a leader in the earliest efforts to win equality for woman, one of the first to champion total abstinence principles, and a preacher of celebrity among the Hicksite Quakers. She was born in Nantucket, January 3, 1793, and was descended from the original proprietors of the island. Her father removed to Boston when she was twelve years old. Although he possessed ample means, he sent his daughter to the public school, desiring that she should esteem herself no better than others. When she had passed beyond the lower grades he placed her in a Friends' boarding-school in New York. There she met James Mott, whom she married at the age of eighteen.

After her marriage, Philadelphia became her place of residence. Here she found abundant work to do in behalf of the slaves and woman's rights. At the age of twenty-five she began her career as a minister, receiving official recognition from her church. In 1883, a convention was held in Philadelphia to organize a National Anti-Slavery Society, and her aggressive speeches had an effect no less stimulating than the impression made by the appearance of a woman on the platform at such an assemblage was sensational. The toleration shown to Mrs. Mott on this occasion was certainly uncommon. Seven years later eight women were among the delegates sent to the World's Anti-Slavery Convention in London, but they were excluded from the floor.

For half a century Lucretia Mott was a pronounced total abstainer. She was quick to realize the full significance of the evils of the prevailing social drinking customs, and her influence, example and pen were devoted to the cause of reform. As a propagandist of radical and unpopular ideas she suffered great persecution, ridicule and denunciation, but in her old age she was regarded with peculiar tenderness and veneration. She died at the age of eighty-seven.

"Far beyond the common limit," said Samuel Longfellow, at the memorial meeting held in the Unitarian Church in Germantown, Pa., "the light of that countenance has been before us and that voice heard wherever an unpopular truth needed defense, wherever a popular evil needed to be testified against, wherever a wronged man or woman needed a champion. There she stood, there she spoke the word that the spirit of truth and right bade her speak. How tranquil and serene her presence in the midst of multitudes that might become mobs. How calm yet how searching her judgment against wrong-doing. No whirlwind of passion or lighting of eloquence; it was rather the dawn of clear day upon dark places and hidden."
—Abridged from *The Cyclopaedia of Temperance and Prohibition.*

BENJAMIN JOY.

By Theodore L. Cuyler, D. D.

Benjamin Joy was one of the most active and indomitable pioneers of the temperance reform. He spent the larger portion of his life in Ludlowville, Tompkins county, N. Y. Being a merchant and manufacturer, his business interests caused him to travel extensively through the central and western parts of his State. In 1827, while visiting the neighboring town of Hector, he learned from Dr. Jewell that a society had been formed there on the pledge of total abstinence from wine, cider and all intoxicants. He returned home and organized a society on the same basis at Ludlowville, December 31 of the same year. This was one of the earliest teetotal societies in the world.

In his frequent trips through all that region, driving from schoolhouse to schoolhouse and church to church, he denounced the drinking usages and formed societies for the promotion of abstinence. His labors of love were without any "pay", except the persecutions of the rumsellers, who cut the harness from his horse and endeavored to break up his meetings. Once they broke a whisky bottle near his head and the old hero shouted with great glee: "Good! my boys, good! served him right! One more devil cast out! I came here to help smash rumbottles!"

Benjamin Joy was a most zealous Christian, and it was at a religious service held at his house, in February, 1843, that the author of this sketch decided to enter the Christian ministry. In 1865, he took a prominent part in the National Temperance Convention at Saratoga and stood with Mr. Delavan and Gerrit Smith in the leadership of the cause in the State of New York. The closing years of his noble life of philanthropy were spent in Penn Yan. His last evening on earth was in a meeting of Good Templars, where he spoke with great power. Before morning he died.

Rev. Dr. David Magee writes:

"No one can forget the addresses of Mr. Joy. How his eye kindled and the tones of his voice deepened as he became more and more engaged, his address overflowing with wit and humor, then melting into pathos, rising at times into the keenest sarcasm and occasionally into terrible invective. For forty-five years he gave, without remuneration, his time and strength and talents to this work. In 1853, he was elected to the legislature on the temperance issue, and of him a journalist of that day (T. W. Brown) wrote: 'No man at the capital, as a man, a temperance advocate, or a legislator, wields more moral power than he. As a debater he is clear-headed, cool, self-poised and ready, and never surprised in any of the strategy which marks the stirring conflicts of the session. His enemies love him while they fear him. As a speaker no man holds in more complete subjection the turbulent elements of the House.' Mr. Joy was especially instrumental in framing the prohibitory law which was finally passed, only to be vetoed by Governor Horatio Seymour. Only three weeks before his death he delivered his annual address to the people of Tompkins county, in which he said: 'By every throb of affection, by every memory of the kindness of the people of Tompkins to myself, I long and pray for their deliverance and the deliverance of their children from the scourge and curse of strong drink. And now, after a world of experience and observation, chastened by many trials, far along in the autumn of life, with the headlands of another world plainly visible, I solemnly declare that the importance of the subject of temperance grows in my esteem with advancing years, and I thoroughly justify every endeavor, every labor, every forced march and exposure, every sacrifice I have ever made for the cause, and I have only to regret that I could not have done more.'"

JOSIAH FLOURNOY.

As a temperance leader, Josiah Flournoy is remembered for his connection with the Georgia agitation of 1839, known as the Flournoy Movement, whose object was to secure the abolition by the State legislature of the liquor license laws. In the spring of 1839, a meeting of citizens of Putnam county, Georgia, through a committee of which Mr. Flournoy was a member, issued an address to the people of Georgia, published in the Atlanta *Christian Index* for March 21, 1839, asking whether the evil of the legalized liquor traffic "ought not to be exterminated." A petition to the State legislature was published in the *Index* in March of the same year, signed by about three hundred citizens of the county. It contained the following words:

"The undersigned, citizens of this State, believing that the retail of spirituous liquors is an evil of great magnitude among us, come to the legislature by petition and ask you, in your wisdom, to pass such a law as will effectually put a stop to it. . . . Your petitioners come with the more confidence, because several states in the Union have already passed such a law as to make penal the retailing of intoxicating drinks."

Mr. Flournoy canvassed the State for signatures to the petition, visiting nearly every part of the commonwealth. His example aroused the people and public meetings were called everywhere. In one of his addresses Mr. Flournoy said:

"I have addressed thousands in public meetings, and spoken to hundreds in private. I find the number of those who favor the plan of a law to banish the tippling-shops from the land to be as eight or nine in ten. No proposition can be offered to the citizens of Georgia that will meet with the same unanimity, nor any ten combined can produce the same good. I have just returned from a trip of ten days to the South. In one of the lower counties I believe every man would sign our petition, and nowhere, even among the worst drunkards, do I meet with opposition. I find more difficulty with men who call themselves politicians than any others; as a class they are least to be expected to do anything to promote the morality of the country. With a few exceptions, they seem desirous to keep back all that would elevate the great mass of society, I suppose for fear they will lose their own importance. I freely warn them that the man who opposes this law, and knows what he is doing at the same time, will deserve and receive the anathemas of the country. He is one who for his own honor's exaltation could drink the tears of female suffering and eat the bread of starving children."

How aptly that speech, though made sixty years ago, fits conditions today! That "there is nothing new under the sun" is illustrated further by what followed. When it became apparent from the indifference of the politicians that the legislature would probably disregard the petition, some of the petitioners began to nominate independent legislative candidates. The political aspect which the movement now took on commanded the attention of partisan leaders and newspapers, and in the contest for Governor, which was decided by a majority of only a few hundreds, party spirit ran high. Shortly before the election the success of the petitioners seemed certain, but the politicians appealed to prejudice by declaring that party interests were endangered, and the popular movement was checked. The legislature refused to act.

Mr. Flournoy's death, which occurred soon after, was attributed to disappointment at the defeat of the cause. —G. M. H.

EDWARD CORNELIUS DELAVAN.

Edward C. Delavan occupied a unique place in the history of the Temperance Reform. He was one of its few financiers. He organized the New York Temperance Society, paid the expense of Hewitt's mission to Europe, controlled the two most influential temperance journals in the United States, paid all expenses of his defense against suits at law instituted by brewers on charges of libel, and paid the cost of the various forms of temperance propaganda which he had introduced. When the American Temperance Union was organized in 1836, he became chairman of its Executive Committee, and contributed $10,000 to the cause. On his visit to Europe in the interest of the movement, he took with him a large supply of literature, including eight hundred volumes of Justin Edward's "PERMANENT TEMPERANCE DOCUMENTS," paid for out of his own purse.

At his suggestion Dr. Edwards prepared a declaration to which he secured the signatures of Presidents Jackson, Madison, John Quincy Adams, Van Buren, Tyler, Polk, Taylor, Fillmore, Pierce, Buchanan, Lincoln and Johnson. It is known as "Delavan's Declaration" and reads as follows:

"Being satisfied from observation and experience, as well as from medical testimony, that ardent spirit, as a drink, is not only needless but hurtful, and that the entire disuse of it would tend to promote the health, the virtue and the happiness of the community, we hereby express our conviction that, should the citizens of the United States, and especially the young men, discontinue entirely the use of it, they would not only promote their own personal benefit, but the good of our country and of the world."

THOMAS L. CARSON.

Thomas L. Carson deserves memorial as one of the most aggressive opponents of the retail liquor traffic in the days before the rise of the "Temperance Tidal Wave." When a young man he observed that, though many towns in his native state, New York, voted "no license," liquor dealers continued their business, unwhipped by the law. That is to say, they defied the people; and the sworn officialdom of the commonwealth perjured itself for the sake of salary, and victory in the next election. Carson conceived a plan of organizing citizens who believed that law should be enforced, that offenders should be duly tried and punished, and that the liquor traffic should be suppressed. That was in 1846, nearly a quarter of a century before the organization of the Prohibition movement. The "Carson League" was organized, composed of persons committed to the enforcement of anti-liquor-selling laws, and pledged to obtain evidence against lawbreakers, and to provide funds for the prosecution of cases against them. This, of course, was a self-imposed burden, because officers had already been elected to "faithfully enforce all laws of the State of New York." But the Leaguers paid their assessments, and performed their extra duties in the spirit of martyrs. The organization spread through many sections of New York, and even into other states.

Not only did Mr. Carson lead his "League" in its campaign, he ran a paper called *The Carson League*, in support of his movement, and in opposition to the so-called "legalized" traffic in intoxicating liquors. By means of this organ Mr. Carson did much toward securing the nomination and election of Myron H. Clark as Governor of New York, in 1854, and the enactment of the prohibitory law of 1855. Believing that his cause had triumphed, Mr. Carson discontinued the publication of his paper, and the League disbanded. But the Court of Appeals discovered a technical flaw in the prohibitory statute and it was repealed. In its stead a license law was reënacted and Mr. Carson resumed his fight against the "legalized outlaw." A new society, known as the State League, was organized, a new paper was established and, from 1857 until his death in 1868, he waged unceasing war against the dram-shop traffic of New York. A brave, energetic, self-denying lover of his fellowmen, he was forced by the compromises of his state government to spend his life in combating an organized trade which the chief executive and all other officials were under obligation to suppress.

Although a true representative of the people, he was stripped of authority to administer government, under that system which converts democracy into aristocracy and plutocracy. The deeds of Carson were the seeds from which have grown the better promise of the present day.

MRS. LULU LOVELAND SHEPARD,
President, Utah W. C. T. U.

MRS. MARION H. DUNHAM,
President, Iowa W. C. T. U.

MISS MINNIE E. NEAL,
President, Florida W. C. T. U.

NEAL DOW—A PROPHET OF GOD.

By John G. Woolley.

An Address Delivered in Willard Hall, Chicago, on the Occasion of the Nineteenth Anniversary of Neal Dow's Birth.

"Yea, I say unto you a prophet."

An old man sits at life's west window; on his head a glorious crown of hoary hair, for he has walked the way of righteousness for seventy years of life and twenty of immortality; in his face the flush of the century's afterglow, and in his eyes the quiet mystery of lights far out at sea. He is a statesman, who years ago pronounced sentence of death upon his own "prospects" for truth's sake, and duty's—a Yankee Cato; a politician who came upon the stage of action when "Drink" was governor, and the church tetrarch to the animalism and moral incapacity of the usurper. And he is a prophet, not one who in a gloomy frenzy seizes a pen and writes he knows not what; or with transcendent vision outwits the future and lays bare its strategies; or, nightly wandering in Egerian groves, hears the gestation of events to come; but one who, having eyes, sees what lies about him here in the open—a seer.

Much of what passes current as "spiritual insight" is strabismus, gotten by trying not to see the shapes that crowd our paths and shame our lust of indolence, claiming consanguinity—and, as to many, rightfully—for that mere introversion of the eyes is all the motherhood the crime-germ needs or knows. And Christian apathy, like a sleeping sow, suckles the saloon and all its loathsome brood; and when, betimes, it looks the "good man" in the face and says: "Speak to me, I am thy child," it is no answer to reply with face averted, "Begone, I love thee not!" It never asked for love, nor wished it, but only recognition, and that it has, for Congress and some forty legislatures vouch today for its legitimacy as our proper offspring, out of wedlock, to be sure, but ours indisputably.

They lie. The brute is none of ours, but a mongrel monster of genealogy untraceable, unclassable, sexless, soulless, something of louse, hog and devil mixed, and only ours by estoppel, because we did not, would not, see that calling us "father" unrebuked, and so being endured and trusted for our sake and upon our credit, it made us liable for its support and all the debts it may incur. God help us at the pay day!

"Where there is no vision the people perish." But this man saw every fact that touched him, and looked into the face of every form that walked his way of life, and to every salutation answered like a man, shirking nothing; and now resting here, wearied by the heat and burden of the day, if the whole peerage of the saloon, the quarter of a million liquor lords, each with his royal letters patent in his hand, should file into the room to taunt and greet him "kinsman," he would look straight into their eyes and say, "You lie!"

What a palatial memory is this, lifting its splendid front here in the gloaming, with the century's sunset beams illumining its window panes! Enter reverently, and let us look about, for there must be some wondrous paintings on the walls. Take off your shoes, walk softly. I will be guide, and where I know the portraits they shall act again and speak to you.

Himself, in the first picture, a young rich man, taking his ease in his own parlor, before an open fire whose piny resins shoot delicious pyrotechnics, odor-laden, into the weak eyes of many lamps. His wife, almost too happy, opposite, with gleaming needles that click like frostbells, knitting a song of her own heart into meshes of soft, bright wools for dainty feet that she has never seen, except in dreams. Entering there, a neighbor woman, young too, and beautiful, a wife and mother, with a face that fairly chills the mind to see it, and eyes dilated to the iris edge by an unspeakable horror, about to speak. Listen! "I can keep my secret no longer; my husband is a drunkard; my children are starving; my heart is breaking; you are his friend; find him for me; bring him home to me quickly, for the love of God!"

What is to be said when a woman talks like that? The terrific calmness of it is noisier than a riot, and confuses sense and banishes speech, except the shallowest. Out into the night he fares, the blindest man in Maine, because the adder "drink" has never stung his heart, nor made him hang his head in shame, nor struck his wife's sweet face with its foul lash, nor goaded him to borrow, lie or steal. He has seen men and women, but as trees walking, and has inhaled the hot breath of the saloon for a generation, and yet not seen it save as one catches glimpses of some slimy, crawling thing, and turns his eyes away no wiser.

A saloon, the squid of life's high sea, with vibrant tentacles that suck the sap of business honor and the pride and strength of youth, and labor's wages, and the blood of human hearts; and squirts ink into the crystal wave of every providence of rescue, while it seeks its cave, and slams the door of Christian law into the face of Christ.

Pyramids of barrels, each monogramed with the nation's signet. Ranks and platoons of bottles dressed to a city license on the right; the liquor laws, militia, bodyguard, each bemedaled on its helmet with federal insignia; the keeper, cuffed and aproned, brusque and business-like, on duty at the bar. In the closet, in the rear, hidden away like a stolen dog, a man, dead drunk in his soul, but in his body writhing on the grill of restlessness, a good man three days since, but now a creature ready to commit murder for a stoup of rum.

His friend, no coward—the blind are brave—though forbidden, finds him out, and in horror turns to the master of the place and says: "Help me to take him away."

And the master replies: "What is it to you? Let him alone to go home when he pleases."

"But his children are crying for food, and his wife weeping her eyes out for love for him; we must get him to them, I tell you. I'll call a carriage. Don't sell him any more drink."

And the man says: "No, not if he hasn't the price."

"What, man! Do you mean to say you would sell him more drink when he is already mad with it, and his home is without a crust, and his wife lies on the floor yonder just a clot of sorrow?"

"Yes. By ——! I sell whisky. It is my trade and as lawful as tanning: more lawful. What have you to show for your tannery? Look at that license, d'ye see, with the names of the selectmen, and the city seal, and the arms of the state of Maine? To —— with your preaching. Get out! Go to the meeting-house and talk through your sleek hat!"

Propped in the corner of the carriage, like a sack of sodden rags, the drunkard and his friend. The clock in the stone tower strikes midnight—tolls midnight—and the moon rolls down behind the pine woods like a tear of God.

Now driver, home; home to the snowy marriage bed with the bridegroom; home to the bride's empty arms, with her lover; home to the true wife, with her husband; home to the prattlers, with their father!

The drunkard in his bed, tossing and moaning, with throat that cracks with its gasping thirst, and blood that crawls like a migration of maggots along the flaccid veins, and breath that sickens and stinks, and makes one look for red-crested grave-worms to crawl out of lips and eyes and nostrils, and burrow into the puffy cheeks of the cadaver, sloughing visibly.

Still the same scene; the night wears on, children sit up in bed and mock the sleepless watcher—crying, "Drink, mamma, drink!" The lamp burns low, goes out; the darkness turns gray. The hot evening horror has boiled down, and the tortured ones are still, at last, rigid, like flies in tar; out of the shadow a form stoops and searches for live coals in the ashes vainly. It is the drunkard's wife.

The young rich man is back by his parlor fire, sitting alone. There is about his mouth that which was not there before. For once a saloon has given value to the world. Neal Dow sees.

Leave the pictures. Sit here, and I will tell you what he saw. Drink, everywhere! Nero—Drink on the throne, fiddling while the city burned; Tarquinia—Drink in the chariot, crushing her dead father's face beneath the bloody wheels; Catherine—Drink at the altar, murdering the innocents; Borgia—Drink in the castle, with butchery and incest; Lucretia—Drink in the home, mad with her wrongs, poisoning her parents; Machiavelli—Drink in the cabinet, publishing lies; Rahab—Drink in the brothel, putting out Virtue's eyes; Barabbas—Drink on the road, robbing the poor; Pizarro—Drink in commerce, plundering the simple; Simon—Drink betraying cities with gifts; Elialtes—Drink leading the enemy through the defenses of his native land; Arnold—Drink selling his country; Belshazzar—Drink scorning Heaven and praising the Gods of Gold; Jeffrey—Drink on the bench, wresting the law; Lord Chancellor—Drink selling injustice; Juror—Drink in the box, ignoring law; Sheriff—Drink in charge of the jail; Alderman—Drink in the council, taking bribes; Mayor—Drink in the chair, selling indulgence to corrupters of the youth; Chief—Drink in charge of the police; Drink—M. C. in the Congress; Drink—M. D. at the cradle; Drink—D. D. in the pulpit; Drink—LL. D. in the college; Judea—Drink with the disciples, selling the Son of God for silver.

You ask me if this is really memory, or pictures painted by a madman's mind on memory's walls? It is memory, true as light, and this man saw it all, and looked at it and pondered it in his heart, and then stood up and said: "By God's help we will stop all this!" And the Quaker went to war, and one honest mayor shook the continent. Had there been then a church, clean-handed, clear-eyed, faithful, militant, to take on board this Viking, it would have swept the sea of licensed pirates, and filled the earth with the knowledge and glory of our God.

Yesterday I heard this gallant man impeached for lack of loyalty to a sect because he took his name from a church book. But he had given his heart to God, aye, and his two hands, and his feet and his shoulders. And his name is written in the sacred history of the holiest warfare ever waged for home and country. Tonight heaven kindles in his soul, universal humanity honors him by public meetings in a thousand cities in his own and foreign lands, and posterity will bless his name when sects have ceased in dusty desuetude. For I do hold that he lifts up the Son of God who lifts another man without a scrap of creed beyond the testimony of the act itself. And he did that not only, but a sovereign state as well, and a great cause. For when Maine's homes were lighted up, and industry revived, and wealth began to flow into her lap, and jails gave way to schools, and saloons to savings banks, the whole world recognized that the time was epochal.

JOHN BARTHOLOMEW GOUGH.

On an October day, 1842, Joel Stratton, a Quaker, persuaded John B. Gough to sign the total abstinence pledge. The famous "Washingtonian" movement was then in full swing, and Stratton, availing himself of the moral enthusiasm created by it, approached poor Gough in the hope of "saving his soul" by rescuing his body from the grip of intoxicating liquor.

Gough had become hopeless. He had entered the domain of that earthly purgatory in which the air is filled with tantalizing threats of a deeper descent to shame, and the sky is black with the sweeping clouds of a coming tempest of death. With a bottle of laudanum in his trembling hand, he had stood at the side of the railway afraid to live, afraid to die. He was only twenty-five years of age, and yet he had become a mere drunken sot—the sodden wreck of body and soul—thrown upon the rocks in a storm bred in the dram-shops of the New World, to which, a boy of twelve, he had come to make his way to fortune.

Born in Sandgate, Kent county, England, his early years had been stripped of boyish freshness and ambition, under the crush of that poverty which exists in the shadow of English aristocracy, pagan in selfishness, Christian in creed. His mother taught the village school, and the government paid a hundred dollars a year to the support of the family, because the father had fought in one of England's wars. Gough was wont to tell in after years, that he had not known in childhood what it was to have a slice of bread with butter, except as the slice was first thinly coated, and then scraped!

In 1829, a neighbor family set sail for the United States, and the boy Gough left home under protection of his mother's friends. Four years afterward he sent back enough money to pay ship passage for his mother and sister—the father having died—and, together, the three set up their home in New York city, where Gough was at work in the Methodist Book Concern as a binder. In 1834, his mother died, and he began to drink—because his "friends" drank. Five years later he married, the young wife hoping to reform him. Unable to make a living at his trade, he went from city to city, doing small jobs, or playing minor parts in low theaters that even then existed in Bristol, Providence, Boston, Newburyport and Worcester.

At Worcester his wife and child died. "Soon it was whispered from one to another," he writes in his autobiography, "that my wife and child were lying dead, and that I was drunk! There in the room, where all who had loved me were lying in the unconscious slumber of death, was I gazing, with a maudlin melancholy imprinted on my features, on the dead forms of those who were flesh of my flesh and bone of my bone. During the miserable hours of darkness I would steal from my lonely bed to the place where my dead wife and child lay, and in agony of soul pass my shaking hand over their cold faces, and then return to my bed, after a draught of rum, which I had obtained and hidden under the pillow of my wretched couch."

He was a murderer! For he had vowed to "cherish" the woman who in 1839 had taken his name. And he had *not* cherished her. Instead of providing for her and her babe, he had spent his wages for drink—always for drink. Instead of making a home for her, he had made a hell. And, now, she was dead—starved to death, and his baby was dead—starved to death.

Then it was that he contemplated suicide, and that Joel Stratton persuaded him to sign the pledge. For several months he kept his promise, then broke it, confessed his fall, signed again, fell again under a devilish scheme to disgrace him as a pledge-breaker, signed again, and kept it until that February day in 1886, when he was stricken with paralysis on the platform in Frankford, Pennsylvania.

After his victory in 1845, he resolved to devote himself to the restoration of men who, like himself, had descended to the depths. Too poor to pay carfare, he tramped through New England, carrying his carpetbag in hand, and telling the story of his life—at seventy-five cents per lecture. Eight years later he was in England, guest of the London Temperance League, one of the most eloquent advocates of temperance in that day or any other. For two years he went to and fro through England, a marvel of oratorical power, and added to his platform appeals the tragic story of his career in an autobiography which sold twenty thousand copies in the first year of its issue. And so, for seventeen years, he traveled abroad and at home, delivering nearly nine thousand addresses on temperance, and lectures on miscellaneous literary and general subjects.

It is just to him as a temperance lecturer to say that, in 1884, he allied himself with that political party which declared itself in favor of prohibiting the traffic in intoxicating liquor. He said:

"I have one vote to be responsible for. . . . This year, however, has seen strange things. Surprising disintegrations have been going on in the two old parties. Both have either open affiliations with, or a cowardly and shameful servility to, the arrogant set of rings and lobbies of this drink trade which lifts its monstrous front of $750,000,000 of money spent directly in it, with an equal sum in addition taxed upon the people to take care of its miserable results."

He had waited long, in hope that he would not be obliged to sever political relations that had become dear to him; but he saw his duty clearly at last, and so, because he believed in prohibiting and annihilating the liquor traffic, he functioned as a citizen with the party that had been organized in 1869, for the purpose of overthrowing it by the organized powers of state.

JOHN B. FINCH,
Lecturer, and Chairman, National Prohibition Committee, 1888-96.

GEORGE W. BAIN,
Lecturer.

Then came the end, and the marvelous voice that had charmed the ear and moved the heart for forty years, was hushed in the mystery of death. —G. M. H.

HENRY A. REYNOLDS.

Red ribbon, white ribbon, blue ribbon! Blue ribbon, Francis Murphy; white ribbon, Frances E. Willard; red ribbon, Henry A. Reynolds.

Reynolds was a graduate of Harvard Medical School, who, during his practice in Bangor, Maine, fell under the influence of that anaesthetic which is known as "alcohol." Again and again he had summoned all his will power to combat with the appetite that had threatened to destroy him, until, at a woman's prayer-meeting he made the supreme effort at self-mastery, and signed the total abstinence pledge. Not content with this achievement, he dedicated himself to efforts for the reclamation of other drinkers of alcoholics, and conceived the plan of organizing a club of self-reformed men— men, who, by sheer effort of will had freed themselves from the enslaving habit. And so, on the tenth of September, 1874, the Bangor Reform Club was organized. The membership increased so rapidly, and the outlook for success in the new movement was so auspicious that Reynolds, believing himself commissioned by God, abandoned his profession and undertook the mission of reclaiming drunkards. In one year, it is said that forty-five thousand men (in Maine!) were enrolled in the Reform Clubs. Reynolds then went to Massachusetts and the West. To those who signed the pledge and joined the club, he gave a bit of red ribbon, and the clubs became known as the Red Ribbon Reform Club—the little bow of red, worn as proudly as a Frenchman wears the ribbon of the Legion of Honor. Among Dr. Reynolds' most efficient associates was John B. Finch, who canvassed Nebraska and secured a hundred thousand signatures to the pledge.

JOHN BIRD FINCH.

It is conceded that, as John B. Gough was the greatest of all moral suasion advocates of the Temperance Reform of the Nineteenth Century, John B. Finch was the greatest of political Prohibition orators and organizers.

Finch's life, in contrast with that of Gough's, was free from the blight of drink. When a boy of fifteen he joined the Good Templars, and soon became Grand Lodge Lecturer for the State of New York; afterwards being elected Grand Worthy Counselor of the Nebraska Grand Lodge, Grand Worthy Chief Templar of Nebraska and Right Worthy Grand Templar of the Order in the United States. During the high days of the Red Ribbon movement, he secured a hundred thousand signatures to the temperance pledge, and, later, founded six Good Templar lodges, three Red Ribbon clubs and one Temple of Honor.

In 1880, Mr. Finch, who, as a Democrat, had stood aloof from the Prohibition party, abandoned his political beliefs because of their lack of harmony with his views as a Good Templar, and identified himself with the organized movement to abolish the saloon by exercise of the state's political powers. His superb powers of oratory and organization were immediately recognized, and he was made chairman of the National Committee in 1884. But, before the next campaign had been organized he was in his grave, dead at thirty-five—but dead at the post of duty. He spoke at Lynn, Mass., on the last night of his life, a martyr to the Great Reform: for physicians had warned him of his danger. He chose to work to the top and climax of his powers, while the day lasted.

Traditions of his eloquence are living and current; those who heard him remember his handsome face, strong and kind, his noble bearing, his fine voice, his clear speech, his magnanimous spirit. He was fit representative of the People against the Liquor Traffic. —G. M. H.

FRANCIS MURPHY.

Francis Murphy was a "moral suasionist." He stood persistently aloof from the Prohibition movement of his time, but lived long enough to see that even his splendid success as a temperance evangelist could not prevent the dominance of the saloon in politics nor destroy the liquor traffic. His career, which began in 1870, at Portland, Maine, where Neal Dow had battled with the dram-shop so spectacularly, terminated in an anti-climax —and the name of "Francis Murphy," which had been so brilliant and magnetic, ceased to attract. Perhaps it was the apparent failure of the police method of dealing with the traffic in drink that suggested his "Gospel" method of treating it; and for awhile it appeared as if, at last, he had found the secret of suppressing it. His mission was even more popular than John B. Gough's and his story of struggle and triumph was almost as marvelous as that of the great Washingtonian. The clubs that he organized were nuclei of wide-reaching influence, and the pledge-signers who accepted his leadership numbered at least ten million. From state to state he went in triumph of appeal to reason and conscience, gaining a hearing where the Prohibition orator was refused audience. Then the clubs began to disintegrate and the crowds lessened, until, at last, he passed away, just on the eve of the great prohibition revival, to which he had contributed so much. His adopted country will remember that, in his young manhood, he fought beneath her flag, and in his later years acted as chaplain in her war with Spain. —G. M. H.

GEORGE W. BAIN.

Born in 1840, George W. Bain began the life that has distinguished him as a temperance reformer, when, in 1869, he joined the Good Templars. A year later, he became editor of *The Good Templars' Advocate*, then Grand Worthy Chief Templar of Kentucky, and organizer. To him, perhaps more than to any other Kentuckian, is due the fact that I. O. G. T. is one of the great governing forces in the moral welfare of his native state.

When the Prohibition party was organized it was natural that Colonel Bain should become a member of it, and quite as natural that his gifts of speech and personal popularity should make him a possible candidate for the highest office in the republic. At the Cincinnati convention, in 1892, his name came before the delegates, but he declined the nomination. Since then he has not been prominent as a party Prohibitionist, but it may be said of him that, while popular as a lyceum lecturer, he is nowhere so much in his element as when engaged in a local option battle.

In the lyceum lecture field no one is more popular than George W. Bain. During the 1907 season, he appeared at fifty-two Chautauquas, and his calls for lectures outnumber the days of the year. He claims to have lived longer than most people, because each day away from his home (he is away from his old Kentucky home eight months out of every twelve) hangs with the weight of two days.

Of him the gifted Gunsaulus, one of America's greatest lecturers, has said:

"Several years back, Colonel Bain took the place in public esteem and affection which was once occupied by John B. Gough. From that time he has been growing in depth of intellectual and spiritual life, and in his effectiveness and charm as an orator. I know of no more wholesome influence in our American public life than the career and message of this rich and vital man."

And Dr. McArthur finely says:

"He and his lectures are the synonym of intelligence, popular power and righteous inspiration."

—G. M. H.

SEABORN WRIGHT.

To this man more than all others, Georgia owes most for obtaining her prohibition law. In his public life he has stood for the most advanced temperance ideas, and everywhere and always these ideas have been put to the fore. Some of the facts in connection with the public life of Mr. Wright are as follows:

He ran for Governor in 1896, favoring state prohibition as against the nominee of the Democratic party favoring "local option." He polled 96,000 votes, but was defeated by the heaviest negro registration ever made in Georgia. He went back into the Democratic party with his prohibition following and won out on the same issue in 1907.

He and his friends did not oppose local option, but contended that the time had come for state prohibition.

He has for many years been in the local option contests throughout the South, in which he has rendered most valuable service.

He has frequently been urged in his state for both Congress and the United States Senate, but has declined in order to work out his ideas in the state legislature.

We asked Mr. Wright for some statement of the ideas and objects of his public life, and what measures he had been interested in procuring. The following is his response:

"Very early in life I became deeply impressed with the idea that the first and highest duty of our government was to make men. If the perpetuity of our institutions depends upon the 'virtue and intelligence of the people,' then it follows that the government is interested above all things in its citizenship. The character of the average man is practically formed by the time he reaches manhood; no influence so greatly impresses the youth of the land as the character and enforcement of the laws under which he lives. If under our laws, drunkenness, gambling, lewdness and kindred vices, are openly tolerated or licensed, in spite of the influence of home and school and church, the average youth follows the standard set by the law.

"The second idea of almost equal importance that came to me was that the people are paying too little attention to the character of the men who compose our state legislatures. Nine-tenths of the laws under which we live are state laws. Therefore it follows that the man who enters public life with the idea of doing good, honestly and faithfully serving the people, can accomplish more in his state legislature than in any other office.

"I have consistently carried out these ideas in my public life. Most of the time for the last twenty years I have been a member of the Georgia legislature. The great measures which have interested me, some of which I have introduced, all of which I have advocated, are:

"1. Local option laws, under which nine-tenths of the territory of Georgia voted dry.

"2. Our public school law, under which we are now annually appropriating $2,000,000 out of the state treasury to public education.

"3. Our pure food law, more rigid than the national law.

"4. Our laws abolishing bucket-shop or exchange gambling.

"5. Drastic laws regulating the sale of dangerous drugs.

"6. Legislation against child labor in factories.

"7. Our great laws, outlawing the manufacture and sale of intoxicating liquors in Georgia.

"In the advocacy of these measures I have been controlled by the one idea—to array the law of my state against the great evils working the destruction of the people.

"This, in brief, is the history of my public life."

It will be seen that the life of Mr. Wright has been crowded actively with efforts for the betterment of humanity. The record is not yet finished, but it already holds enough to be an inspiration to every servant of the public.—*The American Issue.*

RODERICK DHU GAMBRELL.

He was only twenty-two years old when he died in the streets of Jackson, Mississippi, Roderick Dhu Gambrell, journalist. Had he been a mere newsmonger and editor of "Society Notes," he might have lived in peace until his hair whitened on his temples. But he had fight in him, and knew no better use to make of his paper than to attack the "gang" in his town. And so the gang marked him for death.

There are journalists who know the fine art of making attacks without stirring blood, but Gambrell was in to kill or be killed—a true soldier. Perhaps he inherited his instinct for war in the high field of honor, where issues of truth, beauty and goodness are at stake, for both father and mother were temperance workers, charging their child's blood with an infinite and changeless horror of the liquor traffic. The father, the Rev. J. B. Gambrell, made his pulpit a point of attack upon the foul trade, and the mother, because she loved her boy, spoke and prayed with all of a mother's passion against the dram-shop and the heartless vendors of death.

Removing from old Nansemond county, Virginia, where Roderick Dhu was born, father and mother went to Mississippi, and the father became an editor as well as a preacher, and smote hip and thigh, not only with voice but with pen. The boy grew up in an atmosphere of combat. Even his work at the State University and at Mississippi College was only a whetting of a short sword. And so it was fitting that when, only nineteen years old, he became editor, he should call his organ *The Sword and the Shield,* although he had little use for the shield.

As soon as he took the editor's chair he began to write paragraphs that cut to the marrow, and his sword dripped blood. He observed that a saloonkeeper violated the ordinances, and he reported the fact once, twice, thrice, until the reports became offensive, and the saloonkeeper retaliated. At first, threats were employed, but the young editor, being a Virginian, and by descent a Scot, defied the drinkseller, and continued to report violations of the law.

One night an alarm of fire was sounded. The office of *The Sword and the Shield* went up in flames. The saloonkeeper was avenged. Perhaps Roderick Dhu suspected him of setting fire to the plant, but he had no witnesses, and, perhaps, no insurance. In two weeks, however, the publication of the paper was resumed, and the editor, aroused to new energy by the fire, began to gather material for an advance on the hereditary foe. For a score of weeks he pored over the records of legislative proceedings and filled a library of note books with the records of Mississippi politicians, who hoped and believed that the books would never be opened. But Roderick began to publish biographies of eminent representatives of the people, not always welcome to their subjects, and the mail began to bring threats of death, of course always anonymous. Saloonkeepers, unaccustomed to newspaper dictation, grew more and more vicious, and the air grew hot with hatred of the young fellow who had made it his business to interfere with his fellow citizens' "personal liberty."

Meanwhile, the "good people" of Mississippi, having other uses for their medium of exchange, did not subscribe for *The Sword and the Shield* and young Gambrell became not only editor, but compositor, pressman, subscription clerk, bookkeeper, cashier and office-boy.

The crisis began to become acute in 1886. In that year a local option contest was conducted in Hinds county, of which Jackson is capital. Gambrell, of course, went into the combat with his *Sword and Shield*, and, with John Martin, published a daily paper.

One "Colonel" J. S. Hamilton led the liquor forces, a gentleman who was reputed to have been a defaulter to the State, and otherwise interested in suppressing hostile legislation. In spite of his appeal to the negroes and the slum vote, he was defeated in the county option contest and his "influence" declined. However, in April, 1887, he became candidate for State Senator, and the editor of *The Sword and the Shield* set up an anti-Hamilton fight, using the material gathered from the records of the legislature. Hamilton, unable to efface his record, withdrew from the campaign, and the young fighting editor abandoned his opposition.

But, on the night of the fifth of May there were pistol shots heard on a street in Jackson, a cry of "Murder!" the sound of crushing blows. Certain pedestrians passing dared to go to the scene of the tragedy, and found Gambrell dying. Hamilton was there, his coat sleeve on fire and two pistol wounds on his body. Gambrell, it seems, knew how to shoot as well as to write. Albrecht was there, a saloonkeeper and a gambler; Eubanks was there, a henchman of Hamilton. Figures, a gambler, was there. The City Marshal was there, Corraway; but Corraway was a "friend" of Hamilton.

A coroner's inquest was held. Evidence indicated assassination, and there was high talk of lynching Hamilton and his gang, but Gambrell's father appealed to the people to permit the law to take its course. The

MRS. MARY E. CARTLAND,
Vice-President, North Carolina W. C. T. U.

MRS. HARRIET B. KELLS,
President, Mississippi W. C. T. U.

law took its course. At the first trial, Albrecht was released on bond, Figures was discharged, Eubanks and Hamilton were sent to prison. Hamilton was re-tried in an adjoining county, but the deputy sheriff who summoned the jury boasted, it has been charged, of having "fixed" four members of that high tribunal, and Hamilton was acquitted.

This story was published in 1891 in New York, London and Toronto, and no suit for libel has ever been entered against its publishers. The presumption is that it is true, whole truth and nothing but the truth.

But the blood of agitators is the seed of reform.

In 1907, seventy out of seventy-six counties in Mississippi had become dry, and a prohibition campaign was being waged with every indication of success. And in *The Union Signal*, February 20, 1908, this news item appeared:

"The Cavett statutory prohibition bill, which was unanimously passed by the Mississippi house February 7, passed the senate by a vote of 36 to 4 February 14. The Governor's signature is a foregone conclusion, and the law will go into effect January 1, 1909.

"The announcement of the vote was greeted with cheers and general rejoicing from the floor as well as from the well-filled galleries, where young men and maidens awaited as breathlessly as their seniors the result of the roll-call. It had taken but an hour in the house a week earlier to settle the whole matter with a unanimous vote. But the discussion in the senate offered a last opportunity for the liquor members to prove their devotion to their 'wet' constituency; so for two hours the brilliant and impatient audience listened to exhaustive and exhausting arguments that did not change one vote.

"There was practically no opposition in the legislature to a prohibitory statute. The people intended it in the last election. A 'wet' Jackson paper says:

"'It is doubtful if ever before in the history of liquor traffic legislation a law of this far-reaching importance has been enacted with so little dissent. The saloon men surrendered much more cheerfully than the prohibitionists had reason to expect. They foresaw the inevitable and yielded with as much grace as possible under the circumstances.'"

—G. M. H.

GEORGE C. HADDOCK.

He was a preacher, an Episcopalian Methodist, who meddled in politics after the fashion of Isaiah, Ezekiel, Jeremiah, Daniel. After their fashion he paid the price of prophetism by dying at the hands of his enemies.

Haddock came to Sioux City, Iowa, in 1885, appointed to serve a church there. He might have had a "good time" as good times go among preachers who know how to keep things sweet where the dead are. But he was surcharged with moral, political and religious convictions, and therefore likely to shock the parish by his utterance of unwelcome opinions. He was fifty-three years of age when he began his pastorate, having already distinguished himself for hostility to the liquor traffic, and by freedom of thought in theology. At Sheboygan, Wisconsin, in 1874, he had been assaulted by three men for saying things against the saloon, and ten years later he had withdrawn from the Republican party and united with the Prohibition party, voting for John P. St. John and William Daniel— in that crucial year when the vote that had been 12,576 "scattering" in 1880, became 151,809 for the heroic Governor of Kansas. Perhaps he threw his vote away, but he argued that a party which no longer stood for his opinions on the temperance question did not deserve it, and so he went out of one party into another.

Sioux City was under prohibitory law, but its hundred saloons were running as if the liquor traffic were free or licensed. The fifteen churches had been terrified into silence by threats of destruction. Anarchists held sway.

Haddock ignored the saloonkeepers' threats and started a campaign for the enforcement of the law which had been enacted at the demand of the majority of 29,759 citizen voters. He became the leader of anti-saloon forces against a corrupt city press, an inert court and an arrogant liquor league. To his eye it seemed as if Sioux City were in a state of rebellion against the commonwealth, and he said so in a circular letter addressed to his brother preachers. Not content merely to perform the routine duties of a parish minister, he went out into surrounding towns, making eloquent appeals for help in the fight that he had undertaken. Not only so, he did the necessary but unwelcome work of "getting evidence," one of the most difficult tasks under the existing political system. It was while so engaged that he was killed, August 3, 1886.

Weeks passed before the authorities of Sioux City took any steps to avenge the murder, and it was not until the 23d day of March of the next year that the case came to trial. One John Arensdorf was charged with unlawfully killing George C. Haddock, with malice aforethought, aided and abetted by certain other persons described as saloonkeepers and roughs.

It is not difficult to imagine the circumstance of the killing. Haddock, having returned to Sioux City from a trip to Greenville, had taken his horse and buggy to the stable, and was on his way home, when he met a crowd of armed cowards, ready to "do him up" as an open enemy of the Liquor Trade. It is said that Arensdorf thrust a pistol full into the defenseless minister's face and fired. Haddock fell and died.

Arensdorf's "peers," sworn to bring in a verdict according to law and testimony in the case, disagreed, eleven for acquittal, one for murder in the first degree. If the twelfth man had had his price, the verdict would have been unanimous, but he refused to be bought. A second trial was held in November of the same year and a verdict of acquittal was secured, in spite of the fact that a Mr. Munchrath, who had been convicted as one of a band of conspirators against Haddock's life, testified that, at a meeting of the Saloonkeepers' Association of Sioux City, August 2, 1886, the assassination of Haddock had been discussed, and Arensdorf had made the remark that there were funds enough in the treasury of the Association to reward the man who would put the offending preacher out of the way.

The years have come and gone over the grave of George C. Haddock. The Iowa prohibitory law adopted in 1884, was nullified in 1894, and 4491 saloonkeepers do business by paying fines in advance for violating a fundamental laws of the commonwealth. (The mulct law has been declared "null and void" by decision of Judge McPherson.)

Perhaps Haddock threw away his life as he had thrown away his vote, but his martyr blood consecrates Iowa to the outlawry of the liquor traffic. Is there no stone to mark the spot where he fell? Or do the sun and the stars as they look down through the days and the nights shine on a city's shame?

Writing of this, Mr. E. J. Wheeler has said:

"In Sioux City, Iowa, the law had been openly defied, no effort at concealment even being made. The officials of the city and the entire secular press upheld this defiance of the law and opposed any effort to enforce it. The public sentiment of the city, that portion at least which found expression, was in sympathy with the violators of the law, and a public request was made, signed by a large number of representative business men, that no attempt be made to disturb the existing condition of things. Yet with such an unfavorable state of things, a mere handful of determined men and women, with the Rev. George C. Haddock at their head, and with the injunction law of the state behind them, began proceedings, and, in spite of public sentiment and official opposition, soon wrought terror to the entire traffic in that city. It was as much in desperation as in hate that the assault was made by saloonkeepers on Mr. Haddock, resulting in his murder. But the proceedings still went on, and resulted in closing every saloon in Sioux City." —G. M. H.

D. R. COX AND J. W. BEALL.

On a February day, 1907, the public schools in Malden, Missouri, were closed, the churches draped and business suspended. Malden is not a large town and its affairs usually have no wide importance as "news." But there are reasons why all the public schools of the United States should have been closed on that day, all the churches draped and all business suspended. Two citizens, eminent for obedience to the law, devotion to family, and loyalty to church, had been assassinated at the close of a hot local option campaign in which they had taken prominent part—Judge D. R. Cox and Dr. J. W. Beall.

The judge was an able lawyer, widely known through southeastern Missouri, and the doctor was a popular practitioner. Malden had no nobler types of manhood. She knew how to honor them while living, and she knows how to honor them dead. But they had their enemies, created by their impolitic hostility to the liquor traffic. The judge might have saved his life by acting as attorney for St. Louis brewers, but he announced his intention to prosecute boodlers and other criminals as long as he had life and authority. The doctor might have saved his life by preserving a shrewd neutrality.

Instead of compromising, they coöperated with the Anti-Saloon League, contributing money and devoting time to the canvass. They were acting within their civil rights, and, as they thought, were performing a duty to the town, the church, the home. No one could say that they were violating any law of God and man, but one of them at least knew that he carried his life in his hands. For years Judge Cox knew that he was a branded man, and that at any time he might be killed by emissaries of the political gang that dominated Missouri politics. All the same he led the fight that carried his county for local option, and was in his place when, on the night of Monday, eighteenth of February, "Dr." Brannum fired the cowardly shot that ended his life.

A reporter brands the murderer as a "human monster—the spawn of the iniquitous environments of the criminal liquor traffic." Why? Because the liquor traffic refuses to obey any law which interferes with its so-called "rights." Its advocates are afraid of the open field and the fair fight, and accomplish their purpose by inaugurating a régime of terror. It has no real argument. It makes no defense of the saloon. After it has been defeated at the polls, it assassinates, boycotts, runs blind-tigers, blind-pigs, speak-easies, holes-in-the-wall, the jug trade and other dark agencies.

Judge Cox and Dr. Beall were killed at eight o'clock. Brannum was arrested, and the sheriff attempted to take him to jail through the excited crowd. Some one fired a shot and Brannum was dead.

EDWARD WARD CARMACK.

As the pages of this book are closing comes the shocking news of the cruel assassination of E. W. Carmack, stalwart son of the South, truly a hero and martyr of the Great Reform.

EDWARD W. CARMACK,
Ex-United States Senator, Tennessee.

The Nashville W. C. T. U., representing the temperance women of the entire commonwealth, voted the following resolution as an official expression of their attitude toward the assassination of the brilliant gentleman who championed their cause in the arena of politics:

"On Monday, November 9, ex-Senator Edward W. Carmack, as he quietly walked on the streets of our city, was, without the shadow of a chance to defend himself, shot down in cold blood by the murderous hand of an assassin for no other reason than that he stood fearlessly and squarely for civic righteousness as opposed to political frauds and corruptions, and for the protection of the homes of Tennessee from the blighting curse of the legalized liquor traffic."

The *Christian Advocate*, Nashville, one of the official organs of the Methodist Episcopal Church, South, and one of the most influential religious journals in the South, paid this editorial tribute to the memory of the dead editor:

"Tennessee sits in a great shadow. The deadly shot of a personal enemy on the afternoon of November 9 put out the most brilliant light in the public life of this great commonwealth. Not only the state, but the South and even the nation, felt the keenest shock when the news was flashed over the wires of the country that former Senator E. W. Carmack had been killed in Nashville. The sorrow of the best people of the state and nation is profound; for a brilliant editor, a wise and astute statesman, a courageous defender of truth and righteousness, a gallant standard bearer for the cause of sobriety, public morals and clean citizenship has fallen, and the country is robbed of the noble service of one of the most capable and fearless men and one of the most valued and honored leaders which the South has produced in this generation.

"Edward Ward Carmack was born November 5, 1858, near Castalian Springs, Sumner County, Tennessee. He grew to manhood with the opportunities of only an academic education. But he was a reader of good and great books, and he remedied to a great extent the lack of his earlier years. He studied law and began its practice in Columbia, Tenn. At twenty-six years of age he entered the Tennessee legislature, but after one term turned his attention to editorial work, and was a member of the editorial staff of the *Nashville American* from 1886 to 1888, when he founded the *Nashville Democrat*, of which he was editor until it was merged with the *American*, and then he became the editor-in-chief of the *American*. In 1892 he was called to the editor-in-chief's position on the *Memphis Commercial Appeal*. After five years he was elected to the House of Representatives of the United States Congress from the Memphis district. At the end of his second term, in 1901, he succeeded Senator Turley in the United States Senate, where he made a brilliant record and impressed the nation with the superiority of his gifts and the stalwartness of his character. In 1907 he was defeated for re-election to the Senate by Gov. Robert L. Taylor, the most popular politician in Tennessee. In 1908 he was a candidate before the people in a Democratic primary for the office of Governor against the present incumbent, the Hon. M. R. Patterson. The chief issue in the campaign was state-wide prohibition, and Senator Carmack espoused the cause of the people against the sale and manufacture of intoxicating liquors. He was defeated, as he was opposed by the state administration machine and by all the liquor men of the state. He was then made editor-in-chief of *The Nashville Tennesseean*, a paper that had stood nobly with Mr. Carmack for the prohibition of the liquor traffic. In his editorials he has attacked fearlessly the combination that has looked to the overthrow of all legislation on the question of the sale and manufacture of liquors.

"Senator Carmack has died the death of a martyr to the cause of civic righteousness and public sobriety, but his cause is not dead. Tennessee will rise in her majestic strength, and with ten thousand scourging thongs drive from her borders her social enemies who have brought about the lamented death of her most gifted and gallant son. The prohibitionist is dead, but prohibition, the choicest flower in our public life, will spring from his grave to give fragrance and beauty to this fair state of the South."

The *Washington Post* says:

"He would have been an ornament to British parliaments that knew Burke and Fox and Pitt. He would have been distinguished in American senates that contained Clay and Calhoun and Webster. He might have been rich. He had but to stoop. But in the true sense who dares say this American Senator is poor? Where is the man who does not respect him? All the wealth of either Ind would not buy for the base of his lofty character, his unblemished honor."

Of other heroes and martyrs, many of whose names may not have been lifted into the light of fame, there is a history, not less glorious than that which has been recorded. It is known and pondered in quiet places, where hidden souls cherish the memory of faithful men and patient women who have suffered for truth's sake without thought of renown. Should reference be made to some one lowly woman who, from the first days of the Crusade until the last days of her life, faithfully protested against the drink traffic, and regularly attended meetings of her beloved "Union," when her poor body was racked with pain and worn thin by hidden ailment, immediately the names of hundreds of other women suggest themselves—women who could not do more for the Great Reform and would not do less. They also did what they could, and the triumphs of the movement against the saloon are due, not alone to the gifted leaders but to the willing followers, the heroic, loyal rank and file, on whom falls the burden of battle.

WILLIAM H. ANDERSON,
Superintendent, Anti-Saloon League of Maryland.

REV. J. H. DURKEE,
Organizer and Chairman, World's Temperance Centennial Congress, Saratoga Springs, N. Y., June 14-23, 1908.

CHAPTER IX.

EDUCATIONAL ORGANIZATIONS.

AGENCIES, primarily organized to create and crystallize moral sentiment against the liquor traffic, have existed in the United States for a hundred years. Varied in form, their spirit has been identical, and their purpose has affiliated their methods.

Commanding universal confidence by the dignity of their representative men and women, and the logic of their program, they have co-acted with other movements to direct the energies of temperance people on the basis of that craving for fellowship which arises in the soul of every reformer.

At the World's Temperance Congress, held in Chicago, 1893, there were present delegates from twenty-two national bodies, devoted to temperance reform—not one of which was political in organization. Their paramount object was education.

Of these bodies—ecclesiastical, beneficial, medical and military—the history is so important that a volume might be compiled, reciting events in their rise and development. But for lack of space, it is imperative to confine recognition to four of the greater societies.

If it be said that they have directly or indirectly influenced legislation it may be replied that they were logically compelled to demand enactment of law as a means of educating the people and reconstructing the state on the foundation of their ideal.

THE NATIONAL TEMPERANCE SOCIETY.

Compiled from data furnished by JOHN W. CUMMINGS, *Treasurer.*

The full title of the Society is. "The National Temperance Society and Publication House." In the usual sense of the term, however, the Society is not a publication house; it was not organized to make money. Its mission has been to produce a temperance literature for the use of church, Sunday-school and temperance workers generally, and to distribute this practically at cost or free. It has always been a benevolent institution, depending upon free-will offerings for its support.

Through good report and evil report for nearly half a century the Society has been "pegging away," bearing the burden and heat of the day.

Along conservative and dignified lines it has pursued the even tenor of its way, not seeking human plaudits, but desiring to do its part in freeing our beloved land from the thraldom of the rum power, and, particularly, to train children in temperance principles.

The Society was called into existence immediately after the close of the Civil War. Temperance societies had been largely disbanded both north and south, and the temperance sentiment of the country was at its lowest ebb. The land was flooded with drunkenness. The drink habit had become fastened upon hundreds of thousands of soldiers who had just returned to their homes. Work among children had been almost universally abandoned. There was no temperance literature, but little temperance education and few temperance organizations anywhere in existence.

A widespread desire was expressed for something to be done, and a spontaneous call came from all parts of the land, especially from among the churches, that there should be an organization that could rally all good men, women and children to the work of saving the people from becoming a nation of drunkards. The beer and liquor interest had become active and aggressive. It flourished as the war progressed. The beer brewers had organized themselves into a national congress, with millions of money at its command. The friends of temperance saw clearly that something must be done at once if the land was to be saved from all these downward influences.

In August, 1865, a national temperance convention, composed of 325 delegates from twenty-five states and territories, assembled in Saratoga Springs, and organized "The National Temperance Society and Publication House." The convention was composed of representatives from the religious denominations and temperance organizations of the country. The object was to create and circulate a sound temperance literature, and to unify and concentrate the temperance sentiment against the drink habit and the drink traffic.

This Society is genuinely non-partisan in politics and non-sectarian in religion. It avoids all side issues. It bends all its efforts to secure a sound public sentiment in favor of total abstinence and the suppression of the liquor traffic.

Its more than two thousand publications are designed for the education of the people, and especially for the young, in the habits of total abstinence, law and order, and the suppression of the drink traffic. Its catalogue embraces over 2,000 different publications, from the one-page tract up to the bound volume of 1,000 pages. It has printed over 850,000,000 pages of temperance literature, which has been circulated in every state in the Union and in every country on the globe.

It publishes three monthly papers, and has over three hundred first-

JOHN N. STEARNS,
Secretary National Temperance Society.

JOSHUA L. BAILY,
Reformer.

class writers. *The Youth's Temperance Banner* has a monthly circulation of a hundred thousand. *The Water Lily,* with about forty thousand monthly, is suitable for circulation in Sunday-schools. *The National Temperance Advocate,* a 16-page monthly paper, contains arguments, statistics and temperance tables, by some of the ablest writers in the world, and gives a condensed history of the cause everywhere.

The Society has published 189 different books adapted to Sunday-school libraries. Of these books it has printed 510,000 volumes, which are changing hands weekly in many thousands of libraries throughout the land, reaching millions of children who otherwise would have no temperance instruction.

It has published the ablest text-books ever issued upon the nature and effects of alcohol on the human system. Its scientific, economic, religious and legal publications are from the foremost writers of the day.

It published the first "Temperance Lesson Book" for public schools ever issued in the country, and has spent large sums of money in the initial agitation for its introduction into the schools of the land.

It has published fifty-six "Temperance Lesson Leaves," giving Bible texts, questions, notes, teaching hints, etc., of which over 900,000 have been circulated.

Twelve different music and song books have been issued, of which 500,000 copies have been published.

Of the "Temperance Catechisms," the one on "Alcohol and Tobacco" has reached a circulation of over 300,000.

Three American Standard Prize Essays have been published, for which the sum of $1,500 was paid: "Alcohol and Science," 366 pages; "Alcohol in History," 481 pages, and "Alcohol in Society," 398 pages. These volumes cover every phase of the temperance question, and should be in the hands of every temperance worker, student, writer or speaker, and in every library in the land.

It is not only a publication house, but also a great missionary society. In fact, its entire work is essentially a missionary work. The missionary work covers the country, and extends to foreign lands, and consists in part as follows:

1. Work among the colored people in the South, employing colored missionaries, sending literature to ministers, churches, educational institutions, and furnishing libraries for colleges, theological seminaries, etc.

2. Scattering literature in prisons, hospitals, penitentiaries, jails, ships, army posts and other needy localities.

3. The work in Congress for a National Commission of Inquiry and

to look after other national temperance interests at the capital of the nation.

4. Holding conferences, conventions, mass-meetings, congresses, Sabbath-evening services and other public gatherings in different parts of the country.

5. The supplying of special literature to pastors, editors, lecturers, foreign nations, etc.

6. To publish the *National Temperance Advocate*, together with tracts and pamphlets on the medical, religious, economic, social, educational and legislative questions, which as a pecuniary investment never make a return, but which are of great value to the cause.

The Society has called and arranged for the holding of five great National Conventions in different cities of the Nation.

It called an International Temperance Conference to be held in Philadelphia in 1876, during the progress of the International Exhibition, which was attended by 428 regularly appointed delegates. Its results were gathered up and bound in a volume of over nine hundred pages.

A Centennial Temperance Conference was called to meet in Philadelphia in 1885, to celebrate the temperance progress of the country, as related to science, legislation, local option, prohibition, Sabbath and public schools, Congress, literature, etc. Five hundred and nine delegates were registered, and its proceedings were published in a volume of six hundred and fifty pages.

Its great missionary work has been among the colored people of the South. Eight or ten colored missionaries have been employed in different states, visiting churches, schools, families, institutions of learning, to lecture and to circulate a temperance literature among their people. They endeavor to convince and persuade their own race into habits of sobriety and steadfast opposition to the saloon. The weekly and monthly reports from these missionaries are most encouraging. Their services are eagerly sought after, and they are cordially welcomed by their people. Their meetings are largely attended, and their influence is felt all through the community. They have greatly aided in the local option and prohibition contests in different parts of the South.

It has carried on a large educational work in colleges and institutions of learning for the colored people, through the study of Dr. Richardson's "Temperance Lesson Book" and "Alcohol and Hygiene," published by the Society, and by the placing of a great number of volumes in the libraries of schools and colleges accessible to students preparing to be teachers and preachers among their own people.

While the Society is strictly non-partisan, it has persistently fought to secure, in coöperation with other organizations, such federal and state legislation as should protect the native races, among whom our missionaries labor in the territories, in our own colonies, and in foreign lands, from the curse of the liquor traffic; to preserve the sanctity of the Sabbath in our cities, and to defend it against the attacks of the allied forces of rum.

During the last forty-three years there have been few sessions of Congress in which the Society has not been urging restrictive temperance measures, furnishing data for congressmen and senators. In this way, and by the personal efforts of its legislative committee, it has assisted in securing the passage of many bills in the interest of temperance. In the state legislatures it has aided in the passing of local option bills and other restrictive measures.

Several important bills passed by Congress were drafted or initiated by the Temperance Society, such as:

The bill to prevent liquor selling within one mile of the National Soldiers' Home in the suburbs of Washington, D. C.

The bill, in 1891, forbidding the sale of all intoxicating liquors in post exchanges located in prohibition territory, and prohibiting the sale of distilled liquors at all army posts;

The Interstate Liquor Traffic bill, known as the "Original Package Bill," of 1890, to prohibit the shipping of liquor in the original package into prohibitory territory;

The passage by the Senate of the measure ratifying the treaty to protect the native races of the Congo against the white man's rum.

The Society has also had a large part in helping to secure the passage by Congress of several temperance measures initiated by others.

The Society is coöperating with other organizations in pressing before Congress several important temperance measures, among which are the following:

A National Inquiry Commission bill to investigate the effects of liquor on the moral, industrial and political affairs of the United States.

A bill to stop the issue by the Government of Federal liquor tax receipts in no-license or prohibition territory.

The McCumber bill, to suppress liquor selling in old soldiers' homes, and in all buildings owned by the United States Government.

A bill subjecting liquor shipped from another state in the original packages to local authority as soon as it crosses the state line.

A bill restricting the sale of patent medicines containing a large percentage of alcohol.

The submission by Congress to the various states of an amendment to the United States Constitution forever prohibiting the manufacture, sale or importation of intoxicating liquors.

For years the Society has also waged an incessant war against the sale of drink in the army, and has printed and circulated millions of pages of literature among the soldiers in the interest of total abstinence and sobriety.

During the Spanish War it had its agents at various camps, and as a result of their experience and observations published a series of pamphlets which had much to do in arousing the American people and leading Congress to pass the Anti-Canteen law, as the facts contained in the pamphlets were quoted in both the Senate and House by senators and representatives.

It was also the National Temperance Society that started the movement for—

The Temperance lessons in the Sabbath-schools, which are now universally used.

Temperance teaching in the public schools. Through this Society the scientific study of alcohol was introduced, in 1878, into the schools of New York. After this into the schools of New England. Subsequently the noble women of the W. C. T. U. took it up and carried it gradually forward throughout the land.

Stricter temperance qualifications for all Civil Service candidates.

The appointment by the House of Representatives, 1879, of a regular "Committee on Alcoholic Liquors," which has been reappointed at each Congress since.

The Twentieth Century World-Wide Pledge-Signing Crusade, in which the Society sent out, free, over three million pledges and two million pages of temperance literature in response to requests from temperance workers all over the world. To inaugurate this great movement and carry it on cost the Society thousands of dollars.

The Sunday-School Temperance Alliance has for its authority the Word of God. That Word says, "Train up a child in the way he should go, and when he is old he will not depart from it."—Proverbs 22:6.

There should be two divisions of the Alliance—the First Division including all in the Sunday-schools beyond the primary and junior; the Second Division confining itself to all not included in the First Division. It shall be styled "The Water Lilies."

Such well known and prominent Sunday-school workers as the Rev. Theodore L. Cuyler, D. D., LL. D., and the Hon. John Wanamaker, have spoken the heartiest word of approval. Public gatherings have also placed themselves on record regarding the Alliance. At the Annual Convention of the New York State Sabbath-School Association, held at Watertown, N. Y., June 11-13, 1907, the following action was unanimously taken:

"This Convention has heard with satisfaction the plans of the National Temperance Society in reference to its new department, The Sun-

WILLIAM E. DODGE,
First President, National Temperance Society.

JAMES B. DUNN, D. D.,
Vice-President, National Temperance Society.

day-School Temperance Alliance of America, which has recently been inaugurated.

"We heartily sympathize with this effort to provide a common platform on which all Temperance Societies and churches may stand together in the effort to educate and train the members of our Sunday-schools throughout the land in the principles of Total Abstinence for the individual and the entire suppression of the liquor traffic in the State and Nation."

The Sunday-School Temperance Alliance cannot fail to help every existing church and temperance organization. Ten years of persistent Alliance work will solve the liquor problem. The boy who is eleven years old today in ten years will vote. On the Alliance platform all may work together, whatever difference of view there may be in regard to method.

THE SCIENTIFIC TEMPERANCE FEDERATION.

By Cora Frances Stoddard, *Corresponding Secretary.*

When the time is ripe for a great forward movement in the progress of society, it frequently happens that the impulse to such a movement arises about the same time in several minds in different parts of the world. A recent development in the field of temperance effort is a fresh illustration of this fact. For a long time the need had been felt of some organization or agency which would make a specialty of gathering and supplying the concise up-to-date information on the alcohol question which would enable the specialist to put his researches and conclusions on file where they would be sought for and examined, and which would afford a clearing-house of information concerning scientific, moral, economic and social phases of the alcohol question.

To meet this need, the Scientific Temperance Federation came into existence in December, 1906. It was, in part, an outgrowth of the ideals of the late Mrs. Mary H. Hunt for the extension of scientific temperance truth among the people, and its headquarters are at 23 Trull street, Boston, long the headquarters of the work conducted by Mrs. Hunt.

Stated briefly, the object of the Federation is to collect the facts about alcohol and other narcotics in their various relations to the individual and society, to classify these facts so that they will be available for study and consultation, and to use them in stimulating intelligent interest in the alcohol question, in supplying information desired, in counteracting the pseudo-scientific doctrines set afloat by the liquor interests—in other words, to promote in every possible way the education of the public on this subject.

The Federation already has made a considerable classified collection of scientific and other data on the alcohol question. It receives literature and periodicals on this subject from all the leading countries, and has access to the large public, medical and institutional libraries of Boston and vicinity. It is fortunate also in having among its secretaries one who has been engaged for nearly twenty years in this special research work. In the use and development of these resources the Federation will be glad to coöperate with existing organizations, its purpose being to supplement, not to supersede in any sense, the activities already being ably directed by other bodies, and to help supply that working material of scientific fact which is increasingly recognized as an essential element in successful effort. A press circular containing "fillers" of scientific temperance instruction, for use by editors, has already been inaugurated, and editors representing some millions of readers have signified their desire to receive it regularly.

The general scheme of the Scientific Temperance Federation has elicited among representative men and women at home and abroad cordial expressions of interest and of desire to coöperate. A few only can be named. Among those interested are Professor H. J. Berkley, Johns Hopkins University; Professor Winfield S. Hall, Northwestern University Medical School, Chicago; Dr. Charles H. Hughes, Barnes Medical College, St. Louis, Mo.; Dr. T. D. Crothers, Hartford, Conn.; Dr. T. Alexander MacNicholl, New York; Professor John Marshall Barker, Boston University; Dr. Martin G. Brumbaugh, Superintendent of Schools, Philadelphia; Mrs. S. S. Fessenden, formerly President of Massachusetts Woman's Christian Temperance Union, Boston; Mrs. A. J. Gordon, Boston; Mr. William C. Lilley, treasurer of the Presbyterian Permanent Temperance Committee, Pittsburg, Pa.; the Rev. C. L. Morgan, chairman of the National Congregational Temperance Committee, Elgin, Ill.; the Rev. Francis E. Clark, President of the United Society of Christian Endeavor; the Rev. Emory J. Hunt, D. D., President Denison University, Granville, Ohio; Dr. Howard S. Anders, Medico-Chirurgical College, Philadelphia; Dr. J. P. Crozer Griffith, University of Pennsylvania; the Rev. E. O. Taylor, D. D., lecturer on scientific temperance instruction, Boston; Dr. Robert N. Wilson, Jr., secretary of Pennsylvania Society for the Prevention of Social Disease, Philadelphia; Dr. E. A. Winship, editor of the *Journal of Education*, Boston; Dr. Max Kassowitz, University of Vienna, Austria; Mr. Walter N. Edwards, F. C. S., superintendent of department of scientific temperance instruction of United Kingdom Band of Hope Union, London, England; Professor E. Kraepelin, Munich, Germany, famous for his experiments as to the effects of alcohol on mental operations; Professor G. Aschaffenburg, editor of *Criminal Psychology and Penal Reform Monthly*, Cologne, Germany.

About the time the Scientific Temperance Federation was organized, a movement for an international agency for disseminating temperance information developed abroad. This took formal shape in the organization at the Stockholm Anti-Alcohol Congress of The International Temperance Bureau, to be directed by a committee composed of representatives of eighteen countries. Dr. T. D. Crothers, of Hartford, Conn., a United States government delegate to the Stockholm Congress, and one of the official representatives also of the Scientific Temperance Federation at that congress, is the American member of this international movement for the wider dissemination of the facts about alcohol and the alcohol question. The Scientific Temperance Federation will be closely affiliated with the International Bureau as its American branch.

Centralization and specialization are the keynotes of modern progress, and, in social reform at least, knowledge is often both rampart and ammunition. It is believed, therefore, that the organization of the Scientific Temperance Federation, and now of this international agency, with their avowed purposes of collecting and supplying temperance information, is not only timely, but is a necessary step forward in combating the fallacies which so long have held the nations under the power of alcohol, and which the educational bureaus of the liquor interests are doing their utmost to perpetuate.

In addition to the good which it is hoped will accrue to the cause of temperance at large through the membership in the Federation, there will come some direct and personal advantages to members. Anyone may become an associate member through the payment of the annual fee of only two dollars, and will be entitled to receive, gratis, the official organ, while arrangements will be made to supply members correct information on the alcohol question through correspondence, concise printed literature, notices of important facts, references to new books, pamphlets, etc. Membership will also afford access, at a nominal additional cost, to special information desired on topics which involve special research. Frequent and increasing demand is being levied on pastors, teachers, physicians and many others, to prepare papers, addresses or sermons on some particular phase of the alcohol question on which is needed reliable up-to-date information that one has neither time nor facilities to search out for one's self. On such occasions, the resources and assistance of the Federation will be appreciated.

The Federation, accordingly, invites the coöperation of all physicians, pastors, teachers or special temperance workers interested in the objects for which it is organized.

INDEPENDENT ORDER OF GOOD TEMPLARS.
BY MRS. MCCLELLAN BROWN, PH. D., *Grand Chief Templar, Ohio I. O. G. T.*

The International Order of Good Templars is the largest temperance organization in the world, being world-wide in dominion and having initiated over seven million of members and more than seven hundred thousand juveniles in a Junior Order.

Good Templary was organized in Utica, New York, 1851, and was the first organization of any kind to admit women on equal basis with men and make them eligible to any office within the gift of the Order. Its platform of principles was far in advance of anything declared at so early a date:

1. Total abstinence by perpetual obligation.
2. No license in any form or under any circumstances.
3. Absolute prohibition in due form of law for state and nation.
4. Creation of healthy public sentiment through all known modes of enlightened philanthropy.
5. The election of good men to administer the laws.
6. Persistent efforts to save individuals and communities from the direful scourge until success is complete and universal.

While Good Templary is essentially a religious organization, it has no religious test, save the personal belief in a Supreme Being. Its ritual has been translated into fourteen different languages, and the work is instituted in all the United States and all the Provinces of Canada, all the Provinces, Islands and Dependencies of Great Britain, also in Germany, Denmark, Netherlands, Norway, Sweden, Iceland, Switzerland, Belgium, Natal, Central, Eastern and Western South Africa, Burma, India, Madras, Ceylon, Turk Islands, Jerusalem, the Bahamas and Danish West Indies. Nearly all the warships of Great Britain have lodges of Good Templars among the officers and men, and are prepared to introduce the Order wherever they stop for a time.

An estimate of the educational advantages accruing from the Order can be only silhouetted by the men and women whose names have honored the pages of reform, nearly all of whom learned in the Good Templar lodgerooms of the world the fundamental principles of the work, the arts of speech and parliamentary service, the ability to think standing, and to speak spontaneously in any presence; besides the still harder lesson and task of personal sacrifice. This Order has spent more money in the general cause of temperance than all other organizations together, and has in different parts of the world beneficiary institutions for drunkards' children's and orphans' homes, and homes for wives of drunkards, inebriate cures, temperance hospitals, and other asylums for amelioration of the effects of the drink traffic upon innocent parties.

Good Templary is the natural parent of prohibition and the Prohibition Party; also of the Woman's Christian Temperance Union, having through its Grand Chief Templar of Ohio, Mrs. McClellan Brown, organized one hundred and six leagues, afterward called Unions, and called and

MRS. KATE E. WILKINS.
President, Louisiana W. C. T. U.

MRS. ALICE CARY McKINNEY,
Editor, Louisiana "White Ribbon," W. C. T. U.

MRS. McCLELLAN BROWN, Ph. D.,
Grand Chief Templar, Ohio I. O. G. T.

MISS ELIZABETH MARCH,
President, North Carolina W. C. T. U.

organized the first Association of Crusade Women at Columbus, February 24, 25, 1874, having afterwards called the first day of prayer which was observed all over the state, and having called and organized a Committee for National Organization at Chautauqua the following August, to whose first Convention at Cleveland, November, 1874, she gave the "Plan of Work" and "Address to Women of the World." There were at that time ninety thousand pledged Templars in Ohio coöperating with the new women in general work.

Good Templary first organized the children; first started the Fresh Air Movement; set agoing the series of petitions from great Christian bodies for Temperance Lessons in the International Sunday School Series; sent the first woman lecturer around the world on temperance mission, employing two hundred and fifty one interpreters into forty-seven different languages, Mrs. Mary Clement Leavitt of Boston.

It is first in faith of world-wide benefits in its truths; first in hope of the redemption of humanity from the crimes of strong drink; first to extend the hand of charity to the helpless victims; first in arbitration methods seeking now to absolve the nations from the horrors of war. It is an Order which feels the stirring of a common life making the many one, and "will not take a heaven haunted by the shrieks of far-off misery."

THE CATHOLIC TOTAL ABSTINENCE UNION OF AMERICA.

The Catholic Total Abstinence Union of America was formed February 22, 1872, in Baltimore, Maryland. It was organized for the purpose of assisting to stem the tide of intemperance. Following in the footsteps of the glorious apostle of total abstinence, Theobald Mathew, his plan of individual pledges was adopted.

The Union has three objects in view: *First*, to secure to its members the privilege of being received into societies connected with the Union in any part of America; *second*, to encourage and aid committees and pastors to establish new societies; and *third*, to spread by means of Catholic total abstinence publications correct views regarding total abstinence principles.

To accomplish these objects, the constitution of the order requires the practice of the Roman Catholic religion by all members individually; the observance of maxims laid down for spiritual guidance by the reverend clergy; the influence of good example and kind persuasion upon fellow Catholics; the connection with the association of prayer in honor of the sacred thirst and agony of Jesus; and the appointment of a lecture and publication bureau.

The pledge of the Union is as follows:

"I promise, with the Divine assistance and in honor of the sacred thirst and agony of our Savior, to abstain from all intoxicating drinks; to prevent as much as possible, by advice and example, the sin of intemperance in others; and to discountenance the drinking customs of society."

The officers of the Union are a Spiritual Director, President, First and Second Vice-Presidents, Treasurer and Secretary.

While the Total Abstinence Union is the principal temperance organization in the Roman Catholic Church, there are various subordinate and dependent societies in states and dioceses where the Union has not been regularly formed. All these have been approved by the Plenary Council of the Church in America, and the Holy Father has formally commended and blessed the work in which the various total abstinence societies of the church are engaged.

With these approvals the Union has achieved much success. It is earnestly working to have a total abstinence society in every parish; and as a means toward this end, it has provided that the First Vice-President shall appoint an organizer for each diocese. Special efforts are being made to form cadet organizations in order to bring up the youth free from the cravings of appetite. Many societies of women have been formed for the purpose of cultivating the home influence so necessary for the successful continuance of pastoral labors.

The Union has sent out lecturers to all sections of the country, and has disseminated a large number of total abstinence documents, especially the lectures of Most Rev. Archbishop Ireland and the pamphlets of the Rev. Dr. T. J. Conaty. Thus the work of the Union is being carried on from Maine to California and from Minnesota to Texas. Catholics are advised to shun the flowing bowl, and to seek safety for home and family under the banner of the Catholic Total Abstinence Union.

The enrolled membership in good standing is now about 89,400, enrolled in 1042 societies. The President of the Union is the Right Rev. J. F. R. Canevin, Bishop of Pittsburgh, Pa., and the Secretary is J. W. Logue, 1313 Steven Girard Building, Philadelphia, Pa. All state Unions subordinate to the national Union are represented in the great national conventions, and the influences generated in these great gatherings operate for the uplift of the people and the conservation of temperance sentiment in the great Roman Catholic Church. —G. M. H.

MRS. LILLIAN M. N. STEVENS,
President, National Woman's Christian
Temperance Union.

CHAPTER X.

THE WOMAN'S CHRISTIAN TEMPERANCE UNION.

By Lillian M. N. Stevens, *President.*

"*Recognizing the fact that our cause will be combated by mighty, determined and relentless forces, we will, trusting in Him who is the Prince of Peace, meet argument with argument, misjudgment with patience, denunciation with kindness, and all our difficulties and dangers with prayer.*

"*We will lend our influence to that party, by whatever name called, which shall furnish the best embodiment of prohibition principles and will most surely protect our homes.*"—W. C. T. U. Declaration of Principles.

IT HAS been often said and often reiterated that women suffer most because of intemperance. This undoubtedly is true, not because women drink more intoxicating liquor than men, for they drink far less, but because so many of their loved ones—fathers, brothers, husbands, and sons—become victims of that which destroys the highest and holiest interests of the home. Because this destruction of the home had been going on for years and years, the Crusade movement of 1873 was inaugurated, and in 1874 the National Woman's Christian Temperance Union was organized.

In the Crusade, the saloon was besieged with pleading and with prayer, and in fifty days this whirlwind of the Lord had swept the liquor traffic out of two hundred and fifty towns and villages. There had come a great awakening to the women of this nation in regard to the enormous evil of the liquor traffic and the part they ought to take in its overthrow. The need of systematic, organized work was realized, and the National Union was formed.

This society is established in every state and territory, and in more than ten thousand localities there are unions auxiliary to the state and National organizations, which are co-operating to carry out W. C. T. U. plans and purposes, as formulated and adopted at the National annual conventions. These conventions are delegated bodies with representatives from every state.

The Woman's Christian Temperance Union is a total abstinence society. It is also anti-brewery, anti-distillery, anti-saloon, and *anti* all other forms of making and selling alcoholic drink. The society is neither partisan nor sectarian. Its basic principles are: Total abstinence for the individual; and total prohibition for the state and nation. In the promotion of its work it has been led out through the "Do everything" policy of Frances E. Willard into forty different departments of work, ranging all the way from training little children aright, to caring for the prisoner in his cell—the prisoner who in many instances is the victim of strong drink. Each of these national departments is in charge of a superintendent, duplicated in every state and largely in the local unions.

The Department of Organization reaches out to unorganized localities, and has as special national workers in this department (in addition to all the state organizers) forty-two organizers and lecturers; also twenty-five national evangelists whose work is somewhat along the line of organization.

The work among foreign speaking peoples is carried on extensively through literature, public meetings and personal visitation. A W. C. T. U. missionary is kept constantly at Ellis Island, New York, to meet the incoming foreigners.

Through the Department of Medical Temperance, efforts are made to educate the public in regard to the danger of self-medication with powerful drugs. This department teaches that alcohol is dangerous and unnecessary as a medicine, and it also does much to expose fraudulent medicines.

At the organizing convention in 1874, temperance teaching in the public schools was recommended, and the W. C. T. U. has been instrumental in securing laws in every state and territory requiring temperance instruction in all schools supported by public money.

The W. C. T. U., in 1884, used its influence in securing the insertion of the Quarterly Temperance Lesson in the International Sunday School Lesson Series. These lessons are still continued by the Sunday School Association.

The Department of Juvenile Courts, Industrial Education and Anti-Child Labor, works to secure industrial training as a part of the education of our youth, and seeks to prevent improper child labor. This is plainly legitimate temperance work, for a great many of the child laborers are the children of drunken parents, who support saloons instead of supporting their children.

To educate is the first aim of the Department of Anti-Narcotics, and it seeks to instil into the minds of the young the knowledge of the injury produced by tobacco, opium and other narcotics.

Through the Medal Contest Department many thousands of recitations on prohibition, total abstinence, anti-narcotics and other lines of W. C. T. U. endeavor are given before public audiences by young people.

Work among railroad employés, among soldiers and sailors, among lumbermen and miners is extensively carried on. The methods are by visitation and personal effort, organizing temperance societies, securing signatures to the pledge and distributing literature.

The National W. C. T. U. recognizes that intemperance and impurity are closely allied, and that a blow aimed at one falls upon the other. The Purity Department of the W. C. T. U. seeks to lift up the standard of purity in every community, and to establish a single standard of morality for both men and women. Through the Rescue Work it aims to reach the fallen of both sexes, and through Purity in Literature and Art, seeks to elevate the press, to secure the enforcement of existing laws relative to obscene and impure literature and, whenever necessary, to secure better laws.

Even this brief description of the work of a few of the many W. C. T. U. departments will give an idea of the organization's methods and scope. It will readily be seen that the W. C. T. U. is interested in Organization, Prevention, Educational, Social and Legal lines of work, and, in this way, for three decades and four years has been girdling that mighty tree—the liquor traffic. It is true in forestry that a tree completely girdled will die. The liquor traffic is dying out.

An important branch of the W. C. T. U. is the Loyal Temperance Legion. Thousands upon thousands of young people in its Junior and Senior grades in every section of the land, with the pledge in the hand, a reason in the head and conviction in the heart, have been growing up these twenty-five years. Many of them, already grown to manhood and womanhood, in the home, the school and at the ballot-box, have become potent factors in bringing about the recent prohibition victories. The Loyal Temperance Legion, like the Woman's Christian Temperance Union, of which it is a part, is constantly increasing in numbers and in influence.

Twenty-five years ago Frances E. Willard went South with loving kindness in her heart and with loving kindness she was received. Largely through her influence the W. C. T. U. was organized in all the southern states, and it is not at all strange that in the states of the southland which have adopted prohibition, this society and its leaders are now credited with having done much to bring to pass the recent victories. They have been brought about through the patient seed sowing and the application of W. C. T. U. methods and principles to the every day life of the white-ribboner in the home, the church, the school and the state. A popular magazine in a recent editorial well expresses it: "The story of the prohibition victory in Georgia traces back step by step to the doors of its women who taught, prayed, organized, worked and won."

The parade feature in the prohibition campaigns of the last year has attracted much attention. In many papers and magazines these parades have been graphically described and pictured. Women from homes of refinement and luxury, marching with women whose homes and home life have been ruined by drink; children from homes of wealth walking beside the children who are robbed by strong drink of home comforts and loving care. The summing up of the meaning of the mottoes inscribed on their banners is: "To license liquor selling is a sin"; "To prohibit liquor selling is to promote the holiest interests of the home."

Thirty-four years ago, when the Crusaders knelt on the pitiless streets, they did not even dream what the outcome would be. They did not realize that the thousands who came after them, in carrying on a reform more divine than human, would be led to consider the problem from a state or governmental standpoint. These women, and their comrades of later days, who prayed in the saloons have come to be pleaders before legislative and municipal assemblies, not only in every state, but also at our nation's Capitol. It is well known that the W. C. T. U. auxiliaries have been the chief factors in state campaigns for statutory prohibition and constitutional amendments, and for securing the enactment of other reform laws, especially those for the protection of girls.

The principal efforts of the Woman's Christian Temperance Union the past year have been to retain the "anti-canteen" law; to secure the passage of the Littlefield or Bacon bill; to banish the sale of liquor from all government buildings; to secure state laws forbidding the sale of liquor within three or four miles of soldiers' homes, forts, army camps, etc.; to secure a provision for an amendment to the constitution of the United States prohibiting polygamy; to interest all teachers and pupils, especially of Normal schools and colleges, in scientific temperance instruction; to secure at least $2.00 from each local union, or its equivalent from the state, for the Frances E. Willard Memorial Fund; to complete the raising of $10,000 for an emergency fund; to increase total abstinence practice and sentiment, and to promote the prohibition of the liquor traffic everywhere.

The National W. C. T. U. has created a great literature. Nearly every state union has its official paper devoted entirely to W. C. T. U. interests. Each of the forty National superintendents sends out large amounts of literature. The National W. C. T. U. owns and publishes its official paper, the *Union Signal*, a weekly, extensively taken in every state, and also in many foreign lands. The *Crusader Monthly*, also owned and controlled by the National W. C. T. U., is the official paper of the Loyal Temperance Legion. It has a large and constantly increasing circulation, and like the *Union Signal*, goes to every state and to other lands.

The World's W. C. T. U. was organized in 1883, and now embraces about fifty nations. Its aims and principles are the same as those of the National W. C. T. U. of the United States. Frances E. Willard, who for twenty years was president of the National W. C. T. U., was the founder of the World's W. C. T. U. The statue of Frances E. Willard is the first and only statue of a woman to grace the Valhalla of our republic. Under the great dome of our National Capitol she stands.

> "Stand, radiant soul!
> Here, in the center of our Nation's heart;
> Forever of its best life, thou'rt a part;
> Here thou shalt draw thy land to what thou art;
> Stand, radiant soul!"

This recognition was not given because Miss Willard was a great educator or a noble Christian woman, for she was both; but because she heard the cry of the world—the cry of suffering childhood, sorrowing womanhood and wrecked manhood—the result of strong drink. She heard, she heeded the cry, and she became the greatest reformer of the century. The work Frances E. Willard loved and to which she gave her beautiful life, is to go on and on until this nation and all nations are freed from the bondage of the legalized liquor traffic. To help hasten this day has been and will continue to be the mission of the W. C. T. U.

LILLIAN M. N. STEVENS.

Her Introduction to the National Woman's Christian Temperance Union.—Editorial in Union Signal, March 24, 1898.

"As sweet and wholesome as her own piney woods," was Miss Willard's descriptive phrase of the woman who succeeds her to the responsibility of leadership in the National Woman's Christian Temperance Union. As strong as her granite rock, as steadfast as her ocean waves and as easily moved by humanity's needs as her pine treetops, she might have added. Rarely have we seen a character in which the traits of sweetness and strength, steadfastness and pliability, are so blended as in the subject of this sketch. A less gentle nature could never have won for herself such a place in the hearts of our white ribbon women, nor could a less steadfast one ever have been chosen as the closest adviser of Frances Willard.

Mrs. Stevens was born in Dover, Maine, and her home has always been within the borders of the old Pine Tree state. Like so many of our leaders, her first public work was in the school room as teacher, but she early left that sphere, and at the age of twenty-one married Mr. M. Stevens, of Stroudwater, a charming little suburb of Portland. Her husband is in full accord with her principles and life work, and is one of the most genial of hosts to the multitude of her co-laborers who are entertained in their charmingly hospitable New England home. Her only child, Mrs. Gertrude Stevens Leavitt, is a young woman of great promise, an ardent white ribboner and one of the state superintendents in the Maine W. C. T. U.

Her sister-in-law, Mrs. Olive Hanson, who is also, with her husband, a member of Mrs. Stevens' home, is likewise devoted to the interests of the Woman's Christian Temperance Union, and is a woman who brings things to pass with unfailing certainty. The old home, which has been for more than a century in the Stevens family, resounds constantly to the music of children's voices, for, although Mrs. Stevens is prominently connected with the child-saving institution of her state, she believes most ardently that an institution can never be a substitute for a home, and while she urges her Maine women to open their doors to God's homeless little ones, she herself sets them a most practical example. Within the last fifteen years nineteen children have at different times had a home with her, two of whom are at present in her household.

Mrs. Stevens first met Miss Willard at Old Orchard, Maine, in the summer of 1875, and there aided in the organization of the state Woman's Christian Temperance Union, of which she was elected treasurer. She held that position for three years, and then passed, by the process of natural selection, to the position of president. To the latter office she has been elected for the twenty-first time, and in all those years but one ballot has ever been cast for another candidate. Under her wise guidance the Maine W. C. T. U. has come into a position of honor throughout the entire state. Its membership in proportion to the population is very large, one white ribboner to every one hundred and sixty-three and a fraction of the population, and in no other state have we seen greater reverence for the organization exhibited among all classes.

For many years Mrs. Stevens has been reckoned as General Neal Dow's chief coadjutor, and, in the later years of his life especially, he leaned upon her as his trusted friend and adviser. When in Portland, it was her custom to visit him two or three times a week, and since his death she is recognized throughout the entire state as the leader of the prohibition forces. Indeed, in the well-fought battle of 1884, which placed prohibition in the state constitution, Mrs. Stevens won for herself a fame as organizer and agitator hardly second to Neal Dow himself. She visited every county and nearly all the large towns, holding meetings constantly and throwing the whole force of her strong personality into the battle which resulted in such signal victory.

Some of the triumphs of the Maine Woman's Christian Temperance Union under her leadership have been, the school suffrage law, the raising of the age of protection to sixteen years, a strong scientific temperance instruction law, which is well enforced, and the constitutional amendment to which we have already referred.

In addition to her distinctive temperance work, Mrs. Stevens is well known in the other reform and philanthropic enterprises of the state. She

MRS. MARY HARRIS ARMOR,
President, Georgia Woman's Christian Temperance Union.

MRS. ELIZABETH P. ANDERSON,
Recording Secretary, Woman's Christian Temperance Union.

was one of the chief promoters of the Industrial School for Girls, and it was through her efforts largely that a woman superintendent was appointed for this school. She was Maine's choice for the Board of Lady Managers in the World's Columbian Exposition, and served in that Board on most important committees. She was for six years treasurer of the National Council of Women, and has filled many other positions of responsibility and honor. But the Woman's Christian Temperance Union is her first and chief love, and to its interests she has devoted herself with lavish generosity for twenty-four years.

In her own state she has the profound respect of all its citizens. This was especially manifested when a year ago an effort was made to pay for the state W. C. T. U. headquarters. Men gave liberally who had no especial interest in the work or the principles of the white ribbon, but who declared themselves as glad to have such an opportunity to show their appreciation of Mrs. Stevens as a philanthropist and a woman. Her work for the Armenians has already been recorded in the columns of the *Union Signal*. Those who were sent to Maine, found in her not only a benefactor but a warm personal friend, and she is held in almost adoration by those who know her work for this long suffering people. Last summer Mrs. Stevens visited the British Woman's Temperance Alliance Council as the special guest of Miss Agnes Slack. She was shown great honor during her stay, not by Lady Henry Somerset alone, who counts her a valued and trusted friend, but by all who came in contact with her. She was an especial guest with Miss Slack at the Lord Mayor's on the Queen's birthday, and a reception was tendered her by the National Temperance Alliance at which she told the story of prohibition in Maine.

Her present work for the Maine W. C. T. U. is for the enforcement of the prohibitory law, and for the purifying of the state judiciary. The courage of Mrs. Stevens was never more clearly apparent than in this latter work, for she has not hesitated to strike a blow at one long held in official esteem, assured that it is in the interest of purity and morality.

Mrs. Stevens is a woman of radical principles, but conservative in action when conservatism may be trusted to accomplish more than radicalism. She has always stood side by side with Miss Willard in her most advanced steps, from the day of the suffrage agitation until now, and yet so wise and tactful is she in the presentation of advanced thought that she antagonizes very few. She is a woman of strong affections, a devoted friend and a wise counselor. No surer indices can be given of her character than the fact that animals always love her, as she loves them, and that people in all stations of life turn to her involuntarily for advice. Perhaps she holds more secrets of a personal nature than any other one woman in her state, but a secret in her hands is absolutely safe, and her counsel is as wise as it is kindly.

The deep springs of her nature all set toward God and righteousness. She is a woman of profound religious convictions and deep spirituality. Perhaps she may say less on these subjects than some do, but those who know her life best know how truly Christ is her Master and Lord, and how every day and hour of her life are given to humanity for His service and "In His Name."

(Mrs. Stevens was unanimously reëlected President of the National W. C. T. U. at the Denver Convention, October, 1908.)

THE LOYAL TEMPERANCE LEGION.

The Loyal Temperance Legion, senior, intermediate and primary, consists of young folks, organized to build up character, cultivate principles of total abstinence and purity and prepare for efficient service along all lines of reform. Each boy and girl, on entering the society, promises to abstain from the use of alcoholic drinks, including wine, beer and cider, tobacco in any form, and from profanity; and to endeavor to put down indecent language and all coarse jests, and to use every means to fulfil the command, "Keep thyself pure." Although composed of boys as well as girls, the Legion is a branch of the W. C. T. U., its secretary being Miss Anna A. Gordon, noted as Miss Willard's private secretary and one of her nearest heart-friends. It was formed, 1886, of thousands of juvenile societies under care of local Unions, and is conserving a moral force which, when the various states in the Union have abolished the saloon, will coöperate in enforcing law and maintaining ground won during the campaigns for prohibition.

To show what the L. T. L. can do, the story of a boy's battle with the saloon, first told in the L. T. L. monthly, *The Crusader,* is retold:

Into a certain village in Ohio there came one day a bundle of *The Crusader Monthly,* organ of the Loyal Temperance Legion, addressed to students of the High School. Month by month the paper came and, after a year, a Senior Legion was organized. The spirit of the Crusade began to pervade the little town, and sources of saloon supply became reduced. Lack of patronage forced one saloonkeeper out of business. The Loyal Temperance Legion was "doing something." Among the most active members of the society was a young fellow of nineteen. The *Crusader* appealed to him and he awoke to the opportunity of doing duty as a citizen, a duty which it would appear was being evaded by the citizen voters of the village, for the saloons were running full tide and it was up to a boy to resist their subtle call to him. Of fine fiber, a modest, shrinking young

ANNA A. GORDON,
Vice-President-at-Large, National Woman's Christian Temperance Union.

MRS. SUSANNA M. D. FRY,
Corresponding Secretary, 1898-1908, National Women's Christian Temperance Union.

fellow he was, but, when it became clear to him that, if he did his whole duty, he must ask for the enforcement of the law, he no longer shrank. His whole nature absorbed the soul of the nation-wide movement against the saloon—and in his little, obscure village he resolved to play the part of a reformer. He is too modest to tell his own story. His little letter to the editor of this book shows that he had no thought of note, when he began agitation for suppression of the saloons in his village. Two saloonkeepers, who, by common consent, had violated the closing hour law, were arrested and fined. Resenting this interference, they threatened the life of the Loyal Temperance Legion boy—but did not cow him. He knew that the saloonkeepers were cowards, that saloonkeepers had killed Roderick Dhu Gambrell and George C. Haddock and Judge Cox and Dr. Beall. He was not bullet proof, but he and his Legion did duty. Other arrests were made and the little town began to feel the effects of the reformation, inaugurated by a few young people who had read *The Crusader Monthly*.

The Legion went into "politics." Its president was elected Mayor —the old men having abandoned the field—and it brought on a local option election, and the town went dry! —G. M. H.

MRS. SUSANNA M. D. FRY, A.M., PH.D.

NOTE.—*Mrs. Fry has served the National W. C. T. U. at headquarters since 1895. As editor of the Union Signal, and afterwards as Corresponding Secretary she has become known to every member of the Union everywhere. At the 1908 Annual Convention she resigned. The following brief sketch is printed to indicate what a fine type of women are associated in the grand work of this great organization.*—G. M. H.

Mrs. Susanna M. D. Fry, Corresponding Secretary of the National Woman's Christian Temperance Union, brought to the problems of that office in 1898 an unusual equipment as an educator and a reformer. Graduated at eighteen from the Western College and Seminary for Women at Oxford, Ohio, she became a teacher in the primary department of the village school. Her first "declaration" for justice and equality for women was when she declined to accept the "big room" of this same school at one-half the salary paid to male incumbents. Her superior ability as a teacher led her swiftly into positions of greater responsibility. In 1876 the degree of A.M. was conferred upon her by the Ohio Wesleyan University. A little later she took post-graduate work at Syracuse University (N. Y.), and upon examination received the degree of Ph.D.

For nearly fifteen years Mrs. Fry occupied the chair of *Belles Lettres* in the Illinois Wesleyan University at Bloomington. For the greater part of that time she was president of one of the largest literary clubs in the state. For two years she was at the head of the department of

English Literature in the University of Minnesota, and for a similar period she was president of the W. C. T. U. of Minnesota. In 1895 she was elected managing editor of *The Union Signal*, the official organ of the National W. C. T. U. In 1898 she was called from that position to the office of National Corresponding Secretary.

Mrs. Fry's executive ability is coupled with unusual talent as a writer and public speaker. During a year spent in travel and study in Europe with her husband, Rev. James D. Fry, she contributed regularly to several of the leading magazines and newspapers. During her busy life at the desk she has found time to put out one very acceptable book, "A Paradise Valley Girl," and has written a number of leaflets of special interest and help to the work of the W. C. T. U. Mrs. Fry was one of the judges in the Liberal Arts Department of the World's Columbian Exposition, held in Chicago in 1893, and here, as elsewhere, she gave hearty, conscientious devotion to the work in hand.

A distinguishing characteristic of this scholarly woman who has given such honorable and efficient service to the Woman's Christian Temperance Union, is her breadth of vision, her receptive attitude toward all that makes for the development and betterment of humanity, and her unfailing optimism. She is greatly beloved by those who have been privileged to be her co-workers at National W. C. T. U. headquarters. Her sound judgment and keen intuition made her a valued and trusted representative of the rank and file of the white ribbon army.

FRANCES ELIZABETH WILLARD.

CHAPTER XI.

FRANCES ELIZABETH WILLARD.

An Appreciation by The Editor.

WHY a woman, born in an obscure village, should acquire the reputation of doing more for the cause of temperance than any other person of her time, is one of the insoluble problems of psychology. Long before she became famous, however, she was known to be a "genius," and those who knew her were enthusiastically predicting renown for her—even though they did not foresee the Woman's Crusade and the Woman's Christian Temperance Union.

Graduated at the Northwestern Female College in beautiful Evanston, destined to be forever associated with her career, she had already filled her atmosphere with anticipations of some unique and sovereign fate. Her recitations were occasions of wide audience, it is said. Visitors came to the class-room, attracted by the rumor of her astonishing capacity, and professors grew warm with admiration of a girl who promised to make N. W. F. C. a Mecca for aspiring young womanhood.

After teaching school for seven years, she became principal of a seminary; then traveled for that climax of culture which Europe gives to those who are open-minded enough to receive it, and in 1869 returned to Evanston to become Professor of Esthetics, and Dean of the Woman's College. In that year, and only a few miles away, an event occurred which possessed large and critical significance for her. But she had enough to think about as professor and dean, and, it is probable, that her heart was set more on her "girls" than on her future. Her life was fused with that of the bright young womanhood of the college. Perhaps she thought that the goal of her life had been won. She probably had no thought whatever that she was to become so important and potent a factor in the great work which that year brought the Prohibition party into existence.

In the meantime, she had been reviewing the grounds of the religious faith that she had inherited, and revised the creed that she had been wont to repeat. She remained in the "Church," but her faith held more than her church formulas were built to hold. She was no longer a passive reciter of phrases; out of the abysms of doubt she had ascended to a tolerant view of men and things which did her large service in her life as a reformer. For, though she believed in the wide distinctions between evil and good, she believed so profoundly in the All Good as to trust in the ultimate primacy of the Eternal Goodness. So she was sweet and genial among those whose trade she abhorred with all the depth of her angel-like soul.

In 1873, the Woman's Crusade, led by brave women against the skulking cowards who sold drink in the shielded darkness of the dram-shop, stirred the soul of American womanhood, and the Professor of Esthetics felt the pull of another destiny than that of teaching the science of the beautiful in a quiet college town. She resigned, and became corresponding secretary of the organization which sprang into life out of the vanished enthusiasms of that marvelous revolt of women. For five years, not always paid, or paid but ill, sometimes walking the streets of Chicago because she had no money for carfare, she served the Union. Then, in 1879, the sisterhood recognized their God-ordained leader, and she became president of the national organization, and thereafter polled the vote of the annual conventions every year until that year in which her life ended, or ascended—for it has not seemed to end, although there is a grave in Rose Hill cemetery, and in Rest Cottage the room in which she worked may be seen, much as she "left" it.

She dominated the whole order, but the period of her duty was not that of some victorious tyrant, unscrupulous of method, or some astute mistress of the fine art of flattery, or the gross art of purchase; rather, she was the realized ideal of the noble women, who yearned to be all that womanhood may become under culture of holy ambitions and pure purposes. If there was jealousy, it did not appear; it was honor enough to serve her. Anna Gordon was only one of a hundred, or a thousand, gifted girls, glad to be in her service, unsalaried, for the sake of the coveted fellowship of one of the uncrowned queens of American womanhood. She became the guide of the white ribboners, perfecting the organization, enlarging the sphere of its activities. The whole circle of human activity stretched around her, and she attempted everything, because, as she looked abroad, everything needed to be done, if humanity was to be lifted to self-mastery and the high places of the Kingdom of God. For the Christian Union of Women, women of all the churches, there was nothing too hard to try if there were demand for effort to redeem society, in the "mangled shadows" of the liquor traffic, and other unspeakable traffic.

She went into politics, a woman, a subject-citizen, without a vote. And that was one of the dolorous dishonors of the American democracy, which, with her white hand, she sought to remove, but died, unenfranchised. A negro in the southland, bought by a crafty demagogue, may vote, but not Frances E. Willard, professor of esthetics. A scoundrelly tramp, after a night on the floor as a cadger, may go to the polls, with $5.00 in his pocket as price of his suffrage, and exercise the rights and privileges of American citizenship, but not this cultured woman, who stands at the head of American womanhood, with her face angel-touched by faith, hope, love, purity.

But she went into "politics," and in 1882 became a member of the National Executive Committee of the Prohibition party. In that "third party," ostracized, laughed at, denounced, she found fellowship. Clean men, she said. No liquor! No tobacco! There she found fellowship. In 1884, she sought opportunity to speak for ten brief minutes to her "brethren" of the Methodist Church at Cincinnati. The brethren filibustered for an hour to prevent her introduction, but she remained in the "church" until the end. Once she went to a political convention of Republicans at Chicago. She dreamed that they would listen to her plea for a "temperance" plank in the platform. There were good men in the committee, they would give heed to her. The Hon. Henry W. Blair, ardently devoted to the temperance reform, and as ardently loyal to his "party" heard her plead with the committeemen. "She spoke like an angel from heaven," he afterward said. But the Committee on Platform could not see its way to incorporate her resolution in the declaration of Republican principles, and there is a story, that the document which she drafted was found upon the floor, despised, rejected, soiled with dust and tobacco. The disappointment did not embitter her. In 1892, she stood before the Prohibitionists in Cincinnati, still hoping for some wider sweep of political sentiment, hoping that, by some adaptation, the little body of impracticals, idealists, fanatics, might broaden, so as to take in others. So eager, indeed, for reconstruction of the political order was she, that she became a socialist.

It is not difficult to harmonize the two opinions; for, under existing conditions, she could believe that the State *ought* to place the traffic in liquor under the ban of law, and, as an idealist in politics, she could believe that, if the coöperative commonwealth were established, the liquor traffic would cease to exist. She was not "green in judgment," though her eagerness for social reform led her away from the dominant political orthodoxies of her time. Politically, she was a "heretic," unbound by the authorities whose opinions swayed the voting citizenship.

In 1883, she founded the World's W. C. T. U., and, in 1888, she became its president. For American woman there was no higher place; and then, fifty-nine years old, she passed into the silence; and the world echoes yet to the peerless eloquence of her pleas for justice, truth and the Kingdom of God.

Why? Well, she was fearless to speak what the nobleness of her heart prompted. Not less fearless than that Kansas woman who smashed the outlawed dram-shop, but more suave, more winsome. No one was afraid of *her*. Even the so-called liquor men had no word to utter against Frances E. Willard, though their organs were foul with coarse-phrased denunciation of the noble ladies who organized against their truckling trade: fearless with that bravery which enwraps itself in the shield of a self-poise that paralyzes the arm of a foe. She regarded the proprieties, she was so fearless that she dared avoid extremes. No one dared say that she was a wild-eyed fanatic, a woman daft, for she walked to her place like a queen, and, when she wrote, the page was beautiful with the speech of a woman who had known the air of a college and the ways of travel. Fearless, because she trusted that Universal Principle of Truth which, beneath all fraud and pretense, lies in the human soul. She knew that back of all the brutal commercialism of the brewer, distiller and saloonkeeper there was a latent response to her appeal. She was sure of her case because conscience was with her. There was no argument on the other side. No dealer in drink could frame logic into syllogism against the finer argument of her perfect womanhood. No caricature of her, for she possessed that majesty which hedges royalty about, and paralyzes the pencil of a cartoonist.

It is as difficult to solve the problem of her career as to solve the problem of Lincoln's career. He came to his place, first among Americans, out of an environment that bred no hope of eminence; and she began her work in a place and under circumstances that seemed to thwart ambition. Other women had scholarship, oratorical gift, the power of pen to put fine thought in balanced sentence, but she had that subtler quality of soul which gave her the throne among her peers, and she led and ruled, as the old royalty was wont to say, "by the grace of God." She was willing to say that, in all the fine humility of her perfect self-knowledge, she was what she was by the grace of God. It was her gift, as well as her grace.

And so, her influence against the saloon told, even though she did not destroy bars, nor enact laws. She threw the whole light of her thought into the leering face of the saloon, and it fell. Men have asked, "What has the W. C. T. U. done?" But in these years of 1907 and 1908 they no longer repeat the question, for the historians of the Great Reform write that, for a generation, the womanhood of the United States, under the spell of one whom they still call their Glorified Leader, have been "praying" against the saloon. Every day, when the sunbeams fall straight upon the meridian, they lift their souls to Him who is Sun of the

THE WILLARD MEMORIAL,
Statuary Hall, Washington, D. C.

"Ah, it is women who have given the costliest hostages to fortune. Into the battle of life they have sent their best beloved with fearful odds against them.

Oh, by the dangers they have dared, by the hours of patient watching over beds where helpless children lay, by the incense of ten thousand prayers wafted from their gentle lips to heaven, I charge you give them power to protect along life's treacherous highway those whom they have so loved."

sun, Light of the light, and "pray" that the liquor traffic may die, and they believe that, at last, not by might of law nor by power of police, the vile traffic will cease, and men will wonder what hidden force smote it down. Even now, it is not easy to say why, in 1908, there should be so wide a revolution, or why, in spite of all the arts of demagogues there should be such popular interest in the "Liquor Question." Perhaps the noon-tide prayer counts for as much as a vote, perhaps more. For the votes have been cast in favor of the saloon, and yet the saloon has been passing, despite the silence of statesmen. Perhaps Frances E. Willard's life counts for reform, even though her "place" knows her no more. Personality, dedicated to the Moral Right, is put into harmony with the Eternal Forces of progress, and, as the ages pass, it acts more and more potently.

Frances E. Willard believed that, and the Woman's Christian Temperance Union is the body through which her strong, heroic, radiant soul still expresses itself.

MISS WILLARD AS A PATRIOT.

Extract from Funeral Address by MRS. LOUISE S. ROUNDS.

As a Christian, Miss Willard gathered help and spiritual power from all denominations and creeds. She was accustomed to pivot her broad faith and generous charity upon this formula to which her whole life bore never-failing testimony: "No word of faith in God or love toward man is alien to my sympathy."

All countries contributed to broaden her love for humanity and increase her faith in God. It mattered not how far away she wandered, nor under what flag she found temporary protection, she always returned to her native land, and to the flag she loved above all others, with renewed feelings of loyalty and patriotism. The "Stars and Stripes" were to her an emblem of a broader freedom than other countries knew, and thus indicated her own great and grand spirit.

How painfully sad it is that the flag which is displayed from the platform on this sad occasion—this flag which she loved so much to have draped in convention halls where she presided—how unspeakably sad that this flag should today wave over and protect the legalized liquor system! How pitiable that the curse, for the extinction of which she gave her life, should find protection and defense in the laws of our land! He only is a true patriot who is true to the highest and noblest interests of his native land, and we who weep today over her cold, pale face, will cherish her parting message: "Tell the women not to forget their patriotism." And we will not give up the conflict until the Stars and Stripes shall cease to float over a legalized saloon!

Not only was she an American in the noblest sense, but the state of Illinois was loved by her, as perhaps no other state in the Union. In New York she was born and in New York she died, but in Illinois she lived the longest and did her grandest work.

There is wonderful significance in the fact that the ashes of Abraham Lincoln, the grandest man, and the ashes of Frances E. Willard, the greatest woman, in American history, have been committed to the soil of this beautiful prairie state, here to rest until the resurrection morn shall summon all lands and even the sea to give up their dead.

How beautiful as we think of her work and in what harmony with her life are these words which dropped like dew from her pen many years ago: "Lord Jesus, receive my spirit. That is the deepest voice out of my soul. Receive it every instant, voluntarily given back to thyself and receive it in the hour when I drop this earthly mantle and pass onward to the world invisible, but doubtless not far off."

MISS WILLARD AS A LEADER.
Extract from Funeral Address by Mrs. CLARA C. HOFFMAN.

We have not come here to weep. We have come to rejoice. Love is unselfish and must rejoice in the bliss and happiness of its beloved, and we will rejoice though with falling tears and breaking hearts.

Our beloved was a great leader, because within her little hand she held the hearts of all who followed, and with irresistible charm she drew those who lacked the courage to follow. All loved her, because she loved all. All trusted her because she trusted all.

She recognized the best in each, and each reached out and up, and made endeavor because its best was recognized. She had faith in humanity, and humanity believed in Frances Willard. She did not seek her own, but with all her might she sought the greatest good for all.

Multitudes will repeat her words, cherish her memory, emulate her gracious gentleness, follow in her footsteps. Manhood is nobler, womanhood truer, childhood safer because Frances Willard has lived.

> "Ah, she is *not* dead,
> Who in her record yet the earth doth tread,
> With God's fair aureole gleaming round her head."

MISS WILLARD AS A FRIEND.
Extract from Funeral Address by Mrs. KATHERINE LENT STEVENSON.

To my thought, the first thing noticeable in her friendship was its reality. She was the most real person I have ever known. There was absolutely no guile in her. She showed forth her inmost heart with a sweet frankness which seemed to take the whole human family into confidence, saying to them: "I feel all this for you and I believe you feel the same for me."

She was brave in her friendships: she dared to tell her friends their faults. Who of us that have come closest to her does not remember that quaint, pretty way in which she would say, "I think I have a case against thee, dear," and then she would tell out the case without sparing, and yet with such sweetness that no sting was left to rankle in one's mind. She of all others could tell one a fault because she was so constantly telling of virtues. She lived in the "sunshine of commendation" as no one else I have ever known has lived, not the commendation which was showered upon her but that which radiated from her to others.

MISS WILLARD'S PUBLIC LIFE.

Extract from Address by Dr. C. J. Little, *President of the Garrett Biblical Institute.*

Frances Willard reminded me, whenever I listened to her, of Matthew Arnold's definition of religion, "morality touched by emotion." She was conscience aglow with divine light.

Frances Willard had the gift of eloquence. She was a subtle, thoughtful, thrilling talker. Her presence was not imposing, yet it was always tranquilizing at the beginning, and afterwards full of sweet surprises. Her voice was clear and melodious and strong, with a peculiar quality of blended defiance and deference, of tenderness and intrepidity that gave it an indescribable ring. Her diction was studiously simple; her reasoning luminous and homely; her illustrations full of poetry and humor; her pathos as natural as tears to a child. She was wholly unaffected, taking her audience so deftly into her confidence that she conquered them, as Christ conquers, by self-revelation.

There was sometimes a lyric rapture in her utterance that wrought her hearers into a delirium of anticipation. The New Jerusalem of the twentieth century, the transfigured homes of a new commonwealth, seemed to be so near and so real. And there was always when she talked to women and to men such a sublime confidence in their latent nobility and their ultimate righteousness that for a time, at least, they became in their own eyes the beings that she pictured them, and sat enchanted with the revelation.

A NATION'S TRIBUTE.

By Act of the United States Congress, in 1864, each of the states was invited "to send to be placed in Statuary Hall statues in marble or bronze of two of her most illustrious citizens, for permanent preservation." Illinois honored herself by sending a beautiful marble statue of Frances E. Willard, the only figure of a woman in the entire group.

Congress frequently has suspended its ordinary business to pay tribute to the memory of eminent statesmen, but on February 17, 1905, for the first time in its history, the Congress had set apart a day to honor the memory of a woman. On that day the statue of Frances E. Willard was formally presented by the State of Illinois. Following are extracts from a few of the utterances of the occasion.

Prayer by Edward Everett Hale, Chaplain:

"Father Almighty, we remember what Thou hast given this nation in sending such an apostle of Thy word; of Thine own righteousness. She taught this people that the wisdom from above is first pure, and she showed them how to add to their purity peace and gentleness by those efforts by which men shall work with God for the coming of His kingdom.

"Father, we remember her. We preserve the memorials of such a life. But it is not for the past; it is for the future that we pray, that the people of this land may know what it is to be pure in body, pure in heart, pure in soul; that they may offer to Thee the living sacrifice; that men and women may know that they are the living temples of the living God.

"Be with us in the services of today. Be with this nation—north, south, east, west—in the school room, in the church and in daily duty, as men and women seek to draw nearer to God and yet nearer—yes, Father, even though it were a cross that raiseth us—that we may come nearer to Thee. We ask it in His name. Amen."

Senator Cullom, of Illinois:

"Mr. President, I esteem it an honor to have known personally Frances E. Willard during the greater part of her active life. I knew from personal knowledge of the work in which she was engaged, and I witnessed with pleasure the wonderful success which attended her efforts. She was a reformer, but she never shared the usual unpopularity of reformers, and her advocacy of reform in temperance never made her offensive to any class of people. Notwithstanding her public life, she was nevertheless a real woman, with that degree of sincerity and modesty that commanded the utmost respect from all with whom she came in contact.

"The world has been better because Frances E. Willard lived. She devoted her life unselfishly to the cause of humanity, and she brought sobriety into the homes of untold thousands; and at her death she left an organization that has been and will continue to be a potent factor for good in the world."

Senator Beveridge, of Indiana:

"Mr. President—From the beginning woman has personified the world's ideals. When history began its record it found her already the chosen bride of Art. All things that minister to mankind's good have, from the very first, by the general judgment, been made feminine—the

MRS. ELLA A. BOOLE,
National Lecturer, W. C. T. U.

ships that bear us through storm to port; the seasons that bring variety, surcease to toil and life's renewal; the earth itself, which, through all time and in all speech, has been the universal mother. The Graces were women, and the Muses, too. Always her influence has glorified the world, until her beatitude becomes divine in Mary, mother of God.

"Mark how the noblest conceptions of the human mind have always been presented in form of woman. Take Liberty; take Justice; take all the holy aspirations, all the sacred realities! Each glorious ideal has, to the common thought, been feminine. The sculptors of the olden time made every immortal idea a daughter of the gods. Even Wisdom was a woman in the early concept of the race, and that unknown genius of the youthful world wrought triumph itself into woman's form in that masterpiece of all the ages—the Winged Victory. Over the lives and destinies of men the ancients placed Clotho, Lachesis and Atrophos forever spinning, twisting, severing the strands of human fate.

"In the literature of all time woman has been Mercy's messenger, handmaid of tenderness, creator and preserver of human happiness. Name Shakespeare—Miranda and Imogene, Rosalind, Perdita and Cordelia appear; name Burns—the prayer 'To Mary in Heaven' gives to the general heart that touch of nature which makes the whole world kin; name the Book of Books—Rachel and the women of the Bible in beauty walk before us, and in the words of Ruth we hear the ultimate formula of woman's eternal fidelity and faith.

"And so we see that through all time woman has typified the true, the beautiful and the good on earth. And now Illinois, near the very heart of the world's great republic and at the dawn of the twentieth century, chooses woman herself as the ideal of that commonwealth and of this period: for the character of Frances E. Willard is womanhood's apotheosis.

"And she was American. She was the child of our American prairies, daughter of an American home. And so she had strength and gentleness, simplicity and vision. Not from the complex lives that wealth and luxury force upon their unfortunate children; not from the sharpening and hardening process of the city's social and business grind; not from any of civilization's artificialities, come those whom God appoints to lead mankind toward the light."

"And there her statue of purest marble stands today, mutely proclaiming to all the world her own message:

" 'It is women who have given the costliest hostages to fortune. Out into the battle of life they have sent their best beloved with fearful odds against them. By the dangers they have dared, by the hours of patient watching over beds where helpless children lay; by the incense of ten thousand prayers wafted from their gentle lips to Heaven, I charge you give them power to protect along life's treacherous highway those whom they have so loved.' "

CHAPTER XII.

THE NATIONAL PROHIBITION PARTY.

BY SAMUEL DICKIE, *Ex-Chairman Prohibition National Committee.*

NOTE.—For forty years the National Prohibition Party has been the insistent "voice of one crying in the wilderness" on the liquor question. With the heroism of martyrs its advocates have stood steadfastly by its cause through evil report and through good report, even though loyalty has often been at the cost of political, financial, social and (the shame of it!) ecclesiastical ostracism; and, in more than one instance, at the cost of life itself. During its entire history this party has never ceased to press the question of absolute prohibition home upon the conscience of citizenship and the church, and has thus been a prime factor in hastening the day of the final disappearance of the saloon.

In sketching for this book the history and work of the Prohibition Party, Professor Dickie, like Caesar of old, writes of things—"all of which he saw, and much of which he was."—G. M. H.

THE PROHIBITION PARTY.—*In most States, there now exists . . . an active Prohibition Party, which agitates for the strengthening and better enforcement of anti-liquor laws. It deems itself also a National party, since it has an organization which covers a great part of the Union. But its operations are far more active in the States, because the liquor traffic belongs to State legislation. (Congress has, of course, power to impose and has imposed an excise upon liquor.) Since, however, it can rarely secure many members in a State legislature, it acts chiefly by influencing the existing parties, and frightening them into pretending to meet its wishes.*—HON. JAMES BRYCE, in "THE AMERICAN COMMONWEALTH."

THE Prohibition Party not only deems itself a "national" party, but it is so regarded by all students of national political life, because its dominant issue is definitely national. As early as 1854, Rev. Charles F. Deems published, at Greensburg, N. C., a short-lived newspaper, in which he especially urged the importance of independent political action by the advocates of prohibition. But the anti-slavery agitation dominated all other political issues of that period, and, the Civil War coming on, the anti-liquor agitation dropped out of sight for the time.

As a result of the war, the liquor traffic was given a new footing by the Internal Revenue legislation, the United States Government becoming from that time the chief partner in and beneficiary of the manu-

REV. CHARLES H. MEAD,
Lecturer and Singer.

SAMUEL DICKIE,
Twelve Years Chairman National Prohibition Committee.

facture and sale of intoxicating liquors. Being thus "brought into political prominence and schooled in political arts by its close relations with the Federal Government, the liquor element gradually asserted itself in state politics." The liquor interest inaugurated an active campaign for the repeal of such temperance laws as had been adopted in some of the states prior to the war. On June 5, 1867, the National Brewers' Congress, in session in Chicago, adopted the following resolutions:

"WHEREAS, The action and influence of the temperance party is in direct opposition to the principles of individual freedom and political equality upon which our American Union is founded; therefore,

Resolved, That we will use all means to stay the progress of this fanatical party, and to secure our individual rights as citizens, and that we will sustain no candidate, of whatever party, in any election, who is in any way disposed toward the total abstinence cause."

As early as February of the same year, 1867, the State Temperance Convention of Pennsylvania had felt called upon to declare that, "If the adversaries of temperance shall continue to receive the aid and countenance of present political parties, we shall not hesitate to break over political bonds and seek redress through the ballot box."

The Grand Lodge of Good Templars of Pennyslvania passed similar resolutions in June of the same year.

The liquor interests, however, failed to take warning, and continued their course of political aggressiveness. Consequently, in May, 1868, the Right Worthy Grand Lodge of Good Templars, the supreme body of the order, in session at Richmond, Ind., recommended "to the temperance people of the country the organization of a national political party, whose platform of principles shall contain prohibition of the manufacture, importation and sale of intoxicating liquors to be used as a beverage." A year later, in convention at Oswego, N. Y., the same Right Worthy Grand Lodge further resolved, "That we esteem the present an auspicious period in the history of our political affairs for the inauguration of this movement, and therefore we recommend the calling of a National Convention for the purpose at an early date."

Following the adoption of this resolution a meeting was held by those present favoring separate political action, and a committee of five, consisting of Rev. John Russell, of Detroit, Mich.; Prof. Daniel Wilkins, of Bloomington, Ill.; J. A. Spencer, of Cleveland, Ohio; John Stearns, of New York, and James Black, of Lancaster, Pa., was appointed to issue a call for a National political convention, which call was duly issued as follows:

"*To the Friends of Temperance, Law and Order in the United States*:

"The moral, social and political evils of intemperance and the non-enforcement of the liquor laws are so fearful and prominent, and the causes thereof are so entrenched and protected by governmental authority and party interest, that the suppression of these evils calls upon the friends of temperance; and the duties connected with home, religion and public peace demand that old political ties and associations shall be sundered, and a distinct political party, with prohibition of the traffic in intoxicating drinks as the most prominent feature, should be organized.

"The distinctive political issues that have for years past interested the American people are now comparatively unimportant, or fully settled, and in this aspect the time is auspicious for a decided and practical effort to overcome the dread power of the liquor trade.

"The undersigned do therefore earnestly invite all friends of temperance and the enforcement of law, and favorable to distinct political action for the promotion of the same, to meet in general mass convention in the city of Chicago, on Wednesday, the 1st day of September 1869, at 11 o'clock A. M., for the purpose of organizing for distinct political action for temperance.

"All churches, Sunday-schools and temperance societies of all names are requested to send delegates, and all persons favorable to this movement are invited to meet at the time and place above stated.

"R. M. Foust, Philadelphia, Pa.; J. H. Orne, Marblehead, Mass.; Joshua Wadsworth, Cincinnati, Ohio; S. W. Hodges, Boston, Mass.; J. A. Spencer, Cleveland, Ohio; R. C. Bull, Philadelphia, Pa.; H. D. Cushing, Boston, Mass.; Rev. Peter Stryker, D. D., Philadelphia, Pa.; Joshua Nye, Waterville, Me.; Rev. Samuel McKean, Cambridge, N. Y.; T. M. Van Court, Chicago, Ill.; Rev. J. G. D. Stearns, Clearwater, Mich.; William Hargreaves, M. D., Reading, Pa.; D. W. Gage, Ames, Ia.; Rev. J. C. Stoughton, Chicago, Ill.; P. Mason, Somerville, N. J.; Rev. Edwin Thompson, Boston, Mass.; Rev. Elnathan Davis, Fitchburg, Mass.; Ebenezer Bowman, Taunton, Mass.; B. E. Hale, Brooklyn, N. Y.; J. F. Forbus, Cincinnati, Ohio; Samuel Foljambe, Cleveland, Ohio; L. B. Silver, Salem, Ohio; O. P. Downs, Warsaw, Ind.; G. N. Jones, Chicago, Ill.; Dr. C. H. Merrick, Cleveland, Ohio; Jay Odell, Cleveland, Ohio; Rev. William C. Hendrickson, Bristol, Pa.; Enoch Passmore, Kennett Square, Pa.; Neal Dow, Portland, Me.; Rev. John Russell, Detroit, Mich.; James Black, Lancaster, Pa.; Charles Jewett, Pomona, Tenn.; Rev. James B. Dunn, Boston, Mass.; Rev. George Lansing Taylor, New York City; John O'Donnell, Lowville, N. Y.; Rev. William M. Thayer, Franklin, Mass.; Rev. N. E. Cobleigh, D. D., Athens, Tenn.; Peterfield Trent, M. D., Richmond, Va.; J. N. Stearns, New York City; Rev. William Hosmer, Auburn, N. Y.; Rev. S. H. Platt, Brooklyn, N. Y.; S. T. Montgomery, Indianapolis, Ind.; Rev. G. H. Ball, Buffalo, N. Y.; George P. Burwell, Cleveland, Ohio; G. N. Abbey, Cleveland, Ohio; Luther S. Kauffman, Minersville, Pa.; A. T. Proctor, Cleveland, Ohio; George S. Tambling, Jr., Cleveland, Ohio; H. V. Horton, Cincinnati, Ohio; Rev. Moses Smith, Xenia, Ohio; Gen. J. S. Smith, Kingston, N. Y.; T. P. Hunt, Wilkesbarre, Pa.; D. R. Pershing, Warsaw, Ind.; George Gabe, Philadelphia, Pa.; William H. Fries, Clifton, Pa.; S. J. Coffin, Easton, Pa."

I have repeated in some detail the above sketch of the origin of the National Prohibition Party to establish two facts:

1. That the party was forced into existence by the aggressive and persistent political action of the liquor interests themselves;

2. That the call for and the organization of the party was backed by the best moral, temperance and political sentiment of the time.

The organizing convention met in Farwell Hall, Chicago, on the day appointed, September 1, 1869. Five hundred delegates were in attendance, representing California, Connecticut, Delaware, Indiana, Illinois, Iowa, Kansas, Missouri, Minnesota, Massachusetts, Maine, Michigan, New Jersey, New York, Ohio, Pennsylvania, Tennessee, Vermont, Wisconsin and the District of Columbia. Of course, these were all "bolters"—men of moral convictions who had been compelled to withdraw from other parties because of their failure to recognize the justice of their demands in taking position on a great moral issue.

Gerritt Smith prepared an address to the American people which the convention voted to publish. The following is the text of the platform of principles adopted:

"WHEREAS, Protection and allegiance are reciprocal duties, and every citizen who yields obedience to the just commands of his Government is entitled to the full, free and perfect protection of that Government in the enjoyment of personal security, personal liberty, and private property; and

"WHEREAS, The traffic in intoxicating drinks greatly impairs the personal security and personal liberty of a large mass of citizens, and renders private property insecure; and

"WHEREAS, The existing parties are hopelessly unwilling to adopt an adequate policy on this question; therefore,

"We, in National Convention assembled, as citizens of this free Republic, sharing the duties and responsibilities of its Government, in discharge of a solemn duty we owe to our country and our race, unite in the following declaration of principles:

"1. That, while we acknowledge the pure patriotism and profound statesmanship of those patriots who laid the foundations of this Government, securing at once the rights of the States severally, and their inseparable union by the Federal Constitution, we would not merely garnish the sepulchers of our republican fathers, but we do hereby renew our solemn pledges of fealty to the imperishable principles of civil and religious liberty embodied in the Declaration of American Independence and our Federal Constitution.

"2. That the traffic in intoxicating beverages is a dishonor to Christian civilization, inimical to the best interests of society, a political wrong of unequaled enormity, subversive of the ordinary objects of government, not capable of being regulated or restrained by any system of license whatever, but imperatively demanding for its suppression effective legal prohibition, both by State and National legislation.

"3. That in view of this, and inasmuch as the existing political parties either oppose or ignore this great and paramount question and absolutely refuse to do anything toward the suppression of the rum traffic, which is robbing the nation of its brightest intellects, destroying internal prosperity and rapidly undermining its very foundations, we are driven by an imperative sense of duty to sever our connection with these political parties and organize ourselves into a National Prohibition party, having for its primary object the entire suppression of the traffic in intoxicating drinks.

"4. That while we adopt the name of the National Prohibition Party, as expressive of our primary object, and while we denounce all repudiation of the public debt, and pledge fidelity to the principles of the Declaration of Independence and the Federal Constitution, we deem it not expedient at present to give prominence to other political issues.

"5. That while we recognize the good providence of Almighty God in supervising the interests of this nation from its establishment to the present time, we would not, in organizing our party for the legal prohibition of the liquor traffic, forget that our reliance for ultimate success must be upon the same omnipotent arm.

"6. That a Central Executive Committee, of one from each state and territory and the District of Columbia, be appointed by the Chair, whose duty it shall be to take such action as, in their judgment, will best promote the interests of the party."

No presidential campaign being on in 1869, no ticket was nominated at that convention, but in the fall of that year Ohio took the initiative and returned votes for candidates of the Prohibition party as a distinct political organization.

In 1870, six states presented candidates for Governor, the most distinguished of whom was Wendell Phillips in Massachusetts.

This early prominence of Phillips in the movement for political prohibition was especially significant. At the cost of social ostracism, and almost of personal martyrdom, he had led in the anti-slavery movement, and was one of the most prominent founders and leaders of the Republican party. Mary A. Livermore says of him:

"Through obloquy and misrepresentation, defamed by men in his own native city, hounded by the press, mobbed by intolerant opponents, denounced by the pulpit and the politicians equally, for forty years he stood unflinchingly as the friend of the black race and worked for its emancipation till the war accomplished it. When the war ended and the army was mustered out, Wendell Phillips said the last orders were, 'Close the ranks and go forward to new reforms!' He was the first to obey."

In 1870, he was the nominee for Governor of Massachusetts of the Labor Reform as well as the Prohibition party. In his letter of acceptance to the latter he defined his position as follows:

"As temperance men you were bound to quit the Republican party, since it has deceived you more than once. Any Prohibitionist who ad-

PRESIDENTIAL CANDIDATES,
Prohibition Party.

heres to it proclaims beforehand his willingness to be cheated, and, so far as political action is concerned, betrays his principles. The Republican party deserves our gratitude. It has achieved great results. It will deserve our support whenever it grapples with our present living difficulties A party must live on present living service, not on laurels, however well earned. . . . The only bulwark against the dangers of intemperance is prohibition. More than thirty years of experience have convinced me, and as wide an experience has taught you, that this can only be secured by means of a distinct political organization."

This was his position, and he never wavered from it. What he said of the Republican party, and of the necessity for a distinct political Prohibition party, is just thirty-eight years truer in 1908 than it was in 1870.

In 1871, five states returned Prohibition votes.

On February 22, 1872, the first National Convention of the Prohibition Party was held in Columbus, Ohio. Fourteen states were represented. James Black of Pennsylvania, was nominated for President, and John Russell, of Michigan, for Vice-President. The total vote was 5,607.

In 1876, Green Clay Smith, of Kentucky, was nominated for President, with Gideon T. Stewart, of Ohio, for Vice-President. The vote increased to 9,737, and to 43,230 in the various state elections in 1877.

The third national convention was held at Cleveland, Ohio, June 17, 1880. Twelve states were represented. Neal Dow, of Maine, was nominated for President, with H. A. Thompson, of Ohio, for Vice-President. The vote remained almost stationary, 9,678, but increased to 58,688 in the state elections of 1883.

Having attempted to "frighten" the other parties into "pretending" to grant their requests, as Bryce would say, the Prohibitionists of 1884 met at Pittsburg, July 23, and nominated John P. St. John, of Kansas, for President, and William Daniel, of Maryland, for Vice-President. An attendance of 465 delegates from thirty-one states meant that the party was not a mere "balance of power" party. It indicated a genuine independent political party, with a real issue. The vote leaped to 150,626, and the issue was in politics to stay.

Four years passed. On the last two days of May, 1888, forty-two states sent delegates to Indianapolis, and Clinton B. Fisk, of New Jersey, and John A. Brooks, of Missouri, were placed at the head of the ticket. Despite the efforts of the anti-saloon Republicans, and the Woman's Republican League, the vote for the ticket registered 249,945.

The convention for 1892 was held in Music Hall, Cincinnati, Ohio, and nominated General John Bidwell, of California, and James B. Cranfill of Texas. Bidwell had been a Republican member of Congress and also a wine-grower. But, when he realized the effects of a faithless Republicanism and the drink traffic, he had repented and gone out of both lines of business. Cranfill was an editor and preacher, a strong leader in higher politics in his state. The vote ran to 269,191, and the Dominant Issue was still "dominant."

At Pittsburg, in 1896, there was a "split," and the vote for Joshua Levering, of Maryland, and Hale Johnson, of Illinois, dropped to 132,009, though the party never had better candidates.

Four years more passed. The "split" healed, and the brilliant orator, lecturer and editor, John G. Woolley, of Illinois, was nominated, with Henry B. Metcalf, of Rhode Island, as running mate. Woolley made a magnetic campaign, and pulled the vote up to 209,936. Only seven states failed to cast Prohibition votes that year.

When the convention met at Indianapolis, June 30, 1904, a movement was inaugurated to nominate General Nelson A. Miles, of the United States Army, but he declined to act with the Prohibition party, in spite of his anti-canteen sentiments. The convention nominated the "Fighting Parson," Silas C. Swallow, of Harrisburg, Pa., with George W. Carroll, of Texas, for Vice-President. The vote rose to 260,114.

The party immediately began to prepare for the next campaign. In the meantime, anti-saloonism was growing everywhere, and the country was buckling down to a finish fight with the liquor traffic. Undismayed by nine defeats, 1088 delegates met, in this year of grace, 1908, in the city where the party had held its first national convention, and presented Eugene W. Chafin, of Illinois, for the presidency, with Aaron S. Watkins, of Ohio, for the vice-presidency.

Of the convention of 1908 it may be said that the party never met before with stronger confidence in the final and speedy triumph of its cause. When a political party stands faithful and true under the defeats of forty years it may not be charged that such a party is made up of place-seekers moved by a desire for the spoils of office. It is evident that men and women must be governed only by principle and conscience when for so long a time they sacrifice time and strength and money with no hope of material reward or advancement. Yet the delegates of 1908 rejoiced in the abundant evidence to be seen in all parts of the country that the principle of prohibition had won its way over half the territory of the United States and was rapidly encroaching upon the other half.

During all these years, the party has stood true to its original colors, and its demands today remain strictly in line with its original proclamation in 1872, a quarter of a century ago, as witness the platform of this year, as follows:

VICE-PRESIDENTIAL CANDIDATES,
Prohibition Party.

National Platform of the Prohibition Party

Adopted Columbus, Ohio, July 16, 1908.

The Prohibition Party of the United States, assembled in convention at Columbus, Ohio, July 15-16, 1908, expressing gratitude to almighty God for the victories of our principles in the past, for encouragement at present, and for confidence in early and triumphant success in the future, makes the following declaration of principles, and pledges their enactment into law when placed in power:

The submission by congress to the several states, of an amendment to the federal constitution prohibiting the manufacture, sale, importation, exportation or transportation of alcoholic liquors for beverage purposes.

The immediate prohibition of the liquor traffic for beverage purposes in the District of Columbia, in the territories and all places over which the national government has jurisdiction; the repeal of the internal revenue tax on alcoholic liquors and the prohibition of interstate traffic therein.

The election of United States senators by direct vote of the people.

Equitable graduated income and inheritance taxes.

The establishment of postal savings banks and the guaranty of deposits in banks.

The regulation of all corporations doing an interstate commerce business.

The creation of a permanent tariff commission.

The strict enforcement of law instead of official tolerance and practical licence of the social evil which prevails in many of our cities, with its unspeakable traffic in girls.

Uniform marriage and divorce laws.

An equitable and constitutional employers liability act.

Court review of postoffice department decisions.

The prohibition of child labor in mines, workshops and factories.

Legislation basing suffrage only upon intelligence and ability to read and write the English language.

The preservation of the mineral and forest resources of the country, and the improvement of the highways and waterways.

Believing in the righteousness of our cause and the final triumph of our principles, and convinced of the unwillingness of the republican and democratic parties to deal with these issues, we invite to full party fellowship all citizens who are with us agreed.

Samuel Dickie, *Chairman Committee on Resolutions*
Chas. Scanlon, *Chairman of Convention*
Charles R. Jones, *Chairman National Committee*

Facsimile of engrossed platform presented to Messrs. Chafin and Watkins when notified of their nomination.

The history of a political party is not merely the history of its vote: it is a story of its *idea*. Hence, it is that the Prohibition party of the United States has done something more than merely poll a vote of "bolters," "mugwumps" and "independents." It has compelled the general recognition of its issue, a sentiment which has crystallized into a demand, irrespective of party, for that legislation which so long has been thwarted by the machinations of saloon bosses, working through the machinery of the dominant parties.

Different estimates are placed upon the value of the service rendered by the Prohibition party, varied by the standpoints and predilections of observers. Perhaps none will dispute, however, the following finding of a writer in the "Cyclopedia of Temperance and prohibition":

"The party has always been and is today the only national party reliably committed to prohibition and against license; it has done more than has been accomplished through any other purely political agency to keep the issue constantly before the people; it has often been a menace to the stronger organizations and has disciplined and chastened them in not a few instances; it is supported by a large majority of the representative Prohibition leaders; it has engaged in no discreditable intrigues and its characteristic methods have been honorable and straightforward; its development has unquestionably been attended, from whatever cause, by a concentration of organized sentiment, a great extension of prohibitory territory, and an increasing eagerness among the enemies of the cause to effect compromises."

NOTE.—*The character and purpose of a political party is indicated by the type of men called to its official management and direction. In this respect the National Prohibition Party takes high rank. The roll of its National Chairmen is as follows: 1872, John Russell; 1876, James Black; 1880, Gideon T. Stewart; 1884, John B. Finch; 1888, 1892, 1896, Samuel Dickie; 1900, 1904, Oliver W. Stewart; 1905, 1908, Charles R. Jones; not a professional politician nor a time-server among them.*—G. M. H.

MEMORANDUM.

The Rev. John Russell is reputed to be the "father of the Prohibition Party," but there is record to prove that on the second Tuesday night of the month of February, 1861, more than eight years before the Prohibition Party was organized, Bradford McGregor, an initiate of the Good Templars, made the statement, after taking the vows of the order, that he could no longer vote for candidates who did not favor prohibition; and that his obligations as a Good Templar bound him to vote only for prohibition candidates. A week later, the Rev. John Russell was initiated and he, too, reached the same conclusion, under influence of the vows assumed. The two men introduced the subject of political duty under the question, "What

DR. JOHN RUSSELL,
First Presidential Candidate, Prohibition Party.

BRADFORD McGREGOR,
Vocalist; One of the Founders of the Prohibition Party.

may be done for the good of the order?" and the lodge immediately took issue with the two radicals. The Chief Templar announced that if he believed as McGregor and Russell did he would leave the order. "Whereupon," says McGregor, "Russell and McGregor clasped hands on their faith and declared for a third party, and that party a Prohibition party."

Mr. McGregor is still living, a radical Prohibitionist, who has won the respect of his fellow citizens of all parties by his fidelity to conviction and loyalty to a refined moral sense.

History will do right by the Prohibition party and it will be fame enough if it say of us: "They won to their great doctrines, so stubbornly pressed and so faithfully stuck to, loyalty to the church and the absolute destruction of the church's enemy. They won to this doctrine the men and women who won the victory, and they were broad enough not to claim a monopoly of Christian patriotism; and they were big enough to coöperate, when this cause for which they sacrificed got too big for any man or any set of men to lead."

This is higher ground than any other party ever occupied. It presents difficulties, chief of which is the occasional weakening of party organization, by omitting to nominate a full ticket, or any ticket, and putting our power back of candidates who are not of our own party. But I fully believe that such an attitude of party altruism in the interest of a purer patriotism, will multiply the strength of our organization and the weight of our influence.

Finally, let me repeat that the night of the firebell has passed, and the daylight of knowledge and coöperative efficiency is dawning. We set out to compel attention to the lopsided instability of a temperance movement which gave itself wholly to rescue, to warning and to local betterment, and let the fire burn—nay, conceded that it had to burn right on, and fanned it to a whiter, deadlier intensity with the forced draft of high license. We have won that central purpose of our existence.

The rest is not agitation, but constructive statesmanship. The overthrow of the liquor power, not by the fiat of power, nor by shrewd politics, but by the informed and convinced intelligence of the voters, that is our objective. The clang and rattle of alarm must now give way to the modulated voices of reason and fellowship and conscience.

We have got together two hundred and fifty thousand temperance radicals. That is about all there are. The other fourteen million voters are conservatives, of whom the best we can hope is that they will be independent enough to support us when we are reasonable and formidable enough to win. A majority of them will in time accept our reasoning, but it must be reasoning—not shouting and criticism.—JOHN G. WOOLLEY.

CHAPTER XIII.

THE INTERCOLLEGIATE PROHIBITION ASSOCIATION.

By D. Leigh Colvin, *President*, 1899-1908.

THE Intercollegiate Prohibition Association is enlisting large numbers of the brightest intellects in our great colleges and universities in the movement against the liquor traffic. In its membership is a large proportion of the leaders in scholarship, oratory, debate, athletics, Christian work and other activities of college life. These are the young men and women who are destined to be the leaders of thought, the moulders of public opinion and the statesmen of the future. They have been led to the championship of Prohibition by a thorough study of the liquor problem and related problems. They have come to realize that the principle of prohibition is supported by the fundamental principles of economics and political science. Not a few are seeing in the prohibition movement a wide field for service in the betterment of humanity.

There are state organizations in eighteen states extending from New York to California and from Minnesota to Texas, and college leagues in most of the colleges of those states. In the college year 1907-1908, forty-eight thousand students were reached with the principles of prohibition.

The object of the Intercollegiate Prohibition Association, as stated in its constitution, is—

"To promote broad and practical study of the liquor problem and related social and political questions, to advance the principle of prohibition, and to secure the enlistment of students for service and leadership in the overthrow of the liquor traffic."

In accordance with the spirit of educational institutions the Association first of all encourages a thorough study of the liquor problem and related questions. A study is made, not only of its magnitude, not only of its relation to the other great social problems, but special emphasis is placed upon a study of the methods of solution which have been proposed and tried.

The Intercollegiate has prepared a three years course of study which is used in the college leagues all over the country. The first year course is entitled, "Social Welfare and the Liquor Problem." This course makes

INTERCOLLEGIATE PROHIBITION ASSOCIATION OFFICERS AND ORATORS, 1908.

RAPHAEL H. BLAKESLEY.

HARRY S. WARNER,
Secretary.

LEVI T. PENNINGTON.

VIRGIL G. HINSHAW,
President.

D. LEIGH COLVIN,
Treasurer.

CHAS. SCROGGIN PIERCE.

FRED MESCH, Jr.

EVERT L. JONES.

GUSTAVE HOELSCHER.

a study of the effect of the liquor traffic on the fundamental ends of social welfare. Studies are made of the effect of the traffic on public health, covering some of the physiological aspects; also its relation to the public wealth—including the waste caused by the liquor traffic in its various forms, directly and indirectly, its relation to industry and to labor and to wages. In one economic investigation made by a representative of the Intercollegiate, it was found that, by the operation of well known economic laws, there are at least ten ways in which wages are decreased by the liquor traffic. In this course is considered the argument for the saloon as a social center, and the matter of substitutes for the saloon. The course also discusses the relation of the liquor traffic to the city problem, to the race problem, to the family, to political corruption and other related questions.

A second year course is on "The Solution of the Liquor Problem: a Comparison of Methods," in which a comparative study is made of practically the whole range of methods which have been advocated, from the license system up, including high license, local option, the dispensary and Gothenburg methods, state prohibition, the national government and prohibition, the omnipartisan plan, and the plan of the Prohibition party. An unbiased study is made of all the methods, including the principles underlying each of them, the arguments for and against, and the results of the various methods in the different sections where they have been tried. By thus making a comparative study, and by taking into consideration so far as possible the whole range of experience, the student can get a wide basis from which to reach his conclusions. In entering upon the study all students, without regard to their past views, are invited to participate, and there is no commitment to any particular plan or method. All sides are taken into consideration, and the freest expression of opinion is encouraged. This being the case, it is significant that the large majority of those who make a serious and thorough study of the question come out for prohibition and prohibition supported by a political party to enforce it as essential for the ultimate solution.

A third year course deals with "The Legal and Political Aspects of the Problem." The first half year is devoted to a study of the leading court decisions upon the question and the constitutional phases, and the second half year a study is made of the political means and agencies.

All of the courses have appeared in the *Intercollegiate Statesman*, the monthly magazine of the organization, and the course on "Social Welfare and the Liquor Problem" has been published in book form. In the studies given in the *Statesman* three or four sub-topics are outlined for each meeting, a summary of the chief facts is given and a list of references to the leading books and magazine articles is furnished. The references include, not only leading books on the temperance and prohibition question, but also a number of works on sociology, economics, political science and related subjects. In 1907-1908, about 3,600 students were following the courses in the college leagues.

The necessary complement of knowledge is action. The traveling secretaries of the Intercollegiate have urged upon college men the necessity of performing their duties of citizenship. They have done their best to nullify the frequent and too well justified criticism that college men do not perform their part in public affairs. They have urged college men to take the lead against the saloon, and to go into the fight to win. Wendell Phillips has been quoted when he said in his famous address on "The Scholar in Politics" before the Phi Beta Kappa of Harvard: "I urge upon college-bred men that as a class they fail in republican duty when they allow others to lead in the agitation of the great public questions which stir and educate the age. These agitations are the means and the opportunities which God offers us to reform the tastes, mould the characters and lift the moral purpose of the masses on whose intelligence and self-respect rests the state." Late in life, when a young man came to him regretting that he did not live in a time when there was a great cause to champion, Phillips, pointing to a saloon, said that the prohibition of the liquor traffic offered a greater cause than the one against slavery had ever been.

The Intercollegiate has emphasized that to get into the active movement for prohibition offers an opportunity for real social service as replete with the possibilities of achievement for humanity as there is open to the young man in America today.

Some of the brightest students in the colleges are responding to the growing need for trained and consecrated young men and women to enter the prohibition field. In the year 1906, fifty-seven young men and one young woman from the ranks of the Intercollegiate, engaged in the active work against the saloon, under various organizations and committees. In the summer of 1908, more than two hundred college men were thus engaged. In Minnesota, there were about sixty-five; in Illinois, sixty; and a number in Iowa, Indiana, New York, Texas, Washington and other states.

One example of what college students have been able to accomplish is shown by their work in the prohibition legislative campaigns in Minnesota. In 1902, in that state, the vote for the Prohibition legislative candidates was only 4000. In the summer of 1904, four college men were in the field in six counties, and the vote was increased to 12,000, the increase coming mostly from those six counties. In 1906, sixteen college men covered one-third of the state, and the vote increased to 32,000, resulting in the election of three members of the legislature. One additional vote in fifteen would have elected fifteen of the sixteen candidates for whom fights were made. These college men did the hand-to-hand personal work of winning the individual voter. They perfected organization, and stimulated local workers to greater endeavor. They exerted a wide influence, and everywhere the fact that able college men, who had studied public questions, were championing the prohibition issue, gave added prestige to the campaign work.

College men are responding to the call for service with a spirit of sacrifice which is rarely surpassed. One young man, a Norwegian student, working his way through college, in the summer of 1907 earned $140 in prohibition work. Of that he voluntarily contributed $100 to the prohibition cause, and the following winter split wood and washed dishes to pay his way through school. The largest single contribution yet received by the Intercollegiate, came from an officer whose gift of one thousand dollars meant self-denial through several hardworking years. There is scarcely a college man who has entered prohibition work but who could have secured a much larger remuneration in some other occupation, several having declined from two to four times as large a salary.

As a further indication of the spirit of service of college men, one of the state officers of the Intercollegiate, in the summer of 1908, secured the pledge of thirty-five young men, each of whom agreed to be one of one hundred to enlist for service in the prohibition movement for twenty-four months at army wages, namely, thirteen dollars a month and expenses. He secured this number in a few days, without special or widespread effort.

But it is not only in enlisting those who are giving their whole time to prohibition work that the college movement is accomplishing results in bringing about the passing of the saloon. The larger power is exerted by the hundreds and thousands of men and women who, having been influenced by the Intercollegiate, go out from their college halls and, in their respective communities, take an active part against the liquor traffic. For example, in Missouri in 1901, there was but a single county without a saloon. About that time student prohibition leagues were formed in nearly all of the colleges of that state. In the last two or three years county after county has voted out the saloon, until about two-thirds of the counties are dry. The man who, in 1901, visited the colleges in connection with this work, and who is now an attorney in one of the cities of Missouri, says that he finds that in a large number of counties the leadership has been taken by the young men recently out of college, who first became interested in prohibition through the Intercollegiate at that time.

During the college year many of the leagues are active in local campaigns in their respective communities. Often teams of speakers and singers are sent out and hold meetings in neighboring towns and schoolhouses.

Besides the systematic study, and the enlistment of students for service in local and general campaign work, probably the best known feature of the Intercollegiate is its system of oratorical contests. It is the most extensive and most representative system of college oratorical contests in the United States, extending from ocean to ocean, and including not only the colleges but a number of the large universities. The series extends through college, state, interstate and national contests. First is the local college contest, for which students write original orations on some subject related to prohibition. The winner of the college contest represents his college in a state contest. The winner of the state contest goes to an interstate. There are three interstate contests, an eastern, a central and a western, each held annually. Once in two years the winners of the three interstate contests for the two years, six speakers in all, meet in a grand national contest. Professors of oratory in some of the leading universities have said that the winning of the national contest offers the highest honors in American college oratory.

The prohibition oratorical contests have become popular, because they offer a cause to champion. The president of the largest college of oratory in America said that the great orators of history have been developed in the championship of a great cause, and that the greatest cause of today is the cause of temperance and prohibition. The contests usually are largely attended. The attendance at the interstate and national contests has frequently been from three to five thousand people.

In the series leading up to the national contest of 1908, held at Columbus, Ohio, more than six hundred orations were written and delivered. The quality of the orations and the enthusiasm engendered is shown by the fact that the six orators at Columbus were interrupted by applause ninety-four times.

The following is a list of those who spoke in the interstate contests in the years 1907-08, with the state and college from which they came, and the subjects of the orations. Each orator had previously won two contests, first, one in his college, and then his state contest.

Eastern Interstate, 1907—*Indiana*, Gustave Hoelscher, Earlham College, "We the People." *Pennsylvania*, C. Edward Bender, Juniata College, "Bacchus *versus* Columbia." *Michigan*, G. B. Findley, University of Michigan, "The Way Out." *Ohio*, Ray B. Westerfield, Ohio Northern University, "Social Progress." *New York*, Arthur J. Ruland, Syracuse University, "The Crime of the African Coast."

Central Interstate, 1907—*Texas*, Charles S. Pierce, Howard Payne College, "The Price of Victory." *Iowa*, Arthur H. Ayres, Central Holiness University, "The Heroism of Reform." *Kansas*, D. K. Burnham, Baker University, "The Prohibition Party." *Minnesota*, Nelson B. El-

THE INTERCOLLEGIATE PROHIBITION ASSOCIATION. 177

dredge, Parker College, "Christian Citizenship." *Nebraska*, John G. Alber, Cotner University, "The Message of a Martyr." *Illinois*, John A. Shields, Y. M. C. A. Institute, "Unsettled Questions." *Colorado*, Raymond C. Farmer, Colorado College, "The Liquor Problem and Its Solution."

Western Interstate, 1907—*Oregon*, E. L. Jones, Albany College, "The Principles of Citizenship." *Washington*, Warren N. Cuddy, University of Puget Sound, "Our National Foe." *Northern California*, D. C. Boyd, Leland Stanford Jr. University, "Christian Chivalry." *Southern California*, William E. Roberts, Occidental College, "The Conflict of the Twentieth Century."

Eastern Interstate, 1908—*Pennsylvania*, S. Frank Snyder, Pennsylvania College, "The Great Enemy of our Nation." *Michigan*, E. C. Pryor, Albion College, "The Moral Revolution." *New York*, Charles N. Cobb, Colgate University, "The Great American Issue." *Indiana*, Levi T. Pennington, Earlham College, "The New Patriotism." *Illinois*, Charles W. Young, Greenville College, "Freedom's Full Dawn."

Central Interstate, 1908—*Kansas*, James M. Alcorn, Kansas Wesleyan University, "Intemperance *versus* a National Policy" *Minnesota*, John A. Shields, University of Minnesota, "The Victory Year." *Nebraska*, Ford E. Ellis, Cotner University, "The Liquor Traffic a Crime." *Texas*, James C. Boyd, Decatur Baptist College, "The Authority of Law Over Liquor." *Iowa*, Fred Mesch, Jr., Central Holiness University, "The Unconstitutionality of the Saloon."

Western Interstate, 1908—*Washington*, Daniel Dupertuis, University of Puget Sound, "The Coming Victory." *Southern California*, Raphael H. Blakesley, University of Southern California, "The Last Stand." *Oregon*, Miss Mary Gittins, Willamette University, "The Need for Prohibition."

National, 1908—Raphael H. Blakesley, University of Southern California, "The Last Stand." Levi T. Pennington, Earlham College, Indiana, "The New Patriotism." Evert L. Jones, Albany College, Oregon, "Prohibition and Citizenship." Gustave Hoelscher, Earlham College, Indiana, "We, the People." Fred Mesch, Jr., Central Holiness University, Iowa, "The Unconstitutionality of the Saloon." Charles Scroggin Pierce, Howard Payne College, Texas, "The Price of Victory."

The first prize of $100 was won by Mr. Pierce of Texas, and the second prize of $50 was won by Mr. Pennington of Indiana.

The national Intercollegiate Prohibition Association prepares the study courses, publishes the *Intercollegiate Statesman* monthly during the college year, and, from its headquarters in Chicago, keeps in correspondence with and has general supervision over all the college leagues. It sends traveling secretaries to visit the colleges at least once each year, to enlist new members, to secure the adoption of advanced methods in each league and to stimulate greater interest among all the students. In nearly every college the traveling secretaries are invited to speak at chapel before the entire student body, thus wielding a wide influence, and in addition hold from one to five other meetings at each college.

The officers of the Intercollegiate Prohibition Association for 1908 to 1910 are: *President*, Virgil G. Hinshaw, University of Minnesota. *Vice-President*, Harley H. Gill, Morningside College. *Secretary*, Harry S. Warner, University of Chicago. *Treasurer*, D. Leigh Colvin, Columbia University. *Member Executive Committee*, Daniel A. Poling, Ohio State University.

Four of the five officers have had extended post-graduate courses in some of the largest universities.

The organization was incorporated December 12, 1901. The Board of Trustees is composed of Dr. Samuel Dickie, Albion, Michigan; Hon. Oliver W. Stewart, John H. Hill, D. Leigh Colvin and Harry S. Warner, all of Chicago.

The traveling secretaries to visit the colleges in 1908-09 are L. C. Brown, University of Michigan; W. E. Critchlow, Dallas College, Oregon; A. S. Dowdall, University of Minnesota; Hervey F. Smith, Baker University, Kansas; Virgil G. Hinshaw and D. Leigh Colvin.

I.

THE PRICE OF VICTORY.

By CHARLES SCROGGIN PIERCE, *Howard Payne College, Texas.*

First Prize Oration at National Oratorical Contest, the Intercollegiate Prohibition Association, Columbus, Ohio, 1908.

Every victory must be bought. This is the invariable rule in the market-place of the world's affairs. Every achievement of the past has been purchased with its price. None of the great movements that have swept the world God-ward, have succeeded until their advocates paid the price of victory. And God has put a high price upon things of great worth, and the same price to all men and to all ages. He knows no discounts, He holds no bargain sales. Every age has paid in full for its progress. Great principles do not mold the world's thought and character while they lie in God's store-house. They must become living fire in the hearts of their advocates. "Truth is truest when burning."

For four centuries no Spartan ever left a battlefield unless he carried home his shield victorious, or was carried away dead upon it. He paid the price of military glory, and got it.

LESLIE E. HAWK,
Chairman Ohio Prohibition State
Committee.

EDWIN E. HADLEY,
Chairman Kansas Prohibition State
Committee.

REV. A. H. MORRILL, D. D.,
Chairman New Hampshire Prohibition
State Committee.

DAVID B. McCALMONT,
Chairman Pennsylvania Prohibition State
Committee.

Christianity conquered the Roman world because it was not afraid of the price. In the beginning it was the religion of twelve Jewish fishermen; within three centuries it had attained the throne of the Caesars; its symbol, the cross, was carried above the eagles at the head of the army, and its followers constituted the most active, virile and powerful organization in the civilized world.

Switzerland is free, but the story of her struggle is only the old story of liberty bought with a price. From the mythical days of William Tell until the immortal victories at Margarten Pass and Sempach, the Swiss laid themselves on the altar of their country's liberty. At Sempach, when all other means had failed to break the dense line of Austrian spears, Arnold von Winkelreid gathered as many into his bosom as his long arms could reach, and bearing them to the ground, cried out to his comrades: "I give myself to make a way for you."

Science is now free to express her thoughts because her advocates in the past sat in stocks and lay in prisons. Socrates taught his last lesson in prison and drank the fatal poison; Locke wrote his immortal teachings as an exile in a Dutch garret. Roger Bacon was compelled to hide away in manuscripts his more advanced ideas; notwithstanding this, he spent fourteen years in prison, because he was too great for the light of his day. Galileo, old, blind, and forsaken! What great thoughts must have kept him company through the long months in prison! Thomas More died for opinion's sake, that coming generations might live in his land of Utopia where opinion is free. The prison and the stake of the past have paid for the freedom of the present. Thus,

"At the cost of life new truths are taught;
Hate kills the thinker, but it cannot kill the thought."

While the student of affairs watches freedom of conscience, a century old in America, now winning the last foothold of its enemy in the English Parliament, the French Chamber and the Spanish Cortes, let him not forget that this present broad daylight of free conscience was preceded by a long night of religious conformity, lighted only by fagot fires. The veriest novice in the philosophy of history is aware that without the shedding of blood there is no freedom. We follow the lead of our consciences today without pay or penalty, because the men of other days, from John Huss to Roger Williams followed theirs at the price of their lives. Religious persecution scattered the ashes of Wycliffe on the Severn, Jerome on the Danube and Savonarola on the Arno, but its own lifeless body rests beneath an ocean of infamy.

There is no worth without work, there is no success without preparation, there is no victory without its price. History is eloquent with this law, it is written all over the life of man and of movements; and the sooner the enemies of the liquor traffic comprehend its workings and gird themselves to go into the field and pay the full price of victory, the sooner will the clock of man's progress strike the hour of another epoch in the world's approach toward God.

I have here assumed that the destruction of the liquor trade will be a step forward, that this victory is attainable, and that in the not distant future. These three propositions many confess with their lips, and many more believe in their hearts.

II.

And what is this victory over the liquor traffic? Not local option, a system by which the larger political unit notifies the lesser one that it is to have the legal, political and moral right to do wrong if it so choose. No clear-headed, comprehending citizen takes local option to be the "Promised Land," but only that Haran wherein we, Abraham-like, tarry till our father Terah die.

Nor that other hypocritical fallacy called high license, wherein the government, taking a share of the profits, presumes to "respectableize," legalize, civilize and tame the thing, permitting it to look up into our faces and grunt, "I am your offspring." It is a lie. The thing is none of our blood. Man is from God; this thing is from the pit, "half louse and half devil." It is only here on sufferance and must be killed. I am not discussing the making of a truce, or the compensation in a compromise, but the price of a victory, thorough, terrible to the vanquished and eternal. Such a victory can never be until the constitutions, State and Federal, and the statutes throughout our land shall point the finger of scorn at the thing and hiss it from the land as an outlaw and a curse. It can never be until the offices of our land, county, state and national, shall be in the possession of a political party whose palm has not itched for liquor votes, whose fingers have handled no campaign funds from the saloonkeeper's till, whose knees have not bent and whose tongue has not palavered for the liquor dealer's influence on election day—a political party that owes the liquor business nothing but eternal enmity, and stands ready to discharge the debt. This and no less, is our victory—the total and final separation of the government from the liquor trade, and more, the relentless hostility of the government toward the liquor traffic.

III.

There are those who sit aside in a corner and wonder when the final attack is to be made on the liquor forces. Let them awake and come upon the towers, and see that the fight is now on to the finish. The Prohibitionists stand four hundred thousand strong on the firing line. They have said in their hearts: "As for tariff and expansion and government ownership and gold, I know not, but this I do know, that the liquor traffic ought to die." And they stand ready to give and to take blow for blow. They are not conscripts, they volunteered; they are not mercenaries, they joined for the cause's sake; they are not thirty day men, they counted the cost and enlisted for life. Many shall fall like Dow, and Gough, and Finch, and Frances E. Willard with their faces to the foe and with the dew and rust of glory on their unsheathed swords, but no true Prohibitionist will ever come home from the field, or call for a furlough, or a truce, or rest, or peace till the victory is won. If you but look through the smoke of battle you can see the enemy on the retreat. Once he held the trench of respectability, the trench of morality, and the trench of usefulness. Today he holds none of these; he has but one line of defense left, his political power, and this is being viciously assaulted.

IV.

When shall we win? It may be said that public sentiment is not yet ready for a Prohibition law and a Prohibition party. Well and good! There can be no reasonable objection urged against the effort to make public sentiment ready. Does any one fear that a party which must contend for every foot of its ground will come into power before public sentiment is ready? The Prohibitionist is not striving that his plea become law before his country is ready, but that the country may be made ready. And day by day the steady undertow of the truth swings the country farther and farther toward Prohibition. There is no rush of waters, no swish of the currents, no foam, no gale; just the slow move of the mighty waters, regular, continuous, sure.

V.

And there is no abatement in the call for men. From the front comes the cry for more soldiers. The "Old Guard" are falling one by one, they have saluted the flag for the last time, they rest in the trenches, their weapons wait for younger hands. Even the sword of the Lord has a human hilt. Take it up and go forward. Its very steel will give strength to the arm. The world's battles are not all won. The days of faith and courage and the times that try men's souls are not all past. God hath not let us fall on insipid days, when the clear call to a higher duty does not fall on human ears. God is not idle! God is not dead! Put your ear down close to His earth, and hear the tramp of thousands of feet as the young men of America march to their places in the ranks. Sometimes we see no friendly face, we seem to be lone skirmishers on a far-flung battle-line, but our comrades are there in the smoke and heat and dust. Sometimes we can not see even our Great Commander's face; the very smoke of victory may hide Him, but He is there. He stands within the shadow and His reward is with Him. He has the victory in His hands but He will not give it to the half-hearted. It is ours for the price—the full, unstinted, and complete price of victory.

Disciplined to think logically, to speak clearly, and to act wisely, the college man in politics counts for victory of essential issues in the campaign, and for education of the voting citizenship in the intervals. To him the whole range of history is open, and before him lies the broad domain of real politics. He knows what government is and ought to be, and his political activity tells for progress, because his ideas are the incarnation of invincible truth. If he compromises for sake of immediate victory on the plane of business success, he forfeits leadership to the demagogue, and pays penalty in a panic that shakes business to its base. But if, like Emerson, Wendell Phillips, and the men of the Oberlin school, he dedicates himself to reform, he summons to his side the fearless citizens who count not their lives dear to them if they may consecrate them to the universal good. They pay full price of thought, speech and act, of tears and blood, it may be—but they build themselves into the temple not made with hands, that stands forever in the white city of the self-governed people.

If victory has not been won, its price has not been paid. Two hundred and fifty thousand temperance radicals, unconvinced that immediate duty required them to support "good men"—neutral and non-committal on the saloon question—paid the price of "lost" votes on the third day of November, 1908. But fourteen million other citizens "saved" their suffrages by voting for issues and candidates acceptable to the liquor "industry," and the count shows that the "trade" carried the election. Even the Anti-Saloon League candidates went down in defeat. At least five million churchmen declined to pay the price of a victory over the saloon. They went with their "party"—and postponed the solution of the saloon problem until the problem shall solve itself in the slowly unfolding life of the republic. —G. M. H.

CHAPTER XIV.

THE ANTI-SALOON LEAGUE—PURPOSE AND METHODS.

By Bishop L. B. Wilson, D. D., *President*.

THERE need be no misunderstanding of our purpose by either friend or foe. We seek the suppression of the traffic in strong drink as a beverage, whether the place where it is dispensed be legalized or unlegalized, and, except as may be demanded for the harmless purposes of trade, we are pledged to pursue it with hostile zeal from the place of manufacture to the last den from which it may be dispensed. As a League, we will in every lawful way oppose and embarrass the traffic, nor regard our object realized until this foe of humanity has been destroyed. Let there be no question as to this. We are united for the destruction of the rum power.

The method of the League is that of direct attack. No one present at the sessions of our national conventions, or conversant with the conduct of affairs in the state leagues, could fail to note the attitude of our leaders in their dependence upon Almighty God, nor could any thoughtful observer be in doubt concerning our hearty sympathy with every method of moral suasion by which is sought either the deliverance of those who have become the victims of strong drink, or the security of those who are still free from its debauching thrall. More and more would we encourage every effort which in any measure serves to bar the progress of our foe. But, as specialization is the law of largest success, the League has concentrated its endeavors to secure—

First, the execution of existing laws favorable to temperance.

Second, the enactment of laws more adequately meeting the situation.

Inasmuch as the state claims the right to control the traffic, and in so many ways evidences that claim, the League must deal with the constituted authorities, and its methods must, in the nature of the case, be largely political. If it is to influence legislation and promote the fair administration of laws, it must deal with the officials of the state from the moment and manner of their induction into office to the manner and moment of their retirement to private life. Hence it is that the League emphasizes the value of the political franchise, and pleads for the consolidation of temperance sentiment upon every occasion when such action may have special value either in its immediate effect upon legislation or as an education of public sentiment.

But, it is asked, if the League recognizes the importance of political action, why does it decline partisan affiliation? It is a fair question, and we cannot object to giving a reason for the policy to which by our constitution we are committed.

It has seemed the part of wisdom in our plea to the citizenship of the state, as far as practicable, to narrow our contention and so simplify our work. It is surely an easier task to persuade the community that the liquor problem is an issue meriting consideration and justifying practical action, than to convince the people that this is the paramount or only issue. To establish the former proposition a simple recital of facts will many times suffice; but to convince men of the correctness of the alternative contention, one is compelled to argue upon the practical value of almost every conceivable political theorem.

If it be possible to gain the practical end without unnecessarily attacking prejudice, is it not wise to choose for our effort the line of least resistance? The question is not as to our personal conviction relative to the place of this among other political issues, but as to the practicability of convincing other people concerning the matter; and the choice of the easier method cannot in any fairness be deemed a compromise with wrong.

The method adopted by us leaves us free from the necessity of constructing a party platform or of educating statesmen. It is not probable that a platform with a single plank would be accepted as satisfactory by the larger part of the community. Nor would it generally be deemed safe to confide the administration of public affairs to those whose only qualification for office is their hostility to the liquor trade. To deal satisfactorily with such questions as are constantly presented, the men in power ought to represent the best intelligence of the state, its keenest sagacity, its widest practical ability. Increasingly does the welfare of the state demand the presence in office of the broadest and best exponents of our patriotic citizenship.

The formation of a new party is a task so formidable that the League has not regarded its attempt as either necessary or advisable. It is easier to select statesmen than to create them, and there is more hope of winning the battle on the basis of disinterested zeal than if the spoils of office were included among the perquisites of success. With methods flexible enough for every community and every occasion, direct enough to be effective, unembarrassed by affiliation with any political party as such, the League is in position to challenge men of every party who offer themselves for office, to plead with increasing hope for success with every occupant of office,

REV. J. C. SOLOMON, A. M.,
Superintendent Anti-Saloon League of Georgia.

J. B. RICHARDS,
Associate Superintendent Anti-Saloon League of Georgia.

REV. J. L. D. HILLYER,
Anti-Saloon League Worker of Georgia.

however high or low, and to hasten the day when loyalty to right shall be the only guarantee of continuance in office.

If we cannot secure the united action of temperance-loving men in such campaigns as we are conducting, is it likely that an appeal for the permanent severance of party affiliations would meet with satisfactory response? If we cannot hope for victory with the aims and methods which the league has adopted, where shall a ground for hope be discovered?

The difference between a toy watch and a real timepiece is that the latter *goes*. It is of immense encouragement to us to know that the League goes, and that, in the desired way, it is making the saloon go. In Ohio, Rhode Island, Illinois, California, Virginia, West Virginia, Georgia, Indiana, New York, Texas, Washington, Maryland, Pennsylvania, Kentucky, Wisconsin, Tennessee, Connecticut, Massachusetts, the District of Columbia, and other states and territories, we appeal to facts to establish the practical value of our plans. And a study of the liquor organs of the country will prove that our enemies fear the Anti-Saloon League more than any other form of organized opposition to the liquor traffic.

From an address by THOMAS M. GILMORE, President National Model License League, at the Convention at Louisville, Ky., January 21, 22, 1908.

"I want to say that the Anti-Saloon League, which is today directing this prohibition wave, is the most remarkable movement that this country has ever known. . . . In its incipiency it was the personification of modesty, the personification of humility. I say to-day it is the most autocratic, the most dictatorial, as well as the most dangerous power ever known in the politics of this country, and that no man can run for any office, in the majority of our Southern and Western states, without being catechised by some men connected with it. And when he is asked the questions, the answers are given to him, and he is told to respond favorably, or be retired to private life. . . . I say without the slightest hesitation that the Anti-Saloon League is the most dangerous political movement that this country has ever known."

CHAPTER XV.

THE ANTI-SALOON LEAGUE, ORIGIN AND PERSONNEL.

By Louis Albert Banks, D. D.

NOTE.—*This sketch of the founder and the founding of the Anti-Saloon League is taken, upon the recommendation of Howard H. Russell, from Dr. Banks' very valuable book,* "THE LINCOLN LEGION."—G. M. H.

ALL great movements have gathered about some distinct and typical personality. Emerson tells us that every great institution is but the lengthening shadow of a man. Mahomet stands for Mohammedism, Martin Luther for the Reformation, George Washington for the American Revolution, John Wesley for Methodism. When a great task is to be wrought out, God lays the burden of it upon some man's heart, and by inheritance and environment, as well as by discipline and culture, fits him for his work, and drives him forward by a divine impulse until it is accomplished.

The Anti-Saloon League, like every other institution that has been a force for good in the world, has been a growth, and has received into its life great personal sacrifice and service upon the part of many devoted people. While others deserve credit for valuable assistance and unselfish service, without which the results would have been impossible, it still remains true that one man conceived the plan of the organization, as it has finally crystallized into a working engine without material change from the "pattern in the Mount." He saw the visions and dreamed the dreams. By faith he foresaw the coming constituency, the methods of work, and the sure victories of the movement. He was the first missionary in the new crusade utterly to put himself, and all he had, into it. He aroused the needed faith in others, raised the sinews of war, enlisted other leaders, mobilized the army, and conducted such victorious campaigns as have already won the respect of political powers, the fear of saloonkeepers and their allies, the rapidly growing support of all moral agencies, and made the organization a permanent factor in this "noblest conflict of the New Century."

Howard H. Russell from early boyhood had distinct impressions of the evil of the drink habit and traffic. While yet a lad he saw near and dear relatives brought to a premature death through strong drink. It

HOWARD H. RUSSELL,
Founder, Anti-Saloon League of America.

became evident to him that for several generations this habit had been a family weakness. When visiting in Staffordshire, England, Russell found that at least fourteen relatives not far removed, bright young men, several of them trained in the English universities, had all died before reaching forty years of age, and that the drink habit was the assassin in every case. It is no wonder that the subject was always in his mind as of pressing importance.

When a young lawyer in Iowa his firm was employed by a local temperance organization to prosecute lawless saloonkeepers, and to Russell was assigned the prosecution of the cases. He thus learned the perjury and anarchy characterizing such traffickers. He was often called upon for temperance addresses, and, in 1883, he devoted a month to the state campaign for a prohibitory amendment to the Iowa constitution.

During his collegiate course at Oberlin, from 1884 to 1888, he was repeatedly sent as delegate to represent the college at temperance conferences and conventions. While a student, in 1885, he led in the Murphy movement at North Amherst and South Amherst, Ohio, and again, while still a seminarian at Oberlin, but residing at Berea, Ohio, and pastor of the Berea Congregational Church, he organized a local movement which closed eight saloons; and they have remained closed ever since. A vicious physical assault upon him on the street by a saloonkeeper helped to carry the election by six majority.

When the saloonkeepers, thus legally forced out of trade by the village ordinance, continued to sell liquor in violation of law, he secured abundance of evidence and began the prosecution, conducted the trials himself in the mayor's court, and secured such heavy penalties against the lawbreakers that they were compelled to obey the law. When he left Berea to go to Kansas City, in 1888, the citizens generally gave a farewell reception, and a written testimonial with numerous signatures, in recognition of his services in the temperance cause while a citizen of Berea.

In December, 1887, the Oberlin Temperance Alliance requested Mr. Russell to take charge of a movement to secure a needed law from the legislature. They offered to furnish $300 in money towards expenses, and to supply his Berea pulpit when it was necessary to be absent therefrom. He opened a headquarters at Columbus. By working through the pastors and churches a temporary "Local Option League," as it was called, was formed throughout the state, and petitions were circulated in every county for the passage of the Township Local Option Bill.

Previously, in 1886, the legislature, in the enactment of the Dow Law, had given the councils of the various municipalities in the state the power to regulate or prohibit the sale of liquors as beverages. It was under that provision that the Berea saloons were closed. In many localities, when the village council closed the saloons, they opened again for business in the township just outside the line. The enactment of the township local option law was planned so as to enable the farmers to protect the township from the saloon, and incidentally to protect the village or city voting out the saloons.

Under the pressure of the people, stirred up by the Local Option League, the bill was pushed through the house by a small majority and went over to the senate. Here a poll of the senate made by Senator Park Alexander of Akron, who was an earnest friend of the bill, showed a bare majority of one in its favor. On a certain Wednesday morning the bill was to come to a vote. On Monday morning, two days before, Senator Crook, of Dayton, went to Senator Alexander and said that three committees of the brewers, distillers and saloonkeepers of Dayton had called upon him the previous day, and he felt that he must withdraw his promise to vote for the bill. Monday afternoon Mr. Russell went to Dayton, and through friends of the measure, secured the writing on Tuesday of many personal letters to Senator Crook. On Wednesday morning several telegrams were sent him, and when the bill came up, he voted for it and it was passed by a majority of one vote. Senator Alexander remarked afterwards to Mr. Russell that the old prophecy of Isaiah had now been fulfilled: "The crooked shall be made straight, and the rough places plain." This Township law was the entering wedge for local option laws in that state.

This four month's legislative experience led Mr. Russell to believe that a permanent organization of the temperance forces of the churches might make gradual and more rapid headway than hitherto in obtaining anti-saloon legislation. In making his final report to the Oberlin Temperance Alliance in April, 1888, Mr. Russell urged that the temporary organization be made permanent, and that a salaried superintendent be employed to take charge of the work. A county organization was afterwards formed in Lorain county and there the matter rested.

While pastor of the Southwest Tabernacle in Kansas City, in 1890, Mr. Russell sent circular letters to the pastors throughout Missouri, asking their opinion upon the subject, and as the result a largely attended convention was called, and held at Pertle Springs, Missouri, in July, 1890, and a constitution was adopted providing for work in the lines of agitation, law enforcement and legislation by a state organization named the Missouri Anti-Liquor League. Mr. Russell was elected the president for the first year, and he gave his whole two months' vacation without charge to the league, presenting the work at various points in the state. The first fifty dollars expended in printing and postage in working up the state convention in Missouri were furnished by members of the Oberlin Temperance Alliance. Mr. W. J. Reese was appointed organizer, and with a stereopticon which Mr. Russell furnished him, he went out and organized leagues, some of which still continue their work. The state league temporarily ceased its work when Mr. Russell was called early in 1891 to take pastoral charge of the Armour Mission in Chicago.

In 1892, Mr. Russell was invited to deliver a temperance address at Oberlin, and he again advocated the forming of a permanent state organization in Ohio, and tried to induce certain men to take charge of the work, but nothing was done. His pastoral work in Chicago brought before him many tragedies resulting from the drink. Standing upon a box at an undertaker's door, he conducted the funeral of a suicide through drink; the drunkard's home had gone, and his weeping family sat within the door. Again, it was the "only son of his mother, and she a widow," who had been wounded in a saloon brawl on Sunday, and afterwards died in the hospital. In another case it was the mother with seven sorrowing children, who had died in childbirth after being brutally struck by her drunken husband. The doctor gave the man money to buy medicine for the wife and he bought whisky for himself, and on the day of the funeral lay drunk on the floor of the back room. Again, it was a child driven forth by a drunken father to freeze to death.

In the fall of 1892, Mr. Russell talked privately with some of the Oberlin citizens again about the need of State organization in Ohio. They said, "If you will take charge of it, it might be made a success." There was a natural hesitation on his part to leave the regular line of church work in which he was blessed, to be absent most of the time from his family. The question of support was utterly untried and uncertain.

At the time of indecision a new tragedy stirred his heart. He was called as a minister to a home where a drunken mother lay dead. The father was intoxicated, as were also the undertaker's driver and some neighbor women. The little boy of eight years and his little sister of three—worse than orphans—were the only unpolluted objects in the desolate room. "Do you know what caused your mother's death?" he asked. "I do. It was drink," said the weeping boy. "Are you going to drink?" "I'll never touch it!" He pledged the boy, whose clenched hand he raised never to drink that which took his mother's life, and to teach his sister to do likewise. The next morning when he called, the house was vacant and that home like so many others was broken up by rum.

It was there and then he settled the question of his future work as a reformer. He said to himself, "I will go out to my brethren of the churches and demand that they become responsible for an organized activity that shall hasten the day when that kind of tragedy shall be done away." There were two or three conferences at Oberlin between January and May, 1893, and at Mr. Russell's request the Oberlin Temperance Alliance, at a meeting held in the College library on May 24, 1893, formally voted to initiate and to stand officially behind the movement until it should be thought best to expand the work into a state organization. It was voted at that meeting that accounts should be kept and money received and paid by the Oberlin organization for the present, and Mr. Russell was employed as superintendent upon a definite salary to introduce the movement to the people of the state, and as rapidly as possible to organize and federate the churches into a league against the saloons according to plans he had outlined to the Alliance.

As had been voted at the Alliance meeting on May 24, the formal public beginning of the Anti-Saloon League was made the first Sunday evening in June—June 4, 1893—at a union meeting of all the churches in the old First Church, Oberlin. Rev. Dr. James Brand, the pastor, at the opening of the service said among other things that he believed this would prove to be one of the great historic meetings in that church. He spoke of two such meetings already held. One, the Indignation Meeting with reference to the fugitive slave held by his captors in Wellington, which resulted in the rescuing party being sent from Oberlin to take him from them. Another when the two companies were recruited from faculty and students for the Civil War.

Dr. Brand said he believed a movement was to be advocated and begun that night, which would be far-reaching in its influence against the most stupendous and satanic evil in the state and nation. He believed, he said, that in Mr. Russell they saw and were to hear "a man sent from God" for a definite work, who was now about to set in upon his Heaven-ordained task. He called upon all to both hear and then act with reference to the important plans to be presented. Professor G. W. Shurtleff introduced Mr. Russell. He referred to the important work Mr. Russell had already done for the people of Ohio, in managing the campaign in 1888, which had secured the enactment of the Township Local Option Law. He expressed his confident belief that, with the wise and timely plans which Mr. Russell had presented to the Alliance and was now about to advocate to the people, it would be possible under his leadership to develop a permanent and powerful organization against the liquor traffic in Ohio. It was a wonderful meeting. The church was filled to overflowing; students in the great galleries and earnest and attentive listeners in all parts of the house.

Mr. Russell, in his speech that night, called attention to the fact that the saloons were increasing three times as fast as the population, and showed the need of a more powerful organization than then existed in Ohio to antagonize the liquor traffic. He insisted that the churches ought to become responsible for a vigorous and permanent anti-liquor league. He advo-

SAMUEL H. DAVIS,
Superintendent, Anti-Saloon League of Massachusetts.

H. H. SPOONER,
Secretary, State Temperance Union, Connecticut.

HON. FREDERICK FOSDICK,
President, Anti-Saloon League of Massachusetts.

cated an omnipartisan and interdenominational federation, which should overcome the apathy, cowardice and discord then existing among temperance people, and, under the leadership of at least ten competent men employed as experts to devote their whole time to the work, should carry forward a permanent campaign on four distinct lines: *First*, Agitation; *second*, Legislation; *third*, Law Enforcement; *fourth*, an Organization of the Boys. At the close of his speech he appealed for liberal subscriptions to support the movement. Printed three-year pledges were circulated and the aggregate sum pledged was over $600 per year for three years, or nearly two thousand dollars. A private canvass soon increased the subscription to three thousand dollars, and it is an interesting fact that Oberlin, that grand old reform center, with no saloons, and the law well enforced, has given about one thousand dollars per year during the past ten years through the treasury of the Anti-Saloon League, to do missionary work for Ohio and the country in the cause of temperance.

The Ohio Anti-Saloon League was born that Sunday night in the church in Oberlin. It soon spread over the state, and the bold prediction of its founder that the people of the churches would form a mighty league against the saloons was soon fulfilled. Russell was tireless in service and abundant in success. He soon interested men who had both conscience and capital to devote to the cause. Two of them deserve special mention. They are the late E. W. Metcalf, of Elyria, and Mr. A. I. Root, of Medina, Ohio. These men by their counsel and generosity helped give the new venture a rapid start. The League was soon felt in legislation; bad legislation was stopped, and advance measures were taken; laws long disused and disobeyed were brought to light and enforced; until the eyes of temperance people all over the nation were attracted by the Ohio idea of aggressive concentration against the saloon.

In 1894 and 1895, Russell began to have many calls from the outside for information about the Ohio Anti-Saloon League and its work.

Neighboring states began to organize along the same lines. A call for an interstate convention for four or five of the interior states, with a view to forming an Anti-Saloon League, had been prepared and was about to be issued, when a letter came from the Anti-Saloon League of the District of Columbia, inviting the Ohio Anti-Saloon League to join in a call for a convention to organize a National Anti-Saloon League. The Ohio Anti-Saloon League joined in that call and the American Anti-Saloon League was formed at Washington in December, 1895.

The immediate origin of the National Anti-Saloon League may be properly said to have come from four distinct sources. In the first place there had been non-partisan state temperance organizations at work for several years previous to the organization of the Anti-Saloon League.

These were the Total Abstinence Society in Massachusetts, the Connecticut Temperance Union in Connecticut, the Kansas Temperance Union in Kansas and the Maryland State Temperance Alliance in Maryland. At least three of these old state organizations took part in the convention at Washington in 1895 which organized the American Anti-Saloon League, and they have all since as bodies, federated with the national organization. In the second place, a movement had been planned and carried forward by the Rev. A. J. Kynett in connection with his regular work as Secretary of the Church Extension Society of the Methodist Episcopal Church. Dr. Kynett called the organization which he furthered the Interdenominational Christian Temperance Alliance. He printed a monthy magazine in connection with his Church Extension Society work, and this magazine contained a department relating to saloon suppression, in which he advocated the organization of branch Alliances in the different localities throughout the country, and, as far as such branches were organized, he reported their work in that department of the magazine. He advocated the forming of organizations in each local Methodist church, and urged that the churches of other denominations should form like organizations and seek alliance with one another in the various localities and states. To some extent he had succeeded in securing such church and local organizations, and in three states, Pennsylvania, Illinois and Ohio, conventions had been held and officers elected to inaugurate state organizations along the same lines. Not a great deal of work had been done through these organizations, as Dr. Kynett himself stated, for lack of a superintendent who could devote his whole time to the organization and direction of the movement. Dr. Kynett was glad to join forces with the new movement planned at the Washington Convention, and he was, during the early years of the American Anti-Saloon League, one of its most wise and faithful counselors and leaders.

The third source of the Anti-Saloon League movement was found in the federation of the churches and temperance societies in the District of Columbia, which was formed June 23, 1893, under the name of District of Columbia Anti-Saloon League, and which had already at the time of the convention in 1895, done very useful service for the temperance cause at the Capital. Among those who were influential in the District of Columbia League when the National League was formed, may be mentioned Mr. A. N. Canfield, who had called the first conference looking toward the federation of the churches and temperance societies of the District of Columbia in an Anti-Saloon League, and Mr. James L. Ewin, who was the first secretary of the national organization, and is its present corresponding secretary, and who has devoted much time and self-sacrificing service in connection with the calling and management of the various conventions of the League at Washington, and in the furtherance of the League's growth. Rev. Luther B. Wilson, D. D., then a presiding elder of the M. E. Church at Washington, was more than any other man influential in causing the call for a national organization to be issued. He was at that time president of the District of Columbia League, and was elected First Vice-President of the National League. After the death of the Hon. Hiram Price, who was the first President of the National League, Dr. Wilson was elected to succeed him as the League's president, and he has been a most able presiding officer. The fourth source of influence in the forming of the national League is found in the Ohio Anti-Saloon League with its successful history of organization and achievement prior to the convention at Washington in December, 1895, to which it sent its delegates to take part in the forming of the national organization.

Back of or contemporaneous with all these four lines of influence which have been named, were the organized efforts made by temperance workers in all parts of the United States, which had resulted in the agitation of the temperance question and the concreting of the public sentiment thus engendered into statute law, and the obtaining of the enforcement of the law in the various localities throughout the country. The organizing convention adopted a constitution providing for a federation of all organizations pledging coöperation in the suppression of the saloon.

The object of this League as stated in Article Third is as follows:

"The object of this League is the *suppression of the saloon*. To this end we invite the alliance of all who are in harmony with this object, and the League pledges itself to avoid affiliation with any political party as such, and to maintain an attitude of neutrality upon questions of public policy not directly and immediately concerned with the traffic in strong drink."

An executive committee was elected in harmony with the constitution, and provision was made for future annual conventions of the national League. These conventions have been held with an increasing attendance and a growing federation of organizations to promote the objects of the League. The national organization now federates about 250 church, temperance and other bodies in all parts of the country. The Ohio Anti-Saloon League was recognized as the "model" for other state leagues to be formed throughout the country, and the superintendent of the Ohio League was elected first superintendent of the national organization. Gradually the beginning of work has been promoted in the various states since 1895; in some cases by correspondence, but with greater satisfaction and success by a visit to the new state by the national superintendent. In 1897, Superintendent Russell spent three months introducing the work in California and other states in the Far West. For two years after the national League was formed, Superintendent Russell served as Superintendent both of the Ohio League and of the national League, and, during the years 1902 and 1903, he was superintendent both of the national League and of the New York State Anti-Saloon League. During two of the years of his superintendency he traveled over 50,000 miles each year in connection with the work of organization in new states and the fostering of the work in the states where the League had already been formed.

A bright judge of men and great human movements says: "Successful leadership depends entirely upon one's ability to multiply himself through others. Great leaders must not only lay plans which are practical, but must also be able to call around them those who can carry out their orders efficiently and vigorously." This is one of Howard Russell's personal qualities, and has contributed greatly to his success as Superintendent of the Anti-Saloon League of America.

Among many others whom he has chosen and enlisted to coöperate in the expansion of the League, a few names may be mentioned of those who have been longest associated with the work. The Rev. E. C. Dinwiddie, of Springfield, Ohio, was one of the first men called. He was given special charge of the legislative department of the Ohio League, for which work he showed great aptitude. After four years in Ohio he took entire charge of the Pennsylvania League, and then became National Legislative Superintendent. He is a man rarely qualified for such tasks, and his work has met with gratifying success. The Rev. P. A. Baker, D. D., of Columbus, Ohio, was first employed as a district superintendent of the Ohio League, when Dr. Russell resigned to assume the duties of the superintendency of the national League in 1897. Baker carried forward and developed the League in that state with masterly ability and success. He is as brave as a lion, as wise as a serpent and a man of remarkable adaptation to his position. When Dr. Russell became superintendent in New York, Dr. Baker became General Superintendent of the Anti-Saloon League of America. In the expansion of both the state and national Leagues, Baker and Russell have been true yoke-fellows. They are the Cobden and Bright of this mighty movement of reform. Mr. Wayne B. Wheeler was one of the bright men of the class of 1895 in Oberlin College. Upon his graduation from college he began as a field secretary in the Ohio League, and later was admitted to the Ohio Bar, and has since made a brilliant record as attorney for the Anti-Saloon League of Ohio and of the national League. The Rev. Dr. J. C. Jackson was called from an important Columbus pastorate to the League work in 1896, and after assisting Superintendent Russell, both in the state League work, and in organizing new Leagues in other states, he was appointed editor of *The American Issue*, first the organ of the Ohio League, and subsequently that

MISS GLENN WILL,
Field Secretary, Anti-Saloon League of California.

of the national organization. By his voice on Sunday, and his pen during the week, Dr. Jackson is exerting a mighty influence for the cause.

Time would fail to mention other names worthy of record. One after another strong men have been sought out and placed at the head of the various state organizations, and in charge of the equally important district work in many of the states. A particular reference to these leaders and organizers must be omitted for lack of space, but they are exerting a powerful influence in molding public sentiment against the liquor traffic. Nor will it be possible further to recite the wonderful growth and spread of this marvelous movement. Suffice it to say that a little over fifteen years ago Dr. Russell, first privately, then publicly, at the great Oberlin meeting, proposed the League system of state-wide anti-saloon work as it has since been developed throughout the land. At that time, to quote Professor Whitlock, "Russell was the only salaried officer. The League headquarters were in his valise. Its stock in trade was his faith and heroism and the sympathy and prayers of a few friends and advisers." Today, according to Dr. Russell's last annual report, the organization has been started in practically all the states and territories, and nearly five hundred persons are devoting their entire time to the work. The financial support for the past year in the various states and in the national League will aggregate over $400,000.

NOTE.—*In other chapters of the book the great spread of prohibition territory since the Anti-Saloon League began its work is set forth. Where older organizations have sowed and watered the seed so faithfully for so many years, this newer organization, coming in with its practical methods, has gathered the harvest. "And herein is that saying true, One soweth, and another reapeth. . That both he that soweth and he that reapeth may rejoice together."*—G. M. H.

CHAPTER XVI.

THE TEMPERANCE TIDAL WAVE.

By Samuel J. Barrows, *President of the International Prison Commission.*

Abridged and reprinted by permission from *The Outlook*, July 4, 1908.

PART. I.

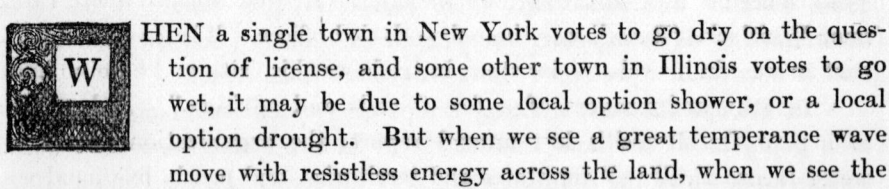

WHEN a single town in New York votes to go dry on the question of license, and some other town in Illinois votes to go wet, it may be due to some local option shower, or a local option drought. But when we see a great temperance wave move with resistless energy across the land, when we see the tide of public opinion against alcoholism making itself felt in England, France, Sweden, Finland, Russia, Switzerland, as well as in Illinois, Oklahoma and the Black Belt, we know just as well that it is not merely a question of local showers—some great moral or social world-force is making itself felt in our civilization.

Logically, as well as historically, it is easy to see why social control of the liquor traffic, in some form or other, has become a recognized principle in modern legislation. When temperance was regarded as an individual and not as a social question, there was a natural protest against the restriction of individual liberty by sumptuary laws. Whether enacted by Lycurgus, Augustus, Charlemagne, or Edward III., they had in them no element of public opinion. They seemed to be the edict of an individual tyrant against individual liberty. Because they were not supported by public opinion they were not observed. Anti-liquor laws in modern democracy are not edicts imposed upon the people; they are laws adopted by the people themselves, and depending upon the people for their execution. In our own day extreme individualism has been modified in every respect by fraternalism, by new conceptions of solidarity and social obligation. "No man liveth to himself." Eating and drinking are private acts, but they may have important social consequences. If the individual is responsible to society for his acts, society is recognizing its responsibility to the individual. It is responsible to some extent for his environment; it must furnish him adequate protection. The state intervenes to protect the individual against diseased meat, impure milk, and adulterations of food of any sort. Individual health may be a personal concern; but the public health is a social concern. Boards of health have sprung up in all civilized countries. Drunkenness is an individual vice; but if it deprives the individual of his self-control, it becomes a social peril; it means theft, assault, wife-beating, social disorder, homicide; it means neglected homes, neglected children, poverty, and pauperism. Alcoholism is a form of temporary insanity. Only the extreme anarchist will deny the right of society to control the man who is socially dangerous because he cannot control himself. If we restrict the liberty of an individual who is drunk or insane, it is because we cannot imperil the liberty of the multitude, and we must also protect the man against himself.

It is too late to ask whether society has a right to protect itself from disorder and indecency, from pauperism and crime; it has been determined to do so in nearly every civilized country; and the great question is not, Shall it be done? but, How shall it be done?

In Europe the most exciting campaign for legislative restriction has been going on at the same time this year in two countries, England and Switzerland, where the conditions are very different. In the United Kingdom the consumption of spirits, wine and beer has become enormous. With a total population of 43,659,000, the expenditure for liquors of all kinds during 1906 reached the sum of $809,681,829, or an average of $18 per capita. In 1907 the expenditure rose to $815,000,000. Deducting children and adult abstainers—about one-half of the population—this means that the drinking half spent on an average of $37.12 per capita, so that a family of two adult drinkers spent on the average of $74.24.

From what source does this enormous supply of liquor come? On January 1, 1907, there were in England and Wales alone 124,189 licensed public houses and 6,907 registered clubs, a total of 131,096 places for the retail sale of drink; that is, one drinking shop or club to every 206 persons. In the same territory in England and Wales 174,049 persons were convicted of drunkenness in 1907, 33,003 of whom were women.

These figures now show, on one hand, why a large number of people in England and Wales are demanding reform, and why it is hard, against the liquor trust, to get a reform through. A vast number of people want to drink, and a vast number of people want to supply them.

Successive Parliaments have tried to bring in satisfactory temperance measures without avail. Mr. Balfour's bill of 1904 left the people in a worse plight than before, as it changed the constitutional order of nearly three hundred and fifty years by making a license to sell liquors a vested interest of the brewer, instead of being, as before, an annual permit liable to be withdrawn for misconduct, and whose renewal might be refused.

This bill also introduced a new element in the granting of licenses; it gave compensation to the owner of the licensed house for the full "monopoly value," often dishonestly inflated, on the withdrawal of the license. Thus a licensed house in the east of London, valued by its owner on the rate-book at £42 for taxing purposes, was valued by him and compensated at £7,560 ($35,800).

The hopes of the temperance reformers are now based on the new license bill for England and Wales (it does not apply to Ireland and Scotland) introduced by Mr. Asquith, then Chancellor of the Exchequer, and now the successor of Sir Henry Campbell-Bannerman. In introducing the bill Mr. Asquith said: "Every one who is interested in social progress will, I am sure, agree that effective reform of the licensing law is now overdue." The bill is not a total abstainers' bill, but a "sober man's bill," which will reverse a part of the policy of Mr. Balfour's "Bless-all-my-dear-friends-and-relations" bill of 1904, by setting up a time limit of fourteen years after the passage of the law when all licenses shall lapse and no further compensation be given for their refusal, and a clear declaration of their annual nature shall be made. The chief aims of the bill are to lessen the present excessive number of public houses and to give to the state unfettered control of the liquor trade. Thirty-two thousand public houses are to be closed in fourteen years. The scale of reduction will depend on the density of population. Compensation is to be paid for all public houses closed within the fourteen years, if closed unnecessarily. The publican, the actual license-holder, is, in addition to the brewer to receive special compensation for the loss of business; previously, the brewers got the lion's share of the compensation. At the end of fourteen years all licenses come under full state control.

One of the most important features of the Government bill is the acceptance of a principle which has wrought such remarkable results in the United States—the principle of local option. When the time limit of fourteen years is reached as to licenses now in force, the people will have the power of local option as to limitation or prohibition. As to new licenses, the people of any given locality after April 5, 1909, are to have the power to prohibit the granting of any new license in that locality. A prohibition resolution can be carried by a simple majority, and the question, whichever way decided, cannot come up again for three years. The hours for opening on Sunday are limited; local magistrates are given power to exclude children from liquor bars and to prohibit the employment of women in public houses. Street beer drinking is made illegal, and the sale of liquor on passenger vessels, heretofore unrestricted, is brought under stringent regulations. Clubs that supply alcoholic drinks are placed on the same footing as public houses. The compensation, as under the Act of

MRS. ADRIANNA HUNGERFORD,
President, Colorado W. C. T. U.

MRS. ANTOINETT ARNOLD HAWLEY,
Honorary President, Colorado W. C. T. U.

1904, is to be raised by a levy "on the trade." The area of the levy is to be the whole of England and Wales, and the full levy is to be raised each year. The money is to be vested in the Licensing Commission, and paid out by them. In the year 1907, 1,716 licenses were extinguished, and the holders under the Act of 1904 were entitled to compensation. The average cost to the compensation fund per license was $4,584, and the compensation levied for the year was $5,363,000.

Both sides regard this as the biggest fight that England has ever had on the liquor question. Mr. Asquith showed that from $500,000,000 to $750,000,000 are invested in the liquor trade. On the other hand, the opponents of the bill, who declare that it is an attack upon property, say that the amount invested equals a billion and a half dollars. The number of employes in the liquor traffic, as given by Mr. Asquith from the census, is nearly 259,000. But the Hon. John Gretton declares that there are 700,000 persons depending upon the direct employment of the breweries, and that more than 1,300,000 depend upon indirect employment.

Thus we have a great industrial force, backed up by an enormous amount of money, opposing the new bill. Many clergymen of the Established Church are lined up with the liquor dealers, the reason for which it is not difficult to discover when we know that 1,280 clergymen have invested their little all in breweries and other licensed establishments. On the other hand, the Primate of all England, the Archbishop of Canterbury, and twenty-one bishops, and the Free Churches, almost without exception, are supporting this bill.

The beautiful lakes of Switzerland are not subject to tidal action, but there is no place in the world where the form of government, with its provisions for initiative and referendum, is so sensitive to tidal movements of public opinion. In the month of April, 1908, public sentiment made a new declaration concerning the regulation of a portion of the liquor traffic. There is no such flagrant intoxication in Switzerland as in England. Women are not seen reeling in public bar rooms; a large portion of the people confine themselves to beer and light wines. Nevertheless, when one studies the sources of crime in Switzerland, he finds there, as in every civilized country, that crime is largely due to alcoholism, the lowest estimate of the relation being thirty-three per cent. and the highest seventy-five per cent.

The control of the system in that land is partly cantonal and partly federal. Switzerland has a population about as large as that of the state of Massachusetts, and is divided up into twenty-two cantons, each of which has its own laws regulating license. The number of saloons is based upon the number of inhabitants. The federal government has a monopoly of the sale of distilled spirits. The cantons receive from the confederation one-tenth of the product of the sale of alcohol, which they use in combating the abuse of alcoholic liquors, applying it to the support of public schools; but many cantons have used this money for public improvements, such as road building, instead of in a direct fight against alcohol. The great danger is from the increased consumption of absinthe, and the temperance societies are making strong efforts for its restriction and prohibition.

During the first week in April of this year all other questions in Parliament dwindled into insignificance compared with the popular demand for the initiative against absinthe, which has already been interdicted by the local legislatures of two cantons, those of Vaud and Geneva. For several days the Swiss Chamber, in the beautiful parliamentary building at Berne, presented an unusual appearance. The galleries were crowded, and the debate, which occupied three days, showed such a ferment as the introduction of alcohol in a legislative program generally produces. There are three official languages, French, German and Italian, in the Swiss Chamber, and all of them were heard in the heated discussion. In Switzerland the initiative was created to enable the people to solve questions themselves, and the petition for the initiative in this case was signed by 168,000 people. Mr. Ruchet, the chief of the Department of the Interior, did not minimize the dangers from absinthe, but maintained that the measure was partial and inadequate, and that the consumption of black coffee, strengthened by schnapps, in German Switzerland is just as dangerous. It is given to children going to schools, and it is used to moisten food for babies to make them sleep better. He confessed that if he had been in Geneva or Lausanne he would have voted for prohibition; but is it worth while, he demanded, to dose all the children of a family because two of them are sick?

The Government, while objecting to the form of the proposition, failed to present any other, and the national assembly gave a majority for the measure which even its most optimistic advocates had not expected. The initiative was carried April 7 by a vote of 82 to 53. An analysis of the vote showed that of the twenty-eight French deputies only ten voted against it; and it was supported by a considerable number of the radicals of German Switzerland, where beer is more popular than absinthe. *La Revue*, of Lausanne, interprets the vote, not as a political manifestation of different groups, but rather as an expression of a current of public opinion marked by the highest idealism. The Upper Chamber ratified the vote of the popular chamber by 24 votes to 12. It seems practically certain that the people will prohibit absinthe, as it has already been interdicted in Belgium.

But a few years ago many temperance leaders in the United States were pinning their faith to the Gothenburg or its companion system in

Norway, and an effort to establish it in Massachusetts failed by one vote in the legislature. An essential part of the system is not merely the state control of the traffic, but the substitution of other attractions for the saloon. The opponents of the system, the total abstainers, point to the fact that the consumption of beer has largely increased, and that arrests for drunkenness have also largely increased, since the establishment of the system. On the other hand, its advocates show that there is less alcoholic drink consumed in Sweden and Norway than in any other country.

My visit in Stockholm preceded by a week the meeting of the International Anti-Alcoholic Congress. Its Secretary, Professor Curt Wallys, one of the most eminent chemists of Sweden, as the result of his scientific studies came to the conclusion that alcohol was not a food, but a source of the deepest social misery. He became a conspicuous leader of the total abstinence movement, and is confident that prohibition will come before long as a legislative measure. As he is a member of Parliament as well as scientific man, his opinion and influence are important.

In Finland, where I had an opportunity to see a number of members of Parliament, including the Baroness von Grippenberg, confidence was strong that Finland would adopt prohibition, but a good deal of doubt was expressed as to the approval of the measure by the Russian Government.

In Russia it was clear that, in addition to political and economic problems, problems of drought and irrigation, problems of ignorance and education, there is also the great burden of alcoholism. Count Witte has recently said that intemperance is the greatest evil from which the country suffers. The Imperial treasury draws a large part of its revenue from the monopoly of alcohol. The income derived from its sale is $368,000,000. Of this sum $1,250,000 is paid out as a grant to various temperance societies to be used in the fight against alcohol. Maxim Kovalevsky, a member of the Council of the Russian Empire, somewhat satirically compares the sum appropriated by the Government to combat alcoholism with that which it derives from the sale of the article it is professedly trying to discourage. Complaint is made that the temperance societies fritter away their money in cheap shows and entertainments. Some of the Council of Bishops have urged that this work be committed to the Church, and point to the fact that in one district, largely made up of working men, eighty thousand had been induced by the Church to sign the pledge, and a million pamphlets against alcoholism had been published at the expense of the Church. The Russian Church is not very active in social reform, and the lower Russian clergy are not shining examples of temperance; and we can hardly expect to see in Russia the Church taking the part in the agitation against alcohol which has been taken by the Baptist and Methodist Churches in our southern states. Kovalevsky pins his faith to political restriction, and reproaches the Government with not knowing that American states had been bold enough to renounce the revenues received from alcohol, and that great independent organizations, without grants from the state, are working for the suppression of intemperance.

In Germany the total abstinence movement was long a subject of ridicule. It has gradually gained strength. Several societies are now working in this particular field, numbering some sixty thousand members, and an organization of moderate drinkers has twenty-seven thousand members. Little has been done in the way of legal restriction. The only thing important in this nature is Section 33 of the *Gewerbeordnung*, which makes the granting of a license dependent upon the proof that there is a necessity for a licensed house. The license may be granted for spirits or simply for beer or wine. The present license law is very unsatisfactory to the temperance leaders. A prominent jurist, Dr. Hermann M. Poppert, a judge in Hamburg, has written a monograph on the subject of local option. It appeals largely to experience in the United States. As the alcoholic liquor trade represents a great organization of capital, attempts will be made to secure the help of the Socialistic movement in this field, and also of the woman suffrage movement, which is more likely to succeed through local option. The present program is to secure a much stricter observance of the existing laws by bringing pressure to bear upon the boards which have the power to grant licenses, and by developing local and social interests to lead the way to local option.

In Roumania the Parliament has recently voted, under the action of a Liberal government, a law concerning the monopoly of village saloons.

In southern France I was struck, last fall, with the contrast presented to conditions in Russia. In both countries there was economic disturbance. In Russia thousands of peasants had been on the verge of starvation by reason of famine; in France the wine-growers were suffering from the excessive bounty of the soil. The crop was so vast that it could not be sold. In Perpignan, one dealer, despairing of selling his wine, concluded to give it away, and placed a large cask on the street with a cup for anybody who came along. Admiring the abundant growth of a vineyard, I said to a peasant woman, "What a beautiful crop!" "Ah!" she said with a sad face, "if rain comes now, the crop will be simply frightful!"

Little intemperance in France can be traced to the use of wine in the home. There, as elsewhere, the danger from alcoholism comes from the saloon and from the drinking of absinthe. A law of 1878 was passed to repress open drunkenness and forbid the sale of alcohol to children under sixteen years of age. A petition lately sent to Parliament for a law forbidding the manufacture and sale of absinthe was signed by three hundred thousand people. A commission was appointed to consider the subject, but thus far without much result. Anti-alcoholic teaching has been introduced in the schools. The Minister of War has forbidden the use of distilled drinks inside the barracks, and has asked the officers to hold lectures on the subject of temperance. A prominent French advocate of total abstinence said to me, "The French army is becoming a school of moderation, if not a school of abstinence."

The French temperance leaders are agitating now to prohibit the manufacture and sale of absinthe, for a law limiting the number of public houses, for the confinement of inveterate drunkards in special asylums and for local option as to license or prohibition.

The method of regulation in the British colonies follows more closely the prevailing method and tendency in the United States than those of the mother country. The passage of the Scott Act in the Dominion of Canada, in 1878, marked an epoch in the history of liquor legislation in that country. It gave to cities and counties the right of local option. The Province of Quebec adopted local option in 1899, and the writer, by a summer residence of thirty years in this province, has noted the gradual development of prohibition sentiment. In Nova Scotia, sixteen out of eighteen counties have local option. In New Brunswick, all but five counties; Prince Edward Island has it in its whole extent; it has made much progress in Manitoba. Temperance sentiment is marked in Ontario. Toronto is a shining example of the effect of public sentiment in reducing the evils of a lax license system. In 1874, with a population of 60,000, it had 530 licenses. In 1907, with 260,000 population, it had but 207.

In New South Wales local option has been in operation since 1882; Victoria adopted it in 1876; New Zealand in 1881, permitting each electoral district to decide the question by a three-fifths vote. Canada shows the smallest per capita consumption of absolute alcohol in the English-speaking world, and New Zealand comes next.

Thus it will be seen from the array of facts here presented, covering Great Britain, the continent of Europe, the United States, Canada, and Australia, that this many-phased problem of liquor regulation is not a local question but a world-wide movement. Local phases may intensify the agitation, but they have not caused it. The whole problem is related to newer and higher ideals of modern civilization, to new standards of personal conduct and of social control, to higher demands of efficiency; it is affected by strong moral and religious impulses and by a determination to attack at their root the diseases and evils of civic and social life.

CHAPTER XVII.

THE TEMPERANCE TIDAL WAVE.

By Samuel J. Barrows, *President of the International Prison Commission*.

Reprinted by permission from *The Outlook*, July 11, 1908.

PART II.

WHEN a flock of curlews fly from Nova Scotia to South America, twenty-five hundred miles in a straight line without a stop, in less than three days, it is a remarkable example of a swift physical transition. The birds were not blown there by a gale of wind; they did not get there by accident. They set out for South America, and every bird got there on his own wings.

Swift transitions in public sentiment are sometimes puzzling because unexpected; but when we analyze them, they come within the accepted laws of cause and effect. They are usually the result of definiteness of aim and a great deal of personal exertion. When the news came to the North that several states in the South had voted for state prohibition, it came to many as a great surprise, especially to people who regarded prohibition as a dead political issue. Some thought it a social spasm, a magnetic brainstorm at the South, and all sorts of guesses were made as to the thing that brought it about. But to those familiar with the history of temperance legislation in that section of the country there is no mystery about it. The manifestation in the South is not the result of any sudden or unaccountable transition of public opinion; it is not due to any hidden causes; they are easily visible when we seek them. It is not the result of an earthquake, nor the eruption of a volcano; it is a ripening process like the blooming of a rose.

Georgia did not have to wait till 1907 to find out that an African negro filled with New England rum is not conducive to social peace or industrial energy; it learned it in 1733. That benevolent penologist, General Oglethorpe, when he founded the colony, got the trustees to prohibit the importation of both the rum and the negro. Fifty years ago in Georgia, as in Maine, state prohibition was a live political issue, and the seed of temperance education was early sown in that fertile state. The fact is that many people at the North have been altogether ignorant of the moral forces which have been working at the South for social renovation. As

W. M. GRAFTON,
Superintendent, Anti-Saloon League of South Dakota.

REV. LOUIS S. FULLER,
Superintendent, Anti-Saloon League of Wyoming, Utah and Montana.

has been shown, however, in a previous article, the movement for social regulation of the liquor traffic is not local or ephemeral; it is felt over the length and breadth of this continent, and even in Europe and Australia.

What are some of the forces and influences which have brought it about? They are personal, organic, educative, industrial, political and moral. So far as our own country is concerned, it is not difficult to trace them.

In December of 1873, the writer was summoned as a journalist to study a temperance crusade, as unique and curious as any of the medieval crusades to capture Jerusalem. It was a crusade of women, and its weapon was prayer. It is odd enough that an *entr'acte* from an opera by Jean Jacques Rousseau should have become a prayer meeting melody in the United States, though unknown in religious worship in France; but it is not more odd than that Dr. Dio Lewis, of Boston, mainly known for his light gymnastics and Turkish baths, should have started a prayer crusade. Nobody knew just what was Dr. Lewis's view of the philosophy of prayer. He was generally thought to be a skeptic; and at Worcester, Massachusetts, in a public meeting some rash ministers tried to corner him with questions as if he were a young theological student at an ordination, but with a superb gesture he adroitly waved them aside, and in a gale of eloquence carried the audience before him as he told how he had received the benediction of a devout and praying mother. Apparently, Dr. Lewis took the modern pragmatist view, that anything is a good weapon that achieves results.

Under his effective inspiration Mrs. Eliza J. Thompson, of Hillsboro, Ohio, started the crusade. The new method was for a band of women to go to the saloon and ask the privilege of praying. If they were not admitted inside, they prayed on the sidewalk. The saloonkeepers, if not converted, were dazed, benumbed; their customers fled. In fifty days the prayer crusade had shut up saloons in two hundred and fifty towns and villages of Ohio. The movement swept to other states. Its failure in Massachusetts was general, not absolute; one victory is recorded. So great was the crowd of curious observers in one saloon at Worcester that the writer of this article took refuge behind the bar. He was solemnly approached by one of the women and begged not to sell any more intoxicating liquor. "I promise you," he said, "that I will never sell whisky again in my life," and the promise has been faithfully kept. As for the real barkeeper, he had made good his escape.

The novelty of the movement, which must not be confounded with that of Mrs. Carry A. Nation and her hatchet many years later, soon passed away. The evil spirits banished from Ohio soon came back, with an even larger percentage of alcohol to the gallon. But in the crusade there was a germ of a wider and greater movement, and in less than a year later, in November, 1874, in Cleveland, Ohio, the National Woman's Christian Temperance Union was organized. It was incorporated in Washington in 1883. It has now 300,000 members in the United States, and is organized in every state and territory in the Union, the District of Columbia and Hawaii.

The State of Illinois chose for one of its two statues to commemorate its greatest citizens in Statuary Hall at the Capitol in Washington the figure of a representative American woman. In the circle of statesmen and soldiers which form an imposing group in that hall the prophetic statue of Frances E. Willard commemorates not only a great personality but the vast organization to which she gave an international impulse. Seated some years ago with her and with Lady Henry Somerset around a tea-table in the home of the latter in London, the writer heard of the plans of these two women to organize the Woman's Christian Temperance Union around the world. Since that time seven international conventions have been held, and there are half a million members in fifty nations.

It is in the United States, however, that the organization has been most effective. Its machinery is simple, well-oiled and coördinated. It can reach by the next mail, if necessary, every legislator in every State in the Union. It is a remarkable illustration of the power of women to organize for moral results. The sphere of its work has broadened into thirty-nine departments. It is agitating for an eight-hour day, for peace through arbitration, the rescue of outcast women, to establish juvenile courts and industrial education, and to promote social purity; but its work for constitutional prohibition and total abstinence for the individual is that for which it is most widely known. Untiring perseverance in prayer and work, a faith which no obstacles can daunt, and a ceaseless persistency in hammering away at an objective point, are characteristics of this organized movement. "Men may get tired and stop," said a political leader to me, "but these women never get tired and never stop, and it is they who did most of the work in our State."

Whenever an election is to be held for local option or for state prohibition, it is the Woman's Christian Temperance Union that forms processions of boys and girls to sing, carry banners, and make personal appeals for temperance. A Congressional Representative from Alabama said that the sight of these children in Birmingham, many of them from the families of drunkards, bearing a banner inscribed, "Please, sir, vote for *us*," "Please, sir, give *us* a chance," was one of the most dramatic and effective weapons in the campaign. Some voters saw the procession with wet eyes, and then went and voted "dry" at the polls.

Systematic and semi-scientific teaching enforced by moral and relig-

ious precept and example, organized and stimulated in the schools throughout the country by the Woman's Christian Temperance Union, together with its Loyal Temperance Legions and Bands of Hope, has been going on for thirty-four years, and the result of this education has been telling in the boys and girls who have since grown to manhood and womanhood. This is one reason of the silent, steady growth of temperance sentiment.

But this organization of women has one limitation. Its members can incite others to vote, but, in the great majority of States, cannot vote themselves. Some organized movement of male voters the country over was necessary to give political effect to these women's petitions to God and man. The organization came when it was needed, and its cradle was the Piedmont Congregational Church, of Worcester, Massachusetts, of which the Rev. D. O. Mears, D. D., was pastor. It was born in 1887, and christened the No-License League. Within three weeks after the League was started in this church there were twenty-five church leagues in the city, and then from this church movement a city league was started. It did not so much create as express a new conviction that the fight for law and order could not be made alone on the lines of the total abstinence movement. It determined to strike at the saloon, the strongest and at the same time the most objectionable intrenchment of the liquor traffic. When a similar movement was formed in Ohio in 1893, Dr. Mears became president of the State organization and suggested the effective name of the Anti-Saloon League. The Rev. Howard H. Russell, D. D., also a Congregationalist clergyman, took hold of the movement about this time, and a National organization was the logical and effective result. It is not tied to the skirts of any political party or religious denomination. The 100,-000 members of the Catholic Total Abstinence Union work with and indorse the Anti-Saloon League, as do the Woman's Christian Temperance Union and the National Temperance Society. Archbishop Ireland and Bishop Watterson, of Columbus, have actively supported its efforts, and help from Jewish leaders has not been wanting. In no moral movement of the country are the organized religious forces so well united as in that of temperance.

The Anti-Saloon League is not, therefore, a single organization, but a league of organizations. It is directed not against the individual but against the saloon; it stands for the largest repression of the liquor traffic. It is opposed to the license system. It is not a political party, but it uses parties to effect its ends. It stands by the men who stand by it. Alert, active, practical, the League cannot always get what it wants, but it gets the best it can.

The growth of the organization has been phenomenal. It has stirred up and united the churches, but, what is more serious to the liquor dealer, it has in many States united the voters under this one issue. While venality in politics has been the discouraging feature in popular suffrage, the Anti-Saloon League has, without spending a dollar for votes, kindled fires of moral conviction which have burned out the saloon even in places where the ballot had been most corrupted. Liquor dealers are beginning to see that the insurance they most need is not against fire, but against the antisaloon forces. For a long time the saloon has been the stronghold of politics, and a good deal of dirty, mean, despicable politics at that. The saloon could not be taken out of politics, but in the South a great deal of politics has been taken out of the saloon, and we have now the politics of the church, the prayer-meeting and the home, and doubtless some "Sunday-school politics" mixed with it. Agitation, legislation and law enforcement is the plan of the Anti-Saloon League.

Still a third great army corps in the organized war on the saloon is made up of the forces of the Christian churches in the South. The reproach so often made against the Church, that it has fixed its eyes too much on a heaven beyond, and is not interested in social salvation, applies less today than formerly to the churches in the South. If Gladstone, John Burns, Carroll D. Wright and the United States Supreme Court have not made a mistake in diagnosis, intemperance is the gravest of all social maladies, and in striking at it the Southern churches are going to the very root of social disorder. Fortunately, they have not been converted to the inverted logic of some of our social philosophers who write their socialistic pellets in capital letters to prove that poverty is the main cause of intemperance.

Alcohol is essentially a product of civilization. Savage tribes have not the machinery, mechanical or commercial, to make and distribute it. Where alcoholism exists in savage communities, civilized man has sent it there. Whether among the Indians in the West, the negroes in the South, or the blacks on the Congo, it is "civilized" rum that is working its ravages. The liquor traffic requires vast machinery for its production and distribution; it employs a great army of men backed up by enormous sums of money. It has taken the advantage of the principle of association in modern life. Against such a mighty organization individuals are as powerless as a straw in the stream. This is not a conflict that can be settled by a duel between David and Goliath, or Alexander and Menelaus. The opposing armies, of Israel and the Philistines, of the Greeks and the Trojans, must settle this in the open field. Millions of men and women and millions of dollars are involved in this fight. The saloon has become the symbol of intemperance, and the church, and the school and the home are set over against it. Politics is the field, ballots the weapons and legislation the objective point in this great fight. Every argument, personal, domestic, racial, economical, moral or religious, that can be brought to bear has been summoned in the conflict.

As to the way the battle is going, it is significant that North Carolina has wheeled into the prohibition column; that the liquor dealers most frankly admit that they have been outstripped in strategy and in effective organization by their opponents; and that official information communicated to the writer from the Treasury Department shows that the revenue of the United States Government for spirits of all characters for the ten months of the fiscal year ending April 30, 1908, have fallen off $11,727,286.94.

No writer going through the Southern states to study present conditions can see in true perspective this great social movement in its historic relations. Personal observation needs to be supplemented, not by random opinion, but by the thoughtful and intelligent testimony of witnesses who have watched the development of social forces for the last twenty or thirty years. The writer has been at some pains to obtain reliable data in the South. It is an exception to find a Southern Congressman who does not know his own district. He is obliged to be a close observer of forces and results. Requests for information were sent to some fifty-three Southern Congressmen, most of whom had the kindness to respond. They were asked to name judges, mayors, chiefs of police, sheriffs and other citizens whose knowledge on this question would be authoritative. One hundred and twelve persons were thus named by the Congressmen. To this qualified jury the following questions were presented:

1. What influences, moral, political, social or economic, led to the passage of the present law?

2. How has this law been carried out?

3. What has been the effect on order in the community?

4. Is it possible to say which form of regulation—state prohibition, local option or the dispensary—has been the most effective?

Responses to these questions have been prompt and numerous, giving highly interesting testimony, showing a first hand knowledge of causes and presenting reliable data as to results. In addition, the local press of the South has been well gleaned for fact and comment. Finally, pains have been taken to get a view of the situation, both local and general, from the standpoint of the brewer, the distiller and the liquor dealer.

I regret that limits of space will not permit me to give more than the briefest review of this interesting testimony.

In Georgia, it is noteworthy that not a single one of the witnesses finds in the Atlanta riot or any spectacular episodes in the campaign the real cause of prohibition sentiment. An able judge of Greene county says: "The real, though remote, cause of the existence of prohibition laws in Georgia is the persistent attitude and teaching of the women for the past thirty years that alcohol is neither necessary nor desirable, and that drunkenness is disgraceful. This sentiment has reversed the ideas of social drinking. Local option laws were passed, and nearly the entire state became dry under them. The shipment of liquors from wet cities into the dry counties persistently was the immediate cause of the exchange of local option for general prohibition. The Woman's Christian Temperance Union and the Church were the organized factors, and in later years the Anti-Saloon League."

Local option was the stepping-stone to prohibition. It was only by a narrow margin that the local option law was passed by the legislature in 1885; but when the legislature met last year and the fight on prohibition was precipitated, only twenty out of one hundred and forty-five counties remained wet. The Atlanta riot furnished an effective weapon for the prohibitionists, and helped to drive the state, already exasperated by the atrocities of the saloon, to the enactment of the most drastic prohibition law of any state.

"Our prohibition law," says a competent witness, "is being more effectively enforced than any other law against a great and general vice." Opponents of the law point to many violations from the secret shipment of liquor into the state, but another observer says, "The consumption of alcoholics now is about as jugs compared to barrels formerly."

As to the effect on law and order, the court records furnish indubitable proof. In Brunswick, after three months' experience, there was a reduction of between 60 and 75 per cent. in the number of cases of disorderly conduct. The Mayor of that city says: "The effect on order in the community has been surprising. The decrease in crime since the passage of the act has been at least 80 per cent."

The Hon. Seaborn Wright, one of the prominent leaders in passing the law, informs me that in Commerce, Georgia, in the first two months after the adoption of the law, the cases in the municipal court fell off 75 per cent. In Macon in the first three months of 1907, under barrooms, there were 322 cases of plain drunks in the Recorder's court; in the same period in 1908 there were only 34. In Athens, in the month of January, 1907, there were 106 cases in the Police court, 50 of them drunks; in the same month in 1908 there were but 29 cases, and but 5 of them drunks.

The Clerk of the Court of Record of Atlanta finds the closing of the saloons a great benefit to the poor whites and the negroes. He sends a copy of the police court records, which show that the court is doing fifty per cent. less business this year than last year. The record of arrests shows the same falling off of about one-half. In spite of the fact that

REV. D. M. GANDIER,
Assistant Superintendent Anti-Saloon
League of California.

REV. I. B. BRISTOL,
Superintendent Fresno District Anti-Saloon
League of California.

DR. W. M. BURKE,
Superintendent Oakland District Anti-
Saloon League of California.

the police are much more strict now in making arrests, but one-fourth as many are arrested for drunkenness and disorderly conduct.

As to the dispensary, Athens, Georgia, was the first city to introduce it. Several other counties established it, and then it was adopted in South Carolina. But it is significant that few dispensaries remained in Georgia when the prohibition law was passed. Dawson county, in which for years the dispensary had paid every expense of the county, so that no county tax was levied, voted it out. Clarke county, operating one of the most flourishing dispensaries in the state, did likewise. The Athens dispensary sold $300,000 a year, and realized in 1907 $55,000 net profit. But the citizens are gladly meeting the deficiency by an increase of one-fourth of one per cent. in tax.

At the meeting of the Georgia State Sociological Society at Atlanta in May, Judge Broyle, of the Recorder's court, showed that under prohibition there had been a decrease of 2,917 cases in the docket of the Police court in four months, as compared with the previous year, and a decrease of 1,484 cases in the number of "drunks." Judge Broyle therefore concludes officially that prohibition does prohibit. He pointed out, however, what he regarded as one serious defect in the prohibition law, and that is the failure to state the exact amount of alcohol in a beverage that will outlaw it. "Under a recent decision of the Georgia Court of Appeals this failure to state the amount of alcohol allows almost any kind of a malt beverage containing two or three per cent. or even more of alcohol to be sold without violating the law, and these beverages can be sold not only to adults but to minors." This opportunity to make "near beer" has been seized upon by the Georgia brewers, some of whom claim to be doing a better business than before. If this be a fact, why should not the brewers be content with the situation? The Savannah Chamber of Commerce, however, is discontented enough to lead a reactionary movement in favor of relaxing the law. On the other hand, in the great fight for the governorship between Governor Hoke Smith and Joseph Brown, his opponent, both men were committed to prohibition and to the strengthening of the present law rather than its relaxation. Has not the time come for the vendors of a much-advertised brand of champagne to transfer their label "extra dry" to the map of Georgia?

In Alabama, sentiment has long been making against the saloon system, and a number of rural counties have had prohibition for years. Some counties established the dispensary system a few years ago, so that the actual saloon area left was but about one-third of the counties of the state when the Anti-Saloon League was organized there about two years ago. The local option law was passed, and the unit of the election necessary to accept it was placed at the county, not the beat or precinct or city. The fire of enthusiasm kindled by this campaign burned further than was expected. The county local option law was all that was adopted by the legislature at its regular session last year and all that was attempted; but when a special session was called by Governor Comer in November, 1907, on the relation of the railways to the state, an opportunity was seized to press state-wide prohibition, and there was no difficulty in getting the two-thirds vote required. This state law does not go into effect in those counties where elections have not been held until January 1, 1909; the results observed are based on the county local option law. Reports are uniform that there is less drunkenness and less crime. "In many counties the jails are practically empty. In several cities the police force has been reduced. The negro croons most pathetically, with strange intonation, 'Old Booze is dead.'"

The Chief of Police of Birmingham reports a decrease in crime and improvement in public order. The State Superintendent of the Anti-Saloon League estimates that general crime has been reduced more than 60 per cent. and drunkenness 85 per cent. The judge of the Criminal Court of Gadsden says the influence which led to the passage of the law was "good women and bad whisky."

Especially interesting from Alabama is the testimony of avowed prohibitionists as to the efficiency of the dispensary. The Rev. Samuel E. Wasson, of Huntsville, says: "The dispensary is an improvement over the saloon. I have seen the operation of both on the same people. I say, without hesitation, that there is not a single exception in the police records of Alabama where the dispensary has followed the saloon that it has not reduced public drunkenness and disorder from 25 to 75 per cent. It also increases the public revenues phenomenally. Where one saloon paid a license of $1,000 annually, the dispensary will pay into the public treasury approximately $10,000 a year, and at the same time improve the public morals at least fifty per cent.; but it has its evils and is by no means the final solution of the liquor question. I am first for prohibition and then for the dispensary." There is other testimony to the same effect, but another observer adds: "The corruption of the dispensary has destroyed it in this Southland." The Hon. Frank S. Moody, President of the First National Bank, Tuscaloosa, Alabama, says: "About 1898, the dispensary was introduced in the state, and spread into twenty or twenty-five counties. A dispensary was in operation in Tuscaloosa four or five years. The old topers drank less and there was practically no making of new topers. Crime due to drunkenness almost ceased in this county. It may be doubted whether a sudden and extreme prohibition law is, all things considered, as good a way of handling the problem as a well-regulated dispensary system. I do not undertake to speak positively about the matter.

It may be that prohibition is best in the rural districts and the dispensary is best in the larger towns and cities."

The Rev. Francis Tappey, minister of the First Presbyterian Church of Huntsville, while maintaining that the dispensary is better than the open saloon, reports that there is less crime in the prohibition counties.

Of all the Southern states, Tennessee furnishes the most interesting illustration of the gradual development of public opinion through local option. Away up in the mountains is Sewanee University. Thirty years ago it felt the need of some protection against the liquor traffic, and in 1877 the so-called "four-mile law" was passed, making it unlawful to sell liquors within four miles of an incorporated institution of learning. It was afterwards applied to all schools in incorporated towns of less than two thousand inhabitants. Liquor was driven from the rural districts to the larger towns. The limit of population was gradually raised so that all towns in the state might surrender their charters and incorporate under the restrictive features of the law. All but Memphis, Nashville, Chattanooga, and a small mining town named La Follette have done so. Thus, legislation in Tennessee has slowly and steadily followed the march of public sentiment. The testimony of judges, police captains, and mayors supports that of Congressmen Padgett, Garrett and Houston that the legislation has been carried out and the effect on law and order is good. Detailed comparison of the criminal court costs in dry and wet counties makes a striking showing in favor of the dry counties. The cost to the wet counties is 12 9-10 cents per capita, and to the dry counties 5 8-10 cents per capita.

Tennessee from the beginning has fought the saloon with the schoolhouse. As a result of prohibition in Knoxville, every public school teacher has had a raise of salary and the school budget has been raised from $63,000 to $106,000. The salaries of policemen and firemen have also been increased. As to the relation of the negroes to the temperance issue in Tennessee, Dr. Edward E. Folk, editor of the *Baptist and Reflector,* of Nashville, says: "As a matter of fact, the effect of strong drink upon the negroes has played a comparatively small part in the passage of these laws. The effect of strong drink upon the white man is just as great as it is upon the negro and even greater: it makes a bigger fool of him. Perhaps the strongest temperance section of our State is East Tennessee, where there are very few negroes. This section gave a majority of 15,000 for the prohibition amendment in 1887."

As to Oklahoma it is too soon to speak of positive results. But the Sheriff of Oklahoma County, in which is situated the stirring metropolis of the State, declares that sixty per cent. of the crime brought about by liquor has ceased. When the writer was in that State in January, public order was good, but the heat of the liquor agitation had not ceased. Although there is constitutional prohibition, the use of spirits and beer is recognized for medical and scientific purposes, and the new Billups law provides for a State agency for the sale, under severe restrictions, of liquor in small packages.

The most thorough study of the relation of the liquor traffic to pauperism, crime and insanity that has been made in any single state was made in Massachusetts and presented in the report of the Bureau of Labor Statistics for 1895 under Mr. Horace G. Wadlin. An examination of the record of arrests and commitments for crimes and offenses in all the towns of the State during the year showed that no thermometer could respond more quickly to changes of temperature than did the record of crime respond to the reduction of the number of the saloons, and the record was always in favor of the no-license towns.

Similar testimony is furnished as to the value of restriction in England. Lord Airedale, in advocating the pending Licensing Bill, said: "As an employer of some fifty years' standing, I can testify to the great improvement in the bearing and the character of the working people with whom I have been closely associated. I attribute some of it to education, but much of it in later years is due to restriction in the hours of opening and to the greater control in matters of licensing."

John Burns said to an audience of workingmen in London: "I believe that the best and most simple remedy for drink is abstinence, but this must be supplemented by local or legislative action. One drink-cursed district, Liverpool, has, since 1889, added 78,000 to its population, reduced its police drunkenness cases from 16,000 to 4,180, its crimes from 926 to 552 per 100,000, its policemen by 100, at a saving of £8,000 to the rates, by the simple remedy of having got rid of 345 licensed places in eleven years."

To my mind, some things are well established by a study of the present great movement for the regulation of the liquor traffic:

1. The sources of the movement are easily discernible. It is not due to local or ephemeral causes; it springs from a public conviction which the United States Supreme Court has well rendered; namely, that "the public health, the public morals and the public safety are endangered by the general use of intoxicating liquors," and that "the idleness, disorder, pauperism and crime existing in this country are largely traceable to this evil."

2. A second public conviction is that expressed by the Supreme Court of Kansas, that "probably no greater source of crime and sorrow has ever existed than social drinking saloons." In addition the saloon has been the polluted sink of gambling, licentiousness and corrupt politics.

3. Educative forces have been working for the last forty or fifty

MRS. MARGARET B. PLATT,
President, West Washington W. C. T. U.

MRS. MARGARET C. MUNNS,
Corresponding Secretary, West Washington W. C. T. U.

years. A new generation has grown up, and found that alcoholic drinks are not necessary for health or happiness.

4. In the movement of the regulation of the liquor traffic in the United States the Woman's Christian Temperance Union, the Anti-Saloon League and the federation of Christian churches have been great factors.

5. Local option has proved to be the most effective legislative or elective measure. State-wide prohibition is a dangerous experiment until the way for it has been paved by local option. Restrictive laws can only be enforced when public sentiment has created them.

6. When public sentiment demands it, liquor laws can be enforced as well as any other laws.

7. A reduction in the liquor traffic is promptly followed by a reduction in crime and by greater social order and tranquillity.

8. The economic results are seen in new evidences of personal and civic thrift.

9. Finally, if I am asked if this movement has come to stay, I may close by quoting the opinion of an interested observer, a prominent leader of the distillers and brewers of this country, the editor of *Bonfort's Wine and Spirit Circular*: "Modern civilization is groping, but it is reaching upward, and it has decreed after a fashion that slums and hopeless poverty and crime due to want and drunkenness shall give way before the doctrine of the brotherhood of man, and that those things and those resorts which degrade must have no place in the civilization towards which the leaders of thought are now aiming."

CHAPTER XVIII.

THE GREATEST PROBLEM SINCE SLAVERY.

By Carrington A. Phelps.

Reprinted by permission from Hampton's *New Broadway Magazine*, New York, July, 1908.

NOTE.—*From time to time you have heard about the great Temperance Movement sweeping over this country. Magazines and newspapers have told the story in parts, presenting a hazy if not confusing picture of the mighty crusade. This article gives for the first time all the tremendous facts of the case in panoramic detail. It tells just who and what are back of the movement; just how a man named Howard H. Russell and his powerful Anti-Saloon League are working, and how a vast army of zealous crusaders are locked in conflict with brewery and distilling interests representing nearly four billions of dollars.*—EDITOR NEW BROADWAY MAGAZINE.

ONE day a little boy heaved a brick. It smashed through the window of a Georgia "white trash" rum-hole. The little boy ran away, the drunken white trash poured out the doors, saw a negro, chased him and—presently Atlanta beheld herself in the throes of "Riot Week." A great red ray of wrath and terror shot across the South. The Negro Question was on every tongue. Various causes were held responsible for the situation. Some declared the outrages upon women were prompting it, others cried, "cocaine," and "racial prejudice." The Anti-Saloon League stepped forward: "Gentlemen," it said, "you are all wrong! The whole trouble is—*whisky!*"

The psychological moment had arrived. The Anti-Saloon League seized the opportunity and swept victoriously over the Southern states.

These Southern victories have been so spectacular that, added to others in various sections of the country, they have brought the anti-saloon movement vividly to the front as a national factor of tremendous importance. For fifteen years the anti-saloon avalanche has been gathering velocity and strength, until today townships and counties are going "dry" by hundreds, perforating their state maps with temperance territory faster than the printers can tabulate them.

Ohio, birthplace of the Anti-Saloon League, and scene of the hardest, oldest fight of all, is winning a rapid-fire victory. This year she wiped out 300 "speak-easies," and passed a county local option law. South Carolina repealed her State Dispensary law this year, and is campaigning with the expectation of reaching prohibition in two years. Of North Carolina's 97 counties 70 are dry, and it is expected the state will go dry within a year.*

Louisiana is another two year contestant. More than two-thirds of her territory and 65 per cent. of her population is dry—two items that may well serve to irritate New Orleans' two thousand saloonkeepers.

Behold Kentucky, the traditional cradle of all good whisky! In less than two years the liquor traffic has been practically obliterated, and yet this state has $160,000,000 invested in distilleries. Only four counties are wholly wet at this writing, and the Jailers' State Association has petitioned the legislature for regular salaries *because under prohibition conditions the empty jails do not bring them fees enough to live on.*

Arkansas is hammering saloons right and left with her "inhabitants" law, by which a majority of the inhabitants, including all women over eighteen years of age, may force a saloon to move four miles from church or schoolhouse. *If there isn't a schoolhouse they build one—and consequently the saloon has to move!* Woman's suffrage scores a point here. To date 58 out of 75 counties are dry in Arkansas, and more are toppling.

Texas, popularly known as the land of lariats and six-shooters, declares with characteristic brevity, "Don't want liquor." She fights quick and sure, and already three-fifths of her counties are dry. Missouri is another lightning change state. Back in 1905, she had only three dry counties. It has been give-and-take, but since then more than half the state has gone dry, and every month sees more spoils brought into the anti-saloon camp.

Virginia, another liquor stronghold, refused licenses to nearly fifty distilleries this year. Three-fourths of her counties are dry, and half the saloons in the state have foundered. The "blind-tigers," too, are doomed under the drastic law just passed. There are here and there places in Tennessee where liquor can be legally sold. It is only a short time before prohibition may be expected.

Indiana is already counting her votes for the anticipated prohibition victory. Two-thirds of her territory is dry, and four miles of saloons are today vacant.

Half of Delaware went dry last November after one of the hottest fights the state had ever known. Liquor interests all over the country

---

*North Carolina has since expelled the saloon by a plebiscite majority of 40,000. —G. M. H.

joined forces in the determination to stop the threatened avalanche, principally for the sake of the tremendous moral effect. They organized, poured a huge and steady stream of money into Delaware politics; fought, bled and came out badly mauled. Everybody is mad now, and the little state is in the fight with its coat off and no time limit.

Vermont has only thirty wet townships out of 238, and she has just closed up over 500 saloons. The state majority is for prohibition, and the next legislature will see things buzz faster than a Kansas cyclone.

Half the towns and cities in Illinois have voted out the saloon. This year's vote closed 1,800 more liquor shops. Of the 1,200 elections held in the state 900 were prohibition victories. Half the area of Chicago, the whisky center of the world, is dry by special legislation. Peoria, which distils as much whisky as any other town in existence, has sent an Anti-Saloon League man to the legislature.

An active fight is on in Massachusetts, 76 per cent. of whose territory is prohibition territory. Illuminative of the power of the Anti-Saloon League in this state is the fact that, of forty legislators whom the League supported, thirty-eight were elected.

In Nebraska, 450 out of 1,000 towns and cities have voted against liquor, and a hard campaign is now on to carry the other half.

New York is the hard nut to crack, and it is here that the final battle will be fought out. The liquor interest in this state is a formidable antagonist with its 35 distilleries, 243 breweries, 30,000 saloons and its consequent political organization and power. Yet out of 933 New York townships the anti-saloonists have made 324 dry.

In the fifteen years of the Anti-Saloon League's activities more than one-half the area of the United States has gone dry; that is, *every minute more than* 150 *acres of United States territory goes prohibition!*

The history of temperance reforms has been one of ups and downs; it has been consistent only in failure; waves of emotionalism have brought about prohibition for a time, but after the excitement had died away the zeal of the reformers has abated, and soon the liquor people have found themselves doing business again, their position apparently the stronger because of this reaction.

Many a grandparent of today remembers the Drunken Period of American history that began after the Revolution and continued for two generations. Everybody drank. The annual consumption of malt and alcoholic liquors was fifty quarts to the family, or about double what it is now.

In 1808, a New Yorker named Clark (Billy James Clark, M. D.) persuaded some forty friends to eschew liquor and confine their attentions to beer alone. Thus was formed the first known temperance society.

MRS. JOHN P. COFFIN,
State Editor for the W. C. T. U., Florida.

HON. JOHN P. COFFIN,
Member, National Committee, Prohibition Party, Florida;
Chairman, Florida Prohibition State Committee.

Sixteen years later Lyman Beecher, father of the famous Henry Ward Beecher, took an aggressive stand against the manifest evil and, after seven years of discouragement, ridicule and fight, forced Congress to place certain restrictions on the liquor traffic. One night a little Baltimore drinking club composed of two blacksmiths, a carpenter and a coachmaker, attended a temperance lecture for amusement. They were converted and at once started touring the country, speaking for temperance. This was the beginning of the "Washingtonians," a movement which soon led to a revolt of 600,000 drunkards.

John B. Gough, a reformed drunkard, was the next leader. Starting in 1844, he was for forty-three years, in this country and Europe, the eloquent voice of the anti-liquor movement. No other man has ever done as much to silence opposition and prepare public sentiment for the educative and legislative work which has followed since his day.

In 1844, five million souls in the United States and Ireland put their names to the pledge under the magnetic exhortations of Father Mathew, an Irish priest, who had been induced to join the temperance workers by a Quaker.

Neal Dow, the fighting Quaker of Portland, Me., was the first to strike at the very root of the liquor evil. Dow preached prohibition first, last and always. In 1846, he began his campaign. He was beaten half a dozen times, but finally forced the state into the position she has never relinquished. A general temperance movement was about to start when the Civil War broke out. After the war the liquor business boomed, for heavy drinking had become the rule again.

Among those who heartily deprecated the liquor evil was President Lincoln. At one time in his youth he had been an active temperance worker, and men are living today who were induced to sign the pledge by Abraham Lincoln's convincing arguments. That he thoroughly appreciated the menace of liquor evils is evidenced by his declaration on the very day of his tragic death that "the next snarl we have got to straighten out is the liquor question."

One morning, three days before Christmas, in the black panic year of '73, the doors of the Presbyterian Church at Hillsboro, Ohio, swung open and out marched thirty women, two by two, singing. They went to drugstores and saloons and hotels; they pleaded and sang and prayed, until saloon after saloon was closed at their entreaties. It was contagion that spread throughout the land, wholly emotional, but from this "Woman's Crusade" sprang the powerful Woman's Christian Temperance Union.

For years there had been growing to womanhood in Illinois a farmer's girl, clean, wholesome and strong—Frances E. Willard. Educated by college, travel and hard work, she was destined, in moulding this great woman's movement, to become "the best beloved woman" of the Nineteenth Century in America. Under her leadership the Woman's Christian Temperance Union bound its bows of white ribbon around the earth's two hemispheres, printed its pledges in every spoken tongue, and presented to mankind the spectacle of the largest organization formed by women since the world began. One of the greatest weapons employed by the W. C. T. U. was the introduction of "Effects of Alcohol" literature into the school books. Every great movement the world has ever known has had its zealots and its pathfinders, its martyrs and its cranks. It has been the fanatic who has preached temperance to the world, but it is the cool-headed, methodical worker who is to-day accomplishing drink reform—reform that has to all appearances the elements of stability.

The anti-saloon movement has found a man and a system. It was in the office of an important brewery that I got my first flashlight view of both. The brewer was tired and hot and mad. He had been holding forth for two hours on the injustice of prohibition. Suddenly he turned and whacked his desk. "My God!" he roared, "this Anti-Saloon League don't sleep. Their people work seven days a week. It's like fighting a presidential campaign twice a year—no rest, no let up, just pound, pound, pound on us twenty-four hours out of twenty-four. We've been dumb and blind and deaf. They've already wiped us off half the map—*and we thought we knew politics!* Now we've got to learn all over again, and what's more, we've got to learn from them! This is none of your brotherly-love-Willie-hold-baby-temperance-tea-parties we're up against! *This is hell!* Everybody is watching the result—watching the single state fights, talking about Georgia, for instance. Now mark my words! All this is deeper than the surface. I don't know who he is and I don't care, but—*somewhere there is a Man Behind!*"

I agreed and—went out to seek the Man Behind. I found him.

He was sitting forward on the edge of an office chair, and he was bounded on the north by a mound of correspondence, on the south by a table with half a hundred reference books, on the east by a desk loaded to the gunwales with information, and on the west by three big maps and a stenographer. He was Howard H. Russell, founder, builder and backbone of the Anti-Saloon League of America.

Before I had talked with him two minutes I began to remember where I had before encountered that intensity of unselfish purpose, that suave but iron attitude, that swift, virile movement in action, that overwhelming concentration. I had met it in the *personnel*, the organization and the every action of the Anti-Saloon League. This man Russell has infused into the work his entire personality. Studying the man means studying the Anti-Saloon League.

But even Russell did not realize the immense potentiality of the live wire he had uncovered. He served as minister in Kansas City and Chicago for several year In 1895, he addressed the temperance forces of Oberlin, advocating a permanent state organization to fight the liquor traffic. His suggestions were met with apathy, but, characteristically undismayed, he continued an active correspondence on the subject among his friends in the little college towns. Finally, they agreed to the scheme, but only on condition that Russell take personal charge of the work. At a meeting of the Oberlin churches Russell outlined his plan. It was approved and that night was formed the Anti-Saloon League of Ohio.

This was the infinitesimal seedling from which the Anti-Saloon League grew to its present national strength. It operated in business-like fashion. Great, nation-wide conditions aided potentially in building up the system.

The first step in an Anti-Saloon League campaign is agitation. This is carried on through the churches and through the women and children, always the women and children. The state is flooded with printed matter, lecturers speak from the street corners, illustrating their arguments with stereopticon views of slum conditions, dives, liquor statistics and effects of alcohol on the physical, as distinguished even from the moral and mental man. People begin to learn; the League continues its campaign of education. Then comes the practical turn to all this community of anti-saloon interest—politics. The League slowly builds up a non-partisan, independent, powerful foe. With this vote it holds the balance of power and can, according to its strength in township, county or state, dictate absolutely to either political party its choice of candidates. Gradually it solidifies its political structure—picking up an assemblyman or state senator one at a time—making him feel that his constituency demands his vote against the saloon. Such a political machine is impregnable, automatic. Once built all it needs is watching. At election time the League votes its candidates into the legislature; compels these men not only to pass its laws but to vigorously follow up their enforcement; watches like a hawk to see that there is no relapse from ground gained.

It is commonly supposed that once a state has swung into prohibition the victory is complete. As a matter of fact, it is only the beginning of a long, tedious, discouraging fight for law enforcement. "Blind tigers," drug stores, hotels and back alley vendors begin a thriving trade in the illicit sale of liquor. Federal licenses to sell liquor are issued to hundreds who are willing to risk the state or local penalty for the illegal selling, but do not dare incur the National Government's drastic punishment. Liquor is shipped in from other states and conditions begin to grow as bad as before prohibition. The State Anti-Saloon League renews its campaign, this time calling for law enforcement. Evidence is procured and cases pushed hotly against the offenders. Legal experts trained in the work are sent into the field to conduct the fight and the struggle is soon brought to a sharp issue. Often it is impossible to get convictions on account of the indifference, incompetence or defiance of officials. These are marked down and active campaigns at once started against their reëlection. It is only a matter of time when officials are procured who will perform their duty.

The headquarters of the Anti-Saloon League is at Columbus, Ohio. The general policy of the movement is arranged by the board of trustees, composed of two men from each state. From this board is selected the national executive committee, which keeps in active touch with each state movement. This committee selects each state superintendent, who is responsible to it for all his acts. He works in conjunction with the state organization, which is managed by a board of trustees consisting of one or more men from every denomination in the state enrolling one hundred and fifty thousand or more members. From this board is selected the executive committee of seven, who carry on the actual fighting in the field. The organization of the Anti-Saloon League numbers over four hundred men who give their entire time to the work, to say nothing of the army of clerks and stenographers necessary to so business-like a system. A press bureau handles all news that is given out and supplies the press with any and all information dealing with the League or with temperance. The active workers get from one thousand to three thousand dollars a year. The expenses of the movement are half a million dollars a year, every cent of which is contributed at meetings or by subscription.

Against this movement is being formed a vast federation of all the liquor interests in America. It is expected that this federation will include the representatives of the 3,632 distilleries and breweries, the 17,111 wholesale houses and the 225,000 saloons—a business that pays an annual tax to the Federal Government of $207,124,000. The entire federation, exclusive of the hotels, represents investments *totaling three and one-half billions of dollars*. In simpler language it is worth *three thousand five hundred millionaires!*

You will, I think, agree that this is to be a struggle between organized forces, a monstrous, inconceivable death-grapple such as the world has never witnessed.

Already the liquor federation has begun its campaign. Tons of literature have been distributed among the farmers of the entire country. Low saloons and dives have been told to close up, have been put out of business by their creators, the big liquor men. All the ancient and modern methods of public-sentiment-building—oratory, lectures, advertising, editorials, etc., are being utilized to their limits.

Let me roughly estimate a part of the profits of the liquor business. According to the government internal revenue reports, taxes were paid last year on 134,031,066 gallons of distilled spirits and on 58,546,111 barrels of fermented liquors. Allow the distiller a profit of 25 cents a gallon and the brewer a profit of $1 a barrel. This gives the former a profit of $33,507,776, the brewer a profit of $55,456,111. *The two profits together amount to $92,053,877 a year!*

But this is only a beginning. The retailer pays the brewery an average price of $6 for a barrel of beer. He sells it for $18. Deducting its cost and $2 for expenses leaves him a net profit of $10 a barrel. Multiply the number of barrels by this and we *have a profit in beer for the retailer of* $585,461,110.

Now take distilled spirits, for which the retailer pays an average price of perhaps $2 a gallon. Estimating 70 drinks to the gallon and 13 cents to the drink gives a gross return of $9.10 on each gallon. Deduct the cost and 60 cents for expenses and the retailer has left $6.50 clear profit per gallon. Multiplying this by the number of gallons of spirits reported last year gives $871,201,929. Now add the wholesaler's and retailer's profits on distilled spirits and fermented liquors. The total reaches the enormous sum of $1,548,716,916.

Suppose now the liquor people spend 25 per cent. of this in the coming fight. This means the tremendous expenditure of $387,179,229 a year. But let us be generous. Let us underestimate their strength. Cut this sum squarely in two and hand it back to the liquor interests for expenses. *This leaves them a campaign fund in their fight against the Anti-Saloon League of over half a million dollars a day!*

And for these reasons the fight may last for fifty years.

CHAPTER XIX.

LIQUOR'S FIGHT AGAINST PROHIBITION.

By Carrington A. Phelps.

Reprinted by permission from Hampton's *New Broadway Magazine*, New York, August, 1908.

Note.—*Six and one half BILLIONS of wealth are involved in the mighty Temperance Movement now sweeping over this country. Five million men, women and children have a bread and butter interest in the outcome. No battle of capital against capital ever compared with this struggle of the Drink Power, backed by billions of wealth, arrayed against Will Power born of Public Sentiment.*—Editor New Broadway Magazine.

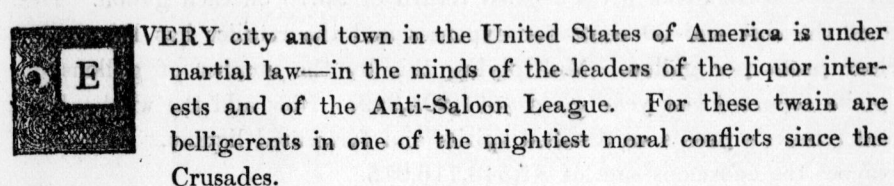

EVERY city and town in the United States of America is under martial law—in the minds of the leaders of the liquor interests and of the Anti-Saloon League. For these twain are belligerents in one of the mightiest moral conflicts since the Crusades.

I have been in the field with the Liquor Army, eye witness of the great battles it has already fought and lost. Also, I have been an observer of the organization of this Liquor Army, and have noted its methods of fighting.

The opposing forces are rallying; are, indeed, in general array from Portland to Los Angeles and from Seattle to St. Augustine. Ordering the campaign on the side of the Liquor Army are captains of industries that are backed by $6,500,000,000. The result is the most terrific war for existence ever fought by any group of businesses in the world. It is the line-up for the life or death struggle of Beer and Whisky and their allied forces—in a general attack on the armies of Prohibition, Temperance and Anti-Saloon.

The battle line of the Liquor Army is different from that which any a war correspondent has ever seen. This is no long, thin line; it is a continental gridiron. And facing this impressive array, at every point on all criss-crossed lines, stands that perfectly disciplined, cold-blooded fighting unit, the Anti-Drink Army.

Necessary to the conduct of a war is a War Department, an army, weapons and ammunition. The Liquor War Department comprises a

REV. W. B. CRUMPTON, D. D.,
President, Anti-Saloon League of Alabama.

REV. BROOKS LAWRENCE,
Superintendent, Anti-Saloon League of Alabama.

number of bureaus represented by the various organizations of brewers, distillers, wine growers and saloon men. There are two secretaries of war. The Secretary of War for Beer is Mr. Hugh Fox, of New York City. He is more actively in touch with the brewers' fight than any other man in America through his connection, as secretary, with the United States Brewers' Association, which carries a membership of more than 500 firms. The Secretary of War for Whisky, Brandy and Allied Alcohols is Mr. Cyrus Turner, of New York City. He knows more about the distillers' fight than any other man in the country through his connection, as general manager, with the National Wholesale Liquor Dealers' Association of America.

These two men, then, are the executive heads of the United States Army of Liquor, 1,200,000 strong—a number of men equal to that of the employés of all the railroads of the land; equal, also, to the total number of troops put under arms by Japan in her war with Russia.

The Liquor Army embraces four divisions of regulars and a great number of brigades of volunteers, or allies. The four divisions of regulars consist of the employés of 1,747 breweries, of 1,200 distilleries, of over 100,000 saloons and of 350 wineries. The wine people, handling principally bottled goods, are not vitally affected by the enemy; hence they are apathetic. As long as the Interstate Commerce Laws permit it, the wine crowd will go right on shipping bottled cheer into the prohibition states.

The volunteers, or allies, of the Liquor Army, include those engaged in the many different trades, industries and callings dependent upon the liquor traffic, such as glass makers, coopers, bottlers, cork and stopper makers, wagon and harness manufacturers, producers of bar fixtures and —the ice man. Other allies are the farmers who supply hops and other raw materials and the 6,600 hotel men of the country, and the 7,000 soda-water makers, and hundreds of thousands of traveling salesmen of the liquor and allied trades. The Liquor Army has also secured the support of those labor unions whose members are employed by the liquor business.

To organize these allies, the Liquor War Department sent out its chief recruiting officer, John A. McDermott. That he was successful is shown by the fact that manufacturers' and dealers' associations, numbering altogether 70,000 members, have been formed in most of the states of the Union to fight the cause of liquor.

The great Why of the successful recruiting in the allied forces lies entirely in the sign of the Dollar Mark. For example, the liquor interests pay $15,000,000 annually to insurance men, $20,000,000 to freight and express men, $5,000,000 to fuel men and $240,000,000 to farmers for hops, barley, rice, rye and horse feed. The liquor forces argue that these business associates are interested most vitally in the continuance of the sale of strong drink. Altogether, the 1,200,000 persons depending for a livelihood directly upon the liquor business and the industries it supports, receive total earnings of $600,000,000 a year. Certain it is, then, that all these will back up the industries that furnish them with daily bread.

As I have indicated, the ammunition used by this mighty liquor force is vast wealth—six and a half billions of property and other business values. That is, an amount of money double that of all the cash in circulation in the United States; it is twice the amount of deposits in all our savings banks. With it, the liquor interests could pay off our national debt and still have over five billion dollars to spare. That campaign fund of the Liquor Army is nearly equal to the total of the capital stock of all our railways; it is one-thirtieth of the aggregate wealth of the nation. And so, $6,500,000,000 is Power.

The money is represented by invested capital in liquor and allied trades, in bonds, wages, plants, real estate and other property, in annual production, good will, brand values, liquor in bond and—certain other things which the tax collector is not supposed to know. The main components forming the grand total are as follows:

Retail investments (real estate, saloons, cafés, fixtures, etc.)	$1,500,000,000
Brewers' investments (breweries, warehouses, equipment, brand values, etc.)	750,000,000
Whisky and liquor investments (distilleries, equipment, brand values, etc.)	600,000,000
Wholesale dealers' investment (real estate, merchandise, good will, etc.)	375,000,000
Allied trades (estimated capital invested)	333,000,000
Wine investments (vineyards, plants, merchandise, etc.)	140,000,000
Total estimated investments	$3,698,000,000
Whisky and other liquors, sales per annum (and whisky in bond)	$1,138,000,000
Beer sales per annum	351,000,000
Taxes (internal revenue, national government, state and city governments) per annum	340,000,000
Wages (brewers, distillers, wholesalers, retailers, etc.) annually	600,000,000
Farm products (annual purchases)	250,000,000
Freight, fuel, insurance, etc., annually	40,000,000
Total annually	$2,719,000,000

I have compiled the foregoing figures after careful investigation among the various liquor interests and with the aid of liquor experts. These estimates are, I believe, conservative. I have given the total investment as $3,698,000,000, and the annual turnover at $2,719,000,000, or a grand total of nearly six and one-half billions of dollars.

An item of special interest in the make-up of this Power is the amount of money paid to government—national, state and municipal. The internal revenue receipts of the United States from the liquor business is a little over $200,000,000 a year. State and city taxation on liquor yields another $140,000,000, making a grand tax total of $340,000,000. Nearly one-half of the revenues of the Federal Government alone come from the liquor traffic. Here, then, are the reasons the Liquor Army hopes to gain recruits from the ranks of the taxpayers.

The aggregation of billions under consideration may be regarded as a Trust. Not a beer or whisky Trust, but a gigantic Drink Trust, consisting of twenty or more real Trusts such as The Distilleries Securities Company, with its 100 plants and its $42,000,000; the American Spirits Corporations, with thirteen companies and $35,000,000; the Kentucky Distilleries, with fifty plants and $32,000,000; the American Malting interests, with thirty-six companies and $30,000,000; the Standard Distilling Corporation, with ten companies and $24,000,000, and the United Brewers, with twelve companies and $6,000,000. These and the other genuine beer and whisky corporations may be said to form one colossal Drink Trust with a power of $6,500,000,000 and therefore with a power that makes Standard Oil and a mere billion-dollar United States Steel Corporation sink into comparative puniness.

The principal weapons employed by the Liquor Army for the use of this ammunition include, *first*, publicity in the form of paid advertising in newspapers and other periodicals; "press agency" work, consisting of the publication of news matter, articles, etc., in newspapers and magazines; *second*, work by mail, letters, circulars, booklets, pamphlets mailed or distributed to individuals, offices or homes; posters and other similar advertising matter; *third*, publications either frankly devoted to the Drink propaganda, or perhaps more often attempting to masquerade as general periodicals publishing articles favorable to the Drink cause; *fourth*, lecturers and public speakers, preferably reformers and ministers, who can be induced to work in the Liquor ranks; *fifth*, politicians and legislators who can exercise influence in places and at times when it is badly needed.

With its War Department, its army, its ammunition and its weapons, what are the liquor people's method of fighting? They divide the methods into two classes, namely, the underground method as practiced for many years, and the open method, which is more or less brand new. Yes, the liquor interests have long known well how to grope their way in the dark under corridors of political and press corruption. But in the past two years they have been compelled to come out into the glare of daylight and fight hand to hand. They knew the uses of smokeless powder and of poisoned arrows made of coin of the Republic, but now they must learn the use of tongue and pen, too, as weapons; and the use of reason, as well as of dollars, for ammunition. Both the underground and the open systems of fighting are today in operation simultaneously.

The open method involves, first, the buying of space in newspapers, in the form of spread advertisements—since the Liquor Army cannot secure publicity on the merits of the case. The most familiar of such advertisements is a full-page affair that is expected to be glitteringly conclusive as an argument in favor of anti-prohibition—because of the statement that George Washington drank wine, or because of the statement that Bismarck was great solely as the result of drinking beer. It is said that one brewing concern is spending a million dollars "placing" an advertisement showing the twelve ages of beer from the harvest field to the table —to run for twelve months in thousands of publications.

Huge posters represent another of the open methods of publicity resorted to by the Liquor Army. One popular poster shows dozens of empty stores resulting, it is alleged, from the bad trade conditions in Kansas City, Kansas, following the advent of prohibition. Sworn statements accompany the pictures, but they do not explain that the great majority of the stores became vacant because situated in the flooded district. The business men of the town vigorously attacked this poster and showed the author to be irresponsible.

Subterranean operations for molding public opinion involve a subsidized press and an intimidated press. Tremendous pressure is being brought to bear on newspapers and other periodicals to force them to work for the Drink cause. The beer and whisky and wine people are good advertisers, and they are exerting all their influence to secure either a favorable attitude or at least neutrality from the daily and weekly press. In some cases their efforts are producing results that ought to be gratifying to the Drink forces. I have noticed recently in several newspapers a whole page article espousing the cause of beer drinking. In other publications I have checked earnest pro-beer arguments printed as "pure reading matter."

As for the intimidated press—the liquor people stop at nothing to crush any newspaper that dares give publicity to the liquor evils. Note this extract from a letter sent to the New Orleans *Times-Democrat* by a Milwaukee brewery:

"We call your attention to the fact that certain newspapers are inclined to boost prohibition. The brewers are keeping a record of such newspapers. As you have had a certain proportion of our business in the past, we advise you that all newspapers who fail to suppress anti-saloon league news hereafter will not only lose our patronage, but also that of most every brewery in the United States. All papers continuing to knock our business can expect to be turned down on any future advertising contracts from both ourselves and all other large breweries."

It is not necessary for me to say that the *Times-Democrat* was not disturbed—perhaps not even annoyed—by this sanguinary communication. Fortunately for the American people the press of this country, taken by and large, is clean and courageous. The Drink forces will undoubtedly find publishers who will print their arguments as "pure reading" when paid enough; but, as a rule, the newspapers will be extremely cautious in adopting any attitude that does not reflect the sentiment of their constituencies.

In making my investigations for this article I found an interesting case, typical of the power and energy the Liquor people are using in their efforts to secure favorable treatment from the newspapers. In one of the large Eastern cities is a newspaper editor whom many men in the profession regard as the greatest daily journalist of the present time. He is a vigorous fighter for the cause that he believes right. His own state recently began a fight for local option—yes, there are two states, Pennsylvania and New Jersey, which as yet have no local option laws—and this man's newspaper surprised and terrorized the Drink forces with a crusade that they knew meant the loss of the state.

They sent a committee to see him—capable, intelligent men who knew how to talk and whose business it is to persuade other men to see things their way. "You see," said the committee, in conclusion, "we don't expect you to advocate our side of it; all we suggest is that you publish only the live news matter on both sides. The other papers in town will treat us right, so that you can be sure that none of them will be printing any news that you won't have."

When they had quite finished the editor said: "For ten or twelve years, at least, I have been trying to get the saloon people to help us clean up some of the worst elements that associate with the liquor business. You have never helped me in these movements. You have been indifferent—at least indifferent—to every reform effort, until now, when the danger of the situation has finally worked its way into your heads, you tell me what you will do in the way of reform. Perhaps you are sincere, perhaps not; at any rate this is the opportunity I have waited for and you can be sure that this paper will do everything it can to secure the passage of a local option law. So far as your advertising is concerned that is a matter you must settle with yourselves. You can use our advertising columns, or you can leave them alone; either course will have no bearing on the paper's policy."

Then the committee lost its temper, and made threats. The editor was optimistic, even cheerful. He opined that his paper would be able to proceed and progress without the friendship of the Drink forces. The committee made good on the threats. Not only was all liquor and beer advertising withdrawn, but allied industries were drawn into the boycott until finally the newspaper lost even the advertising of the pickle manufacturers!

The liquor interests may be made unhappy when I tell them that the editor has proven himself a very good business man. The circulation of his paper has steadily advanced, his advertising receipts have increased, and his monthly net profits are larger than they were before the boycott began.

A still craftier method of reaching the public is through the columns of apparently religious or reform publications that are either owned or "influenced" by the liquor interests. These papers piously take the stand of law enforcement in regard to closing saloons on Sunday, and so forth, appearing thus to be the true friend of public morality.

I have mentioned lecturers and pulpit orators in the Drink service. These are the fighting chaplains of the Liquor Army—cleric allies who serve the Demon Rum. A score of preachers who are identified with the liquor interests could be mentioned, but the record of two or three will suffice.

First, there is the Rev. Charles F. Taylor, late pastor of a church in Amsterdam, New York. He is now the editor of *The True Reformer*, in which publication frequent attacks are made upon the Anti-Saloon League. T. De Quincy Tully, secretary-treasurer of the society publishing this paper, is a favorite orator at liquor conventions, and his speeches are reproduced in pamphlet form and used as ammunition by the Drink Army. Howard H. Russell tells me that at one time Tully applied for a position with the Anti-Saloon League, and failed to get it.

One issue of *The True Reformer* advocates leaving the prize fight law "as it is," and devotes many pages of its space to an earnest effort to prove prohibition impracticable. I am told that *The True Reformer* is mailed regularly to ministers in various sections of the country. *The True Reformer* frankly states that it "is not published to make money, or with the expectation of even paying the cost of its publication, but as a medium for conveying valuable information to the people not otherwise obtainable."

Another of the chaplains, the Rev. E. A. Wasson, is pastor of St. Stephen's Protestant Episcopal Church, at Newark, New Jersey, and edi-

MRS. W. A. LAWSON,
President, Wisconsin W. C. T. U.

DR. ELLEN J. WETLAUFER,
President, Wyoming W. C. T. U.

tor of *The Crown*, a religious monthly with the following motto: "'True religion is true humanity, and true humanity lies in loving and serving others. To love man is to love God; and to serve man is to serve God.'"

That the services of the Rev. E. A. Wasson are highly appreciated by the United States Brewers' Association is evidenced by the fact that under the title of "The Anti-Saloon League Sham" they issue in pamphlet form an article from his *Crown*. Further appreciation is indicated by page 24 of the *Crown* for March, 1908, upon which appears an anti-local option argument signed "Press Bureau German-American Central Alliance, Newark, N. J.," and bearing the three stars that mean nothing to the lay reader but which the newspaper man interprets as "paid advertising."

I came upon a third chaplain of the Liquor Army, through receiving a pamphlet containing this item: "Rev. William A. Wasson, rector of Grace Church, Riverhead, Long Island, says: 'The church cannot longer afford to have its name exploited by the prohibitionists. The church and the liquor trade should stand shoulder to shoulder in this great fight. *We need each other.*'" I found the Rev. William A. Wasson to be a brother of the clergyman above mentioned, and an ardent representative of the liquor traffic at legislative hearings. His addresses before liquor conventions are all published in pamphlets by the liquor people, and scattered over the country as "representing the views of prominent clergymen on the liquor question."

A fourth chaplain of the kind is the Rev. O. M. Muller, who edits that ambitious liquor paper, *The Tribunal of Reason*. This publication contains a paying assortment of liquor advertisements and is owned, so I am told, by a Brooklyn dealer named Schwab.

The most potent of all the underground methods of the Liquor Army are those followed in securing control of state legislatures. In legislative liquor fights, the power of money can, as a rule, be brought to bear upon votes. Legislators can be controlled, too, on the strength of past favors. And the good will of the ruling political ring can be secured for a consideration.

Despite both open and underground methods in operation in state legislative bodies, the Liquor Army has seven times gone down to defeat in the seven great decisive battles of the war—Maine, Kansas, North Dakota, Georgia, Alabama, Oklahoma and North Carolina. The Liquor Army did not fight hard, to be sure, in the battles of Maine, Kansas and North Dakota. The sensation produced upon the Liquor Army in losing, in turn, those three states, was that of a flea on a lion. The lion roared—that was all. But in the other four states the liquor legions fought tooth and nail.

Yet the Liquor Army was defeated in Oklahoma, its losses there numbering 540 saloons. It was defeated in Alabama, its money losses amounting to $1,385,000 of capital invested in that state in the brewery and distillery business. It has more recently been defeated in North Carolina, with pecuniary losses aggregating $308,000.

Generals of the Liquor Army thought they would win sure in Georgia, where the very Governor of the State, Hon. Hoke Smith, was one of the owners of the Piedmont Hotel, in Atlanta, a hotel with a bar. The great expectations of the generals of Liquor were not realized, however; for with courageous pen Governor Smith signed the Prohibition Bill, thereby personally losing many thousands of dollars through the closing of this bar. The loss to the Liquor Army in that Georgia campaign involved $1,680,000 of invested capital.

A series of defeats with tremendous losses has befallen the Liquor forces in all the other states of the Union, too. In Kentucky, where $100,000,000 is invested in distilleries, the Liquor Army has fought, step by step, ever backward, always in retreat, till it has lost every county in the state excepting four. In Texas it has lost half the state, county by county, together with $2,500,000.

As for defeat and loss in other ways—during the spring of 1908 seventy-five carloads of fixtures were returned to one Western brewery—from closed saloons. A million railroad men have been sworn to total abstinence through rules of their own brotherhoods.

On constant guard are those sentries of the Liquor Army, the saloon-keepers. These live with their ears close to the ground. They are trained in close political work, are in direct contact with the people, are immensely powerful. They are freemen, yes. But a freeman can be a slave. He can sell himself to debt. *The average saloon man is owned body and soul by the brewers.* In nine cases out of ten he is in the hands of the brewery that advances his license, that puts up his bond, and that furnishes him with beer on credit. It is estimated that the breweries own fully seventy-five per cent. of the saloons of the country.

The progeny of the saloon is the dive. Last year the generals of the Liquor Army were forced to acknowledge at last that the dive was bad for the liquor business. And forthwith the Liquor Legion began a movement that is called "cleaning house," which meant wiping the dives from municipal maps. Definite action was taken by the formation of the New York State Lager Beer Association, which made an agreement with the bonding companies whereby the brewers were to refuse beer, and the bonding companies to refuse to give bonds to disreputable saloon men. As a result, on the first day of May, 1908, revelry by night was no longer heard in saloons of the dive class in New York State. This "looked good" to the people as divisions of the Liquor Army in other States perceived. Forthwith, throughout the Union, a general house-cleaning movement began.

The first to take an active step in the great anti-prohibition fight was the United States Brewers' Association, the most powerful body of its kind on earth. It was the heads of this body who promulgated the order to add the open method of fighting to the underground. The distillers, meantime, were not idle. Cyrus Turner, shrewd observer and tactician, took hold of the Wholesale Liquor Dealers' Association and of the National Protective Bureau, both comprised of whisky men, and made the work of these bodies effective. Later, the distillers got together and formed what they call the Model License League, the purpose of which was and is to get before the people a so-called model license bill limiting the number of licenses and severely punishing excise infringements. Instantly every hanger-on in the distillery business, realizing the cloak the new organization afforded, rallied around the standard of Model License and assumed a sanctimonious attitude.

But the Liquor Army lacks *esprit de corps*. Its own camps are riven by internecine warfare—by strife in its own ranks. Between the brewers and distillers there has always existed the bitterest rivalry.

Then, too, there is fierce competition among the brewers themselves, incessant factional feuds and vendettas. Moreover, manufacturers of pure whisky are opposing the "blenders"—the makers of blended whiskies. And the dealers in bottled goods not only actually welcome prohibition, but in some cases contribute to its campaign expenses, because it booms their business and kills the barreled beer and whisky shipments—the laws permitting the shipment of bottled goods into dry territory. Lastly, the American Wine Growers' Association is fighting alone. And here is one more squabble within a squabble: for the wine people are at swords' points with the importers who bring into the country vast quantities of foreign wines.

And so the war goes on, this war which is destined to be the greatest national struggle the United States has ever seen. Upon the one side stands the Anti-Saloon League, with its myriad Temperance allies, and that mighty, imponderable force, Public Opinion. It is this that is setting in against liquor drinking the world over.

On the other side stands the Liquor Traffic, monstrous, inconceivable in its strength and craft, facing possible confiscation of its great interests, loss of its billions, fighting against extermination. Coolly it is distributing its forces, strengthening its ramparts, plotting and counterplotting, alert, forceful, menacing. It is prepared for any sacrifice, any price—for it is fighting for life, and in that balance all else counts as nothing. *Six million dollars a day it receives from the people in exchange for its wares.* It can well afford to be lavish in its defenses, even though the fight cost it half a million dollars a day for many months to come.

In endeavoring to gain an idea of the results of this vast struggle I have talked with the biggest leaders on both sides, and their composite view seems to be much as follows: The Anti-Saloon League will continue its devastating, machine-like victories, sweeping perhaps half a dozen more states into prohibition. It will ignore as false and untrustworthy the protestations of the drink forces that their intentions toward reform are sincere. Finally, the Liquor Army will be compelled to *prove* its sincerity by purging their trade of its evils, by eliminating that American institution, the saloon, by adopting some other social substitute like the German *Bierhallen*, and by actively aiding in decent legislation and law-enforcement. Then and only then will Public Opinion be satisfied. And once Public Opinion is satisfied the Anti-Saloon League will have no further cause for activity.

Among the Italians there is an organization called the "Black Hand." This secret, oath-bound band selects a victim for assassination, and details some member to carry out the sentence. The assassin waylays his victim and drives the dagger to his heart. These men are not choice in their methods of murder, but accomplish their deadly designs by any and every means.

This new "Black Hand" society has invaded an entirely different realm. As a rule, the deadly methods of the brewers, maltsters and distillers are as secret as are the underground plans and purposes of the other "Black Hand" society. While the purpose to kill is not boldly stated, it yet remains the truth, as announced by Shylock, that "You do take my life when you take that which doth sustain my life." The maltsters and brewers are to secure the names of all friends of temperance, and propose to use all the strength and power at their command to destroy the business enterprises with which these men are connected.

This has always been the plan and spirit of the liquor trade. It was revealed to me a quarter of a century ago when, as a young editor out in West Texas, I began my fight for temperance and prohibition. We had had two saloon fires in our little town, and it was believed by many that the owners started these fires for the purpose of collecting the insurance. I denounced the whole liquor business as a crying evil against society and a menace to the public good. I was immediately waited upon by a leading saloonkeeper, who informed me that if I did not let up on the whisky business my enterprise would be destroyed. I knew that the threat meant very much more than this saloon man expressed, and was not surprised when afterward I was waylaid to be shot, and my life was saved only by a Providential intervention.—Dr. J. B. Cranfill.

CHAPTER XX.

THE SOUTHLAND'S WINNING FIGHT.

By Harris Dickson, *Judge of Municipal Court, Vicksburg, Mississippi.*

Note.—Judge Dickson is an author of wide popularity. One of the most interesting and valuable contributions to the literature of the great movement for the prohibition of the liquor traffic is his series of articles under the title "The Battle of the Bottle," published in The Saturday Evening Post, *October, 1907, to January, 1908, from which the following chapter is condensed by permission.*—G. M. H.

EVERY Southern state today has vast areas of dry territory: South Carolina, North Carolina, Florida, Mississippi, West Virginia, Kentucky, Tennessee, Alabama, Oklahoma, Georgia, Texas, Louisiana, Arkansas.

The farmers went about getting rid of doggeries in their good old-fashioned way. Nowhere on all the statute books of the world is the ancient Anglo-Saxon principle more clearly writ than in those early liquor laws of the South. "Local self-government" and "community rule" were guide-posts for their simple legislation. If a cross-road doggery interfered with a schoolhouse, or disturbed the worshipers at a church, the people of that locality had their representative in the legislature secure an act forbidding the sale of liquor within four miles of that particular church or school. The schoolhouse of the South is almost as much a sanctuary as the church, and the people plant them thickly. This throttled the doggery.

When the slaves were freed the planter closed his big house and moved to town—poverty and protection the reasons. This changed the whole structure of southern society. Out of the wreck and the ruin a new society grew up.

Somebody had to work. So the white man stepped into the furrow. When conditions settled down the negro began to rent land and till it. The plantation store sprang up. Each share hand or tenant drew his weekly rations.

"Gimme a quart o' whisky," says the negro on Saturday night, and thus he wasted his wages and crippled his efficiency.

"Yes," the planter admits, "it's a bad business. But if I do not sell whisky, the next plantation will. Negroes won't trade at a store where they can't get it."

This system worked very well in prosperous years, but hard times came. Mortgage company and factor shut down on the planter, and he cut off the negro's whisky.

After that the negro went to town for liquor. There were saloons for negroes who left the fields and flocked to the cities—dens of unspeakable infamy with dance halls, crap games, opium, cocaine and all the rest. In many cities these dives existed long after stringent laws had been enacted for their suppression. Men higher up in the business protected them; rich brewers paid their licenses. They constituted the political machine, grinding out officials who bore their stamp. They dictated the election of sheriffs, tied the hands of prosecuting attorneys, packed the juries, and tugged at the judicial ermine. And they built up a power so great that it held itself above the law. Instead of the law regulating the liquor traffic, the traffic regulated the law. The protest against this has been gathering for many years; now it is irresistible. Thousands of citizens believe that a traffic which cannot be regulated ought to be destroyed.

I.

THE FIREWATER CRISIS IN ALABAMA.

As in other southern states, the cross-roads doggery was first attacked and demolished. By special acts of the legislature prohibiting the sale within five miles of certain schoolhouses and churches the bar room was driven out of the country into the incorporated towns where it would be under police restraint. Very early in this conflict it developed that many people were opposed to the saloon itself, not only in the country districts, but in the towns as well. As they did not then feel strong enough to vote, they steered a middle course and adopted a local dispensary law. This gave the people in each town of five thousand inhabitants the choice between saloons run by individuals and a dispensary run by the community. It was a municipal monopoly of the liquor traffic, and the profits were used for public improvements.

Many good people regarded this system as a step in advance of the open saloon and supported it while waiting for something better.

One system brings on another. The dispensary brought on the drinking-room near by. Growlers began to say rude and angry things concerning the dispensary, even to whisper "graft." The dispensary system began to wane.

Prior to the meeting of the legislature in 1907, state-wide agitation

REV. J. L. HARLEY,
Superintendent, Anti-Saloon League of South Carolina.

JOHN A. OATES,
Chairman Anti-Saloon League of North Carolina.

was begun for a local option law. Some one suggested a state prohibition law, but it did not pass, many Anti-Saloon League leaders opposing it. They feared the time was not yet ripe for state prohibition; they thought it better to capture county by county, building up strength and weakening the opposition.

On February 26, Governor Comer signed the local option bill. An even greater victory was yet to come, the Sherrod Anti-Shipping Law. This drastic measure makes it unlawful for any person, firm or corporation to accept any liquors for shipment, transportation or delivery into a prohibition district. As the law now stands, a dealer in Mobile or Birmingham cannot ship a thimbleful of whisky to a dry town in the state, but the dealer at Pensacola, Florida, Chattanooga, Tennessee, or Louisville, Kentucky, may dump it into Alabama by the car load. That is interstate commerce, which the state of Alabama is powerless to restrict. Bills are pending, however, in the Congress of the United States, the effect of which will be to leave each particular state in full control of this traffic, as a part of its police power. The chief interest of the Alabama fight centered in Jefferson county and the Magic City of Birmingham. From this community the Anti-Saloon League sought to rout its ancient enemy. Petitions for a special election were circulated and signed by 5,538 voters, more than a sufficient number. The election was held on October 28, 1907.*

II.

AN INQUEST ON THE GEORGIA SALOON.

When the whites were again in the saddle (after the reconstruction period), one of their first legislative acts was to forbid any bar-room within three miles of a church or school house in the state. Several years afterward local option laws were enacted, the first ever passed in the South, if not in the United States. Almost at once the different counties began to hold elections, and in a decade 125 out of 145 counties in the state were dry. Agricultural communities almost without exception voted against the sale. The larger cities remained wet.

This concentrated the liquor traffic in the cities. In 1896, certain prohibitionists determined to make a straight fight for state prohibition—but were defeated. After their defeat most of the prohibitionists returned to the Democratic party and began to work for state prohibition within the party.

For it was discovered that local option was no longer safe. The cry was raised, "local option won't do any longer, because the liquor deal-

---
* Alabama has since become a prohibition state.—G. M. H.

ers will come down to our dry counties where there are negro majorities, pay their taxes and put liquor back into their hands." Then came the riot—brought about, as many believe, by the negro saloons on Decatur street, and the congregation of negroes at low dives. The mad purpose at the beginning was to go down to these dives and tear them to pieces. These establishments were closed for a number of days, and the people of Atlanta discovered that there was scarcely a need for a Recorder's Court.

Such were the appalling facts suddenly thrust upon the people of the state who had been taught to believe that Atlanta was one of the best regulated cities in the South, with a low percentage of crime. Later, the City Council, at the instance of big liquor dealers, put a number of these negro saloons back on Decatur street. Indignation spread and the people of the entire state roused themselves against the traffic. Men who had never before been prohibitionists placed themselves squarely in the ranks.

The prohibition giant awakened to a realization of his strength. The legislature being in session, the prohibitionists began to clamor for a state prohibitory law. Petitions began to pour in to the country members from clubs, anti-saloon leagues, the W. C. T. U., churches and several chambers of commerce. Bills were introduced by country members for state prohibition, and, after a fiery debate there was introduced in a most spectacular manner that obstructive engine known as the filibuster.

Very early of the morning when the bill was put upon its final passage ten thousand people assembled around the capitol. The bill was called and a filibuster began. It seemed practically impossible to force a vote. Night came, nine o'clock, and though an overwhelming majority was in favor of the bill, no action had yet been taken. The House adjourned. Next morning the filibusters agreed that if the bill were deferred until the following Tuesday it should come to a vote after six hours of debate. This final vote stood 139 for to 39 against. When Governor Hoke Smith attached his signature to the prohibition law, he is said to have signed away $30,000 from his private revenues. Governor Smith is quoted as saying: "Congress should provide by law that liquor shall not be shipped from a wet state into a dry state. Interstate commerce, regulated by Congress, should not tolerate the shipment of liquor into a state where the people have voted against the sale of liquor in that state. The greatest thing that can be done for the temperance cause is to forbid the shipment of liquor from wet states into dry states. Let that once be stopped and the argument of non-enforcement of the law is gone, and the states will go stumbling over each other to enact prohibition laws."

(When Congress was granted power to regulate commerce among the several states, it was not intended that the so-called "United States Government" should possess authority to force a traffic upon a state which had legislated against it. The original thirteen States had been sovereign, free and independent, and when they founded the "more perfect union" of 1787, they did not for a moment consider that the regulation of commerce "among" them involved the right to coerce them into tolerating a prohibited traffic. Seaborn Wright once said that if the Federal Government persisted in forcing the Liquor Traffic upon the Southern states, they would exterminate the negro! He should have said, they would wage another war for the dissolution of the Union!—G. M. H.)

III.

THE OBITUARY OF KENTUCKY AND THE EPITAPH OF TENNESSEE.

In 1905, the County Unit Bill was passed, which excepted those counties where there is a city of the fourth class, of 3,000 population. This law went into effect June 11, 1906. Under it there have been thirty-eight campaigns, thirty-six of which the prohibitionists have won. In the territory thus voted dry there is a population of 600,000 people, nearly 13,000 square miles. There is one solid block in southeast Kentucky with but one saloon town. Ninety-eight per cent. of Kentucky territory is dry. Seventy-five per cent. of Kentuckians live in dry territory. Ninety-two counties are entirely dry. Fourteen counties have one saloon town. Seven counties have two saloons each. Two counties have three saloons each. Four counties are almost solidly wet.

The slate has been wiped so clean in Tennessee that little can now be done except to write obituary. There are now only three cities in the State of Tennessee where liquor may be legally sold: Nashville, Chattanooga and Memphis. Nashville has a restricted saloon district; Chattanooga will reduce her saloons to 67. Memphis alone does business in the old way at the old stand.

IV.

FROM THE OLD DOMINION TO THE LONE STAR STATE.

There are one hundred counties in Virginia, seventy-two of which have no saloons. Forty-six counties have no form of license whatever. Twenty-six counties have no saloons, but have dispensaries, or some modified form of license. Twenty-eight counties have saloons in the cities. Out of one hundred and forty incorporated towns one hundred and twenty are dry; out of nineteen cities six are dry. There are but thirty-three municipalities in the state where the open saloon exists. Of the 1,060 saloons two-thirds are in four counties around Richmond and Norfolk.

The temperance forces are thoroughly united and propose to amend the defective election laws.

West Virginia came into the world as a child of war. Its first feeble cry was a feeble wail against the cradle's insatiate enemy. As the babe grew stronger its anti-liquor legislation became more stringent. There are fifty-five counties in the State; twenty-nine of these are dry. Nine counties have saloons in one town each; five in two; two in three; two in four, and eight in five towns or more. Two years ago the prison report showed that thirty-two dry counties had 106 men in the penitentiary while Fayette county alone, with eighty-three saloons had 159!

Florida has had local option since 1887, by an amendment to the constitution of the state. One peculiar feature of the law is that although the county, as a whole, may vote wet, yet, if a single precinct in the county shows a majority against the sale, then no liquor can be sold in that precinct.

The growth of straight-out prohibition sentiment has caused a curious change. In cities like Pensacola the most pronounced local optionists are the men who bitterly denounced it ten years ago. Then they were clamoring for the privilege of selling in counties that did not want it, overriding local opinions and desires. They fought local option when the state was trying to get it. Now they claim to be inventors of the plan, preaching the beauties of the time-honored Anglo-Saxon principle of local self-government.

The Governor of Florida is an outspoken prohibitionist.* He makes one striking statement:

"It was observed by merchants in dry communities that their bills were paid more promptly, that the volume of business was greater, that the people became more prosperous and the towns improved more rapidly, until now people look upon the question both from a moral and a business standpoint, as their observation has confirmed them in the belief that it is better from every standpoint that the country should abolish the sale of liquor."

Mississippi, in 1880, had open saloons throughout the State. Since 1886, the State has had an effective county local option law, under which many elections were held with varying results. As early as 1890, forty counties had gone dry. In 1890, the constitutional convention was held —its paramount purpose being the disfranchisement of the negro. When the convention assembled many ardent prohibitionists regarded it as their golden opportunity and pressed vigorously for an amendment, but it was voted down. Subsequently the brazen defiance of law in the saloon coun-

---

* There ought to be a recognized style of distinguishing a Democrat or Republican advocate of prohibiting the liquor traffic from a party Prohibitionist. For instance, Seaborn Wright, of Georgia, is a "red-hot Southern Democrat" who favors the prohibition of the dram-shop—but he has no sympathy with the party of which Chafin and Watkins are candidates for the Presidency and Vice Presidency.—G. M. H.

ties converted thousands, and in 1908 Mississippi took her place among the eight prohibition States of the Union.

Louisiana is divided; the north is largely dry; in the southern parishes it is generally wet. A strong temperance sentiment is developing and liquor men are taking time by the forelock in an effort to weed out the most objectionable members of their class. The state had a slightly modified form of local option under which twenty-three parishes are dry, seven partly dry and twenty-seven wet. This situation is changing, always toward the dry side.

There is a petition law in Arkansas peculiar to that State; a majority of the "inhabitants" may petition for the removal of all saloons within three miles of any church or schoolhouse. This applies to cities. As "inhabitants" include wives, mothers, daughters over eighteen years of age, it would seem that this is a most effective weapon. Indeed, it is difficult to imagine how any further legislation could be needed. There is one element of certainty in Arkansas. A test of strength has been made and measured. If state prohibition be submitted to the people, it will carry.

The local option law of Missouri permits counties to vote as a whole, except cities of 2,500 or more, which vote separately. Prohibition effort is being focused on the legislature which will meet in 1909. The plan is to carry the state, county by county, as was so successfully done in Georgia, Alabama and Mississippi.

Political conditions in the Lone Star State have changed since 1887, when the prohibition amendment to the constitution was voted down by an enormous majority. At that time any man twenty-one years of age could vote and no questions asked. One hundred thousand negro ballots were probably cast against prohibition. Today there are not ten thousand negro votes in the State, out of a total vote of 900,000. Poll tax and registration requirements are so strict that very few illegal votes could possibly be cast. This puts a different face on the matter.

The liquor interests are wide awake to their danger, but in Texas, as in other States, they are taking notice too late. Long continued violations of law have built up such bitter opposition to the entire traffic that nothing short of annihilation will satisfy its foes.

CHAPTER XXI.

THE WOMAN'S CHRISTIAN TEMPERANCE UNION IN ACTION.

HISTORY is composite biography. When the final story of the Woman's Christian Temperance Union shall have been written, it will be largely a recital of facts and experiences in the lives of thousands of women, who, in many places and stations, have discharged duty in the spirit of faith, hope and self-sacrificing love. From every part of the country have come to the editor of this book, stories of achievement in the face of apparently insurmountable difficulty, triumphs in tribulation, and victories through invincible effort that read like the eleventh chapter of Hebrews. These stories, bits of biography and personal experience, are athrill with tragic interest. To print them all would require a volume. Sufficient extracts are reproduced to present a fair picture of this magnificent working force in action.

Tennessee will probably be the ninth Prohibition state by the uplift of the prohibition wave of 1907-8. Mrs. Silena M. Holman, President of the State Union, in her résumé of conditions, says:

"At this writing, August, 1908, a strong fight is being made for a legislature in favor of state prohibition. We believe we are going to win, but if we fail, we shall not be discouraged, for we think all the powers of darkness cannot delay the matter longer than the meeting of another legislature.

"The question naturally arises as to what causes led to this condition of affairs in the state. What influence led the people to a hatred of the saloon, and abolished it from so much of the state, with good promise of driving the traffic from the entire state at an early date? I would say that the 'Four-mile Law' has been a fine educator. Then the early temperance societies, the Sons of Temperance and the Good Templars did much to set the people thinking. But I think that no force has done quite so much to educate the people of the state as to the evils of the saloon as the Woman's Christian Temperance Union.

"The Union was organized in this state in 1882. In the years since its organization, its speakers have visited almost every city, town and village, speaking to people along temperance lines. In 1887, when the campaign was made for constitutional prohibition, their speakers canvassed the entire state, organizing hundreds of unions, and helping under local

MRS. CORA D. GRAHAM,
Corresponding Secretary, New York
W. C. T. U.

MRS. ELLEN L. TENNEY,
Treasurer, New York W. C. T. U.

MRS. C. A. G. FAIRCHILD,
Recording Secretary, New York W. C. T. U.

MRS. H. L. BULLOCK,
First Vice-President, New York W. C. T. U.

option. Twenty-nine out of a total thirty-two is surely progressing. There is not a county in the state that has not more or less dry territory.

"Since the fact has been demonstrated that cities can be run and prosper financially without the revenue of the saloon, the prohibition sentiment is growing rapidly among business men, and particularly among managers of large industries.

"Everything points to the wiping out of the saloon root and branch in the near future. The fact that we have but one large city is greatly in our favor. Our watchword is: State-wide Prohibition in 1910!"

From the far away West, Mrs. Lulu L. Shepard, President of the Utah W. C. T. U., writes:

"The saloons of Utah feel that they have seen their best days, and realize that the death knell has been sounded. The State Convention just closed was the most successful in the history of our Union. Never has enthusiasm for our cause been so great. Many rural communities are already planning for the closing of all saloons. Joseph Smith, President of the Mormon Church, has pledged the support of that great organization to the cause of temperance. There is but little doubt but that county local option will carry at our next legislature."

From the far Northwestern region, Mrs. E. C. Bodwell, President of the East Washington W. C. T. U., writes:

"For twenty-five years our Union has been protesting against the license system of the State. We have worked for local option and hope to secure a law at the next session of the legislature. Recently, many towns in the eastern part of the state have driven out the saloons by local popular vote. We have secured an anti-cigarette law, and our Union did much work for the Juvenile Court law passed in 1905. Wherever our Union has been active there is a strong growing public sentiment in favor of prohibition. As a consequence the Sunday-closing laws are better enforced now than ever before. We are asking our legislature for a resolution favoring an anti-polygamy amendment to the Federal constitution."

From Arkansas Mrs. Lulu A. Markwell, President of the State W. C. T. U., writes:

"We have sent out over 600,000 leaflets, also 45,000 posters which now adorn all the highways. In Pulaski county, a package of 'Convincing Logic' has been sent to every voter. This work is in connection with our approaching local option election. On election day we will hold all-day prayer meetings. In some precincts our women will stand guard to prevent ballot-box stuffing."

Mrs. Mamie M. Claflin, editor and publisher of the *Union Worker*, Nebraska, writes:

"For thirty-five years the W. C. T. U. has been taking higher ground constantly, and leading the way for other organizations not so strong in the faith to follow. As a consequence we now have faithful working allies in our work for county local option. We expect the same legislature which gives us the local option law also to provide for the submission of a prohibition constitutional amendment. The Union has secured 75,000 names to a petition to the legislature. We have about 5,000 members, and were never more aggressive and determined intelligently to fight the battle to a victorious issue."

From the "Mountain" state, or the "Treasure" state as its inhabitants like to call it, Montana, Mrs. W. E. Currah, State President, writes:

"The steady campaign of the small band of members of the W. C. T. U., the I. O. G. T., the Anti-Saloon League, the Prohibition party, the church societies and of fraternal organizations, is gradually bringing results calculated to protect our homes and children from the ravages of the legalized saloon. Like all good women everywhere, our Montana women never know defeat so long as there is a loved one to fight for. That the present 'temperance wave' will bring permanent results is the freely expressed opinion throughout the State."

From Massachusetts, Mrs. Janette Hill Knox, Corresponding Secretary, and editor of *Our Message*, writes:

"The Massachusetts Union was organized in 1874, with Mrs. S. A. Gifford, familiarly known as "Mother Gifford," a sweet-spirited Friend, as its president. Mrs. Mary A. Livermore, of national fame, succeeded her after two years, and held the position for ten years. For the remainder of her life Mrs. Livermore was retained as honorary president, and her marble bust adorns the state headquarters. She was succeeded by Miss Elizabeth S. Tobey, who served for six years. Then Mrs. S. S. Fessenden served for ten years. Her successor was Mrs. Katherine Lent Stevenson, the present incumbent, just rounding out her tenth year of service. During all these years the Union has been pushing the work of organization and education. Massachusetts furnished the first round-the-world white ribbon missionary in the person of Mrs. Mary Clement Leavitt. Ten years ago, Miss Elma Gowen started on a white ribbon missionary tour. Mrs. Stevenson, the President, is to make a world tour the coming year, her special mission being to visit educational institutions in the interest of temperance. We have at present nearly 250 local unions, with a membership of 10,000, including the Young Women's branch. There are 100 Loyal Legions with a membership of over 3,000. The Union is carrying on thirty-one departments of work. We have succeeded in securing a scientific temperance instruction law, laws prohibiting the sale of tobacco to minors and a cigarette law, and have been instrumental in preventing laws favorable to the liquor interests. Through its various departments, the Massachusetts Union has been a power for good not only in its own state but beyond."

As all know, Iowa has been the seat of a most bitter war between the liquor and the anti-liquor forces. Of the situation there Mrs. Marion H. Dunham, President of the State W. C. T. U., writes in the following statesmanlike way:

"In Iowa, which originally prohibited the sale of liquor except through state agencies, a Republican legislature, in 1855, inserted in the law the phrase, 'excepting wine and beer.' Under cover of this all liquors were sold freely. But in 1882, after a campaign of three years and a half, the voters (by constitutional amendment) declared against the manufacture and sale of liquor in the state. In December of that year, in an agreed case among the liquor dealers, the Supreme Court declared the amendment null and void, on the technicality that the wording of the resolution passed by the second legislature was not precisely the same as that passed by the first, though the journal which alone could have proven it, was not to be found.

This setting aside the will of the people aroused the state, and when the legislature met in 1883, a mass meeting was held in Des Moines, and such demands made that a prohibitory law was passed, going into effect July 4, 1884, which was strengthened in the next legislature.

"When prohibition had been enforced the results were all that were ever claimed for it, but the politicians plotted to bring it into disrepute, and many officials have refused to enforce it, and the State Temperance Alliance which attempted it at last had to give it up.

"With the violation of the law as an excuse, in April, 1894, our so-called 'mulct' law was passed, which, while not repealing or modifying the prohibitory law, allowed its waiving, if a certain per cent. of voters in counties or cities of over 5,000 population should petition for liquor selling, and a minimum fee of $600 should be paid, half to the city and half to the county. Under the shelter of that law saloons were thrust into nearly half our 99 counties, in most of which there had never before been a saloon. The flagrant violation of law still kept on. The petitions had no time limit, but two years ago we succeeded in getting a five-year limit placed on them. This is the present legal condition. Last January a mass meeting was called in Des Moines, and the different temperance organizations entered into a federation to work for constitutional prohibition. As a resolution to submit the question to the people has to pass two succeeding legislatures it means a three and a half years campaign, but we mean to win.

"Immediately after the mass meeting the liquor forces organized, and are carrying on a wide distribution of literature, etc. So it will not be a one-sided battle as it was so largely before." *

For thirty-five years the W. C. T. U. has been in operation in Ohio. Miss Frances H. Ensign, President, says:

"We have 25,000 members and about 1,000 local unions. We are carrying on thirty-three departments of work. We have sent out this year a very large amount of temperance literature—more than one and one-half million pages. Our State paper is the *Ohio Messenger*, Lillian Burt, Editor, with a circulation of 10,000.

"The Ohio Union secured our state scientific temperance instruction law, and helped to secure the passage of all the temperance laws on our statute books, including those introduced by the Anti-Saloon League.

---

* Since the above was written, the mulct law has been declared null and void by a judge of the United States Circuit Court.—G. M. H.

"We will work at the next session of the legislature to secure a bill providing for franchise for women in local option elections."

Pennsylvania has the labor question complicated with the liquor question. Mrs. Ella M. George, President, describes the conditions from the viewpoint of a disfranchised woman in politics. She says:

"The temperance conditions are not what we wish. There are two reasons for this: First, we have been ruled by 'bosses' who are under the influence of the whisky dealers, and, second, we have so many foreigners who, by illegal means, get the use of the ballot when only a short time in the country.

"In 1889, the prohibition question was submitted to the people. The Boss said 'No,' and the temperance cause went under. But Pennsylvania was never so stirred on this question as at the present time. We are going to break the yoke of the Boss and free ourselves from the hand of this oppressor. We are organizing Citizens' Schools for the education of our foreigners, where we will teach them the pernicious effects of the drink habit. The temperance sentiment has grown rapidly this last year.

"The work done more recently by the Union and other organizations in securing votes for local option candidates stirred the state from center to rim. The clouds are breaking, the dawn is coming. Pennsylvania will soon be free!"

New York has a membership of 30,000 in the W. C. T. U. Mrs. Frances W. Graham, President, says:

"Each year shows a splendid increase over the preceding, not only in membership but in achievement. For the future we plan still more work along the lines of organization, preventive, educational, social and legal work, building on the evangelistic foundation, realizing that it is only by united and consecrated effort that we can accomplish the work to which we are called.

"We have driven fermented wine from the communion table; alcohol in all its forms must go from the culinary department, and from the medicine chest. We shall work for the complete prohibition of the traffic in strong drink through legal enactment, so that, instead of selling to men the right to deal in this unholy stuff, the selling of it shall be a crime and the seller a criminal. Until this is accomplished, the work of the Woman's Christian Temperance Union will not be complete. This, then, is our plan for the future."

In Oregon, the lost powers of democracy have been restored. By their exercise a law providing for local option was adopted by the people in 1906. The President of the State Union, Mrs. Henrietta Brown, surveying past, present and future in the life of the commonwealth, says:

"Our state has been under the license system, regulated by city charters. The use of intoxicants has been very general, but not notably inordinate. Moderate drinking rather than excessive drunkenness has been the rule. Our large lumber camps, mills, canneries and other industries have suffered greatly by the open saloon being in close proximity to their

MRS. BELLE M. WELCH,
Recording Secretary Minnesota W. C. T. U.

MRS. DELLA R. MANDIGO,
Treasurer Minnesota W. C. T. U.

MRS. BESSIE LAYTHE SCOVELL.
President Minnesota W. C. T. U.

plants. The usual demoralization has followed in the wake of the saloon in Oregon as elsewhere.

"A vigorous system of education, setting forth the pernicious influence of the saloon, the disastrous effect of the drink habit upon the individual, the home and business, has resulted in a great awakening of our people in the last ten years. Result: Two years ago, under the initiative and referendum law, local option was submitted to the people. Twelve counties voted dry, and many precincts in other counties. This year another vote was taken, and now we have twenty-one counties under local option. After the battle was fought and lost, the work lagged somewhat for awhile, but later took on new life again. During the past eight or ten years it has steadily increased in numbers, financial ability and influence for good, until today it has come to be reckoned as one of the strongest forces for temperance and righteousness.

"In these years many of the ablest women in our national work have visited and worked in the state, lecturing and building up the organization. Altogether, a force is kept in the field averaging about six or eight months of organizing work each year. Can anyone estimate the tremendous influence this continuous lecturing along temperance lines from able people, traveling in all parts of our state for months and years, has had in creating and keeping alive temperance sentiment?"

Washington is so big that its W. C. T. U. is sub-divided into Eastern and Western. Mrs. Margaret B. Platt, of the Western Branch, writes:

"License has prevailed in this state and, until within the last two years, the 'wide-open' policy has existed practically everywhere. There have been small towns where liquors have been excluded by popular sentiment, but in numerous instances saloons have finally been forced upon such communities by connivance between saloon men and county commissioners. The saloon power has been dominant. Four years ago one of the leading brewers of the state was a member of the State Senate. For years any proposed temperance legislation was considered merely as a joke by most of the members of the legislature. Local option has been before the legislature at four successive sessions and failed each time. It is now *the* issue of the campaign, and there is little doubt that the next legislature will pass some kind of a local option measure.

"A great arousement of public sentiment has taken place during the last few years, notably the last four. Sunday-closing has been compelled in most of the state, and the 'wide-open' policy will never again prevail. There is a breaking away from the saloon dominance, and the *brewer* will not again be a member of the legislature—is not a candidate, though some of his henchmen are. The Republican party has declared in its state platform for local option; the Democratic party has declared for submission of a prohibitory amendment to the people, and the Prohibition party is in better fighting trim than ever, waging war for straight prohibition.

"The W. C. T. U. of Western Washington has increased from a few hundred members to probably about 3,500, including 'Y's' and 'L. T. L.'s.' We have over 150 local unions. The Union maintains state headquarters in Seattle, and is a recognized power in the state. This is the west side only. The eastern side has its own organization; that is, each side ranks as a separate state organization.

"There are two unorganized counties, sparsely settled, mostly heavily wooded, and practically impossible of organization at present. We meet here the difficulty of keeping up local unions among a *moving* population. Sometimes a whole union will move, the members seeking to find or make homes in other places.

"Through the persistent efforts of the Union the saloons have been banished from Pullman, the seat of the State College."

A very interesting phase of the W. C. T. U. work is that which has been conducted in Indian Territory, now a part of the State of Oklahoma. Of this work Mrs. Lilah D. Lindsey, herself an Indian, President of the Indian Territory W. C. T. U., writes:

As many know, we have had the most rigid prohibition laws enforced by the United States government from the time the Red Man took up his home upon the land now known as Indian Territory. All Indian treaties with the government bound the United States, through her courts established in the Territory, to enforce the prohibition law, provided for in these several treaties. In proper keeping with the spirit of those former treaties when the passing of the Tribal Government came, the Enabling Act providing for our evolution from Indian Territory to the State of Oklahoma, prohibition was one of the terms of the act. Immediately upon the dawn of Statehood, through a united effort of Indian Territory and Oklahoma Territory, an effort was made to make prohibition state-wide. Under the local option laws of Oklahoma Territory enacted by their Territorial Government, many saloons had come into that territory. In the election for the adoption of our constitution uniting these two territories into one state to be known as the state of Oklahoma, by a majority of more than 18,000 we made prohibition state-wide, and the saloons have gone from our midst, we hope forever.

Throughout Southern California, rich in flowers and historic associations, the W. C. T. U. is growing like the fairest of Pasadena roses. Mrs. Hester T. Griffith, formerly President of Los Angeles county, has become President of the State Union. At Los Angeles, in the May days of 1908, a county Union convention was held, reported to be the most interesting and successful since the beginning. Seventy-one Unions were reported, with a membership of 2,650.

In the April elections, anti-saloon victories were won in Imperial, Corona, Oceanside, Whittier, Elsinore, Santa Paula and San Jacinto. In all these elections fair progress against saloons has been shown wherever the question is made an issue.

The New Mexico Union held its "silver anniversary" at Roswell, September, 1908. The first Union was organized in 1883, at Albuquerque, by Frances E. Willard. Mrs. S. C. Nutter, the President, writes:

MRS. LULU A. MARKWELL,
President, Arkansas W. C. T. U.

MRS. LILAH D. LINDSAY,
President, East Oklahoma W. C. T. U.

"Through our efforts scientific temperance instruction in the public schools has become a law. Many reform measures have been aided for legislation. Protests against the sale of liquor to Indians, and petitions of varied nature have been sent to Congress. Money has been raised and sent to help suffering humanity everywhere. Aid has been given to rescue work and children's homes. Lectures have been given by noted speakers, and it is conceded by people who are interested in the welfare of New Mexico, that, if it were not for the courage and influence of the W. C. T. U., temperance sentiment could not have reached the point it assumes today. The growth of public opinion in favor of the abolition of saloons during the past two years has been nothing less than marvelous. With all the losses by removal, the Union has more than doubled its membership, and has added six new Unions, and three L. T. L.'s to its ranks. A few short years ago this section of the country was wide open, licensing other evils as well as the liquor traffic. Now there are several prohibitory laws, which will soon be strengthened and enforced."

Miss Elizabeth March, President North Carolina W. C. T. U., writes:

"From the most correct information I can get, I am impressed that the Friends, originally called Quakers, who have ever been the exponents of peace, purity and temperance, were the earliest promoters of the temperance cause in North Carolina. Especially is this true of the interest and activities of the women in the state, to educate public sentiment up to the principles of 'Total abstinence for the individual and prohibition for the State.' As early as 1880, the women of the Friends' church organized a 'Woman's Temperance Society' at Guilford College, an educational center established by the denomination, where many of the young people of other denominations have received, no doubt, their very best moral training that shaped their course for useful, happy lives.

"Other temperance influences and organizations had, of course, also helped to develop a wholesome sentiment in the State, giving sufficient faith and courage to undertake a campaign for state prohibition in 1881. But the time was not ripe, as was proven by the result of the election—116,072 majority votes cast against state prohibition.

"The following year Frances E. Willard came into the state in the interest of the cause, organized a few unions, and effected the state organization by calling a convention which was held in Greensboro. The 'Woman's Temperance Society' of Guilford College, but a few miles away, affiliated with the organization, under the name of 'The North Carolina Woman's Christian Temperance Union.' A comprehensive plan of work, including a number of educational departments for study and practical application, under an approved constitution and by-laws was adopted.

"The official duties from the beginning have been chiefly in the hands of the women of the Friends' church, capable, willing workers in the righteous cause. They at once put into practice our watchwords, 'Organize, Agitate, Educate.' Favorable sentiment grew steadily despite much opposition and criticism; but experience proved to the women the truth of Mrs. Mary H. Hunt's assertion, 'The star of hope for the temperance reform stands over the schoolhouse'; hence the need of a law requiring scientific temperance truths to be taught in the schools that would make the young people intelligent in reference to the poisonous effects of alcohol and other narcotics on the human system. That need was met in the splendid scientific temperance instruction law, enacted by unanimous vote in both houses of the General Assembly in 1891. The law was strengthened by the General Assembly in 1907, and now has the hearty endorsement and commendation of the State Superintendent of Public Instruction.

"Pulpit and press had become earnest, outspoken champions of the temperance cause. The W. C. T. U., supplemented by the Anti-Saloon League, an aggressive re-enforcement, were a united force against the liquor power. With confidence and hope the temperance people of the state thought the time had fully come for action. The League, taking the initiative, representatives of home protection, memorialized the General Assembly in its extra session last January asking that the people be granted the privilege to vote on the question of state prohibition. The request was granted, the campaign was inaugurated and brought to a glorious consummation on May 26, 1908, in the gratifying victory of 44,196 majority votes for state prohibition."

From Washington, D. C., Mrs. Clinton Smith, President of the District of Columbia Union, writes:

"The liquor traffic has been pressed hard towards its death in the District of Columbia. For many years we had low license. Now we have an $800 license fee. We have some 600 saloons. Every license is reported to Congress, both House and Senate, early in the session each year. The Congress of the United States, through its agent, the Excise Board, licenses these saloons one by one as fast as the licenses expire, so there is no lack of licensed places. Besides, there is an equal number of unlicensed places, which are constantly checked and closed by the police, and as constantly resumed. There is a serious movement on foot to have the Federal Government provide an inebriate asylum to provide shelter and sustenance for the poor wrecks that have produced the revenue.

"No one votes here besides members of Congress. Congress makes all laws, good and bad. In the District no citizen has a voice in any governmental matters—for instance, whether there shall be a new school building; who shall teach his children in the public schools; at what salaries, and how or what. His taxes must be paid regularly; but how much they shall be, and how they shall be used, is not for him to say. There has been a lively agitation whether license or prohibition of the liquor traffic should prevail here, but no person has any power to register his opinion upon it. All that he can do is to appeal to Congress as a petitioner. Last season many hearings were held by congressional committees; many public mass meetings addressed by noted speakers in the largest churches in the city packed by the populace to the doors, where the evils of the liquor traffic were fearlessly handled.

"The advocates of the liquor traffic, too, have met and depicted 'The Horrors of Prohibition,' and declared that they would save the nation from it. The liquor league has brought its brightest lights to bear, the brewing interests, the Wholesale Liquor Dealers' Association, the Retail

Liquor Dealers' Association, their attorneys and their national presidents, have appeared and spoken at the hearings. Miss Phoebe Couzins, of St. Louis, Mo., has come to Washington more than once to combat the Union, but the sentiment for prohibition is a recognized power. Several thousand children have been enlisted, equipped and enthused, to help win the bloodless victory, and take part in the peaceful war.

"The liquor traffic, its backers and promoters, have succeeded in deceiving the most valuable and conservative force opposed to drink, the church. For years the political power of the liquor traffic has been boasted of until many good people believe that it is invincible. This belief is our greatest obstacle. In what can this great strength lie? Not in numbers. Heaven forbid! How great a showing can it muster at the polls? If its political power should be tested it would crumble like a rope of sand. There are a great many saloonkeepers, bartenders and drunkards and moderate drinkers who will not vote for liquor *per se*. Political affiliation depends upon other things. Besides, a large proportion of these people desire to see the passing of the liquor traffic, which means more than the fall of the saloon.

"This spring the Anti-Saloon League appealed for local option for the District of Columbia. The W. C. T. U. did not join in this work as we believe that a place where there is no voting is an unreasonable place to ask for local option."

HAWAII.

By Mrs. Mary S. Whitney, *President W. C. T. U. of Hawaii.*

In the year 1802 an English ship, "The Margaret," visited this group. One of the officers, John Turnbull, wrote an account of the voyage. He found that convicts from Botany Bay had previously escaped to these islands, and had been put in possession of tracts of land, upon which they raised sugar cane, and from this contrived to distill a sort of liquor. The King made some mild remonstrance, but, before long acquired a relish for spirits and navigators carried on a lively trade in liquors. Not long before his death, however, he tabooed all distilleries, but, upon his death, in 1819, all restraint was thrown aside. The chiefs and common people abandoned themselves to drunkenness and all kinds of excess.

Among such a people as this the first missionaries arrived in April, 1820. The habits of the young king were an especial hindrance to success, and great efforts were made to induce him to change them. In 1823, his mother died, and for a time he seemed to reform. But the influence of profligate white men overcame his better principles. Not long after he departed for England, where he died and the good queen mother resigned.

In 1829, the first criminal code was enacted by the chiefs against retailing ardent spirits, and in 1831 a native temperance society was formed at Honolulu, having about a thousand members—four years before the first National Temperance Convention in the United States declared in favor of total abstinence, and nine years before the great Washingtonian movement.

In 1832, the queen regent died. She was succeeded by the young prince, and for a time the restraints upon the manufacture, sale and use of intoxicating liquors were relaxed.

In 1835, at a great temperance meeting a committee of natives was appointed, who drew up a memorial to the king, protesting against the distilling and retailing of spirits. This was signed by six of the chiefs and nearly three thousand of the people, and the government was almost entirely freed from responsibility for the traffic.

About this time a prohibitory law was enacted. In 1838 the first license law was enacted, and in 1840 a law prohibiting the manufacture and use of intoxicating drinks was signed by king Kamehameha III.

These were the halcyon days of the Hawaiian mission. Upon this quiet scene there appeared, July 9, 1839, a French ship of war, and traffic in French wines and brandy was forced upon the islands under threat of bombardment. But the king and chiefs of their own accord formed a temperance society, and for many years afterwards drunkenness was almost unknown among the natives. But this was not true among the foreign population, and in 1844, the first temperance society among foreign residents was formed. In 1859 a new society was organized, and for twenty years, except in Honolulu, the islands were under practical prohibition. But in 1882 the prohibitory law was repealed against the protests and petitions of thousands of our best citizens.

In April, 1881, the "Committee of Twenty-one" was appointed to conduct public meetings, solicit signatures to the pledge, and endeavor to enforce more perfectly existing laws relating to the manufacture and sale of intoxicating drinks. A year later a great wave of religious interest swept over all the islands. Meantime, the W. C. T. U. had grown strong, and the leaders were desirous of extending its influence to other lands. In 1884, Mrs. Mary Clement Leavitt, world organizer, arrived, and held a series of meetings. The Committee of Twenty-one was disorganized, and Miss Mary E. Green was elected President of the W. C. T. U. of Hawaii, and performed the duties of the office until her death, in 1901.

Francis Murphy, E. S. Chapman, and John G. Woolley have visited the islands in the interest of the great reform, and a branch of the Anti-Saloon League has been established, the present effort of which has been to secure local option.

Two years ago we came within one vote of obtaining local option from our legislature, and a strong fight is being put up to elect men who will carry the measure next spring (1909).

MRS. EMOR L. CALKINS,
President, Michigan W. C. T. U.

MRS. A. S. BENJAMIN,
President, Fifth District Michigan W. C. T. U.

CHAPTER XXII.

THE PROHIBITION PARTY AT WORK.

THE National Prohibition party has been one of the earliest and strongest "educative" forces in the United States on the evils of the liquor traffic, though some writers seem disposed to ignore this fact. As early as or even before the "No License League" of Massachusetts, or the "Local Option League" of Ohio, or the "Anti-Saloon League" of the District of Columbia, or the "Interdenominational Christian Temperance Alliance" of Washington, D. C., or the "Connecticut State Temperance Union," or the "Kansas State Temperance Union" (out of which organization the Anti-Saloon League of America sprang), the National Prohibition party had been organized, had raised aloft its high ideal and instituted its vigorous and unremitting propaganda. As early as 1884 Frances E. Willard was a member of its National Executive Committee, and had aligned with it her great organization.

If the men who have been conducting campaigns of that party since 1869 had been dumb, and if the women who have coöperated with them had been idle, there would have been no "tidal wave" in 1907-1908. If there had been no *Voice* in New York—with the echoing Prohibition press, there would have been little story to tell of the anti-saloon sentiment that has incorporated itself in the national movement of the first decade in the twentieth century.

Walter Wellman, the newspaper correspondent, as he sat in Memorial Hall at Columbus, Ohio, and looked out over the 1,500 delegates who had met to formulate a Prohibition platform, and nominate candidates for the national campaign of 1908, wrote as follows:

"Earnestness, conviction to a high ideal of duty, the proselyting, reforming, crusading spirit, the spirit that has helped in all ages to make the world what it is through moral force rather than through physical conquest, the spirit of the liberators, of the champions of human rights—all these are dominant notes in this convention. It is impressive in its love for humanity, its singleness of purpose. Unthinking, superficial, ribald persons might sneer at them, but the fineness of them is in their good faces, bespeaking intelligence, refinement and work for a cause in which their souls are warm. The men—many of them are ministers of the gospel, many are business men, some of them of more than ordinary success, while many more are of that stamp of earnest, courageous men you always find in a great moral movement, in a cause which has altruism and not any sort of selfishness whatever at the back of it."

Perhaps no better illustration can be given of the attitude, hopes and prospects of the Prohibition party than is reflected in the addresses notifying the candidates, this year, 1908, for President and Vice-President, of their nomination, and their responses.

The notification address to Eugene W. Chafin was delivered by Hon. Charles Scanlon, of Pittsburg, who was chairman of the convention. In the course of the address he said:

"It is an honor worthy of any man to be chosen as standard-bearer for such an exalted position by a company of men and women as unselfish in motive, lofty in aim, patriotic in spirit, sound in principle, firm in conviction, strong in faith, persistent in effort and logical in method, as ever stood forth in God's name to give battle to a mighty foe.

"You are not asked to lead a forlorn hope. The final issue of this struggle is not now nor ever has been in doubt. The principles advocated by the Prohibition Party are as certain to prevail as time is to continue.

"We do not claim that intemperance is the only sin in the world, or that the liquor traffic is the only subject demanding attention. There are many vitally important questions before the American nation, moral, social, religious, industrial, economic, sanitary, scientific—all pressing for solution. Among them are the race problem, impurity, bad literature, Mormonism, marriage and divorce, the prevention and treatment of crime, pauperism, insanity, degeneracy, disease, trusts, immigration, capital and labor, municipal government, political corruption, the development and preservation of our natural resources and others. But all of these would be greatly simplified, and some of them completely settled, by the extermination of the liquor traffic.

"Recognizing those other questions, the Prohibition party has framed a platform which is clear and concise, conservative, constructive and comprehensive. It contains everything of value in all of the others without their evasions, technicalities, obscurities, false issues, sophistries and subterfuges.

"But some one asks, What have the Prohibitionists done? They have unmasked the liquor traffic, and made it a by-word and a hissing throughout the world; they have taught every man, woman and child in the nation that one strong, simple word—PROHIBITION—on the lips of honest men, is the death warrant for the most atrocious criminal that ever preyed upon the human race; without deal or dicker, without compromise or confusion, and with unsullied garments they have moved through the political mire of nearly forty years, 'as conspicuously beautiful as a star riding solitary through the night'; under a galling fire of ridicule from opinionated opponents, up steep and stony paths which could be tracked only by the feet of fearless faith, they have borne aloft the banner of righteousness and planted it upon the ramparts of truth; they have stormed the citadel of antiquated science, and dispelled the medical superstitions of centuries; they have won verdicts from the courts which the liquor inter-

HON. EUGENE W. CHAFIN,
Presidential Candidate, Prohibition Party, 1908.

HON. AARON S. WATKINS,
Vice-Presidential Candidate, Prohibition Party, 1908.

ests would give millions to have reversed; they have expounded the word of God, so that on this great issue the church has harmonized its position with His revelation of Himself in his works of creation and in the life and teaching of His Son.

"These, Mr. Chafin, are the people and the principles you are commissioned to represent. If you command the support you deserve, you will have the praise, the sympathy, the assistance and the vote of as many as have votes, of the one hundred and sixty thousand ministers in the United States, of the one and one-half million Sabbath-school teachers, of the thirty million church members, of the four hundred and sixty thousand public schoolteachers, and of all others who love virtue and hate vice; and you will be the next President of the United States. If you do not get the support, you will deserve it, and that is better than to get the office and not deserve it."

Following are extracts from the response of Mr. Chafin:

"On the fourth of March, 1909, our National Government will have completed its 120th year of constitutional history. During that time twenty-five men have occupied the presidential office. All have been men of high distinction, and a few of them of eminent ability. For the first time since the death of Washington, December 14, 1799, we are without a living ex-president. When Lincoln took the oath of office five former presidents were living—the greatest number in our history. They did nothing to help him in the great struggle which resulted in the passage of the Thirteenth Amendment to the Constitution, which marked a higher standard of Christian civilization. They were the representatives of two dominant political parties, Whig and Democrat, which, for about fifty years, opposed the bringing of any great new question into the political arena.

"We are now approaching the close of another fifty years, where two dominant political parties, Republican and Democratic, have allied themselves with the most gigantic crime that ever cursed the world, and by their attitude make known to the American people that they do not propose to permit them to have a chance, even though the majority may favor it, to destroy the liquor traffic, and add another amendment to the Constitution which would mark the highest achievement of civilization in the world's history.

"Twenty-seven presidential campaigns have been more or less fiercely fought to gain control of the Government. Most of them have been battles over fictitious issues which had little or nothing to do with the administrations which followed. In not more than six instances would a line of American history have been changed if the defeated candidate had been elected instead of the successful one.

"For a long time there has been a disposition on the part of the leading politicians of the old parties to belittle and ignore the liquor problem. This has now reached an acute stage, which amounts to a conspiracy on the part of the leaders of these parties to coin up the conscience of the people into liquor license revenue and offices. To show that these parties are wrong and that the Prohibition party is right, and that we are justified in pressing this issue as by far the greatest in American politics, I will call but one witness. He was the greatest man who lived in the nineteenth century, Abraham Lincoln. He made five speeches in his lifetime, which constitute his political creed. One of them was upon the liquor question, for he was a life-long total abstainer and a prohibitionist. It was delivered at Springfield, Illinois, February 22, 1842. In the course of that speech he said:

" 'If the relative grandeur of revolutions shall be estimated by the great amount of human misery they alleviate and the small amount they inflict, then, indeed, will this revolution be the grandest the world shall ever have seen. Of our political revolution of '76 we are all justly proud. Turn now to the temperance revolution; in it we shall find a stronger bondage broken, a viler slavery manumitted, a greater tyrant deposed; in it more of want supplied, more disease healed, more sorrow assuaged. And when the victory shall be complete—when there shall be neither a slave nor a drunkard on the earth—how proud the title of that land, which may truly claim to be the birthplace and the cradle of both these revolutions that shall have ended in victory! How nobly distinguished that People who shall have planted, and nurtured to maturity, both the political and the moral freedom of their species!'

"I consider my nomination the highest honor that will be conferred upon an American citizen this presidential year. With a firm reliance upon Divine Providence, I accept your commission, and will hold high the banner of our party, and defend the only national platform made this year that recognizes Almighty God, and give all there is of me in thought, strength and soul, until these great reforms are crystallized into law, and the victory is complete."

The address to Aaron S. Watkins, notifying him of his nomination for the Vice-Presidency was delivered by Robert H. Patton, of Springfield, Ill., chairman of the notification committee. Among other things he said:

"As you, sir, are to be our leader for this distinguished national office, it is most appropriate that I here place, and that you and the party in this campaign place, the most emphasis upon that part of our platform which declares upon the burning question of the hour, the national prohibition of the traffic in intoxicating liquors. There can be no final, effective solution of the drink problem which stops short of the fullest recognition of the fact that this question is a national political issue. There may and will be local victories, resulting in relief of great value, but no permanent cure without the national death warrant to the liquor traffic.

"For this reason the Prohibition party, for the tenth time, has taken its stand for the national prohibition of the manufacture, sale, importation, exportation and transportation of alcoholic beverages. Local and state prohibition must be reinforced by national legislation. There is not a community or state which has outlawed the traffic but what knows and feels the necessity of such national action. There is a universal conspiracy to break down all prohibition laws, which can be met only by the concerted action of all the states backed by the power of the national government.

"In the first place the national government must change its attitude. It now stands as an interested party in its perpetuation, by sharing in the profits of this traffic. The government was not instituted for this, but 'to secure life, liberty and the pursuit of happiness.'

"The Constitution vests in Congress the control of interstate commerce. This makes this question a national issue of first magnitude today. All of our prohibition territory, state and local, lies helpless before the flood of liquors imported from other states. By newspaper advertisements and the United States mails, the distillers and brewers carry on this guerrilla warfare upon our homes in utter defiance of all local sentiment and laws.

"The Prohibition party in its platform declares there is a remedy for this condition, the constitutionality of which no good lawyer will question. The power of the national government to entirely prohibit the interstate traffic in liquors is conceded. For this we declare.

"From the exalted pinnacle of the home of Abraham Lincoln, out of the noise of tumult, riot and lawlessness, the blood of innocent victims cries today in unmistakable tones, and gives us a new revelation of the necessity for the speedy national outlawry of this traffic. The race riots of the past, of which our recent one at Springfield is without parallel in its atrocities, have written across the sky of both the North and the South the inevitable conclusion that peace, law and order cannot be perpetuated side by side with the saloon. The state of Georgia read this lesson in the riots of Atlanta, heeded it, and banished the saloon. The rest of the nation must do the same thing or reap the harvest they have sown."

Mr. Watkins, in accepting the nomination, made an address, from which the following extracts are taken:

"I am glad to be the nominee for Vice-President of this the greatest party now concerned in American politics. The question of the saloon is nation-wide in its scope. The liquor question affects every grade and form of government in this land. This of itself constitutes the liquor question, the greatest question in American politics, and the party that faces this question boldly and takes a stand upon it thus becomes the greatest of all political parties in America.

"The party which I represent is not only the greatest party in the breadth and scope of its principles, but it is the greatest in the unselfish devotion of its members to a high moral principle without any hope of reward, graft or emolument of any kind. Never before has the attention of our nation been directed with such keen interest to the doings of the Prohibition party as in this year of 1908. The press is anxious to secure copies of our addresses and to give prominence to our meetings and to our plans. The people hear us gladly and thoughtfully, and all this largely because they appreciate our unselfishness and admire the heroism of the movement.

"It is often assumed that a third party Prohibitionist has no confidence in any method of solution of the liquor traffic except the political one. Nothing could be further from the truth. In the State of which I am a citizen, hundreds of municipalities have voted out the saloon. In every case, no matter who had the management of the contest, the third party Prohibitionists were always in line, and always voted and usually worked with whatever influence they might possess for the ridding of their community of the saloon. In my own case, I have never allowed any temperance organization to exist anywhere within range of my influence without giving it my hearty support.

"We are shut up to one method of dealing with the question, and that is the method of prohibition. But the more serious problem arises, Shall prohibition be accomplished by means of a political party, or shall it be left to some non-partisan organization or effort? We insist that the partisan method is the only true method under existing circumstances.

"There are many well meaning temperance men who refuse to unite with the Prohibition party, believing that more immediate and practical results can be obtained through the influence of non-partisan organization. We refer such friends of the cause to recent events in the state of Ohio and other states. Men who have taken a very prominent position on the temperance question have, with almost uniform regularity, been relegated to private life, although we believe they had the good wishes of a majority of their constituents. The non-partisan method has disappointed its warmest advocates. It has not achieved the immediate and practical results that were predicted.

"But there are many who are dissatisfied with this method who still do not unite with the Prohibition party. They have their excuses or reasons for refusing to do so. One of the most common is, 'I do not want to throw away my vote.' In the state of Pennsylvania this year there is not one chance out of a thousand that Mr. Bryan will receive the electoral vote, and, since the votes of the individual citizens count for nothing unless they have achieved a plurality and obtained the electoral vote of the state, therefore, according to this principle, every Democrat in the state of Pennsylvania is now reasonably certain of 'throwing away his vote' at the coming election. Mr. Bryan will probably receive the electoral vote of Georgia; therefore, every Republican in Georgia will 'throw away his vote.'

"I confidently expect that many who are now before me will live to see the saloon an outlaw in all the states of the American Union. It may be that Mr. Chafin will not be elected President of the United States this year; it may be that I will never preside over the Senate; but some day a Prohibitionist will be occupying each of these positions. And when the record of the great temperance reformation is written by the impartial historian of the future, the convention which nominated Mr. Chafin and myself will take its place, along with the Virginia Convention and the Continental Congress, as a landmark of American progress and of worldwide reform."

In reports from representatives of the Prohibition Party in different states, one reads of heroic efforts in the face of almost overwhelming odds. Mr. John P. Coffin, State Chairman of Florida, says:

"Prohibition has taken hold of our state with such force that it will never again go back to the old status. Each day adds to the great army of those pledged to the utter extermination of the liquor traffic in the 'Land of Flowers,' and it is certain that, with the legislature and senate now nominated and sure of election, a constitutional amendment will be submitted to the people. When this is done we can

NATIONAL EXECUTIVE COMMITTEE, PROHIBITION PARTY, 1908.

A. A. STEVENS.    FELIX T. McWHIRTER.    J. B. CRANFILL.

CHARLES R. JONES.    W. G. CALDERWOOD.    A. G. WOLFENBARGER.

OLIVER W. STEWART.    SAMUEL DICKIE.    FINLEY C. HENDRICKSON.

rest assured of victory by an overwhelming majority. Many of the wholesale liquor houses and distilleries are flocking to our large cities from neighboring states which have driven them out. They are locating here in the hope that, with the power of their combined wealth, they can put off the evil day. But they are building upon an insecure foundation, for the people of Florida have made up their minds that this great evil shall not overshadow them and spread a blight upon the youth and maidens of this sunny land. More than this, the employers of labor, the merchant and the farmer, have found out that the way to bring and keep prosperity is to banish that which tends only to destroy it. They see that the great love professed for them by the dealers in liquor is only for the dollars they may take from them. The rank and file of the state is solidly against the manufacture and sale of the stuff in Florida.

"We expect to cast the largest vote for the Prohibition Party that has ever been cast in the state at the next election. But no matter what the Prohibition Party as a party does or does not do, it is certain that the people of all parties will join hand to hand to drive liquor out. Victory is assured, even before the gage of battle has been cast."

The Chairman of the State Executive Committee, Idaho, Mr. Aaron M. Bray, says:

"Idaho has had a law on her statute books for several years giving the different cities and towns the right to prohibit the liquor traffic. The last legislature gave county commissioners the right to refuse license in rural districts, and this has been done in some cases. Through the labors of Mr. Nichols and others a number of towns have closed the saloons.

"The Prohibition Party stands for statewide prohibition, and, in the meantime, advises its members to take advantage of the laws we now have. Some counties have in their own conventions declared for local option, in some cases declaring for the county as the unit. Opposition to the liquor traffic is growing fast, and will doubtless result in something before long. The *Sunday Morning Statesman* is conducting a forum on the liquor question, in which all kinds of arguments are given on all sides of the question."

On the face of the statutes Georgia is a saloonless state. Colonel W. S. Witham, Chairman Prohibition Party Executive Committee, says:

"The prohibition law works beautifully in Atlanta and the state, and is a success everywhere except in two or three cities where the mayor and other officials by negligence encourage the whisky people, who have sworn to bring the law into disrepute.

"When the legislature passed the law the present wet city officials were in office and will hold over this year. Certain members of the legislature from some city districts have given notice to the legislature and the people of Georgia that the law would not be upheld in their towns. One of these cities has kept the promise.

"The whisky people openly state that their success has always been, and will continue to be, through bringing the law into disrepute.

"Twenty years ago the city of Atlanta went dry, and the Prohibitionists immediately folded their arms and went to sleep, as is the custom of Prohibitionists everywhere, while the whisky people diligently worked the *disrepute* trick, and whisky came back.

"The chief of Atlanta police stated, at a mayoralty convention, that whisky drinking and crime has been reduced about fifty per cent. in Atlanta since the prohibition law went into effect.

"The saloon has been and is now charged with having been the direct cause of the riot which occurred in our city last year."

In little Delaware, where the anti-saloon sentiment has been developing and crystallizing into laws, there has been a Prohibition Party organization since 1888. Mr. R. M. Cooper, Chairman of the State Committee, says:

"The state has been under a moderate license law for many years, license granted by the court on petition of applicant endorsed by twenty-four respectable citizens—respectability often questionable.

"The party has had an active working force in the state. We have barely held our own all these years, because the two old parties have tried to freeze us out. The better class of old party men would say, 'You are all right,' but they continued to vote the license ticket.

"Numerous efforts were made to secure the passage of a local option bill by people of all parties, but all efforts proved failures until 1903, when a prominent Democratic lawyer openly announced himself in favor of such legislation. When the bill was passed and the way open, the better class of voters organized for local option, sentiment grew in strength, and friends of the cause in numbers, even the colored voters falling in line, till unexpected majorities won the election for the two southern counties, and reduced the license vote in lower New Castle so that a little more effort would have won it also.

"Regardless of party, the better class of citizens openly avow themselves in favor of men for state officers who stand firmly for enforcement of present laws and further legislation for prohibition in the state, and national legislation to stop interstate traffic. The candidates who stand for these things will get the votes, all other issues being out of the question for the time being."

Many of the men who made the Prohibition Party, and who still are making political history in the United States as pioneers of reform, are still living. One of them, Mr. T. B. Demaree, of Kentucky, a member of the National Prohibition Committee, gives a bit of his life story:

"I was one of the organizers of the party in Kentucky, in 1876. Gen. Green Clay Smith and myself were the organizers and the first members of the National Committee, and I have been honored with that position continuously up to the present.

"The Independent Order of Good Templars was the first to strike for a law prohibiting the sale of liquor in this state. In 1872 the Grand Lodge appointed a committee to secure petitioners asking the legislature to submit the question to a vote. Nearly 200,000 names were secured, and the writer was one of a committee to present it. The House passed the measure, but it hung fire in the Senate after the liquor dealers sent tens of thousands of dollars to defeat it. But they gave us a local option law as a compromise, and in a very short time we had over one-half of the state under local prohibition. And this is all the legislation we have ever been able to secure. But with it we have voted out the saloons in ninety-seven of the one hundred and nineteen counties in the state, and in all except four or five counties there are saloons in the county-seats only.

"There were only four persons present at the organization of the party, and I believe that I, alone, remain. The others have crossed over the river."

W. G. Calderwood, Secretary Minnesota Prohibition Committee, writes:

"The first movement in this state looking toward a party that would take up the prohibition question was inaugurated about 1876. In the election of 1877 a temperance ticket was in the field and received 2,396 votes. Subsequently this was increased to 9,030, and in 1888 the Prohibition Party polled 17,026.

"After suffering repeated defeats, at the close of the campaign of 1902 the State Executive Committee determined that the usefulness of the Prohibition Party as a mere protest or political purity organization had passed. It had taught the lesson of the evil of the saloon, and it now confronted the new problem of delivering political results commensurate with the purpose of the party. It was determined to concentrate the entire force on the legislature, and in 1904 this was carried into execution. The legislative vote in 1902 was only 4,000. Nominations were made in twelve districts, and the legislative vote increased 12,000. In one instance, the Prohibitionists lacked only sixteen votes; in another fifty. In 1906 the party nominated candidates in thirty-two districts, pushed the legislative vote to 32,000, and elected three men to the legislature, without the advantage of any cumulative system of voting, such as Illinois enjoys, a record equaled by no other state in the Union. The value of this achievement is accentuated by the fact that a clean party fight was made in every instance, and that no endorsement in any district was given by any other party or organization. In no other state did the Prohibitionists elect three out of a total of one hundred and nineteen. 'Out to Win' campaigns were conducted, not so much as party campaigns as 'good men' campaigns.

"In the 1908 campaign nominations were made in forty-eight out of sixty-three legislative districts of the state with seventy-one candidates out of a total of one hundred and eighteen. "Out to Win' campaigns were conducted in thirty-nine districts."

Edwin C. Hadley, Chairman of the Kansas Prohibition Committee, writes:

"Prohibition (state constitutional) in Kansas twenty-eight years well enforced in four-sixths of the state, partially enforced in one-sixth of the state, poorly enforced in one-sixth of the state. Wherever poorly enforced it is because of public officials (sheriffs, prosecutors, mayors, etc.) who have no regard for their oaths of office. Open joints (saloons) in probably not over a half dozen places in the state. In most places where the law is not enforced the trouble is with the drug stores which do not obey the law as to selling for medicinal purposes only.

"In Kansas City, Kansas, formerly most hostile as far as public opinion was concerned, the law has been well enforced for two years, owing to the courage of Assistant Attorney General C. W. Trickett. Kansas City, Kansas, last year had the largest proportionate increase in building operations of any city of the Union, according to a Federal census bureau report.

"Political parties, as such (except Prohibition Party), have never stood for prohibition in Kansas, and not until the last and present campaign have they stood for law-enforcement.

"Thousands of grown men and women in the state never saw a saloon. The sight of a drunken man is very rare in any of the Kansas cities and towns. Even lax enforcement of a prohibitory law is much better than open saloons.

"The Prohibition Party has had slow growth in Kansas, because the voters, having state prohibition, have not realized the additional importance of national prohibition.

"Continual attempts of brewers to get the question re-submitted in Kansas have always failed. Nine-tenths of the people are in favor of prohibition.

"Thirty-five counties of the state have empty jails, and thirty-seven counties have no criminal cases on the docket. Forty-four counties are without a single pauper, and twenty-five counties have no poorhouses."

In New York state is a good illustration of what earnest effort systematically directed will accomplish. In 1907, Mr. C. E. Pitts, a young attorney of Oswego, N. Y., was made Chairman of the State Committee. Mr. Pitts had had experience in connection with a very successful organization of Oswego County. He introduced the methods learned there in the state work with excellent results. In a brief account of the work in New York state, he says:

"At the time of the birth of the Prohibition party in this state, which occurred at Oswego in 1869, the state was blessed with strong men in the Prohibition line. After 1882, the vote increased rapidly, to 25,000 in 1884, and to 41,000 in 1891, we holding a large balance of power in the state. Then came the free silver split in our party ranks, and our vote dropped down to 17,000, and we were nearly wiped off the ballot.

"Then for years after that disastrous campaign, amid great discouragements, State Chairman J. H. Durkee fought for the advancement of the party, and got the vote back to 22,000, but, since we had not a vestige of real working organization, the vote again began to slump until it dropped below 16,000 in 1906. We had no organization worthy of the name, no systematic enrollment, no election district, town and ward committees, except in rare cases.

"In the meantime, Oswego County had been organized and enrolled

A. U. COATES,
Member, National Committee, Prohibition Party, Iowa.

F. W. LOUGH,
Chairman, Indiana Prohibition State Committee.

ALONZO E. WILSON,
Member, National Committee, Prohibition Party; Chairman, Illinois Prohibition State Committee.

HURAM W. DAVIS,
Chairman, Kentucky Prohibition State Committee.

by election precincts, fighting organizations builded, towns swept by the Prohibition party, four score Prohibitionists elected to office over their Republican and Democratic opponents. The county conventions had increased in size from 11 delegates in 1900 to 335 in 1906. This led to a demand for the same kind of organization and work in the entire state, since a similar *pro rata* vote in all the counties would mean 250,000 votes in the state, and over 4,000 officials elected to office.

"In March, 1907, the writer was elected State Chairman. We at once inaugurated Oswego County plans in the balance of the state, and have been cheered by scores of our discouraged men rallying to the fight. At present we have over three-fourths of the 4,522 election districts of the state enrolled so that we know every Prohibition voter and can place our hand on him at any time. We have over one-half of the election districts organized. We are placing in our county and district workers' hands over sixty kinds of supplies for organization and work. As a result, the entire party organization is becoming uniform, and our men all along the line are moving forward.

"Our county conventions this year have run from three to fifteen times the usual size. Our state convention was three times as large as usual, and ten-fold more enthusiastic, over one thousand Prohibition workers being present.

"We have tickets in every one of the over 550 judicial, congressional, senatorial, county, assembly and school commissioner districts of the state where candidates are voted for this fall. Full tickets everywhere and one continuous word of cheer comes from the counties, east, south, west and north. Our men are working like beavers. We shall poll 50,000 votes in the Empire State this fall.

"We are also pushing the "Venango Plan" (named from the county of its birth), by which the voters sign a pledge-card agreeing to vote the Prohibition ticket in the given town or county when a specified number (enough to make a majority) have signed. We are pushing this in two 'concentration districts,' and seven out of every ten voters approached are signing. Illustration—the town of Wilna, Jefferson County, has 1,050 voters, and with but five-sixths of the town canvassed, we have six hundred and fifty signatures to the Venango pledge; Champion, with 512 votes has 381 signed. The state committee will concentrate enough work in these counties to sweep them, then branch out into others.

"We shall hold 10,000 meetings in the rural schoolhouses and churches of the little hamlets and villages, reaching scores of thousands of voters who never before heard our issues discussed. We have placed in the county chairman's hands nine kinds of supplies, and matters are nicely started and will be kept going.

"We have an extraordinarily strong ticket this fall, headed by the Hon. George E. Stockwell for Governor, and Marshall A. Hudson for Lieutenant Governor."

The following table shows the votes cast in the different states for Presidential and Vice Presidential candidates from the first campaign in 1872 up to the election of 1904. It is but fair to say that the small votes polled by the party are entirely out of proportion to the strong and wholesome influence it exerts:

PROHIBITION PARTY'S VOTE, 1872 TO 1904.

STATE	1904 SWALLOW	1900 WOOLLEY	1896 LEVERING	1892 BIDWELL	1888 FISK	1884 ST. JOHN	1880 DOW	1876 SMITH	1872 BLACK
Alabama	612	2,762	2,147	239	583	613			
Arizona	125								
Arkansas	993	584	839	113	641				
California	7,380	5,024	2,573	8,096	5,761	2,960	61		
Colorado	3,438	3,790	1,717	1,652	2,191	761			
Connecticut	1,506	1,617	1,808	4,026	4,234	2,305	409	378	205
Delaware	607	538	355	564	400	64			
Florida	5	2,234	1,778	561	423	72			
Georgia	685	1,396	5,613	988	1,808	168			
Idaho	1,013	857	179	288					
Illinois	34,770	17,626	9,796	25,870	21,695	12,074	443	141	
Indiana	23,817	13,718	3,056	13,050	9,881	3,028			
Iowa	11,061	9,502	3,192	6,343	3,550	1,472	592	36	
Kansas	7,245	3,605	1,921	4,553	6,779	4,495	25	110	
Kentucky	6,609	3,780	4,781	6,442	5,225	3,139	258	818	
Louisiana					160	328			
Maine	1,510	2,585	1,570	3,062	2,691	2,160	93		
Maryland	3,044	4,582	5,918	5,877	4,767	2,827		10	
Massachusetts	4,274	6,202	2,998	7,539	8,701	9,923	682	84	
Michigan	13,302	11,859	5,025	20,857	20,942	17,403	942	767	1,271
Minnesota	6,199	8,167	4,348	14,017	15,311	4,684	286	144	
Mississippi			485	910	218				
Missouri	7,181	5,965	2,169	4,298	4,539	2,153		64	
Montana	327	298	186	549					
Nebraska	6,326	3,655	1,193	4,902	9,429	2,899		1,599	
Nevada				89	41				
New Hampshire	749	1,270	779	1,296	1,566	1,570	180		200
New Jersey	6,838	7,183	5,614	8,136	7,904	6,153	191	43	
New Mexico									
New York	20,787	22,043	16,052	38,193	30,231	24,999	1,517	2,329	201
North Carolina	361	1,006	675	2,636	2,789	454			
North Dakota	1,105	731	358	899					
Ohio	19,339	10,203	5,068	26,012	24,356	11,069	2,616	1,636	2,100
Oklahoma	1,544								
Oregon	3,795	2,536	919	2,281	1,677	492			
Pennsylvania	33,717	27,908	19,274	25,123	20,947	15,283	1,939	1,319	1,630
Rhode Island	768	1,529	1,160	1,654	1,250	928	20	68	
South Carolina							43		
South Dakota	2,965	1,542	685						
Tennessee	1,889	3,900	3,098	4,856	5,969	1,131			
Texas	4,244	2,644	1,786	2,165	4,749	3,534			
Utah		205							
Vermont	792	368	733	1,424	1,460	1,752			
Virginia	1,382	2,150	2,350	2,798	1,682	138			
Washington	3,229	2,363	968	2,553					
West Virginia	4,604	1,585	1,203	2,145	1,084	739			
Wisconsin	9,770	10,124	7,509	13,132	14,277	7,656	96	153	
Wyoming	207		136	530					
TOTALS	260,114	209,936	132,009	269,191	249,907	150,626	10,366	9,737	5,607

CHAPTER XXIII.

SYMPHONY OF THE STATES.

THE following statements of the anti-liquor situation in each of the states and territories are condensed from reports furnished by the official representatives of the Prohibition Party, the Woman's Christian Temperance Union, the Anti-Saloon League, and other active workers in the field. Limitations of space have compelled condensation to the lowest terms. It is unfortunate that the flavor of personality, and the fragrance of faith, courage, patience and triumph that characterizes these reports, must be lost. Changing the simile, it may well be said of them that they do indeed constitute a *Symphony*, a sounding together of a song of faith, gladness and triumph.

A careful endeavor has been made to make these reports accurate and up to date. But the battle is in progress everywhere, victories are being won daily, and progress is so rapid that it is difficult to keep the record even with the events.

It was the original plan to print, in connection with these reports, maps showing wet and dry territory in each state, but it was found that, owing to the rapid additions that are being made to dry territory, the maps would be out of date by the time they could be printed. For the same reason it is found impossible to present a summary showing in totals the wet and dry territory and population for the whole country.

ALABAMA.

Alabama is soon to become one of the *dry* states. In 1908, the legislature enacted a state prohibitory law, to take effect January 1, 1909. Local option had previously driven the saloons out of fifty of the sixty-seven counties. At the last previous session of the legislature, laws were enacted giving county local option and preventing shipment of liquor from wet territory to dry. Under this law there are, at latest advices, only four counties in the state where saloons are located, one with barrooms and dispensary saloon, and twelve with dispensary saloons. These will disappear when the new law goes into effect. B. B. Comer, Governor, utters these hopeful words:

"It is not the man who does the drinking and commits the deed who suffers most. The man in prison is cared for; his victim, God knows where! It is the mothers, wives and orphans of these men who do the suffering. Suffering is not caused by these criminals within the walls of the penitentiary only, but by those at home who frequent the saloons, spending their money for drink, leaving their wives and children in squalor without the protection of their rightful guardian.

"Our larger towns, Birmingham, Decatur, Gadsden, Huntsville and Dothan, under prohibition, have greatly decreased their criminal record. We estimate that with a few years of prohibition our penitentiaries will show a marked decrease in the number of their inmates.

"I think the above statement of facts would be sufficient to make any humane party do all he can for prohibition. Aside from this, we think our state will have several millions a year that has hitherto gone for liquor. This leaves a margin for illicit and other sales."

CALIFORNIA.

In 1898, Sutter County and ten small towns were under prohibitory law. Outside of this area every square foot in the state was practically under domination of the liquor traffic. There was then no legislative provision for the banishment of existing saloons, no public official seeking to obtain such legislation, and apparently no one else who had any hope of seeing the liquor traffic dethroned. However, the state had given John Bidwell, as Presidential candidate on the Prohibition ticket in 1892, the Woman's Christian Temperance Union and other organizations were at work, and the anti-saloon sentiment did exist. But, with the organization of an Anti-Saloon League, under the leadership of Rev. Ervin S. Chapman, D. D., author of "THE STAINLESS FLAG," the tide turned. With him in command, the forces rallied, and apparent defeat was turned into victory. There are now over fifty incorporated cities and scores of towns and villages which have driven out the saloon. Five counties have prohibitory ordinances, and others would have if the popular will could find expression in a referendum. Five counties have precinct option ordinances, under which there are more than 150 "dry" precincts.

On "Stainless Flag Day," 1907, 1,000 pastors delivered addresses appropriate to the occasion, and distributed 135,000 copies of the Stainless Flag Address in their congregations.

ALASKA.

NOTE.—*The following statement was prepared specially for this book. It is significant and important because it proves that an executive can enforce law without consulting so-called public sentiment. The dance halls and gambling saloons were closed by exercise of police powers, and*

MRS. IMOGENE F. H. LaCHANCE,
President, Arizona W. C. T. U.

MISS CHRISTIANNA G. GILCHRIST,
Vice-President, Arizona W. C. T. U.

MRS. S. D. WILBUR,
Treasurer, Arizona W. C. T. U.

MRS. LUELLA E. THOMAS,
Corresponding Secretary, Arizona W. C. T. U.

MRS. ANNA THOMPSON,
Recording Secretary, Arizona W. C. T. U.

the laws proposed, while in advance of public opinion, are crystallizing an attitude hostile to the traffic in intoxicating liquors.—G. M. H.

By Hon. W. B. Hoggatt, *Governor.*

I have to state that since I became Governor of this territory, two years ago, we have succeeded in closing all dance-halls and gambling halls, both of which had heretofore flourished in all parts of the territory in connection with the saloons.

We are now making a strong effort to prevent the licensing of saloons, except in incorporated towns and places where we have a United States Commissioner or marshal resident. I asked Congress for an amendment to our code which would enable us to effect this reform, and a bill, H. B. 21,957, passed both houses of Congress at its last session, and is now on the Speaker's table ready for conference at the beginning of next session. If this becomes a law, as I think it will, the number of saloons in Alaska will be reduced by one-half.

These reforms are as yet somewhat in advance of the public sentiment of the territory, but, when in effect, I am satisfied will be sustained by growing public sentiment.

ARIZONA.

Arizona has a local option law, but it requires a two-thirds majority to expel the saloons. At an election held in May, 1908, in Maricopa County, there was a majority of 203 against the saloons, but not a two-thirds majority. A movement is on foot to secure a change in the law, making a mere majority sufficient under local option to eradicate the saloon. The Anti-Saloon Leagues of New Mexico and Arizona are under the same management. Since 1900 there has been a Prohibition party contingent in Arizona, but its vote has been small.

ARKANSAS.

Of the 75 counties, 58 are dry. Eighty per cent. of the population is in dry territory, and 68 per cent. has been in dry territory for ten years. In 1894 the license majority was 52,358. In 1906 the no-license majority was 15,618. The people vote by wards, townships and counties on the question of selling liquor. All applicants for license must pay $400 county tax, $300 state tax and from $50 to $200 in addition to the county fund. Saloons can be prohibited within three miles of a church or school by petition. Under provision of this law a campaign was instituted during 1908, and the Church Temperance Association, under the leadership of a commissioner, was in the front of the fight. He predicted that in six months Arkansas would be without licensed saloons.

Election returns (September 17, 1908) indicate that Little Rock, Pine Bluff, Helena, Texarkana and Newport have gone wet, the large number of negroes being voted like sheep for license candidates. St. Francois and other interior counties voted dry. Claims of fraud are made on every hand, the election officials being charged with ignoring the requirement that negroes shall show poll tax receipts before being allowed to vote.

COLORADO.

In Colorado there are eight general regulatory laws against the saloon which, if enforced by the authorities or voluntarily obeyed by the saloon men, would close all the dram-shops in the state. The saloon-keeper is prohibited from selling after midnight and on Sunday. He is not permitted to sell to minors, nor are women permitted to frequent his place of business. Wine rooms are prohibited. He cannot sell to Indians, idiots or drunkards.

Previous to the passage of the local option law in 1907 there were a large number of prohibition and no-license communities in the state. In the two largest, Colorado Springs and Greeley, there is a clause in the title deeds prohibiting forever the manufacture, sale or giving away of intoxicating drinks as a beverage on the property, subject to forfeiture of property right to the Townsite Company if the regulation is violated. Other communities of this class are Fort Morgan, Steamboat Springs, and, during the current year, still other places have been organized subject to the same property conditions.

The passage of the local option law last year gave each municipality, ward or voting precinct the right to settle the saloon question by majority vote. In the elections which have been held under this law, twenty towns gave majorities against the saloon, among them suburbs of Denver, such as Highland, South Denver, University Park, Berkeley, Barnum and Harmon. Other places already had no-license ordinances.

A fight under county local option is under way, and several counties are dry.

CONNECTICUT.

In 1854, a prohibitory law was enacted, but repealed in 1872. Then followed local option laws. Licenses are granted by county commissioners selected by the legislature. A vote on the question, saloon or no saloon, may be taken annually upon petition of twenty-five voters. Of 168 municipalities, 96 are dry. The tax levied on the retail liquor traffic is $450 in towns of over 3,000, and $250 in all other places. In small towns a license may be issued to a well-regulated hotel at not less than $150.

The temperance forces are working harmoniously by their different methods toward state prohibition. The Connecticut Temperance Union is the oldest state temperance organization in the United States, and antedates the National Temperance Society by nearly a year. It does the work of the Anti-Saloon League, with which it affiliates, and carries the burden of other reform movements. The W. C. T. U. is a decided force, and the Good Templars, Sons of Temperance, Catholic Total Abstinence Union, etc., are all working well in their special fields. Annually, in September, a "get-together meeting" is held. All shades of opinion are freely and frankly expressed, and a friendly discussion of differences produces a closer union.

DELAWARE.

In 1897 the Constitutional Convention adopted a provision for local option on prohibition or license, which hostile legislatures rendered abortive.

After ten years of effort by the Delaware State Temperance Alliance and affiliated bodies a general local option law was enacted in 1907. As a result, Kent and Sussex counties, embracing two-thirds of the geographical area of the state, were delivered from the saloon. New Castle county and the city of Wilmington, the metropolis of the state, were not so fortunate.

The anti-liquor forces are now making vigorous efforts to secure law enforcement in Kent and Sussex counties, to elect legislators in New Castle county favorable to re-submission of the question to voters, to influence the selection of a congressman from Delaware favorable to national temperance legislation, and to end the domination of the saloon and its agents in all parts of the commonwealth. There will be no rest until state-wide prohibition is secured.

DISTRICT OF COLUMBIA.

The Anti-Saloon League was organized in the District of Columbia when there were 1,100 saloon licenses, with the number increasing every year. Had the rate of increase continued, there would be 1,400 saloons in the District. They have decreased to about 600.

The anti-liquor forces of the District are seeking prohibitory legislation. A local option bill, recommended by the commissioners of the District at the session of Congress 1907-1908, while not as far reaching as desired, will, if passed, greatly lessen the evils of the traffic in the national capital.

FLORIDA.

A local option provision was incorporated in the constitution in 1887. Of 46 counties, 37 are dry. Only twenty-two incorporated towns have saloons. Nearly three-quarters of the population live under prohibitory law, and the laws against the sale of liquor are very stringent. There are only about 240 saloons left in the state, and a law forbidding saloons within four miles of a church or school building, except in incorporated towns, has enabled the citizens to extend dry territory.

There is a state license of $500, but counties, towns, and cities, may impose an additional license not to exceed $250.

There is a growing sentiment for state-wide prohibition. N. B. Broward, Governor, says:

"When my opinion is asked on the subject by any member of the legislature, I do not hesitate to say that I believe in prohibition, and if the resolution were passed and before the people, I should favor its adoption and speak in its favor. I would suggest that the ministry of the state urge each member of the Senate and House to vote for the measure, and in that way the woods, so to speak, may be fired to that extent that whatever the motive may have been that prompted the introduction, the resolution will be forced to a successful conclusion."

GEORGIA.

As a result of one of the most remarkable campaigns in the history of the anti-saloon war a prohibition bill was passed by the Georgia Senate, July, 1907, by a vote of 34 to 7; the House passed the bill by 139 to 39; and Governor Hoke Smith signed it on August 6. The law went into effect on January 1, 1908, with a strong legislative backing, and an overwhelming prohibition sentiment among the white people. One hundred and twenty-five out of 148 counties were already dry, and practically 93 per cent. of the state was under prohibitory law.

The results of prohibition are most gratifying. The courts have almost nothing to do. A drunken man is seldom seen, and sometimes in the city of Atlanta, with a population of 100,000, there is not a prisoner in the station house. Drunkenness has decreased 50 per cent., and crime 75 per cent. Another noticeable feature of improved conditions is a marked decrease of the jug trade.

Prohibition has come to stay, and Georgia will enforce her law at all hazards. Hoke Smith, Governor, says:

"It is absolutely impossible to have a permanent, decent municipal government where the saloon dominates municipal politics. The elimination of the saloon will help municipal politics everywhere, even in those places where the saloon does not dominate municipal politics.

"Over one hundred counties in the state have had prohibition for years. They have outgrown counties situated similarly which permitted the sale. There is no doubt that prohibition is wise from an economic standpoint. The overwhelming sentiment of the white people of Georgia is for prohibition, and the law will be enforced."

HAWAII.

By John G. Woolley.

NOTE.—*During the year 1907, Mr. John G. Woolley lectured in the islands in the interest of the Anti-Saloon League. He resided in Honolulu and from that city wrote several articles which were published in* The Daily News *of Chicago. In one of these he gives a very interesting account of the conditions and prospects.*—G. M. H.

"Since the treaty of annexation and the consequent increase in tourist traffic, and especially the increased number of warships and transports that put in here, saloons have multiplied in number, influence and malign results—the native having become not only a customer but also a possible commodity in liquor legislation and law non-enforcement. The saloons have been tolerated by the good but futile 'leading class' on the hoary misconception that the military and tourist visitors are against unfermented hospitality in all its possible and delightful forms, when almost any tourist, and an increasing number of soldiers and sailors would testify that they drink because they run up against the goods and the custom, rather than because they seek to do it.

"The white population is small, intelligent, reputable, prosperous and benevolent, but greatly weakened in its political influence by a certain South Sea, unconscious holier-than-thou-ness, which, along with a splendid inheritance of good blood, good sense, good training and good fortune, has come down from missionary times; and paralyzed in its political efficiency by inter-marriages.

"Long contemplation of the immoralities of the natives has induced a prevalent strabismus in the whites as to immoralities of their own; and civic courage has gone glimmering in a mesh-work of affinities and consanguinities. The basest job-chaser is likely to be son-in-law or brother-in-law to the best and cleanest; the wine and the spirit merchant is likely to be cousin to the deacon; and brewery stock spreads like the Russian thistle through the assets of the pious. All this of course is fatal to clean administration; but only for the time being, for a sounder substratum of good character than there is here is nowhere. The federal and territorial officials have been and are, with rare exceptions, men of unblemished integrity; but the county and city organizations are molasses barrels to the blue-bottle flies of tainted politics.

"In the native mind white society is missionary society, and the inconsistency of missionary preaching with 'missionary' practice is the *pons asinorum* of native progress. In the old missionary days the chiefs were absolute and the people something worse than serfs. The teachings of the missionaries took strong hold of the King and the chiefs, with such effect that the islands came by fiat under complete prohibition more than half a century ago, and even the great chiefs poured out their fluid deviltry upon the sand. Then crime and disorder all but disappeared, and the wonderful little christendom enjoyed its golden age. Afterward came the constitution, with representative government, freehold lands, and the seven-devilness of a reinstated liquor trade; and finally, American rule with moneyism, partyism, and the infamous doctrine that saloons and slums and crimes are normal symptoms of human liberty.

"Thus 'missionaries' were, relatively, as unfit for suffrage as the natives. They had learned to think of themselves as wheat-kernels in bins of chaff, and before they had quite awakened to the phenomenon that what seemed shucks to them was grain too, the political liquor-dealer had preempted the mill-site.

"It is a land of principle and of good deportment. But the only conviction I could see that was red-hot and ready for the anvil, was that the natives are amiable, unstable, and desperately in need of temperance work. But the natives not only bear the brunt of the liquor evil, they have the votes by which to banish it. The population of the islands is about 155,000, of which there are native Hawaiians 54,000, white 13,000, Chinese 26,000, Japanese 62,000, and a few thousand negroes and Porto Ricans. Of the Orientals only those born here are entitled to vote.

"I visited several conventions of native ministers, and found them very intelligent as to conditions and very receptive as to ways and means. My interpreter was the Rev. Stephen Desha, a half-white grandson of the old Governor of Kentucky, a man of power in whose glorious eloquence my small speeches became sheaves of thunderbolts, whereat my pleasure was made humble and my humility pleasant. But the problem was to reach the native masses. Accordingly, at the time this letter is written, I am *en route* around Robin Hood's historic barn to the ballot-box *via* the school-house.

"Armed with permission from the territorial superintendent of public instruction I have spent eight days circumnavigating this island of Oahu in a road-wagon, and speaking in every public school on the island about how to mix drinks and good gray matter to produce success in life.

"Teachers and pupils received me with enthusiasm, and I knew instantly when beginning to address them that the soil was ready to be sown. A few questions brought out clearly that the case against the liquor traffic is made out in every nook and corner of the country. Practically every child old enough to understand was keen to sign the pledge of total abstinence. But I asked them to postpone the decision until they had talked it over at home, when, if they wished, they could write me a letter.

"I go now to make a similar tour of the other islands. Then, having met all the teachers and pupils and got the subject into the homes in that way, I go over the same routes, holding public meetings for the adults, and finally close the campaign with a series of meetings for the whites in Honolulu. It is the most elementary work I have yet had, but very interesting and good in my opinion for great returns. Great prohibition news is coming from the Mainland. Before many months the Mainland shall hear good news from us."

IDAHO.

Idaho has been a license state, although she has had a law on her statute books for several years giving cities and towns the right to prohibit the traffic. But few persons knew anything about it, and no advantage was taken of it until Mr. Emmett D. Nichols called attention to it and began agitating the matter of getting municipalities to act within their statutory rights. County commissioners have power to refuse license in rural districts, and in some cases this has been done. Meridian was the first town which closed its saloons. Malad, and Moscow—seat of the State University—and other towns in the same county have passed prohibitory ordinances. Opposition to the traffic is developing rapidly, and soon will find expression through a direct local option law.

In 1904 there was no dry territory. In 1908 many towns are under no license and saloons are closed on Sunday by state law.

ILLINOIS.

In Illinois the minimum license is $500, but there is no limit on the maximum license which may be exacted, and in many municipalities the license fee is placed at a $1,000.

The law of 1907 provides for local option by townships and municipalities, and by precincts and counties not under township organization. In the spring election of 1908, out of 1,250 townships voting, 900 abolished the saloon. Of the 1,400 townships in the state 1,053 are now "dry." Twenty-five counties were voted dry, making a total of 36 dry counties in the state. Of the 40 larger cities voting upon the question 22 were carried by the anti-saloon forces. The largest city which voted dry was Rockford, with a population of 40,000, where 53 saloons were suppressed. The large vote cast in cities like Springfield, Bloomington, Joliet, Danville, Elgin, Aurora, Rock Island, Moline, means that there are multitudes of people living in these cities who are seeking relief from the presence of the saloon. This should be granted in the form of a resident district bill.

Among the most effective forces in the creation of anti-saloon sentiment is the system of Chautauqua Assemblies conducted by the Prohibition Party.

INDIANA.

By Governor J. F. Hanly.

Three years and a half ago I recommended to the General Assembly that it pass a law giving the majority of the legal voters of a township or city ward the right to remonstrate against the traffic in intoxicating liquors at retail, and making it unlawful for the Board of County Commissioners, after the filing of such a remonstrance, to grant a license to any person within such territory for a period of two years. Under this law 830 townships have inhibited this traffic.

Public sentiment has been created in behalf of this law, and public opinion has advanced under the demonstration of the benefits derived from the inhibition of the dram-shop in these communities, until, today, the people of the state would, in my judgment, overwhelmingly favor the enactment of a county local option law that will preserve without impairment the present remonstrance law and be additional and supplementary thereto. Personally, I am so fully persuaded of the moral, economic and financial value of such legislation that I shall recommend and earnestly insist upon the enactment of such a measure.

The Moore remonstrance law, enacted 1905, is in effect local option by a majority petition of voters in townships and city wards, the township including all incorporated towns, but not cities. Forty-three county-seat towns, 20 cities, 250 incorporated towns and 23 counties are dry. Eight hundred and nineteen townships are dry. And, in the wet cities, 53 wards and 37 residence districts are dry, making a net population of 230,000 living in dry territory in cities which are partly wet. There are 1,579,775 people of the state living in dry territory; 600 saloons were closed during the first six months of 1908, and 80 per cent. of the territory of the state now grants no license.

NOTE.—*In September, 1908, Governor Hanly convened the legislature in special session for the adoption of a county local option law, which was passed by a handsome majority.*—G. M. H.

IOWA.

In 1883 a prohibitory amendment to the constitution was secured, but it was declared void by the state supreme court. The legislature then enacted a prohibitory law. This was afterwards amended by a mulct provision, which practically nullified the prohibitory law in any community upon petition of 65 per cent. of the voters. Of the 99 counties in the state 77 are dry; of the 1,112 municipalities 975 grant no license. The minimum tax is $600. In 1906 2,000 saloons were operating in Iowa; in 1908 there were only 1,600. A total of 1,225,000 of the population live in dry territory.

A campaign for a re-submission of the constitutional amendment has been inaugurated, but it will be necessary to pass the bill in two general assemblies before it can be submitted to the people for special election. In January, 1908, a mass meeting was held in Des Moines, and the different temperance organizations—W. C. T. U., Prohibition Party, Anti-Saloon League, etc.—entered into a federation to work for the amendment. These forces are enlisted for the three and a half years campaign necessary under the law.

SYMPHONY OF THE STATES.

KANSAS.

By Hon. E. W. Hoch, Governor.

Note.—*The governor of Kansas very kindly has contributed the following brief statement of the situation in his state. Kansas is one of the pioneers in the prohibition movement, and the magnificent results that have followed her successful experiment are a most valuable object lesson for the citizens of other commonwealths.*—G. M. H.

In 1880 Kansas adopted a constitutional amendment prohibiting the manufacture and sale of intoxicating liquors in this state, except for medicinal, scientific and mechanical purposes. Kansas was a pioneer in this prohibition movement. It proceeded upon two fundamental assumptions:

First, we claimed that the logical attitude of government toward a recognized evil is that of prohibition. That the liquor traffic is a recognized evil is attested by every license law high or low. For, we insisted, if the liquor traffic is good, it should be as free as the grocery business, or the blacksmith business; but, if it is bad, then the government should have no partnership with it.

Second, we held that a business which decreases the earning capacity of a large number at least of its patrons cannot, in the nature of things, be a good thing financially for a community, state, or nation.

Upon these lines we have fought our battle for a quarter of a century, and the result has been most gratifying. I believe Kansas is today the soberest, most orderly state in the union, and I believe no similar number of people anywhere on earth are relatively more prosperous. Without great banking centres containing accumulations of outside money, we have over one hundred dollars per capita in our banks. One third of our counties are without prisoners in their jails and without paupers in their poorhouses. One half of our counties have not sent a prisoner to the penitentiary in the past year. More than one half the prisoners in our penitentiary never lived in Kansas long enough to gain a residence. The state is practically free from saloons, and the sentiment is overwhelming in favor of maintaining this condition. No political party dare antagonize this policy, and no politician who wishes success dare espouse the cause of the saloon in Kansas.

Prohibition has been a great success in Kansas morally, educationally, and financially, and abundant facts can be produced to substantiate all these statements.

Indisputable testimony proves that constitutional prohibition was not enforced in Kansas under an administration of party government which, for the sake of retaining power, compromised with illicit liquor dealers in Kansas City, Leavenworth, Wichita, and other cities and towns. The Mercantile Club, of Kansas City, says:

THE PASSING OF THE SALOON.

"Prior to July 1, 1906, Kansas City for many years had from one to two hundred 'joints' selling liquor in open violation of law. . . The proprietors of these places were technically arrested and fined, once a month or once every two months, according to the custom in vogue. . . . The amount of money collected from 'joints' and not paid into any public treasury will never be known. Enough is known of unofficial collections to make the system remembered as a public disgrace."

To party Prohibitionists, as well as liquor dealers, this was proof that the saloon was safe in the hands of political organizations which refused to commit themselves against it in their declarations of principles.

However, in 1906, the moral influences in the state, which had been so long suppressed by political compromise, suddenly became operative, and an Assistant State's Attorney, Hon. C. W. Trickett, emerged from the official body of the commonwealth as an administrator of law. In an address, delivered at the No-License Conference, Indianapolis, December 3, 1907, this attorney said:

"With many misgivings I accepted my office. I went to Topeka, and, in the presence of the Attorney General, Governor Hoch said, 'I do not believe it can be done. . . But we will make one more attempt; we will try again.'"

The Assistant State's Attorney did try again—*and succeeded*. Open saloons, blind tigers, dives and joints disappeared. A limited clandestine trade, however, was still conducted in back lots and sheds! The Mercantile Club says:

"The people of Kansas City do not yet claim to have a model city in every way. But they do claim that no other city in the United States can present such a record of progress made."

In his Indianapolis speech Attorney Trickett said further:

"Two years ago, the word went forth to sound retreat on the temperance question. Out in Kansas they were organizing 'Re-Submission Temperance Societies.' People were discouraged, but, when the notes were heard, it was, instead of 'Retreat,' 'Forward! Charge!' And the Old Guard, the Woman's Christian Temperance Union, the Christian Endeavorers, swung into line, and the saloon has been driven out of Kansas. And, in my judgment the day is not far distant when it will be decreed that governmental sanction cannot be given to a traffic which destroys the morals, peace and safety of the people."

Kansas has a strong and efficient working organization of the W. C. T. U. The Kansas State Temperance Union (now affiliating with the Anti-Saloon League) has long been a great moral power in the state. The attitude of the dominant political parties in the state being friendly to prohibition, the Prohibition party has had no strong organization or following. The church, the schools, and the public press all reflect the high moral sentiment of the state against the liquor traffic. It is safe to predict that hereafter as heretofore Kansas will be found in the front rank of the Great Reform.

REV. W. Z. ALLEN,
Field Secretary Anti-Saloon League of Iowa.

REV. W. C. BARBER, B. D.,
Superintendent Anti-Saloon League of Iowa.

M. S. ODLE, LL. B.,
Attorney for Anti-Saloon League of Iowa.

The pro-saloon forces consist of the Personal Liberty League, the Anti-Resubmission League, the German American Alliance, the Wholesale and Retail Liquor Dealers' Association and the Brewery Association. They are carrying on a wide distribution of literature, etc.

The campaign this time will be a fight to a finish.

KENTUCKY.

A local option law was enacted in 1906. In the first 37 local elections all went "dry." Out of the 119 counties, 92 are dry, 4 are wet, 2 have three wet towns in each, 7 have two wet towns in each, and 14 one wet town each. There are less than sixty localities in the state where intoxicating liquors can be legally sold. Seventy-seven per cent. of the population live in dry districts, and 98 per cent. of the territory is under prohibition. There is also a law in force prohibiting the wholesale traffic in dry territory. All cities of 3,000 or more are separate units.

The Mayor of Louisville was removed from office by the Governor because he would not enforce the Sunday-closing law.

The I. O. G. T. was the first organization in the state to advocate a law prohibiting the sale of liquor. In 1872 the Grand Lodge appointed a committee to secure petitioners asking the legislature to submit the question to a vote of the state, and nearly 200,000 names were secured. The House passed the measure but it hung fire in the Senate, after the liquor dealers had spent tens of thousands of dollars to defeat it. Other organizations have since lent their aid.

LOUISIANA.

In 1882, when Frances E. Willard organized a Woman's Christian Temperance Union in New Orleans, it was very unpopular, and its representatives found it difficult to get a hearing even in a church. In 1888, when the Prohibition Party made its first appearance in the state, it polled only 188 votes. But these two organizations, aided by others, began a course of agitation and education which gradually worked a great revolution in conditions of the state. In 1905, Rev. P. A. Baker organized the Anti-Saloon League in the state, and secured a state superintendent, who was compelled to carry on his work for three years without money and without an office.

From these unpromising beginnings the work has progressed until in the spring of 1908 there were 34 parishes out of 59 which had gone dry, thus placing three-fourths of the territory and 40 per cent. of the population under prohibition.

The Shattuck bill recently enacted, if enforced, will destroy all the viler saloons remaining in the state; if it is not enforced state-wide prohibition will surely follow in 1910. Prohibition sentiment is growing rapidly, and it is believed that, with or without the enforcement of the Shattuck bill, the whole state may be carried for prohibition within two years by a systematic campaign. Governor Sanders says:

"Prohibition has worked well in those sections of the state where popular sentiment is behind the law, and some of the most prosperous towns and parishes are those where prohibition has prevailed for a period long enough to afford fair tests of its merits."

MAINE.

In 1851 a prohibitory law was enacted, repealed in 1856, and re-enacted in 1858. In 1884 it became a part of the constitution. All efforts for re-submission have been defeated, and, despite the violation of law in certain cities, popular opinion is so largely in favor of the constitution that repeal would be impossible.

At the present time the law is very well enforced in nearly every section of the state. The result of practically every election held in the state in the past quarter of a century has hinged upon the question of prohibition. According to government statistics, the amount of liquor sold in 50 illegal places in Maine is not equal to the amount sold in one average saloon in a license state. W. T. Cobb, Governor, writes:

"So long as I am governor I shall oppose nullification, shall insist upon law-enforcement, and so long as the Sturgis law remains on our statute books and officials fail to do their duty, I shall use that law to enforce prohibition with all the power, influence and resources at my command."

Valuable testimony in favor of the efficiency of Maine's prohibitory law appears in the *Bar and Buffet*, one of the ablest and sanest of the liquor journals:

"Deputy Commissioner Sturgis Goss is at work on a song which will be a parody on 'Locked in the Stable With the Sheep,' only he will call it 'Found in the Hide With the Booze.'

"Deputy Goss' inspiration comes from a seizure which Deputies Beaulieu and Stevens made in a stable on Lincoln alley early Friday morning. They took a peek into things at their leisure before the proprietor showed up, and discovered one of the most ingenious and best concealed hides which has been unearthed by the officers of late.

"Entrance is made by first going up two flights of stairs and then down one. But the flight that you go down is so carefully concealed that it was only by the merest chance that the officers found it. The stairs creaked with each step, which was the only noise except that of scampering rats as large as pet poodles and with tails as long as a train of cars.

"At the foot of the stairs the officers found an open room which apparently was a part of the stable. A lamp with a smoky chimney was on a box beside which were a number of glasses. Near by were a ten-gallon keg, a two-gallon jug, a gallon measure and a pint measure, all containing whisky. This booze den was evidently the retreat and source of supply of the pocket peddlers.

"Liquor selling in Lewiston and other Maine cities which have been invaded by the Sturgis deputies has been reduced to such an exact science that those who take chances are being called professional booze vendors. As doctors can tell whether a person is ill by the look of his face, so can these peddlers tell whether a man wants to buy whisky when he shows up at a resort where the stuff is dealt out on the sly.

"Only one question is asked a customer by the pocket pedler. He simply walks up to the man and says: 'Big or little?' and soon produces the goods ordered.

"'Big or little?' means more than the words indicate. If the customer says big, he gets a pint, and if he says little, he gets half a pint. He isn't asked what kind of stuff he wants, for only one is carried. He gets whisky or nothing."

This is a good example of the much talked-of "blind-pigs" or "blind-tigers" that are said to flourish in dry territory. Such a place cannot be very popular and is a great improvement over a wide open, attractive, legitimatized saloon. It illustrates also the length to which this anarchistic trade will go in law-breaking.

MARYLAND.

The state contains 23 counties and the city of Baltimore. Ten counties are dry, 3 have saloons in only one place each; 2 counties are almost free; 6 have some dry territory, and only two are wholly wet. Baltimore has several dry residence districts.

A campaign is on for a uniform local option law for counties, election districts, municipalities and wards. The anti-liquor organizations are all active, prohibition sentiment is growing, and the time seems not far distant when the whole state will be dry.

MASSACHUSETTS.

Massachusetts is a license state, with provision for municipal and city local option. The license cannot be less than $1,000 per annum, and is determined by the local licensing board, except that the minimum fee is in all cases $1,000. In one case the fee was made $1,000,000 in a town which had accidentally voted "yes." The various towns and cities are allowed to vote on the question once a year.

The present local option law of Massachusetts was passed in 1881. The high-license feature was enacted in 1888, and many towns and cities have remained dry under this law for over twenty years. It is estimated that about 45 per cent. of the entire population is now under no-license.

Among the large cities of Massachusetts which are now dry under the local option law are Worcester, population of 130,000; Cambridge,

100,000; Lynn, 50,000; Quincy, 30,000; Brockton, 50,000, and Haverhill, 40,000. There are 277 dry municipalities to 77 wet ones. Seventeen cities are under no-license, while 16 still retain the saloon.

MICHIGAN.

Although Michigan is the home of the father of the Prohibition party, and there is record to show that the nucleus of that organization was formed in a compact between two members of the order of Good Templars at a lodge meeting in 1861, yet, prior to 1908, there was but one dry county in the "Wolverine" state. On that date ten additional counties voted dry, and at this writing, out of 84 counties 11 are dry, and 90 municipalities out of 412 grant no license.

The Michigan law provides only for county local option, except that in an incorporated village a council may pass a prohibitive ordinance. The retailer's state license is $500 in addition to the special United States tax. The total receipts from liquor license in 1907 averaged about one dollar for each person in the state.

The anti-liquor organizations are carrying on a vigorous prohibition propaganda which will soon result in additional dry territory. F. M. Warner, Governor, takes this strong stand:

"The people certainly have a right to expect officials of the counties which have voted dry, to do away with the selling of liquor, to see that the liquor law is enforced. In the event of violation of the law, I should certainly take such steps as may be necessary to bring about a change in that regard, even if it made necessary a change in those holding the offices. The law has been placed upon the statute books by the people themselves, and it is going to be enforced in those counties where that action has been taken, and those who believe otherwise have no business holding official positions."

MINNESOTA.

Minnesota has a township local option law, also local option for municipalities organized under a village charter. Out of the 525 municipalities, 160 are dry; of the 1,800 townships, 1,200 are without saloons, while 400 of the remaining 600 have saloons only in incorporated villages. Forty-five per cent. of the population, 900,000 persons, are in dry territory, which includes the patrol limit of Minneapolis, under which saloons are limited to a small section in the business district. There is a reasonably strict enforcement of the law closing the saloons on Sunday and at 11 p. m.

The minimum state license in cities of 10,000 or more is $1,000; elsewhere the license fee is $500. But any municipal or county board, having authority to grant license, may impose higher license fees, or even refuse to grant license.

At this date a campaign is on for the election of a legislature which will enact a county local option law.

MISSISSIPPI.

During the present year, 1908, a state-wide prohibition law has been adopted.

Local option prevailed in the state as early as the 50's It then applied to beats, supervisors' districts, and towns. In 1880 a county option bill was passed, and in 1886 a more liberal local option law was adopted. Under this the saloon was speedily removed from rural districts and small towns. As a result of this law, 69 counties (90 per cent. of the territory) out of the 76 in the state are dry. Edmund F. Noel, Governor, says:

"In Mississippi unlawful retailing is generally less frequent than gambling or carrying concealed weapons. None but anarchists contend that other criminal laws tempt commission of what they prohibit, yet human nature is the same in its results and workings in regard to all classes of prohibited acts. The men, the money, and the literature that are being provided by the liquor manufacturers and dealers for their bitter and relentless war against prohibition prove that they do not believe, in the slightest, that prohibition does not greatly lessen the use of stimulants.

"Upon this question the judgment of the dry counties as to what is good within their own borders is to be made equally applicable to the whole state. The right of the majority to voice public policy is even more unquestionably possessed by the state than by its smaller subdivisions; and its condemnation of the liquor traffic being clearly expressed, it is for us to make it effective. Method and time are the only questions for real discussion."

MISSOURI.

Missouri has a local option law with a county unit, excepting cities having a population of 2,500, which vote independently. Of the 114 counties, 77 are now dry, and 10 other counties have but one saloon town each. About 700 saloons have gone out of existence in St. Louis on account of Governor Folk's strict enforcement of the Sunday-closing law the last three years. The first four months of 1908, 308 saloons were closed by local option and public sentiment. The state license is $200, and applicants for license must have a majority petition of taxpayers in the block in cities of over 2,000; and in towns or cities under 2,000 population, must give bond in the sum of $2,000 with two sureties, and must be of "good moral character," and pay $600 to $1,200 for county purposes each year at the discretion of the county court. The town or city may impose additional license, which varies from free to $5,000 a year, averaging throughout the state about $1,200 city license. The average total license in the state is about $2,000 a year.

Prohibition sentiment is very strong and growing. Further legislation will be demanded. J. W. Folk, Governor, reports:

"When I became governor and had the power to put an end to saloon lawlessness in the cities, I endeavored to have the law enforced. For doing this I have been constantly abused and vilified by the liquor interests and their allies."

MONTANA.

The temperance sentiment in Montana is confessedly sluggish, owing to wide territory and scattered population. But, since Montanans are progressive people, the prospects are that the moral standard of the state will be elevated and the Indian reservations will not long be the only dry spots in the state. Prohibitionists, Anti-Saloon Leaguers, the I. O. G. T., the W. C. T. U., and various church societies and fraternal organizations are coöperating to charge the atmosphere with enough lightning to smite the liquor traffic. A campaign for a municipal local option law is under way.

NEBRASKA.

For fifteen years sentiment against the saloon has been intensifying as a result of agitation and legislation. Out of the 90 counties of the state 21 are now dry, 13 have one wet town each, and 4 have two each. There are approximately 1,000 towns in the state. Of this number, 150 are merely post-offices and stations. Of the remaining towns, 450 are without saloons. In the city of Lincoln saloons are not allowed to sell after 7 o'clock in the evening, nor before 7 o'clock in the morning.

In 1890 a constitutional prohibitory amendment was adopted by popular vote, but by treachery and chicanery the liquor forces defeated it.

A campaign for a county option law is in progress, with promising prospects of success. It seems very probable that Nebraska will soon be numbered in the list of prohibition states.

NEVADA.

Nevada has the unenviable distinction of having a larger number of liquor dealers in proportion to population than any other state or territory in the United States. Many of the mining camps have more saloons than all other places of business combined. Nevada has a license system for saloons and gambling. Towns in the state are all wide open. There is no Prohibition party in the state, because election laws require ten per cent. of the voters to sign a petition in order to get a place on the official

J. W. HILTON, A. M.,
Secretary Anti-Saloon League of
Nebraska.

SAMUEL Z. BATTEN,
President Anti-Saloon League of
Nebraska.

REV. J. B. CARNES, Ph. D.,
Superintendent Anti-Saloon League of
Nebraska.

ballot. It is thus far impossible to secure the requisite number. Many men come to Nevada to exploit the mines, and expect to go elsewhere to live when they have accumulated sufficient wealth. Of course, such men do not have as much interest in the moral condition of the state as permanent residents. However, thoughtful citizens who see what other states are doing contemplate the possibility of some legislative action. A resident of the state suggests that a Prohibition party would be a good thing to gain and hold the balance of power.

The W. C. T. U. maintains an organization in the state, and the Anti-Saloon League has a superintendent for Nevada, Wyoming and Utah combined.

NEW HAMPSHIRE.

For nearly fifty years this state was under the prohibition policy, until the legislature of 1903 passed a law, known variously as the "local option" law, and the "license" law, by which it was made legal to sell liquor in any town or city which should vote for license.

There was strong opposition to the enactment of this law, but, despite it all, a legislature strongly Republican enacted the law, and the Republican Governor gave it his approval. Prior to this legislation, some of the cities and larger towns had been very lax in the enforcement of the prohibitory law.

At a special election held in the spring of 1903 57 towns and 11 cities voted for license, the total popular majority for license being 7,700, only two of the ten counties returning a majority against license.

In 1904 the towns again voted upon the question, and 45 towns voted for license and 177 against. The cities continued for another two years under the license policy.

In 1906 the whole state again voted on the license question, and 42 towns and 5 cities voted for license, while 182 towns and 6 cities voted against, making, in the aggregate, a popular majority of 513 in favor of license in the whole state, only three of the ten counties giving a license majority.

A slight study of the situation as revealed by these election results shows that the tendency of the voters since the first election has been steadily toward no-license.

The people have found that the effect of license has been steadily to increase drinking and drunkenness, and all the disorder that usually accompanies the saloon. The old prohibitory law has never been repealed. Its provisions are simply suspended in those towns and cities that vote for license. The temperance sentiment is growing in favor of the repeal of the license law, which would then leave the state under a good prohibition law, with greater stringency than it possessed before the passage of the license law.

The Anti-Saloon League has decided that the license law must be repealed; the Prohibition party demands the same action and is working to that end; the W. C. T. U., and probably every other temperance organization in the state, demand its repeal. The religious organizations heartily favor the same action.

NEW JERSEY.

New Jersey is a license state. The law provides for a minimum fee of $100 in townships and in places of less than 3,000 people; $150 in townships of between 3,000 and 10,000, and $250 in townships of over 10,000. But any town may impose an additional tax by direct local vote.

The state has no local option law and none of the counties are dry. Ocean Grove, famous as the Methodist Camp Meeting Grounds, is, of course, free from saloons and so are the towns of Vineland, Millville and Bridgeton, in Cumberland County. These are the only municipalities of any size free from saloons. The number of smaller municipalities that are dry is variously estimated.

There is a Sunday closing law. During August, 1908, the Governor threatened to call out the militia to close the notorious resorts at Atlantic City on Sunday. But the proprietors surrendered, and the saloons and gambling places for the first time during the season were closed on Sunday. An agitation for a county option law has been started and the anti-liquor forces are coöperating to secure its passage.

MRS. EMMA L. STARRETT,
Corresponding Secretary Nebraska W. C. T. U.

MRS ANNETTA NESBITT,
Treasurer Nebraska W. T. U.

MRS. FRANCES BEVERIDGE HEALD,
President Nebraska W. C. T. U.

CHAPTER XXIV.

SYMPHONY OF THE STATES—CONTINUED.

NEW MEXICO.

NEW MEXICO is practically a license state. The statute books show little restrictive legislation. The only notable exception is an old law which forbids the issuing of licenses in any but incorporated cities and towns, or in villages of less than 100 population. The license fee is from $100 to $400, according to the location, but an incoporated city or town may require any additional license tax which the council may see fit to impose. The license thus exacted in some of the towns is as high as $2,400.

In a few cases the town councils have passed ordinances prohibiting the granting of licenses, but the greater number of municipalities are governed in the interests of the saloon. The anti-liquor forces are agitating for a local option law and other restrictive legislation.

NEW YORK.

NOTE.—*New York being the most important of the northern states, and presenting conditions that are or have been repeated in the other states of that section, the situation as reported by representatives of the Woman's Christian Temperance Union, the Anti-Saloon League, the Prohibition Party and other organizations is given at some length.*—G. M. H.

Under the provisions of the Raines law, adopted in 1896, an excise commissioner, appointed by the Governor with the advice and consent of the Senate, has control of the liquor trade. The term of the commissioner under this law is five years, and he appoints his own administration staff. Under the provisions of the law, townships only are given the right of local option.

About 315 townships, with an aggregate population approximating 600,000 persons, are dry, and 296 others, with a population of 500,000, are under partial license. The remaining townships of the state, 322, comprising a population of about 1,200,000, together with all the cities, are wet.

The license fee in any city with a population of 1,500,000 or more is $1,200. In any city with a population of 500,000 to 1,500,000, $975.

In cities and towns from 50,000 to 500,000, $750; 10,000 to 50,000, $525; 5,000 to 10,000, $450; in cities, towns and villages of from 1,200 to 5,000, $300; in all places with a population of less than 1,200, $150.

The form of local option under the Raines law provides for the submission of four questions:

1. Whether the sale of liquor to be drunk on the premises should be permitted.

2. Whether the sale of liquor not to be drunk on the premises should be permitted.

3. Whether the sale of liquor in a drug store, under a prescription from a physician, should be permitted.

4. Whether the sale of liquor in connection with a hotel should be permitted.

There are in New York State at this time 243 breweries, 35 distilleries, and about 30,000 holders of liquor tax certificates, or, upon the average, one to every 300 people, and one to every 60 voters in the state.

In 1856 the constitutional prohibition idea as it is now understood, was definitely broached, and then the necessity of including the manufacture as well as the sale of liquors seems not to have been perceived. In that year William H. Armstrong, Grand Worthy Patriarch of the Grand Division of Sons of Temperance of Eastern New York, proposed and discussed the plan. In 1857 he secured a unanimous endorsement from the Grand Division, which was renewed at three subsequent sessions. Mr. Armstrong printed in the New York *Witness* for May 29, 1858, a very thorough article defining the new program, suggesting that an amendment worded as follows be added to the Constitution of the State of New York:

"The sale of intoxicating liquors shall not be licensed or allowed in this state excepting for chemical, medicinal, or manufacturing purposes, and then only under restrictive regulations to be made by the legislature. It shall be the duty of the legislature to prescribe proper penalties for the sale of liquors in violation of this provision, such liquors being hereby declared a *common nuisance* and liable to confiscation."

Although some temperance organizations joined with the Sons of Temperance of Eastern New York in favoring constitutional prohibition, no practical steps were taken until the legislative session of 1860, when the following joint resolution was introduced into the New York Senate (see the New York *Tribune* for April 9, 1860):

"*Resolved* (if the Assembly concur), That the Constitution of the State be amended as follows:

" 'The sale of intoxicating liquors as a beverage is hereby prohibited, and no law shall be enacted or be in force after the adoption of this Amendment to authorize such sale, and the Legislature shall by law prescribe the necessary fines and penalties for any violation of this provision.'

"*Resolved* (if the Assembly concur), That the foregoing amendment be referred to the Legislature, to be chosen at the general election of Senators, and that, in conformity to Section 1 of Article 13 of the Constitution, it be published for three months previous to the time of such election."

The Senate approved this joint resolution on the 13th of March, 1860, by a vote of 30 yeas (29 Republicans and one Democrat) to 6 nays (all Democrats), and the Assembly concurred on April 5, 1861, by 69 yeas to 33 nays. The endorsement of the next Legislature was required before the proposed amendment could go to the people; but the exciting events of the Civil War caused the abandonment of the plan.

The Woman's Crusade movement probably originated at Fredonia, this state. There is record that the women of that town moved against the saloons for eight days before the women of Hillsboro, Ohio, inaugurated their campaign of prayer and of appeal to the saloon-keepers.

The State Woman's Christian Temperance Union was organized October 14, 1874, and from that day to this has been one of the most effective factors in the political life of the commonwealth. Through the efforts of the Union—

Scientific temperance instruction has been introduced in the public schools.

A law prohibiting the giving or sale of cigarettes to boys under sixteen years of age has been secured.

A law raising age of protection for girls from 12 to 16 and then to 18 years has been enacted.

A successful protest against the introduction of the English barmaid system has been embodied in legislation.

A successful demand for the enforcement of the law which prevents society women from serving intoxicating liquors at the Langtry tea, in New York City.

Indecent, vile, and immoral shows at state and county fairs have been prohibited.

Curfew laws through ordinances have been enacted in at least seventy-five villages and cities.

A bill giving tax-paying women the right to vote in towns and villages on propositions submitted to taxpayers has been secured.

A drinking fountain was erected on the Pan-American grounds.

The Union maintains the Mary Towne Burt free bed in the National Temperance Hospital in Chicago.

The Union assisted in securing the passage of the Anti-Canteen Law in Congress, and also the state law prohibiting the sale of liquor on state and county fair grounds.

The repeal of the Horton law which legalized prize fighting was due, in part at least, to the Union's influence.

Legislation looking to legal opening of the saloons of New York City on Sunday has been successfully prevented.

The Union assisted in securing the passage of the bill prohibiting the sale of intoxicants in government buildings and at Ellis Island, added its protest to that of other women's organizations which resulted in the unseating of Brigham Roberts, representative in Congress from Utah, and in the effort to secure an amendment to the federal constitution that shall prohibit polygamy. The Legislature of the State of New York was the first to adopt a resolution to that effect.

In 1900 the Union had a bill drawn up and presented to the Legislature to provide for local option in cities. Every year since then a similar bill, with some changes and modifications, has been introduced through the efforts of the Anti-Saloon League. In the effort to secure its passage the Union has heartily co-operated.

NORTH CAROLINA.

The state adopted a prohibitory law in May, 1908, by a majority of 44,000 in a total vote of 292,669. Five years earlier, in 1903, the Watts bill was passed, by which prohibition was given to the rural districts, and a local option election was granted to municipalities upon petition of one-third of the voters. Under the operation of this law 68 counties adopted no-license, and only 30 favored the saloon. Nine-tenths of the state was under prohibitory law before the vote of 1908. There was no saloon outside of an incorporated town. Governor Glenn led the fight for statutory prohibition. He declared:

"The last bridge is burned behind me, and I stand squarely with the great temperance forces to drive out this hideous monster from our fair state. A man must take a square and unmistakable stand for the right or for the wrong, for righteousness or for evil, for happiness or for misery, for justice or for oppression. As for me, I am heart and soul against the liquor traffic.

"But some one says money derived from the liquor business is necessary to run the schools. I say it is not. The schools do not depend on blood-money. Wipe out the liquor business and, if necessary, the state can well afford to increase the tax on property to sustain the schools and save the boys and girls of this land.

"You have all heard the old cry that prohibition will not prohibit; blind-tigers and all forms of unlawful sale will flourish. Prohibition can be enforced as effectively as other laws are. Let the officers of the law,

REV. JAMES W. COOL, D. D.,
Asst. Supt. and Business Manager, Anti-Saloon League of New York.

REV. T. M. HARE,
Superintendent, Anti-Saloon League of the District of Columbia.

backed up by the moral sense of the community and the coöperation of good citizens, do their duty; let the men who break the law be sentenced to the roads, and let no government grant them a pardon, and you will have prohibition in full force."

NORTH DAKOTA.

North Dakota was admitted as a state in 1889 with a constitutional prohibitory provision. The state, largely settled by men with little capital, has obtained a degree of prosperity under prohibition which is little short of marvelous, when the shortness of time and other circumstances are considered. The United States census report shows that North Dakota has the greatest wealth per capita of any state in the Union. Farm earnings per capita are the greatest in the nation. The state has a $100 per capita in savings banks, second only to Maine, six times the amount per capita in the savings banks of the great state of Pennsylvania, seven times that of Illinois, and ten times that of Ohio. Population has increased seventy-five per cent. in ten years.

Public sentiment would not re-admit saloons under any conditions, and prohibitory requirements are more and more strictly enforced. John Burke, Governor, writes:

"We have had prohibition so long in North Dakota that in some counties there are no jails. There is not much crime in the state."

OHIO.

On February 22, 1872, the first national nominating convention of the Prohibition Party was held at Columbus, Ohio.

In December, 1873, the Woman's Crusade sprung into public notice at Hillsboro, Ohio.

On November 17, 1874, the Woman's Christian Temperance Union was organized at Cleveland, Ohio.

On June 4, 1893, the Anti-Saloon League was organized at Oberlin, Ohio.

While the State of Ohio thus has the distinction of having been the scene of the inauguration of these great anti-liquor organizations and demonstrations, yet the state has also had an unenviable notoriety for its truckling to the liquor trade, its connivance at the violation of its constitutional provision against the traffic, and its industrial and political subserviency to liquor behests. There is hardly any phase of the pro and con of the liquor question that has not had its illustration in the state.

In 1851 the licensing of the retail trade in liquor was specifically prohibited by a clause of the Constitution of the State. But, by subterfuge, the General Assembly long ago established what is practically a license system by the passage of the so-called "tax" law. In 1883, by a popular majority of more than 82,000, the voters of the state adopted an amendment to the constitution, reading—

"The manufacture of and the traffic in intoxicating liquors, to be used as a beverage, are forever prohibited; and the General Assembly shall provide by law for the enforcement of this provision."

At the same election another proposed amendment conferring upon the General Assembly the power to regulate the traffic in intoxicating liquors was voted down by a majority of over 92,000.

Yet by various legal technicalities and court influences resorted to by the liquor interests, the people of Ohio again were robbed of the fruits of their victory. But the moral sentiment has continued. In no other state perhaps have the pro-liquor and the anti-liquor forces been more fiercely arrayed against each other. Gradually victory is being won by the anti-liquor forces.

In 1888 a township local option law was passed, and in 1902 another law giving local option to cities and villages, as a whole, was adopted, and in 1906 still another law giving local option to residential districts in cities was secured, and in 1908 a new residence local option law was adopted, providing that saloons may be wiped out by petition instead of by election.

Under these laws 500 villages and cities grant no license, while 1,155 out of 1,371 townships are "dry." About 68 per cent. of the territory in the state is without a saloon. City residence districts, with an aggregate population of 425,000, are free from the saloon under the Jones law.

At the last session of the legislature a county local option law was passed, which went into effect September 1, 1908. Andrew L. Harris, Governor, said:

"You believed that slavery was a crime. There are other reforms, such as the question of temperance. I believe today that the sentiment of the nation is of such a character that there is but one feeling in either of the great political parties of this country, and that is that there should be restrictive laws, at least in regard to temperance; that public sentiment is reaching such a point when such a thing as laws permitting the dealing in intoxicating liquors will not be known upon our statute books. We may differ as to progress and methods, but I believe there is in every section a sentiment in favor of temperance, and in favor of stopping the evils resulting from the sale of intoxicating liquors."

Addendum.—There are 88 counties in Ohio. When the county option law went into effect, September 1, 1908, five counties were already dry through township and municipal option. Since September 1, and up to November 24, 1908, 49 counties have voted dry and 7 wet under the new law, and 1,658 saloons (seven miles frontage) have been closed. In the 49 dry counties the average majority was 1,214, while the average wet majority in the other 7 counties was 518. Elections are pending in other counties. The indications are that all but the few counties containing the larger cities will soon be dry.

Through the efforts of the liquor forces Governor Harris was defeated for re-election. Curiously enough, some of the counties which gave majorities against Harris have now given dry majorities. This seems to indicate that some of the personal liberty advocates, after all, do not want saloons next door to themselves.

Public sentiment has become so aroused that it will not be surprising if a state-wide movement for constitutional or statutory prohibition follows. Undoubtedly Ohio would give a decided popular majority for prohibition.

OKLAHOMA.

On a certain day in the summer of 1908 some of the state officials of Oklahoma were seen emptying bottle after bottle, keg after keg, barrel after barrel of beers of various brews, wines of many kinds and whiskies of different brands, into a wooden trough that carried the liquor into a sewer. The different liquors mixed in the trough flowed harmoniously into the man-hole.

What was the meaning of this "destruction of property"? The people had brought their commonwealth into the Union under a constitution absolutely prohibiting the manufacture, sale, barter, giving away, or otherwise furnishing, except for medicinal and industrial purposes, of intoxicating liquors within the state. Regardless of the constitution and the laws adopted under it, the liquor trade had persisted in its efforts to distribute its contraband goods in the state. The liquors destroyed on this day had been confiscated throughout the state and shipped to the headquarters in Guthrie. All of it had been examined and found to be below the state's standard for medicinal purposes, and under the provisions of the law it must be destroyed. Altogether on that one day 30,000 pint bottles and 25 kegs of beer were emptied, as were several dozens of cases of whiskies, wines, etc.

The liquor dealers will testify that "prohibition does prohibit" in Oklahoma.

As Oklahoma also includes what was formerly known as Indian Territory, and the state includes a large Indian population, a brief account of the adoption of prohibition is interesting.

Indian Territory had been under the most rigid prohibitory laws enforced by the United States Government from the beginning of its jurisdiction. All Indian treaties bound the United States to enforce the provision against the sale of intoxicating liquors incorporated in these various contracts. When the tribal government ended, the enabling act providing for the erection of the State of Oklahoma included prohibition as one of the conditions. Immediately upon the inauguration of statehood an effort was made both in Indian Territory and Oklahoma to make prohibition *state-wide*. Under the local option laws of Oklahoma enacted by the territorial government, many saloons had been introduced. In the election for the adoption of the state constitution a majority of more than 18,000 electors declared in favor of prohibition. The people had so thoroughly canvassed all aspects of the case that the new commonwealth begins its history under a *régime* which assures its freedom from the evils so apparent in states where the dram-shops exist. The first state legislature has enacted a suitable code of enforcement laws and the constitutional provision is being well deserved. C. N. Haskell, Governor, says:

"Prohibition is argued as being an infringement on personal liberties. Is there a single law in the broad length of our land that would permit any man to commit suicide? If the kisses of the wife and the clinging embraces of your babies are to be conducive to happiness, then begin there in your search for pleasure. Is the promotion of such pleasures as that an infringement on personal liberties?

"They say: 'Oh, don't destroy the progress and prosperity of our town.' Not for a minute does the existence of a saloon assist the substantial prosperity of any town. You said in your constitution that the governor shall be charged in his oath to enforce its provisions, and by the Heavens eternal, you've elected one who will see that they are enforced."

OREGON.

The State of Oregon has one of the best local option laws in the country, passed by the people under the initiative amendment to the constitution in 1904, the majority for the adoption of the law being about 1,600. In the spring of 1906 the brewers and liquor dealers of the state submitted to the people under the initiative an amendment to this law which, had it been adopted, would have killed the measure. After two years' experience under the old law the people of Oregon rejected the amendment and sustained the law by an increased majority of almost 10,000.

MRS. HESTER T. GRIFFITH,
President, Southern California W. C. T. U.

MRS. MARY C. SAMPSON,
Corresponding Secretary, Southern California W. C. T. U.

MRS. S. W. PLIMPTON,
Treasurer, Southern California W. C. T. U.

MRS. MARY ALDERMAN GARBUTT,
Treasurer of Temple, W. C. T. U., Los Angeles, California.

MRS. CHARITY WAY,
Recording Secretary, Southern California W. C. T. U.

Eight entire counties of Oregon are dry. Seventy precincts in other counties are dry, and five college towns in the state do not have a single saloon.

In the local option contests during the spring of 1908 the anti-saloon forces won victories in favor of local option. Of the 33 large counties 21 voted dry, thus excluding the saloon from more than two-thirds of the state's area.

PENNSYLVANIA.

Pennsylvania and New Jersey are the only states east of the Rocky Mountains having no prohibition or local option law. A local option bill was introduced in the legislature of 1907-1908, but was defeated by a small majority. The question was again submitted at the primary elections in April, 1908, and candidates were asked to pledge themselves to vote for a local option bill. The local option question will come before the next session of the legislature.

The Brooks High License law gives local judges the power of granting licenses. The people have the privilege of remonstrating and proving violations of the law against an applicant for license, but results depend upon the personal attitude of the judge. A bond of $2,000 is required from each licensee. Applicants must have signatures of twelve reputable electors of ward, borough, or township. The license tax in cities of the first and second class is $1,100; third class, $550. In all other classes, $350; in boroughs, $200; in townships, $125. The operation of the law in very many cases is a tragical farce, and the anti-liquor forces are combining to secure local option.

Green County has no saloons, and there are many towns that never have had one.

RHODE ISLAND.

A prohibitory law was passed in 1852, and was re-enacted in 1853 to overcome the effect of a decision of the United States Court. The question of its repeal was submitted to the next election and resulted in retaining the law. This law provided for what has since been known as the "dispensary system." In 1863 the law was repealed, and a license law enacted in its stead. Another prohibitory law was passed in 1874, but was repealed in 1875, when the former license law with some modifications was re-enacted.

In 1884 a prohibitory amendment to the constitution was adopted. The liquor interests secured the appointment of one of their tools as the chief of the state police, whose duty it was to enforce the law. Such scandal and confusion arose in consequence that, in 1889, a large majority voted to repeal prohibition, and a license system, with local option features, was adopted.

The license fees run from $300 to $1,000 for retailers, and from $700 to $1,500 for wholesalers. Under the local option features 16 of the 38 cities and towns have no saloons. These 16 towns include 8 per cent. of the entire population of the state.

SOUTH CAROLINA.

For years after the Civil War South Carolina was cursed with the open saloon, which was to be found everywhere, even at the cross-roads and grocery stores throughout the state. So much of vice and crime and misery resulted that a sentiment against the open traffic was aroused and rapidly crystallized. A law was secured under which the saloon was driven from the rural districts and was confined to the incorporated towns and cities, where it would be under police regulation. The time soon came when the towns and cities began to ask for relief, and, under a system of local option, a number of these corporations banished the saloon.

In 1892 the famous "Dispensary Law" was enacted. A state liquor dispensary was established at the capital city, Columbia, from which county dispensaries were supplied with liquor to be retailed to the people. This system led to such serious abuses that in 1907 the dispensary law was repealed, and a bill adopted granting to communities local option as to dispensaries or prohibition. Of the 41 counties 23 now have dispensaries and 18 are dry. Fifty per cent. of the territory of the state is dry.

A vigorous campaign for state-wide prohibition is now under way.

SOUTH DAKOTA.

South Dakota entered the Union as a prohibition state. An amendment to the prohibitory law, however, has been passed, which provides for its nullification by a majority vote of a municipality at an annual election. In order to maintain saloons in any community this vote must be taken each year, and, unless the vote is taken, or a majority of the voters decide otherwise when the vote is taken, the prohibition feature remains in effect. Of the 64 counties in the state 13 are dry; and of the 136 towns and cities 42 are without saloons.

The license fee, provided in communities where the saloons are installed by a majority vote of the citizens, is $1,000, $400 of which goes to the county and $600 to the municipality. There are 547 licensed saloons in the state, and about 1,500 places that have federal tax receipts or certificates which renders them immune from federal punishment.

County option is now the issue. Two years ago a county option bill was defeated in the legislature, but an appeal was made to the people under the referendum clause of the constitution.

It is interesting to note that the campaign now in progress turns not so much upon the rightfulness or wrongfulness of the saloon, as upon the privilege of the American voter to determine for himself by a majority vote as to what he wants. This illustrates the strength of the argument for the initiative and referendum.*

TENNESSEE.

At the close of the Civil War one of the first plans of hundreds of the men of the state for retrieving their fallen fortunes was by making and selling liquor. Small distilleries were established all over the state, and at every cross-road settlement liquor was retailed. Naturally, crowds of dissolute men congregated at such places, and children going to and from school were exposed to danger. It was necessary, as early as 1865, to adopt laws forbidding the sale of liquor near school-houses. These were special acts applying to particular schools, and many such were adopted.

In 1870 the constitution was revised, and such special laws prohibited. In 1877 a law was passed forbidding the sale of liquor within four miles of any incorporated school outside of incorporated towns. The result was that small towns surrendered their charters and incorporated their schools. Little log cabins in remote country places were incorporated.

Ten years later, in 1887, the four-mile law was so amended as to include all schools, public or private, incorporated or unincorporated. In 1899 the law was amended so as to apply to incorporated towns of 2,000 inhabitants and under. Such towns then re-incorporated—of course, without the saloon. In 1903 the law was amended to include towns running up to 5,000 inhabitants. In 1907 it was amended to include all towns in the state. When this last amendment was passed liquor had been abolished in all the towns of the state excepting 12. After the passage of this law the saloon was outlawed in all the towns excepting 4—Nashville, Chattanooga, Memphis and LaFollette.

Early in 1908 a movement in favor of state-wide prohibition was inaugurated. This question became involved in the canvass of the two Democratic candidates for the governorship, with the result that the temperance vote was divided, and state prohibition apparently failed. A campaign was then immediately started to elect legislators who will favor

---

* By a majority of 1,000 this measure failed to receive the endorsement of the people at the election in November, 1908.—G. M. H.

state-wide prohibition, resulting, November 3, 1908, in the election of safe prohibition majorities in both the House and the Senate.

TEXAS.

By REV. B. F. RILEY, *Superintendent Anti-Saloon League.*

From the foundation of Anglo-Saxon supremacy in Texas there has been a conflict with the liquor traffic. More than seventy years ago deliverances were made in church assemblies against it, and sermons were preached in opposition to the saloon.

After the Civil War conditions became such as to make it a matter of necessity to stem the tide of demoralization. As a life-long friend of the negro, I desire to say that he has a natural thirst for strong drink. Restrained from its use during his bondage, he became its easy victim after his emancipation. Corrupt politics in the South was coupled with the saloon in compassing the depression and demoralization of the great black race.

But the saloon was not confined to the negro in its ravages of demoralization and ruin. Mexicans and Anglo-Saxons were equally its victims. By 1887 the inroad on society was so serious that there was an upheaval of public sentiment in favor of state-wide prohibition. Sufficient force was brought to bear on the legislature of that year to compel the submission of the question to the people relative to a prohibitory amendment to the constitution.

The result of this contest was a defeat of the measure by more than 90,000. It is a matter of history that Ex-Governor Lubbock, the chief representative of the liquor men, procured a letter from Jefferson Davis just prior to the election, in which letter Mr. Davis advised against state prohibition as a curtailment of personal liberty. This served to win many votes in favor of the saloon.

At that time the election law of Texas was exceedingly lax, of which fact the liquor men took advantage, and in the crowded centers had thousands of repeaters on election day. In addition to this they imported thousands of Mexicans across the border and voted them, together with other thousands of negro women whom they dressed in the garb of men. If a fair election could have been held, prohibition would have begun in Texas twenty-one years ago.

It is worthy of comment and reflection just here that every public and prominent man who engaged in behalf of liquor during that contest, in 1887, afterwards was relegated by the people to oblivion. Both United

States Senators, Roger Q. Mills and Richard Coke, passed forever from public view.

The result of the election aroused interest afresh in the hearts of the people, and they forced the legislature to give the best local option law perhaps in existence. At that time there were only three dry counties in the state. As the result of local option we have now 156 dry counties, 77 partly dry and for the most part dry, and only 25 wet counties.

Local option proved to be both too local and too optional, and the liquor men began rapidly to ignore and defy public sentiment by every possible species of lawlessness. Liquors were smuggled in, officers were controlled in the non-enforcement of the law, and in a number of counties it was made of no effect. The local option law provides for a possible election every two years, on application of 250 signers of a petition. As a result of the demoralization nine counties were won back to the liquor traffic, but, within the same period, fifteen others were carried for prohibition, giving the result just stated.

In June, 1907, the Anti-Saloon League began work in the state. The presence of a state-wide organization which proposed the extirpation of liquor and the full enforcement of the laws, quickened and stiffened public confidence at once. Illustrations of its ability to bring about the enforcement of the law made the Anti-Saloon League at once a popular institution, and public confidence grew rapidly.

In January, 1908, there was a spontaneous demand for a mass meeting of the prohibitionists of the state, the result of which was a general movement looking to state-wide prohibiton. After a thorough discussion of the matter, it was resolved to avail ourselves of the provision for such action in the election law of the state. That law provides that on application by petition of one-tenth of the voters to the Democratic executive committee for the submission of any measure to a primary referendum on the part of the party thus petitioning, it shall be thus submitted, the result of which primary shall determine whether it be made a platform demand or not.

There being practically but one party in Texas, that of the Democracy, the condition was complied with, and the names of many more than one-tenth of the voters were presented. In order to circumvent this action and to confuse the public thought, the liquor men, through their attorneys, presented at the same time a larger petition in behalf of local option, although local option was already grounded in the constitution. They were prompted to this action by the following reasons:

First—They recognized the utter impossibility of success in case of a square issue between liquor and prohibition.

Second—Local option is a cherished principle to the people, and the liquor men realize that it would be better to retain that than to lose all, and they hoped sufficiently to disguise the fact that it was already constitutional from a sufficient number to cause submission to be defeated.

Third—If the majority should declare in favor of local option as against submission, that would have the effect of subduing public sentiment. The executive committee, in compliance with the request of the liquor men, granted this concession. Thus the ticket was loaded with four propositions: One for submission; another against submission; still another for local option, and yet another against local option. The effect of this was very confusing, but the purposes of the liquor men were gradually exposed to the public, or at least sufficiently exposed to enable submission to prevail with about 5,000 majority. Doubtless thousands were confused, or the majority would have been much greater.

Beaten at the ballot-box, the attempt was made to nullify the result on a technicality. Every attempt was made to evoke an opinion of the attorney general favorable to the contention of the liquor advocates, but he declined to give such opinion. Then the contest was transferred to the Democratic executive committee, which committee declined to declare the result sought.

This was followed by a contention on the floor of the Democratic state convention, in which the prohibitionists outnumbered the opposition two to one. The result of the entire contest was the following plank in the platform:

"We demand the submission by the Thirty-first Legislature of the State of Texas of a constitutional amendment to the people of the State of Texas, for their adoption or rejection, prohibiting within the State of Texas the manufacture, sale, gift, exchange, and intra-shipment of spirituous, vinous, and malt liquors, and medical bitters capable of producing intoxication, except for medicinal and sacramental use."

This was followed by the speech of Governor T. M. Campbell, who was, at this time, renominated to succeed himself. He said:

"The platform of the Democratic party means something in Texas to-day. It is a covenant with the people of this state, and it will be redeemed by those intrusted with power in this state. The duty of the Democratic party now, and the duty of the Democratic legislature, has been defined by this convention, and I pledge you that I will use every effort that legitimately belongs to the office of governor to the end that the platform demands adopted by this convention shall be carried out in letter and in spirit."

This prohibition demand is the only one made in the platform. Meanwhile the Texas Brewers' Association has appropriated $300,000 with

CALEB E. BURCHENAL,
Chairman, Wilmington Anti-License League, Wilmington, Delaware.

REV. JOHN M. ARTERS,
Superintendent, Anti-Saloon League of Delaware.

which to defeat prohibition, and announces that it will control the next legislature. Of the effects of prohibition Governor Campbell says:

"About fifty of the totally dry counties, and many of the precincts in the others, have become so since 1903. The effect has been to greatly decrease the consumption of intoxicants and has greatly decreased the amount of crime."

Texas is well equipped with anti-liquor forces. The W. C. T. U. is well organized, active, and influential, with an efficient colored branch. The churches and the colleges and schools of the state are unusually strong factors.

UTAH.

Utah is a license state. A campaign for county local option is now in progress. This has the endorsement of all the church organizations, including the Mormon church. Economic conditions in the Mormon community are almost ideally perfect, and the influence of Mormonism is in itself hostile to the drink traffic.

VERMONT.

In 1904 there were 138 prohibition towns. In 1908, 216. The original prohibitory law of 1852 was repealed in 1902. Town local option for prohibition or license was adopted. In March, 1908, 265,584 of the people were living under prohibition. Only 77,047 were under license. The vote in the state has changed from 5,222 license majority, 1903, to more than 9,000 no-license majority in 1908. In the first year of license in the saloon towns drunkenness increased 200 to 840 per cent. All the temperance forces of the state have combined in a campaign for the restoration of the prohibitory law of 1852.

VIRGINIA.

A local option law was passed in 1903. Under its operation 80 counties have expelled saloons, 14 have saloons in only one place, and in 50 counties no form of license is issued. Under the new liquor law all distilleries as well as saloons have been removed from dry territory. Since 1904, 1,500 drinking-places have been abolished. The spring campaign of 1908 closed up 375 saloons, distilleries, and social clubs. A movement for state-wide prohibition will soon be undertaken.

WASHINGTON.

Until within the past two years the wide-open policy has existed practically all over the state. Councils in incorporated cities and towns, and the board of commissioners in counties, have the power to regulate or prohibit saloons. The license law provides for fees running from $300 to $1,000.

The town of Pullman, forty-five square miles of residence section in the city of Seattle, and the Indian reservations, are the only dry territory. With half the population of the state living in cities, and with the liquor traffic wealthy and well entrenched and very active, the temperance forces have a hard struggle. A local option bill has been defeated in four successive sessions of the legislature.

The anti-liquor organizations, however, are active, and growing stronger, and public sentiment is advancing so rapidly that it is believed a local option bill will be adopted at the next session of the legislature, and that within the next eighteen months at least half of the geographical area of the state will become dry territory.

WEST VIRGINIA.

The constitution authorizes county commissioners to grant or refuse liquor licenses. The legislature grants to councils of certain towns and cities the right to issue licenses. License fees run from $300 to $2,000.

Out of the 55 counties 32 grant no licenses, 12 grant licenses in one town each, and 11 grant licenses wherever an application is made.

There were 748 prisoners in the penitentiary in 1904. Of this number, 106 came from the 32 no-license counties, 104 from the twelve one-town license counties, and 458 from the 11 wide-open license counties. From Fayette County (wide-open license), which has 3 per cent. of the population, came 159—or 20 per cent. of the inmates of the penitentiary, 53 more than from the 32 no-license counties. The criminal expenses of the no-license counties average 72 mills for each inhabitant. For Fayette County, 491 mills for each inhabitant, and for McDowell County (also wide-open license) 919 mills for each inhabitant. Hancock County, which has not had a saloon for sixty years, had not one cent of criminal expense for the year ending October 1, 1904.

State prohibition was defeated at the last session of the legislature by a narrow margin, but the campaign is on anew, with the prospect that the next legislature will submit a constitutional amendment to the voters. Wm. M. O. Dawson, Governor, writes:

"Do men talk of graft? It is the saloon that furnishes the scene and atmosphere where bribery is easy and secure from interference. Do men deplore the rule of corrupt political bosses? It is the saloon that rallies the mass of venal and unpatriotic voters who constitute the phalanx of the bosses' power. Has crime become rampant on the streets? The saloon is the refuge of the criminals. Does vice seek protection? The saloon effects the arrangement with the policemen who are familiar with its dark secrets and comrades of its debased fraternity. Do gamblers wish to ply their demoralizing trade among the young? The saloon affords them not only the shield, but brings them the susceptible patronage of inexperienced youths. Is there a movement afoot for any measure of civic betterment? Its opponents foregather in the saloon, and if any chicanery can beat the better will of the majority, the fraud will be devised in the saloon.

"These are no wild charges from crazed fanaticism, but a statement of conditions that can be demonstrated out of any year's history in any American municipality of importance. To emblazon this responsibility of the saloon so manifestly before the eyes of the public that it cannot escape the notice of any man who thinks at all or be ignored by any person who professes the slightest concern for a pure civic life, is the immediate next task of the saloon's enemies. And it is a task that should be discharged without rant or railing, but simply with calm resort to the inevitable logic of common experience in America."

WISCONSIN.

Wisconsin has a tax law, with a provision for city, township, and village local option. In 1907 an additional law was passed, providing for district option. The minimum state tax is $100 in rural districts, and $200 elsewhere. By popular vote, at a special election, the former may be increased to from $350 to $500, and the latter to from $500 to $800. Elections for this purpose however cannot be held oftener than once in three years.

There is not a county in the state entirely dry, but, of the 1,454 towns, villages, and cities, about 800 are dry under local option. County local option is the next step in the way of advance temperance legislation.

WYOMING.

License laws are in operation, and the state is practically wide open. The evil results of the traffic are so apparent, however, that a strong temperance sentiment exists, although far in advance of any present organized effort. The anti-liquor forces are organizing, and progressive legislation against the liquor evil undoubtedly will soon be found upon the statute books.

CHAPTER XXV.

THE CLEANSING OF KANSAS CITY, KANSAS.

By C. W. Trickett, *Assistant Attorney General, Kansas.*

NOTE.—*No other event in the anti-liquor warfare has been more spectacular and significant than the attack upon the saloon forces in Kansas City, Kansas. This battle was initiated and carried to successful issue by C. W. Trickett, an attorney of Kansas City, appointed Special Assistant Attorney General by Governor E. W. Hoch. In this chapter is given Mr. Trickett's own story of his successful campaign against the saloons of his city.—G. M. H.*

MR. TRICKETT'S remarkable achievement of closing two hundred and fifty-six saloons, two hundred gambling dens, and sixty houses of social evil, in Kansas City, Kansas, in the short space of thirty days, immediately attracted national attention to him.

At the annual convention of the Kansas State Temperance Union, held at Topeka, Kansas, February 5, 1907, Governor E. W. Hoch, in delivering the address of welcome, said:

"I shall be especially sorry that I shall not be able to stay to share with you the pleasure and profit which I am sure is in store for you, especially in the address that is to be made to you to-night by the man, I was about to say, who has wrought a miracle in Kansas—Mr. Trickett, of Kansas City. I do not believe that as great a single achievement for temperance, for sobriety, for good government, for the home, for everything we hold dear, has ever been wrought in the state of Kansas, or in the Union, as great for all these interests, as has been wrought by Mr. Trickett and his associates in Kansas City."

Commenting on the above, Mr. J. K. Codding, attorney for the Kansas State Temperance Union, says:

"Subsequent events have verified the Governor's statement that the closing of the Kansas City, Kansas, saloons by Mr. Trickett was the most important forward step for state-wide prohibition of this generation. Not only has Mr. Trickett's work been important to the nation, but it came at an opportune time in the fight for law enforcement in Kansas, and from the day that he successfully closed the Kansas City, Kansas, saloons, the permanency of the prohibitory law in Kansas was assured."

S. E. NICHOLSON,
Secretary, Anti-Saloon League of America.

HON. C. W. TRICKETT,
Assistant Attorney-General, Kansas.

In the following address, delivered by Mr. Trickett at the Chautauqua Assembly, Winfield, Kansas, Mr. Trickett gives his own account of his victory over the saloons and the beneficent results that have followed.

Every thinking person has often asked himself the question, "What is Life?" and the answer which satisfies depends upon the point of view of the questioner.

Many have attempted to answer the question, and the answer invariably reflects the speaker's point of view. For instance, one will say that life is a "gala day," while another describes it as "a vale of tears." One will say it is "a dream in the night," and another will define it as "the mist in the morning." One says "Let us eat, drink and be merry, for to-morrow we die," and another says, "Life is a great battle with constant engagements."

Perhaps this last definition is the only one that will apply to universal mankind. The world is one great encampment, wherein each man and each woman is a soldier. We did not enter the service as volunteers, but each one is drafted. We were given no voice in the matter of enlistment, and no choice of place in the ranks.

There is no end to the days of our service until we are mustered out by death. Neither the wealth of a Rockefeller, nor the power of the mightiest monarch can procure for us a substitute.

No greater battle ever raged in the world than that now in progress between the friends and foes of a higher standard of civic righteousness in our municipalities.

As I stand here to-day I am looking in the face of a battalion of the Great Commander's army. Some of you are going to be heroes in that engagement, and will receive badges of honor for service well done. Some of you will be deserters, and some will prove cowards and slip to the rear and out of sight. Some may even be traitors and go over to the enemy and fight under the black flag of wrong. Woe unto this state and nation if it contains many such sons, and woe unto that person who proves such a son.

We naturally pause to ask, what is at stake in this engagement? Is this a skirmish or a general engagement? Is it epoch making—is it to be one of the great decisive battles in our national progress?

I venture the assertion that this engagement is of the utmost importance. That its result will determine whether a government of the people, by the people and for the people can long endure.

Eighteen centuries ago we are told that "When He beheld the city, He wept over it." And the world still weeps over its cities. When this government was founded, Thomas Jefferson declared cities to be "ulcers upon the body politic." But the situation is tenfold more alarming now than when Jefferson made the remark. At that time there were but two cities in this nation as large as Kansas City, Kansas, is to-day.

It has been declared by our wisest statesmen that our most alarming situation is the gravitation of population to the city. We are nearing, if we have not already reached, the point where one half of the population of the country can be found in our cities.

There is no problem more grave than that of rescuing our municipalities from the corrupt and corrupting influences that are threatening our very civilization.

The slightest investigation will convince any intelligent person that the American Saloon is the one great and corrupting influence of our city life.

You would probably discount the statement of ministers and temperance orators as to the evils flowing from the use of intoxicating liquors, but you cannot question the judgment of our supreme court, before whom come the criminal cases of every county in the state, and who have actual knowledge of that which caused the crime. I read from the case of the State of Kansas vs. Crawford, 28 Kansas, 733:

"Probably no greater source of crime and sorrow has ever existed than social drinking saloons. Social drinking is the evil of evils. It has probably caused more drunkenness and has made more drunkards than all other causes combined, and drunkenness is a pernicious source of all kinds of crime and sorrow. It is a Pandora's box, sending forth innumerable ills and woes, shame and disgrace, indigence, poverty and want; social happiness destroyed; domestic broils and bickerings engendered; social ties sundered; homes made desolate; families scattered; heart rending partings; sin, crime and untold sorrows; not even hope left, but everything lost; and everlasting farewell to all true happiness and to all the nobler aspirations rightfully belonging to every true and virtuous human being."

The Supreme Court of the United States, in the case of Mugler vs. Kansas, 123 U. S. 205, says:

"We cannot shut out of view the fact, within the knowledge of all, that the public health, the public morals and the public safety are endangered by the general use of intoxicating liquors; nor the fact established by statistics accessible to every one, that the idleness, disorder, pauperism, and crime existing in the country are largely traceable to this evil."

The Supreme Court of Indiana, in the case of Beebe vs. State, 6 Ind. 542, says:

"That drunkenness is an evil both to the individual and to the state all must admit. That its legitimate consequences are disease, and destruction of mind and body, will also be granted. That it produces four-fifths to nine-tenths of all the crime committed is the united testimony of those judges, prison-keepers, sheriffs, and others engaged in the administration of the criminal law, who have investigated the subject. That taxation to meet the expenses of pauperism and crime, falls upon and is borne by the people, follows as a matter of course. That its tendency is to destroy the peace, safety and well being of the people, to secure which the first article in the Bill of Rights declares all free governments are instituted, is too obvious to be denied."

Bearing in mind these decisions, and the declaration of every supreme court in our Union, that the saloon is a menace to the health, happiness and morals of the community, listen to what the Supreme Court of the United States says:

"No legislature can bargain away the public health, or the public morals. The people themselves cannot do it, much less their servants." Stone v. Miss. 101 U. S. 816.

And again: "No legislature can bargain away the public morals or the public health, or the public peace." Phelan v. Va., 8 Howard 163-168.

In the light of this declaration by the highest court in our land, how can any legislature pass a law that is constitutional that licenses those dens which every court says are the prolific source of crime, and are destructive of the morals, health, and happiness of the community?

I presume there is no intelligent person who will defend the saloon upon moral grounds. We have passed that point in the discussion. The excuse given for the enactment of license laws is that prohibition does not prohibit; that high license is the better method of control; that liquor will be sold anyway, and that the city ought to derive a revenue from it to take care of the expense made upon the public by the traffic.

Then again, they say prohibition may work in rural districts, but cannot be enforced in a large city; that dens of vice are necessary in a large city, and to wipe them out will destroy the prosperity of such city. These statements have been so frequently and persistently made by the friends of the liquor traffic, that a large number of good citizens have come to believe them.

Temperance advocates have answered by saying if liquor will be sold anyway, it must be sold without our license—we will not be partners in the crime—we will not accept part of the blood-money.

About a quarter of a century ago the people of this state said that they would not legalize a traffic which, as our Supreme Court says, produces innumerable ills and woes, shame and disgrace, indigence, poverty and want.

Twenty-five years ago we discovered a precious jewel, and we hid it away. It has been hid so long the world was denying we possessed it;

so it became necessary to polish it, and hold it forth to prove we owned it, as well as its great value.

Kansas is to-day the experimental station of the world. In this State is to be determined and forever settled whether prohibition can be enforced in large cities as well as in rural districts. Kansas proposes by actual experiment to demonstrate whether dens of vice are necessary for the prosperity of large cities. Peculiar circumstances caused the selection of Kansas City, Kansas, as the first experimental station. It was a city of nearly one hundred thousand inhabitants, and the metropolis of the state. It was a manufacturing city, and the home of the wage-earner. It had a large population of foreigners—the pauper labor of the old world. It possessed a larger number of undesirable citizens in proportion to its population than any other large city in this nation. Time and again has the slum broken forth like a volcano, burning property, wrecking trains and destroying lives. It is a city that elected by two thousand majority a mayor whose platform was "Damn the constitution and laws of the State of Kansas;" a city that was regarded throughout the world as the most law-defying community on earth—the Sodom of the age.

Surely if prohibition could be enforced in such a city, it could be enforced in any other large city in the world. If such a city could get along and prosper without its dens of vice, surely any other large city might do likewise. If the closing of the saloons in such a city lessened crime, and elevated the morals of the community, then it would be a good thing for any other large city. These are the reasons why the people of Kansas, and of the nation have kept their eyes upon Kansas City for the past year.

Eight days from to-day will be the anniversary of the closing of the last open saloon in Wyandotte County. It is a coincident that the anniversary of the birth of the nation should be the day of the redemption of the metropolis of our state. July 4, 1906, was the first day since that county was settled that the inhabitants lived, moved, and had their being, without an open saloon.

I am not here to-day to preach to you the beauties of temperance. I am here to read to you a chapter covering twelve months in the life of Kansas City, Kansas, and let those unvarnished facts present their own moral. I shall tell you how the saloons were closed, and what was the effect on business, crime, and morals, and leave you to your own conclusions.

I was appointed Special Attorney General for Wyandotte County on June 8, 1906. At that time there were 256 open saloons, 200 gambling dens, and 60 houses of social evil.

Of these saloons, 210 were in Kansas City, 22 in Argentine, 10 in

ALFRED L. MANIERRE,
Attorney. Prohibition Party Worker of New York.

REV. C. J. C. SCHOLPP,
Editor, "The Sentinel," Frewsburg, New York.

WM. SCHALBER,
County Chairman, Prohibition Party, Rochester, New York.

FRANCIS E. BALDWIN,
Ex-Chairman, New York Prohibition State Committee.

Rosedale, and 14 in other localities. Thirty days later there was not a saloon in the county. It will be hard for you to realize that so many could be closed in such a short time, but when you have heard how it was done, you will wonder why it took so long.

For two weeks no outward movement was made. The saloon-keepers were in high glee, and temperance people in sackcloth and ashes, each thinking nothing would be done. But during those two weeks scouts were sent into every joint in the county to gather evidence, and court records were examined to ascertain the condition of old suits.

During the last five years something like fifty or sixty suits had been filed, but in no instance was the judgment entered of record. Wherever the petition was broad enough, a journal entry was prepared and recorded providing for a "writ of abatement."

The first public act was to issue these writs in four cases. Those were selected which contained costly fixtures, and located in different parts of the city, in the hope that, when the power of the law was demonstrated, the others would take the hint and quit. But no such result followed, and the business continued. The next day we issued writs in all remaining cases where judgment would permit, and there were publicly destroyed fixtures of the estimated value of $25,000. But even this did not cause a ripple, and the saloons continued business just the same.

Having exhausted all cases where there were judgments, injunction suits were filed by the wholesale, and at the commencement of these suits the saloon-keeper and his bartenders, and the owners of the property, were enjoined from maintaining a place where intoxicating liquors were sold or kept for sale. This had not the slightest effect, and the saloon business continued just the same. The arresting of violators of these injunctions for contempt of court was the next move. Six bartenders were taken, one after another, from one saloon, and placed in the county jail, but that saloon continued business just the same with new bartenders, and the breweries boasted they could get new men as fast as the old ones were put in jail, and that they would be doing business when I was in my grave. It should be borne in mind that, as the rich breweries owned the saloons, they would pay the fines of the men arrested, continue their salary while they lay in jail, and put new men in their places behind the saloon bar.

It was very evident that life was too short to close the saloons by the contempt method. At this juncture, the situation looked gloomy indeed. Some new plan had to be devised. Was it possible that in this enlightened day a court of equity was powerless to compel obedience to its orders and decrees? I remembered that some three years prior, when the citizens of the sixth ward of our city threatened to destroy a railroad bridge that was obstructing the flow of water in the Kansas river, an injunction was granted by Judge Pollock, of the Federal court, and then, upon an affidavit being filed that it was believed that the people would disregard and refuse obedience to his order of injunction, the said judge called the United States Marshal before him and commanded him to go and take possession of said bridge, and see to it that his order was obeyed. It seemed reasonable that if, upon the filing of an affidavit that it was believed an order would not be respected, the court could take possession of the property to enforce obedience, then surely when the order was being openly and flagrantly disobeyed, the court could take possession so as to compel obedience. With this thought in view papers were prepared in ten test cases, and presented to the judge, and it was argued and urged that a court of equity had the right and power to do anything that was necessary to compel obedience to its orders; that if necessary the court could place a receiver in charge, or order the premises locked up, or do anything else that might be necessary for the purpose of compelling respect for the order of injunction. The court after due and careful deliberation sustained this contention, and the order of the court, after reciting the formal preliminaries, read as follows:

"Now, therefore, said application is granted, and it is considered, ordered, adjudged, and decreed, that the Sheriff of Wyandotte County, Kansas, be and is hereby directed to immediately proceed to said premises and see that the order of this court is literally obeyed, and if necessary place locks upon all doors to said premises, or place a custodian in charge thereof with instructions to see that the said order is obeyed, and bring before this court any person found violating said order."

Armed with these writs, the sheriff and his deputies went post-haste in every direction, and, if there was no legitimate business being conducted in any saloon, the premises were left decorated with padlocks; but if any legal business was being carried on in addition to the selling of liquor, for instance, such as barber shops, cigar stands or pool tables, then a custodian was placed in charge day and night to compel obedience to the court's order.

After the granting of the first ten orders prepared, new and additional ones were prepared as fast as possible, and within three days more than sixty buildings were padlocked. Then it began to dawn upon the breweries that costly fixtures were being locked up in these rooms to abide a day when final judgment would order the sheriff to take them forth and publicly destroy them; and the saloon-keepers caught the padlock fever and padlocked their own buildings, so that they might carry the key rather than the sheriff. Then for days and weeks traffic was suspended in our city because every dray and transfer wagon was pressed into service to haul all fixtures that were not locked up by the sheriff, out of the State of Kansas. I recall one day looking out of the window of my office seeing nine transfer wagons, one behind the other, all loaded to their utmost with saloon fixtures, making a bee line for the state line. One who did not witness the sight cannot comprehend it. Every saloon contained from two to four wagon-loads, and when you remember that there were more than two hundred saloons, you can in a measure imagine why it took so many transfer teams.

It had been said by some that new law, and new rules of procedure have been used in this contest. If it be true that it is new law, then we say it is good law. But we deny it is new law. The right of a court to take possession of property if necessary to enforce a court order, is as old as jurisprudence itself. There is no limit to the power of a court of equity. If an extraordinary situation arises, then an extraordinary remedy may be applied. If the time ever comes when a court cannot enforce its orders, then has civil government ended, and it is time for military occupation. The life and property of the citizen is secure just so long as courts have the power to enforce their decrees and orders, and no longer.

After the saloons were closed, we were bothered by boot-legging. In the beginning this was largely by bartenders who had been thrown out of a job. The President of the Liberal League, thinking he must show his followers the way out, pulled the padlocks from his former place of business and opened up at the old stand. He was allowed to continue for two days in order to get evidence, and then arrested for contempt of court on five charges. He was tried and convicted on three, and given eighteen months in jail, fined $1,500 and costs, and required to give bond to obey the injunction in the future, and the other two charges are still pending for trial. His conviction and punishment put an end to any further attempt to run an open saloon. From that time on we have been bothered only with secret selling in back alleys, dark area-ways, and kindred places, but this is but a drop in the bucket compared with what it was.

The publicity given to the closing of the saloons in our county has brought letters from all over the world, making inquiry. There is a marked contrast in the information requested. From foreign countries the inquiry is: "How does it affect the morals of the people; what effect did it have on crime?" The inquiry from the several states is universally: "What effect does it have on business?"

I shall try to answer both of these questions. There are a number of good people in the world who believe it is impossible for a large city to exist without the saloon. Kansas City, Kansas, had its share of such people. When I was appointed, delegation after delegation visited my office to protest against closing the saloons, because they said it would ruin business. There were bankers and merchants, real estate men and lumbermen, and in fact all classes and professions. The bankers said it would lessen deposits, and cause a tight money market. The merchant said it would cause the people to go to Kansas City, Missouri, to trade where they could get their drinks. The real estate man said it would decrease our population, render vacant many houses, cause rents and prices of real estate to fall, and otherwise ruin the town. The lumbermen said it would stop the progress of the town, and the erection of new buildings would cease.

It is now twelve months since there was an open saloon in the county, and what is the result? Have any banks failed? Has the price of real estate declined? Are there vacant houses? Has work on new buildings stopped? Have taxes increased? Has our city ceased to grow, and are we losing in population? No man can truthfully say that any of the prophesied evils have happened.

The bankers who said it would injure their banks have returned to admit their mistake, and now say it has helped them. The real estate man says rents are higher than ever before. The lumberman says so many new buildings are being erected that it almost impossible to supply the demand, and this in mid-winter. The taxpayer finds that it has put money into the public treasury instead of increasing taxes. The furniture dealer finds that he is selling more furniture than ever before. The shoe man reports likewise. Recently Mr. Newton, of the firm of Dengel & Newton, stated to me that one astonishing feature of the increase in their line was that it was largely in footwear for women and children. Why is it that when the saloons are closed the women and children buy more shoes?

The timekeeper of one of the large packing-houses tells me that if the saloons are kept closed, they could afford an increase in wages, because of the increased efficiency of the men. Similar statements have been made to me by the superintendents and managers of other large institutions. I have personally talked with many of our business men, and almost without exception they report an improvement in business since the closing of the saloons. There are some lines that unquestionably were injured. For instance, the ice man was injured. The proprietor of our local plant said the closing of the saloons decreased his sales thirty tons a day. But he was patriotic enough to add that he hoped they would be kept closed even if he had to shut down his plant. I find that nearly every gent's furnishing goods establishment reports a loss of business, and that the same is true of the tailors. The reason for this was explained to me by a clerk in one of these establishments. He said that men were more liberal in their purchases when drinking, and that many times they would spoil a suit of clothes in a drunken revel and buy a new one before going home. The saloon-keeper and gambler always patronize the tailor for expensive suits, while those of legitimate professions must be content with "hand-me-downs." The barbers who were located in or near a saloon have been injured, but those in the rural districts report a greatly increased business. I do not know a single groceryman, dry goods merchant, or furniture dealer but that has an increased business. But it is needless to speculate as to various lines, when there is one source from which we can secure absolute evidence as to all lines.

In every community the banker is the index to business conditions. He sits at the ticker and hears the telegraphic news from every avenue of business. He is the nerve center, and feels the slightest interference with business conditions. If any line of trade is injured, he knows it almost before the owners thereof. Day in and day out, week in and week out, year in and year out, the banker sits with his finger upon the pulse, counting the heart-beats of business. Upon the testimony of those experts I will rest this case. We bid them take the witness stand and tell us of conditions both before and since the saloons were closed.

In the twelve months since the saloons were closed, the combined deposits of our banks have increased one and a half million dollars.

Does that indicate a ruined business and a bankrupt city? I hold in my hand the written testimony of these bankers, and offer it in evidence. Here is what they say:

HOME STATE BANK.

KANSAS CITY, KANSAS, Feb. 1, 1907.

Mr. C. W. Trickett, Kansas City, Kansas.

Dear Sir: With reference to your inquiry concerning conditions of our business as compared with that of June, 1906, we beg to state that our deposits have grown from $95,000.00 on June 30, 1906, to $132,000.00 on the 30th of January, 1907, an increase of 40 per cent., and the volume of our business has increased in a greater proportion.

The month of January just closed has shown a large increase in business as compared with the depressing month of January last year when the joints were in full blast. During the month three times as many new savings accounts were opened as in the month of January a year ago.

Respectfully yours,

J. W. HULLINGER, *Cashier.*

ARMOURDALE STATE BANK OF COMMERCE.

ARMOURDALE, KANSAS, Jan. 25, 1907.

Mr. C. W. Trickett, City.

Dear Sir: Enclosed find statements of the bank June 30 and January 25 as requested. Our deposits have increased more than 20 per cent. since the joints were closed. I have never been able to figure out how open saloons would benefit business, or closed saloons injure business. So far as our business is concerned, the statements speak for themselves.

Respectfully,

W. T. ATKINSON, *Vice-President.*

INTER-STATE NATIONAL BANK.

KANSAS CITY, KANSAS, Jan. 26, 1907.

Mr. C. W. Trickett, Kansas City, Kansas.

Dear Sir: Replying to yours of recent date I wish to give it as my opinion that there has been an improvement in the business of Kansas City, Kansas, since your successful warfare against the joints, and that the moral tone of the city is certainly much better than it ever was.

Yours truly,

WM. C. HENRICI, *Cashier.*

CITIZENS STATE SAVINGS BANK.

KANSAS CITY, KANSAS, Jan. 30, 1907.

Mr. C. W. Trickett, Kansas City, Kansas.

Dear Sir: In reply to your inquiry as to relative condition of our business now and at the time of the closing of the saloons in this city June 30, 1906, will say that our deposits since that time have increased 30 per cent., which we attribute largely to this cause.

We arrive at this conclusion from the fact that we are gaining so rapidly in new accounts, many of which we are positive are from that element which formerly spent their earnings for liquor. It is with great satisfaction that we can report to you that our business has been wonderfully increased, and I think I voice the sentiment of all the bankers in the city when I say that the banks have been wonderfully benefited by this procedure. Very truly yours,

J. D. WRIGHT, *Cashier.*

I come now to our largest bank, the one that carries the accounts of a large majority of the business men, and I ask you to note carefully what they say:

THE COMMERCIAL NATIONAL BANK.

KANSAS CITY, KANSAS, June 22, 1907.

Mr. C. W. Trickett, Assistant Attorney General, Kansas City, Kan.

Dear Sir: Referring to your enquiry with reference to general conditions since the closing of the joints in this city, I am pleased to state that the joints have now been closed for a year, that one year ago our deposits were $2,263,344.75 and at the close of business last night, one year later, our deposits were $3,032,832.65, an increase of $769,487.90 in twelve months, the largest increase of new business that we have had in any period of the same length of time since beginning.

We think we have the accounts of more than 50 per cent. of the business houses of this city, and have talked to a large number of them with reference to the effect of the closing of the joints on their business, and with but very few exceptions they have expressed themselves as pleased, and many of them are more than pleased with the result. Many of them have stated that it has been the best year they have ever had, and I believe that this feeling is shared by a large majority of the professional men and other intelligent citizens of the city. I have heard many of our best citizens, who were formerly inclined to think that closing of the joints would hurt the city, now express themselves as hoping we would never go back to the old *régime*, and others have proposed that, if the state administration lets up, we raise any amount of money necessary to prevent such catastrophe.

During my residence of nearly seventeen years in this city, conditions were never so good as they are at present time in every department of our civic life.

I hope that the conservative business men of every city in the state may be convinced of the truth of these statements.

Yours truly,

C. L. BROKAW, *Cashier.*

The change in public opinion in Kansas City, Kansas, is simply marvelous. A few months before the saloons were closed a mayor was elected by almost 2,000 majority, and his platform was "Damn the constitution and laws. The saloons shall run."

He was ousted from office, and on December 11, 1906, a new election was held. The politicians of both old parties put forth candidates that were allied with the crushed saloon element. A meeting was called and Dr. Gray was placed in the field as an independent candidate, upon a platform that demanded the enforcement of law, and especially the prohibitory law. If closing the saloons had injured business we would have found the business men arrayed against Dr. Gray, but instead of this the business men subscribed $2,000 to cover the expense of his campaign, and 152 business men signed a public appeal to the voters to support Dr. Gray, and the voters did support Dr. Gray, and he was elected mayor.

Since that time another election was held, and again the candidate declaring for law enforcement, and the keeping of the saloons closed was elected by an overwhelming majority.

If the testimony of our bankers and business men, and the recorded votes of our citizens do not convince you that the people of this community from actual experiment believe it a good business proposition to get rid of dens of vice, then you are not open to conviction, and further words of mine are useless.

An examination of the criminal docket of our court reveals the fact that since the saloons were closed we are running at a reduced expense of criminal prosecutions of more than $25,000 a year. The closing of the saloons has so lessened crime that a much smaller police force is required, making possible another saving of $25,000. The fact is that we are saving now in the various departments for the suppression of crime more than we ever received in revenue from the saloons.

An examination of the criminal docket of the District Court will reveal the fact that before the joints were closed it required six or more weeks to try the criminal cases. Since the closing of the joints, at no term has it required to exceed three weeks. The same proportion holds good in every other court having criminal jurisdiction.

The Police Judge of Argentine in a published interview says he is without a job. The Police Judge of this city was quoted in the *Star* as follows on September 11:

"Since the closing of the joints in Kansas City, Kansas, there has been a large reduction in crime. Before the joints were closed they had from ten to thirty in the police court every morning, since then the arrests have been very few. When Judge John T. Sims came to police court this morning, and was informed that the docket was clean, that there were no prisoners to be brought before the court, he spoke as follows: 'What! Do you mean to say that in this city of 85,000 people we are getting so good that not a single arrest has been made in twenty-four hours? That is a record breaker!'"

On the 23d of January, the chief of police of Kansas City, Kansas, gave the following interview for publication in the *Kansas City Star:*

"The joints were the greatest crime producers this city has ever known. Since the closing of these places there has not been half as much crime as under the old system of a wide-open town. Under the old system of a wide-open town the police court was crowded with offenders every day, and many of them were turned over to the state, charged with serious offenses. Now the police court has little business, and few men are carried into the state courts for prosecution. Drunkenness, wife-beating, cases of destitution, thieving and other offenses are not half so numerous. It is wonderful what a change has taken place.

"In the two city courts few suits have been filed to collect debts. Men who have been in the habit of spending their earnings in joints now pay their grocery bills and house rent, and make better provision for their families in other ways. Some of these people who were never known to pay a debt are getting to be very respectable people. This is all very significant. It shows what respect for law will do for a community. Everybody seems to be better satisfied. The only people who want to return to the old system are joint-keepers and those who rented their buildings for joints. The day of the open joint is past."

And this is the testimony of one who has spent his life on the police force and in the sheriff's office in our county, and knows every crook and tough in town.

MRS. MARY WILDER BARNES,
Corresponding Secretary, New Mexico, W. C. T. U.

MRS. S. C. NUTTER,
President, New Mexico W. C. T. U.

The *Kansas City, Kansas, Globe*, on Dec. 20, 1906, said editorially:

"With the exception of the Kentucky hotel murder and the burglarizing in three private residences, there has been practically no crime in the city in the past two months. As to petty offenses, the city was never cleaner. Where the police docket was formerly blackened by the written names of dozens of offenders daily, it is now barren, with but an occasional exception."

Last fall the business men of our city gave a week's carnival. Every day and night 50,000 people gathered in the heart of the city and paraded the streets. There was no drunkenness, no picking of pockets, no rowdyism. It was the common comment of all that the greatest marvel of that week of marvel was the absence of these things, and the committees of business men having it in charge frankly admitted that it would have been impossible to have held it if the joints had been running.

We no longer need a detective force. Thieves and burglars have followed the saloon out of our city. The great daily newspapers of Kansas City, Missouri, have kept close watch upon the situation in our city, and have daily and weekly chronicled the result. A few of the statements may interest you.

Last January the Police Judge of Argentine, a city of more than ten thousand population. said in an interview published in the *Kansas City Star:*

"They can talk all they want to about the closing of the joints in this county making conditions worse, but anyone who looks over my docket will find there is not one case now where there were fifteen before the crusade against the joints began."

The *Kansas City Journal* of April 18, 1907, contained the following:

"Police Judge John M. Woodward, of Argentine, is the most disconsolate official in Wyandotte County. He doesn't like to say it, but he feels that his friends handed him a lemon when they elected him police judge at the last election. He promptly opens court each morning at 8 o'clock, and clearing his throat says to the marshal:

" 'Call the first case.'

" 'There is no first case,' responds the marshal.

" 'Nothing doing?' says the judge.

" 'Nothing doing,' says the marshal.

" 'Pshaw,' sighs his honor climbing down from the bench.

"There has been only one case in the Argentine police court in three months, and that was a Kansas City, Missouri, man who became intoxicated, and took the wrong street car, and landed in Argentine drunk. Argentine's one patrolman was discharged last Tuesday night."

In Kansas City, Kansas, the record in police court is just as marvelous. One year ago our city officials were trying to find a way to spare the money to enlarge the city jails. To-day, the doors of our jails swing idly on their hinges and we have no use for those we have.

On September 11 of the last year, for the first time in the history of our city, there was not a case in police court. The press gave the following account:

"The police judge adjusted his glasses and said, 'Call the first case, Mr. Bailiff.' 'There ain't no first case,' responded the grinning bailiff. The judge remarked as he left the bench, 'This is the first time within the memory of our oldest citizens that the usual row of drunks and disorderlies failed to appear.' The guards at the rock pile have been discharged and the jails are idle."

Again on February 23, 1907, the *Kansas City, Kansas, Globe*, said:

"Yesterday being a holiday one would imagine that a large number of people would celebrate the occasion and there would be a large docket in police court, but such was not the case yesterday. Not one arrest was made during the twenty-four hours ending at eight o'clock this morning. As there were no continued cases, no police court was held."

On the 4th of May, 1907, the following item appeared in the *Kansas City Star*:

"I walked right in and turned around,
And walked right out again."

"John T. Sims, Police Judge of Kansas City, Kansas, was humming this song this morning as he walked from the city hall at 8:05 o'clock. He explained to the questioner: 'There wasn't a case tried in the police court this morning.' Kansas City, Kansas, has a population of 90,000. There has been a light docket since the joints were closed."

On the 5th day of February the papers said:

"Only fifteen prisoners are in the Wyandotte County jail. Before the joints were closed, there were from twenty-five to thirty all the time. The police force in Kansas City, Kansas, is smaller than it has been for years, yet there are few holdups or thefts, and, instead of a long police docket each day, only one or two cases are tried."

"Wyandotte County affords an instance which may be in point. Formerly, from fifteen to twenty young men were sent annually from Wyandotte County to the reformatory. This year, with the joints in Wyandotte County closed, the reformatory population has been augmented by only two prisoners from Wyandotte County."

I have brought you the records of our criminal courts, the declaration of our daily press, the record of police courts, jails, and reformatory, and if these things do not convince you that saloons and crime go hand in hand, no words of mine will do so.

It should not be overlooked that there has followed in the wake of law enforcement a great benefit to our city that cannot be measured in dollars and cents.

Our sanitarium had many cases of *delirium tremens* every week when joints were in operation, but Dr. S. S. Glasscock, the head physician, tells me there have been but two cases in the past six months.

The judge of the Juvenile Court recently told me that when the joints were in operation many children had to be assisted every month, but that with the closing of the joints this had totally disappeared, and that during the past six months there were but two applications and these were the children of a mistress of a disorderly house who abandoned them when she followed the saloons out of the city.

Our public schools reported an abnormal demand for admission to the public schools last fall. While formerly eight new teachers were sufficient each year for the increase in attendance, last fall eighteen new teachers had to be employed. Inquiry reveals the fact that since the saloons were closed, fathers are providing for their families and the boys are trying to get an education who formerly had to work to support their mothers and drunken fathers. Dollars and cents cannot measure this, but in the future life of our city it will weigh heavily in the balance for good government.

The manager of the Children's Home says there has been a large decrease in the number of dependent poor and cases of destitution.

The county poor commissioner says that not so many poor persons are being sent to the county farm, and that the hundreds of cases of destitution due to the husbands spending their money and time in the "joint" have almost entirely disappeared.

Teachers in the public schools report that children are now well clothed who formerly were in rags because their parents spent their earnings in the "joints."

Festus Foster, secretary of the Associated Charities, in a published interview on January 23, 1907, said:

"Although the population of our city is rapidly increasing, the number of cases of destitution is decreasing materially. We trace this directly to the fact that the joints have been closed and that a better condition prevails on all hands. A person who has not been actively connected with charity work cannot appreciate the wonderful change that has taken place since the 'joints' were closed."

More than a score of cases have come under my personal observation where individual drunkards have become sober and industrious citizens since the closing of the "joints."

Periodically for some three or four years a lady, poorly dressed, called upon us to file a divorce suit for her, because her husband spent all his earnings for drink. Upon each occasion it was the same story. Her husband earned $6 a day, and yet his wife had to earn the living for the family. Disliking to file divorce suits, we kept putting off the evil day. During the past six months I had not heard from her. On Christmas day while sitting at my desk her husband called, and said his wife wanted to see me. Supposing it was the same old story I pleaded business, but he refused to take no for an answer and said his wife must see me. I stepped into the buggy waiting at the door, and we were soon at a neat cottage. When the door opened I beheld a room neatly carpeted, with new furniture, and there stood the wife neatly dressed. The children were clothed like the children of well-to-do citizens. In the center of the room stood a Christmas tree, still glittering with its decorations.

Noticing that I was puzzled, the wife remarked, "I just wanted you to see, Mr. Trickett, what the closing of the joints has done for our home." And then the husband explained by saying: "Yes, this is what closing the saloons has done for us. At first I was bitter because I was deprived of the right to go in, purchase, and drink what I pleased, and for a while I went across the State line; but I did have American manhood and pride left, so that, when I could not walk in at the front door, I would not sneak into back alleys, or into dark areaways, or into a room with bolted doors and drawn curtains, where each one looked like a thief watching and expecting officers. We have purchased this little home on payments, have furnished it, and are happy and content."

These are matters that in my judgment weigh heavily in the scale, and yet cannot be measured in dollars and cents. It is needless to comment upon such matters.

It may be proper for me to say that the contest in Wyandotte county, so far as I was concerned, was not a temperance move. It did not present itself to me as primarily a question of prohibition or anti-prohibition. It was a question whether the state in which I lived was a sovereign state, and whether law reigned in Kansas City, Kansas. It was not a question whether it would help or hurt business, but it was a question whether treason would be tolerated.

When Kansas City, Topeka, Leavenworth, Wichita and other cities say they will not obey the constitution and laws of this state, it is treason. Nullification can never have an abiding place in this city. We will no more tolerate "city rights" today, than "state rights" in former days.

Kansas has blazed the path in many crises. It was in Kansas that the scuffle in the vestibule of the greatest drama of all time took place. It was a Kansas boy that led the relief army and first scaled the walls of Pekin. It was a Kansas boy that went into the jungles of Cuba and taught the Cubans how to fight for their rights. It was Kansas boys that first plunged over the ramparts in that awful charge at San Juan hill It was Kansas boys that, at the close of battle in the Philippines, being far in advance of the rest of the army, and being questioned how long they could hold their advance position, sent back the reply, "Until we are mustered out." And that which Kansas boys have done in the past, Kansas boys will do in the future. Having put our hand to the plow we will not look back, nor count the cost. A Kansas boy occupies the Governor's chair. A Kansas boy is Attorney General. Kansas boys are in the legislature, and Kansas boys all over this state are now saying to the world that the upas tree of nullification and treason cannot thrive upon the fertile fields of Kansas and in the very heart of the nation. If it ruins business, let it be ruined. If it increases taxes, we will foot the bill. Never shall it be said that Kansas weighs her honor in the scale with business and taxation. Never shall it be said that Kansas is trying to bribe eternal justice into writing a false inscription over its name; but rather let it be said that Kansas cut out the cancers upon her body politic, and asks the historians to place a finger of charity over the wound, and write only of the glories that will be.

Up in Portland, Maine, Samuel F. Pearson of kindred spirit to Mr. Trickett, immortalized himself, as other men have done, by keeping faith with conscience and doing duty. He had been an obscure Methodist mission worker in the city of Portland, and had seen how prohibition did not prohibit, under a *régime* which elected men who connived with liquor dealers to nullify a strong and faultless law. Having seen this condition of lawlessness, he announced that if he, an humble Methodist preacher, were elected sheriff, he would enforce the law at all hazards. The people took him at his word, and elected him. Having tried preaching the gospel, with the usual results known to most mission workers in cities, he now proceeded to administer a discredited law.

One of his first problems was to find men who would obey orders. He found them, even in Cumberland county. Then the Maine prohibition law worked, because he and his deputies worked. By night and by day, fighting all sorts of schemes of the liquor dealers, defied, threatened, handicapped, he continued until the criminals gave up the battle.

Pearson has passed on. There are whispers that he died of the strain of his term as sheriff. To go up and down the streets of a city day and night in peril of ambush wears on the nerves. Pearson was in danger. Any man is in danger who is in favor of the enactment and enforcement of the law against the saloon trade. Carmack, of Tennessee, for instance. Pearson was in danger, and knew it. He took office knowingly at the risk of his life. The men who voted for him knew that he would be in peril. But while he was sheriff, he was sheriff; the law was enforced, and the saloon and the blind tigers and the bootleggers disappeared in Portland. —G. M. H.

CHAPTER XXVI.

CARRY A. NATION—HEROINE OF THE HATCHET.

Introductory Sketch, By Will Carlton.

SOME years ago, the American public, always longing for "something new," was treated to an absolutely unique sensation. A woman armed with a hatchet had gone into a Kansas liquor saloon and smashed up its appurtenances in a very thorough and unconventional manner. After this, she went into and through another, and another; and it began to look as if all the bibulous paraphernalia of Kansas were about to be sent into the twilight.

When the smoke had somewhat cleared away, and time elapsed sufficient to garner these circumstances into authentic news, it transpired that the woman who had done this was Mrs. Carry A. Nation—utterly obscure and unknown until that week.

This raid among decanters was a very singular and startling act, for a woman; but, somehow, people found it refreshing. It represented precisely what many had imagined in their minds, what thousands of women had wished they themselves could or dared do, what myriads of confirmed drinkers, even, had wished might be done. News of Mrs. Nation's swift and decided action went all over the country, like a stiff, healthy gale. She was sharply criticised—but there lurked very often a "dry grin" behind the criticism. This smashing was all very direct and unique; and Americans are in general fond of directness and uniqueness. It was, technically, illegal, but, even so, it was remarkable that the saloons which Mrs. Nation wrecked, were themselves in brazen defiance of the laws of the state of Kansas—unenforced on account of the fear or venality of public authorities.

The work of this determined woman went on with a thoroughness and promptness that made it ultra-interesting. She was imprisoned again and again, and became an inmate, at one time and another, of some thirty-two different jails. She had trial after trial—in which was developed the fact that her tongue was as sharp as her hatchet; she often addressing even the judge presiding, as "Your Dishonor," while prosecuting attorneys she treated with supreme scorn. Not much mercy was shown her in the county bastiles: she was often bestowed in cells next to insane people—in the hope, she thinks, that she might become really

MRS. CARRY A. NATION,
The Heroine of the Hatchet.

crazy, as well as reputedly so. One sheriff, finding that the fumes of cigarette smoking made her ill, treated all her fellow-inmates to the little white cylinders and set them at work puffing vigorously. Chivalry and humanity seemed, for the time being, to have faded from men's minds.

In these different immurements, she had time to write to her friends, and even to publish a paper, called *The Smasher's Mail.* She told how she came to do this work; it was, she claimed, by the direct command of God. She had promised Him that if he would forgive her many sins, she would work for Him in ways no one else would; and He took her at her word—ordering her to go and smash saloons. This, of course, provokes a smile among most people, but Mrs. Nation is not the first one that has worked under God's command—whether real or supposed.

At last, so many fines were heaped up against her, which must be paid before she could be liberated, that it seemed to her as if she would never get free. But, in this dark hour, a lecture agent appeared, and said he would pay the amount if she would give him some "dates." She laughingly says now that she did not know what he meant, and actually wondered if he thought she was a fruit-dealer. But when he explained what he meant by "dates"—a chance to go on the platform and give the people a reason for the hatchet that was in her hand—she saw the gates were opened—and enthusiastically went from jail to the lecture platform.

She became immediately a drawing card—in assembly halls, in some churches and even at county fairs. She worked, tirelessly and industriously, to pay back the lecture agent for the sums he had advanced; and after a time found surplus amounts on hand.

She did not hesitate very long as to the purpose for which they were to be applied. Her personal expenses were very small; she dresses plainly; and believes that God is entitled to her financial gains.

A "Home for Drunkards' Wives" was her first thought after paying the fine money, and she set about establishing it, and is working for it now.

After her platform work had proceeded for a time, it was decided that she should star in the play "Ten Nights in a Barroom." As all know, who have witnessed this simple but powerful drama, every act of it is a prohibition lecture, and Mrs. Nation's part, that of the mother of the murdered boy, was a lecture of itself. In one scene, she was represented as smashing a saloon, most thoroughly; and this business was the most popular of anything in the play—even at theaters that drew most of their patronage from habitués of saloons.

Mrs. Nation's reasons for stepping from the churches to the footlights is not without its logic in these days. "People go to the theaters more than they do to the churches," she says, "and I want to go where there are plenty of people to hear me, and where they need me."

From the regular theater she passed, and for the same reasons, to the vaudeville, and did her regular "stunts" along with the singers, the dancers, the harlequins, acrobats and the burnt cork humorist. The writer of this has seen her in one of these performances, and considers it entirely unique and unmistakably commendable. It was in one of the most "free and easy" vaudeville shows in Greater New York, and the audience, composed of men and boys, was a hilarious one, and could have even become a turbulent one, if anything had occurred that did not please them. Many were half drunk, or nearly so. "Smoke, if you want to," was lettered on a conspicuous sign, and most of this audience wanted to. In the midst of the exercises an interlude occurred in which the audience was invited to a saloon downstairs where they could proceed still farther in the liquid burning out of their bodies. On the same stage of this same vaudeville theater John L. Sullivan, the retired prize fighter, had, only a week before, appeared "in monologue," and had sometimes been so drunk that he could not go through with his part.

In the midst of all this, Carry Nation was announced, and she stepped upon the stage, unattended by any glare of colored lights or fanfare of music. A quiet, motherly-looking woman, plainly dressed, with a Bible in her hand, she commanded almost immediately the respect of that large crowd—from the men in the orchestra stalls to the gallery gods. One half-intoxicated fellow began to scoff at her, but was almost immediately hushed by the scarcely less drunken ones around him. It was a sight that hushed them all into respectful silence, for a respectable, earnest woman, with the Holy Book in her hands, will have a subduing effect upon almost any company of people.

Mrs. Nation announced her text and preached a sermon and delivered a temperance lecture, both within the half hour. (The latter she calls a "prohibition lecture"—hating the word temperance, as applied to drink.)

She said words, such as had probably not been heard by most of those there, for a great many years. She told them what sots they were making of themselves, and made her points so emphatic that they cheered her—almost in spite of themselves. She commenced her speech as an experiment, so far as that day's audience was concerned; she closed a heroine. She did not remain idle during the time between her appearances on the stage, but cultivated the acquaintance of the actors and actresses, and, it is said, to their good. It would be hard to see how one woman could do more good in half an hour, than she does; and that among those that need it most.

Mrs. Nation's whole name is Carrie Amelia Nation, but, having noticed from old records that her father wrote the first name "Carry," she now does the same, and considers the name portentous as concerns what she is trying and means to do. She believes, she says, that it is her mission to *carry a nation* from the darkness of drunken bestiality into the light of purity and sobriety; and if she can do this, or in any great measure contribute to it, there are millions of people in the world that will bid her God speed.

Against the charge of illegality, Mrs. Nation has defended her drastic mode of campaign on the ground, *first*, of common law right, and, *second*, of her divine vocation. On the point of legality she says:

"It it is not only the privilege of the patriotic citizen to abate a dangerous nuisance, but it is commendable. Bishop on *Criminal Law*, paragraph 1081, says:

"'The doctrine (of abatement of a public nuisance by an individual) is an expression of the better instincts of our natures, which lead men to watch over and shield one another from harm.'

"1 Bishop's *Criminal Law*, 828; 1 Hilliard on *Torts*, 605:

"'At common law it was always the right of a citizen, without official authority, to abate a public nuisance, and without waiting to have it adjudged such by legal tribunal. His right to do so depended upon the fact of its being a nuisance.

"'In abating it, property may be destroyed, and the owner deprived of it without trial, without notice and without compensation. Such destruction for public safety or health is not a taking of private property for public uses, without compensation or due process of law, in the sense of the constitution. It is simply the prevention of its obnoxious and unlawful use, and depends upon the principle that every man must so use his property as not to injure his neighbors, and that the safety of the public is the paramount law. These principles are legal maxims or axioms essential to the existence of regulated society. Written constitutions presuppose them, are subordinate to them and cannot set them aside.'

"Judge Baker sums up the case thus:

"'The women who destroyed such property are not criminals. They have the right to abate such common nuisances as men have to defend their persons or domiciles when unlawfully assailed. As the women of that state are denied the right to vote or hold office, I think they are fully justified, morally and legally, in protecting their homes, their families and themselves from the ravages of these demons of vice in the summary manner which the law permits.'"

On the same ground Abraham Lincoln once defended women charged with a similar offense.

MRS. NATION'S OWN STORY.

In an autobiography as unique as her own personality, Mrs. Nation describes her call of God and the beginning of her career as a saloon-smasher. Her first husband, Dr. Gloyd, had died after a downward career of drunkenness. She had married Mr. David Nation and removed to Kansas.

While at Medicine Lodge, in that state, she had been appointed jail evangelist. In this capacity she would invariably ask the men in prison, young and old, "Why are you here?" The answer was, "Drink, drink." To quote her own words:

"They told me that they got their drink in Kiowa. This town was in Barber county, a county right on the border of Oklahoma. I went to Mr. Sam Griffen, the county attorney, time after time, telling him of these men being in jail from drink. He would put the matter off and seem very much annoyed because I asked him to do what he swore he would do, for he was oathbound to get out a warrant and put this in the hands of the sheriff who was oathbound to arrest these divekeepers, and put them in jail; and the place or dive was to be publicly abated or destroyed. Mr. Griffen was determined that these divekeepers should not be arrested. I even went down to Kiowa myself and went into these places and came back, asking this county attorney to take my evidence, and he would not do it. Then I wrote to Mr. A. A. Godard, of Topeka, the state's attorney, whose duty it was to see that all the county attorneys did their duty. I saw he did not intend to do anything; then I went to William Stanley, the Governor, at Topeka. I told him of the prisoners in jail in our county from the sale of liquor in the dives at Kiowa, told him of the broken families and trouble of all kinds in the county, told him of two murders that had been committed in the county, one alone costing the taxpayers $8,000; told him of the brokenhearted women and the worse than fatherless children as the result. I found out that he would not do his duty. I had gone from the lowest to the chief executive of the state, and, after appealing to the governor in vain, I found that I could go to no other authority on earth.

"Now, I saw that Kansas was in the power of the bitter foe to the constitution, and that they had accomplished what the whisky men and their tools, the Republican party and politicians, had schemed and worked for. When two-thirds of the voters of Kansas said at the ballot box—about 1880, I think it was—'We will not have a saloon in our state.' This was made constitutional by the two-thirds majority. Nothing could change this or take it out of the constitution except by having the amendment resubmitted and two-thirds of the people voting to bring the saloons back. They intended then with their bribes and otherwise to buy votes. The first act was to organize the state into what they called the 'Mystic Order of Brotherhood.' Of course, this was kept very quiet and few of the people in the towns knew of this order and organization. When the Devil wants to carry out his deepest plots he must do, through a secret order, what he cannot otherwise do. He does his work through, by and in the kingdom of darkness. For this one reason he must hoodwink the people to make them his tools.

"God has given me a mean fight, a dirty and dangerous fight; for it is a war on the hidden things of darkness. Through this 'Mystic Order of Brotherhood' managing the primaries and elections, they got into office from constable up to the governor, the tools of the liquor power. The great question that was then discussed was *resubmission*. Every representative at Topeka was in favor of the resubmission without an exception. Money was sent into Kansas by the thousands from brewers and distillers to be used by politicians for the purpose of bringing about resubmission. Kansas was the storm center. If the liquor men could bring back saloons into Kansas then a great blow would be struck against prohibition in all the states. This would discourage the people all over. Their great word was, 'You can't.' 'Prohibition will not prohibit.'

"I do not belong to the *Can't* family. When I was born my father wrote my name *Carry A. Moore;* then later it was *Nation,* which is more still. *C. A. N.* are the initials of my name; then C (*see*) A. Nation! And altogether *Carry A. Nation!* This is no accident, but Providence. This does not mean that *I* will *carry a nation,* but that the roused heart and conscience will, as I am the roused heart and conscience of the people. God's crowd and the Devil's crowd: one gains the battle by *can,* and the other loses it by *can't.*

"My Christian experience will give you the secret of my life; it is God indwelling. When I found I could effect nothing through the officials, I was sad, indeed. I saw that Kansas homes, hearts and souls were to be sacrificed. I had lost all the hopes of my young life through drink; I saw the terrible butchery that would follow. I felt that I had rather die than to see the saloons come back to Kansas. I felt desperate. I took this to God daily, feeling that He only could rescue.

"On the 5th of June, 1899, before retiring, I threw myself face downward at the foot of my bed at my home in Medicine Lodge. I poured out my grief and agony to God, in about this strain: 'O Lord, you see the treason in Kansas. They are going to break the mothers' hearts. They are going to send the boys to drunkards' graves and a drunkard's hell. I have exhausted all my means, O Lord. You have plenty of ways. You have used the base things and the weak things. Use me to save Kansas. I have but one life to give you. If I had a thousand, I would give them all. Please show me something to do.'

"The next morning I was awakened by a voice which seemed to be speaking in my heart these words: 'Go to Kiowa'; and my hands were lifted and thrown down—and the words, 'I'll stand by you.' The words, 'Go to Kiowa,' were spoken in a murmuring, musical tone, low and soft; but 'I'll stand by you,' was very clear, positive and emphatic. I was impressed with a great inspiration. The interpretation was very plain. It was this: 'Take something in your hands, and throw at these places in Kiowa, and smash them.' I was very much relieved and overjoyed, and was determined to be 'obedient to the heavenly vision' (Acts 26:19). I told no one what I had heard or what I intended to do.

"I was a busy homekeeper, did all my housework, was superintendent of two Sunday-schools—one in the country; was jail evangelist, president of the W. C. T. U., and kept open house for all of God's people, where all the Christian workers were welcome to abide at my house. When no one was looking I would walk out in the yard and pick up brickbats and rocks, would hide them under my kitchen apron and would then take them to my room, and wrap them up in newspapers, one by one. I did this until I got quite a pile. . . .

"At half past three that day I was ready to start. I hitched up the buggy myself, drove out of the stable, rode down hill and over a bridge that was just outside the limits of Medicine Lodge. . . . I expected to stay all night with a dear friend, Sister Springer, who lived about half way to Kiowa. When I arrived near her home the sun was almost down, but I was very eager to go to Kiowa and I said: 'Oh Lord, if it is Thy will for me to go to Kiowa tonight, have Price (my horse) pass this open gate'; which I knew he would never do unless God ordered it. I gave him the reins, and when I got opposite the open gate my horse jumped forward as if someone had struck him a blow. I got to Kiowa at half past eight, and stayed all night.

"Next morning I had my horse hitched and drove to the first dive, kept by a Mr. Dobson, whose brother was then sheriff of the county. I stacked up the smashers on my left arm, all I could hold. They looked like packages wrapped in paper. I stood before the counter and said: 'Mr. Dobson, I told you last spring to close this place. You did not do it. Now I have come down with another remonstrance. Get out of the way; I do not want to strike you, but I am going to break this place up.' I threw as hard and as fast as I could, smashing mirrors and bottles and glasses, and it was astonishing how quickly this was done. These men seemed terrified, threw up their hands and backed up in the corner. My strength was that of a giant. I felt invincible. God was certainly standing by me. . . .

"I broke up three of these dives that day, broke the windows on the outside to prove that the man who rents his house is a partner also with the man who sells. The party who licenses and the paper that advertises, all have a hand in this and are *particeps criminis*. I smashed five saloons with rocks before I ever took a hatchet.

"In the last place, kept by Lewis, there was quite a young man behind the bar. I said to him: 'Young man, come from behind that bar. Your mother did not raise you for such a place.' I threw a brick at the mirror, which was a very heavy one, and it did not break, but the brick fell and broke everything in its way. I began to look around for something that would break it. I was standing by a billiard table on which there was one ball. I said: 'Thank God!' and picked it up, threw it and it made a hole in the mirror.

"By this time the streets were crowded with people; most of them seemed to look puzzled. There was one boy about fifteen years old who seemed perfectly wild with joy, and he jumped, skipped and yelled with delight. I have since thought of that as being a significant sign, for to smash saloons will save the boy. I stood in the middle of the street and spoke in this way: 'I have destroyed three of your places of business, and if I have broken a statute of Kansas, put me in jail; if I am not a lawbreaker, your mayor and councilmen are. You must arrest one of us, for if I am not a criminal, they are.'

"One of the councilmen, who was a butcher, said: 'Don't you think we can attend to our business?' 'Yes,' I said, 'you can, but you won't.

As jail evangelist of Medicine Lodge, I know you have manufactured many criminals, and this county is burdened down with taxes to prosecute the results of these dives. Two murders have been committed in the last five years in this county, one in a dive I have just destroyed. You are a butcher of hogs and cattle, but they are butchering men, women and children, positively contrary to the laws of God and man; and the mayor and council are more to blame than the jointists, and now if I have done wrong in any particular arrest me.' When I was through with my speech I got into my buggy and said, 'I'll go home.'

"The marshal held my horse and said: 'Not yet; the mayor wishes to see you.' I drove up to where he was, and the man who owned one of the dive buildings I had smashed was standing by Dr. Korn, the mayor, and said: 'I want you to pay for the front windows you broke of my building.' I said, 'No, you are a partner of the divekeeper, and the statutes hold your building responsible. The man that rents the building for any business is no better than the man who carries on the business, and you are party to the crime.' They ran back and forward to the city attorney several times. At last they came and told me I could go. As I drove through the streets the reins fell out of my hands and I, standing up in my buggy, lifted my hands twice, saying, 'Peace on earth, good will to men.' This action I know was done through the inspiration of the Holy Spirit. 'Peace on earth, good will to men' being the result of the destruction of saloons and the motive for destroying them.

"When I reached Medicine Lodge the town was in quite an excitement, the news having been telegraphed ahead. I drove through the streets and told the people of my work in the jail here, and the young men's lives that had been ruined, and the broken-hearted mothers, the taxation that had been brought on the county, and other wrongs of the dives of Kiowa; of how I had been to the sheriff, Mr. Gano, and the prosecuting attorney, Mr. Griffin; how I had written to the state's attorney general, Mr. Godard, and I saw there was a conspiracy with the party in power to violate their oaths, and refuse to enforce the constitution of Kansas, and I did only what they swore they would do. I had a letter from a Mr. Long, of Kiowa, saying that Mr. Griffin, the prosecuting attorney, was taking bribes, and that he and the sheriff were drinking and gambling in the dives of Kiowa.

"This smashing aroused the people of the county to this outrage, and these divekeepers were arrested, although we did not ask the prosecuting attorney to get out a warrant, or sheriff to make an arrest. Neither did we take the case before any justice of the peace in Kiowa or Medicine Lodge, for they belong to the Republican party and would prevent the prosecution. The cases were taken out in the country several miles from Kiowa before Moses E. Wright, a Free Methodist and a justice of the peace of Moore township.

"The men were found guilty, and for the first time in the history of Barber county, all dives were closed."

Mrs. Nation has explained that she found her first method of "smashing" with stones and brickbats unsatisfactory from the fact that when her ammunition was once used it was gone beyond recovery and she was left helpless and empty-handed without an instrument with which to pursue her work. She then tried using an iron rod which also proved unsatisfactory. Then she fell afoul a hatchet, and found it so peculiarly well adapted to her purpose that she adopted it permanently, and it has become the universally recognized emblem of her strenuous form of missionary service. Mrs. Nation says of her first use of the hatchet:

"I was in a meeting of the W. C. T. U. in Wichita, of which Mrs. Summers was president. I wanted to have these women go with me and destroy the places there that were murdering their sons. Many present were in favor of it, but Mrs. Summers was bitterly opposed. I had not up to this time taken a hatchet in my work, nor did I do so until I reached Sister Evans' house, just before starting in my second raid in Wichita. Three went out in the hall with me, Mrs. Lucy Wilhoite, Miss Muntz and Mrs. Julia Evans. The husband of the latter was a great drunkard, otherwise a capable physician. Those three women said they would go with me. We went to Mrs. Evans' home. I took a hatchet, and Mrs. Evans carried a piece of iron. We marched down to the first place, kept by John Burns. We walked in and began to smash right and left. With my hatchet I smashed in the large plate glass windows and also the door. Sister Evans and I then attacked the show case, then went behind the bar and smashed everything in sight. The bartender came running up to me with his hands up. I said, 'Don't come near my hatchet; it might fall on you, and I will not be responsible for the results.'"

John Brown, an eccentric, a product of Kansas, by methods unconventional, illogical and in themselves futile for accomplishing his purpose, nevertheless aroused and inspired a nation, and achieved immortality in history, tradition and song, and is and ever more shall be credited with a large part in the great drama which resulted in the overthrow of slavery.

Likewise in some measure, Carry A. Nation, an eccentric, a product of Kansas, holds and shall hold a permanent and prominent place in the annals of the anti-liquor crusade. Caricatured, buffeted, the theme of jest and cartoon, imprisoned more than thirty times by the "powers that be," she has aroused and centered attention upon the lawless liquor saloon, and has greatly stimulated the agitation which is resulting in its downfall.

In her biography, frank to the point of nakedness, one gets a glimpse into that type of courageous and prophetic soul which stands before the king and with unwavering finger and tongue proclaims, "Thou art the man," and which makes a whip of small cords and scourges the money-changers out of the temple of God, and smashes their tables.

HON. JOHN T. SHEA,
Secretary, Anti-Saloon League of Massachusetts; Vice-President
Catholic Total Abstinence Union, Boston.

WILLIAM E. JOHNSON,
U. S. Special Indian Agent

CHAPTER XXVII.

FIGHTING FIREWATER.

THRILLING EXPERIENCES OF WILLIAM E. JOHNSON, *Special Indian Agent*.

NOTE.—*The early wars to* EXTERMINATE *the Red Man furnished no more thrilling—and far less noble—episodes than are found in the incidents related here from the experiences of Mr. Johnson in his efforts to* SAVE *the Indians. For the material used in this chapter credit is due principally to "The Associated Prohibition Press," F. D. L. Squires, Editor.*—G. M. H.

WHEN the white man came to the New World he brought with him a doctrine that puzzled the red man, and a drink that poisoned him. For every Indian converted to the doctrine, a score were killed by the drink. With zeal born of love of lucre, five white men pushed the traffic in rum, where one missionary preached religion. And so, robbed of land and ruined by liquor, the tribes receded before the advance of the pale face, until only remnants of once mighty nations are now corraled in the reservations. Of course, there have been prohibitory laws—but there has been only a half-hearted enforcement of them. For nearly three centuries the tribes have been plagued by the white man's drink—three centuries of liquor dishonor even blacker than that century of land robbery of which Helen Hunt Jackson tells in her "Ramona." Some time the awful drink story will be told, and the world will shudder at the tale of greed and graft—of woe and waste.

This chapter summarizes the record of conditions as they existed prior to the appointment of William E. Johnson, as United States Special Agent or Inspector, and the changes that came about after he had begun his campaign against the scoundrels who had been selling liquor to the tribes.

Old John Heckewelder, the missionary, who wrote a history of the manners and customs of the North American Indians, says that they were totally ignorant of the processes of distillation and fermentation. They were *uncivilized*. It was not until civilized Europe, nominally Christian for a millennium, "discovered" them, that they first learned the qualities of intoxicating liquor. Heckewelder says that the mysterious drink was at first taken with hesitation and fear. The Indians perhaps suspected poison, but being deceived accepted the proffered cup eagerly—and then asked for more—and more. Having created a demand, the European traders, hungry for profits, furnished the supply; and, the market expanding, the "Indian problem" emerged. This created prompt necessity for governmental and missionary activities among the red men of the forest. In 1629, only nine years after the sacred ark of the Mayflower had touched the rock at Plymouth, old Governor Endicott said, speaking for the authorities in London: "We pray you endeavor, though there be much strong water for sale, yet so to order it as that the savages may not, for our lucre's sake, be induced to the excessive use, or rather, abuse of it, and at any time take care our people give no ill example."

Governor Endicott "endeavored" to "order" the traffic—but failed—the "lucre" was too potent a motive. From his day until the Federal Government was organized, the colonial "states" endeavored to "order" the business, but failed. The "more perfect union" of 1787 began its history with legislative endeavors to suppress the trade among Indians, because of their tendency to "excess and drunkenness," but failed. Always the "lucre" was more powerful than the "law," and the Indian furnished a market to the steely-souled dealer in drink.

Of course the real philanthropists deplored the fact that European civilization had brought to their shores the drink of death with its advance agents and representatives, and began to organize agencies to extinguish the nefarious trade. As early as 1685, the Quakers "agreed" and gave as their "judgment" that it was not "consistent with the honor of truth for any that make profession thereof to sell rum or any strong drink to the Indians, because they use them not to moderation." That seems to have been the beginning of a movement for the prevention of cruelty to Indians. Since then all sorts of societies have been organized to instil principles of hostility to distilled drink among the natives of North America—resulting in more or less dismal failure.

And the government of the United States has expended hundreds of thousands of dollars in the futile effort to protect their "wards" against degraded whites, who have taken malicious delight in getting Indians drunk for the sake of lucre. Always lucre!

The story of the efforts to "regulate" the traffic, or to suppress it, would require the publication of a special volume. Our purpose is to describe, first, the situation as it existed in 1904; and then, as it exists in 1908, after four years under an administration of law which places in power a man who has a heart to fight the traffic to death—or die in the attempt.

A condition of affairs has existed among the Indians in the United

States which is an infamous disgrace to the so-called government at Washington. The United States Indian Commissioner, in his report for 1904 says:

"Civilization is not an unmixed blessing. It carries with it grave responsibilities and some undesirable tendencies. The Indian, while being fitted for citizenship, is absorbing vices as well as virtues, and weakness as well as strength. This is especially true in relation to his physical well-being. It is always easy for the Indians to get liquor."

From the beginning of Anglo-Saxon supremacy in America, it has always been easy, or comparatively easy. The following extracts from official reports illustrate present-day conditions.

One of the farmers in charge of the Navajo extension says:

"I am convinced that one of the greatest drawbacks to the moral progress of these Indians is the influence exercised over them by the traders. Another demoralizing agency is the practice of Indians leaving the reservation to work on the railroads. While away they have free access to liquor, and most of their wages are lost in gambling. Out of several hundred who were at work on the Santa Fé railroad last year, none of them returned with any money so far as I could ascertain, and, with but few exceptions, they were more degraded than before they left the reservation. Nearly all their women who accompanied them on these trips became prostitutes."

A special disbursing agent says:

"The sale of liquor to Indians in the city of Tucson, Arizona, San Xavier Reservation, is still causing considerable trouble; in fact, no arrests of Indians have been made by city or county officials or by the Indian police, except for disturbing the peace or other minor offenses committed when under the influence of liquor. No intoxicants are sold at or brought to the reservation, but the Indians can always find some miscreant in Tucson, who, for a small consideration, will procure it for them. During the past year I made fourteen complaints against persons who sold liquor to Indians, and was fortunate enough to obtain eleven convictions."

The Disbursing Agent at Hoyt, Kansas, Pottawatomie Agency, says:

"This reservation is environed by small villages, and the Indian can procure, with less trouble than any other person, all the whisky or other intoxicants he may want. Notwithstanding prosecutions in the United States district courts, and under the prohibitory law of Kansas, the ubiquitous 'boot-legger thrives and prospers at the expense of the Indian.'"

The Indian Agent at the Leech Lake Agency, Minnesota, says:

"The unlawful sale of alcoholic liquors to Indians by saloon men still continues in all the small villages adjacent to the Indian country. An Indian has but little trouble in getting all the liquor he wants, so long as he has the money to pay for it. While the law is adequate and plain, it is difficult to convict any one under it. Public opinion fails to recognize that it is more harmful to permit traffic which tends to debauch and destroy the Indian than to permit it among the white people. And, while a great majority of white people in these towns are law-abiding citizens and do not approve of selling intoxicating liquors to Indians, much of the revenue by which the town is supported is derived from the saloon element. To antagonize this element would cut off the revenue, and evidence cannot be obtained from local citizens for this purpose."

At Winnebago Agency a similar state of things exists, but worse:

"The liquor traffic at the town of Homer, nine miles from this agency, is very bad. These Indians spend a great deal of their money at this town for whisky. It seems to be a very easy matter for them to get all the liquor they want. I have endeavored to stop this liquor traffic, but so far have met with little success. The people at Homer claim they do not like the state of affairs there, but at the same time they are not doing anything to stop the sale of liquor because they say it would interfere with their business. I have reported cases to the United States court, but they were not acted upon for the reason that there was not sufficient money to pay witness fees, etc. I am of the opinion that the judge of the United States district court imposes too light a sentence on bootleggers when convicted. If a few of them would be given the limit of the law as a sentence, I believe the liquor traffic at Homer could be stopped."

At the Sac and Fox Agency, the disbursing agent says:

"Drunkenness exists among the Kiowa Indians generally, and among the Sac and Fox to a large extent. The Sac and Fox women are very much opposed to the use of liquor among their people and assist greatly in preventing an increase of drunkenness. It is comparatively easy for an Indian to secure what whisky he wants in any of the small towns in the vicinity where they live. The Indian has the money and the whisky seller the whisky. Many of the towns are filled with tramps who do not hesitate to buy whisky for an Indian if they are promised a drink, or are given a little money over and above the cost of the whisky. These are the most difficult offenders to detect, since they are at one place today and at another tomorrow, and no one knows their names. The Indians as a rule are unwilling witnesses, and will not tell the truth about these matters, unless for some reason they desire revenge. Two whisky sellers were prosecuted and convicted during the year. In addition to this number, five others were prosecuted but not convicted. Twenty-one cases of drunkenness were punished by confinement in the Agency jail and compelling the offenders to work a number of days."

The Superintendent of the Klamath Agency says:

"The evil has grown with the increase of facilities for getting liquor, and the greatest vigilance is necessary at all times to prevent serious trouble from it. Some success has been achieved in the punishment of offenders, but, since the rapid development and settlement of the extensive country adjacent to the reservation by white people, much greater facilities are offered than existed formerly for the Indians to procure whisky."

At the Warmspring Agency in Oregon, the Superintendent says:

"Intemperance is fast becoming a menace to the peace and happiness of these people, and promises to be as troublesome here as at other reservations. Drunken quarrels and carousals are becoming more frequent. During the last ten years the country north and east of the reservation has been settling up rapidly, and some half dozen saloons have been opened. This brings whisky within the reach of any Indian who wants it. Confederates retail it outside of the saloon to the Indian in large or small quantities as desired. This illegal traffic is carried on in such a way as to evade the law or to make it impossible to get sufficient evidence to convict the offender."

At Greenville, California, the Superintendent of the Industrial School, fearing that liquor was being sold to pupils, sought for evidence himself and got it. He saw a dealer delivering whisky over a bar, and had him arrested. The fellow was found guilty, fined $100, and will forfeit his permit.

The authorities generally agree that it is very difficult to obtain convictions, and impossible to suppress the traffic among Indians, and that, despite the coöperation of authorities, the traffic is actually increasing. It is *white* men, members of the "superior" race, "Christian" liquor-dealers, who thus defy and ignore the laws of God and man. However, 631 whisky sellers were prosecuted during the year 1903-1904.

In 1905-1906 the Osage Agent said:

"The whisky pedler upon the reservation has not thrived. Considerable quantities of liquor have been confiscated and destroyed at the various railroad stations, most of which presumably belonged to persons who intended it for their own use. The Indians as a whole have been sober and contented, except a small per cent. of those living near Greyhound, Fairfax and Ralston, who repair to the latter place on every occasion, and there find saloons with high board fences surrounding the yard in the rear, termed 'bull-pens.' Small rooms are partitioned off in the rear of the buildings, fitted up with dumb-waiters and various other contrivances to prevent the Indian customer from seeing the person who delivers the liquor. It is no uncommon sight to see fifteen or twenty drunken Indians on the streets of Ralston at a time, some of them almost naked, having bartered their blankets for whisky, or they were stolen from them while drunk. The real criminal, the saloon proprietor, so far has gone scot free. The difficulties in the way of procuring evidence against these saloonkeepers are many."

While Anti-Saloon League attorneys have been conducting a legislative and law-enforcing campaign in the neutral territory between Republicans and Democrats, and the W. C. T. U. women have been praying at the noontide hour, and holding conventions, and prosecuting their forty different lines of work, and the Prohibition party has been organizing and operating in the open field where elections are lost and won, the United

States government, in the person of its special agent, William E. Johnson, has been engaged in a lurid conflict with all sorts and conditions of liquor sellers among the Indians. Johnson, long before this appointment, had acquired a national and even international reputation as an author and editor, a fearless detective, and an acute investigator of conditions in so-called prohibition territory.

As an illustration of the special agent's compaign methods, this story may be told. The saloons of Oklahoma City were thrown into wild tumult when, very unexpectedly, forty-two rum-sellers were arrested and put under bonds to await the action of the Federal grand jury. Of this a press correspondent wrote:

"The saloons of Oklahoma City have been in the habit of violating the law in every respect they choose to do. It seems that some days ago, William E. Johnson, Special Agent of the Interior Department, 'threw out his lines' to catch the scamps for selling to Indians. A few expert operators, working under Johnson's personal direction, soon had the necessary evidence, and Tuesday night United States Commissioner Spitler sat up till midnight making out the warrants. Wednesday afternoon United States Marshal Abernathy, with a couple of deputies, was summoned to this city from Guthrie, and early in the evening began to gather in the delinquent rumsellers. Before the saloonkeepers realized what was going on, they were being picked up all over the city and hurried to Commissioner Spitler's office for arraignment. Some of the early birds had gone to bed, and there was a wild scrambling for bonds and cash bail. Spitler demanded a gilt-edged $1,000 bond in each case, and 'straw bail' did not 'go' for a minute.

"Thursday the work of arresting the forty-two erring drink-sellers was completed, and there is wailing and gnashing of teeth. As high as $20 was offered for a glimpse of the man who was responsible for the 'outrage.' 'I am mighty glad that the saloonkeepers are finding that there is a God in Israel,' said a banker here today.

"In the United States District Court, Judge Meeks has just refused an application for an injunction to restrain the Santa Fé Railway from further refusing shipments of low-grade beers into the Indian Territory. This decision has been bitterly fought, and is of prime importance to the enforcement of the prohibitory law in the Territory.

"Some months ago, through the efforts of Mr. Johnson, all of the express companies and railways doing business in the Territory issued general orders to all agents to refuse shipment of all brewery products as well as spirituous liquors to Territory points. A furious contest followed, in which Johnson smashed up nearly 25,000 bottles of these beers which were sneaked into the Territory by tricks and deceptions on the railway agents. For some weeks the air all over the Territory was full of injunction suits, replevin suits, damage suits and flying beer bottles. This medley finally resulted in W. R. Wilson, backed by the Dallas Brewery of this place, filing an application in the United States District Court here for an injunction to restrain the Santa Fé Railway from further refusing these shipments.

"Johnson was at once notified by the railway company's counsel, and hastened to Dallas where he arranged with William H. Atwell, United States District Attorney, to intervene in behalf of the government. Johnson worked up the necessary evidence and a desperate legal battle followed. It was regarded as a test case; because, if it was decided adversely to the railways, all the other railways and express companies would be subject to similar suits, and would probably have been compelled to resume shipments of the various low-grade beers. Yesterday, Mr. Atwell fought the brewers' attorneys all day in the United States court here, with the result that Judge Meeks, before whom the case was heard, refused the application. The result is a striking victory for the government, as it will fortify the railways in their position of refusing to receive the stuff for shipment."

Another correspondent says:

"The vigorous war which has been waged on the liquor outlaws in the Indian Territory during the past ten months by Special Agent William E. Johnson of the Interior Department, has reached the assassination stage. Gradually, in one way and another Johnson has drawn the net closer about the unlawful traffic until the price of twenty-five-cent 'nigger' whisky has gone up in most parts of the territory to two and even three dollars per pint. The meeker class of bootleggers have almost wholly been driven out of the business, and only the most desperate class remain. A two weeks' hand-to-hand contest has followed with this element, with whom the issue has been fought out at the point of the rifle and revolver.

"Since May 28, Special Officer Johnson has led this contest, with a price of $3,000 on his head from one gang of desperadoes at Porum, besides similar plots at Sapulpa, Mill Creek, and other parts of the Territory. In his stay here, Agent Johnson has gathered about him a company of kindred spirits, ready to follow him anywhere and meet the desperadoes on their own ground.

"During the last two weeks, mostly in midnight battles, two whisky pedlers have been shot dead, one shot through the arm, one horse shot to death, one of Johnson's officers, Sam Roberts, has been killed, and another, E. J. Sapper, shot through the side of the head, but he is recovering. This disaster happened a week ago at Porum, the center of a section of Indian Territory wilderness famous in western criminal annals for cold-blooded murders. It was in the heart of this section that Johnson, last fall, single-handed and alone, held up a camp of outlaws, and at the point of his revolver arrested John Harris and his daughter Nora, who are now in jail at Vinita, charged with the famous murder at Paw Paw in which Harris beat out the brains of his son-in-law with a bar of iron.

"This section is dominated by two young desperadoes, Eugene and Ben Titsworth, of Porum. Some time ago Johnson set out to 'clean up' this gang which had intimidated the whole section. In this work Johnson's chief helper was Dr. E. J. Sapper who, besides being Johnson's deputy, was also a United States Marshal for that section. Sometime ago, Johnson caused a warrant to be sworn out for Eugene Titsworth for selling whisky. The warrant was served by Dr. Sapper, but Titsworth made his escape from the officer and fled to Ft. Smith. Johnson then placed one of his 'Indians' on the trail and he was finally rounded up at Ft. Smith, landed in jail and brought back. In the meantime, Johnson and Sapper made a night raid on Titsworth's joint gambling layout in the woods near a camp of railway construction laborers at McMurray Crossing. The raid was made near midnight in a driving thunderstorm, and the outfit and drinkables destroyed. Johnson alone next made a descent on Ben Titsworth's joint at Warner, and destroyed it in the teeth of Ben's threats.

"While in the Fort Smith jail, Ben Titsworth made the acquaintance of one Jim Patman, *alias* Jack Baldridge, and with several other *aliases*. Patman's term had about expired, and Titsworth, who is a man of wealth, hired Patman to kill Johnson and his assistant Sapper, agreeing to pay the murderer $3,000 for the job. After their release from jail, the toughs returned to Porum where Titsworth made a murderous assault on a young man whom he suspected of giving information to Sapper. Johnson at once went to Porum to arrest Titsworth for the assault. Titsworth resisted arrest, and assaulted Johnson. In the struggle Johnson threw Titsworth upon the floor, placed handcuffs on him and brought the prisoner in irons to jail at Muskogee, forty miles away. Patman was in town at the time and weakened at carrying out his murder compact with Titsworth.

"Titsworth again wiggled out of jail, and at a picnic near Porum following July 4, set up a 'spiked cider' stand. Johnson had intended to be present at this picnic but was called away on a chase of some outlaws in the Choctaw mountains, and Dr. Sapper with an assistant, Sam Roberts, went to Porum by Johnson's direction to keep order. It was there that the Titsworths got Patman half drunk on the 'spiked cider,' and goaded him into the murder that followed. As Sapper and Roberts entered the booth to seize the cider, the crowd of ruffians closed in. 'Kill him, —— —— ——!' shouted Eugene to Patman, who immediately sent a bullet crashing through Sam Roberts' brain. At the same time Ben Titsworth shot Dr. Sapper through the side of the head, and he fell unconscious. The assassins then fled.

"Later the Titsworths gave themselves up, with the intention of laying the whole affair on to Patman, and cheating Patman out of his $3,000 reward as well. A dozen officers at once entered the jungle and soon captured Patman, who became angered at the treatment meted out to him by the Titsworths, and confessed to the whole plot.

"All the desperadoes are now in jail, being held to the grand jury investigation and denied bail. The capture of the desperadoes and their confinement in jail has operated to discourage others who are still devising schemes to smuggle liquor into the Territory.

"Since the traffic has been cut out of the railways, attempts have been made to transport it overland by teams at night. Agent Johnson has been checkmating this by waylaying and seizing teams, smashing the liquor, putting the driver in jail and confiscating the team. Thirty-two horses, fourteen wagons, four saddles and forty men have so far been captured in this way, and several thousand dollars worth of liquor seized."

At the Indian conference at Lake Mohonk in 1907, Mr. Johnson graphically described some details in his contest with the railroads entering the territory. He said:

"When I reached Indian Territory two years ago, I discovered that the supply of liquor at that time was coming in chiefly by express and freight. The railways had issued orders years ago forbidding their agents to accept shipments of intoxicating liquors for points in the Indian Territory, but those orders had long since been forgotten. Practically every train that came into the Indian Territory brought with it a considerable supply of intoxicating liquors. My first attempt, therefore, was to break down this source of supply. I did it by inaugurating a system of searching these trains. At first I found myself confronted with the orders from the superintendent not to allow officers in the express cars. I would go into the express cars at night, usually at first, and notify the messenger that I had come for the purpose of examining that express car. I would tell him that if he permitted me to examine the car, all right; if he did not permit me to examine the car, I would do it anyhow, and if I found any intoxicating liquors I would take him off at the next station and put him in jail. He usually saw the point. By following that policy for a short time I have managed to break down this opposition to searching the express cars; and, within a few months it was a common practice of all deputy marshals throughout the Territory, to search these express cars.

"Then came the problem of robbers getting on the express cars in the guise of officers. I have met that by issuing a letter of identification to deputy marshals and my own deputies who were authorized to search these cars. The express companies on the other hand instructed their agents and messengers to honor these letters of identification. That solved the railway transactions as far as whisky was concerned.

"But we were confronted with another problem than that of whisky. The brewers were making a species of beer, theoretically less than two per cent. alcohol, but actually more than two. This beer was sold under various names, like 'Uno,' 'Ino,' 'Hiawatha,' 'Mistletoe,' 'Pablo,' 'Tip-top,' and various *aliases* of that sort. In order to make the fight the stuff would be actually less than two per cent., and after the trade was established they would jump it to four per cent. and five per cent., just like any other beer. These agents dealing in these low-grade beers were well fortified financially. They had arrangements with banks and financial institutions to go on their bonds immediately after arrest. Their cases, owing to the congested conditions of the dockets, would never come up to trial, and these people were practically immune from prosecution for those reasons. I had analyzed by government chemists all of these two per cent. low-grade beers which were being sold in the Indian Territory; and I had in my pockets the opinion of each of the four district attorneys in the Indian Territory that these products were contraband under the act of 1895.

"I then went out upon a little pilgrimage to St. Louis, Chicago and New York, and had a heart-to-heart conference with each of the traffic managers of the railway companies doing business in the Indian Territory, and each of the superintendents of the express lines doing business there. I showed them the law. I showed them the opinions of the district attorneys. I showed them the analysis of the government chemists. I put it up to them as to what they were going to do about it, whether they were going to make a mockery of this matter, or whether they were going to coöperate with the government in enforcing the law. I assured them that in case they took the former course the United States attorneys of the Territory would coöperate with me and make trouble for the railway companies. The result of the conference was that each of the railways without exception, and each of the express companies without exception, sent out most positive orders to all agents in and out of the Territory to refuse shipments of anything that came out of a brewery or distillery to points within the Indian Territory. They not only sent those orders, but they sent out instructions to their route agents to see that their orders were carried out, and they also told me that if I would call their attention by telegraph to any infractions of these orders that they would summarily dispose of the offending agents. The result was that within ten days this traffic was practically eliminated, and, further, half a dozen or so of the agents who had attempted to make sport of these orders found themselves looking for other positions. That settled the beer business in the Indian Territory for the time being. There were 353 beer joints which paid their special taxes as retail dealers in liquors in the Indian Territory and probably 40 or 50 who had not paid taxes. Approximately 400 establishments were closed in this way, and they remained closed for quite a long time.

"Finally they sprung a new scheme on me. Under the Interstate Commerce law the railways could not refuse to receive shipments of intoxicating liquors from a point out of the state to some point through the Territory in another state. So they began shipping this stuff, for instance from Kansas City to Dallas, Texas, in car lots. When the car got to a point where they wished to sell the stuff, for instance at Muskogee, they would replevin it in some local court, and then they would have the stuff put on the market again. I was up against this proposition. I could not arrest those men and make successful prosecutions for the reason they were simply going to give bond and go on selling the stuff again. Section 2140 of the Revised Statutes, which was enacted in 1836 and revised at some intervals since then, gave extraordinary powers to the Indian agents, subagents or the commanding officers of the post in a military reservation. These two powers were of two classes. *First*, there was power to search and seize; *second*, there was the power to sell teams and goods and peltries, and sell them under libel proceedings. The latter part of that section made it the duty of any officer or any employé of the United States, or any Indian agent to seize and destroy ardent spirits and wine. The Act of 1895 extended the contraband of goods to cover all sorts of fermented and malt liquors in the Indian Territory. The Court of Appeals construed that to mean that if a beverage was either malted or fermented it was contraband, irrespective of the proportion of alcohol contained therein.

"While the act of 1895 said nothing about the authority of an officer to summarily destroy malt or fermented beverages, I took the view that it was the intention of Congress to extend these powers of an officer to cover all inhibited beverages, and that, inasmuch as malt or fermented beverages could not be introduced without a crime having been committed, no one could acquire property rights in them in the Indian Territory. We therefore set out upon a policy of seizing and destroying all of those liquors, irrespective of the amount of alcohol contained therein. Later the court of the Western District, Judge Lawrence presiding, decided that the policy was according to law.

"In this contest, myself and deputies were arrested many times in municipal courts that were controlled by whisky pedlers, and damage suits aggregating about $170,000 were piled up against me. They even sued the Secretary of the Interior for $75,000 on my account. But after I had obtained twenty-three indictments from grand juries against the plaintiffs, they found themselves holding the hot end of the poker and dismissed all these cases at their own cost. Two of my men, Sam Roberts and John Morrison, have been murdered by the liquor outlaws, both while in the discharge of their duty. Another of my deputies, E. J. Sapper, was shot through the side of the head while making a raid, but recovered. I have been especially fortunate in my assistants; they are as brave and loyal a band as ever lived at any time or anywhere."

Supplemental to the above statement by Mr. Johnson, a correspondent writes:

"On November 19, the Special Agent gave out to the newspapers a signed statement that he proposed to leave the Territory that night for a few days, and that on his return he proposed summarily to seize and destroy all of the low-grade beers found in the Territory regardless of the name and where found. This sensation of the hour was telegraphed into every hamlet in the Territory, and was known in every joint within twenty-four hours. . . .

"Johnson suddenly appeared back in the Territory, and the fiercest kind of a six-weeks contest began. The dealers had hurriedly shipped out most of their supplies, but kept a few on which to base a fight. One wholesale dealer emptied his whole stock of about 10,000 bottles in order to save his glassware. Lawyers were ready to serve injunction suits on the agent should he appear, but Johnson generally came at night, smashed everything up, and got out of town before a judge could be gotten out of bed to sign an injunction order. The last and biggest of these raids was at Ardmore, where Johnson swooped down on the express office at four o'clock in the morning, and in a driving rainstorm seized and broke 1,920 bottles of 'Tintop' amid the maledictions and threats of four beer lawyers. When the destruction was complete, Johnson challenged them to go with him to Judge Townsend and he would help them to get an 'injunction.' The judge, however, after hearing all sides of the case, flatly refused to help the beer lawyers even by granting them a temporary injunction, and the coterie left. Since then no other attempt at 'injunction' has been made.

"In these raids, Johnson smashed up nearly seven thousand bottles of beer. The destruction of the costly patented bottles cut the brewers far worse than the destruction of the sloppy beer.

"Defeated in the injunction schemes, attempts were made to swamp Johnson in damage litigation, and suits amounting to nearly $100,000 damages were piled up against him. The Department of Justice promptly instructed the United States attorneys to take charge of his defense in this little litigation and fight the suits to the bitter end. Johnson's fight attracted wide attention and commanded the respect of the people. This was apparent especially in the change in the attitude of the grand juries toward him. As fast as these damage suits were filed, the Special Agent would present the facts to the first grand jury. The result was that the juries promptly returned criminal indictments against every one who brought one of these damage suits.

"There were plenty of sidelights to the great fight. The postmaster at McKey filed charges against Johnson with the Secretary of the Interior for destroying 100 gallons of respectable cider in his postoffice. Johnson's reply was simply to secure a criminal indictment from a grand jury against the postmaster for bootlegging, and file counter charges against him with the Postoffice Department at Washington. The postmaster is now out of jail under $500 bond and trying to 'explain' to the Postoffice authorities in Washington and save his job.

"The Oklahoma Vinegar Co., of Fort Smith, Ark., took a hand in the fray and filed charges against Johnson in Washington for breaking up their business in the Territory. Johnson's reply was to secure criminal grand jury indictments against seven of the Vinegar Company's best customers for selling their 'spiked cider' which was guaranteed to be 'absolutely non-alcoholic.' The Vinegar Company is now busy defending these criminal indictments.

"Then a systematic attempt was made to wear out the Special Agent by sneaking in small shipments of beer labeled 'cranberries' or 'potatoes,' here and there through easy express agents who regarded their orders as a joke. Johnson met this attack by having all such express movements promptly reported to him by his agents by telegraph, giving the points of origin and destination. Telegraphic complaints were at once filed against such agents, who would immediately get from their superintendents a telegram demanding an explanation for their disobedience of orders. After a few agents had thus nearly lost their jobs, this trouble was adjusted.

"Then a systematic attempt was made to flood the Territory with whisky just before Christmas, and inaugurate a general drunk and thus discredit the whole law-enforcement movement. Mr. Johnson checkmated this by posting twenty of his best Indian police at points where the railways enter the territory, with instructions to search all trains coming in and seize all liquors. The result was that the newspapers declared it to be the 'dryest' Christmas that the Territory had ever experienced.

"On Christmas day, the fight had practically been won, but the six weeks' contest, in fully one-half the nights of which the Special Agent had been wholly without sleep, drew heavily upon his strength. In a three-o'clock-in-the-morning raid a few days before, he had cut his hand in smashing up a seizure of 200 bottles of whisky on a Santa Fé train. Blood poisoning resulted, and a week's dangerous illness followed. During this illness, two reckless brewers took advantage and shipped in nearly two carloads of beer, which was quickly scattered about the Territory. It was shipped in closed barrels as 'potatoes,' and consigned to fake commission houses. As soon as he was able to be out, Johnson presented the evidence to the grand jury in session in the Chickasaw Nation, which promptly voted indictments against the brewers responsible for the trick. It is understood that the brewers have now given up the fight, and that practically every one of the more than four hundred beer joints is closed. Only a few are attempting to run as pool-halls and cider shops. A dozen papers in the Territory have announced in big headlines recently, 'THE BEER PERIOD IS OVER.'

"The contest has wrought remarkable changes in six weeks. The newspapers, that at first treated the whole matter as a joke, are now noting the improved conditions and are generous in their praise. The thirty Indian policemen who had been leaderless, neglected and laughed at, are now active, earnest and eager for assignments to hunt booze, and many of them are doing splendid service. The 125 deputy marshals, then discouraged and listless, are now full of life and full of fight. In a recent special article describing the improved conditions, the *Daily Oklahoman* said: 'Within the last few months the presence of Mr. Johnson seems to have redoubled the efforts of the deputy marshals all over the Territory, and there has developed a sort of rivalry to see which can locate and destroy the most liquor. This has always been the duty of the marshals, but at this time there is spice in their zeal, and as the federal *régime* draws to a close they fight on bootleggers harder.'

"While the beer fight has made the joint-keepers ugly, and several gunplays, fisticuffs and attempts on the lives of officers, have been made, only one man has been seriously hurt during the six weeks' fight. A couple of desperate bootleggers shot Deputy Marshal W. E. Strickland of Tulsa, the 44-caliber bullet entering his cheek and coming out the back of his neck. Strickland will live, but it was a close call. Strickland is a Prohibitionist, and one of Johnson's best helpers for whom he was instrumental in securing a place on Marshal Bennett's staff some time ago."

The Federal government prohibits the sale of liquor to Indians, and employs agents like Johnson and his associates to enforce its regulations, and at the same time accepts revenue from and issues receipts to the very people who are violating this law.

The liquor dealers, on their part, ignore and defy law, even committing murder in their open rebellion. What consideration can be due to a "business" which begets such a spirit in its followers? What would happen if grocers, or blacksmiths or any other line of industry or trade should assume such an attitude of anarchy?

Finally, this story is but one more evidence that, to enforce prohibition, Prohibitionists must be elected and appointed to office.

It is for the citizenship, the voters, to say how long such work as Mr. Johnson has done and is still doing must be required.

CHAPTER XXVIII.

THE NEGRO PROBLEM AND THE LIQUOR PROBLEM.

I.

THE founders of the American Republic declared that "all men are created free and equal"—and introduced African slavery. The American people declare in their magna charta that "all men are entitled to life, liberty and the pursuit of happiness"—and go into partnership with the liquor traffic, the greatest enemy the world has known to life, liberty and happiness. Thus this country has a "Negro problem" and a "Liquor problem" both of its own making. A nation, like an individual, must suffer for its mistakes and its sins. For its wrongs toward a defenseless and dependent race this nation has suffered its awful baptism of blood. For their abhorrent compacts with the still and the vat the American people are paying a penalty in disease and vice and crime and pauperism and degradation and death beyond expression.

From the nature of social conditions these original twin evils today present twin problems. Indeed, it might be said that in some respects the two problems are identical. In the southern states where the negro population is so large, and in those northern cities where large bodies of the black race have congregated, the liquor question becomes acute. It has been found that ignorant and shiftless negroes plied with bad whisky by bad white men make a combination fraught with the gravest danger and the greatest evil.

There is no question that very many advocates of prohibition in the southern states were impelled to demand the enactment of laws for the suppression of the liquor traffic, because the black man, made drunken by unscrupulous white men engaged in the liquor trade, had become a peril to the womanhood of the dominant race. At the National Woman's Christian Temperance Union Convention, in Denver, October, 1908, the State President for Florida said:

"The negro question has its bearing, as it does on nearly every movement in our section of the country."

The State President for Texas said:

"I think that the prohibition movement has a direct bearing upon the negro question, and has had a most salutary reformatory effect in those

THOS. E. TAYLOR,
Secretary, The Colored Anti-Saloon League of America.

REV. C. W. McCOLL,
President, The Colored Anti-Saloon League of America.

parts of the South where the colored population is so heavy. Of course, in our state the class distinctions have been preserved, and are now as much in evidence as they were before the war. But I will say for the negroes that they take to the prohibition idea most kindly, and we have a most active association of colored women as a branch of our Union."

Mrs. Margaret Dye Ellis, of Washington, D. C., said:

"The purging of the country of the rum curse was a dire and pressing necessity in some quarters of the South, because of the prevalent population of improvident negroes and dissolute whites. Of course the efforts of our organization proved of inestimable benefit to such communities and, equally, of course, the moral status of the South is raised in proportion to the spread of the gospel of prohibition."

Mrs. C. J. Vayhinger, State President of Indiana, said:

"While I am not exactly from the South, I understand conditions there. They are partly the same in my state. While it is a question of pure morality, there is no doubt that the good effects of prohibition extend to all branches of society, and those in the lower levels will be the greatest gainers from the abolition of the traffic in intoxicating liquors."

On the other hand, Mrs. Frances E. Beauchamp, President of the Kentucky Union, said:

"I do not think the negro question has anything to do with it. I know it did not in our state. Of course the good example of the white people will necessarily have its effect upon the negroes, but it was not with this particular end in view that we have kept up the agitation which is bringing about such great results. Pure morality, and the saving of the people who suffer and die because of the fatal sway of King Alcohol, is our motive, and that only is what actuates us."

Mrs. Beauchamp speaks for herself and perhaps for the typical W. C. T. U. woman. But Hon. Seaborn Wright, and scores of representative southerners, frankly say that the liquor traffic was hastened under ban of law, because it had made the negro tenfold more than ever a menace to the safety of the white man's home and the peace of the community. This they claim was the determining factor in inducing and hastening radical action.

Booker T. Washington once said that, "If the white man will keep the negro in the gutter, he must stay there with him." The same thing is true of the state in its attitude toward the saloon. If it tax the saloon "to provide against evils," it must lie down in the gutter with the saloon, a partner in perpetuating its evils. And the peril of it is that when the saloon dies in the gutter of its own evils, the State must die there, too.

II.

PROHIBITION AND THE NEGRO.

By BOOKER T. WASHINGTON, *in The Outlook, March,* 1908.

I have read much in the northern papers about the prohibition movement in the South being based wholly upon a determination or desire to keep liquor away from the negroes and at the same time provide a way for the white people to get it. I have watched the prohibition movement carefully from its inception to the present time, and I have seen nothing in the agitation in favor of the movement, nothing in the law itself, and nothing in the execution of the law that warrants any such conclusion. The prohibition movement is based upon a deep-seated desire to get rid of whisky in the interest of both races because of its hurtful economic and moral results. The prohibition sentiment is as strong in counties where there are practically no colored people as in the Black Belt counties.

If I mention these facts here, by way of introduction to what I have to say in regard to the results of prohibition where I have been able to observe them, namely, two typical Southern cities, Birmingham and Atlanta, it is because I want to emphasize the fact that the contrary is true: prohibition in the South is essentially a moral movement, the first effect of which has been a remarkable reduction in crime. Putting it roundly, according to the reports of the police magistrates, prohibition has reduced the amount of crime in Birmingham one-third and in Atlanta one-half, since January 1, when the law went into force.

The significance of these facts will be appreciated when you consider the extraordinary number of people who are arrested and sent to the mines and penitentiaries every year by the criminal courts of these two cities. During the year 1907 the police of Atlanta, according to a report in the *Atlanta Constitution* of January 1, made 24,332 arrests. This means that during the year, on an average, one person out of every six in the city of Atlanta was arrested. And this number has been increasing. There were 2,630 more persons arrested in 1907 than in 1906. This is an increase of considerably more than twelve per cent. in one year.

Of course this does not mean that one person in every six in Atlanta is a criminal, because a good many persons represented in these statistics were arrested several times during the year, and a good many others were arrested but not convicted. Putting the best construction upon the facts, however, they indicate an abnormal drain upon the ranks of the peaceful and law-abiding people of the city into the classes that fill the penitentiaries and supply recruits to the chain gangs, which are already doing too large a portion of the work of the State. It should be taken into account also that, under present conditions, Southern prisons are conducted too largely for the purpose of punishing men rather than reforming them, and they are therefore constantly discharging back into the ranks of the industrious and law-abiding populations a stream of hardened and embittered men and women, which in turn pollutes the masses of the people with which it mingles.

Prohibition has attacked this evil at its source, and the results which the enforcement of this law brought about serve to indicate to what extent evils that the South has accepted as human and inevitable, can be modified and cured, if proper measures are taken and these measures are backed by the will of the people.

In his report to the mayor at the end of the first month of prohibition, Judge N. B. Feagin, of Birmingham, makes the following statement:

"The decrease in arrests averages about as follows, in comparing January, 1908, under prohibition with January, 1907, with saloons: Aggregate arrests decrease 33 1-3 per cent.; for assault with intent to murder, 22 per cent.; gambling, 17 per cent.; drunkenness, 80 per cent.; disorderly conduct, 35 per cent.; burglary and grand larceny, 33 per cent.; vagrancy, 40 per cent.; wife-beating, 70 per cent."

There were 33 arrests for drunkenness in January, 1908, as against 174 for the same month of 1907. There were 56 arrests for disorderly conduct in January, 1908, as against 90 for the same month of 1907.

Several times during the past eight weeks there has not been a single prisoner before the Recorder's Court at Atlanta charged with drunkenness. The first instance of this kind was January 4, when there were but 17 cases on the docket; nine of these were cases of children. On the same day a year ago 63 cases were tried in that court, of which 32 were for drunkenness and 28 for disorderly conduct. Wednesday, January 29, at the session of what was called by the local papers "the smallest police court ever held," there was only one prisoner at the morning session. It was about this time that the newspapers recorded another extraordinary event in the history of the city. For the first time in many years, the jail was for several days empty.

The records of arrests for the month of January show a more extraordinary decrease in Atlanta than in Birmingham. For the month of January, 1907, 1,653 cases were put on the docket of the Recorder's Court in Atlanta. During the month of January, 1908, on the other hand, there were but 768 cases on the docket, a decrease of considerably more than 50 per cent. During January, 1907, there were 341 cases of drunkenness tried, but in 1908 only 64, a decrease of more than 80 per cent.

The justices of the peace, before whom warrants in minor criminal cases are issued, report a similar falling off. Three classes of warrants ordinarily taken out by negroes and the poorer class of whites show, according to reports in the newspapers, a falling off equal to that of the Recorder's Court. These are the warrants charging abandonment of minor children, dispossessory warrants—taken against people unable to pay their rents—and warrants charging various kinds of larceny. A good many of these cases grow out of family quarrels, and serve as a sort of a barometer of the condition among the poorer classes in the city. These evidences indicate that the closing of the saloons and the breeding-places of crimes and disorders has brought a remarkable change into the homes of the poor, where, finally, the effects of crime and disorder are always most keenly felt.

Commenting on the situation as it is in Atlanta and Birmingham, the *Birmingham News* says:

"For ten years Birmingham has not enjoyed so orderly a period as it has since the first of January. The moral improvement in the city has been marked since prohibition went into effect. The newspapers are no longer giving space to reports of murders, shooting and cutting scrapes, personal altercations and other disorders, as they formerly did, for the reason that the regard for law and order in this community is very much more in evidence since the removal of the whisky traffic."

In Birmingham, the demand for reform has not stopped with the closing of the saloons. Since January 1 seventeen gambling houses, many of which had been running for years in a more or less public way, have been closed. A Law and Order League has been formed, and vigorous measures are being taken throughout Jefferson county to do away with the "blind-tigers" and to suppress the vices that have centered about and in these moral cess-pools.

The interesting thing about the prohibition movement in the South is that it goes out from and is supported by the churches. The campaign in Jefferson county, Alabama, which changed Birmingham from wet to dry began, as I have been informed, in a ministers' meeting. The superintendent of the Anti-Saloon League in Alabama, Mr. Brooks Lawrence, is a minister and a Northerner. One of the charges brought against him during the campaign was that he was a carpet-bagger, and that the prohibition movement was an attempt "to dump Northern ideas" upon the South, where they did not fit conditions.

It was predicted that prohibition would demoralize business. In Birmingham alone one hundred and twenty-eight saloons, fourteen wholesale liquor stores and two breweries were closed as a result of the law. But the predictions do not seem to have been fulfilled. It has recently been announced that a fourteen-story building was to be erected on the site of one of the oldest saloons in Birmingham; and Atlanta is preparing to pave and improve the notorious Decatur street, on which the larger part of the dives of the city were located. It is promised that it will soon become one of the best streets in the city.

Prohibition has been the popular issue, and it has the South behind it. Many of those, I am informed, who voted for prohibition were men who themselves belonged to the class that had supported the saloon. On the other hand, many of those who opposed prohibition were men who rarely, if ever, entered a barroom.

Directly, and indirectly, the members of my own race have suffered, perhaps more than any other portion of the population, from the effects of the liquor traffic. But the educated men and the leaders of the race have been quick to see the advantages that would come from the total suppression of the saloon. Everywhere in the South this class has given its votes to the support of prohibition, even where it brought them in opposition to the men whom they have been disposed to regard as their friends, and in support of those whom they have been accustomed to regard as their enemies. In Birmingham the negroes formed an organization, and cast nearly all of the registered colored vote for prohibition.

Prohibition in the South is to a certain extent a woman's movement. In the campaign in Alabama it was the women, the mothers and the wives and the children of the men who supported the saloon with their earnings, who marched in the processions, and stood all day at the polls to see that their husbands, sons and fathers voted "right."

No one who is at all acquainted with the conditions in the South can doubt the depth and the genuincness of the feelings that are behind prohibition, which is in no way a political maneuver, but an inspired movement of the masses of the people. Its great importance, it seems to me, consists in the fact that it is bringing the ordinary conservative elements in the community, the women, the ministers and the people in the churches, into close and intimate contact with actual conditions and with the real problems of the South. It is at the same time, if I may say so, an intellectual awakening and a moral revolution.

III.

THE NEGRO AND PROHIBITION.

By J. C. Price, *President National Afro-American League.*

Remembering the circumstances in which the Afro-American was placed by the dreadful institution of slavery it is not to be wondered at that he now cultivates a taste, even a love, for alcohol. Yet it is remarkable to note the progress toward sobriety that the race has made in the later years of its emancipation. A colored total abstainer is not a rare person in any community nowadays. The various temperance societies, and nearly all the other secret organizations supported by the Afro-American race, uniformly require those who seek admission to pledge themselves to be sober men and women, and in most cases to be total abstainers. The drift is more and more in this direction, and hence soberness in the race is constantly on the increase. It is remarkable, too, to observe the steadfastness and persistency with which colored teachers, as a rule, hold to the idea that the race is to be uplifted morally, as well as materially and religiously improved, through total abstinence as a chief instrument. It is the rare exception, not the rule, to find a colored teacher who does not hold to this doctrine. The result is that many boys and girls in the schoolrooms all over the South, and in other sections as well, are being trained to habits of temperance, and will in all probability develop into consistent temperance men and women.

And it must not be forgotten that the true and most influential leaders of the race, the ministers, are molding and shaping the opinions of both old and young in favor of soberness and total abstinence. The unanimity with which the churches of all denominations declare for the temperance reform is most encouraging. It is a very rare thing to find any considerable proportion of the ministry of any religious denomination exerting an influence in behalf of the extension and perpetuation of the liquor traffic. The church, as a factor in this race development and elevation, is laboring steadfastly and earnestly for the right. It is the one force that checks and holds the individuals of the race from following the evil propensities of their own hearts when every other force proves unavailing. In it is the chief hope for the present, as well as the eternal salvation of the negro. If the church is kept pure it can lift up and give honor and perfect freedom to the freedmen. The race has implicit confidence in the truth and value of God's Word. This confidence must not be shaken, but must be cultivated by the selection of clergymen well qualified by special training to teach wisely, acceptably and properly. Along with such cultivation will inevitably go a determination to strengthen the temperance cause more and more.

I have watched closely the men who are recognized as the race leaders in various states and localities. It is acknowledged that they are generally shrewd, calculating, and hard to circumvent when they attempt political manoeuvres. It is my observation that these leaders are strictly reliable and trustworthy when confided in, and—however surprising the statement may be to some—they are generally sober, upright and honest. I confess that in some localities this rule does not apply, but on the whole a more sober class of leaders does not exist in any race than in the Afro American.

OFFICERS, COLORED WOMAN'S CHRISTIAN TEMPERANCE UNIONS.

MRS. F. E. W. MORRIS, A. M.,
Cor. Secretary, Thurman W. C. T. U., Texas.

MISS CORA L. EUGENE,
State Organizer, Thurman W. C. T. U., Texas.

MRS. ELIZA E. PETERSON,
President, Thurman W. C. T. U., Texas.

MRS. FRANCES JOSEPH GAUDET,
President, Willard W. C. T. U., Louisiana.

MRS. M. R. BARNES,
Vice-President, Thurman W. C. T. U., Texas.

One of the evils against which our people have had to contend is the crossroads grocery store, to be found all over the Southland—the bane of this section. Here, with no city or town ordinance to make drunkenness an offense and to threaten certain punishment, they have been accustomed to congregate and drink their fill, carouse, engage in free fights, and do other hurtful and equally unlawful things, while no one dares molest or make afraid. And the grocery-keeper, finding his trade benefited, encourages the debauchery. This evil, instead of becoming less, increases. The business of many prosperous towns and villages is being injured seriously by the competition at the crossroads, and the resulting vice, violence and impoverishment.

The records of the courts would show that crime among our people is traceable in a large majority of cases to a too free exercise of the liquor habit. Of the men belonging to the race who are hanged, I think it entirely reasonable to say that at least four-fifths committed their offenses while under the influence of liquor. But, speaking of the race broadly, and duly considering all the unusual circumstances that ought to be taken into consideration, I think it cannot fairly be charged with anything like gross intemperance. It is something out of the usual order to come upon a case of *delirium tremens* among the negroes. Comparatively few of them drink anything of consequence during the week, but excessive imbibition is mostly indulged in on Saturdays. With their vigorous physical constitutions they are able, in six days of comparative temperance, to resist the undermining effects of the seventh day's spree. Therefore, this is not a race of drunkards, and there is abundant reason for believing that, with proper education and training, it may be made a race of sober people and abstainers.

In all the Prohibition and Local Option contests in the South, numbers of colored men have been on the side of temperance, and fought valiantly for its success. Many others would have thrown their influence the same way had they not been duped by misguided leaders who raised false cries of alarm, declaring that Prohibition was a device to take away their dearly-bought liberty. It is customary to blame the negroes for the defeats of Prohibition in Texas, in the second Atlanta contest, etc.; but it must be remembered that, without a large share of the negro vote, Prohibition could not have carried in Atlanta at the first trial and would have been lost in hundreds of other fights.

In order to strengthen the cause of temperance in the South nothing is more important than to treat the negro fairly, to keep faith with him, to permit no pledge to be broken. Once won, the colored man is the most faithful and reliable of allies. It is of course needless to add that the supply of temperance literature should be kept up and increased. Especially valuable is the work of arousing total abstinence enthusiasm among the students in the various educational institutions—young men, and women, too, upon whom the future of the race, and its influence for good or evil, so largely depend. The tracts and other publications of the National Temperance Society have had and are having a most helpful effect; and the literature emanating from the publishers of the *Voice*, from the Woman's Christian Temperance Union, and from other societies and organizations bears good fruit.

I am indeed hopeful for the future of the Afro-American race, and particularly hopeful that it will become a positive and influential contributor to the triumph of the temperance reform.

The above article was written some time ago, but is introduced here as reflecting conditions which are largely influential in bringing about the adoption of state-wide prohibition in the South.

A very hopeful feature of the situation with reference to the negro race is found in the efforts of negroes themselves for their own redemption and salvation.

Typical organizations with this object in view are "The Colored Anti-Saloon League of America," which affiliates with the white organization, and the "Willard W. C. T. U," of Louisiana, the "Thurman W. C. T. U." of Texas, both of which affiliate with the National Union.

IV.

THE COLORED ANTI-SALOON LEAGUE OF AMERICA.

In February, 1905, Rev. C. W. McColl was employed by the Pennsylvania Anti-Saloon League as "Superintendent of Anti-Saloon League Work Among Colored People." Four months afterwards Mr. McColl organized the "Pennsylvania Colored Temperance League" as an auxiliary to the Pennsylvania Anti-Saloon League, and inaugurated movements among the people of his race in harmony with the methods adopted by the "Federated Church in Action."

After two years the Pennsylvania organization broadened its scope, and became "The National Colored Temperance League"—the headquarters being transferred from Philadelphia to Indianapolis. In August, 1908, the "National Colored Temperance League" changed its name to that of "The Colored Anti-Saloon League of America."

It is the policy of the League to unite for the realization of its object, the efforts of all colored citizens who are identified with churches, temperance societies, and organizations devoted to political righteousness, comprehending all in one active federation, directing their total influence by practical methods to specific ends. The League binds itself to affiliate with no political party, and to be neutral on all public questions not touching the traffic in strong drink or civic corruptions springing therefrom; provided, however, that this pledge shall not hinder the indorsement of candidates for public offices whose election will further the objects of the League.

The membership of the League is composed of one delegate from each church, Sunday-school, Society of Christian Endeavor, Baptist Young People's Union, Epworth League, the Woman's Christian Temperance Union, the Prohibition Alliance, affiliating with the League throughout the United States.

The officers are Rev. C. W. McColl, President; Rev. E. S. Shumaker, Chairman Headquarters Committee; Thomas E. Taylor, Secretary; Rev. C. H. Winders, Treasurer—all located at Indianapolis. The members of the National Board of Trustees are Mrs. Lucy Thurman, Jackson, Mich.; James A. White, Columbus, Ohio; Mrs. E. E. Peterson, Texarkana, Texas; Miss Mary A. Lynch, Salisbury, N. C.; Mrs. Rosetta E. Lawson, Washington, D. C.; Rev. B. H. Tilghman, Burlington, N. J.; H. L. Billups, Sedalia, Mo.; Rev. W. G. Parks, Philadelphia, Pa.; Rev. G. C. Sampson, Indianapolis, Ind. There is a long list of associate members embracing the most prominent members of the race in sixteen different states.

Any person (colored or white) may become an associate member by paying one dollar into the League's treasury, and it is desired that many become associate members for the twofold assistance such act will afford the League.

V.

WORK AMONG THE NEGROES IN TEXAS.

By Mrs. E. E. Peterson, *President Thurman W. C. T. U. (Colored)*

During the state campaign of 1886-'87, the colored people were largely ignorant of the meaning of prohibition. Saloon men told them the common falsehoods that voting against liquor was taking their rights away from them, voting against their personal liberty, that it was only a ruse of the white people to get them back into slavery. And although the saloon men were and are all white, with not enough exceptions to be counted, they succeeded in misleading the colored people, and in buying the leaders among them—preachers and teachers, politicians, and all whom they could get who had influence in the community or town in which they (the leaders) resided.

There were few temperance men in those days, but they kept at work. At every association and conference and Sunday-school convention, there was one or more who would persistently make temperance reports. Many times it was argued by some that there was no good in temperance reports, that everybody drank just the same. But they continued to make reports.

Twelve years ago, the National Woman's Christian Temperance Union sent into the state Mrs. Lucy Thurman, National Superintendent of colored work. She organized the women, and found quite a few to take hold. The first President was a teacher, Mrs. Fannie Hall, of Dallas, who could not continue the work, and resigned in two years. The second, Mrs. Dodson, of Palestine, also a teacher, then took up the work and was making rapid headway with it, but died after a few months' service. At the third convention I was elected, and for nine years have given my entire time to the work.

At first I found strong opposition to the cause, but by persistent Christian effort, and by living at the feet of the blessed Master for constant support, the sentiment is changed almost entirely. Not a leader, teacher or minister, of any standing in the state, of any denomination, will now offer one word in favor of the liquor traffic. None of the best men of the race will allow saloon men to pay them to work for the saloon in prohibition campaigns as we have had them over the state, and many are only waiting for the state campaign to come which we expect next year, since submission carried about a month ago in the Democratic primaries, and also was endorsed two to one in the Democratic convention which met in San Antonio.

We have fourteen colleges, academies, a state normal, and the presidents of all save one declare in favor of prohibition; and some of them are making speeches for it this summer in their summer campaigns for their respective schools.

In some of the counties in the eastern part of the state, where the colored people outnumber the whites two to one, prohibition carried by more than a thousand majority. In Matagorda county, in the southern part, when prohibition was voted upon the second time, after two years of prohibition, every colored box in the county carried for prohibition. Only one box lost, and that was where the whites were in majority. There are some instances where the colored people have not done so well, but even then the corrupt leaders are responsible for it. The masses would always vote right if the leaders were true. There are two Baptist Conventions in the state, and both endorsed state-wide prohibition, or rather expressed themselves in favor of it when submitted, which we hope to see done next year.

The liquor men have many intrigues to play upon the more ignorant ones of the race. For instance, in one county, a strong liquor man, not a saloon man, but one who was in favor of the traffic, and no doubt was paid to be, had always been an "anti," saw that the colored people were receiving enlightenment on the question in the county campaign, came over to the prohibition side and announced through the papers, and in circular form, that they (the prohibitionists) were not going to allow the negroes to have anything to do with the election; that the white men of that county would not have black men running over their wives, and they all had better stay away from the polls on election day—and more of that kind of sentiment. The saloon men went to the colored people all over the county, showed them the papers and literature, and said, "We are going to stand by the colored people. You come to the polls on election day and you can vote for your rights," etc. Thus they pretended to show where they, the saloon men, were the negroes' friends. Sad pity! The poor colored people fell into the trap, and voted the curse back, and within two weeks after, in the county seat the calaboose was filled with men and women, all colored. Before that the calaboose was empty, and hogs were staying in it.

However, the leaders of the race and the people generally are becoming more and more incensed against the saloon. Where there are no saloons there is little or no race trouble, but where there are saloons there is often trouble. There have been nearly three hundred lynchings in the state, and not five of them have occurred in prohibition counties. In two counties last year, the saloon was brought back, and both have had lynchings since. Grimes county is one, and Milam county is the other.

Our white prohibitionists and Woman's Christian Temperance Union have ever stood by me and given me the greatest encouragement in counties where our own people were utterly unable to appreciate the effort. And many times, where the whites have come to the meetings and spoken and talked of it to the colored people, they too have been helped, through believing that if the best white people are with me, they too have a right to take hold. This is not true of the more enlightened ones. These have been interested all along, and now as a whole are in favor of the prohibition movement.

Our Teachers' State Convention endorsed prohibition in its last session in Dallas. Two M. E. Annual Conferences—Texas and West Texas, and one A. M. E. Conference—Northeast Texas, always endorse prohibition.

VI.

Here is an incident in the experience of Mrs. F. A. J. Gaudet, President of the Louisiana Willard Woman's Christian Temperance Union (Colored). The Union had started a campaign against the sale of liquor to minors. In the slum district of New Orleans Mrs. Gaudet intercepted a boy leaving a saloon with a pail of beer. She called a policeman and requested him to arrest the barkeeper. This he refused to do, and also declined to take the boy into custody, saying that he (the policeman) had witnessed no violation of the law. He said:

"If you want a charge made you must go with me and the boy to the station."

"All right," she replied, "I will go."

"You will have to ride in the patrol wagon," he said.

Meanwhile the usual street crowd had gathered. She said to Mrs. Hill, one of their women:

"How embarrassing! How humiliating! But, if it takes this to win, God helping me, I will submit. We will ride."

The wagon came, and with the officer she, still holding to the boy with the liquor, climbed in, and rode away to jail. Here she had the boy and herself paroled. She took him to his home, and on the steps of his mother's house, at one o'clock Sunday morning, she read her a serious lesson, and turned her boy over to her, she to bring him to court Tuesday morning. On Monday morning a committee from the Saloonkeepers' Union waited on her, and promised if she would not prosecute the case they would keep every boy under eighteen years of age out of the saloons. She agreed to this, and they have kept their word partially.

It is notorious that the "race riots" in the cities of the north are the outgrowth of the saloon. There has never been such a "riot" except where "dives" flourish.

From the facts and conditions set forth so briefly and partially in this chapter, two things are evident.

1. That if liquor is entirely prohibited, the race problem at once loses its most threatening element of danger.

2. That the colored people respond as readily to good influences as to evil, and under favorable environment are faithful and dependable.

3. That if rightly led and encouraged they will themselves be of the greatest aid in overthrowing and destroying the liquor traffic among them.

CHAPTER XXIX.

UNCLE SAM THE BIG BARTENDER.

"And now also is the axe laid unto the roots of the trees."

IT cannot well be denied that the attitude of the United States government towards the liquor traffic is as anomalous as was its attitude towards negro slavery. Founded to establish justice, it denied justice to the negro on the basis of a compromise with slave-owners, as even now it denies justice to countless thousands of men, women, and children who suffer indescribable wrongs on account of the traffic in intoxicating liquors. Founded to provide for the general welfare, it ignored, under the slavery system, the highest well-being of a vast body of "persons" to whom it denied "personality," and in this day it still ignores the rights of men to be born into an environment free from peril to the fullest human life. Founded to secure the blessings of liberty to "ourselves and to our posterity," it inconsistently denied to the negro the title of freedom, and it still imperils the liberty of large numbers of citizens by tolerating the existence of a traffic which degrades the entire social and political life of the Republic.

The guilt of the government is infinitely more, however, in reference to the liquor traffic than it was in the matter of the slave trade. For with reference to the latter it had only a moral responsibility, while with the liquor busines it has established an open alliance and has made itself the chief beneficiary of this "trade of death."

Under its constitution, this government, at its own instance, without coöperation of the states, or, even in spite of their opposition, has power to protest against the liquor traffic, to discountenance it, to tax it, or to prohibit it. This power lies in its authority to legislate upon questions of national revenue and expenditure, and to regulate intercourse with other nations and commerce between the states.

As early as 1790, despite Alexander Hamilton's opinion, expressed in the *Federalist*, that the spirit of excise laws, "inquisitive and peremptory," is inconsistent with the genius of the American people, a bill, providing for the taxation of distilled spirits was introduced in Congress.

It was defeated mainly by the representatives from Pennsylvania. In 1791, Mr. Hamilton, first Secretary of the Treasury, receding from his theoretic opposition of the year before to the "inquisitive and peremptory" characteristics of the excise, advocated the imposition of a tax upon distilled spirits, and the tax was laid. The western counties of Pennsylvania immediately opposed the tax in an armed rebellion. A federal army, composed of the militia of adjoining states, was led into the region, and, at the expenditure of $1,500,000, quelled the insurrection. Federalism was strengthened. Popular sympathy for the administration of Washington was aroused, and the "democratic" clubs which he had denounced as the real instigators of the revolt against the federal government, became objects of general suspicion as treasonable organizations and ceased to exist.

Thomas Jefferson, sympathizing with the opposition to excise laws, secured the overthrow of the entire internal revenue system of the government, and, from 1802 to 1813, no inland taxes were levied upon articles grown or manufactured in the United States.

In 1813, to meet the cost of the war of 1812, the system was revived, and it continued until 1817, when again the internal taxes were repealed. Then, for a period of forty-three years, from 1818 to 1861, no internal tax of any kind was levied by the federal government. During this period the public debt had decreased from $127,334,933.74 in 1816 to $33,733.05 in 1835, and had again increased to $90,580,873.72 in 1861.

To provide for expenses incurred in prosecuting the war for the preservation of the Union, Congress, in 1862, once more adopted an internal revenue law, and created the Bureau of Internal Revenue. Almost everybody and everything was taxed. By act of May 31, 1868, however, all manufacturers, except those of distilled spirits, tobacco, and fermented liquors, were relieved of all special tax. Acts of 1870 and 1872 made other reductions. At present, the United States Government continues to derive revenue from taxes upon spirits, tobacco, fermented liquors, oleomargarine, filled cheese, mixed flour, adulterated butter, process or renovated butter, opium and playing cards.

The existing system of internal revenue, therefore, dates from July 1, 1862, and Abraham Lincoln, total abstainer and prohibitionist though he was, was a reluctant party to its adoption. He consented to its establishment as a means of raising money for prosecuting the war, hoping, in his great soul, that, when the Union had been saved, he might organize the moral forces of the republic in a movement to overwhelm the liquor traffic. We know that, on the day before his assassination, he anticipated the inauguration of such a movement. There is every reason to believe that, having freed the country from the horrors of slavery, he fondly hoped that he might also emancipate it from the horrors of the traffic, which, from his boyhood, he had hated as he hated slavery. However, in harmony with his policy of doing one thing at a time, he devoted his energy and authority to the preservation of the Union, not realizing that the liquor industry, submitting to special tax, instead of rebelling against it after the manner of the early whisky insurrectionists, would become a most serious peril to the public welfare, and a menace to domestic tranquility and political liberty.

The distillers of 1862 were wiser than those of 1794. Accepting the tax receipt as a *quasi*-license, despite the government's disavowal of the principle of license, they organized to intrench themselves and to secure "favorable" legislation. However, there are three classes of distillers: (1) Those who pay the special tax and submit to government supervision; (2) Those who defraud or attempt to defraud the government; (3) Those who deny the right of government to impose any tax upon distilled spirits, and operate illicit stills.

Against the illicits, or, as they are picturesquely called, "moonshiners," the government wages perpetual warfare. With the second class, there has been conflict ever since the law of 1862 went into effect. With the first class, a *modus vivendi* exists—a compromise, under the terms of which the United States (In God We Trust) government absolutely superintends the business, and collects $1.10 tax per gallon upon an article for which the actual producer receives but 20 cents. Every step of the distillation process, from the grinding of the grain to the final act of sale is supervised by the United States officials, not for the purpose of guaranteeing purity, as the distillers affirm (See Hayner's advertisements), but solely for the collection of the excise. As an internal revenue auditor once remarked, "The government has no interest in the question except for the money that is in it." That is to say, its attitude is wholly mercenary, and, both non-moral and immoral, because all moral issues involved are ignored by it.

In 1907, the Federal Government collected $215,904,720.07 special tax on spirits and fermented liquors, more than half of its aggregated receipts on account of internal revenue.

Of course, the government has power to impose and collect this tax, because the Congress has so ordered. It has power to levy and collect any tax which it may see fit to impose. This was settled once for all when the federal troops entered the State of Pennsylvania and collected the whisky tax at the point of the bayonet. Even now, federal officials are on the hunt through the mountains of Kentucky for illicit stills. And in every brewery and distillery of the United States there are agents of the government, appointed to supervise the processes of brewing and distillation from the day on which the first bushel of grain is delivered at the plant until the last drop of the product is ready for the market.

Technically, the government at Washington does not license the traffic. Technically, there is no contract of partnership between the Government on the one hand, and the brewer, distiller and saloon-keeper on the other. But the Government assumes the right to appropriate the lion's share of the proceeds, under implied threat of drenching the ground with illicit liquor, smashing illicit stills, and closing the doors of illicit places of sale. It does not confer a license, but it passes a "tax certificate," commonly known as a "government license."

Now, when two or more persons unite their property and labor in the business of making spirits and fermented liquors, they agree to divide the profits, and bear the loss in certain proportions. By this contract each party acquires an interest in all the partnership property, becomes responsible for the partnership engagements, and is empowered, in transactions relating to the partnership, to bind by his acts the other partners as well as himself.

Suppose, now, that Doe and Roe, regarding the business of distilling spirits from corn as lawful, propose to form a partnership. A contract is drawn by an attorney at law; capital is invested in a plant, and grain is purchased in open market. Yet, before a grain of corn is ground for the mash, a third partner must be taken in, a United States Internal Revenue collector must be seen, and a rake-off for Uncle Sam must be arranged. He puts weighers, gaugers and storekeepers in charge, and the business is watched day and night by these hawk-eyed gentlemen in the name of the Federal government. The government assumes no risk in the enterprise. Yet it practically takes possession of the product and holds it as a guaranty for the payment of the special tax.

And it does this by virtue of an act passed during the war between the States, when the government, pressed for money, was forced to enter into a deal with the liquor men. For the sake of protection, the brewers and distillers consented to place their business under governmental supervision, and, for the sake of getting ready money, the government was willing to become sponsor of vat, still and worm. The war ended, but the government was still in debt, and so the special tax remained in force, and the liquor men have taken good care that it should continue.

Liquor advocates argue that it is more than ever a necessity to the maintenance of government and that an attack upon excise is an attack upon the flag. Most adroitly they have identified the liquor industry with political interests, and forced the great political parties to adopt a program of silence on issues that are dominant in every state in the Union.

It may be well to note somewhat specifically at this point the very intimate and friendly relations that have been established and maintained between the government and the liquor interests under the internal revenue resumé. When the federal tax on liquors was first proposed, in 1861, it was resisted by the representatives of the liquor traffic. At that time, however, the "trade" was not organized. Under the operations of the new law the distilling and brewing interests soon got together, established good working organizations, and were strongly capitalized. These organizations found it advisable to establish friendly relations with federal officials and influential politicians. This led to the establishment of the "Liquor Lobby," which for so many years has been such a familiar and powerful feature in Washington and elsewhere. The influence of the lobby, and official subserviency to its influence, have led to many scandals.

The system of federal regulation and taxation has resulted in a phenomenal increase in the manufacture and consumption of liquors, and has been disastrous in every way to the interests of the temperance movement. Naturally, therefore, the liquor trade has resisted every attempt to repeal the internal revenue law. Indeed, at times when the government was in receipt of surplus revenues, they have favored the repeal of the tariff system and customs duties rather than the internal taxes.

In 1887, John M. Atherton, President of the National Protective Association of Distillers and Liquor Dealers, said:

"Under the Government supervision there are certain marks, stamps, gauges, etc., put on every barrel of whisky, which serve to identify it. These form an absolute guaranty from the Government, a disinterested party of the highest authority, to the genuineness of the goods. There is such a tendency to adulteration that this guaranty is of great value. Next, if the general Government laid no tax upon whisky the States almost certainly would. As they are under no compact to lay the same tax, the rate would almost certainly be unequal. For instance, with a tax of 25 cents a gallon on the whisky produced in Kentucky the State would have an abundant revenue for all her needs, without taxing anything else at all. But it might happen that Ohio and Indiana would lay no tax, or a very light one, upon whisky. In that case Kentucky distillers would be compelled to manufacture at a very great disadvantage, and would, in fact, be compelled to close altogether. A tax by the National Government bears on all States alike, and affords a fair field for competition."

In the following year, 1888, The United States Brewers' Convention, in an official utterance, said:

"The old objection urged against excise could not at present be revived, seeing that those who have to bear the tax and all the inconveniences that are said to grow out of its alleged obnoxious features, are perfectly satisfied with their present status, so that, as we have stated on another occasion, whatever commiseration may be felt for them by certain theorists, is just so much sympathy wasted. As far as the brewers of this country are concerned, it is well known that, so far from opposing an excise, they materially aided the Government during the incipient stages of the system in making the tax collectible as cheaply and conveniently as possible. Their action at that time was not only prompted by the intention to prevent injustice being done them, but also, in a very large measure, by patriotic motives; while their present course (of non-interference with the Federal tax) is dictated not only by industrial considerations, but also by the conviction, sustained by the experience of our own people and the people of many other civilized countries, that the present system, while perfectly justifiable when viewed from the standpoint of political economy, promotes temperance more effectually than any other measure yet proposed or executed for that purpose. . . . To judge from present indications, there is no danger of a reduction of Internal Revenue, other than that derived from articles which do not concern us industrially."

On the other hand, the Government, through its official representatives, has been equally friendly and considerate toward the trade. As early as 1865, a representative of the Internal Revenue office attended the Brewers' Convention, and said:

"It is the desire of the Government to be thoroughly informed of the requirements of the trade, and I will give information on all questions, in order to bring about a cordial understanding between the Government and the trade."

The following year another Internal Revenue official assured the Brewers' Convention thus—

"Let us take no backward step. I say us, for I am with you. The Commissioner of Internal Revenue is with you. The President is with you."

In 1877, Green B. Raum, the Commissioner of Internal Revenue, wrote to the Brewers' Convention:

"I am glad to learn that the conduct of this Bureau has been satisfactory to such an important body of taxpayers as the brewers of the United States, and I trust that nothing will occur to disturb the friendly relations now existing between this office and your Association."

In 1890, Commissioner John W. Mason addressed the Convention in session at Washington. He said:

"Our business relations for the last year have been quite extensive, and I may say—speaking for the officers of the Commission of Internal Revenue—that they have been of a pleasant character. In order that they may continue so, and that the pleasant features of the connection may as far as possible be increased, it is very desirable that the Commissioner should know you all personally and that, personally, he should know your wishes. . . . Having paid that amount of money (revenue) you are entitled to expect that such restrictions only shall be imposed upon you as are necessary to enable the Government to secure the regular revenue. . . . You are all business men, engaged in a lawful business and entitled to pursue that business untrammeled by any regulation of the office of the Commissioner of Internal Revenue, except in so far as may be necessary for the purpose of collecting the revenue. . . . If there be any regulations or anything whatever pertaining to the office which you may deem unreasonable or unnecessary, I beg that you will not hesitate to express your views."

As a result of the fostering influence of the Internal Revenue system, the manufacture of whisky was so stimulated that at times there was a heavy over-production. To meet an exigency of this kind, in 1885, Hugh McCulloch, Secretary of the Treasury, made a ruling from which the following paragraph is taken:

"The manufacture of whisky is one of the largest and most important branches of domestic industry in the United States, and is at the present time, like other manufacturing interests, greatly suffering from over-production. A legitimate business, from which large revenues are derived, it is not only depressed by over-production, but by being burdened by heavy taxes, the payment of which, as is the case with no other article, is required within a fixed period whatever may be the condition of the market. . . . Under existing laws the manufacturers or holders of whisky are compelled to pay a tax amounting to nearly five times its cost on the article before it is withdrawn from the warehouse for consumption, or to export at great expense, to be held in foreign countries until there is a home demand for it, or to be sold in such countries to the prejudice of our public revenues."

Thus, from year to year, for almost half a century, the liquor trade has continued to intrench itself and to dominate the Government and the politics of the country. It is evident, therefore, that it can never be overthrown until it is attacked and defeated in this the very seat of its power.

In actual practice, the legal aspect of the traffic does not emerge until the product of the still is placed upon the market for sale as a beverage. Upon this point the Supreme Court of the United States has decided that—

"1. There is no inherent right in a citizen to sell intoxicating liquors by retail; it is not a privilege of a citizen of the state or of a citizen of the United States.

"2. The sale of such liquors in this way has been at all times by the courts of every state considered as the proper subject of legislative regulation.

"3. By the general concurrence of opinion of every civilized and Christian community, there are few sources of crime and misery to society equal to the dram-shop, where intoxicating liquors in small quantities, to be drunk at the time, are sold indiscriminately to all parties applying. The statistics of every state show a greater amount of crime and misery attributable to the use of ardent spirits obtained at these retail liquor saloons, than to any other source.

"4. A license may be exacted from the saloonkeepers, imposing restrictions—
   a. As to persons to whom intoxicating liquors may be sold.
   b. As to the hours of day during which sales may be made.
   c. As to the days of week on which sales may be made.

"5. The retail sale of intoxicating liquors may be absolutely prohibited as a business attended with danger to the community."

This decision, written by Justice Stephen J. Field, is not wholly satisfactory to those who believe that the government ought to prohibit the traffic so far as its powers operate, but it settles several questions which, prior to 1890, were supposed to be open.

However, it exposes the anomalousness of the government's attitude more completely than could be done by mere criticism of its failure to realize the political ideals of socio-political reformers, because it shows that the nation, through its Supreme Court, is cognizant of the actual effects of the liquor traffic upon society, for the court recognizes that a greater amount of crime is attributable to the use of ardent spirits in retail liquor saloons than to any other source.

That is to say, *the saloon is the chief source of crime in the United States.* This being true, government is morally bound by all the interests which the state is organized to conserve, to employ its powers in its overthrow.

If, therefore, the government has authority to summon the militia to suppress a rebellion against the excise in Pennsylvania, or to commission Internal Revenue officials to arrest moonshiners and destroy their stills, because they have not paid tax, there would seem to be no reason why it should not destroy by mere force (government in its last analysis is simply organized force), all places where intoxicating liquors are sold, because they are sources of crime.

And the government cannot divest itself of this responsibility on the plea that, although it collects a tax, it does not "foster" the traffic by a system of license. "The special-tax stamp issued," says the Commissioner of Internal Revenue, "is not a license." Section 3243, Revised Statutes of the United States, provides that:

"The payment of any tax imposed by the internal revenue laws for carrying on any trade or business shall not be held to exempt any person from any penalty or punishment provided by the laws of any state for carrying on the same within such state, or in any manner to authorize the commencement or continuance of such trade or business, contrary to the laws of such state, or in places prohibited by municipal law; nor shall the payment of such tax be held to prohibit any state from placing a duty or tax on the same trade or business, for state or other purposes."

See also the opinion of the Supreme Court of the United States, in the *License Tax Cases*, 5 Wall. 462.

Technically, therefore, the United States government does not license the traffic. But, in view of the Supreme Court's decision in the Christensen case, it would appear that it ought to prohibit it in all places where its power is supreme. And, because it is a question of public morality, it ought to be a matter of Federal law, and not merely of public expediency or state action. This is a prohibitionist's answer to Lincoln Steffens' question, "What do you expect of your government?"

But the liquor tax policy of the Federal government is forcing an issue in the states, which will ultimate, either in repeal of the internal revenue laws so far as they relate to intoxicating liquors, or in a conflict between the commonwealths and the so-called government at Washington. Citizens of prohibition states, who, for a generation have persistently struggled to free themselves from the tyranny of heartless, blasé, saturnine saloonkeepers, will not long submit to the defiant nullification of laws which have cost so much to enact. Conflict between the taxing power of the Federal government and the police powers of the state is inevitable. Powers, which the Supreme Court of the United States has pronounced sufficient to deal with the liquor traffic, cannot be annulled by a tax policy administered in contempt of those powers.

The saloon problem will be solved. The saloon will cease to exist. But the problem of the saloon will not be solved until the problem of the Union also is solved, until the compromises of 1787 have been swept away, and a new Union established, founded on principles of a unified national life. If the nation is one, then the dual system must cease to exist or its operations must be harmonized, as the "Departments" of France are administered from Paris as capital of the republic.

Long ago the hour arrived for the reconstruction of the American Republic upon a self-consistent basis. The nation cannot live half drunk and half sober. A constitutional convention ought to be called for the purpose of revising the constitution so as to meet the needs of the modern age. When that convention shall meet, representatives from prohibition states will demand recognition of their right to exclude intoxicating liquors from their boundaries. They will demand protection against a traffic which the so-called "Federal" government is bound to prohibit, and out of the discussions of the convention will emerge a "more perfect union," in which the liquor traffic shall have no place.

In the meantime, the Chief Executive of the nation, by the strict enforcement of existing laws and constitutional provisions, could go far toward closing every dram-shop in the territories, in the Philippines and other insular possessions; to abolish saloons in national parks, soldiers' homes and all government property; to enforce liquor laws in the District of Columbia and the anti-canteen law. He could also appoint as judges and district attorneys citizens who shall administer law in accord with the ideals of a great political brotherhood, organized in recognition of the rights of the obscurest member of human society.

To show to what extent the United States as a nation, "We the people," participates in the profits of the liquor trade, the following figures are given:

United States Internal Revenue Collections on Liquors 1863 to 1907.

Fiscal Years Ended June 30.	Distilled Spirits	Fermented Liquors
1863	$ 5,176,531	$ 1,628,934
1864	30,329,150	2,290,009
1865	18,731,422	3,734,928
1866	33,268,171	5,220,553
1867	33,542,952	6,057,501
1868	18,655,631	5,955,869
1869	45,071,231	6,099,880
1870	55,606,094	6,319,127
1871	46,281,848	7,389,502
1872	49,475,516	8,258,498
1873	52,099,372	9,324,937
1874	49,444,090	9,304,680
1875	52,081,991	9,144,004
1876	56,426,365	9,571,281
1877	57,469,429	9,480,789
1878	50,420,815	9,937,052
1879	52,570,285	10,729,320
1880	61,185,509	12,829,803
1881	67,153,975	13,700,241
1882	69,873,408	16,153,920
1883	74,368,775	16,900,616
1884	76,905,385	18,084,954
1885	67,511,209	18,230,782
1886	69,092,266	19,676,731
1887	65,829,321	21,922,187
1888	69,306,166	23,324,218
1889	74,312,206	23,723,835
1890	81,682,970	26,008,535
1891	83,335,964	28,565,130
1892	91,309,984	30,037,453
1893	94,712,938	32,527,424
1894	85,259,252	31,414,788
1895	79,862,627	31,640,618
1896	80,670,071	33,784,235
1897	82,008,543	32,472,162
1898	92,547,000	39,515,421
1899	99,283,534	68,644,558
1900	109,868,817	73,550,754
1901	116,027,980	75,669,908
1902	121,138,013	71,988,902
1903	131,953,472	47,547,856
1904	135,810,015	49,083,459
1905	135,958,513	50,360,553
1906	143,394,055	55,641,859
1907	156,336,902	59,567,818
	$3,323,349,763	$1,143,015,584

A grand total of $4,466,365,347.

When one remembers that every penny of this immense "revenue" is blood-money, taken out of the life and health, and food and shelter, and brain and brawn, and virtue and manhood of the people; that it is the price of vice and crime, of disease and death, of pauperism and starvation, of shame and debauchery, of the woe and misery and suffering and degradation of innocent mothers and wives and little children, it should stir even the most stolid citizenship to revolt and action. Study these figures. They are stubborn and concrete facts.

So detailed and far-reaching are the commercial relations between the government and the liquor industry that distillers brand boxes containing their products: "Bottled at the distillery under the supervision of the United States Internal Revenue Department, for account of ————————————." This does not necessarily imply that the whisky is virginally pure, nor that it will not produce the effects which ordinarily follow imbibition. Indeed, it does not absolutely guarantee the supervision; for commissioners of Internal Revenue have stated, on their honor as representatives of a government—which trusts in God for protection against the Japanese, and in the liquor industry for fifty per cent. of its income—that distillers have been known to offer money to gaugers, watchmen and supervisors for their "absence" at the crucial period of "bottling."

However, the "United States Government"—that great "artificial person" which exists in international law and cartoons as a corporation with a soul—consents to be known as an endorser of the goods produced in breweries and distilleries. And this is the open shame of it all, that, on the 4th of March, 1909, one more good citizen will take the oath of office as President on the big Bible, and, for the next four years, share officially with the Internal Revenue department in guaranteeing the intoxicants which the Supreme Court declares beyond the right of one citizen to sell another by retail in dramshops!

Against these concrete and stubborn facts the political idealist and the social reformer utters protest in the name of the "general welfare" which the government is pledged to conserve, in full assurance of hope that "Uncle Sam" will some day cease to attend bar.

CHAPTER XXX.

ON TO WASHINGTON.

A SYMPOSIUM BY THREE ABLE WRITERS.

PART I.
By GEORGE F. MAGOUN, *D. D.*

OUR Federal government being complex, each of its three branches, executive, judicial, legislative, has plural relations to the liquor traffic in place of the single one; and each group of these relations is exercised through the person or persons nationally authorized for the purpose.

1. The official relations of the President of the United States, being in their nature executive, are controlled by those of Congress and the Supreme Court. His responsibility thus modified is the least belonging to the three branches; but in the exercise of it he may grievously fall short of what is legislatively and judicially laid upon him. There may often be times, even under Federal statutes inadequate for the protection of the people and rules for the service very imperfect, when negligence or malfeasance in his official subordinates, traceable to the liquor traffic and resulting in vast national loss and dishonor, might be readily reached by him, arrested and punished, but which remain undisturbed.

2. Of the Supreme Court something more positive can be said. Its later decisions are its better ones. More and more this flagitious traffic has been rebuked by our highest tribunal. Though not perfectly self-consistent, it has sometimes favored the manufacturer, the importer and the vender against the people and their local institutions, yet the Court has been coming closer to the principles of natural life and morality. It has buttressed the republican government, guaranteed to the states by the constitution on the side of the police power. By the pen of an associate justice it has declared that there is no inherent right in a citizen to sell intoxicating liquors by retail. Already it had decided that every state has a right to prohibit the sale and manufacture of intoxicating liquors, but in this decision the court reaches high water mark and its decisions henceforth rest upon an ultimate principle of natural ethics. Coupled with its descriptions of the traffic, as the source of most of the poverty, disaster, and vice of the nation, this declaration against any traffic right

MRS. CLINTON SMITH,
President District of Columbia W. C. T. U.

MRS. J. W. ROBINSON,
W. C. T. U. Worker, Washington, D. C.

MRS. CLAYTON E. EMIG,
Corresponding Secretary District of Columb'a W. C. T. U.

MRS. HANNAH E. CROSBY,
An Early W. C. T. U. Worker, Washington, D. C.

prepares the way for its extermination. Reached through many compromising questions and conflicting decisions, this fundamental principle plants our court of last resort where it will need to stand in that good time coming, when Congress and the people shall have outlawed the traffic.

3. The most material relations of our general government to the traffic are necessarily through Congress. Here we encounter the theory that the life of the traffic is in the hands of the states exclusively and cannot be reached by the national law-making power. This theory grew up naturally in colonial times; the last recognition of it seems to have been in later decisions of the Supreme Court which place all intoxicating liquors upon arrival in the states or territories under laws enacted in the exercise of the police power thereof. From this fact interesting consequences follow. One is, that neither Congress, Supreme Court, nor President, can be insensible to disastrous and shameful results to states forced to self-defense against national action. Another is, that revenue from imported liquors is not essential to a national government; as the number of prohibition states increases, the enormous internal liquor revenue will also dwindle and taxation be re-adjusted.

But there are other important national interests affected by the traffic, the responsibility of Congress for which is affected by no theory of power. The District of Columbia, having no local legislature but Congress, the drunkard-making which goes on throughout the ten miles square, as well as in the capitol grounds and building, is by its express permission and sanction. The nation is thus committed to and chargeable with every local dram-shop in the district. Congress has passed a license law freed from some pernicious features of preceding laws, but by the same token it has left its duty undone in not sweeping the traffic from the seat of government altogether.

The result of our study of the subject is, that the multiform and complicated relations of our government to the liquor traffic are anomalous; some of them working a measure of good, others frightful and universal harm. The general condition produced is local option on the national scale, remorselessly sacrificing the interests of temperance states. It needs to be logically and legally and practically unified. It needs to be brought under one principle of national right. Congress must be first corrected, its relations being largely obstructive. This done, we need feel little concern for the attitude of the Federal courts or the executive. Personal relations do not fall into this subject, and would doubtless be cured by the thorough curing of official ones. Though on principle a majority of the people of the land are against the saloon, there is this day a working majority of all in its favor.

This accounts for the frequent defeats of reform. Vast numbers of temperance people are timid and torpid, never lifting a finger or uttering a word against the dram-shop, however they and their fellows suffer from it. Unfortunately, they give a character to the whole people, and render such a paper as this possible and true. It is they who have tacitly put drinking men into Congress, the courts and the White House, and will yet again unless better temperance men than themselves prevent. Sometime it will all be impossible. But must we wait until there is a declared and working majority in the land against dram-shops? I think not. We need not even wait for constitutional prohibition in the majority of states.

All great reforms are carried by minorities soon to become majorities. The educating power of law lies here. It outruns popular habits, feelings, convictions even. We are slowly approaching the time when fifteen, twenty, then a half or more of our forty-six states will be for constitutional prohibition; but before we reach that time our national triumph will be assured. Our moral civilization must yet largely advance before we shall be ready for that grand consummation—prohibition throughout the Union by amendment of the United States Constitution. But progress and the process of it lie in four words of Tennyson, "sweeter manners, purer laws." The order of his thought is the order of logic and of events.

PART II.

By PERE G. WALLMO, *in The Arena, October,* 1908.

The importance of the "temperance wave" of 1907-8, may be gauged by the large number of "temperance" bills introduced during the session of Congress which ended March 4, 1908. Sixty-odd measures were presented during the first session. The most talked-of bill is the "Littlefield Bill." There are something like twenty-five bills of the same character, all seeking to place intoxicating liquors, shipped from one state into another, absolutely under the police powers of the state into which they are shipped. Representative Acheson, of Pennsylvania, has presented a bill which provides that no intoxicating liquors shall be transported from any state, territory or district of the United States into any other state, territory or district.

The Littlefield Bill was considered by the Judiciary Committee of the House, while seven bills of a similar nature were considered by a sub-committee of the Senate Judiciary Committee. The question of allowing each state to regulate its own liquor traffic was dwelt upon considerably, and appealed to Senators Knox, Clay and Bacon, who favor the rights of the states. After listening to the arguments on both sides, Senator Bacon drew up a bill, which, however, was not acceptable to a majority of the Senate Committee on the Judiciary, and Senator Knox framed another which was reported to the Senate, prohibiting express companies and other carriers from acting as agents of liquor dealers, from delivering liquors to fictitious persons, and from shipping any package containing liquor from one state to another, unless such package be so labeled on the outside cover as to show plainly the nature of its contents and the quantity contained therein.

The second group of bills relates to the issue of special tax receipts by the U. S. Internal Revenue office. Of these bills there are twenty-five providing that no such tax receipts shall be issued in prohibition territory. Senator Gallinger and Representative Hill have introduced bills which provide that no U. S. government tax receipt shall be issued to any firm or individual until such person or firm shall first have secured a valid license from state, county or municipality.

Of the other bills the one to stop the manufacture and sale of all intoxicating liquors in the District of Columbia is of more than local interest. But there is a very serious obstacle to the passage of this bill. Realizing the difficulties of securing any legislation on these lines for Washington, Mr. Gallinger has introduced a bill providing for high license.

Other bills prohibit the sale of liquors in all buildings owned or controlled by the United States government—upon warships, in navy yards, in parks—in fact, everywhere that the government has control. Representative Acheson has a bill forbidding the transmission through the United States mail of any publication of any kind containing an advertisement of any intoxicating liquors.

The prohibitionists have introduced a constitutional amendment which would leave the entire question in the hands of the citizens of the various states and would relieve Congress of all further temperance legislation.

There are other measures on the other side, relating to the reëstablishment of the Canteen.

It is not to be presumed that the temperance people are having things their own way before Congress. The liquor men, especially the wholesalers and the brewers, realize that they have to fight for their lives. The organization known as the "German American Alliance" has made a special appeal to Congress against all temperance measures, because, in their opinion, the restrictions imposed by these measures interfere with "personal liberty." Efforts have been made to enlist the aid of the labor unions, notably, the American Federation of Labor, against temperance legislation, on the claim that such legislation would tend to injure industries that employ many men.

While none of the bills presented has become law, the two most important ones are in such shape that they are almost sure of getting attention at the next session of Congress—*unless the bill introduced the last week of the session, providing for a commission of five Senators and five members of the House to investigate the whole subject is pushed through Congress.* Such a commission would probably spend two years investigating, and in the meantime all legislation on the subject by Congress would be postponed.

Beyond doubt the creation of this commission to investigate is designed to ward off all legislation adverse to the interests of the Liquor Trust. If it shall be appointed in 1908, there will be no report before 1911. The report would then be referred to some other committee, and, if Lieutenant Totten's mathematical interpretation of the signs of the times is correct, the Millennium will have arrived before the bill sees daylight again. Under the Alexander Hamilton system of government, the "people," who fancy themselves sovereign, will be thwarted and manacled, and the Liquor Lobby will still have its way with Congress.

Evidently the time has arrived in the history of the United States when a change of system is needed, and not merely a change of administration. When Congress ceases to respond to the demand of a moral movement that is as wide as the republic itself, the hour has struck, not merely for a new alignment of political parties, but for the reconstruction of government in such a way as to make Congress representative of real issues.

Condemnation of a tyrannical "Speaker" is not sufficient; much less the shifting of power from one liquor-dominated party to another. There must be reorganized a true democracy, self-ruled in the love of highest good, and fearless of the lowest evil.

Under pressure of moral sentiment, as pure as the Decalogue and as clean as the Sermon on the Mount, sixty bills have been presented in Congress, providing for restriction of the liquor traffic. If by some hocus pocus, all legislation on this most important question is to be dodged and opposed for another presidential term, it will be the supreme duty of the people to organize a new commonwealth which shall express the principles of a true liberty, a true equality and a true fraternity.—G. M. H.

PART III.

STATES' RIGHTS VS. FEDERAL RIGHTS.

NOTE.—*Perhaps no man in the country has given more careful and intelligent study to the relations of the general government to the liquor traffic than Finley C. Hendrickson of Cumberland, Maryland. Mr. Hendrickson is an attorney at law of high standing, chairman of the Maryland Prohibition Committee, and member of the National Prohibition Committee. In the three following contributions Mr. Hendrickson presents conclusive reasons why the government should not only divorce itself from its wicked connection with the liquor traffic, but should coöperate in measures to prohibit and destroy it—G. M. H.*

By Finley C. Hendrickson.

(Argument before the Ways and Means Committee of Congress, February 3, 1906, in favor of House Bill No. 8768, to prohibit the sale of Federal tax receipts to applicants who are prohibited by state laws from engaging in the liquor traffic.)

"Mr. Chairman and Gentlemen of the Committee: Strictly speaking, this measure has nothing to do with the relative merits of license and prohibition. It is designed to rectify a dangerous conflict between the procedure of the Federal government and the states, as relating to the liquor laws.

"The present action of the Treasury Department in selling Federal tax receipts to those who are defying state law, in both license and prohibition territory, has done and is doing much to encourage lawlessness in the states. In low license territory the number of those who hold Federal tax receipts exceeds the number who hold regularly issued licenses. In high license districts the difference is more marked. In prohibition districts, every dollar paid for tax receipts is gotten from outlawry.

"The right to raise this internal revenue was vested in Congress, under Section 8 of Article I of the Constitution, which provides that Congress shall have the right to raise such revenue 'to pay the debts of the United States, and for the common defense and general welfare of the United States.'

"It is clear, therefore, that the framers of the Constitution never intended that the taxing power should be exercised, except when it could be done not only to raise revenue, but to subserve the highest interests of law and order.

"It is interesting to note how Congress in previous years regarded the rights of the states when acting under their reserved police powers, as they clearly do when pursuing the policy of license or prohibition.

"In 1794, Congress first exercised the right to tax retailers of intoxicating liquors in the states. Section 3 of the act contained the following provision: 'Provided, always, that no license shall be granted to any person to sell wines or foreign distilled spirituous liquors who is prohibited to sell the same by the laws of any state.' That act was repealed about eight years later. In 1813, Congress again exercised the right to tax retailers of liquors in the states, but again recognized the sovereign police powers of the states by the following provision: 'Provided, always, that no license shall be granted to any person to sell wines, or distilled spirituous liquors, or merchandise as aforesaid, who is prohibited to sell the same by any state.' That act was repealed a few years later.

"No further exercise was made of the power to raise internal revenue from retail liquor sellers in the state until the passage of the act in 1862, now under consideration. That act also clearly recognized the police powers reserved within the states by the following provision: 'No such license shall be construed to authorize the commencement or continuance of any trade, business, occupation, or employment therein mentioned within any state or territory of the United States in which it shall be specially prohibited by the laws thereof, or in violation of the laws of any state or territory.'

"To say that Congress in 1862 meant to override any of the police powers reserved in the states would be to do violence to the lawmakers of that memorable period. All that can be claimed for the wording last quoted as a matter of interpretation, which is supported by the debates of that period as shown by the "Congressional Globe," under date of May 25 and 28, 1862, is that inasmuch as the police powers in some of the states had yielded to military necessity, and it was believed by all that such a war revenue measure would be soon repealed, there was no need of any clearer recognition of the right of the states to act within their police powers, untrammeled by any procedure on the part of the Federal government. The previous revenue acts had been repealed shortly after their passage. A long interval had intervened from 1817 to 1862, in which there was no exercise of the taxing power as applied to retailers of liquors in the states. It was believed that this measure would soon be repealed. Those who framed it and those who voted for it, certainly never intended that it should be used to encourage and protect lawlessness within the states.

"But the Treasury Department has interpreted the act to mean that it *must* treat those who defy state liquor laws with the same consideration and afford them the same protection that is accorded those who are engaged in a legal business. The bill under consideration is designed to cure that bad procedure.

"The present practice of the Treasury Department is without precedent and without analogy, inasmuch as the possession of the tax receipt can be no legal protection against the penalties of the state laws, if the possessor is unable to obtain a state license, and there is no principle on which the Treasury Department has a right to demand that such persons shall pay a 'tax.' The very basis of taxation is protection, and where full and adequate protection cannot be accorded, no 'tax' should be demanded.

"The present procedure is very detrimental to law and order, since it fosters lawlessness in both license and prohibition territory. Those who are denied a local license or permit, but who determine to trample state liquor laws under foot, purchase the tax receipt, call it a 'government license' and go in to defy state authority under the guise and declaration that the Federal government is with them in their contempt of such state laws.

"The anomalies are marked. The states try to suppress outlawry; the Federal government encourages and protects it. The Federal government prosecutes 'moonshiners' who violate Federal law, but from the very building where such laws are executed, internal revenue collectors are dealing 'hand in glove' with the enemies of state law.

"The logical conclusion of the wrong premise and the wrong interpretation by the Treasury Department of the act of 1862 is to be noted by a rule of that department sent out to its collectors on the 13th of August, 1903, (Treasury Decisions, Vol. VI, No. 33, page 13), whereby:

" 'Collectors and deputy collectors are not only prohibited from giving out copies from their records, but also from testifying orally, in cases not arising under the laws of the United States, as to facts that have come to their knowledge as the result of information contained in the records.'

"This rule was issued sixteen days after one district judge in a habeas corpus case decided that internal revenue officers need not answer in the state courts as to who were the holders of tax receipts.

"The true doctrine would seem to be that where the Federal government is given sovereign power, as in the matter of tariff, foreign policy, etc., the states should support at every point the chosen policy. The converse of this should be equally true. Where the states have retained sovereign powers, as they have done with reference to police powers, the Federal government should give every support to those powers. Thus both state and Federal government will add strength and dignity to the whole and no conflict result.

"Suppose the states were to interfere with the execution of Federal law, as the ruling of the Treasury Department interferes with state laws? Would Congress look kindly upon such procedure? Suppose the states would pass a law that certain state officers having in their possession valuable records should not testify in Federal courts as to who were smugglers and 'moonshiners?' How would Congress regard that? But is it any less censurable that the Treasury Department should stone the police powers reserved in the states and stand with the lawless and against the administration of state liquor laws?

"Some may think the states do not pursue a proper policy when they experiment with Prohibition. But the states have the constitutional right to pursue that policy, and they should be permitted to exercise that right untrammeled by Federal powers. But whether you consider license or prohibition the best policy for the states to pursue, all must agree that *lawlessness*, whether aimed at state or Federal laws, is highly detrimental to the 'common defense and general welfare of the United States.' This spirit of lawlessness and increase of crime is becoming a serious question. In free governments, where those who have come out from oppression are all too liable to mistake license for liberty, there is every reason for all the functions of government being united in support of law and order. Lawlessness encouraged in one direction against a particular law will sooner or later manifest itself against all law. If the lawless are to be encouraged by the Treasury Department in their opposition to state liquor laws, the same lawless spirit will manifest itself against Federal law, and all law, as soon as occasion arises. The highest interest of government can only be subserved by all branches uniting for its suppression.

"We respectfully urge the favorable recommendation and passage of this measure."

IS THE REPUBLIC SELF-SUFFICIENT?

By Finley C. Hendrickson.

(Written originally for *The New Voice*.)

The cry of the brewers and distillers that "Prohibition doesn't prohibit," involves one of the gravest questions ever presented to the American people. When this Republic threw down the challenge to the monarchical forms of earth in the adoption of the Declaration of Independence, and afterwards adopted the Federal Constitution, the people selected the very forms through which they hoped to demonstrate that there was nothing inherently weak in a free government, such as they were then establishing, but that it would prove self-sufficient for every test. Monarchy was brought to a standstill in 1776 in its attempts to crush out the liberty for which the Revolutionary patriots contended. Later the nation triumphed over and was preserved through sectional civil war. And now a third and no less critical epoch is aproaching, in which it is to be demonstrated to ourselves and to the world to what extent a government under freedom can cope with and triumph over this internal evil of the drink traffic. The task before us is not less delicate nor of less momentous import than others that have gone before. If the brewers and distillers can finally make good their boast that "Prohibition doesn't prohibit," and cannot be made to prohibit, then over the face of civil liberty must be written the failure of free government. Then it must follow that the apologists of monarchy will declare with renewed vigor that there is no form of government but monarchy.

Hence it is that the brewers and distillers have thrown down the challenge to the American people on the self-sufficiency of the Republic. It is founded on majority rule, but the liquor interests pervert the power of our government, so long as it is accorded them to defy the power and jurisdiction of the government which they have abused, so soon as it is withdrawn from them. If a county passes a local option law, they ship their liquors in from adjoining license counties; if a State passes a prohibitory law, they flood the "dry" State with interstate liquor shipments. They purchase tax receipts, commonly known as "government licenses," from the Treasury Department, and boast the rule of the department which forbids internal revenue collectors testifying against their lawlessness in the State courts. They care little whether a hamlet, a town, or even a county, goes "dry" or not, so long as they can centralize in and exploit the functions of the Federal Government to defeat the will of the majority.

But some may say that in the sale of liquors in defiance of State law, under the plea that the lawless seller holds a "government license," and in the shipment of interstate liquors through common carriers into "dry" territory, the liquor interests are not defying and challenging the self-sufficiency of the Republic, since what they do they do through the consent of at least one part of the Republic, the Federal branch. But it is a matter of boasting on the part of the brewers and distillers that they, within our very doors, defy the will of the majority which we are determined every foreign interest shall respect and obey. Suppose any foreign government should declare that they meant to land a shipload of goods at the harbor

MRS. EMMA SANFORD SHELTON,
Recording Secretary, District of Columbia
W. C. T. U.

MRS. S. M. WESCOTT,
District of Columbia W. C. T. U. Worker.

MRS. M. E. COHEN,
Vice-President, District of Columbia
W. C. T. U.

MRS. CHAS. P. GRANDFIELD,
Treasurer, District of Columbia W. C. T. U.

MRS. W. F. CRAFTS,
District of Columbia W. C. T. U. Worker.

of New York without paying the tariff duty on them? Would the American people consent to that? No, indeed. Congress would be convened at once, and the American people would respond as one man, even to the call of arms, if necessary, to maintain respect for our laws. But the brewers and distillers ship carloads of liquor into Kansas and other prohibition states, through interstate commerce, and declare that they mean to continue to do so, no matter what the people of those states may say, and Congress looks on with indifference. Is not the defiance of the laws of a sovereign state, passed in the interest of highest citizenship, of more importance than the landing of a shipload of goods in the harbor of New York contrary to tariff laws?

Let us bear in mind that the perverting of functions of government may be a far more serious matter as affecting our experiment as a republic among the nations of the earth, than the open defiance of our institutions by some despotic foreign power against which freemen are prompt to guard themselves. The action of the liquor men consists now both of perversion of government as well as defiance of it. They defy the authority of the will of the people of the states, while at the same time they pervert the functions of the Federal government. They will thus be stronger and quicker to defy both state and federal government when occasion arises. The national lawmakers are not making smooth the future path of human liberty by smiling upon the defiance of the liquor interests directed against law and order. They do but sow to the wind in the circumvention of the state law through the perverting of federal functions, but to-morrow or in the days to come the nation will reap the whirlwind harvest of lawlessness directed against federal law.

In the final analysis the prohibition question is not solely as to whether prohibition does or does not prohibit. It is not a question as to whether one does or does not drink. Far deeper and more important is the challenge which the brewers and distillers, exploiting federal power, have flung to everyone who believes in civil liberty, that a government built on that foundation is not self-sufficient to make itself respected by those who, partaking of the "blessings of liberty" for themselves, wish to deny it to all others as against the evil which they promote.

LIQUOR "CENTRALIZATION BY CONSTRUCTION."

By Finley C. Hendrickson.

(Written for "The Passing of the Saloon.")

While the liquor movement has thus far embraced no larger political divisions than separate states, and most of the dry area was secured through county, township and district contests, it is inevitable that the nation will soon become, by the very logic of the situation, the battle-ground on the prohibition question. The theory of our dual form of government suggests it, and the whole trend of the prohibition reform moves towards it.

This broader battle-ground can be anticipated by noting how the prohibition reform has moved from the mile or two limit for churches and schoolhouses, and the protection of residential districts, up to election district and township and then on to the county. That attained, many who had favored the county movement rested from further agitation, and often refused to join in any movement for statewide prohibition.

But the prohibition counties soon found that the liquor traffic was camped at their doors in the way of a jug trade, liquor being brought in from adjoining license counties, or through interstate commerce from nearby states. Thus express offices, steamboat landings and railroad depots were turned into substitutes for the saloons which had been voted out.

Once more the prohibition forces have taken up the march, now making their slogan statewide prohibition, and state after state already has swung into line, to be followed in the near future by others, more particularly perhaps in the South.

The contest in these states, being confined to this single issue, and with record votes polled, it no doubt has appeared to the mass of citizenship that, the entire state being freed from the saloon, nothing further remained to be done, and they now could rest in peace and enjoy the fruits of their prohibition labors. But the noise of battle hardly had ceased in any state until the mails were flooded by the liquor men with information how the bibulous, without regard to sex, race, age, color or personal habits, could be supplied with their favorite tipple through the medium of interstate commerce carriers.

Although nearly half the population, and over half the area, of the forty-six states have passed into the dry column, revenue statistics show only a considerable but not a relative decrease in the consumption of liquor. A C. O. D. jug, paying as it does a revenue into the coffers of the United States treasury, weighs heavy in the governmental scale as against state sovereignty. The bibulous are encouraged to part with their coin and hand it over to agents of common carriers, who find that it does not interfere with their salaried positions to act also as agents for the brewers and distillers for additional compensation. The agent naturally reasons that the common carrier, whose interest he is supposed to promote, gains commercially by a stimulated C. O. D. jug trade in dry territory.

Thus the matter stands at the present day, the states finding it impossible, under Supreme Court decisions, to pass any law to correct the interstate jug trade. Jurisdiction of the federal government over the interstate shipment does not end until the liquor has reached the hands of the consignee. At that point the states find it utterly impossible to prevent the lawlessness which the federal government aids through interstate commerce. The liquor interests, the common carriers and the lawless are a powerful triumvirate, holding open the door which the states have sought to close. Then the cry goes up that "prohibition doesn't prohibit," and the liquor interests parley with the citizenship of the states, and challenge them to make choice between the open licensed saloon *with* revenue or the interstate jug trade *without* revenue.

Let us turn now to the Federal point of view. While the prohibition fight was being carried on from the one-, two-, three- or four-mile limit, or residential district, to the election district or township, then to the county, and from the county to the state, the brewers and distillers were centralizing their power in the federal government, knowing that, so long as they could hold that citadel of power, they might be harassed by local option and prohibition laws in the states, but could not be made to surrender altogether. Then there is always the hope that, from behind such federal fortifications, they may sally forth at some time when the attention of the people in the prohibition states is directed to some other overshadowing issue, and retake all the lost territory.

The means adopted by the liquor interests in order to centralize their power in the federal government were, after all, simple. The procedure consisted for one thing, in the retention of the fiscal policy of the Federal government adopted during the Civil War relating to taxation of liquors. The liquor dealers, instead of demanding the repeal of the war revenue measure of 1862 when the cause for its passage had ceased to exist, favored its retention, and they now boast that through its operation the traffic they represent pays large sums into the federal treasury. From 1880 to 1907, the government received $3,639,172,297.00 in taxes on spirits and fermented liquors. Having thus exploited the fiscal policy of the government, under which a purely war revenue measure has been retained in times of profound peace, they advanced the doctrine that prohibition states should be denied federal appropriations, because the adoption of prohibition by the states interfered with the federal fiscal policy. The brewers boldly said to each senator and representative—

"But when a state, after successive legislative acts, shuts down the manufacturing establishments paying the internal revenue, asks from the federal government appropriations for river and harbor improvements, rural free deliveries, public buildings, and expects protection against lawlessness and against foreign enemies, does not the question arise: Can the prohibition states expect that the monies paid into the United States treasury by anti-prohibition states in the form of internal revenue, shall be expended for the benefit of prohibition states?"

While recognition of this doctrine was not embodied in law, it received no rebuke at the hands of the national lawmakers, but rather a friendly countenance in the refusal by Congress to pass a proper interstate commerce act to permit the states to protect their dry territory from the interstate jug trade. In this way a politic Congress could say to the prohibition and temperance forces: "We refuse to embody into law this suggestion of the brewers that Congress punish the prohibition states by withholding from them federal appropriations." At the same time they could say to the aggressive brewers: "While Congress did not adopt the policy of punishing prohibition states by withholding federal appropriations as you desired, it did refuse to pass a law to permit the states to protect their dry territory from your interstate jug trade." Just how long Congress can extend the right hand of fellowship and aid the liquor interests, while it extends the other hand to state sovereignty with empty declarations of friendship, without losing its precarious balance, remains problematical.

A wheel within a wheel of this fiscal policy is found in the sale of Tax Receipts, commonly known as "Government Licenses," to approximately eighty thousand violators of state liquor laws who persist in selling in defiance of the state laws of their respective localities, whether in dispensary, license, local option or prohibition territory. Not only that, but internal revenue collectors are forbidden by the Treasury Department to testify in the state courts against these lawless characters. Thus the liquor interests have centralized and fortified in the fiscal policy of the federal government to the detriment of the judicial processes of all the states.

But the interstate jug trade, solely within the control of Congress, is the chief bulwark of the liquor forces. Should Congress remain inactive, and the Supreme Court refuse to reverse its former decisions denying to the states the right to regulate or prohibit this interstate traffic in intoxicating liquors, all of the forty-six states could adopt the prohibition policy, and yet the liquor interests could, by centralizing in the District of Columbia alone, for instance, virtually nullify the operation of the prohibition laws of all the forty-six states, limited only by the cost of freight and express charges to points of destination. The states are powerless now as against "outside nullification." An interstate jug trade is more sacred to Congress than the laws of a sovereign state. A saloon is stationary and its evils may be dealt with by local authorities, but the United States mails and interstate carriers are wings and feet to the brewers and distillers of the license states. Their eyes perceive no state boundaries in their deliveries.

Thus, by using the interstate jug trade as a sword, and the fiscal policy of the federal government as a shield, the brewers and distillers have not felt it necessary to bend all their energies to defeat the adoption of local option laws, knowing that so long as they could centralize in the federal government, and act through a well organized force of express agents and a stimulated C. O. D. trade which pays ready cash, their business could go merrily on. It is natural the big brewers and distillers consider it far more dignified and strategic to guard their federal outposts and husband their resources beneath the federal rooftree than to hazard all in the many local option contests on the question of saloons or no saloons, requiring in the aggregate the expenditure of large sums of money, and getting knocked on their shins by a pronounced dry majority.

While the American people have spurned the general doctrine of "centralization by construction," because they instinctively feel that its adoption would prove a doorstep to despotic power, they are rapidly awakening to the fact, as to the drink traffic, it is not a mere theoretical discussion but an accomplished fact. If "centralization by construction" is ever to be adopted as a general policy by the American people, and the reserved powers in the states shall, because of weakened constitutional safeguards, set their united currents to the swelling of federal power, the brewers and distillers will be able to boast that they had anticipated this action, and, at the very time when the general doctrine of centralization had been utterly repudiated by the American people, it had been carried to the farthest limits for the benefit of the liquor interests.

Late in October, 1908, a newspaper writer said:

"Probably the most surprised of all persons who have felt the effect of the wave of prohibition which has swept over the southern and some other states are Treasury Department officials. Liquor dealers were aware of what would be coming to them, but the Internal Revenue Bureau had no suspicions of the great monetary loss the government would sustain until the reform had begun to operate.

"The losses are piling up so rapidly that a serious deficit is being created in the government resources, and Congress will have to take up the matter at the coming session and cover the loss from some other source. At the Treasury Department it was said that indications point to a deficit of $2,000,000 for October, and more will follow as the prohibition movement spreads.

"Just what method is to be suggested to Congress to make up the loss has not been decided, but it may be thought necessary to advise further increases in whisky and beer taxes. This, it is thought, will cause a hard fight before Congress.

"The wholesale liquor dealers of Washington, who were asked about the matter, said the distillers and others had lost so much already that they could not stand any further taxation and remain in business.

"The Treasury Department officials said the greatest loss in income has been sustained in Kentucky, Tennessee and Louisiana, the three big distillery states. It is there that stamp fees are collected in millions. Those distillers have lost 90 per cent. of their trade in the southern states, and are now practically sending nothing into the dry districts, depending for business on the North and West. And now, reports assert, the temperance wave is making its way slowly north from Texas into Arkansas, Colorado, Nebraska and South Dakota. Liquor men prophesy that all of these states are going dry, or will pass practically prohibitive laws.

" 'With this condition in view,' said a Washington wholesale dealer, 'it is certain that there will be a protest that will be heard from the Atlantic to the Pacific if they try to increase taxes. Why, the distillers can't pay them unless they, in turn, increase prices.'

"The loss in revenue last month, Treasury figures show, on spirituous liquors alone, was $1,506,819. The total since July has been $5,542,958, and figures so far received for October show that the loss will be $2,000,-000 or more. The loss on beers and other fermented liquors in September amounted to $1,796,914.28, and this loss is also increasing."

To offset revenue losses caused by enactment and enforcement of prohibitory laws, the Prohibition party proposes equitably graduated income and inheritance taxes. These may not be as scientific as the Single Tax on Land Values, but they are more defensible than the tax on intoxicating liquors.

It is plainly apparent that political parties can no longer ignore the liquor question on the plea that "it is not a national issue." It is up in a peremptory way for discussion and settlement, and parties, willy-nilly, must recognize it, and formulate and declare their policies and attitude toward it. The fight is on to a finish. It can not be doubted that ultimately and speedily the same great people that freed themselves from slavery will also free themselves from the saloon. —G. M. H.

CHAPTER XXXI.

THE ANTI-LIQUOR FIGHT IN CANADA.

By Ben H. Spence, *Secretary Ontario Branch The Dominion Alliance.*

GREAT in area, but with vast territory yet undeveloped, Canada, with a population of about seven millions, is today a great nation-in-the-making.

Canada's 3,745,574 square miles give to her 178,011 square miles more territory than the United States, including Alaska. Millions of acres of this is most fertile land, and is destined to be the granary of the world.

The great natural wealth of Canada is attracting to her borders vast numbers of immigrants. Indeed, the problem of foreign-born population is already being acutely felt and is causing patriotic Canadians to have grave concern as to what moral and social conditions will obtain in this new growing land.

The population of the Dominion, according to the last census, taken in 1901, was 5,371,315. During the last seven years there has been added to the population about a million and a half people. Approximately this population might be grouped as follows:

Maritime Provinces (consisting of Prince Edward Island, New Brunswick and Nova Scotia	1,000,000
Quebec	2,000,000
Ontario	2,500,000
Western Provinces (consisting of Manitoba, Saskatchewan and Alberta)	1,000,000
Pacific Coast (British Columbia)	500,000

These groups are distinct in many respects, and indeed form nations of themselves. Each province is autonomous and is in many particulars self-governing. The Federal Parliament has jurisdiction over matters relating to commerce, revenue, militia, postal service, railways, etc. In the provinces is vested the police power, education, the administration of provincial lands, and the control of legislation creating and regulating municipalities. These municipalities are governed by practically the same laws that obtain in all such political divisions.

These legal divisions, and this apportionment of legislative functions, has a direct relationship to the temperance question throughout the Dominion of Canada. The Dominion Parliament, and the Dominion Parliament only, has full power to prohibit the manufacture, importation and sale of intoxicating liquor. The provinces have very large powers regulating and prohibiting the sale, but must not interfere with inter-provincial trade. In all the provinces, except British Columbia, the legislatures have delegated to the municipalities power to prohibit the sale of liquor within their bounds by the enactment of local option by-laws. This power is being effectively used today in many places.

TEMPERANCE SOCIETIES.

The first temperance society in Canada, as far as known, was formed at Brockville, Ontario, in the year 1828. Thereafter for many years the temperance reform was confined largely to the activities of what were called "temperance societies" of one kind and another.

In 1846, the secret temperance society movement began with the formation of a division of the Sons of Temperance at Montreal, Quebec. A central body of this order began a systematic temperance propaganda in 1847, which was very successful. The year 1853 marks the advent of the Independent Order of Good Templars with the distinctive features of that body. At that time Harmony Lodge No. 1 was organized at Merrickville, Ontario. The first Council of the Royal Templars of Temperance, "Pioneer No. 1," was organized at Toronto on the third day of October, 1878. For a time all these orders flourished and the aggregate membership ran up to over 100,000.

The Woman's Christian Temperance Union was established in Canada in 1874 when a local union was formed in the town of Owen Sound. This particular society is still flourishing and has been a most important factor in the securing of local option in that place.

The "Y's" were organized in 1881 and have since done good work.

A Dominion Union of the Woman's Christian Temperance Union was formed in 1885, and today there is not only the Dominion Union, but Provincial Unions in practically every province.

Great and lasting work has been done by the consecrated womanhood of Canada through the W. C. T. U. Their indefatigable efforts and thorough consecration have been of incalculable value in the upbuilding of the strong temperance sentiment which now prevails.

Largely through the efforts of the Woman's Christian Temperance Union, legislation has been secured by which scientific temperance instruction is given in Canadian schools. The control and management of the public schools is in the hands of provincial legislatures, and in nearly every

REV. J. C. SHEARER, D. D.,
General Secretary, Board of Temperance and Moral Reform of the Presbyterian Church, Canada.

JOSEPH GIBSON,
President, Ontario Branch, The Dominion Alliance, Canada.

province provision is made for thorough instruction regarding the physiological effects of alcohol.

EARLY LEGISLATIVE EFFORT.

During this era of the temperance societies, the first definite attempts were made to secure prohibitory legislation. Attempts were made in the various provinces to secure the passage of prohibitory laws. A prohibition measure was passed by the Province of New Brunswick about fifty years ago, but was repealed by the next legislature. Some years later in the legislature of the Provinces of Ontario and Quebec, which were at that time united, a similar measure was defeated by the casting vote of the Speaker.

These attempts at legislation were made before the union of all the provinces into what is now known as the Dominion of Canada, which federation was formed in 1867.

Shortly after the federation of the different provinces an agitation was inaugurated looking towards a law of total prohibition for the whole Dominion. The House of Commons was flooded with petitions from every part of the country. Legislatures in the different provinces passed resolutions asking the national body to enact such a law. A call for a Prohibition Convention was issued by sixteen members of the House of Commons in the year 1875, and in response to this 280 representatives from different provinces assembled at Montreal. The late Hon. Senator Alexander Vidal presided at the meeting, while helping in the organization were the Hon. Neal Dow, of Portland, Maine, and John S. Stearns, of New York.

Among the resolutions adopted by this Convention were the following:

"1. That the manufacture, importation and sale of intoxicating liquors to be used as common beverages are found by the Parliamentary Committees, as well as the experience of society, to be a fruitful source of crime and pauperism, alike subversive of public morality and social order.

"2. That all attempts to restrict the traffic by license law are unsatisfactory, inasmuch as intemperance and all the evils connected therewith are constantly increasing.

"3. That nothing short of the entire prohibition of the manufacture, importation and sale of intoxicating liquors as beverages would be satisfactory to this Convention.

"4. That in order that a prohibitory liquor law when passed, may have the sympathy and support so indispensably necessary to its success, it is the opinion of this Convention that the Dominion Parliament should be urged to frame such a law, subject to ratification by popular vote."

One result of this Convention was the formation of what is known as the Dominion Alliance for the Suppression of the Liquor Traffic, which organization is still the recognized representative body of the Dominion of Canada, uniting all churches of all denominations together with all temperance and moral reform organizations in a powerful federation for practical action along carefully considered lines.

A branch of the Alliance was formed in every province with a general council for the whole Dominion. A branch of the Alliance or some organization similarly constituted, is at present actively at work in every province. The present Dominion officers are John Dougall, Esq., of Montreal, President; F. S. Spence, Esq., Toronto, Secretary.

The proposals of the Montreal convention cited above were not acted upon by the Dominion Parliament, although the matter was discussed from year to year. Committees were appointed to consider the question, and one year a special Board of Commissioners was sent to investigate the prohibitory laws of the United States. The only results, however, to the research of this commission were a Blue Book and a resolution by the House of Commons assenting to the principles of prohibition.

In 1878, the Canada Temperance Act, popularly known as the Scott Act, was enacted. This was really a local option prohibitory law applying to cities and counties, and which could only come into force upon being ratified by a vote of the electors of the territory affected.

The Canada Temperance Act was immediately taken hold of by the temperance people. The city of Fredericton, the capital of New Brunswick, was the first place to vote, and a large majority was recorded in favor of the law. The measure is still in force in that city, being again sustained by an overwhelming majority in May, 1908. Other cities and counties fell into line and in a short time the great part of the Maritime Provinces, and large sections of Ontario, Quebec and Manitoba were brought under the operation of the law.

The measure was to an extent a disappointment. The machinery for enforcement was inadequate. Political complications interfered with its success. There was dispute between the provincial and Dominion authorities in regard to enforcement. This was aggravated by the fact that the Scott Act being a Dominion measure, repealed, so far as the territory it affected was concerned, the liquor license laws of the different provinces. The result of all was that the law was repealed in every place in Ontario, Manitoba and Quebec, in which it was adopted. It is, however, still in force in a large part of the Maritime Provinces.

While the Scott Act was to some extent a disappointment, it certainly was effective in reducing the consumption of liquor, and in lessening drunkenness and crime. In the Province of Ontario, taking a period of three years before the adoption of the measure, the three years during which it was in force, and the three years following its repeal, we find the commitments for drunkenness during the Scott Act period were very much less than in either of the other periods. The following are the figures:

During three years before the Scott Act............2144 commitments.
During three years of the Scott Act................ 977 commitments.
During three years after the Scott Act............1531 commitments.

In the other provinces equally good results followed.

With the repeal of the Scott Act there seems to have been for a time a lull in regard to temperance work. This was the time when the great Christian Endeavor movement was inaugurated. One of the effects of the growth of the Christian Endeavor idea was to swing into the line of Christian activity, in a distinctively Church organization, the moral enthusiasm and activity, which before had found expression and an avenue of usefulness in organizations such as temperance societies outside of the church. With the growth therefore of the Christian Endeavor movement, there was a decline in the strength of the temperance societies, but yet an undoubted ultimate gain in regard to temperance work. The result has been that the "Christian Endeavor" idea has laid hold upon the Church itself, and the churches have become temperance societies.

Practically every church in Canada today is a temperance society of the strongest and best kind, and nearly every preacher of the Gospel an advocate of temperance in its sanest form. Today the churches are practically vying with one another for leadership along the line of temperance reform.

The Presbyterian Church has its Temperance and Moral Reform Department with Rev. Dr. G. C. Pidgeon as chairman and Rev. Dr. J. G. Shearer as secretary. The Methodist Church has its Temperance and Moral Reform Department with Rev. Dr. S. D. Chown as general secretary and Rev. H. S. Magee as associate. The Baptist Church has a Moral and Reform Department with Rev. Dr. A. T. Sowerby as chairman. In the Anglican Church there is the Church of England Temperance Society; in the Roman Catholic Church, the League of the Cross; and in all the churches unprecedented activity along temperance lines. These are all united in the Dominion Alliance for legislative work.

THE DOMINION ALLIANCE.

The purpose of the Dominion Alliance is set out in the following Declaration of Principles:

"1. That it is neither right nor politic for the State to afford legal protection and sanction to any traffic or system that tends to increase crime, to waste the national resources, to corrupt the social habits and to destroy the health and lives of the people.

"2. That the traffic in intoxicating beverages is hostile to the true interests of individuals, and destructive of the order and welfare of society, and ought therefore to be prohibited.

"3. That the history and results of all past legislation in regard to the liquor traffic abundantly prove that it is impossible satisfactorily to limit or regulate a system so essentially mischievous in its tendencies.

"4. That no consideration of private gain or public revenue can justify the upholding of a system so utterly wrong in principle, suicidal in policy and disastrous in results as the traffic in intoxicating liquors.

"5. That the total prohibition of the liquor traffic is in perfect harmony with the principles of justice and liberty, is not restrictive of legitimate commerce, and is essential to the integrity and stability of government, and the welfare of the community.

"6. That, rising above sectarian and party considerations, all citizens should combine to procure an enactment prohibiting the manufacture, importation and sale of intoxicating beverages as affording most efficient aid in removing the appalling evils of intemperance.

Its organization is simple yet comprehensive and affords full scope for the thorough coöperation of all moral reform agencies in temperance work.

FURTHER LEGISLATIVE ACTIVITY.

The revival of interest in temperance work again precipitated the situation in the Dominion Parliament and in the various provincial legislatures.

The pressure became so strong that in 1891 another Royal Commission was appointed by the Dominion Parliament, and after a long, exhaustive investigation the majority members brought in a flabby and meaningless report. A minority report was also presented which declared unhesitatingly and emphatically for nation-wide prohibition.

POPULAR VOTES.

Something further had to be done by the politicians to relieve the situation, and in the Provinces of Manitoba, Prince Edward Island, Ontario and Nova Scotia plebiscites were taken upon the prohibition question. The result of these votes was as is set out in the following table:

PROVINCE	VOTING.	VOTES FOR PROHIBITION	VOTES AGAINST PROHIBITION	MAJORITY FOR PROHIBITION
Manitoba	July 23, 1892	19,637	7,115	12,522
Prince Edward Is	Dec. 14, 1893	10,616	3,390	7,226
Ontario	Jan. 3, 1894	180,087	108,494	71,593
Nova Scotia	March 16, 1894	46,756	12,355	31,401

Following these various provincial plebiscites, further efforts were made to secure something practical and definite in the form of a prohibitory law.

There was a change of administration at Ottawa, the Liberal party came into power. A plank in their platform was the submission to the people of the question of national prohibition. In consonance with this a Dominion plebiscite was taken on September 29, 1898, the result being that 278,380 votes were cast for prohibition and 264,693 against, a majority of 13,687 for prohibition.

The peculiar feature about this vote, however, was that the Province of Quebec, which is largely French Canadian and Catholic, gave a majority of 94,324 against prohibition, while the rest of the Dominion gave a majority of 108,111 in favor of such a measure. The Premier, Sir Wilfred Laurier, a French Canadian Catholic, took the ground that in the face of such a vote, to pass such a law would amount to the coercion of the Province of Quebec by the rest of the Dominion. Nothing was done.

By this time, however, it was found that the individual provinces had large prohibitory powers, and in the year 1900 a provincial prohibitory law was enacted by the legislature of Manitoba. Political and legal complications, however, arose which deferred the coming into operation of the law for a time, with the final result that the question of the coming into force of the measure was submitted to a referendum. This was done in spite of strong protests from the temperance people, many going so far as to declare that they would have nothing to do with a referendum submitted in this way. The whole proceeding was one of the most despicable political tricks ever perpetrated.

Under the most unfair conditions, and with the most open and barefaced electoral corruption, a majority was polled against the coming into force of the Act, and the legislation indefinitely shelved.

In 1902, a bill similar to the Manitoba Act was introduced into the Ontario legislature. To this also there was a string. The question was to be submitted to a vote with a provision that the aggregate vote in favor of the measure must be equal to a majority of the votes polled at the preceding elections.

The result of the poll was: For the Act, 199,749; against the Act, 103,548; majority for the Act, 96,201. By the requirement of the law the aggregate vote in favor needed to be 212,739. The temperance people therefore, while polling an enormous majority, were 12,990 votes behind the required aggregate. The government refused to put the law into force.

The unfair character of this legislation is seen by the fact that if the temperance people had polled 12,990 votes more and the liquor men had polled 109,190 votes more, yet nevertheless the temperance people would have won.

Disgusted at the political perfidy of a Government which was supposedly temperance, the people of Ontario rose in their might and turned them out at the general elections of 1904. The people in that province are now turning to local option, and are doing for themselves what their representatives in Parliament refused to do for them; and, indeed, all through the Dominion the local option method is being effectively used by the temperance workers as the immediate means at their hand in the great warfare they are waging.

THE SITUATION TODAY.

The following may be said to be a bird's-eye view of the situation throughout the Dominion in all the provinces at the present time.

In the Dominion Parliament, legislation is being sought to enable the provinces to enact a more effective prohibitory measure than they have now power to pass and also to prevent the shipment of liquor into prohibition areas and to regulate the common carriers in regard to this.

The Province of Prince Edward Island is the pioneer prohibition province of the Dominion. Prior to 1902, local option in the form of the Scott Act was put into force through the entire province except in the capital city of Charlottetown, and a campaign was then brought on and a province-wide prohibitory law was secured. The situation was then a peculiar one. The Scott Act, a Dominion local option law, was in force all through the province except in Charlottetown, where the provincial Prohibitory Act applied. The provincial law was found to be much stronger and more satisfactory in its working than the Scott Act. The temperance people then brought on a campaign for the repeal of local option. As soon as the country repealed the law it immediately came under the operation of the provincial act.

The whole province is now under provincial prohibition with the result that a short time ago every jail in the entire province was empty save one, where a single offender was in durance. And for what offense? Actually for selling liquor contrary to law!

Temperance sentiment is exceedingly strong in the Province of Nova Scotia. A very rigid license law is in force throughout the entire province, but licenses are only granted in the city of Halifax, the county of Halifax and the county of Richmond. The other nineteen counties of the province are without the legalized sale of liquor, and an effort is now being made to secure a provincial prohibitory law.

The Province of New Brunswick shows encouraging progress also. Of the fifteen counties and cities in the province, nine, including the capital city of Fredericton, are under local option by the Scott Act.

The Provincial Temperance Organization is now entering upon a

F. S. SPENCE,
Honorary President, Ontario Branch, The Dominion Alliance, Canada.

REV. S. D. CHOWN, D. D.,
General Secretary, Board of Temperance and Moral Reform of the Methodist Church in Canada.

G. F. MARTER,
Ex-President, Ontario Branch, The Dominion Alliance, Canada.

determined campaign to bring the entire province under prohibition by provincial enactment.

To those who have looked upon the Province of Quebec as hopeless from a temperance standpoint, recent events are indeed amazing. This province, which voted by an overwhelming majority against Dominion prohibition, is today ridding itself of the curse of the liquor traffic more rapidly than any other province in the Dominion.

Within the past two years over 100 municipalities have come under local option and at the present moment out of 994 municipalities over 700 have freed themselves of the licensed liquor traffic.

This great movement is largely due to the splendid work of the Franciscan Fathers under the leadership of Archbishop Bruchesi. Tremendous pledge-signing campaigns have been carried on throughout the province. These have been followed by the passing of local option by-laws.

In Ontario, the banner province of the Dominion, a tremendous fight is now on. Prior to 1906, the people in the various municipalities had the power to pass local option by-laws by simple majority of the votes polled. The temperance people were just beginning to use this power largely, and at the preceding municipal elections had succeeded in abolishing the traffic from fifty-eight municipalities. At the session of the legislature in 1906, however, an act was passed making it impossible to carry by-laws except by a three-fifths vote of the electors. The effect of this arbitrary unfairness has been to tremendously hamper reform efforts. During the years 1907 and 1908, only seventy-three municipalities have been able to abolish the liquor traffic, although in 145 places majorities were polled for local option by-laws.

Another campaign is on this year but the results are not likely to be any more encouraging and the determination of the temperance people is growing stronger than ever that the three-fifths injustice must be removed. Today there are 312 municipalities in Ontario entirely free from the liquor traffic. Licenses are still granted in 492.

The Province of Manitoba is also a scene of great activity. At the last session of the provincial legislature an act was passed enabling municipalities to enact local option by-laws upon a majority vote of the electors. Already twenty-seven out of 128 municipalities are dry. Campaigns are on, voting to take place in December next in about seventy-five more. It is entirely likely that the result of this fall's campaign will be that more than one-half the province will be under prohibition.

Saskatchewan and Alberta, the two new provinces in "The Last West" are beginning well. At the recent session of the Saskatchewan legislature a strong license law was enacted providing for local option by majority vote, and already the forces are lining up for the fight.

The Alberta License Law is perhaps stronger in some respects than that of Saskatchewan, but does not provide for local option, this being only obtainable under the old regulations. There is little doubt, however, that the next session of the legislature will give such a law.

It must be remembered, however, that in both these provinces there are immense areas without licenses, because owing to the rigid provisions of the law, would-be license holders cannot obtain the necessary number of signatures to their petitions or comply with the legal requirements.

West of the Rocky Mountains is British Columbia, the largest province in the Dominion, with great problems of its own. British Columbia is perhaps not so far advanced as other provinces along temperance lines, but at the present time a great campaign led by the W. C. T. U. is in progress, having for its object the securing of local option. This campaign is meeting with most encouraging success.

THE CHURCH VS. THE BARROOM.

The temperance battle in the Dominion of Canada has practically become and is today a fight between the Church and the Liquor Traffic. The churches are taking high ground. The traffic is fighting hard.

There were in the Dominion of Canada, according to the last census, 11,943 churches with 2,209,392 communicants. In addition to these there were 8,470 Sunday-schools with 75,846 teachers and officers and 646,455 scholars.

There are in the Dominion of Canada 9 distilleries, 96 breweries, 14 wineries, 6,000 wholesale and retail liquor dealers.

The brewers and distillers of the Dominion of Canada have invested in their establishments a fixed capital of $10,076,906, a working capital of $14,456,175, making a total capital of $24,533,081.

There are 3,692 employés. The wage bill is $2,144,157. The product is valued at $12,167,045.

The "trade" is most perfectly organized in each province, and lately a subsidiary organization has been formed as an Allied Trades Association led by a prominent manufacturer of bar fixtures. In spite of all, however, temperance sentiment is advancing rapidly.

The churches are on record in no uncertain way.

The Roman Catholic Church is perhaps leading in the temperance fight today as has already been indicated. The pastorals of the archbishops have contained many earnest warnings to their people against the evil power of the drink habit and against the common traffic in intoxicants.

The Church of England in its various synods has strongly declared itself. The New Brunswick Synod has adopted the following resolution:

"*Resolved*, That this Synod recognizes the evil of intemperance as one of the greatest obstacles to the spread of Christ's kingdom; and, further resolved, that in the opinion of this Synod, the Church of England should be found in the front ranks in the contests against this gigantic evil, and that the clergy and laity of this diocese be called upon resolutely to oppose the evil, and to encourage every legitimate effort to suppress it."

The General Assembly of the Presbyterian Church in July, 1908, said:

"The Assembly would reaffirm the deliverance of former Assemblies that nothing short of the prohibition of the traffic in intoxicants for beverage purposes can satisfy as the goal in temperance reform, and would recommend our people in those provinces where there is no immediate prospect of carrying and enforcing prohibition, to unite with others in working towards this end by—

a. The curtailment of the traffic by local veto.

b. The abolishment of the barroom (*i. e.*, the sale for consumption on the premises) and the public treating system associated therewith."

The Methodist Church is on record as follows:

"That the liquor traffic of today is the greatest stumbling block to the church's progress, is fraught with untold evils to humanity and spreads desolation over the length and breadth of our fair Dominion.

"That the efforts put forth by the governments to restrain, by license laws, this cyclone of destruction, have failed in their purpose; be it therefore

"*Resolved*, (1) That we are unalterably opposed to all efforts to regulate the liquor traffic by taxation or license, high or low. These afford no protection from its ravages, but on the other hand, entrench it in the commonwealth, throw around it an artificial garb of respectability, and make the people partakers of and responsible for the evils resulting therefrom. 'It is impossible to legalize the liquor traffic without sin.'

"(2) That we declare the complete and immediate prohibition of the manufacture, importation and sale of alcoholic liquors for beverage purposes to be the duty of the civil government."

The Congregational Church has said:

"*Resolved*, That as ministers and delegates we are in a position to feel the pulse of the best sentiment of our Dominion, that is gradually moulding public opinion; and we feel that the tax-paying and thinking element of the Dominion would be glad of prohibition of the liquor traffic, enforced by officers who are willing to enforce the expressed wish of the people. We thank those representatives in Parliament who were firm in demanding immediate prohibition in accordance with our resolution of last year."

The Baptist Church has said:

"Whereas the traffic in intoxicating liquor is a recognized evil producing a large proportion of the poverty, suffering, disorder and crime in our Dominion, and unnecessarily adding much to the taxes of our people; and whereas we believe that a law enacted by the Dominion Parliament prohibiting the importation, manufacture and sale of all alcoholic liquors, except for use in medicinal, mechanical and sacramental purposes, and containing ample provision for its strict enforcement by the proper authorities, will greatly diminish these and other evils, and largely increase the prosperity and promote the health, peace and morals of our country, it is therefore resolved, that in the opinion of this convention, it is now the duty of the Dominion Parliament to enact such a prohibitory law."

The Churches are practically one in their present campaign for barroom abolition.

The traffic, however, is strong and its influence great.

The per capita consumption of liquor in the Dominion of Canada for the year ending March 31, 1908, was 6.624 gallons.

The commitments for drunkenness in the Dominion of Canada for one year, 1906, the last for which figures have been published, were 25,110.

CANADA'S DRINK BILL.

A recent summary of the drink bill of Canada is as follows:

Direct Cost.
Paid for liquor by consumers.................................$ 59,126,549

Indirect Cost.
Labor lost and producing power destroyed by
    Intemperance $60,515,977
Deaths through Drink, $4000 to $5000 each... 20,000,000
Grain destroyed (in manufacture of liquor).... 2,000,000
Indirect labor (in manufacture, carriage and
    sale of liquor)........................ 6,784,400
Public cost for crime, lunacy................ 3,534,608   92,834,985

Or a grand total that the liquor traffic cost Canada last
    year.......................................$151,961,534
The Revenue received from the Traffic by the Dominion was.$ 12,871,537
By the various Provinces............................. 1,250,000
By the various Municipalities........................ 1,250,000

Total ....$ 15,371,537

CANADA'S PROBLEMS.

Some phases of the temperance problem in Canada call for special note. One is the growth in recent years of the treating system.

Drinking has largely disappeared from the homes of the people and from private and public social functions, but barroom drinking has enormously grown. If the aggregate consumption of liquor in the Province of Ontario were divided into ten parts, it would be found that nine of the ten parts were consumed by the men standing in front of the bar there and then in the barroom, and only one-tenth by the people outside the barrooms in private and social functions.

The great reason for this is the treating system. This is especially prevalent amongst young men, and the barrooms are filled with groups of young fellows who stand the treats until they cannot stand.

Another feature is the linking together of hotels and bars. There are practically no saloons in Canada, but licenses are granted to barrooms in hotels and the hotel business of the country has been practically handed over to liquor dealers. This is bad for the hotel and bad for the country, and gives to the liquor trade a standing and prestige in the community it would not have were it confined to saloons and shops. Indeed, in the Province of Ontario it would be difficult to find a man who called himself a "liquor dealer." All are "hotel keepers," and the cry in the local option campaigns is never, "How will the community get on without the bar?" but "What will we do for hotel accommodation?"

This has been recognized by the temperance people, and at the last Convention, by unanimous vote, resolutions were passed asking for legislation prohibiting the issuing of licenses to sell liquor to any house or place of public entertainment.

There is little or no public drinking by women in Canada, and, indeed, in many parts women are prohibited from entering the barrooms where liquor is sold.

The separation of Canada into many different geographical divisions with the long boundary line makes the enactment of a Dominion law very difficult. This is aggravated by what has already been referred to, the racial and religious difference between Quebec and the rest of Canada. The change that has taken place in Quebec recently, however, is likely to mean the reviving of activity and a strengthening of the demand for legislation that will be Dominion-wide in its operation.

Canadian temperance workers are perhaps more conservative and certainly less spectacular in their campaign methods than their brethren in many parts of the United States. Literature, public meetings, church services and organized personal work are the methods used. Parades, bands, stereopticons, do not seem to influence the public mind and are little used for campaign purposes.

The particularly satisfactory aspect of the temperance movement in Canada at the present time is the practical unanimity of moral reformers in regard to the line of action to be pursued. An eminently wise policy has been adopted which, while distinctly progressive, is also reasonable, and appeals to the judgment of the average man. The cry, "extremists," "fanatics," "sentimentalists," is little heard, nor is there much occasion for it. While unswerving in their loyalty and endeavor after the utter annihilation of the liquor traffic, the Dominion Alliance is today more concerned in the next step to be taken than with the last. The campaign policy is well voiced in the campaign cry, "Banish the barroom, destroy the treating system!" That is the next step in the temperance reform in Canada.

In a determined, systematic, persevering way the churches of Canada are unitedly pressing forward, and are winning all along the line.

We will win. We must win. We are right.

> "For life shall on and upward go,
> Th' eternal step of progress beats
> To that great anthem, calm and slow,
> Which God repeats."

CHAPTER XXXII.

SIGNS OF THE TIMES.

"THE PASSING OF THE SALOON" is the product of a careful survey of public opinion in reference to the liquor business in the United States and Canada in the year nineteen hundred and eight. The editor has been in communication with women and men in all the states, and in the Dominion, whose relation, either to the government or to the various organized movements against the liquor traffic, qualifies them to speak authoritatively. Convictions on this subject long cherished by the few have become the demands of the many.

The problem which confronts the American people is the administration of government so as to realize the ideals of the moral aristocracy. If, as a famous purveyor of popular amusement says, "Ninety-five out of every hundred people are good," the government will be pure and good when the ninety-five have control of the governmental machinery. But, if the five, composing the impure and evil minority, obtain control of the legislative and executive functions of government by terrorism or by appeal to greed, the majority will be under foot.

Something like this has been the status of things in the United States, at least, since the liquor interests consolidated as a political power. The anti-saloon movement, of which this book is the story, is an effort of the great majority to recover their lost rights and powers, and is, therefore, not merely the history of a moral reform. It is rather, as the Hon. Seaborn Wright has said, "the history of a political revolution." In the Anti-Saloon League the "federated church" has entered the domain of politics for the purpose of rescuing legislatures from control of liquor lobbies, and creating conditions in which the moral sentiment of the commonwealth may find expression in practical law-making.

The campaign of 1908 is not merely "a fight between democracy and federalism," as Professor Giddings says. It is the beginning of the final struggle between the ninety-five and the five, which will result in the evolution of a system of self-government based upon the right of the best citizenship to administer law for its own protection. As one of the speakers said at the Louisville meeting of the Model License League: "People have become tired of finding the saloon in the way of every movement they have undertaken in the name of reform, and they are rebelling!"

"The Passing of the Saloon" is a report of a rebellion which will never end until the powers of government are wrested from the gangs that have governed through the saloon, and they have been driven from their seats of stolen power.

Yellow journalism, the muck-rakers and panics to the contrary notwithstanding, the first decade of the twentieth century must be regarded as an era of ethical progress. The world is better than it used to be. Political conscience, business conscience, social conscience and ecclesiastical conscience, each is more sensitive. Though politicians, business men, society people, and even churchmen may have cause to fear the "yellow" reporter, in their hearts they, too, condemn the things that have been under the ban of the prophets and moralists for a thousand years.

Evidences of this appear all around the globe. If, on the Western continent there is a "temperance" tidal wave, sweeping up out of the depths of the world's sense of the truth and justice and destroying an evil traffic in liquor tolerated too long, there is also in the Orient a movement on foot for the suppression of the century-old opium trade. The vast development of this "industry" of the Far East is chargeable in no small degree to England, which has sanctioned and fostered the production and consumption of poppy-juice for revenue, with as little regard for human welfare, as the United States government has protected the traffic in intoxicating liquors for revenue.

From the day that the first pound of opium was sold until now, there have been voices raised against its use. From the day that the first glass of intoxicating liquor was distilled until now, there have been voices lifted against the drink traffic. But the moral intelligence of the few of the past has become the wisdom and conviction of the people of the present; and there are fore-gleams of a coming era in which the trade in drug and drink will be branded universally as criminal, and banished by decree of the awakened people.

Long before Lord Chief Justice Mansfield, of the English Court, in 1770, pronounced negro slavery unlawful, there had been one-ideaed reformers who had denounced human slavery as a violation of fundamental right and law. But it was not until after Mansfield had uttered his decision in the famous case of *Somerset vs. Stewart* that slavery ceased to exist in the British Empire. But the institution was doomed as soon as one conscience-dominated man dared open his mouth and pronounce upon it the judgment of God.

And so, in this same great empire, the opium trade now is doomed, despite the shameless wars which Great Britain, for purposes of revenue, prosecuted in the past to compel China, a "pagan" nation, to abandon a policy of prohibition, under which she had sought to protect her millions against the opium drug habit. For, at last, the world-rising ethical tide compels England—"Christian" England—to give aid to the anti-opium crusade. In like manner, in America, a public conscience finally aroused compels the prohibition of the revenue-producing liquor traffic.

Never before has the watchword of peace among the nations of men been so persistent and dominant as now. In spite of a sensation-loving press and jingo politicians, the better thought of the world turns more and more from the bloody pomp and barbaric paraphernalia of war, and finds fit and impressive expression in peace congresses and arbitration and reciprocity treaties. A war between nations is now seen to be as senseless as a brawl between two families in the city street. There is as much reason why Smith and Taylor should settle a "ditch" question by a duel in the public road, as that France and Germany should settle a boundary question or any question upon the so-called "field of battle." The war spirit dies hard, but the time approaches when swords shall indeed be beaten into plowshares and spears into pruning hooks, and the nations of the world shall learn warfare no more.

Invention, science, education, industry, trade, commerce, have welded the races into a family. Human interests have become one. Steam and electricity have destroyed the barriers between the peoples. The day of the Federation of the World and the Parliament of Man is at hand.

In all ages mankind has been stirred to real development and progress by moral questions alone. At bottom every impulse which has aroused peoples to their larger activities has been inspired by questions of right and wrong. It is the urge of conscience that lifts humanity upward.

The questions that grip the public mind at any period are reflected in current periodicals, in the acts of legislative assemblies and in political campaigns in which moral issues force political parties into real combat for control of government. The party "machine" may endeavor to suppress discussion of issues based on real distinctions of truth and error and right and wrong. But students of true public opinion in this present time, know that the questions which take real hold upon public attention in the United States especially, are the suppression of "graft", resistance to the aggressions of predatory wealth, and the abolition of the liquor traffic. Almost every local campaign hinges upon some phase of the liquor question. Candidates everywhere have been compelled to declare themselves for or against the saloon, in spite of the famous announcement of a brilliant Ohio Senator that he was "neither for nor against," for in his judgment the liquor question had been settled for all time according to "the eternal principle of taxation."

Never before has the newspaper press opened its columns so freely as now to reports of the anti-saloon agitation and to discussions of the liquor problem. Even the much berated party Prohibitionists are treated with respect by reporters. There are no longer the sneering references to the sparseness of men and the plentitude of women at temperance and anti-saloon meetings.

Salient among the moral forces that are driving the saloon out of existence, should be noted specially the high-class monthly magazines and the "Chautauqua" assemblies. Readers of current literature have found in their favorite magazines brilliant stories of the anti-saloon movement, north and south, east and west; stories as fascinating as the lightest fiction, and athrill with the valor that makes battle stories interesting reading. Students of social life discover that common folk everywhere are hungry for knowledge of the first and last fact in history and science. Hence they flock more and more each summer to the Chautauqua, by the riverside and in the woods.

The monthly magazines as a whole reflect the highest ideals in current periodical literature. In like manner the Chautauquas represent the highest ideals in public intellectual entertainment. There is no more astonishing fact in recent times than is seen in a great multiplication and vast expansion of monthly magazines, many of them growing in but a short time into business enterprises of great profit and value. In like manner the Chautauquas multiply and prosper. It is a most promising sign of the times when undertakings based upon these high ideals become so popular that they *pay*.

Through these channels the higher life of the time is exhibiting itself, and by these admirable agencies the progressive elements of thought are reacting upon thinking women and men everywhere. It is evident that the "plain" people and the "cultured" people alike, open-minded to the largest visions of truth that make for the fullest life, are advancing to strategic points in the long conflict with anti-social forces. More, perhaps, than ever before, *the life that now is* assumes eternal and universal meaning, and the Kingdom of God is discerned to be the Kingdom of Man. The brightest magazine writers are most earnest advocates of human rights, the rights of the child toiler, the sweat-shop worker, the day laborer, the disfranchised woman citizen. Likewise the most popular Chautauqua lecturers are the heralds of a better day for the great masses, the real wealth producers, heralds of an emancipation that will bring purest pleasure of life to every human being in the commonwealth.

People read the newspapers for news, but they read the magazines for discussion of the vital questions of the day. They go to "Coney" for an "outing" but they go to Chautauqua for an uplift, for a wider horizon, for a greater impulse to life worth while. The hunger for true art, true literature, craves satisfaction. As the Magazine and the Chautauqua *come*, the Saloon will *go*.

The most widely read and discussed article in the Magazine is the story of the anti-saloon crusade, or the one depicting the evil influences and effects of drink. In like manner "Temperance Day," or "Anti-Saloon Day" is the one great day at the Chautauqua. And so it comes about that readers of the magazines, and the Anti-Saloon League, constitute the Federated Church in action against the saloon.

To an account of one special phase of the moral progress of today this volume is devoted. Some of the men and women who contribute so interestingly to its pages, who, today sit in seats of honor, but a little while ago were denounced as fanatics, dreamers, cranks, impracticable persons, heretics, and unwarranted disturbers of the social order.

But in religion and in politics the reformer is always pronounced a heretic—at first. Martin Luther, John Wesley, George Fox, were heretics. Paul was a heretic. Jesus of Nazareth was a heretic. Wendell Phillips, Lloyd Garrison, Abraham Lincoln were political heretics. The great Republican party was, in its beginning wholly heterodox according to the prevailing political standards of that period, and was as bitterly denounced and hated by the "vested interests" of that time as are the radical parties of the present by the "predatory wealth" of today.

Whoever and whatever disturbs the Established Order in any time or place is always heretical. Hence, the New must always find its expression outside of the Old. Moral sentiments, which develop according to their own laws force new alignments. Fundamental reforms of this era, originally declared unpopular, are based on eternal principle, inspired by high ideals. They are indices of the better day that is to come, even as the feeble and despised efforts of the "Anti-Slavery Society" of 1833 presaged the universal liberty of today, and as the little "Temperance Society" of 1808 was the forerunner of the triumphing movement of the present time.

The most marked feature of political conditions the world over today is seen in the rise of democracy. In republican countries like our own, in limited monarchies like England and Germany, in retrogressive, despotic countries like China, Russia, Persia and Turkey, is witnessed the growth of the spirit of democracy. In our own country more and more the tendency is to get the government back into the hands of the people. Everywhere there is an outcry against the political machine, bossism, graft, centralization and so on. In all countries having popular government, the movement toward the initiative and referendum is growing in strength.

In ancient monarchies constitutions with representative democratic government is demanded.

In other words, one of the most promising signs of the times is the tendency everywhere among all nations and peoples toward realizing the idea of government of the people by the people for the people.

When responsibility for the liquor traffic in any particular community is thrown directly upon the people of that community themselves, they abolish it. No man not personally engaged in the traffic, wants a saloon next door to his residence or place of business. This principle is well illustrated in the success of the local option contests everywhere. Politicians will deal and dicker with and pander to an evil, but the people, when made responsible, abolish it.

Another most encouraging sign of the times, is the increasing openness of mankind everywhere to receive and adopt the true principles of Christianity. Never before were Christian missionaries so welcome and so influential in all parts of the world as they are today. Their influence is gradually—very gradually it may be in many cases—leavening the lump of humanity. Thus the thought of all races is being lifted toward the high ideals of the Man of Nazareth, and these ideals are finding their expression in improved laws and customs of the nations. An illustration of this is set forth in a recent address by Rev. John Howard Melish, rector of the Holy Trinity Church, Brooklyn, who said:

"A Pentecost seems to be taking place in Korea. Forces, no doubt in large part political and commercial, but also supremely religious and educational, are bringing that Eastern nation to a new birth. Men everywhere are inquiring about the 'new religion.' Churches are crowded many times a day. Teachers and preachers cannot meet the need. We seem to be witnessing what has not been seen for centuries, a nation turning Christian.

"What is of great significance in the religious awakening and conversion of Korea, is the kind of Christian religion which is receiving this overwhelming response. If the reports are true, it is a religion with two sides. Those who have received it and who are extending it among their fellow countrymen know only 'The Father' and 'Our Elder Brother.' The names which have been and are to multitudes of us Western Christians of value have no existence to those Eastern followers of Jesus. God and Jesus they know, but 'Christ' and the doctrines of the Trinity, the incarnation, the atonement, are not even names. Their religion is without dogma."

Recognizing the law of reform, the principle of progress, it is safe to say that any declaration of moral truth, any announcement of universal law must finally ultimate in recognition and find formal expression. And so, it is safe to predict that the social ideals portrayed by some of the so-called Socialists, whether Christian or secular, are destined sometime to realization. Especially must this be true as these ideals relate to the liquor traffic. They contemplate the development of a coöperative commonwealth, from which the liquor traffic and all similar evils will be excluded, not by arbitrary exercise of power according to the law of public necessity, but by the presence of the spirit of altruism, and the economic principle of coaction in production and distribution of wealth. The saloon could not exist in a community in which all men live and act in the spirit of Jesus. Nor could it exist in a community where all productive forces coact in creating *economic* goods. If all citizens of the United States were to aim at realization of the Christ-ideal of manhood, and devote their powers to the production of things that make for life, the dram-shop would die. The growth and spread of the propaganda of socialism is rapid, and is making an impress upon the political and the church life of the world today. It offers a radical cure for the liquor evil. The current local option contests illustrate principles of socialism; also, the referendum, in practice.

Another significant phenomenon of the religious world of the present day is seen in the remarkable growth of what is known as the Christian Science movement. Without passing judgment upon the tenets or practices of that organization, it is worthy of mention here from the fact that it proffers a radical cure for the drink habit and the drink traffic. It is a moral force of singular refinement. It does not operate drastically, but none the less effectively it frees the individual life from grossness of thought, speech and action. By the process of realizing the *truth* of existence, all *evil* disappears from the domain of consciousness and conduct, because the identity of the real man with God has been discerned. Saloonkeeping becomes impossible, because personal life is lifted to a plane on which pure, unselfish and refined motives are dominant. To pass from a Sunday service, or from the testimony meeting, or from the reading of "SCIENCE AND HEALTH" to a dram-shop is unthinkable. Existence has become moralized, spiritualized—and the gross elements of it fall away from the spirit which knows its identity with the Universal Principle.

Christian Science does not obtrude itself as an ally of the Anti-Saloon League movement, but, nevertheless, its spirit and its literature are permeating the inner life of the American people. Therefore, in taking account of the real resources of prohibitionism, the Church of Christ, Scientist, must be regarded as one of the gentle, persuasive influences which mean the establishment of a social order in which men will not need prohibitory legislation.

"By their fruits ye shall know them." This recognition is rendered here because investigation shows that drunkards by hundreds and thousands are being restored to manhood, and health, happiness and usefulness by this regenerating agency. A distiller, brewer or saloonkeeper cannot long continue so—and be a Christian Scientist.

NOTE.—*In other chapters of this book are re-published articles from a number of the current weekly and monthly periodicals, which show the very high order of work these agencies are doing for the Great Reform. We reprint here by permission an editorial article from McClure's Magazine of October, 1908, which further illustrates what a great factor the periodical press is becoming in this movement.—G. M. H.*

The great wave of temperance which is now sweeping Europe and America has its chief impulse, no doubt, in ethical and religious sentiment. But a new force is operative—the force of an exact knowledge of the evil physical effects of alcohol.

The story of the modern series of scientific experiments with alcohol, begun about twenty-five years ago and still in progress, is given by Dr. Henry Smith Williams in this number of *McClure's Magazine*. These investigations, largely conducted in Continental Europe, include experiments on the senses, upon the muscles and upon the different human intellectual activities, from the simplest to the most complex. Without exception they show that every function of the normal human body is injured by the use of alcohol—even the moderate use; and that the injury is both serious and permanent.

This knowledge is of concern to all the world. But there is in America a particular and special concern over a condition which may be believed to be unparalleled in human history—certainly in modern civilization: the power of the saloon in American government, especially the government of cities.

The fact is notorious; yet the condition is not clearly understood. Sixty years ago, with the first flood of European immigration, the character of American city governments changed suddenly and entirely. A great proportion of the peasantry who arrived here from the farms of Europe stopped in our cities. They were isolated from the rest of the population; their one great social center was the saloon. And out of this social center came their political leaders and the manipulators of their votes. The European peasant saloonkeeper, for more than half a century, has been the ruler of a great proportion of American cities.

The case of Tammany Hall, for so many years the real governing body of New York, is most familiar. Its politicians for half a century have graduated into public affairs through the common school of the saloon. Its leaders at the present time are perfect examples of the European peasant saloonkeeper type, which has come to govern us. The same condition exists to a large extent in nearly every one of the larger cities in the country. An analysis of the membership of the boards of aldermen in these cities for the past few decades shows a percentage of saloonkeepers with foreign names which is astonishing.

A government necessarily takes the character of those conducting it. The business of saloonkeeping, which produced the present management of our cities, involves, from the conditions which surround it, a disregard for both law and proper moral ideals. Ordinary commercial motives urge the proprietors, as a class, to increase the sale of a commodity which the state everywhere endeavors to restrict; and a savage condition of competition drives them still further—till a great proportion break the provisions of the law in some way; while a considerable number ally themselves with the most degraded and dangerous forms of vice.

The government by this class has been exactly what might have been expected. A body of men—drawn from an ancestry which has never possessed any knowledge or traditions of free government; educated in a business whose financial successes are made through the disregard of law—are elevated to the control of the machinery of law and order in the great cities. Another type of citizen—men of force and enterprise unsurpassed in the history of the world—by adapting the discoveries of the most inventive century of the world to the uses of commerce, have massed together in the past half century a chain of great cities upon the face of a half savage continent, and left them to the government of such people as these. The commercial enterprise of these cities has been the marvel of the world; their government has reached a point of moral degradation and inefficiency scarcely less than Oriental.

The debauching of our city life by this kind of government has been frequently pictured in this magazine. A government by saloonkeepers, and by dealers in flagrant immorality, finds both its power and profit in the establishment of vice by its official position. The progress of such a government is shown in George Kennan's description of the former *régime* in San Francisco, published in *McClure's Magazine* of September, 1907:

"Instead of protecting the public by enforcing the laws, it devoted itself mainly to making money by allowing gamblers, policy-sellers, brothel-keepers and prostitutes to break the laws. Its honest officers and men tried, at first, to do their duty; but the police commissioners, under the influence or direction of Ruef, interfered with their efforts to close illegal and immoral resorts; the police court judges, allowing themselves to be swayed by selfish political considerations, released the prisoners whom they arrested."

Conditions similar to this have been shown in this magazine to exist in New York, Chicago, St. Louis, Pittsburg and other great cities of America. The results have been a general disintegration in the moral fiber of cities. Life itself is much more unsafe than under the well-ordered governments of European cities. The murder rate in Chicago and New York is six or eight times as great as in London and Berlin. Even such a primary necessity of civilization as the safety of women is lost sight of. A leading Chicago newspaper said, in 1906:

"It has ever been our proudest boast as a people that in this country woman is respected and protected as she is in no other. That boast is becoming an empty one in Chicago. Women have not only been annoyed and insulted in great numbers on the street within a very short time, but not a few have been murdered. In the year before the Hollister tragedy, there were seventeen murders of women in Chicago, which attracted the attention of the city."

The system of government which produces this result was well described some years ago by the late Bishop Potter, speaking of conditions in New York:

"A corrupt system," he said, "whose infamous details have been steadily uncovered, to our increasing horror and humiliation, was brazenly ignored by those who were fattening on its spoils, and the world was presented with the astounding spectacle of a great municipality, whose civic mechanism was largely employed in trading in the bodies and souls of the defenseless."

Aside from giving direct encouragement and propagation to the more terrible forms of vice, the European peasant saloonkeeper government of our cities furnishes a fitting field for so-called respectable men—but really criminals of the worst type—who help organize and perpetuate saloon government for the purpose of securing, by bribery, franchises for public utilities without paying therefor. Thus American cities have been robbed as well as badly governed.

There are signs of amelioration of these conditions in most of the great cities of the country. But every advance is made against the fierce antagonism of just such systems as Bishop Potter described; and those systems exist in every large American city today—either in direct control or ready to take control at the slightest sign of relaxation by the forces which are opposing them. And the foundation of this evil structure is the European peasant saloonkeeper.

McClure's Magazine, in the next year, will consider the horrible influence of the saloon on American life. Dr. Williams will follow his article in the present number by studies of the influence of alcohol upon society at large, upon racial development, and upon the state. The author is especially equipped for the work. He is, in the first place, perhaps the greatest living popularizer of national science and history in America; and he has himself made life-long observations upon the influence of alcohol—both physical and social—first as a medical practitioner in the treatment

ANTI-SALOON LEAGUE DAY, LANCASTER, OHIO, CAMP-MEETING, AUGUST 19 1908.

SEABORN WRIGHT,   PURLEY A. BAKER,   WAYNE B. WHEELER,
Attorney and Legislator, Georgia.   Superintendent Anti-Saloon League of America.   Superintendent Anti-Saloon League, Ohio.
ANDREW L. HARRIS,   BISHOP LUTHER B. WILSON,   J. FRANK HANLY,
Governor of Ohio.   President Anti-Saloon League of America.   Governor of Indiana.

of the insane at the great asylums at Bloomingdale and Randall's Island, and later by study and observation in the chief capitals of Europe, where he has lived the greater part of the last ten years. The sound judgment and impartial temper which have characterized his work in other fields will be found in his treatment of this great subject.

THE STORY OF A GROUP PICTURE.

A typical illustration of the magnificent educational work of the Chautauqua Assemblies, is seen in one day's observation and experience by the Editor.

On the 19th of August, 1908, by a coincidence which gives moral and political significance of the most critical character to a place and a day, six men sat for a group picture: Rev. Luther B. Wilson, D. D., LL. D., one of the General Superintendents of the Methodist Episcopal Church, and President of the Anti-Saloon League of America; Honorable Andrew L. Harris, Governor of Ohio; Honorable J. Frank Hanly, Governor of Indiana; Honorable Seaborn Wright, of Georgia, "Father of Prohibition in the South"; Rev. Purley A. Baker, D. D., General Superintendent, and Wayne B. Wheeler, attorney, for the Anti-Saloon League of America.

More than five thousand men and women gathered on that August day on famous old Lancaster (Ohio) Campground, to celebrate "Anti-Saloon League Day," and to inaugurate in the state the local campaigns under provisions of the new County Local Option law. Senator Rose, who presented the original bill which passed the legislature of 1907-1908, and became law by assent of Governor Harris, was present.

The glorious summer day seemed electric with excitement as the crowds filled the immense auditorium and awaited the appearance of Bishop Wilson; electric with applause as the Fairfield County Teachers' Institute entered the assembly and took seats on the platform. Bishop Wilson's address was devoted to definition of "the flag," the flag of the American Union. What does it stand for? For religion, for education, for the home, for industry, he declared in sentences that thrilled with protest against the elevation of the American standard above an institution that stands against religion, against education, against the home, and against all the interests of a normal industrial life. While he spoke, the music of the Cadets' splendid band was heard down the aisles of the wood, and the governors of Ohio and Indiana entered, the audience rising and tendering the Chautauqua salute.

At two o'clock Governor Hanly delivered an address which gripped body, brain and conscience for well-nigh two hours, an address which can never be reported. He vivisected the "personal liberty" claims, the arguments in favor of license, and all other defence of the liquor traffic.

His tribute to Abraham Lincoln was one of those utterances of stalwart loyalty to high ideals of patriotism which deserve record on marble tablet in the halls of fame. And the audience listened while the afternoon sun was dipping into cloud, forgetful of everything but duty in the political crisis rapidly becoming acute in Ohio.

Then the picture was taken. Preceded by the band, the Governor of Ohio went to "Guest Cottage" and met the other gentlemen who had consented to sit. Fittingly, the President of the Anti-Saloon League of America sat in the center of the front row, with Governor Harris on his right and Governor Hanly on his left—and they three represent the harmonies of church and state in the moral activities of the commonwealth. Back of the President of the League stood its General Superintendent, Rev. Purley A. Baker, on his right the Hon. Seaborn Wright, of Georgia, and on his left Wayne B. Wheeler, of Ohio.

In all the country that day, it is to be doubted if six other men met —grouped together—whose work and influence meant more for the welfare of the nation. No one who looked at them as they fronted the camera failed to discern the almost tragic meaning of the scene. For Governor Harris had been marked for defeat by the so-called "Personal Liberty League," and the "German-American Alliance," and all other leagues and alliances in Ohio which despise and defy laws in restraint of the traffic in intoxicating drink. He had done his duty as governor. A General Assembly had enacted a law conferring upon the people of the state the right to vote by counties on the question, Shall the saloon continue to exist? There was no reason why he should refuse to sign the bill—and every good reason why he should sign it. *And he signed it.* And because he signed it, the combined pro-saloon forces arrayed themselves against him. On that August day, he openly identified himself with the work of the Anti-Saloon League, and throughout the state the telegraph bore the tidings to brewer, distiller and saloonkeeper everywhere—and again he was marked for slaughter.

In like manner Governor Hanly had burned his bridges behind him, and risked future political preferment for himself and his party, that he might come out in the open and fight against the greatest enemy of the commonwealth.

In another chapter of this book is told the story of Seaborn Wright, who, putting aside offers of political and official advancement, chose to fight the fight for his beloved Georgia until the hated saloon was driven from her borders.

Wherever the fight against the saloon is fiercest there the names of Purley A. Baker and Wayne B. Wheeler are best known, and they need no further introduction here.

And thus the picture illustrates the federation of the North and the South, the Republican and the Democrat, the statesman and the churchman, for the siege against the saloon.

The evening fell and the lights flashed out along the avenues of the city in the woods. At half past seven Seaborn Wright came upon the platform—a man of gentle soul, one would say, mild and suave. He spoke on the relation of the saloon to the Race Problem in the United States. He spoke, he declared, as "a red-hot Southern Democrat." Hot with hatred of the vicious and abominable traffic, he branded it as the direct cause of all the conflict that had ever arisen between whites and negroes, not only in the South but in the North. He described the condition of the negro under the prohibitive *régime* of the slave period, and that which was produced by the introduction of the saloon at the close of the war for the Union. Then he recited the history of anti-saloon legislation in Georgia, beginning with the "three-mile law," and ending with statutory prohibition. As framer of the first local option law in the country, he described his relation to state prohibition, and the progress of anti-saloonism, from hostility to the doggery at the crossroads up to the dive in the streets of the city.

The saloon being driven from the country, the negro followed it to the city, to meet there the degraded white man and woman. Together they descended into the underground and developed the vicious impulse that gave birth to the Atlanta riots. The real cause of causes, whisky—whisky shipped from Chicago and Cincinnati; whisky in bottles labeled with obscene pictures indescribable. Not content with filling the black bottle with the liquid of death, distillers, high in the life of their cities, made appeal on their labels to the lowest brute-lust of the drinker, careless of the fate either of woman or man. The speaker reached almost a frenzy of horror as he described the "woman victim's scream" in the city streets. He had no word in defense of the mob, but, crazed by liquor and inflamed by thirst for revenge, nothing could curb it but guns. A drunken mob—in Atlanta! A drunken mob—in Springfield!—home of Abraham Lincoln—smiting down not only some vile wretch guilty of crime, but the innocent, the helpless, even the industrious, thrifty negroes in their lowly homes.

Roused to indignation most intense, the South demands protection from the North, demands protection against that government of the Nation which recognizes and shares in the profits of the traffic that the state prohibits, and gathers in its excise despite the will of the commonwealth. The old question of "states' rights"? Has the state any right that the Federal government is bound to respect? Can the republic live, divided on an issue so vital, so big with peril?

The stars shone down on the old campground. Crickets chirped in the fields. Just beyond in the little city there were saloons brilliant with light and filled with men, drinking, gambling.

Was the speaker mistaken when he begged in the name of all that is good and holy, that North and South join in battle against the common enemy, the Saloon, if the Nation should live? The stars shone on through the night. A thousand slept in quiet places of the woods. But in the shadows, the echoes of predicted peril lingered. And, in the wakeful moments, men and women heard again the terrific denunciation of the "red-hot Democrat" from Georgia, the Southern orator stirred to cyclonic eloquence by vision of the dram-shop's crimes against the home, the manhood and womanhood, the childhood of the republic.

Six men sat together for a while under the trees on old Lancaster campground. Before the morning of the next day had come, they had gone out, by various ways, to stern duty and to manifest destiny. They may never meet again, but no hostile destiny shall ever blot out the splendid significance of the little group that they formed—by request of him who edits this story of "THE PASSING OF THE SALOON."

And the words they have spoken and the deeds they have done, shall spread and leaven and ferment, and hasten the day of regeneration for the nation. Such is the splendid work of the Chautauqua.

NOTE.—*Illustrative of the assistance the Socialists are rendering, the following extracts are presented.*—G. M. H.

Dr. Richard Frohlich, in an address on "Drink and Social Misery," said:

"What is the significance of all this for the working-class? There is no doubt, first of all, that the well man is better fitted for every task than the sick man; that the man who has no beer liver, beer kidneys, or beer heart can be used to better advantage in the work of organization and the struggle of the proletariat. Furthermore, there is no doubt that all the forces which keep the standard of living of the working class so low are strengthened by the consumption of alcohol; that poor nourishment is made a graver danger by the resort to alcohol, and that the evils of overwork are increased by it. *Everything that tends to plunge the workingman into misery is encouraged by alcohol—everything that is working to bring him out of his wretchedness is discouraged by alcohol.*

"If we have been right in rejecting the middle-class preaching of temperance because their *dilletante* methods only waste time, money and men, we must also in justice add: That form of alcoholism which is accepted as a matter of course by society also costs time, money and men—and hence it must be combated.

"Everyone of you knows better than I the difficulties which organization meets among those working men who cling stubbornly to their customs of drinking. It cannot be said in these cases that the condition of the class is the cause; for the member of the organization has the same wages at the turning-lathe as the non-member. But if the workman is addicted to drink, and seeks his pleasure in drink, all the arguments of the organized members of the class have little force with him, because he is not in a position to appreciate his situation as a member of the class to which he belongs. The rise in his spirits which is obtained at the expense of a few cents for alcohol prevents such appreciation. The brain, the prime factor in the battle for organization, is affected even by very small quantities of alcohol, and *against the alcoholization of the brain the worker must wage relentless war.*"

Edward Lind, Socialist of Chicago, writes:

"While the international Socialist movement is organized primarily for the purpose of dethroning 'King Capital' by destroying the sources of his power, viz., Rent, Profit and Interest, we should not overlook that great enemy of the people, 'King Alcohol,' whose source of power is the organized liquor traffic.

"The history of the saloon is a gruesome story of crime, misery and woe. And now that a wave of prohibition is sweeping the country, the Socialists should point out that Socialism will dethrone 'King Alcohol' by destroying the saloon as a private institution. By socializing the sale of liquor you destroy the 'incentive' of every saloonkeeper, because there would be no 'profit' and therefore no saloon.

"Prohibition will not abolish *involuntary poverty*. Socialism will not only abolish involuntary poverty but the saloon also.

"We should endeavor to get those indefatigable workers of the Prohibition party into the party that is world-wide in scope and fundamental in its philosophy, untiring in its efforts to organize the world's disinherited; its motto is: '*Workers of the world, unite!*' I refer to the International Socialist Party."

Of the Socialists' scheme our own Frances E. Willard, speaking to her comrades in National Convention in 1897, said:

"Look about you; the products of labor are on every hand; you could not maintain for a moment a well ordered life without them; every object in your room has in it for discerning eyes, the mark of ingenious tools and the pressure of labor's hand. But is it not the cruelest injustice for the wealthy, whose lives are surrounded and embellished by labor's work, to have a superabundance of the money which represents the aggregate of labor in any country, while the laborer himself is kept so steadily at work that he has no time to acquire the education and refinements of life that would make him and his family agreeable companions to the rich and cultured? The reason why I am a Socialist comes in just here.

"I would take, not by force, but by the slow process of lawful acquisition through better legislation as the outcome of a wiser ballot in the hands of men and women, the entire plant that we call civilization, all that has been achieved on this continent in the 400 years since Columbus wended his way hither, and make it the common property of all the people, requiring all to work enough with their hands to give them the finest physical development, but not to become burdensome in any case, and permitting all to share alike the advantages of education and refinement. I believe this to be perfectly practicable, indeed, that any other method is simply a relic of barbarism."

This book treats of the visible reasons, social, industrial, political and economic, why the saloon should perish from the face of the earth. But there are other reasons, individual and social, which may not be discussed in the open page of a book. Physicians, father confessors, heads of asylums for inebriates and the so-called "fallen," city missionaries, rescue workers, deaconesses who stand guard at the city's gates—these know, but cannot tell. Were these reasons known, as they ought to be, the Prohibition tidal wave of 1907-1908 would never recede until it had overwhelmed every dram-shop in the republic. Drunkenness is bad enough, but, deep below drunkenness and the traffic in drink, are evils that prey upon the springs of human life, so foul that they may never be portrayed. Down in the depths, the underground, they grovel. And the saloonkeeper *knows*, and fosters them! For reasons deeper than they ever tell, the temperance and prohibition agitators plead for the ostracism of the saloon! For reasons deeper than they divulge, the "old boys" in the inebriate asylums plead with the new boys *not* to go to the saloon!

This book also treats of the visible agencies enlisted for the overthrow of the saloon and the liquor traffic. It is a vast host, marshaled in divisions and battalions under able leaders, all enlisted for a common purpose. Whether involved in a local option skirmish or a statewide battle, all rally under the same banner, and raise the same battle cry—"Total Abstinence for the Individual, and Total Prohibition for the State!"

But, whether in camp or in the field, on the picket-line or on the march, every soldier, every officer, every company, regiment, or division, under whatever form or name, is drilling and preparing for the early day when the nation-wide engagement shall be on, and the final victory draw near.

As the pages of this book have taken shape, it has been given to us to glimpse the vision of the prophet's servant in the mount. They that be for us are greater than they that be against us. There is a God in Israel. The Moses, the Lincoln, will appear—and, in the fulness of time, the Emancipator shall issue his decree, and—*the saloon shall cease to be.*

CHRONOLOGICAL HISTORY OF THE GREAT REFORM.

This table has been compiled on the basis of authoritative sources, and covers the most important dates in the history of the Temperance, Prohibition, and Anti-Saloon League movements in the United States.

1676—June. The new reform Assembly absolutely prohibits the sale of wines and ardent spirits, if not at Jamestown, Virginia, yet elsewhere through the whole country.

1681—November. The West Jersey Assembly prohibits the sale of ardent spirits to red men.

1685 The Yearly Meeting of Friends for Pennsylvania and New Jersey declares against intemperance.

1763 The English introduce the rum traffic, which the French had prohibited among the Indians along the lakes and the Valley of the Ohio.

1777 The United States Congress recommend the state legislatures to pass laws for the prohibition of distilling grain.

1779—April. The Methodist Conference at Baltimore proposes to disown all persons who engage in the practice of distilling grain into liquor.

1785 Benjamin Rush, M. D., publishes his "Inquiry into the Effects of Ardent Spirits on the Human Body and Mind." This date is the starting point in (American) temperance literature. Dr. Rush (1808) was made an honorary member of Dr. Billy J. Clark's Society at Moreau, N. Y.

1789 Agreement among the farmers in Litchfield County, Conn., to abstain from use of intoxicants during harvest.

1790—December 29. A bill is introduced in Congress taxing distilled liquors.

1790—December 29. The College of Physicians, Philadelphia, memorializes Congress to impose such heavy duties on distilled spirits as shall restrain their intemperate use.

1802 Congress authorizes the President to take steps for the prevention of the liquor traffic among Indians.

1805 The Sober Society formed at Allentown, N. Y.

1808—April 30. The Union Temperance Society of Moreau and Northumberland, N. Y., organized by Billy James Clark, M. D. The first "temperance" society in American history.

1810 Heman Humphrey, of Fairfield, Conn., preaches six sermons on intemperance—believed to be the first ever given on the subject.

1812 The Rev. Mason L. Weems, rector of Alexandria Parish, Va., author of a "Life of Washington," publishes "The Drunkard's Looking Glass."

1812—May. The M. E. General Conference *votes down* the resolution, "That no stationed nor local preacher shall retail spirituous or malt liquors without forfeiting his ministerial character among us."

1812 The first delegated Conference of the Methodist Episcopal Church recommends the Annual Conferences to make a firm and constant stand against dram-drinking, etc., "so common among Methodists."

1812—June. At a meeting of the General Association of Congregational Churches, Sharon, Conn., Lyman Beecher inaugurated a temperance movement, after moving the discharge of a committee which "did not see that anything could be done."

1813 The Massachusetts Society for the Suppression of Intemperance, at Boston.

1825 Lyman Beecher preaches his famous "Six Sermons" at Litchfield, Conn. Repeats at Hanover Street Church, Boston, 1826. "The Proposed Remedy for intemperance—the banishment of ardent spirits from the list of lawful articles of commerce by a correct and efficient public sentiment."

1826—February 13. The American Society for the Promotion of Temperance.

1826—September 1. Total Abstinence Society in the United States organized at Andover, Mass.

1828—First Woman's Christian Temperance Society organized in Ohio.

1828—March 4. *The National Philanthropist,* the first paper ever published to advocate entire abstinence, appears in Boston, Mass., afterwards edited by William Lloyd Garrison.

1829—August 22. Young People's Temperance Society organized at Hector, N. Y.

1831 or 1832. The Board of Health, Washington, D. C., requests the Council to prohibit the sale of intoxicating liquors as a public nuisance during prevalence of cholera.

1832 Wilbur Fisk publishes his "Address to the Members of the Methodist Church" urging Methodists to abandon the traffic in intoxicating liquors.

1832—November 5. General Cass, Secretary of War, prohibited the introduction of spirituous liquors into any camp, fort or garrison of the United States.

1833—February 26. Mass meetings in behalf of temperance held throughout the United States.

1833—February 26. The American Congressional Temperance Society organized. The Hon. Lewis Cass, Secretary of War, President.

1833—May 24-27. First National Temperance Convention meets at Philadelphia. Four hundred delegates from twenty-two States.

1833 The first local option law for the suppression of intemperance is granted by the Georgia Legislature to the inferior courts of Liberty and Camden counties.

1834 Kentucky Legislative Temperance Society organized.

1834—Delavan's Declaration issued. Afterwards signed by twelve Presidents of the United States. Total abstinence.

1834 By vote of Congress and approval of President Jackson, the sale of liquor among Indians is prohibited.

CHRONOLOGICAL HISTORY OF THE GREAT REFORM.

1835—February. The Rev. G. B. Cheever, of Salem, Mass., publishes "Deacon Amos Giles' Distillery: A Dream." Cheever is arrested for libel by a distiller. Defended by Rufus Choate, but punished with fine and imprisonment for thirty days. But public sentiment was aroused, and the distillery closed.

1836—August 4. Second National Temperance Convention in Saratoga, N. Y.

1837 General James Appleton, a member of the Maine legislature, advocates prohibition of the liquor traffic. He is the real "Father of Prohibition."

1838 Rhode Island and New Hampshire leave the license of the liquor traffic optional with the towns.

1839—March 29. Abraham Lincoln appeared as counsel for fifteen women, indicted for smashing a dram-shop—the Carry A. Nations of that day.

1840—April 6. The Washingtonian Temperance Society organized.

1841—June 12. John Henry W. Hawkins signs the pledge and becomes the Major General of the Total Abstinence army or Washingtonian movement.

1842—February 22. Abraham Lincoln delivered a temperance address at Springfield, Illinois, in which he said: ". . . In it (the Temperance Revolution) we shall find stronger bondage broken, a viler slavery manumitted, a greater tyrant deposed; in it more of want supplied, more disease healed, more sorrow assuaged. By it no orphans starving, no widows weeping; by it none wounded in feeling, none injured in interest. Even the dram-maker and dram-seller will have glided into other occupations so gradually as never to have felt the change, and will stand ready to join all others in the universal song of gladness. And what a noble ally this to the cause of political freedom." (A pamphlet containing this address was bought of Mr. Oldroyd, in the room in which Lincoln died, during my visit to Washington, 1892.—G. M. H.)

1842—August 2. The Independent Order of Rechabites founded in New York City.

1842—September 29. The Sons of Temperance organized in New York City.

1842—October 31. John B. Gough signs the pledge.

1843 Oregon passes a prohibitory law.

1843 Cadets of Temperance organized.

1843 Theodore L. Cuyler dedicates himself to the Temperance Reform.

1845—December 5. The Order of the Temple of Honor founded, one of its objects being the ultimate prohibition of the liquor traffic by constitutional law.

1846—August 7. The Democrats enact a prohibitory law against the drink traffic.

1848—May. The M. E. General Conference forbids members buying, selling, or drinking intoxicating beverages.

1849—July 2, to July 23, 1853. Father Mathew tours the United States in behalf of Temperance.

1851 Illinois enacts a nominal prohibitory law.

1851—June 2. The "Maine" law signed by Governor Hubbard.

1851 The Independent Order of Good Templars founded in Central New York.

1851 Michigan adopts a Constitution which forbids the Legislature to enact license laws.

1852 Vermont enacts a prohibitory law.

1853—September 6-10. World's Temperance Convention in New York.

1855 New Hampshire enacts a prohibitory law.

1855 New York enacts a prohibitory law.

1855 Indiana enacts a prohibitory law.

1861—February. John Russell and Bradford McGregor, members of the Good Templars, constitute themselves the nucleus of a Prohibition party.

1862—July 14. Abraham Lincoln signed the law prohibiting the use of spirituous liquors in the navy.

1865 The Fifth National Temperance Convention, first after the close of the War for the Union, held at Saratoga. "Total abstinence for the individual—total prohibition for the State."

1865 National Temperance Society organized.

1866—March 26. The Supreme Court of the United States decides that a federal tax receipt for the retailing of liquors does not operate as a license or right to sell in defiance of state laws.

1868 The Right Worthy Grand Lodge of Good Templars declares for the formation of a political party, pledged to enact and enforce laws against the liquor traffic.

1868—December 9. The first unqualified prohibition party resolution adopted by the State Temperance Convention, Bloomington, Illinois.

1869—April 24. Prohibition party of Ohio organized at Crestline.

1869—September 1. The National Prohibition Party organized, Farwell Hall, Chicago.

1869 Royal Templars of Temperance organized. (Reorganized in 1877 as a beneficiary society.)

1872 At Osborn, Ohio, Mother Stewart organized the first woman's union against the saloon, antedating the W. C. T. U.

1872—February 22. The Catholic Total Abstinence Union of America, formed in Baltimore, Md.

1872—February 22. The first National Prohibition Convention held, Columbus, O.

1872 T. S. Arthur, author "Ten Nights in a Barroom," published "Three Years in a Mantrap."

1872—January 19. The first Reform Club formed at Gardiner, Maine.

1873 Blue Ribbon movement inaugurated by Francis Murphy.

1873—December 23. The Woman's Crusade organized at Hillsboro, Ohio.

1873—December 27. The first surrender of all his stock in trade made by a saloonkeeper "in answer to prayer."

1874—September 10. The Red Ribbon Movement inaugurated by Dr. Henry A. Reynolds.

1874—November 17. The National Woman's Christian Temperance Union founded at Cleveland, Ohio.

1876 The Hon. Henry W. Blair, of New Hampshire, first introduces into Congress a joint resolution, proposing an amendment to the Constitution, prohibiting the traffic in spirituous liquors.

1876—June 12. Woman's International Temperance Congress, Philadelphia.

1876 The Loyal Temperance Legion organized.

1876—June 13-14. International Temperance Congress, Philadelphia.

1877 The Citizens' League of Chicago, for the suppression of the sale of liquor to minors, organized.

1877 The National Prohibition Alliance organized.

1879 Frances E. Willard elected President of the W. C. T. U.

1879 A committee on Alcoholic Liquor Traffic in the Lower House of Congress ordered. Subsequently appointed. The Speaker, however, "packed" the committee with Representatives known to be hostile to action.

1880 Department of Scientific Temperance Instruction in Public Schools. W. C. T. U.

1880—November. Prohibition constitutional amendment adopted in Kansas by a vote of 92,302 for, to 84,304 against.

1881 The Church Temperance Society organized in New York City, to promote temperance, to rescue the intemperate, to remove the causes of intemperance by preaching the Gospel, establishing coffee-houses, improving dwellings for the poor, and circulating wholesome literature.

1881 Nebraska enacts a high license law, under encouragement of radical temperance men and prohibitionists.

1881—May 1. Constitutional amendment prohibiting traffic in intoxicating drink, goes into effect in Kansas.

1882 Vermont legislature enacts a law providing for compulsory scientific temperance instruction in public schools. First state legislature in the Union so to act.

1882—June 27. The people of Iowa voted for constitutional prohibition by a majority of 29,759—155,436 for, 125,677 against.

1883 Anti-license campaign conducted in Ohio. William McKinley declares that the license voter makes himself responsible for all evils that flow from the liquor traffic.

1883—February 22. The Citizens' Law and Order League of the United States organized in Boston, Mass.

1883—June 16. The Templars of Temperance organized in New York.

1884—July 4. Kansas legislature enacts prohibitory law.

1884—July 23. John P. St. John nominated for President on Prohibition ticket.

1884—September. The people of the State of Maine voted for constitutional prohibition—70,783 for, and 23,811 against.

1885—January 1. The National League for the Suppression of the Liquor Traffic, Boston.

1885 The Dominion W. C. T. U. organized in Canada.

1886 Local option adopted in Mississippi.

1886—April 7. The people of the State of Rhode Island voted for constitutional prohibition: 15,113 for and 9,230 against.

1886—May 17. Law for compulsory temperance education in public schools (D. C.) passed by Congress.

1886—May 19. Congress enacts a National Temperance Education law.

1886—May 3. George C. Haddock assassinated by pro-saloon men in Sioux City, Iowa, while engaged in an anti-saloon campaign.

1887 The United States Supreme Court hands down a decision denying the right of compensation to liquor dealers.

1887—May 5. Roderick Dhu Gambrell assassinated by pro-saloonists in Jackson, Mississippi.

1887 Local option law adopted in Florida.

1888—May 30. Clinton B. Fisk nominated President on the Prohibition ticket.

1888—July 9. Senator Blair, of New Hampshire, reported favorably a joint resolution proposing an amendment to the Constitution of the United States, in relation to the manufacture, importation, exportation, transportation, and sale of alcoholic liquors.

1890—November. The Supreme Court of the United States renders decision in the Christensen case: "No inherent right to sell intoxicating liquors by retail."

1890 The non-partisan W. C. T. U. organized.

1890 The Dakotas admitted into the Union as prohibition States.

1890—April 9. Senator Wilson, of Iowa, reports favorably a bill drawn by the National Temperance Society to prevent the importation of intoxicating beverages into prohibitory States.

1893—July 1. The Dispensary System introduced in South Carolina.

1893—June 4. The Anti-Saloon League of Ohio organized at Oberlin, Ohio.

1893—June 5. A World's Temperance Congress held in the "Hall of Columbus," World's Fair, Chicago. Delegates from twenty-two national bodies.

1895—December 18. National organization of the Anti-Saloon League effected, at Washington, D. C.

1898 The American Institute for Social Service, in New York.

1900 Samuel F. Pearson, a Prohibitionist, elected sheriff in Portland, Me. "The saloons closed up business."

1900 National Federation of Churches organized in New York.

1901—February 2. The Anti-Canteen Law passed.

1902—November 23. The Twentieth Century Pledge-Signing Crusade inaugurated.

1905 The Anti-Saloon League in Ohio defeats the Republican candidate for Governor and elects John M. Pattison, a Democrat. Pattison died in office, but Andrew L. Harris, Republican, co-operated with the League and the majority of the Assembly in passing anti-saloon measures.

1905 The Moore remonstrance law passed in Indiana.

1906 Local option law enacted in Kentucky.

1906—June 16. The Christian Social Fellowship organized, Louisville, Ky.

1907 Judge S. R. Artman rendered his decision against constitutionality of license.

1907 The Iowa Anti-Saloon League begins prosecution of law-breaking saloonists in Sioux City.

1907 Municipal and ward local option bill passed by Colorado legislature.

1907 State dispensary in South Carolina abolished.

1907—September 16-19. Tenth Annual Convention of the Anti-Saloon League of America.

1907—September 17. Oklahoma adopted a constitutional amendment providing for prohibition.

1907—October 17. Prohibition goes into effect in Oklahoma.

1907—November 1. Knoxville (Tenn.) placed under prohibitory law.

1907—November 16. President Roosevelt signed proclamation announcing admission of Oklahoma into the Union—without a legalized saloon.

1907—November 19. The Senate of Oklahoma, by a vote of 32 to 2, passed the House bill providing for state prohibition to go into effect December 31, 1908.

1907—November. The Alabama legislature enacted a state-wide prohibition law.

1908 North Carolina goes 40,000 majority in favor of prohibition.

1908—January 1. The Baltimore & Ohio Railroad Company prohibits the use of intoxicants on duty or off duty by employes charged with the direction or operation of trains.

1908—January 1. State-wide prohibitory law adopted by the Georgia legislature.

1908—January 21-22. The Model License League Convention held at Louisville, Ky. The saloon excoriated as a menace to the "Trade."

1908—April. Local option elections in Colorado. Twenty towns banish the saloon, and more than half the residence district of Denver.

1908 Illinois abolishes 900 saloons at the Spring election.

1908—June 2. The International Supreme Lodge of Good Templars met in Washington, D. C.

1908—June 17-18. The National Division of Sons of Temperance of North Carolina held 64th Annual Session in Saratoga, N. Y.

1908—June 14-23. The World's Temperance Centennial Congress in session at Saratoga Springs, N. Y.

1908—July 1. Residence district local option law goes into effect in Wisconsin.

1908—August 18. Eugene W. Chafin receives formal notification of his nomination as President on the National Prohibition platform.

1908—August 19. Anti-Saloon League Day at Lancaster, Ohio. Addresses by Bishop L. B. Wilson, President of the Anti-Saloon League of America; Governor J. Frank Hanly, of Indiana, and Hon. Seaborn Wright, of Georgia. Five thousand persons present. The Rev. P. A. Baker, General Superintendent of the Anti-Saloon League, and Wayne B. Wheeler, Attorney for the League, took part in the program.

1908—September 1. Under provision of the Rose County Local Option Law, the Anti-Saloon League inaugurates petition-signing movement for county elections in Ohio. Elections, begun September 26, result, by November 24, in the suppression of 1,658 saloons in 49 countries. Five counties had previously voted "dry" under the Beall law. Seven counties retain 413 saloons.

1908—September 8. A conference of the National organization of Church Temperance at Little Rock, Arkansas. General Missionary Abbott announces movement to abolish all saloons in the State under provision of the 3-mile law.

1909—January 1. Prohibitory law goes into effect in Alabama.

BIBLIOGRAPHY.

I.

CONGRESSIONAL LIBRARY LIST.

ACROYD, WILLIAM.—The History and Science of Drunkenness. London: Simpkin, Marshall & Co., 128 pp. 8vo.

ADAMSON, WILLIAM C.—Regulation of the Liquor Traffic. Speech in the House of Representatives, January 31, 1908. (*In* Congressional Record, 60th Congress, first session, vol. 42, Jan. 31, 1908, current file, pp. 1446-1447.) Appended is the letter on the subject by Mr. Clayton, of Alabama.

AMERICAN PROHIBITION YEAR BOOK FOR 1907.—Compiled by Alonzo E. Wilson. Chicago: Published by Lincoln Temperance Press, 1907. 96 pp. 12 mo.

AUSTIN, H.—The Liquor Law in the New England States. Boston, 1890. 8vo.

BARKER, JOHN MARSHALL—The Saloon Problem and Social Reform. Boston, Mass.: The Everett Press, 1905. vii, 212 pp. 12 mo.

BILLINGS, JOHN SHAW, *ed.*—Physiological Aspects of the Liquor Problem; Investigations Made by and under the direction of W. O. Atwater, John S. Billings, H. P. Bowditch, R. H. Chittenden and W. H. Welch, sub-committee of the Committee of Fifty to Investigate the Liquor Problem. Boston and New York: Houghton, Mifflin and Company, 1903. 2 vols. 8vo.

BLACK, H. C.—A Treatise on the Laws Regulating the Manufacture and Sale of Intoxicants. St. Paul: West Publishing Co., 1892. 8vo.

CAINE, WILLIAM SPROSTON.—Local Option, by W. S. Caine, William Hoyle and Rev. Dawson Burns. London: S. Sonnenschein & Co., 1885. (4), 132 pp. 12 mo. (The Imperial Parliament, *ed.* by Sydney Buxton, vol. 6.)

CALKINS, RAYMOND—Substitutes for the Saloon: An Investigation Made for the Committee of Fifty, under the direction of F. G. Peabody, E. R. L. Gould and W. M. Sloane. Boston and New York: Houghton, Mifflin and Company, 1901. xvi, (2), 397, (1) pp. Diagrams. 12 mo. Bibliography, pp. 389-391. "South Carolina Dispensary System," pp. 31-33.

COLLINS, BAILIA WILLIAM.—The Restriction of the Liquor Traffic in Relation to the Diminution of Drinking, Drunkenness, and Crime, as Illustrated in the Working of Forbes Mackenzie Act. (*In* National Association for the Promotion of Social Science. Transactions, 1874, pp. 922-931. London: Longmans, Green & Co., 1874. 8vo.

DORCHESTER, DANIEL.—The Liquor Problem in All Ages. New York and San Francisco: Phillips and Hunt, 1888. 8vo.

FANSHAWE, EVELYN LEIGHTON.—Liquor Legislation in the United States and Canada. Report of a Non-partisan Inquiry on the Spot into the Laws and Their Operation, undertaken at the request of W. Rathbone, M. P. London, Paris and Melbourne: Cassell & Co., limited, 1893. viii. 432 pp. 12 mo.

FEHLANDT, AUGUST F.—A Century of Drink Reform in the United States. Cincinnati: Jennings & Graham; New York: Eaton & Mains, 1904. 410 pp. 12 mo.

FERNALD, JAMES C.—The Economics of Prohibition. New York: Funk & Wagnalls, 1890. xvi, (2), 515 pp. 12 mo.

FOCHIER, EMANUEL.—Le système de Gothenbourg et le monopole de l'alcohol en Russie et en Suisse. (*In* Questions pratiques de législation ouvrière et d'économie sociale, vol. 1, June 1900, pp. 200-204; July, 1900, pp. 213-219. Lyon, Paris, 1901. 8vo.

GOULD, ELGIN R. L.—Popular Control of the Liquor Traffic. Baltimore: Friedenwald Co., 1895. 102 pp. 12 mo.

GREAT BRITAIN. *Colonial Office.*—Local Option (colonies). Return to an address of the House of Commons, dated 1 May, 1906. Colonial Office, February, 1907. F. J. S. Hopwood. London: Printed for H. M. Stationery Office, by Eyre & Spottiswoode, 1907. iv, 489 pp. Fol. (Great Britain. Parliament 1907. House of Commons, reports and papers, 47.)

————. *Foreign Office.* Diplomatic and Consular Reports. Miscellaneous series, No. 324, United States. Further report on Liquor Traffic Legislation of the United States since 1889. London: Harrison & Sons, 1894. 82 pp. 8vo. *See also* Miscellaneous series, Nos. 78-154.

————. ————. Diplomatic and Consular Reports. Miscellaneous series, No. 657. United States. Report on Liquor Traffic Legislation of the United States. London: Harrison & Sons, 1907. 111 pp. 8vo.

GUSTAFSON, AXEL.—The Foundation of Death: a Study of the Drink Question. Boston, etc.: Ginn, Heath & Co., 1884. 12 mo.

INDIANA. *Circuit Court (20th Circuit).*—Indiana Circuit Court Decision Relative to Liquor Licenses. Decision in full of Judge Samuel R. Artman, of the Circuit Court of Indiana, concerning the unconstitutionality of liquor licenses. Washington: Government printing office, 1907. 14 pp. 8vo. (U. S. 59th Congress, 2d session. Senate document 284.)

INTERNATIONAL CONGRESS AGAINST THE MISUSE OF STRONG DRINKS.—Proceedings. 1st, Antwerp, 1885. 2d, Zurich, 1887. 3d, Christiana, 1890. 4th, The Hague, 1893.

JOHNSON, J. A.—The Gothenburg System of Regulating Saloons. (*In* League of American municipalities. Proceedings 6th annual convention, 1902. pp. 36-40.) Des Moines, Iowa, 1902. 8vo.

KELYNACK, THEOPHILUS NICHOLAS, *ed.*—The Drink Problem in its Medico-Sociological Aspects, (by four medical authorities). London: Methuen & Co., 1907. viii, 300 pp. Diagrams. 8vo. (The new library of medicine.)

KOREN, JOHN.—Economic Aspects of the Liquor Problem. An investigation made for the Committee of Fifty, under the direction of H. Farnam. Boston and New York: Houghton, Mifflin & Co., 1899. x, (2), 327 pp. 12 mo. Bibliography, pp. 313-322.

MCVEY, FRANK L.—The Martin Mulct Law of Iowa. (*In* Social Economist, vol. 8, March, 1895, pp. 156-163.)

MADDEN, JOHN, *of Milwaukee.*—Shall We Drink Wine? A Physician's Study of the Alcohol Question. Milwaukee: Owen & Weihbrecht Co., 1899. 220 pp. 8vo. "Alcohol as a Factor in the Production of Insanity," pp. 117-127.

MASSACHUSETTS. *Bureau of Statistics of Labor.*—Tenth Annual Report. Boston: Rand, Avery & Co., 1879. 8vo. "Statistics of Drunkenness and Liquor Selling Under Prohibitory and License Legislation, 1874 and 1877," pp. 165-180.

――――. ――――. Eleventh Annual Report. Boston: Rand, Avery & Co., 1880. 8vo. "Statistics of Crime, 1860, 1879," pp. 123-195.

――――. ――――. Twenty-Sixth Annual Report. Boston: Wright & Potter Printing Co., 1896. 8vo. "Relation of the Liquor Traffic to Pauperism, Crime, and Insanity," pp. 1-416.

――――. *General Court.*—House of Representatives. Document No. 192. 1894. Report to the General Court of Massachusetts on the Gothenburg and Norwegian systems of licensing the sale of intoxicating liquors, by John Lowell, H. P. Bowditch and John Graham Brooks. 187 pp. 8vo.

MELLOR, JOHN.—The Local Option Situation in Pennsylvania (with colored maps and diagrams, showing at a glance the position of the movement in 1889 and in 1907; a list of the members of the legislature of 1907 who voted for and against the resolution on the Craven local option bill; together with a copy of the said bill and other pertinent election statistics.) Pittsburgh, Pa.: J. Mellor, c. 1908. 49 pp. Maps. Diagrams. 8vo.

OREGON. *Laws, Statutes, etc.*—Local Option Liquor Law enacted by the People upon Initiative Petition at the General Election held June 7, 1904. Salem, Ore.: J. R. Whitney, state printer, 1905. 12 pp. 8vo.

PATTEN, S. N.—The Economic Basis of Prohibition. (*In* Annals of the American academy of political and social science, vol. 2, July, 1891, pp. 59-68.)

PEABODY, FRANCIS GREENWOOD, *ed.*—The Liquor Problem; a Summary of Investigations conducted by the Committee of Fifty, 1893-1903; prepared for the committee by John S. Billings, Charles W. Eliot, Henry W. Farnam, Jacob L. Greene, and Francis G. Peabody. Boston and New York: Houghton, Mifflin & Co., 1905. ix, 182, (2), pp. 12 mo.

PEASE, EDWARD R.—The Case for Municipal Drink Trade. London: P. S. King & Son, 1904. viii, 166 pp. 12 mo. Bibliographical note, pp. 159-162.

PRATT, EDWIN A.—The Licensed Trade; an Independent Survey. London: J. Murray, 1907. ix, 329 pp. 12 mo.

REID, GEORGE ARCHDALL O'BRIEN.—Alcoholism; a Study in Heredity. London: T. F. Unwin, 1901. xvi, 293 pp. 8vo.

ROWNTREE, JOSEPH.—British "Gothenburg Experiments and Public-house Trusts. 2d ed. London: Hodder & Stoughton, 1901. vi, (2), 176 pp. Plates. 12 mo.

――――. Public Control of the Liquor Traffic, being a Review of the Scandinavian Experiments in the Light of Recent Experience. London: G. Richards, 1903. xxx, 296 pp. 8vo.

――――. The Temperance Problem and Social Reform. 9th ed. London: Hodder & Stoughton, 1901. xxxi, 777 pp. Tables. Plates. Maps. Diagrams. 12 mo.

SITES, CLEMENT MOORE LACEY.—Centralized Administration of Liquor Laws in the American Commonwealths. New York: Published for Columbia University by the Macmillan Company; London: P. S. King & Son, 1899. xii, 13-162 pp.

8vo. (Columbia University, New York. Faculty of Political Science. Studies in history, economics and public law, vol. 10, No. 3.)

SOUTH CAROLINA.—Report of the State Board of Directors of the South Carolina Dispensary, for the fiscal year 1904. (*In* South Carolina. Reports and resolutions of the General Assembly, 1905, vol. 2, pp. 959-974. Columbia, S. C., 1905. 8vo.)

———. Report of Standing Committee of the Senate and House of Representatives on financial transactions of the State Dispensary, 1905. (*In* South Carolina. Reports and resolutions of the General Assembly, 1906, vol. 2, pp. 23-32. Columbia, S. C., 1906. 8vo.)

———. Testimony taken at Spartanburg, Sumter and Columbia by the Committee appointed to investigate the dispensary. (*In* South Carolina. Reports and Resolutions of the General Assembly, 1906, vol. 1, pp. 966-1571. Columbia, S. C., 1906. 8vo.)

STEHR, ALFRED H.—Alkoholgenüss und Wirtsschaftliche Arbeit. Jena: G. Fischer, 1904. xii, 235 [1] pp. 8vo.

STUART, GEORGE RUTLEDGE.—The Saloon Under the Searchlight. New York, Chicago, etc.: F. H. Revell Co., c. 1908. 64 pp. 12 mo.

UNITED STATES. COMMISSIONER OF LABOR.—Fifth Special Report. The Gothenburg System of Liquor Traffic. Prepared under the direction of Carroll D. Wright, by E. R. L. Gould. Washington: Government printing office, 1893. 8vo.

———. ———. Twelfth Annual Report. 1897. Economic Aspects of the Liquor Problem. Washington: Government printing office, 1898. 8vo.

———. Fifty-seventh Congress, 1st session. Senate document No. 435. Editorial clipping from the Press and Banner, Abbeville, S. C., of Wednesday, June 25, 1902, headed "Florida Seeking Light on the Dispensary Law," and describing the effect of the law in South Carolina. June 27, 1902. 3 pp. 8vo.

VANCE, JOSEPH ANDERSON.—American Problems. Chicago: The Winona Publishing Co., 1904. 252. pp. 12 mo. "The Liquor Problem," pp. 121-167.

WADLIN, HORACE G.—Relation of the Liquor Traffic to Pauperism, Crime and Insanity. Boston: Wright & Potter Printing Co., 1896. vii, 416 pp. 8vo.

WALDRON, GEORGE BURNSIDE.—The Prohibition Handbook, with numerous tables and diagrams. New York, London and Toronto: Funk & Wagnalls Co., 1896. 158 pp. Illustrations. 16 mo.

WARNER, HARRY S.—Social Welfare.

WHEELER, EDWARD J.—Prohibition: the Principle, the Policy and the Party. New York: John R. Anderson Co., 1889. (2), ii, 227 pp. 12 mo.

WINES, FREDERIC HOWARD.—The Liquor Problem in its Legislative Aspects, by Frederic H. Wines and John Koren. An investigation made under the direction of C. W. Eliot, S. Low, and J. C. Carter. 2d. ed. Boston and New York: Houghton, Mifflin & Co., 1898. viii, (2), 425 pp. 12 mo.

WISCONSIN.—Bureau of Labor and Industrial Statistics. The Liquor Traffic in the United States and in Wisconsin. (*In its* Twelfth Biennial Report, 1905-1906. pp. 149-266. Madison, 1906. 8vo.)

WITTENMEYER, ANNIE.—History of the Woman's Temperance Crusade. Boston: James H. Earle, 1884. 805 pp. 8vo.

II.

ADDITIONAL LIST.

ARTMAN, SAMUEL R.—The Legalized Outlaw. Indianapolis, Ind.: Press of Levy Bros. & Co. 1908.

BANKS, LOUIS ALBERT.—The Lincoln Legion.

BEAUMONT, T.—The Nature, Uses, and Effects of Ardent Spirits. London: 1831.

BLACK.—"Intoxicating Liquors," secs. 25-26, 31, 37, 39-43, 82-83.

BLAIR, HON. H. W.—The Temperance Movement.

BLISS.—The New Encyclopedia of Social Reform. Funk & Wagnalls Co. 1908.

BURNS, DAWSON; CAINE, WM. S., and HOYLE, WM.—Liquor Laws, 3d Edition, 136 pp. 12 mo. London: Imperial Parliament: 1896.

CHAPMAN, D. D., LL.D., E. S.—A Stainless Flag. Chicago: 162 Ohio St., Anti-Saloon League.

CHERRINGTON, E. H.—Anti-Saloon Year Book, 1908. Chicago: Cor. LaSalle Ave. and Ohio St., American Anti-Saloon Press Bureau.

CLUBB, HENRY S.—The Maine Liquor Law: Its Origin, History and Results, including the Life of Neal Dow. 12 mo. New York: 1856.

CRAFTS, WILBUR F., PH. D., and MRS. CRAFTS.—Intoxicants and Opium in All Lands and Times. International Reform Bureau: Washington, D. C.

CROTHERS, DR. T. D.—The Relations of the Doctor to the Alcoholic Problem. Published by the author, Hartford, Conn. The Insanity of Inebriety. The Alcoholic Problem in Europe. The Clinical Study of Inebriety.

CUMMING, A. N.—Public House Reform, an Explanation with an Appendix. London, 1901.

CUTTEN, DR. GEORGE B.—Psychology of Alcoholism. Charles Scribner's Sons, New York.

DEWAR, DAVID.—The Liquor Laws for Scotland. Edinburgh: 1884.

DEWITT, E. L.—The Dow Liquor Tax. Ohio State Reports, N. S., Vol. XXXVIII., pp. 199-242. The State vs. Hipp.

EDDY, RICHARD.—Alcohol in History: An Account of Intemperance in All Ages. New York: 1887.

EVERT, REV. J. G.—The Bible and Total Abstinence. The Germans and Temperance. The Principles, Aims, and Results of Prohibition (In German). Hillsboro, Kansas.

FINCH, JOHN B.—The People vs. The Liquor Traffic. New York: 1887.

FOREL, PROF. AUGUST.—Hygiene of Nerves in Health and Disease. G. P. Putnam & Sons, New York.

GEORGE, DR. GEORGE N.—The Seven Deadly Sins of Civilization.

GEORGE, J. E.—The Saloon Question in Chicago. New York: 1897.

HAMMELL, GEORGE M.—The Passing of the Saloon. Cincinnati: The Tower Press, 1908. Illustrated. 600 pp. 8vo.

HARGREAVES, WM., D. D.—Worse than Wasted.

HAWEIS, H. R.—Drunkenness (In "Current Coin"). 1883.

HEATH, A. R., and WILSON, HON. A. E.—American Prohibition Year Book, 1908. Chicago: 92 LaSalle St., Lincoln Temperance Press.

HOPKINS, PROF. A. A.—Wealth and Waste.

HORSELEY and STURGE.—Alcohol and the Human Body. 23 Trull St., Boston, Mass.

HOYLE, WM.—Our National Resources and How They Are Wasted. London: 1871.

HUNT, DR. REID.—Studies in Experimental Alcoholism.—Bulletin No. 33. Hygienic Laboratory of the Public Health and Marine Hospital Service of the United States. (Not for sale. Apply to Surgeon-General, Washington, D. C.)

ILES, GEORGE.—The Liquor Question in Politics. New York: 1889.

IRELAND, JOHN.—Intemperance and Law. Buffalo: 1884.

JAMES, W.—Wine Duties, Considered Financially and Socially; Being a reply to Sir James E. Tennent. London: 1855.

JEROME, WM. TRAVERS.—The Liquor Tax Law in New York—A Plea for the Opening of Saloons on Sunday. New York and London: G. P. Putnam's Sons, 1905.

JOYCE, C. H. The Alcoholic Liquor Traffic. New York: 1880.

JUTKINS, A.—Hand-book of Prohibition. Chicago: 1884.

LEAVITT, THOS. H.—Liquor Legislation. Lincoln, Neb.: 1885.

LECKY, W. E. H.—Democracy and Liberty. 1896.

LEES, F. R.—The Temperance Bible Commentary.

————. Text Book of Temperance.

LEVI, LEONE.—Consumption of Spirits, Beer and Wine, and Its Relation to Licenses, Drunkenness, and Crimes; A Report. London: 1872.

————. The Liquor Trades; A Report on the Capital Invested and the Number of Persons Employed. London: 1871.

LEWIS, DAVID.—The Drink Traffic in the Nineteenth Century; Its Growth and Influence. London: 1885.

LEWIS, DIO.—Prohibition a Failure: or the True Solution of the Temperance Question. Boston: 1875.

LILLY.—"The Saloon Before the Courts," 12-17, 30-31.

MCCARTHY, JUSTIN.—Prohibitory Legislation in the United States. London: 1872.

MCDOUGALL, T., WALDEN, J. M., REDKEY, M.—The Liquor Question in the Ohio Campaign of 1883: The Scott law and its principles vs. the second or prohibition amendment. The discussion as carried on in the columns of the Cincinnati Commercial Gazette, with a supplement in reference to prohibition in Maine.

MCKENZIE, FRED. A.—Sober by Act of Parliament. London: 1896.

MITCHELL, KATE.—The Drink Question. London: 1890.

MOREWOOD, SAMUEL.—A Philosophical and Statistical History of the Inventions and Customs of Modern Nations in the Manufacture and Use of Inebriating Liquors. Dublin: 1838.

OKEY, G. W.—The Dow Liquor Tax. Ohio State Reports, N. S., Vol. XLIV., pp. 539-576—Adler vs. Whitbeck.

PATTON, D. D., WM.—Bible Wines: or the Laws of Fermentation and the Wines of the Ancients.

PITMAN, R. C.—Alcohol and the State; A Discussion of the Problem of the Law Applied to the Liquor Traffic. New York: 1877.

ROWNTREE & SHERWELL.—The Taxation of the Liquor Trade. Macmillan & Co. 1906.

———. The Temperance Problem and Social Reform.

RUSSELL, JOHN.—Is a Prohibition Party a Feasible and Reliable Agency for Securing the Enactment and Execution of Prohibitory Laws?

SHADWELL, ARTHUR.—Drink, Temperance and Legislation. London: Longmans, Green & Co.: 1902.

SHEEN, J. R.—Wine and Other Fermented Liquors, from the Earliest Ages. London: 1864.

SMITH, GOLDWIN.—Prohibition in Canada and the United States. (In "Essays on Questions of the Day"): 1893.

SPENCER.—"The License Question," in Stephens' "Prohibition in Kansas."

STARKE, DR. J., Translated from the German.—Alcohol—The Sanction for Its Use Scientifically Established and Popularly Expounded by a Physiologist. New York and London: G. P. Putnam's Sons. 1907.

STEARNS, J. N., Edited by.—Temperance in All Nations. The National Temperance Society and Publication House: 1017 pp. 2 Vols.

STEBBINS, J. E.—Fifty Years' History of the Temperance Cause. Hartford, Conn: 1874.

STELZLE, CHARLES.—The Workingmen and the Saloon. Chapter III., "The Workingmen and Social Problems."

TENNENT, SIR. J. E.—Wine: Its Use and Taxation. London: 1855.

THOMANN, GALLUS.—Liquor Laws of the United States: Their Spirit and Effect.

———. The System of High Licenses: How It Can Be Made Successful. New York: 1885.

———. Colonial Liquor Laws. Part II of Liquor Laws of the United States; Their Spirit and Effect.

———. Real and Imaginary Effects of Intemperance. A statistical sketch. New York: 1884.

———. Inebriety and Crimes. New York: 1889.

WALKER, JOHN.—The Commonwealth as Publican: An Examination of the Gothenburg System. Westminster: A. Constable & Co. 1902.

WARNER, HARRY S.—Social Welfare and the Liquor Problem. 250 pp.; cl. 75; paper 35. The Intercollegiate Prohibition Association. 151 Washington St., Chicago.

WEEDEN, W. B.—The Morality of Prohibitory Liquor Laws. Boston: 1875.

WELLS, D. A.—Our Experience in Taxing Distilled Spirits. (*In* "Practical Economics.") 1885.

WILLARD, FRANCES E.—Glimpses of Fifty Years—Autobiography of Frances E. Willard. Chicago: H. J. Smith & Co.

WOOLLEY, JOHN G., and W. E. JOHNSON.—Temperance Progress in the Nineteenth Century. Hyde Park, Chicago: The New Voice Company. (For all publications of The New Voice Company, address John G. Woolley, 5535 Cornell Ave., Hyde Park, Chicago.)

MISCELLANEOUS.—Citizens' Law and Order League of the United States. Proceedings of the National Convention. 1883.

―――――. Congrès international pour l'étude des Questions relative á l'alcoholisme. 1879-1880.

―――――. "Mida's Digest of State Liquor Laws and Court Decisions." Published by the Criterion Publishing Company, Chicago, Ill. Price. $6.00.

―――――. National Retail Liquor Dealers' Convention of the U. S. A., 12th Annual Convention. 1893.

―――――. One Hundred Years of Temperance. Proceedings of Centennial Temperance Conference. Philadelphia: 1885.

―――――. Public Control of the Liquor Traffic. New York: The Macmillan Co.

―――――. State Prohibition and Local Option.

―――――. The Prohibitionists' Year Book. New York: 1880.

III.

ARTICLES IN PERIODICALS.

1895.—President Roosevelt and the Liquor Traffic. McClure's Magazine: 1895.

1901.—Liquor Habit in Russia. The Outlook: New York, July 13, 1901.

1903.—Fight Against Alcoholism Abroad. Review of Reviews. December, 1903.

1903.—Government Control of the Liquor Traffic. Slaymaker. New Voice, August 13, 1903. Same: Central Law Journal, June 5, 1903.

1904.—The Liquor Problem. John Brisben Walker. Cosmopolitan, vol. 37 (Oct., 1904): with advertising matter.

1905.—Collapse of the Subway Tavern. National Temperance Advocate, October, 1905.

1905.—The Temperance Problem and the Subway Tavern. International Magazine, January, 1905.

1905.—Public Control of the Liquor Traffic in Sweden and Norway. M. Alger. Arena, vol. 33 (Feb., 1905): 134-142.

1906.—Summary of Temperance Laws.—American Issue, January 30, 1906.

1906.—The Norwegian System of Liquor Control. James Seth. Contemporary Review, vol. 90 (Dec., 1906): 861-872.

1907.—The City of Chicago. Turner. McClure's, April, 1907.

1907.—The Rising Tide of Temperance. Charles Frederick Carter. Harper's Weekly, vol. 51 (Dec. 7, 1907): 1790-1791.

1907.—A New Plan for State Control of the Liquor Business. Justus Newton Brown. Bibliotheca Sacra, vol. 64 (Oct., 1907): 693-712.

1907.—Notes on Current Legislation: Liquor Legislation. John A. Lapp. American Political Science Review, vol. 2 (Nov., 1907): 62-64.

1907.—The Battle of the Bottle: The South's winning fight for prohibition. Harris Dickson. Saturday Evening Post, vol. 180 (Oct. 26, Nov. 9, 23, Dec. 28, 1907, Jan. 25, 1908): 3-5, 35: 11-13. 22; 15-17, 44; 15-17, 29; 18-22.

1908.—The March of Temperance. Pere G. Wallmo. The Arena, October, 1908.

1908.—Does Prohibition Pay? Rev. C. F. Aked. Appleton's Magazine, July, 1908.

1908.—Prohibition's Failures. Literary Digest, vol. 36 (Mar. 21, 1908): 397-398.

1908.—The South and the Saloon. W. G. Brown. Century Magazine, July, 1908.

1908.—Foreign Anti-Liquor Movements. Nation, vol. 86 (Mar. 12, 1908): 230-231.

1908.—Does Prohibition Pay? George C. Lawrence. Appleton's Magazine, July, 1908.

1908.—The Geography of our Liquor Laws. World's Work, vol. 15 (Feb., 1908): 9842-9844.

1908.—The Government and Temperance Reform. Albany Review, vol. 3 (Apr., 1908): 11-22.

1908.—The Temperance Tidal Wave. Rev. Sam'l J. Barrows. The Outlook (N. Y.), July 4, 11, 1908.

1908.—Temperance in America. W. C. Jenkins. National Magazine, vol. 37 (Feb., 1908): 574-581.

1908.—Prohibition and the Negro. Booker T. Washington. Outlook, vol. 88 (Mar. 14, 1908): 587-589.

1908.—Prohibition in the South. Frank Foxcroft. Atlantic Monthly, vol. 101 (May, 1908): 627-634.

1908.—Prohibition and Social Psychology. Prof. Hugo Munsterberg. McClure's Magazine, August, 1908.

1908.—Alcohol and the Individual. Henry Smith Williams, M. D., LL. D. McClure's Magazine, October, 1908.

1908.—Scientific Temperance Federation. The School Physiology Journal (Monthly), 23 Trull St., Boston, Mass.

1908.—Environment and Drink. North American Review, Vol. 161, 460.

1908.—Liquor and Labor. Smith. Catholic World, 47, 539.

1908.—Shall Prohibition Laws be Abolished. Crothers. Popular Science Monthly, 45, 232.

1908.—Temperance Special. Fourth Edition. The Christian Socialist. Chicago: The Co-operative Printing Co., 5623 Drexel Avenue.

1908.—Ethics of Prohibition. Fraser. International Journal Ethics, 9, 350-359.

1908.—Temperance or Prohibition. Gustave Pabst. Cosmopolitan Magazine, vol. 44 (Apr., 1908): 558-560.

1908.—The Fight Against Alcohol. Arthur Brisbane. Cosmopolitan Magazine, vol. 44 (Apr., 1908): 492-496.

1908.—Why I am a Total Abstainer. Alexander Alison. Cosmopolitan Magazine, vol. 44 (Apr., 1908): 554-558.

1908.—Does Prohibition Pay? The Test of a State that has Persisted. Holman Day. Appleton's Magazine, August, 1908.

1908.—Sixty Years Futile Battle of Legislation with Drink. Philip Rappaport. Arena, vol. 39 (Mar., 1908): 315-318.

1908.—The Moral Dignity of Prohibition in the South. John E. White. Southern Workman, vol. 37 (Mar., 1908): 174-180.

1908.—The New York Saloon. Arthur Huntington Gleason. Collier's, vol. 41 (Apr. 25, May 2, 1908) : 16-17, 31; 12-13, 27-28.

1908.—The Nation's Anti-drink Crusade. Ferdinand Cowle Iglehart. **American Review of Reviews**, vol. 37 (Apr., 1908) : 468-476.

1908.—Local Option and State Prohibition in the South. A. J. McKelway. **Charities and the Commons**, vol. 19 (Jan. 25, 1908) : 1452-1453.

1908.—Prohibition: the New Task and Opportunity of the South. John E. White. South Atlantic Quarterly, vol. 7 (Apr., 1908) : 130-142.

1908.—The History of Liquor Legislation in Iowa. 1846-1861. Dan Elbert Clark. Iowa Journal of History and Politics, vol. 6 (Jan., 1908) : 55-87.

1908.—The Fight Against Alcohol. World-wide Significance of the Movement. Arthur Brisbane. Cosmopolitan Magazine, vol. 44 (May, 1908) : 549-554.

1908.—The Fight Against Alcohol. Georgia Pioneers and the Prohibition Crusade. John Temple Graves. Cosmopolitan Magazine, vol. 45 (June, 1908) : 93-90.

1908.—The Law of the White Circle. A Story of the Atlanta Riot. A Study of the Race Problem and the Saloon Problem. The **Taylor-Trotwood Magazine**, June-August, 1908, Nashville, Tenn.

INDEX.

A.

Abbey, G. N., 164
Abel, John J., 54, 60
Abolition Society, The, XVIII
Abbott, Dr. A. C., 64
Abbott, Dr. Lyman, 42
Absinthe, 200, 202, 203
Abstinence Union, The Catholic Total, 141
Ach, Professor, 56
Acheson Bill, The, 366
Advocate, St. Louis Christian, 8
Afro-American, The, 345, 346
Ainu, The, 39
Airedale, Lord, 214
Alabama, 211, 212, 231, 235, 236, 265, 344
Alaska, 266, 267
Alber, John G., 177
Alberta, 379, 387, 388
Alcohol, 53, 54, 60, 61, 62, 208, 210, 400, 402, 406
Alcohol and Cancer, 66
Alcohol and Epilepsy, 66
Alcohol and Heredity, 66
"Alcohol and Hygiene," Richardson's, 134
Alcohol and Pneumonia, 65
Alcohol and Tuberculosis, 65
Alcoholic degeneration, 62
Alcoholic insanity, 60
Alcoholism, 65, 68, 197, 199, 201, 202, 208
Alliance for the Suppression of the Liquor Traffic, The Dominion, 381, 383
Alliance vs. Joyce, 101
Altgeld, Governor, 20
Amendment, The Fourteenth, 88
Anti-Alcoholic Congress, The International, 201
Anti-Canteen Law, The, 136
Anti-Saloon League of America, The, 33, 42, 43, 185, 186, 190, 207, 208, 211, 215, 216, 218, 220, 221, 222, 224, 233, 234, 266, 274, 275, 287, 295, 393, 403
Anti-Saloon League of America, The Colored, 348
Anti-Slavery Party, The, XVIII
Anti-Slavery Society, The, 397
Arizona, 267
Arkansas, 217, 235, 241, 243, 267
Artman, Judge Samuel R., 81, 98, 99

Aschaffenburg, Prof. Dr., 58, 59, 138
Asquith, The Hon. H. H., 198, 199
Atherton, John M., 357
Atkinson, W. T., 310
Atlanta, 260, 342, 343, 344 . . . Riot, 209, 210, 211, 216, 238
Ayres, Arthur H., 176

B.

Baily, Joshua L., 3
Bain, George W., 3, 121
Baker, Rev. Purley A., D. D., 194, 275, 403, 404
Balfour, Hon. A. J., 197
Ball, Rev. G. H., 164
Banks, Rev. Louis Albert, D. D., 8, 186
Baptist Church, The (Canada), 389
"Bar and Buffet, The," 276
Barker, Rev. John Marshall, D. D., 138
Barrows, Rev. Samuel J., D. D., 196, 205
Baudron, Dr., 65
Bayer, Prof. Dr., 59
Beal Local Option Law, 102
Beall, Dr. J. W., 127, 151
Beauchamp, Mrs. Frances E., 341
Beebe vs. State (Indiana) 95, 302
Beecher, Henry Ward, 3, 219
Beecher, Lyman, 219
Beer, The Nature of, 77
Bender, C. Edward, 176
Benedict, Roswell A., 3
Bennett, Rev. Albert Arnold, 38
Berkeley, Prof. Dr., 62
Berkley, Prof. H. J., 138
Beveridge, Senator Albert J., 160
Bidwell, General John, 167, 266
Bidwell Presidential Vote, 264
Billups, H. L., 349
Billups Law, The, 214
Birmingham, (Ala.), 212, 237, 342, 343, 344, 345
Bishop's Criminal Law, 321
"Black Hand," The, 234
Black, James, 163, 164, 167, 170
Black Presidential Vote, 264
Blair, Hon. Henry W., 155
Blakesley, Raphael H., 177
"Blind Tigers," 277

INDEX.

Bodwell, Mrs. E. C., 243
"Bonfort's Wine and Spirit Circular," 14, 215
Booth, General William, 8
Bourneville, Dr., 66
Bowman, Ebenezer, 164
Boyd, D. C., 177
Boyd, James C., 177
Bradley, Justice, 96
Brand, Rev. James, 190
Bray, Aaron M., 259
Breweries, 225
Brewers' Association, U. S., 233
Brewers' Congress, National, 163
Brewers' Convention, U. S., 357, 358
British Colonies, 203
British Columbia, 379
Brokaw, C. L., 311
Brooks, Bishop Phillips, 8
Brooks High License Law, 29
Brooks, Rev. John A., D. D., 167
Brotherhood, Universal, XIV
Brouardel, Dr., 65
Broward, Gov. N. B., 270
Brown, Mrs. Henrietta, 246
Brown, John, 326
Brown, L. C., 178
Brown, Mrs. M. McClellan, Ph. D., 139
Brown, Van Wert, vs., 101
Broyle, Judge, 211
Bruchesi, Archbishop, 387
Brumbaugh, Martin G., 138
Brunswick, New, 203, 379, 381, 382, 386
Brussells Act, The, 36
Bryan, William J., 26
Bryce, James, 162
Buchtel, Gov. Henry A., 10
Buckley, Rev. James M., D. D., 8
Buddhist Temperance Society, 39
Bull, R. C., 164
Bullitt, Marshall, 2
Burke, Gov. John, 287
Burnham, D. K., 176
Burns, John, 208, 214
Burwell, George P., 164
Butchers' Union Slaughter-House Co. vs. Crescent City Live Stock Lndg. Co., 96
Butler, Amos W., 13
Butler, Judge, 14
Buxton, Charles, 14

C

Calderwood, W. G., 261
California, 51, 248, 266
Calmette's Laboratory, 64
Campbell-Bannerman, Sir Henry, 198
Campbell, Governor T. M., 296
Canada, Dominion of, 203, 379, 380, 381
Canada, First temperance society in, 380

Canada Temperance Act, The, 382
Canada's Drink Bill, 389
Canadian Presbyterian Mission, 38
Cancer, Alcohol and, 66
Canevin, Rt. Rev. J. F. R., 142
Canfield, A. N., 192
"Canteen," The, 367
Canterbury, The Archbishop of, 199
"Capital Sins," 21, 22
Carmack, Edward Ward, 3, 128
Carnegie, Andrew, 3
Carroll, George W., 168
Carson League, The, 112
Carson, Thomas L., 112
Catholic Total Abstinence Union, 141, 207, 269
Cavett Law, The, 125
Centralization by Construction, 377
Chafin, Eugene W., 24, 28, 168, 254, 255
Chalmers, Rev. James, 38
Chamberlain, Joseph, 3, 36
Chapman, Rev. Ervin S., 452, 266
Chautauqua Assemblies, 273, 403, 396, 397
Chelsea, 25
Chesterfield, Lord, 4
Chicago, 20, 21, 22, 25, 47, 218, 402
China, Emperor of, 13
Chown, Rev. Dr. S. D., 383
Christensen, Crowley, vs., 93, 361
Christian Church, The, 31
Christian Endeavor, 383
Christian Endeavorers, 275
Christian, Judge Ira W., 101
Christian Missions and Social Progress, 33
Christian Science, 399
Church, The Established, 199
Church, The Federated, 393
Church, The Free, 199
Church, The Russian, 201
Church Temperance Association, 267
Cincinnati, 15
Cincinnati Chamber of Commerce Report, 47, 48
Civil Law and Moral Law, One, 100
Civil War, The, XIX
Claflin, Mrs. Mamie M., 243
Clark, Sir Andrew, 4
Clark, Billy James, M. D., 218
Clark, Francis E., 138
Cleveland, President, 20
Club, The Poor Man's, 78
Cobb, Charles N., 177
Cobb, Governor William T., 276
Cobden, Richard, 10
Cobleigh, Rev. N. E., D. D., 164
Codding, J. K., 300
Coffin, John P., 258
Coffin, S. J., 164

INDEX.

Colorado, 268
Colored Anti-Saloon League of America, The, 348
Colvin, D. Leigh, 172, 178
Comer, Governor Braxton B., 10
Commerce, Interstate, Laws, 225
"Commoner, The," 27
Commonwealth, (Kentucky) vs. Douglas, 99
Compensation, 87, 198, 199
Conaty, Rev. Dr. T. J., 142
Congress and the Liquor Traffic, 369
Congress of the United States, 365, 376
Congress, The Continental, XVII
Congress, World's Temperance, 131
Connecticut, 268
Constitution, The Federal, 29
Contract, License, Not a, 85
Cooper, R. M., 260
Court, The Supreme, of the United States 80, 359, 360
Courts, Findings of, 80, 81, 359, 360
Cowan, Prof. Dr., 62
Cox, Judge D. R., 127, 151
Craig Colony for Epileptics, 66
Cranfill, Rev. Dr. J. B., 167, 234
Cregier, People ex rel. Morrison vs., 84
Crime, Liquor Traffic and, 95
Critchlow, W. E., 178
Cross, League of the, 383
Crothers, T. D., M. D., 65, 138, 139
Crotty, People vs. Village of, 87
Crowley vs. Christensen, 93, 361
Crusade, The Woman's, 28, 205, 219, 285, 287
Cuddy, Warren N., 177
Cullom, Senator Shelby M., 160
Cummings, John W., 131
Currah, Mrs. W. E., 244
Cushing, H. D., 164
Cuyler, Theodore L., 108, 136

D

Daniel, William, 167
Dante, XIV
Davis, Rev. Elnathan, 164
Davis, Jefferson, 294
Dawson, Gov. William M. O., 10, 298
Dayton, Judge Alton G., 13
Deems, Rev. Charles F., D. D., 162
Delavan, Edward Cornelius, 111
Delavan's Declaration, 111
Delaware, 217, 218, 260, 269
Delirium Tremens, 60
Demaree, T. B., 260
Dennis, Rev. James S., D. D., 33
Dickie, Samuel, 162, 170, 178
Dickinson's Lectures, Dr. Baillie, 65
Dickson, Judge Harris, 235

Dietl, Prof. Dr., 55
Dinwiddie, Rev., E. C., 194
Dispensary, 211, 212, 217, 236, 291, 292
Distilleries, 225
District of Columbia, 269
Doane, Rev. E. T., 37
Dominion Alliance for the Suppression of the Liquor Traffic, 381, 383
Dominion of Canada, 381, 387, 388
Dominion Parliment, The, 380, 384, 386
Dougall, John, 382
Dow, Neal, 4, 113, 164, 167, 219, 381
Dow Presidential Vote, 264
Dow-Aiken Law, 97, 101, 102
Dowdall, A. S., 178
Downs, O. P., 164
Dramshop Act, 84
Drink and Social Misery, 406
Drink Bill, Canada's, 390
Drink Bill, United States', 197
Drink Trust, The, 227
Drunken Period, The, 218
Drunkenness, 95, 197, 210
Dunham, Mrs. Marion H., 244
Dunn, Rev. James B., D. D., 164
Dupertuis, Daniel, 177
Durien vs. State (Kansas), 95
Durkee, Rev. J. H., D. D., 262

E

Economic goods, 49
Economics, 48
Edwards, Justin, 106
Edwards, Walter N., 138
Eldredge, Nelson B., 177
Ellis, Ford E., 177
Ellis, Mrs. Margaret Dye, 341
Emerson, Ralph Waldo, 182
England, XIII
England, Church of, Temperance Society, 383
Ensign, Miss Frances H., 245
Epilepsy, Alcohol and, 66
Ewin, James L., 192
Exner, Prof. Dr., 55
Expenditure for Liquors, 197

F

Farmer, Raymond C., 177
Farris, Hon. Frank H., 2, 28
Farwell Hall, 165
Federal Rights, States' Rights vs., 368
Federal Tax Receipts, 369, 372
Federated Church, The, 393
Fehlandt, August, 97
Fessenden, Mrs. S. S., 138, 244
Field, Justice, 81, 93, 96, 360
Filipinos, 41

Finch, John Bird, 119, 170
Findings of Courts, 80, 81
Findley, G. B., 176
Finland, XIII, 201
Fisk, Clinton B., 167
Fisk Presidential Vote, 264
"Flag, The Stainless," 266
Florida, 235, 240, 269
Flournoy, Josiah, 110
Foljambe, Samuel, 164
Folk, Dr. Edward E., 213
Folk, Governor Joseph W., 10, 279, 280
Forbus, J. F., 164
Formosa, Island of, 38
Foss, Bishop Cyrus D., 9
Foster, Festus, 315
Fourteenth Amendment, 88
Foust, R. M., 164
Fox, George, 397
Fox, Hugh, 225
Fraizer, Samuel, 107
Frame, State vs., (Ohio) 96
France, XIII, 202
Franklin, Benjamin, XVII
Fredericton, City of, 382
Fries, William H., 164
Frohlich, Dr. Richard, 406
Fry, Mrs. Susanna M. D., 151
Fürer, Prof. Dr., 57

G

Gabe, George, 164
Gage, D. W., 164
Gambrell, Roderick Dhu, 123, 151
Garrison, William Lloyd, 397
Gaudet, Mrs. F. A. J., 351
Gauld, Rev. W., 38
George, Mrs. Ella M., 246
Georgia, 205, 209, 211, 231, 237, 259, 270
Gerhardt, State vs., 85
Germany, XIII, 202
Gifford, Mrs. S. A., 244
Gilbert Islands, 37
Gill, Harley H., 178
Gilmore, Col. T. M., 1, 185
Gittins, Miss Mary, 177
Gladstone, William E., 4, 208
Glasscock, Dr. S. S., 315
Glenn, Governor Robert B., 11, 286
Goldie, Sir George T., 36
Good Templars, 269
Good Templary, 140
Gookins, Judge, 95
Gordon, Anna A., 150
Gordon, Mrs. A. J., 138
Gothenburg System, 200
Gough, John Bartholomew, XIV, 116, 219
Gowen, Miss Elma, 244

Grady, Henry W., 4
Graham, Mrs. Frances W., 246
Great Britain, 203
Greeley, Horace, 4
Green, Miss Mary E., 252
Gretton, Hon. John, 199
Griffis, William Elliot, 32
Griffith, Mrs. Hester T., 248
Grippenburg, Baroness von, 201

H

Haddock, Rev. George C., 125, 151
Hadley, Edwin C., 261
Hale, B. E., 164
Hale, Edward Everett, 5, 160
Halifax, 386
Hall, Mrs. Fannie, 350
Hall, Winfield S., 138
Hamilton, Alexander, 353, 354, 368
Hammell, George M., XIII
Hanly, Governor J. Frank, 11, 273, 403, 404
Hargreaves, W., 164
Harlan, Justice, 87
Harris, Governor Andrew L., 288, 289, 403, 404
Harris, Townsend, 40
Haskell, Governor Charles N., 290
Hawaii, 251, 271
Haynes, L. M. D., 17
Heath, A. R., 49
Heckewelder, Rev. John, 327
"Hell of the Pacific," The, 37
Helmholtz, 54
Hendrickson, Finley C., 368, 369, 371, 373
Hendrickson, Rev. W. C., 164
Henrici, W. C., 310
Heredity, Alcohol and, 66
Hill, John H., 178
Hillsboro, (Ohio), 205
Hinshaw, Virgil G., 178
Hoch, Governor Edward W., 10, 274, 275, 300
Hodge, Prof. C. F., 59, 60, 66
Hodges, S. W., 164
Hoelscher, Gustave, 176, 177
Hoffman, Mrs. Clara C., 158
Hoggatt, Hon. W. B., 267
Holman, Mrs. Silena M., 242
Honolulu, XIV
Horton, H. V., 164
Hosmer, Rev. William, 164
Hudson, Marshall A., 263
Hughes, Charles H., 138
Hullinger, J. W., 309
Hunt, Emery J., 138
Hunt, Mrs. Mary H., 137
Hunt, T. P., 164

I

Idaho, 259, 272
Illinois, 51, 206, 218, 273
Inalienable Right, To pursue lawful business, 96
Inalienable Right, To sell intoxicating liquor, Not, 85, 93, 94
Income and Inheritance Tax, 378
Indian Commissioner, The U. S., 329
Indian Problem, The, 328
Indian Territory, 248, 290, 335, 336, 337
Indiana, 217, 273
Indiana, State of, vs. Edward Sopher, 101
Indiana, Supreme Court of, 302
Ingersoll, Robert G., 5
Inherent right, To sell intoxicating liquors by retail, not, 85, 93, 94
Initiative and referendum, 17, 18, 199, 293, 397
Intercollegiate Prohibition Association, 172, 178
Intercollegiate Statesman, 173, 177
Interstate Commerce, 93
Interstate Commerce Laws, 225, 238
Internal Revenue, U. S., XX, 227, 354, 358, 362, 363, 367, 377
Intoxicating Liquors, Retail sale of, cannot be legally licensed, 98
Iowa, 244, 274
Iowa, Liquor legislation in, 97, 98
Ireland, Archbishop John, 9, 142, 207
Issue, The People's, XV
Ito, Kazutaka, 39

J

Jackson, Rev. J. C., 192, 193
James, Prof. William, 55
Japan, 38
"Japan Evangelist," 38
Jay, John, 6
Jefferson, Thomas, 354
Jesus of Nazareth, 397
Jewett, Charles, 164
Johnson, Hale, 167
Johnson, Rev. Dr. Samuel, 6
Johnson, William E., 327, 332, 333, 335, 338, 339
Jones, Charles R., 170
Jones, E. L., 177
Jones, G. N., 164
Jones, Lief, 14
Jones, Sam P., 6
Joy, Benjamin, 108
Joyce, Alliance vs., 101
Jug Trade, C. O. D., 374
Juvenile Courts, Department of, 144

K

Kansas, 87, 88, 91, 231, 262, 274, 275, 316, 317, 318, 322, 323
Kansas City, (Kansas), 228, 275, 300, 302, 304, 307, 312, 313, 314, 316
Kansas City (Kan.) Mercantile Club of, 275
Kansas, Mugler, vs., 83, 84
Kansas, Supreme Court of, 95, 214
Kansas vs. Crawford, 302
Kansas vs. Ziebold & Hagelin, 88
Kansas City (Missouri), 70, 76, 308
Kansas State Temperance Union, 275
Kauffman, Luther S., 164
Keane, Archbishop John J., 9
Kennan, George, 401
Kentucky, 217, 232, 235, 239, 275
Kentucky vs. Adams Express Co., 98
Kentucky vs. Douglass, 99
Ketterling vs. Jacksonville, 103
Khama, 34
Kipling, Rudyard, 6
Klondike, The, XIV
Knights of Labor, 44
Knox, Mrs. Janette Hill, 244
Knoxville, (Tenn.) 213
Kovalevsky, Maxim, 201
Kraepelin, Prof. Dr., 55, 56, 57, 58, 138
Kurz, Prof. Dr., 58
Kynett, Rev. A. J., D. D., 192
Kyofukwai, (Temperance Union, Japan), 39

L

Labor, Knights of, 44
Labor, Massachusetts Bureau of, 12
Lager Beer Association, N. Y. State, 232
Laitenan, Prof. Dr., 64
Lancaster, Camp-meeting, 403
Laurier, Sir Wilfrid, 385
Lawrence, Rev. Brooks, 344
Laws, Interstate Commerce, 225
Lawson, Mrs. Rosetta E., 349
Lawton vs. Steele, 96
League, The Carson, 112
League of the Cross, 383
Leavitt, Mrs. Mary Clement, 141, 244, 252
Legal and Political Aspects of the Liquor Problem, 173
Levering, Joshua, 168
Levering Presidential Vote, 264
Lewis, Dio, M. D., 205
Liberal Party, The, 384
License, 199, 202, 299
License, High, 1
License League, National Model, 1, 28, 31

INDEX.

License, Limitations of, 100
License, Not a Contract, 85
License, U. S. Government, 376
License, U. S. Special Tax Receipt, Not a, 360
License Tax Cases, 361
Licensed public houses, 197
Licensing Bill, The, 198, 214
Licensing Commission, 199
License, Power to, dormant, 85
Lilley, William C., 138
Lincoln, Abraham, XVII, XIX, 6, 30, 219, 256, 321, 354, 397, 403, 405
Lind, Edward, 407
Lindsey, Mrs. Lilah D., 248
Little, Rev. Charles J., D. D., 159
Littlefield Bill, The, 366
Liquor Business, Capital of, 226
Liquor Business, Profits of, 223
Liquor Industry, The, 46, 47, 48, 49
Liquor Interests, Amounts paid by, to other businesses, 225
Liquor Interests, Federation of, 222
Liquor, Intoxicating, not an ordinary commodity, 95
Liquor League, The, 19
Liquor Lobby, The, 357
Liquor Power, The, XIII
Liquor Problem, The, 46, 340
Liquor Traffic, a recognized evil, 274
Liquor Traffic, Congress and the, 369, 370
Liquor Traffic, Dominion Alliance for the Suppression of the, 381
Liquor Traffic, Socialism and the, 399
Liquor Trust, The, 368
Liquor, Transportation of, from one local option county to another, illegal, 98
Livermore, Mrs. Mary A., 166, 244
Liverpool, 214
Lobby, The Liquor, 357, 368
Local Option, 198, 203, 206, 210, 212, 217, 237, 267, 268, 269, 273, 275, 277, 278, 279, 290, 295, 296, 297, 382, 386, 398
Local Option League, 187
Logue, J. W., 142
London Missionary Society, 38
Long, John D., 6
Louisiana, 217, 235, 241
Lowell, James Russell, XIII
Loyal Temperance Legion, 145, 150, 207
Lubbock, Governor, 294
Luther, Martin, 7

M

Macgregor, Sir William, 38
Mackay, Rev. Dr., 38
MacNicholl, T. Alexander, 138
Madagascar, Queen of, 14
Madagascar, W. C. T. U., 37
Madden vs. Smeltz, 101
Magee, Rev. H. D., 383
Magoun, Rev. George F., 364
Maine, 28, 50, 51, 205, 231, 276
Malagasy, W. C. T. U., 37
Manila, 40
Manitoba, 379, 382, 384, 387
Manitoba Act, The, 203, 385
Manning, Cardinal, 9
Mansfield, Lord Chief Justice, 394
Maori-land, 38
March, Miss Elizabeth, 249
Markwell, Mrs. Lulu A., 243
Maryland, 277
Mason, P., 164
Massachusetts, 50, 218, 244, 277
Massachusetts Beer Co., 83
Mathew, Theobald, XIV, 104
Mattingly, Senator, 13
McCleod, Prof. Dr., 64
McClure's Magazine, 400, 401, 402
McColl, Rev. C. W., 348
McCumber Bill, The, 135
McDermott, John A., 225
McElroy, Rev. W. F., 23
McGregor, Bradford, 170, 171
McKean, Rev. Samuel, 164
McKinley, William, 7
McPherson, Judge Smith, 97
Mears, Rev. D. O., 207
Medal Contest Department, 144
Melish, Rev. John Howard, 398
Merrick, Dr. C. H., 164
Merwin, Col. J. B., 30
Mesch, Fred. Jr., 177
Messmer, Archbishop Sebastian C., 1
Metcalf, E. W., 191
Metcalf, Henry B., 168
Methodist Church (Canada), 389
Methodist Episcopal Mission (Japan), 39
Michigan, 278
Miles, General Nelson A., 168
Milles, Prof. Dr., 64
Minnesota, 261, 278
Missions, Christian, and the Liquor Traffic, 34
Mississippi, 235, 240, 279
Mississippi, Stone vs. 82, 90, 100, 303
Missouri, 217, 241, 279
Miyama, 39
Mohammedism, 32
Montgomery, S. T., 164
Montana, 244, 280
Moody, Hon. Frank S., 212
Moonshiners, 355
Moore Remonstrance Law, 274
Moreau Temperance Society, XVIII
Morgan, C. L., 138
Mott, Lucretia, 107

INDEX.

Mugler vs. Kansas, 83, 88, 92, 302
Muirhead, Dr., 25
Mulct Law, Iowa, 97, 274
Muller, Rev. O. M., 231
Munn vs. Illinois, 89
Murphy, Francis, 119, 120, 252

N

Nagasaki, 39
Napoleon, The Little, XIII
Nation, Mrs. Carry A., 27, 205, 318, 319, 320, 321, 325, 326
National Temperance Society, The, 207
Nazareth, The Man of, 398
Nebraska, 218, 243, 280
Negro and Prohibition, The, 345
Negro Problem, The, 340
New Brunswick, 203, 379, 381, 382, 386
New Brunswick Synod, The, 388
New Hampshire, 281
New Jersey, 282
New Mexico, 248, 283
New South Wales, 203
New York, 218, 246, 283, 402
New Zealand, 203
Nichols, Emmett D., 273
Noel, Governor Edmond F., 12, 279
No-License Conference, The Indianapolis, 275
No-License League, The, 207
North Carolina, 209, 231, 235, 286
North Dakota, 231, 287
Nova Scotia, 203, 205, 384, 386
Nuisance, Common, 91
Nuisance, The Saloon, a Public, 101
Nutter, Mrs. S. C., 248
Nye, Joshua, 164

O

Oberlin, 221
Oberlin Temperance Alliance, 187
Odell, Jay, 164
O'Donnell, John, 164
Oglethorpe, 205
Ohio, 51, 205, 216, 245, 287
Ohio, Liquor Tax, 97, 98
Ohio, Supreme Court of, 96
Oklahoma, 213, 231, 235, 289
Ontario, 203, 379, 381, 382, 384, 387
Oratorical Contests, Prohibition, 176
O'Rear, Justice, 98
Oregon, 246, 290
Original Package Bill, 135
Orne, J. H., 164
Ottawa, 384

P

Parks, W. G., 349
Parliament, The Dominion, 380, 382, 384, 386

Passmore, Enoch, 164
Patton, Robert H., 256
Paul, Saint, 397
Pauperism, 95
Pearson, Samuel F., 317
Pennington, Levi T., 177
Pennsylvania, 51, 246, 291, 354
Pershing, D. R., 164
Personal Liberty League, 403
Peterson, Mrs. E. E., 349
Peterson, Dr. Frederick, 56
Phelan vs. Virginia, 303
Phelps, Carrington A., 216, 224
Philippine Islands, 40, 41
Phillips, Wendell, XIX, 7, 166, 174, 182, 397
Pidgeon, Rev. Dr. G. C., 383
Pierce, Charles S., 176, 177, 178
Pitts, C. E., 262
Platt, Mrs. Margaret B., 247
Platt, Rev. Dr. S. H., 164
Platform, National, of the Prohibition Party, 169, 253
Plebiscite, Dominion, 385
Pneumonia, Alcohol and, 65
Police Powers, 81, 82, 83, 85, 86, 89, 90, 92, 96
Poling, Daniel A., 178
Pollock, Judge, 306
Poor Man's Club, The, 42
Poppert, Prof. Herman M., 202
Portland (Maine), XVI., 317
Potter, Bishop, 402
Powderly, T. V., 12
Presbyterian Church, General Assembly of, 389
President of the United States, 364
Price, Hon. Hiram, 193
Price, J. C., 345
Prince Edward Island, 203
Privilege, The Grant of License, special, 96
Presidential Vote, Prohibition, 264
Prisons, U. S. Commission, 12
Proctor, A. T., 164
Prohibition, 28, 254, 258, 266, 270, 274, 275, 366, 373
Prohibition and License, 50
Prohibition in the South, 345, 347
Prohibition party, XVIII, 33, 43, 153, 165, 166, 167, 170, 181, 253, 262, 274, 275, 287
Prohibition party vote, 264
Prohibition Press, The Associated, 327
Prohibition State Constitution, 81
Prohibition States, 205, 206, 210, 231
Prohibition, The Negro, and, 345
Prohibition Tidal Wave, 408

INDEX.

Property rights, Prohibitory Law violates no, 87
Protective Association, Mutual, 45
Pryor, E. C., 177

Q

Quakers, The, XVIII, 327
Quebec, Province of, 203, 379, 381, 382, 385, 387

R

Race Riots, 352
Raines Law, 283
Rauber, Prof. Dr., 62
Receipts, Federal Tax, 369, 376
Referendum, Initiative and, 199, 266
Reform, The Great, XVI
Regulation in the British Colonies, 203
Regulation, Meaning of, 102
Remonstrance Law, Moore, 274
Republican Party, 397
Restraints, Prohibition violates no constitutional, 86
Retail Sale of intoxicating liquors cannot be legally licensed, 98
Revenue, Internal, 209, 227, 377, 378
Reynolds, Henry A., 119
Rhode Island, 291
Richards, Rev. Henry, 36
Richardson's "Alcohol and Hygiene," 134
Riley, Rev. B. F., D. D., 294
Ritter, Judge Eli J., 100
Roberts, William E., 177
Roman Catholic Church, The, 388
Roosevelt, Theodore, 7, 16
Root, A. I., 191
Rose, Senator Isaiah, Ohio, 403
Roumania, 202
Rounds, Mrs. Louise S., 157
Rousseau, Jean Jacques, 205
Ruchet, Mons., 200
Rudin, Prof. Dr., 57
Ruland, Arthur J., 176
Rush, Benjamin, M. D., XVII, XVIII
Ruskin, John, 7
Russell, Miss Elizabeth, 39
Russell, Howard H., 186, 187, 188, 189, 190, 191, 194, 195, 207, 220
Russell, Rev. John, 163, 164, 167, 170
Russia, XIII, 201

S

Saloon, The, XX, 18, 21, 22, 44, 45, 76, 79, 208, 225, 400
Saloon, Municipalities have power to regulate, 101
Saloon, The Passing of the, XVI, XXI

Saloon Problem, The, 361
Saloon Vote, The, XV
Saloon's Attraction, The, 77
Saloonkeeper, The, XIV, 18, 20, 22, 46, 69, 70, 71, 72, 73, 400, 401, 408
Sampson, Rev. G. C., 349
Sanders, Governor, 276
San Francisco, 26
Saskatchewan, 379, 387
Savannah, 211
Scanlon, Hon. Charles, 254
Scheffer, 54
"Science and Health," 399
Scientific Temperance Federation, 137
Scott Act, The, 203, 382, 383, 386
Sewanee University, 213
Shattuck Bill, The, 275
Shearer, Rev. Dr. J. G., 383
Shepard, Mrs. Lulu L., 243
Shields, John A. (Illinois), 177
Shields, John A. (Minnesota), 177
Shumaker, Rev. E. S., 349
Sibree, Rev. James, 37
Silver, L. B., 164
Sims, Judge John T., 313, 314
Slack, Miss Agnes, 149
"Smasher's Mail, The," 319
Smith, Mrs. Clinton, 250
Smith, Gerritt, XVIII, 165
Smith, Green Clay, 167, 260
Smith, Hervey F., 178
Smith, Governor Hoke, 12, 211, 232, 238, 270
Smith, Gen. J. S., 164
Smith, Rev. Moses, 164
Smith Presidential Vote, 264
Snyder, S. Frank, 177
Socialism and the Liquor Traffic, 399, 407
Social Misery, Drink and, 406
"Social Welfare and the Liquor Problem," 172, 173
Socrates, 7
Soltau vs. Schuyler Young, 98
Solution of the Liquor Problem, 173
Somerset, Lady Henry, 206
Sommer, Sheriff, 72
Sons of Temperance, 380
Soper, Rev. D. S., 39
South Carolina, 211, 217, 235, 292
South Carolina, Supreme Court of, 95
South Dakota, 292
Sowerby, Rev. Dr. A. T., 383
Special Tax, U. S., 355
Special Tax, U. S., not a license, 360
Special Tax Receipts, 367
Spence, Ben H., 379
Spence, F. S., 382
Spencer, Rev. D. S., 39
Spencer, J. A., 163, 164
Spratling, Dr., 66

INDEX.

Springfield (Illinois) riots, 23, 24, 25
Squires, F. D. L., 327
"Stainless Flag, The," 266
Starr, Rev. Dr. D. J., 12
States Rights vs. Federal Rights 368
Stearns, John N., 163, 164, 381
Stearns, Rev. J. G. D., 164
Steele, Lawton vs., 96
Stevens, Mrs. Lillian M. N., 143, 147, 150
Stevenson, Mrs. Katherine Lent, 158, 244
Stewart, Gideon T., 167, 170
Stewart, Oliver W., 46, 170, 178
Stier, Prof. Dr., 56
Stockwell, George E., 263
Stoddard, Cora Frances, 137
Stone vs. Mississippi, 303
Stoughton, Rev. J. C., 164
Stuart, Sherlock vs., 85
Sullivan, John L., 7
Sumner, Charles, XVIII
Supreme Court of the U. S., 93, 96, 100, 302, 364, 374
St. Augustine, (Fla.), XIV
St. John, John P., 167
St. John Presidential Vote, 264
Swallow Presidential Vote, 264
Swallow, Rev. Silas C., 168
Sweden, XIII
Switzerland, VII, 199, 200

T

Taft, William H., 27
Tambling, George S., Jr., 164
Tammany Hall, 400
Taney, Chief Justice, 81
Tappey, Rev. Francis, 213
Taro Ando, 39
Tax Certificate, The U. S., 356, 367, 369
Tax, Income and Inheritance, 378
Tax, U. S. Special, 30, 227, 355, 376
Taylor, Rev. Charles F., 230
Taylor, E. O., 138
Taylor, Rev. George Lansing, 164
Taylor, Thomas E., 349
Temperance Act, Canada, 382
Temperance Advocate, National, 134
Temperance Alliance, Sunday School, 137
Temperance Association, Church, 267
Temperance Congress, World's, 131
"Temperance Documents, Permanent American," 106
Temperance, Royal Templars of, 380
Temperance Societies, Buddhist, 39
Temperance Societies, Industrial, 39
Temperance Society, First in Canada, 380
Temperance Society, Church of England, 383
Temperance Society, National, 131
Temperance, Sons of, 380

Temperance Union, Connecticut, 269
Temperance Vote, The, XV
Temperance Wave, The, XIV
Templars, Independent Order of Good, 139, 269, 380
Tennessee, 213, 235, 239, 293, 442
Texas, 217, 232, 235, 241, 294
Thayer, Rev. William M., 164
Thompson, Rev. Edwin, 164
Thompson, Mrs. Eliza J., 205
Thompson, H. A., 167
Thoreau, Henry D., 43
Thurman, Mrs. Lucy, 349, 350
Tilghman, Rev. B. H., 349
Tobey, Miss Elizabeth S., 244
Todhunter, Oscar B., XVI, XVII
Township Local Option, 187
Travelick, R. F., 12
Treasury Department, U. S., 370, 371
Trent, Peterfield, 164
Trickett, Hon. C. W., 262, 275, 300, 301
Trust, The Drink, 227
Tuberculosis, Alcohol and, 65
Tully, T. DeQuincy, 2, 230
Turner, Cyrus, 225

U

Union Signal, 146, 149, 152
United Societies (Chicago), 21
United States Census, 50
United States, Internal Revenue Collection of, 362
United States, Supreme Court of, 93, 100, 208, 214
Utah, 243, 297

V

Van Court, T. M., 164
Van Wert vs. Brown, 101
Vayhinger, Mrs. C. J., 341
Venango Plan, The, 263
Vermont, 218, 297
Versailles, XIII
Vested Right, License gives no, 86
Victoria, 203
Vidal, Hon. Alexander, 381
Vintschgau, Prof. Dr., 55
Virginia, 217, 239, 297
Virginia, Phelan vs., 303
Voice, The California, 13
Voit, Prof. Dr., 54

W

Wadlin, Horace G., 214
Wadsworth, Joshua, 164
Waite, Chief Justice, 82
Wallmo, Pere G., 366

INDEX.

Wallys, Prof. Curt, 201
Wanamaker, John, 136
Warner, Governor F. M., 278
Warner, Harry S., 178
Wasson, Rev. E. A., 230, 231
Wasson, Rev. Samuel E., 212
Wasson, Rev. W. A., 231
Washington, 297
Washington, Booker T., 341, 342
Washington, D. C., 250
Washington (East), 243
Washington (West), 247
Washingtonians, 219
Watkins, Rev. Aaron S., D. D., 168, 256, 257
Watterson, Bishop, 207
Watterson, Henry, 8
Welch, Prof. William H., 61, 63
Wesley, John, 9, 397
Westerfield, Ray B., 176
West Virginia, 235, 240, 298
Wheeler, E. J., 46, 127
Wheeler, Wayne B., 192, 403, 404
White, James A., 349
Whitney, Mrs. Mary S., 251
Wilberforce, Canon, 10
Wilkins, Prof. Daniel, 163
Willard, Frances E., 33, 119, 145, 146, 148, 155, 156, 157, 158, 159, 160, 161, 181, 206, 219, 248, 249, 275, 407
Williams, Henry Smith, M. D., 52, 400
Williams, Rev. John, 37
Wilson, Henry, XIX
Wilson, Bishop Luther B., 183, 193, 403
Wilson, Robert N., 138

Winders, Rev. C. H., 349
Wine Growers' Association, American, 233
Wineries, 225
Winship, E. A., 138
Wisconsin, 299
Witham, Col. W. S., 259
Witte, Count, 201
Woman's Christian Temperance Union. 33, 140, 143, 149, 151, 153, 206, 207, 215, 219, 220, 242, 266, 269, 274, 275, 287, 350, 351, 380
Woman's Crusade, The, 153, 154
Woodhead Dr. Sims, 62, 63, 64
Woodward, Judge John M., 313
Woolley, John G., 28, 113, 168, 171, 252, 271
Woolley Presidential Vote, 264
World's W. C. T. U., 146
Wright, Carroll D., 12, 208
Wright, J. D., 310
Wright, Seaborn, 121, 210, 239, 341, 393, 403, 405
Wyoming, 299

Y

Yajimo, Mrs. 39
Young, Charles W., 177
Young Woman's Christian Temperance Union, 39

Z

Ziebold & Hagelin, Kansas vs., 88